Teaching with

The Bedford Guide for College Writers

2. Background Readings

Teaching with

The Bedford Guide for College Writers

FIFTH EDITION

X. J. Kennedy, Dorothy M. Kennedy, and Sylvia Holladay

---

2. Background Readings

Edited by

T. R. Johnson
Boston University

Shirley Morahan
Northeast Missouri State University

Bedford/St. Martin's   Boston   New York

For information, write: Bedford/St. Martin's
75 Arlington Street, Boston, MA 02116

ISBN: 0–312–19737–3

Acknowledgments

David Bartholomae, "Writing with Teachers: A Conversation with Peter Elbow," *College Composition and Communication,* February 1995. Copyright 1995 by the National Council of Teachers of English. Reprinted with permission.

Richard Beach, "Demonstrating Techniques for Assessing Writing in the Writing Conference," *College Composition and Communication,* February 1986. Copyright 1986 by the National Council of Teachers of English. Reprinted with permission.

James A. Berlin, "Poststructuralism, Cultural Studies, and the Composition Classroom: Postmodern Theory in Practice," *Rhetoric Review,* Volume 11, Number 1, Fall 1992, (pp. 16–33). Permission granted by publisher. "Rhetoric and Ideology in the Writing Class," *College English,* September 1988. Copyright 1988 by the National Council of Teachers of English. Reprinted with permission.

Ann E. Berthoff, "Dialectical Notebooks and the Audit of Meaning." Reprinted by permission of Ann E. Berthoff. From *The Journal Book,* edited by Toby Fulwiler, Heinemann-Boynton/Cook Publishers, a subsidiary of Reed Elsevier Inc., Portsmouth, N.H., 1987.

Patricia Bizzell and Bruce Herzberg, "Research as a Social Act," *The Clearing House* 60, March 1987. Reprinted with the permission of the Helen Dwight Reid Educational Foundation. Published by Heldref Publications, 1319 Eighteenth Street, N.W., Washington, D.C. 20036-1802. Copyright © 1987.

Wayne C. Booth, "The Rhetorical Stance," *College Composition and Communication,* October 1963. Copyright 1963 by the National Council of Teachers of English. Reprinted with permission.

Kenneth A. Bruffee, "Toward Reconstructing American Classrooms: Interdependent Students, Interdependent World." From *Collaborative Learning* by Kenneth Bruffee (chapter four). Johns Hopkins University Press, 1993. Copyright 1993. Reprinted by permission of the Johns Hopkins University Press.

Suzanne Clark, "Review: Women, Rhetoric, Teaching," *College Composition and Communication,* February 1995. Copyright 1995 by the National Council of Teachers of English. Reprinted with permission.

Lisa Ede and Andrea A. Lunsford, "Audience Addressed/Audience Invoked: The Role of Audience in Composition Theory and Pedagogy," *College Composition and Communication,* May 1984. Copyright 1984 by the National Council of Teachers of English. Reprinted with permission.

Acknowledgments and copyrights are continued at the back of the book on page 386, which constitutes an extension of the copyright page. It is a violation of the law to reproduce these selections by any means whatsoever without the written permission of the copyright holder.

Preface

This selection of readings can help you acquire or broaden a theoretical and practical background as you use *The Bedford Guide for College Writers*, Fifth Edition. Although we've selected the readings with first-time instructors in mind, we also hope that veteran instructors in community colleges and four-year institutions will find helpful perspectives, important ideas, and practical suggestions.

Our discipline's conversations have always been spirited, whether about philosophical issues, learning and writing theory, or pedagogical assumptions that influence our work with writers. From such conversations — public and private, in scholarly journals or faculty lounges — and from our own classroom experience and reflection, we can gain confidence in our vision of the nature and purpose of writing courses. We hope your "conversation" with these readings will help you to become an adept and creative teacher of writing.

The readings in this volume address major concerns of *The Bedford Guide for College Writers*. Chapter 1, "Teaching Writing: Concepts and Philosophies for Reflective Practice," examines, describes, and reflects on the beliefs and assumptions that inform writing pedagogies. The readings in Chapter 2, "Thinking about the Writing Process," discuss ways that writers shape thought into words when they explore ideas, plan, draft, consider (or ignore) audiences, and revise. Chapter 3, "Responding to and Evaluating Student Writing," focuses on teachers' strategies for responding to writers' needs and working with students at diverse writing sites. Chapter 4, "Issues in Writing Pedagogy: Institutional Politics and the Other," focuses on classroom and faculty diversity. Many of the readings offer you helpful citations, and an annotated bibliography lists many helpful articles that could not be included here. These pieces offer the opportunity for further reflection on and research into composition and the artful teaching of composition.

You can, of course, just jump in anywhere and read the article that best suits your needs that day. But know that there are rich interconnections among these readings that build a recursivity into the collection. If you are reading the article by Mara Holt, you might find yourself dropping back to see what Kenneth Bruffee says about collaborative learning for the construction of knowledge. The articles by Peter Elbow and Nancy Sommers are referenced frequently in other readings in the collection, so you might find yourself stopping in the middle of one reading to refer to another.

Each writer in this collection has teachers as his or her primary audience, so you will find in the readings very practical recommendations about teaching strategies. A headnote to each reading focuses on key assumptions and consistent themes of the writer. Two kinds of "apparatus" follow each selection: "The Writer's Insights as a Resource for Your Teaching" and "The Writer's Insights as a Resource for the Writing Classroom." We wrote the first set of recommendations to prompt you into "reflective practice" as a writing teacher. We based these recommendations on our experience working with writers, our training and supervision of novice writing instructors, and our work with colleagues across the curriculum. The second set of suggestions describe some strategies that have worked for professors and graduate writing instructors alike, as we apply the insights of a reading to our classrooms.

Several instructors commented on the fifth edition with thoughtful and detailed comments. Though we were unable to incorporate all of the reviewers' suggestions, we know that this edition benefited from their responses. We wish to thank Fred

D'Astoli, Ventura College; Janice Mandile, Front Range Community College; Scott Stankey, Anoka-Ramsey Community College; and Patricia White, Norwich University.

Background Readings, the second volume of the instructor's manual that accompanies *The Bedford Guide for College Writers,* includes both theoretical background and practical advice for composition instructors. The first volume of the instructor's manual, on the other hand, provides practical suggestions about interconnecting the readings and writing assignments of *The Bedford Guide* with the discussion of the large discourse community of writing teachers. We recommend that you use these two volumes together so that you can best take advantage of the information in *The Bedford Guide for College Writers.*

Contents

3. Responding to and Evaluating Student Writing   196

4. Issues in Writing Pedagogy:
Institutional Politics and the Other   285

1. Teaching Writing: Concepts and Philosophies for Reflective Practice

In Chapter 1 of this ancillary, you can find readings that provoke you to reflect on your own practice as a writing teacher and also to understand the unique features of *The Bedford Guide for College Writers*. The readings have been chosen for two reasons: to illuminate major assumptions, implicit and explicit, about why and how we teach students to grow as writers; and to illustrate pedagogic strategies used by writing instructors who organize their courses with various foci, such as writing as a recursive process, the writer's resources, writing as critical thinking, evaluation for revision, and so on. We recommend that you begin your research into composition theory and pedagogy with these readings and that you return to them when you want to reflect on the experiences of the writing community that you foster.

INITIATING REFLECTIVE PRACTICES AS A WRITING TEACHER

Every choice you make as a writing instructor is informed by some philosophy of composition and of teaching composition, even if you're not fully aware of the philosophy you hold. The more aware you become of your assumptions and premises, the more you can look at, rethink, and improve your teaching. Notice how each of the writers in this section challenges us to examine the assumptions that govern the ways we teach. To begin this process of reflection, we recommend that before you begin to teach a writing course, or early in the semester, you sit down and freewrite or brainstorm for about fifteen minutes, listing your "I believes" about writing and about the teaching of writing. Periodically, shape those beliefs into some prose that you can refer to as you plan assignments, structure sequences of assignments, build or redesign a syllabus, ponder a writing curriculum, propose support services for writers across the curriculum, or discuss your pedagogy with teaching colleagues. You might also want to consult *Teaching with* THE BEDFORD GUIDE FOR COLLEGE WRITERS. *1. Practical Suggestions*, which offers a number of essays to help you shape your teaching philosophy. Reading the essays crafted by experienced writing teachers like those whom you meet in this book will also be a resource for your reflecting and your teaching. All the writers of essays in this collection care deeply about serving students, improving the quality of learning experiences, and sharing their concepts, philosophies, and advice with colleagues.

Many first-year instructors keep a "reflective journal" in which they log and reflect on what occurs in class and how students respond to assignments. Those instructors use the journal to describe their own reactions and responses to the class dynamic, to the process of building a writing community, and to the connections they make among what they are reading outside the classroom and actual events within the classroom. Two or three times a semester they read over their entries and chart their own learning and growth as instructors. By the end of the first semester, most new instructors can see some dramatic change in confidence, attitudes about writing communities and student writing, use of teaching strategies, and understanding of how the parts of the syllabus or the course connect.

The reflective journal is a very useful resource for writing about teaching, for developing a final draft of a philosophy for teaching writing, and for designing syllabi for second-semester or second-year courses. It could be an important part of a "teaching portfolio," a collection of products that demonstrate your practice and improvement as an instructor. That portfolio could include assignments given, copies of student responses, syllabi, descriptions of classroom activities, notes on reading journal entries, student feedback, printouts of e-mail and e-conference conversations of student writers, copies of the summative comments you write students, and hypertext documents. From that collection, you might on occasion select representative materials for others to view, read, hear, and evaluate. Your teaching portfolio both fosters and reflects your "reflective practice" as a writing instructor. You will use it to assess your progress as a professional educator. You can also use it to identify strengths, areas for improvement, and new visions and goals for your writing community; it will be helpful in your construction of knowledge about writing and about teaching writers. It is a primary document to use when you apply for teaching positions, fellowships, research grants, tenure, and promotions.

GEORGE HILLOCKS *Some Basics for Thinking about Teaching Writing*

The college writing classroom can seem disarmingly complex, especially for new teachers. How does one formulate a flexible approach that will evolve and improve as it must in order to succeed? This chapter from George Hillocks's Teaching Writing as Reflective Practice *offers a concrete, step-by-step strategy for making the classroom a viable place to learn more about the teaching of writing. Hillocks begins by discussing in broad terms the nature of "theory" and how it provides our classrooms with coherence, purpose, and a meaningful way to gauge our success. Hillocks distinguishes practice-as-routine from practice-as-reflective-inquiry and sets up a six-phase model for improving our teaching: first, we evaluate a particular practice; next, we project a desired change in student performance; third, we devise strategies that might bring about the desired change; fourth, we implement the strategies; fifth, we evaluate the results; and finally, we consider the incidental or unexpected results that derive from the new practice. By making reflective inquiry a part of our daily practice as teachers, we transform our classrooms into dynamic spaces of constant change and growth — for teachers as well as students.*

In various projects that my students and I have been conducting to discover how teachers think about their teaching, one distinct profile has emerged so far that hinges on a common set of attitudes toward students, teaching, and learning. While our sample is drawn from teachers in a large urban community college system, experience indicates that the same profile appears at other levels. I present this profile as representative of beliefs shared by several teachers in the sample, but certainly not all.

This representative professor holds a Ph.D. in English from a prestigious university. He believes that the primary task of his freshman composition class is to teach the "modes of writing." Of his students, he says, "I'm always surprised at how little the students do know about a given subject or a given approach to writing about something." He believes that, after mechanics and editing, "Perhaps their second weakest area . . . is what I would loosely call reading between the lines, thinking for oneself, thinking, using analogy, being creative."

Classes observed begin with the professor making an assignment followed by a presentation of information about the mode of writing represented in the assignment. This complete, he turns to the previous assignment and asks several students to read their papers aloud. After each reading the professor comments. This goes on until class ends. In one class he presents the mode of writing he calls "extended example." He explains at some length that it will not be the same as classification or narrative.

> The essay that I am about to put on the board, where we use example as a way of developing a paper, will be somewhat closer to the classification one, but not the same. There will never be a paper that is exactly like the last one. Don't you see? Don't think that just because you did that last time, that somehow you've got to do it this way this time and if you can't fit it, there is a problem. Don't *try* to fit it. It's a different assignment. It has an entirely different set of problems that you have to work on solving. When you tell your story, it's just like if I turn on the television and I had missed the commercial. I am seeing characters developing some conflict. I'm seeing them change as a result of the pressures they are under. It's a *story*. I'm trying to say that over and over again, it is a story. It is not a classification of anything. You are telling us a story. So there's no first, second, and finally. There is a plot, which may have a beginning, a middle, and an end. That is not first, second, and finally. There is no conclusion; there is an ending.

He continues for thirty lines of transcript, talking more about narrative, which students have already written and will read aloud later, and contrasting it with news commentaries on TV. He says he wants to "take a minute and throw some things on the board so you have a sense of where we're going." He says, "Do not hesitate to ask questions if the assignment is still not clear to you. I'm not trying to rush you. I thought it was fairly well understood, but if it's not, I can only know unless, you know, you ask me questions and indicate what's not been made clear. OK. Just copy what's on the board, but don't copy anything yet. Some of this is just a reminder, which you probably already know." Perhaps not surprisingly, no one asks questions. He writes several assignments in abbreviated form, including one for "theme three," the next composition that students will write.

Theme 3 (extended example)
　　Choose only one:
　　(1)　What are three dangerous drugs?
　　(2)　What are three situations where we should not drink and drive?
　　(3)　What are three jobs for the future?
　　(4)　Who are three well-known illiterates?

After thirty-nine lines of transcript and a period for role taking, he turns to theme three:

> Now the expository mode, we call an example. Really, example is not an expository mode, but I'll make it one anyway. Secondly, example is used in all the various modes to get the point across. And we are concentrating on using example very explicitly this time, so I think we will just say the expository mode is example. You have to decide who the audience is and who you are as a speaker, what your attitude is, and if you're having some difficulty with that, we can discuss it on Thursday. Give it some thought before Thursday. For number six I have given you four questions which will force you to write a paper in which you have an introductory paragraph, three developmental paragraphs, each of which will have one example in the second form, and then you will have a fifth paragraph, which is a conclusion. Now this time you are *not* telling a story. You are explaining something. You must use one of the four, only one. If you choose number one, I'll see your topic is drugs.

The professor continues for sixty-five lines of transcript, which include a lecture on famous illiterate athletes, before asking volunteers to read their narratives.

The Basics of Practice

Any teacher of writing is faced with a wide variety of possibilities for teaching that range from the imposition of little or no structure to very tight constraints on students, from teacher lecture to free-flowing class discussion with no limits on topics students may wish to mention, from daily free writing to daily drill on usage, from the use of computers to the use of chalkboards, from curricula based on the writing types of current traditional rhetoric to those that seem to admit to no important differences among writing tasks and sometimes no curricula at all. In this welter of possibilities how can we know how to proceed in making decisions about both curriculum and specific classroom practice? What prevents classrooms from becoming a hodge-podge of activities: ten minutes of free writing, five of sentence combining, fifteen of lecture about "description," twelve on vocabulary, and, assuming a fifty-minute class, eight minutes of small-group discussion on a topic of the students' choice?

What is it that renders the classroom process coherent? What can be the basis of future practice with particular students? I think the answer to both these questions is *theory*. Every teacher of writing has a set of theories that provide a coherent view of the field and means of approaching the task of teaching. Leon Lederman, the physicist and Nobel laureate, says simply that theory is "the best explanation of the data," taken to include their nature and relationships. Theories may be based on a combination of assumptions, constructions derived from empirical research, and argument. They vary in quality with the care exercised in establishing each component. One such "explanation" for writing teachers has to do with written discourse, some explanation of the features of writing, their occurrence, and relationships.

The profile with which this chapter opens illustrates several theories. Let us look at four. The most obvious is the explanation of discourse that leads to the teacher's opening discussion about how "extended example" differs from "classification" and narrative. In this teacher's theory, written discourse includes many such "types." He will teach ten of them in the course of the semester. Each is characterized by a structure that he endeavors to explain to his students, contrasting it with others that may be similar in certain ways. Thus, he says, of narrative: "There is a plot, which may have a beginning, a middle, and an end. That is not first, second, and finally. There is no conclusion; there is an ending." Further, he believes that the central features of each type are adequately represented in his chalkboard outline of the assignment. He believes that if students understand these features, they will be able to generate an example of the type.

The second theory underlying this profile is pedagogical and quite straightforward. Simply stated, it holds that teaching is tantamount to telling. It is based on the assumption, which Lindley Murray states in the 1795 preface to his venerable grammar, that people can, using appropriate language, "transfuse . . . sentiments into the minds of one another" (5). In the classes of these teachers, observations reveal that their talk dominates the available time by wide margins, not infrequently 100 to 1. In the class transcript excerpted above, the teacher has 229 lines while one student speaks for two lines up to the point that students read their essays aloud.

A third theory, one of epistemology or knowing, appears to underlie both of the above. It appears to be what post-modern critics would call a "positivist" epistemology, one that holds reality and knowledge to be directly apprehensible by the senses without interpretation, almost without ambiguity. Such a theory endorses teaching as telling. The professor simply needs to "infuse" his ideas of "extended example" into the minds of students. Further, those ideas can be adequately represented simply by means of the outline on the chalkboard. The same epistemology is implicated in the theory of representational discourse the professor holds. He seems to believe that the substance of at least some kinds of discourse may be directly apprehended without the filters of persuasion on the part of the writer or interpretation on the part of the reader. Thus, he says, "example is used in all the various modes to get the point across." For him, the import of an example is self-evident.

These three theories are closely tied together so as to support one another. Their interlocking results in the smooth functioning of the class, which rolls along under the professor's direction without any apparent difficulty.

The fourth theory is based on the assumption that students have weak backgrounds that render them unlikely to learn. This assumption is taken as fact, as the epistemology might lead us to expect, and statements about student weakness tend to the absolute; for example, "No matter what I do, there is very little improvement." Because they perceive students as very weak, they adopt the corollary that whatever is taught must be simplified and "highly structured." That simplification and structure should enable them to "transfuse" the necessary information directly into the minds of students who cannot think for themselves and "want to be force fed." They say, "The more structure they have, the more comfortable they are with an assignment." Note the simple structure of the five paragraph theme assignment above.

The basic assumption about students and the theory of teaching in this profile, taken together, form a very tight syllogistic system for thinking about teaching. If teaching is telling, then proper teaching has taken place when the proper basic formulas about writing have been presented. If students do not learn much even when proper teaching has taken place, it is not surprising because they are weak and cannot be expected to learn. The teaching has not failed; the students have. Therefore there is no reason to change the method of teaching. Teaching writing becomes a protected activity. There is no need to call assumptions about methods into question, no need to try something new, no reason to doubt oneself as a teacher. Of course, not all teachers in our sample conform to this profile. Many believe that students can learn, and this belief appears to influence what they do. The point is that *the assumptions we make and the theories we hold have a powerful effect on what and how we teach.*

I believe that teachers of written composition must work from at least four major, interconnected sets of theories: (1) composing processes, (2) written discourse, (3) invention or inquiry, and (4) learning and teaching. These theories will necessarily be the basis for the content and organization of students' experiences in any program intended for helping people learn to write.

This is not to say that theory is the only source of what we do as teachers. Two other sources are equally important: what has been called reflective practice, and the teacher's general fund of life experience.

The Nature of Reflective Practice

Many people believe that research and theory govern practice. The relationships, however, seem far more complex than that, particularly if we think of "practice" in more than the simplest sense of the word as, according to the *Oxford English Dictionary (OED)*, "the action of doing something." What I intend here is more akin to the third and fifth definitions offered by the *OED:* "the doing of something repeatedly or continuously by way of study; exercise in any art, handicraft, etc. for the purpose or with the result of attaining proficiency" (3) and "the carrying on or exercise of a profession or occupation" (5). Taken together, these suggest a kind of practice that is reflective, that permits the practitioner to learn through practice, not simply through *trial and error,* an expression that suggests a kind of randomness that does not allow for the building of knowledge. Others suggest that practice is essentially routine.

Practice as Routine

Stephen North writes of the knowledge of practitioners as a body of lore that he characterizes as "the accumulated body of traditions, practices, and beliefs in terms of which practitioners understand how writing is done, learned, and taught" (22). He argues that "practice is largely a matter of routine. . . . Practitioners operate within the bounds of lore's known: they approach the matter of what to do by reducing the infinite number of new situations into familiar terms, then handling them with familiar strategies" (33).

North allows, however, that under three conditions "practice becomes inquiry" but only

(a) when the situation cannot be framed in familiar terms, so that any familiar strategies will have to be adapted for use;
(b) when, although the situation is perceived as familiar, standard approaches are no longer satisfactory, and so new approaches are created for it; or
(c) when both situation and approach are non-standard. (33)

North speculates that, judged by these standards, with the normal freshman composition teaching load, "practice qualifies as inquiry less than ten percent of the time" (34).

These guidelines for thinking about what constitutes inquiry in practice are useful. To use them for the analysis of inquiry in the practice of teaching writing would require definitions of the key terms, of course. What constitutes standard and nonstandard situations? What constitutes "an approach" in the teaching of writing? When is an approach standard or nonstandard? North's examples suggest that a nonstandard situation represents a shift in circumstances comparable to the advent of the open admissions policy that brought underprepared students into Mina Shaughnessy's classroom, prompting the inquiry that resulted in *Errors and Expectations.* In the same way, a nonstandard approach is one that leaves behind most, if not all, of the teaching tactics previously used.

Reflective Practice as Inquiry

It seems to me, however, that inquiry occurs in practice on a far less grand scale. Assume that a teacher who has been using a story from the classroom anthology to exemplify specificity in writing has decided to dump it because she feels her students are unenthusiastic about it and do not seem to care about its specific imagery. Instead she selects a passage by a ninth-grader from the student magazine, *Merlyn's Pen,* as a model of effective, specific writing, asks a ninth-grade class to read and respond to it, and examines students' responses to it in some way to determine its impact on students' understanding of what specific prose is. Does that sequence constitute inquiry? The sequence will not allow the teacher to explain the kind of cause-and-effect relationship that North talks about. She will not know if there is a more or less effective passage. And if she uses other activities to promote specific imagery in the writing of her ninth-graders, she will not be able to judge how important her prose model was in that effort.

Her evaluation of the impact of the passage is likely to sound something like this: "I think the kids liked the passage a lot. They were very attentive while I read it aloud, they had lots to say about it when I asked what they liked about it, and they were able to find many examples of specific details. I think it has given them a better idea of what it means to be specific in their own writing." Clearly, the teacher has engaged in a kind of practical inquiry that includes the identification of a problem (an ineffective model), the hypothesis of a reasoned solution (that a piece written by a student might have greater appeal), the informal testing of the hypothesis, and an arrival at some resolution of the problem. In Dewey's terms, this process that originates in doubt and moves in a rational way to resolution constitutes inquiry.

If the teacher uses the same model with many ninth-grade classes over a period of several years, does the practice become what North calls routine? The *OED* defines *routine* as "of a mechanical or unvaried character; performed by rule." To say that teaching is routine is to suggest its comparability to operating a punch press, without having to set the press up. If our teacher is aware that no two groups of students are the same and uses the selection in an interactive way, monitoring responses, responding to students as individuals, and evaluating the effectiveness of the selection, then the teaching cannot be mechanical, unvaried, or performed by rule. (By the same definition, the kind of teaching represented in the profile that opens this chapter is routine.)

If the teacher remains open to the possibility that the piece of writing may not have the desired effect for one reason or another, if she monitors student response to determine how it is or is not working, then the teacher maintains the basic posture of inquiry in teaching, regarding actions as hypotheses to be assessed. If, on the other hand, the teacher presents material without regard to any student response and makes no attempt to assess student understanding as teaching proceeds prior to grading assignments at the end of teaching sequences, then the teaching must be regarded as routine: mechanical and unvarying. We may call the former by Donald A. Schön's term: reflective practice. And such reflective practice is the basis for inquiry in teaching. Indeed, reflective practice becomes inquiry, in North's sense, as it becomes more formal and systematic.

The Priority of Reflective Practice

Quite clearly, in the case of teaching writing (and perhaps in other cases as well), research and theory would not exist if practice were entirely unreflective. More than creating a need, however, reflective practice can provide the foundation for research. A number of research projects, for example, seem to have been instigated by classroom practice. Teachers have noticed something interesting, curious, or unexpected in the process of interacting with students and have developed and examined those possibilities with great care, using a variety of research strategies from case studies to quasi-experiments designed to examine hypotheses (e.g., Atwell; Cochran-Smith and Lytle; Hillocks "Effects," "Interaction"; Olson; Sager; Troyka).

At the same time, practice appears to generate important ideas for theory. For example, some teachers were using small student-led group discussions long before Vygotsky was translated into English. The success of small-group collaborative learning has a potential for adding to Vygotskian theory. The success of the practice drives a need to develop an explanatory theory.

Further, practice may give us cause to question theory. For example, I recently witnessed a teacher attempting to capture the interest of what had been designated by the school as one of its lowest-level ninth-grade groups. She had asked them to write journal entries about their own personal experiences or whatever concerned them, to share entries they liked with others, to revise them, and so forth. So far as I could see, she was doing everything she could to follow Donald Graves's recommendations. Nonetheless, these African American inner-city youngsters were not buying it. They saw no value, at the time, in writing about their own personal experience. Several students had even asked the teacher if they could go back to doing fill-in-the-blank exercises. This they regarded as "real" English. What does one do if the theoretical stance recommends an open approach to topics and structures but the students view such an approach as silly? Such situations wrestle us into rethinking theory.

If practice can lead us to reexamine theory, it must be the case that practice may take a theoretical stance. Reflective teachers develop a stance based on sets of ideas about their students and their subject, ideas that may be more or less systematically developed but that are able to provide tentative hypotheses about how students will react and what they are likely to learn under certain conditions. As the initial profile of this chapter indicates, even the least reflective teachers operate on the basis of some theories of learning and subject matter.

Frame Experiments

When teachers move beyond the automatic and begin to consider the effects of their actions on students and to devise alternatives, they find that, as Schön points out, they "deal often with uncertainty, uniqueness, and conflict. The non-routine situations of practice are at least partly indeterminate and must somehow be made coherent" (157). To do that, Schön argues, they "frame" the "messy" problem by attending selectively to certain features, organizing them, and setting "a direction for action" (4), which becomes a "frame experiment."

Between the body of knowledge and theory available in a field and its skillful application in a concrete situation, there is always a "gap of knowledge." Bridging that gap requires "a thoughtful invention of new trials based on appreciation of the results of earlier moves. The application of such a rule to a concrete case must be mediated by an art of reflection-in-action" (158). "Skillful practitioners learn to conduct frame experiments in which they impose a kind of coherence on messy situations and thereby discover consequences and implications of their chosen frames" (157). For Schön, the "frame experiment" is the essence of reflective practice. I argue that it is also the basis of inquiry in teaching.

What would such a frame experiment look like in the teaching of composition? Over thirty years ago, well before the current popularity of "process instruction," my friend and colleague, James F. McCampbell, was teaching a class of ninth-graders, mostly boys, whose reading in a remedial reading class had improved enough to move into a regular English class. Because other students making this shift had experienced so much difficulty in expressing themselves in writing, we had decided to keep them together as a group to try to help them become more fluent as writers. At the time, no one was doing much of anything about the teaching of writing, let alone with students who were particularly weak as writers. The automatic response to weak writing for most teachers at the time was to go for the grammar book, reasoning that if only students knew their parts of speech, their syntax, and usage, they would be able to write adequately. Making this assumption required ignoring the fact that these means did not bring about the desired end, not even with students who did not experience inordinate difficulty with writing (Braddock, Lloyd-Jones, and Schön; Hillocks, *Research*).

Jim McCampbell noted that the papers attempted by these students were characterized not so much by poor spelling and lack of proper punctuation as by brevity. Most students in this group would not write much more than three or four lines for any assignment, no matter how much time had been involved in what we would call "prewriting" today. Jim was using our normal literature program, one that had been developed by the faculty over a period of several years (Hillocks and McCampbell). Generally, writing activities grew out of unit activities. For example, in a unit on the "Outcast," students wrote about their own feelings of being ostracized, their responses to and interpretations of events and situations in stories and poems, and a story in newspaper format about a case of ostracism.

Normally, our instructional emphasis was on the development of content as students wrote, shared drafts, provided feedback in small groups, and revised. Because these students normally wrote so little, McCampbell decided to jettison the usual emphasis and adopt one that concentrated on encouraging students to write more. After a classroom discussion that began with student reaction to a recent news story about a child who had been locked away in a trunk for many months and ended with students telling about how at one time or another they had felt left out, if not ostracized, he asked his students to write whatever they wished as long as it related somehow to the topic they had been discussing. As he circulated among the class as they wrote, he complimented students on what they had written and asked them to write more. He reported that students did produce more. In fact, after a few weeks, they were producing ten to fifteen times the amount they had prior to his beginning this "frame experiment." At the time, we all thought this appeared to be a remarkable result, one that we could attribute to Jim's having simplified the task and reinforced students as they wrote more.

Six Dimensions of Frame Experiments

What Jim did in this instance exemplifies at least six basic dimensions of the "frame experiment" essential to reflective teaching: (1) analyzing current student progress in relation to general course goals; (2) positing some change or range of possible changes sought in the writing of students; (3) selecting or devising a teaching strategy or set of strategies to implement the desired change; (4) devising a plan for implementing the teaching strategies; (5) assessing the impact of the teaching strategy in order to "discover consequences and implications of [the] chosen frames"; and, perhaps most important, (6) confirmation or change of the strategies used. For it is easy to imagine a teacher who, while noting the failure of students to learn what was taught, simply proceeds with more of the same, assuming that the "consequences and implications" of the "chosen frame" are the students' problems, not the teacher's. Let us examine each of these six in somewhat more detail.

The first dimension of reflective teaching appears to be an ongoing analysis of student progress in terms of the course goals. By *ongoing* I mean the daily consideration of student progress as indicated in responses during teacher-led discussions, participation in small groups, and the full variety of writing that is part of an active composition class. Most of these judgments will be informal, concerned with the quantity and character of individual responses in classroom talk and signs of understanding and change in pieces of writing at various stages of development; fewer will be formal, based on fully developed, final pieces of writing.

In reflective practice, assessment asks the extent to which the teaching and goals have been appropriate and effective for the students. Such assessments will be generated from the teacher's store of relevant theory and ideas garnered from practice and life experience. For assessment to be reflective, it must grow out of theory related to the particular teaching problem and students. In that sense, testing programs mandated by states and school districts or college English departments have nothing to do with reflective practice; nor do teacher-made tests that are administered without regard to specific teaching or learning problems.

In the example above, Jim McCampbell assessed the character of student writing in a way not foreseen by the existing course and unit structures. Those structures had assumed that students would have the ability or disposition to develop more extended pieces of writing. When Jim realized that his students did not, rather than simply bewailing the luck of the draw as others might well have done, he assumed that his students could move beyond their present stage and asked himself what he might do to help them. He also assumed that the problem was not one of intelligence or knowledge, but one of disposition. These students, he knew, had met with anything but success in the English classroom. Therefore he concluded that the ordinary goal of the unit (elaboration of ideas in different writing tasks) was inappropriate for his students. He adopted a modified goal. Students would still elaborate ideas, but developing a disposition to write would take priority.

The second dimension of reflective teaching is the envisionment of some desired change in light of the teacher's available theory. It requires deciding *in advance* what will be taken as evidence of success and generally means that the teacher can let the students know the purpose of instruction so that they can work toward the goal thoughtfully. To begin a personal narrative in the middle of an event (*in medias res*) might be such a goal, one that is based on a reasoned conception of personal-experience writing, an understanding of what students can already do, and some idea of how to help students reach that goal.

In the teaching of writing it is not possible, nor would it be desirable, to specify in advance precisely what success entails for any given piece of writing, certainly not with the precision engineers expect in specifying the characteristics and tolerances, let us say, for the construction of a bridge. Such standardization is antithetical to what most of us regard as good writing. At the same time, that we have and use criteria for judging writing is evident in a variety of settings. In Jim McCampbell's case above, the problem was rather a simple one, to write more words in connected discourse, at least loosely connected. . . .

The third feature of reflective teaching is selecting or inventing particular strategies for particular purposes and particular students. Jim McCampbell's strategy above, though simple, is a good example of reflection-in-action. Jim assessed the students' writing, brought to bear his knowledge of what life in classrooms is like for students who have difficulty, recalled a study or two reported at National Council of Teachers of English meetings that indicated focusing on "correctness" resulted in shorter and simpler sentences, and decided that what he really wanted was to encourage students to write more. He decided to allow students to write what they wanted following class discussions and to encourage them, however he could, to write more.

Many strategies that teachers adopt are quite complex. Often, they seem simply to work from a good idea, an insight into what students might enjoy and could do with some support in the form of a model, a special activity, perhaps simply clear directions and support from the teacher during the process. When teachers have the support of theory, they can invent many "good ideas." Processes of inventing, sequencing, and validating activities will be examined in later chapters.

Because Jim's strategy was so simple, the plan for implementing it (the fourth dimension) was also simple: (1) Circulate among students while they worked in class and make such statements as, "That's great! You've written a lot. Try to write some more." (2) Write comments on papers in the same vein: "Terrific! You have written more than you usually do. Keep it up!" Unfortunately most plans for implementation are not so simple.

The fifth and sixth dimensions involve assessing the impact of the strategies and deciding whether the plan might be worth using again. As with the first dimension, judging the impact of the teaching strategies on students' learning will be based on the goals and the theory underlying them. But to focus only on the goals and nothing more is to ignore too much that may occur incidentally. For example, research suggests that a focus on "correctness" may result in a general degradation of writing including fewer words and simpler sentences as students strive to avoid error (Adams; Hillocks, *Research*). Teachers who focus on "correctness" tend to ignore decreases in complexity of thought and syntax in favor of their selected goal.

On the other hand, unexpected benefits can be ignored as a result of the excessive myopia that a mechanical adherence to goals might foster. My students and I discovered that about twenty-one of the twenty-nine African American seventh-graders assigned to what is called in Chicago a "low-level" language arts class began to produce interesting and lively figurative language when they were involved in writing descriptions of sea shells so that one of their classmates could pick out the shell described from the whole batch of twenty-nine shells. Serendipity at its best. All we had hoped for was concrete detail.

In McCampbell's case, assessment was relatively simple. There was certainly no need for elaborate counting. A glance at earlier and later papers told the story clearly. Volume had increased enormously. Several students were producing between two hundred and three hundred words at each writing. The strategy was confirmed. Quality would be another question.

Frame Experiments and Theory

At the time of this success, we attributed the change in student production to Jim's having simplified the task and provided positive reinforcement on a regular schedule. These moves made good pedagogical sense, simply on the basis of our experience with students who had difficulty with reading. At the time, we thought of this as an essentially Skinnerian interpretation, one that is out of fashion now, rejected as mechanistic and shallow. But it is interesting that other, more recent theories also make use of the idea of positive reinforcement, for example, Csikszentmihalyi's *Flow: The Psychology of Optimal Experience.*

In retrospect, we can add a layer of interpretation. Bereiter and Scardamalia's studies of young children writing reveal that they knew a great deal more about given topics than they use in writing. In one study, students wrote about as many words as they would say in a conversational turn (Bereiter and Scardamalia). In a second study, the researchers urged the youngsters to write as much as they could, and they wrote about three times more than the students in the first study. When a researcher asked them simply to write more, they wrote about as much again as they had after the initial prompt. Additional requests to "write some more" yielded more (Scardamalia, Bereiter, and Goelman). These researchers reason that children have learned a schema for conversation but not one for writing. In their responses to assignments, they are fulfilling what they see as a conversational turn. It is possible that Jim's promptings to write more were serving the same function as that of the researcher in Bereiter and Scardamalia's studies.

Whatever the case, the point is that the act of considering such reasons in relation to experimental frames provides the theoretical base for reflective teaching. When teachers reason about choices, plan in light of those reasons, implement those plans, examine their impact on students, and revise and reformulate reasons and plans in light of all that experience, that conjunction constitutes theory-driven teaching. Such teachers are engaged in reflective practice and inquiry.

By definition, then, teachers who try new ideas, whether their own or those of others, without considering them in light of some organized body of assumptions and knowledge (including their own experience) that acts as a kind of preliminary testing ground for those ideas, cannot be considered reflective. A reflective practitioner will analyze a new idea in light of its appropriateness to the students and their present knowledge; its fit with available theory, experience, and the goals of teaching; and its probability for success as judged from the teacher's experience and knowledge. All parts of these theories may not be explicit, and those that are may not be fully tested or examined critically. But for reflective practitioners, the working or action theories they hold continue to grow as they conduct new "frame experiments."

Life Experience and Teaching

Our ideas and beliefs about teaching come not only from theory, practice, and research, but from a variety of perhaps disparate sources. Ideas for some of my activities that have been most popular with students came from watching my own children at play. Many have come from news stories of various kinds. Some I have been able to tie to theory; others have seemed atheoretical in their early uses but aided in the development of theories that I have worked with over the years. My students report similar experiences. Some have said that they seem always on the lookout for materials that will be irresistible to their students. That kind of search appears to become part of the life pattern of teachers who invent materials and activities. It is habit forming.

Other influences on teaching come from sources that we can no longer identify: values, attitudes, beliefs. Sometimes it seems important to take stock of these, to say "What is it I believe and why?" These personal beliefs are difficult to explain and even more difficult to pass on to another. One of the most important beliefs for my teaching comes, at least in part, from my father's firm faith in the value of struggling to succeed even in the face of defeat. It is embodied in his favorite story of Robert the Bruce. Legend says that after suffering six defeats at the hands of the English, the Bruce lay in a cave one night, discouraged, even considering giving up the struggle against the English. He watched a spider as it painstakingly climbed a fine thread to its web, only to fall back and start over again. Six times the spider made its way slowly up the thread. Six times it fell back. But on the seventh try, the spider succeeded. The Bruce took this lesson to heart, gathered his forces, and began a successful campaign against King Edward crowned by the Battle of Bannockburn, where Bruce succeeded in crushing the English even though he was outnumbered three to one.

No doubt the story of the spider is apocryphal. The Bruce did not keep a journal, after all. But there is truth in it. Though someone has failed any number of times, there is no evidence that the next try will not succeed. For with every trial we reinvent ourselves. Only the failure to try assures failure.

Works Cited

Adams, V.A. *A Study of the Effects of Two Methods of Teaching Composition to Twelfth Graders.* Unpublished doctoral dissertation. University of Illinois at Urbana-Champaign.

Atwell, N. *In the Middle: Writing, Reading, and Learning with Adolescents.* Portsmouth, NH: Heinemann, 1987.

Bereiter, C., and M. Scardamalia. "From Conversation to Composition: The Role of Instruction in a Developmental Process." *Advances in Instructional Psychology.* Ed. R. Glaser. Vol. 2. Hillsdale, NJ: Erlbaum, 1982. 1–64.

Braddock, R., R. Lloyd-Jones, and L. Schoer. *Research in Written Composition.* Champaign, IL: NCTE, 1963.

Cochran-Smith, M., and S. L. Lytle. *Inside/Outside: Teacher Research and Knowledge.* New York: Teachers College, 1993.

Csikszentmihalyi, M. *Flow: The Psychology of Optimal Experience.* New York: Harper, 1990.

Dewey, J. *Logic, the Theory of Inquiry.* New York: Holt, 1938.

Graves, D. *Writing: Teachers and Children at Work.* Portsmouth, NH: Heinemann, 1983.

Hillocks, G., Jr. "The Effects of Observational Activities on Student Writing." *Research in the Teaching of English* (Feb. 1979): 23–35.

Hillocks, G., Jr. "The Interaction of Instruction, Teacher Comment, and Revision in Teaching the Composing Process." *Research in the Teaching of English* (Oct. 1982): 261–78.

Hillocks, G., Jr. *Research on Written Composition: New Directions for Teaching.* Urbana, IL: National Conference on Research in English / ERIC Clearinghouse on Reading and Communication Skills, 1986.

Hillocks, G., Jr., and J. F. McCampbell. *An Introduction to a Curriculum: Grades 7–9.* Euclid, OH: Project English Demonstration Center / Euclid Central Junior High School and Western Reserve University, 1964.

Lederman, L. "Scientific Literacy." Lecture presented at the Workshop on Dimensions of Literacy and Numeracy, University of Chicago, 15 March 1991.

Murray, L. *English Grammar.* New York: Raynor, 1849.

North, S. *The Making of Knowledge in Composition: Portrait of an Emerging Field.* Portsmouth, NH: Heinemann, 1987.

Olson, C. B. *Thinking Writing: Fostering Critical Thinking through Writing.* Irvine, CA: HarperCollins, 1992.

Sager, C. "Improving the Quality of Written Composition through Pupil Use of Rating Scale." Diss. Boston U, 1973.

Scardamalia, M., C. Bereiter, and H. Goelman. "The Role of Production Factors in Writing Ability." *What Writers Know: The Language, Process, and Structure of Written Discourse.* Ed. M. Nystrand. New York: Academic P, 1982. 173–210.

Schön, D. A. *Educating the Reflective Practitioner: Toward a New Design for Teaching and Learning in the Professions.* San Francisco: Jossey-Bass, 1987.

Shaughnessy, M. *Errors and Expectations.* New York: Oxford UP, 1977.

Troyka, L. Q. "A study of the effect of simulation-gaming on expository prose competence of remedial English composition students." Diss. New York U, 1973.

Hillocks's Insights as a Resource for Your Teaching

1. Off the top of your head, list the key assumptions that shape your approach to teaching writing. Study the list, and pinpoint a pattern of connection among the key assumptions. Draft a statement that links and organizes these assumptions into a theory — a kind of mission statement for your classroom. What are the sources for your beliefs about writing pedagogy? Do you see gaps in these sources or perhaps conflicts between them? How have you been negotiating your way through these gaps in your daily practice of teaching? Do they suggest windows into possible areas of growth and improvement for either your theory or your practice?

2. In your journal, describe a classroom situation in which a particular pedagogic "routine" is not working. Describe exactly what comprises your practice, and, as closely as you can, pinpoint how and why it is missing the mark. Using what Hillocks calls the "six dimensions of frame experiments," try to explore ways to improve the situation you have described.

Hillocks's Insights as a Resource for the Writing Classroom

1. Share Hillocks's ideas about the teaching of writing as a reflective practice with your students. Explain in your terms how you might see the classroom as a scene of ongoing inquiry, adjustment, and improvement. Have the students write a brief account in their journals of classroom routines that they have experienced in the past that have fallen short of their intended goals. Ask the students why they thought the routine was less than successful. Discuss with them your own thoughts about what they have described.

2. Share your own theory of writing pedagogy with your students. Discuss the particular ways it informs your classroom practice — from the overall structure of your syllabus to the details of your briefest assignments. Discuss with them the ways you hope to fine-tune this theory — the dimensions of it that you hope to explore further with them via particular assignments.

ERIKA LINDEMANN   *Three Views of English 101*

In her description of three perspectives on the purpose of a writing course, Erika Lindemann challenges all writing instructors to identify and redefine "those institutional practices that we, as a community of English 101 teachers, find essential to our work." She borrows a method of inquiry from Young, Becker, and Pike, who in 1970 borrowed from physicists a practice of thinking through phenomena by shifting from one model of interpreting and explaining to another model (Do I see this as particle? Wave? Field?). Young, Becker, and Pike combined that practice with linguistic and rhetorical theories to invent heuristic strategies, particularly their "tagmemic grid" to help writers discover and generate ideas. Lindemann's argument gives a clear and practical overview of the pedagogical implications of our beliefs about writing and the roles of student writers.

This essay resumes a discussion that began in 1992, when Gary Tate and I debated the place of literature in Freshman English during the annual meeting of the Conference on College Composition and Communication. Those presentations, revised for *College English,* appeared in the March 1993 issue and generated several responses, four of which were published in the October 1993 issue. At that time, neither Tate nor I wished to respond to the responses, for our purpose had been to engage teachers in an important discussion about the nature and purpose of the first-year course. Having taken our turn in the conversation, we wanted others to have their say.

What they said was revealing. Most of the responses in *College English* take exception, not to Tate's position (that literature belongs in Freshman English) but to mine (that it does not). Though you will want to read the four responses as they originally appeared, let me abstract their principal claims here:

- If literature does not belong in the first-year writing course, then the first-year writing course does not belong in the English department.

- Reading books has become the occasion for [students'] own questions about human growth and change.

- Thus, combining composition and literature in required freshman English classes makes sense not only because it introduces first-year students to the type of writing necessary to succeed in college but also because, if it is done right, it is practical, enjoyable, an efficient way to develop critical thinking and the easiest way to introduce large numbers of students to cultural diversity.

- We should not allow the misuse of literature to discourage us from "right use."

Both Tate and I find these and other responses to our debate engaging but also puzzling. Colleagues invite us to lecture on their campuses or to appear together at conferences; they include the *College English* essays in their course packs for graduate classes; they urge us to make up our differences, unaware that we have been friends for many years and have co-edited a book. What began (I thought) as a discussion about the nature and purpose of the first-year course appears now to be part of a much different conversation. In this essay, I propose to examine the "event" begun by the Tate-Lindemann debate. Though it signals an important opportunity to explore what English 101 is, or could become, it also illustrates significant differences in the assumptions teachers make about the course. Unless we take into account these differences in perspective, we will be unable to establish sufficient common ground for moving the discussion forward.

To continue the conversation requires me to write more than a response. It requires new arguments, based perhaps but not necessarily on those already advanced. I now realize that many readers regarded the Tate-Lindemann debate as a political argument. In advocating that poetry, fiction, and drama be excluded from English 101, I created the perception that I was anti-literature, had sided with the compositionists in the so-called lit/comp split, advocated removing the course from English departments, and found misguided those students and teachers who love books. Writers are responsible, of course, for the impressions they create, but readers too construct texts, and their ways of reading my original essay have reminded me again how truly beleaguered writing and literature teachers sometimes feel in each other's company. Nevertheless, reducing my essay to a political claim disparaging the use of literature in a writing course allows readers to co-opt the larger pedagogical argument I was making. Regarding me as one of "them," a politically suspect, anti-literature compositionist, makes my argument easier to dismiss, especially by those who love literature and regularly teach it in English 101. Reading the essay politically shifts the ground just enough so that we do not have to deal with the "prior question" I posed at the beginning of my original essay: "We cannot usefully discuss the role of imaginative literature (however defined) in freshman English without first asking what the purpose of a writing course is."

To my mind, we still have not addressed the prior question. In the rest of this essay, I wish to return to it. I propose to advance three ways of seeing English 101. I am interested primarily in exploring why we hold such different opinions about the course, but I also believe that whether or not we include literature in English 101 depends on how we see it. Though it is difficult to sort pedagogical arguments from political, historical, and theoretical ones, I intend to focus primarily on *instruction*, not institutional relationships, departmental politics, or rhetorical theories. What we do in the classroom, it seems to me, reveals most clearly our different ways of seeing English 101, and these pedagogical differences remain the greatest obstacle to defining a common ground that helps us explain the course to one another, to our students, and to people within and outside the academy. Until we can find some common ground in instructional practices (or articulate our differences when we cannot), other discussions seem irrelevantly secondary. Until we can say why teachers and students meet together to read and write in a place called college, we cannot address other practices — placement tests, teacher training, program administration, hiring, and so on — meant to advance this work.

Each view of English 101 outlined here proceeds from a definition of *writing* — what it is and how we teach it — that varies among teachers. I want to examine the term *writing* and the consequent perspectives that shape our notions about English 101 by borrowing a method of inquiry described in Richard E. Young, Alton L. Becker, and Kenneth L. Pike's *Rhetoric: Discovery and Change:*

> We have found three perspectives particularly useful in exploring a unit of experience. These three perspectives are identified in Maxim 4: *A unit of experience*

can be viewed as a particle, or as a wave, or as a field. That is, the writer can choose to view any element of his experience *as if it were static, or as if it were dynamic, or as if it were a network of relationships or a part of a larger network.* Note carefully that a unit is not *either* a particle *or* a wave *or* a field but can rather be viewed as all three. (122)

In fairness to Young, Becker, and Pike, the heuristic procedure they describe makes it theoretically possible to generate nine, not just three, views of *writing*. To select only three, as I do here, oversimplifies the ways in which they overlap. For my purposes, however, three approaches illustrate that, despite our different ways of seeing English 101, we can still engage in a constructive conversation about the nature and purpose of the course.

Regarding writing as a particle, wave, and field generates three views of English 101, each perspective depending on whether we see writing *primarily* as a product, a process, or a system of social actions. Each view is "right" for the person who holds it, but each view also is partial and calls up quite different assumptions about the course and our reasons for teaching it as well. Each view has its own historical antecedents, its own theory of language, its own notions about how students learn, and its own political implications. Each view also assigns different values to literature, reading, and the role of texts. Individual teachers do not need to know *consciously* what these antecedents, theories, implications, notions, and values are, but each of us customarily assumes that others share our perspective — until some difference of opinion reminds us that other views are possible. A teacher who regards writing primarily as a product is likely to encounter problems talking to a teacher who sees writing as a system of social actions. Neither teacher may be conscious of the difference in perspective, but unless they both can create an appreciable space for some shared assumptions about the term *writing*, their conversation about English 101 is likely to be unproductive.

In what follows, I want to explain these three views in greater detail and, for each one, examine the following four questions: Given this view, what is the principal focus of English 101? What roles does each perspective assign teachers and students? What function does reading have in the course? Why do students write, and by what standards do we judge their work?

Writing as Product

The view that writing is a product is the oldest and most prevalent. Though its antecedents appear in classical rhetoric, its contemporary incarnation is not altogether classical because it slights invention and treats audience, language, and style differently. Even so, this view predominates among parents, students, many teachers, and most college administrators. Many product-centered teachers do not read *College English;* they may be unfamiliar with professional developments that have changed English 101 since they themselves took the course. Though teachers who regard writing as a product probably received no formal training in teaching either literature or composition, their coursework prepared them to be intelligent readers. They teach English 101 by remembering the writing courses they took (or what they heard about them) but do not rely on memory alone. Their instructional practices have changed in their encounters with students, in responding to their students' and their own successes and failures.

Seeing writing as a product appeals to these teachers because they already are oriented toward texts. They tend to be biographical or philosophical critics, who regard writing as a moral or aesthetic act. They believe that poetry, fiction, and drama convey important messages to readers about how to live well: "Reading books has become the occasion for [students'] own questions about human growth and change."

Product-centered or so-called traditional pedagogy regards English 101 as a content course centered in texts. If students read enough, they will encounter sufficient ideas to write about and eventually will write better. Given this view, reading texts, especially important works of belletristic literature, is essential to teaching writing well because literature offers ideas for students to write about and stylistic models to emulate. Students read these works, discuss them with the teacher and their classmates, and then address comparable subjects in their own essays.

Thinking is the most important form of invention in product-centered courses. Though what is meant by *thinking* is not always clear, many traditional teachers attempt to teach this skill by discussing logical fallacies and syllogistic reasoning or by designing exercises in "critical thinking." Other invention strategies receive scant attention perhaps for historical reasons, Renaissance rhetoricians having divorced invention from rhetoric to realign it with logic. Be that as it may, students in a product-centered English 101 course typically plan their responses to an assignment by reading a text and then thinking about it. Their reading and thinking may culminate in writing an outline, a "product" with its own formal requirements that nevertheless is intended to help writers arrange their material in some "logical" order.

When students write in a product-centered course, they usually write essays. The essay is the "product" traditional English teachers know best because it is a conventional form for interpreting poetry, fiction, and drama. However, other products are alive and well in traditional English 101 courses: outlines, five-paragraph themes, practice paragraphs, sentence diagrams, and workbook exercises. Because product-centered courses assign primacy to texts, teachers pay considerable attention to form. They assume that proficiency in constructing essays depends on developing confidence about "lesser forms." First, students may examine small units of language — parts of speech, for example — then practice writing sentences and paragraphs before composing whole essays. This sequence of instruction proceeds from studying the smallest units of language to constructing increasingly larger ones. It assumes that students must command the parts of a text — words, sentences, and paragraphs — before constructing the whole, before doing "real" writing. This piecemeal approach is especially common in community colleges where an entire course may focus exclusively on parts of speech or on writing paragraphs. In product-centered courses, literary texts support invention, but the building blocks of language provide the "content" for discussing arrangement and style.

Product-centered courses advance a notion of style defined rather narrowly to include principles governing sentence structure, word choice, mechanics, and usage. The stylistic principles students learn may derive from the study of literature, grammar, or a handbook. The teacher discusses these principles in class and encourages their imitation through exercises and eventually essay writing. Presumably, by imitating these principles, students will learn to apply them to forms of writing required in other college courses and beyond. Imitation is the watchword. Most traditional teachers accept without question the value of imitation as a pedagogical principle. Pedagogies based on imitation have never been subject to the scrutiny or controversy that attend newer teaching methods such as group work.

The teacher in this course assumes the role of an expert, a literary critic imparting knowledge about texts, ways of reading them, and principles governing their form and style. She uses primarily lecture and discussion to convey these subjects. She may give tests and pop quizzes (other products) to ensure that students have learned the material. Her writing assignments carefully spell out formal and stylistic requirements expected in students' final drafts. Because the topics of these assignments tend to derive from readings, invention or planning receives less attention than revision, an activity that enables students to correct their drafts and bring them closer stylistically to the models under study. Avoiding plagiarism is a concern because the teacher rarely sees early drafts; the focus is on the students' final product.

Because students write primarily for the teacher-as-critic, the teacher's standards for "good writing" apply. Teachers, in turn, often express frustration that their students' writing rarely exhibits the formal or stylistic competence of the models explicated so patiently in class. Given the evidence of students' writing, many product-centered teachers conclude that students do not command the knowledge of subject matter, form, and style to succeed, that they seem unable to learn by imitation, or that they are deficient in the expertise the teacher brings to class — a command of literature, or of grammar, or of the essay form. A few teachers may question altogether the legitimacy of the course. Though they believe in the timelessness of good writing, they rarely see it in students' papers and may persuade themselves that their expertise has fallen on deaf ears.

Because students are regarded as novices, deficient experts, or worse, unruly and incorrigible people, many traditional teachers mark students' papers as copyeditors would, rarely commenting on content but copiously "correcting" the text, generally at the level of the word or sentence. They attempt to note all errors, in part to justify the grade but also perhaps to signal to students (by referring them to the handbook) that they still have much to learn about style, usage, and mechanics. The teacher-as-critic works from a tradition of rules about form and style, matching students' texts against exemplary models characterizing this tradition. Annoyed by students who still haven't learned these principles after twelve years of schooling, the traditional teacher may express students' grades in tense mathematical formulas: three misspelled words or one comma splice earns an F. Though no points get added back for making sense or saying something meaningful, split grades sometimes reward content, even though mechanics are flawed.

Teachers who regard writing as a product make English 101 a product-centered course. Though such a course may draw its content from essay anthologies, newspapers, or television and movies, the majority of product-centered courses require students to read and write about literature. Literature provides ideas for students to contemplate, enables the teacher to assume the role of expert, and determines which stylistic principles are worth emulating. The curriculum moves students through discussions of principles, terminology, and subject matters that represent things to *know,* not what writers *do.* The exercises and assignments progress from the smallest to increasingly larger units of discourse, from the study of grammar to sentences to paragraphs to essays. Through practice based largely on imitation, students eventually should understand the etiquette of these forms and duplicate them. Though traditional teachers hope to make students sensitive to the possibilities of language, they generally focus on forms, formulas, terminology, and rules.

Writing as Process

The view that writing is a process has antecedents in classical rhetoric too, but in American education its intellectual parents are Ralph Waldo Emerson, Henry David Thoreau, and American Romantic writers. It enjoyed a resurgence during the late 1960s and influenced writing courses primarily through the work of Janet Emig, Ken Macrorie, Peter Elbow, and Donald M. Murray. To see writing as a process is to be concerned not so much with what writers *know* but with what they *do.* This view assumes that all writers negotiate similar processes in planning, drafting, and revising their work, yet every writer also approaches composing with unique cognitive abilities and strategies for solving the problem a writing task presents. Teachers who regard writing as a process may have training in literature or in composition, but what attracts them to the approach is that it focuses primarily on students.

Process-centered or so-called expressivist teaching assumes that, if students write often, on subjects of interest to them, they will discover who they are as writers and will gain confidence in making their ideas and feelings known. The student writer is the expert, commanding subjects and strategies for composing that the teacher has no access to because they are born of the writer's experience. The student has a self to discover, some truth to express, a unique language and voice. The assignments in process-centered courses encourage self-expression and the discovery of self. Though students write essays, they also may write letters, dialogues, journal entries, autobiographical material, personal reactions to reading assignments, or exploratory pieces that examine career goals, life goals, and interpersonal relationships.

The teacher in a process-centered course does not see himself as an expert in literature, style, or some other "content." Instead, he considers himself a more experienced, confident writer, giving students permission to reflect self-consciously on their composing and providing opportunities for students to explore the self and the world. He tries to give writers confidence by encouraging honesty and by respecting what students have to say. He also writes with his students from time to time, sharing with them his own wars with words.

Process-centered courses pay considerable attention to invention. Journals, freewriting, heuristics, analogies, and other ungraded prewriting activities enable students to discover what they want to say. Unlike traditional courses that begin with the study of a genre or a unit of language, the parts leading to the whole, process-centered courses begin with a student-self who must discover her message. Planning permits her to find her purpose, audience, and voice. Each assignment offers her an opportunity to plan, draft, and revise. Students repeatedly practice solving problems in writing, making decisions, and experimenting with linguistic and rhetorical options. Practice, not imitation, is the watchword. Because process-centered courses also are student-centered, they encourage students to discuss with one another their plans for tackling assignments or successive drafts. These workshops not only help students talk out their ideas and find an authentic voice but also make public the criteria for good writing, students helping other students attain them.

The most important text in such a course is student writing. Though reading is important, belletristic literature is not. Primarily, students read one another's work, their own creative acts, not works appearing in anthologies of essays or collections of poetry, fiction, and drama. Occasionally, published works may serve as examples of forms students are practicing (journal entries, dialogues, or autobiography) or of subjects they are exploring (growing up, learning about the self and others). Nevertheless, process-centered courses avoid large doses of literature for two reasons: it displaces the focus on student writing, and imitation, so central to traditional courses, has negative connotations.

Imitation is suspect because it can lead to dishonest uses of language and substitutes another's style for the writer's own fresh, original voice. Expressivist pedagogy supports a broad definition of style, defined as all of those choices writers make to create an honest voice expressing a message to an interested reader. Though writers must conform their messages to reasonable conventions of spelling, mechanics, and usage, these same rules and principles may prove confining. So students in process-centered courses have permission to play with language, especially meta-phor and analogy, figures that help readers understand the writer's personal world. An individual style that avoids cliché, jargon, and stereotypes is preferable to pre-tentious or derivative language (Macrorie calls it "Engfish"). Only by regarding lan-guage as suspect and sometimes stifling can students pierce Emerson's "rotten dic-tion" and learn to develop their own voices.

Because process-centered courses assume that students have important mes-sages to share, students write for one another as well as for the teacher. The criteria for good writing do not always derive from literary standards applied to finished drafts. Process is more important than product, so teachers may review (but do not grade) the scratchwork and multiple drafts for evidence of thoughtful planning and revision. Students see a great deal of writing as they discuss their work-in-progress and comment on classmates' drafts. The teacher guides these discussions by means of sample student drafts, training the class to appreciate a writer's strengths and to offer constructive responses to guide revision. When it comes to evaluating the final draft, sometimes simply "publishing" the piece is sufficient. Students may read their work to one another or send it to an appropriate audience. They may contribute their best writings to a class-produced anthology distributed at the end of the term.

When the teacher evaluates students' work, he may write comments only on a draft, not the final version. This feedback establishes a dialogue, the voice of the experienced teacher-writer engaging the student's voice and suggesting changes to consider for the final version. Or the student and teacher may discuss the draft in conference. In either event, the teacher will note strengths as well as weaknesses, will react to the message as a sympathetic reader, and will offer guidance about particular strategies and processes to try in the next draft. He responds to students' writing, not with mathematical formulas or corrections, but with questions, sugges-tions for further writing, and encouragement. Though students may write and re-write their work throughout the term, only some of it receives a grade; much of it remains ungraded. Eventually, students may add their finished pieces to a portfo-lio, which will receive a single grade at the end of the term. If the teacher grades individual assignments, he is likely to reward the honest voice, the truthful insight, and language that takes risks.

One important goal of a process-centered English 101 course is self-discovery, encouraging students to compose a self in language. Some teachers, however, find it difficult to balance the freedom and discipline necessary to cultivating truth-telling authentic voices. Some students quickly learn what sorts of selves the teacher would like to see in their writing. They invent a *dis*honest persona who will carry them to an A. Other students, those who remain truthful, may disturb the teacher even more. Their voices betray bigoted selves or selves so abused as children or so confused by experience that their writing embarrasses classmates and leaves the teacher won-dering how to respond. Though English 101 is not the place for saving or improving souls, process-centered courses have contributed much to the teaching of writing. They have renewed our appreciation for invention and given us respect for the mes-sages of our students.

Writing as System

The view that writing is a system emerged in the mid-1980s. Though it is as old as Aristotle's *Rhetoric,* its recent reappearance seems to be, in part, a reaction to the process-centered approach. It also reflects efforts to consolidate our understanding of how people write in contexts outside English 101. By studying writers in various professions as well as students writing for college courses, some teachers concluded that the process approach had oversimplified matters. In portraying writers as isolated individuals, it had divorced them from the social contexts in which language always operates. By restricting audience primarily to the self, expressivist pedagogy had stripped rhetoric of its important cultural, often political, force. Writers, these teachers claimed, live in a culture shaped by language, and language is always a form of social interaction. Writing, then, is a way of living in social groups, of interacting with others and having them interact with us. Though we write to make meaning and discover the self, we also write to make a difference in the world.

In an important essay first published in 1986, Marilyn Cooper responds to the process-centered view, with its images of the solitary author, by proposing instead an ecological model for writing. Just as natural environments comprise dynamic interlocking systems, in which organisms both respond to and alter their surroundings, writers are "continually engaged with a variety of socially constituted systems" (367). The ecological model usefully complicates the learning and teaching of writing because it reminds us of the social context in which all writers work. Cooper identifies at least five systems that every writer is necessarily involved in:

> The system of ideas is the means by which writers comprehend their world, to turn individual experiences and observations into knowledge. . . .
>
> The system of purposes is the means by which writers coordinate their actions. . . .
>
> The system of interpersonal interactions is the means by which writers regulate their access to one another. . . .
>
> The system of cultural norms is the means by which writers structure the larger groups of which they are members. . . .
>
> The system of textual forms is, obviously, the means by which writers communicate. (369–70)

Teachers who find the ecological model appealing are still defining its pedagogical implications. Their primary goal is to empower writers to membership in various discourse communities. Their classrooms are not always in a building on campus. They may teach writing in a community literacy project, a shelter for battered women, or a prison, where definitions of *community* and *empowerment* are complicated by social alienation and economic disenfranchisement. On campus, they may realize their goal best in cross-curricular courses that help students negotiate the demands of writing in varied disciplines. For these teachers, writing-across-the-curriculum is not a course in reading and then writing essays about issues such as global warming; such courses can be just as product-centered as traditional writing-about-literature courses are. Instead, these teachers encourage students to understand the systems that comprise the diverse discourse communities in which students find themselves. The ecological model suggests that, if students learn the systems and conventions characterizing particular discourse communities, they can successfully participate in and eventually even alter these communities.

To understand the discourses of the academy and gain confidence in approximating them, students must learn new ways of reading and writing. David Bartholomae's "Inventing the University" and Bartholomae and Anthony Petrosky's *Facts, Artifacts, and Counterfacts* help teachers understand how students encounter the academy and begin to find their place in it. No one seriously proposes that English 101 can prepare a first-year student to read and write the discourse of physics with the fluency of an experienced physicist. But English 101 can introduce students to some disciplinary assumptions about using language to make knowledge.

Seeing writing as a system contextualizes these disciplinary perspectives and raises questions student writers inevitably must answer for every course they take: What is a legitimate subject to write about in this discipline? What assertions and proofs are appropriate? What options do I have for defining my point of view and organizing my material? What should my writing look like, what conventions of form and style apply? Through careful reading and the analysis of a variety of texts, students examine how writers in the sciences, social sciences, and humanities handle these matters. Then they practice creating similar texts: journalistic essays, interpretations of music or art, case studies, analyses of data, and investigations of problems a discipline seeks to address. Assignments in this kind of English 101 course rarely call for self-expressive writing; instead, tasks resemble those that students encounter in the academy. They usually call for referential and persuasive writing because informing and persuading members of academic discourse communities (including professors) are significant functions of academic literacy.

Teachers adopting the ecological model attempt to forge their English 101 classes into a community of writers. They act as facilitators. Though students may begin the course having been schooled in the strategies of individual competition, the teacher deliberately fosters collaboration so that students must now learn from one another. In this model, students are always members of a stable writing group, working together for the entire term so that they develop trust in one another, accept responsibility for the group's successes and failures, and appreciate one another's diverse abilities and interests. Every class meeting involves group activities: developing schedules for a project and assigning research tasks, sharing information gained from independent reading and research, talking out plans for a draft, responding to and revising drafts, sometimes writing collaboratively. Discussions of readings also may begin in groups, each group talking about and writing out what it wishes to say about a text, then reporting its findings to the rest of the class. The teacher assumes responsibility for setting tasks that require learning by consensus, for monitoring students' work (intervening only to clarify tasks or help groups work efficiently), for synthesizing discussion, and for reporting on the quality of the work the groups have done. Community, collaboration, and responsibility are the watchwords.

System-centered courses treat invention, arrangement, and style as conventional, as practices admitting considerable variability. Each discourse community advances its own principles of good writing, which initiates must infer by reading and analyzing models intelligently and then imitating them. Because the opportunities for misreading are plentiful — as any student struggling to make sense of a difficult course knows — focusing exclusively on texts is not enough. Textual forms, as Cooper notes, are only one of several systems characterizing any discourse community. Students also must understand the community's culture, what subjects it finds worth writing about, how readers and writers relate to one another, what value people place on experience, observation, interpretation, speculation, objectivity, and so on. In the process, students learn how flexible such concepts as audience, purpose, and style are. Students come to understand that "good writing" requires making effective choices in juggling the demands of a task, a language, a rhetoric, and an audience.

Because most writing teachers feel at home in the humanities, they can "know" firsthand only some of the conventions governing academic discourse communities. They may find it next to impossible to judge what a biologist might call "good writing." While this obstacle altogether prevents some teachers from adopting the approach, other teachers have developed ways to learn more about the ecology of the academy. They learn much from talking with their students. They discuss writing with colleagues in other disciplines, requesting samples of their students' work and using their training in how to read texts to deduce rhetorical and linguistic principles that need attention in English 101. They invite faculty members to class to explain their expectations for effective student prose. Sometimes they team-teach writing courses linked to courses in other disciplines.

Adhering to the model can be difficult when it comes to evaluating students' writing. Ideally, the ecological model suggests that those most familiar with the system should judge the student's work, just as our own writing gets judged by those audiences for whom we intend it. By this logic, if an English 101 assignment asks students to approximate the discourses of the social sciences, social science faculty members should assess the responses. In some team-taught or linked courses they do, but for other types of system-centered English 101 classes, this arrangement is impractical. As a result, most teachers adopt an unhappy compromise. They maintain a faith that their students *eventually* will succeed in writing for other faculty members, but they adopt traditional methods of grading students' papers or borrow strategies that have worked well for process-centered teachers — a portfolio system, for example.

Dissatisfied with the compromise, a few teachers have explored an alternative emphasizing communal standards for good writing, standards developed in the context of the English 101 class itself. These teachers, trained in methods of holistic assessment, teach their students how to evaluate one another's work holistically. Guided by the requirements of a fully contextualized assignment, the class develops a scoring guide or a rubric. Because this rubric makes clear and public the criteria that will be used to assess students' responses, it also helps students plan, draft, and revise their work. After the teacher has collected the final drafts, students practice scoring actual responses (identified only by a "student number" such as the last four digits of a social security number) until they become calibrated to the rubric. Then they read and score their unidentified classmates' work. Anyone familiar with the literature on assessment understands the inherent dangers in such a system of evaluation. Nevertheless, with proper training, students can be as capable and conscientious as teachers in evaluating student writing responsibly. The method helps students internalize and apply criteria for effective writing much more quickly than teacher-controlled assessments do, and it reinforces the principle that students really are writing for one another, for the class-as-discourse-community, which will eventually judge their work.

Collaborative writing, group work, even students' evaluating one another's writing are not new. Nineteenth-century college students engaged in such practices in their debating societies, communities they formed to prepare themselves for the pulpit, the bar, and the lectern in ways that they believed their courses could not. While they are methods new to English 101 and likely to concern product- or process-centered teachers, pedagogies that foster active, communal learning nevertheless also enjoy the sanction of tradition. Moreover, the ecological model finds growing support among those faculty members and administrators outside English departments who believe that English 101 ought to prepare students for the writing they must do to succeed in the academy. In "Writing and Knowing: Toward Redefining the Writing Process," James A. Reither concludes that "writing and what writers do during writing cannot be artificially separated from the social-rhetorical situations in which writing gets done, from the conditions that enable writers to do what they do, and from the motives writers have for doing what they do" (621). Teachers adopting the ecological perspective have helped us direct writing back into the world, reminding us of the social context of all rhetorical activity.

A Common Ground?

All three views of *writing* exist simultaneously in our profession. Yet each perspective promotes an English 101 course that differs from the others with respect to its principal focus, the roles it assigns teachers and students, the function reading has in the course, the reasons why students write, and the standards by which we judge their work. Reading, for example, is important in all three models, but reading literature may not be. To see writing as product is to assert the primacy of texts; consequently, reading and discussing belletristic literature may occupy considerable prominence in a traditional English 101 class. To see writing as process is to advocate the importance of what people do *as* they read and write; so *how* students read may matter more than *what* they read in a process-centered English 101. Expressivist pedagogy supports a definition of *literature* enlarged to include genres other than poetry, fiction, and drama and at the same time also narrowed to focus on texts that have a self-expressive aim. To see writing as a system is to value the complicated contexts in which writers and readers use language to interact with one another; reading, like writing, offers a way into the conversation. A literary text, however, may not be a form by which writers and readers communicate in a particular discourse community, or it may be only one of many forms. So an English 101 course that examines the function of reading in the academy (or in a community outside it) may omit belletristic literature, primarily because reading and writing about literature are activities peculiar to only one discourse community students encounter. To omit literature, however, is not to ignore reading or the multitude of interpretive practices disciplines use to make knowledge. Because all disciplines comprise dynamic interlocking systems, we cannot assume that the ways of reading practiced in one discipline necessarily apply to any other.

What then is our common ground? I would argue that it is teaching. Regardless of which perspective shapes our peculiar brand of English 101, we all seek to give students practice with reading and writing. We hope to guide this practice in constructive ways, designing assignments and class activities that encourage students to see the power and possibility of language. We hold students responsible, not only to themselves, but also to an audience, a larger society of readers. As surrogates for this audience, we offer feedback on the reading and writing students do, not only to help them improve their performance but also to make familiar and useful the standards by which they may judge their own work. We do all this in the belief that what we teach is worth knowing and that our students are worth our respectful attention.

At the same time, if these statements characterize our common ground, they are too general to govern consistent instructional practices. For example, while we might agree on the value of "designing assignments and class activities that encourage students to see the power and possibility of language," we disagree about how best to implement this goal. As we have seen, the assignments and class activities in product-, process-, and system-centered courses all look quite different. Similarly, every sentence in the preceding paragraph admits diverse possibilities for giving students practice with reading and writing, holding students responsible to themselves and an audience, offering feedback on the reading and writing students do, and so on. Though teaching may not be shabby common ground on which to stand, our divergent views of English 101 may promote greater disagreement than consensus about pedagogical issues. Even so, I do not believe that English 101 teachers hold such disparate views of the course that they cannot talk with one another, a conversation it seems to me increasingly urgent for us all to participate in.

I am not suggesting that all English 101 courses must look alike or that all teachers must hold the same view of writing, teaching, or learning. But we also cannot justify our work as a profession by giving every English 101 teacher licence to do as he or she pleases. Some of the instructional practices I have described make sense, and others are ineffective. How do we best evaluate them?

It is clear to me that private criteria will not help us identify teaching strategies that merit either applause or condemnation. We now have access to considerable research and scholarship that deserves further discussion — in our journals, our conferences, and our classrooms. The pedagogical implications of this work need our collective, not merely our individual, attention. We need to adopt some of the strategies beginning teachers use to discuss with one another what they read and how it affects their teaching. In deciding what kind of teacher they wish to become, in developing a rhetoric of teaching, they not only ask questions about themselves, their students, and the purpose of English 101, but also keep testing their assumptions against the collective wisdom of a local as well as a national professional community.

Experienced teachers, however, too often suppose that the provisional answers they settled for after a year or so in the classroom will serve a lifetime. Because every writing teacher approaches his or her initiation into the profession individually, uniquely, each eventually comes to believe that "whatever works for me and my students is best." But such self-expressive assertions ignore the larger institutional and professional culture that in fact also has shaped our understanding of what it means to teach English 101 well. Private definitions of good teaching, persistent inconsistencies between what we say and what we do, and resistance to approaches that seem alien to us prevent the sort of communal thinking necessary to identifying our common ground and explaining our work to others, especially students, parents, and colleagues outside and within the profession.

In outlining here three views of English 101, I have tried to avoid arguing that one is "right." Making such a claim would amount to substituting my preference for judgments I believe we should make collectively. It would serve to close a conversation rather than continue it. My purpose instead has been to define in the differences I have described some important tensions to resolve. We ought not regard these differences as either a matter "simply" of personal taste or as implied criticisms of how some teachers conduct their classes. Paradoxically, pedagogical differences may represent opportunities to discover shared assumptions. Our differences may help us redefine those instructional practices that we, as a community of English 101 teachers, find essential to our work.

Works Cited

Bartholomae, David. "Inventing the University." *When a Writer Can't Write: Studies in Writer's Block and Other Composing Process Problems.* Ed. Mike Rose. New York: Guilford P, 1985. 134–65.

Bartholomae, David, and Anthony Petrosky, eds. *Facts, Artifacts and Counterfacts: Theory and Method for a Reading and Writing Course.* Portsmouth: Boynton, 1986.

Cooper, Marilyn M. "The Ecology of Writing." *College English* 48 (Apr. 1986): 364–75. Rpt. in Marilyn M. Cooper and Michael Holzman. *Writing as Social Action.* Portsmouth: Boynton, 1989.

Elbow, Peter. "The War between Reading and Writing — And How to End It." *Rhetoric Review* 12 (Fall 1993): 5–24.

"Four Comments on 'Two Views on the Use of Literature in Composition.'" *College English* 55 (Oct. 1993): 673–79.

Lindemann, Erika. "Freshman Composition: No Place for Literature." *College English* 55 (Mar. 1993): 311–16.

Reither, James A. "Writing and Knowing: Toward Redefining the Writing Process." *College English* 47 (Oct. 1985): 620–28.

Tate, Gary. "A Place for Literature in Freshman Composition." *College English* 55 (Mar. 1993): 317–21.

Wiener, Harvey S. "Collaborative Learning in the Classroom: A Guide to Evaluation." *College English* 48 (Jan. 1986): 52–61.

Young, Richard E., Alton L. Becker, and Kenneth L. Pike. *Rhetoric: Discovery and Change.* New York: Harcourt, 1970.

Lindemann's Insights as a Resource for Your Teaching

1. Notice how Lindemann reminds her teaching colleagues, "We need to adopt some of the strategies beginning teachers use to discuss with one another what they read and how it affects their teaching. . . . In developing a rhetoric of teaching, they not only ask questions about themselves, their students, and the purpose of English 101, but also keep testing their assumptions against the collective wisdom of a local as well as a national professional community." Lindemann describes, in effect, "reflective practitioners" who consciously and continuously identify, define, and refine both the philosophical basis of their pedagogies and the teaching practices they use to assist writers.

   To prompt reflective practice as an instructor, begin and maintain a double-entry or "dialogic" journal in which you focus on your experiences, feelings, discoveries, insights, and questions about the processes of teaching writing. In Chapter 2 of this volume, Ann E. Berthoff describes such a journal as a "dialectical notebook" and emphasizes how this technique assists writers to clarify, discover, and reflect on the meaning of what they encounter.

   Label one side of a notebook — or a computer screen if possible — "earlier." Use the other side for "later." On the "earlier" side, record impressions, anecdotes, and insights about your students; list and pose questions that occur to you about teaching writing; and respond to readings or to conversations you have with colleagues. Now and then, review entries, and use the other side to think about and respond to your earlier entries.

   Such a journal gives you a set of lenses for analyzing and evaluating your own teaching, becomes a cumulative record that might prompt a scholarly essay or research proposal, motivates you to look for professional writing that might respond to your questions, and prompts an ongoing dialogue with yourself about the recursive process of teaching — and learning to teach even better.

2. In your journal or elsewhere, list your assumptions about writing and writing courses, including any you might have that were not mentioned by Lindemann. Sketch out a description of your view of English 101. This early draft can be helpful as you clarify and shape what might be your "philosophy of teaching writing." It can also give you some ready responses when students ask, "Why do we have to do this?" If you share your beliefs, students might become more comfortable with you, the course, and class activities.

Lindemann's Insights as a Resource for the Writing Classroom

1. These three ways of viewing English 101 have also influenced writing courses and writing assignments from kindergarten through high school. Your students already have beliefs about the purpose of a writing course and about what writing is and how writers work. Ask them to draft letters in class the first week, defining the ways they view writing and their fears and expecta-

tions about the purpose and practices of the course. Ask for volunteers to read their letters, and follow up with a discussion, either in small groups or to the entire class. Then ask students to respond in their journals to something they heard that confirmed or challenged what they thought about writing, writers, or writing courses.

2. Lindemann lists "the study of grammar" as a recurring issue only for teachers who see writing as product and English 101 as a content course focused on texts. But, of course, whichever models we teach from, we all must think through and plan how to focus on the grammars students use in their texts. Many of your students will expect the course to emphasize correct grammar; some introductory letters will state, "I need to work on my grammar" and not much else. A primary concern of many faculty across the curriculum is whether grammar is taught in English 101. Some administrators will call you up as a kind of "grammar hotline" to resolve some grammatical choice their assistants questioned while word-processing memos.

   The issue is simple: not whether we work with grammar in the course, but when and how. By 1950, the *Encyclopedia for Educational Research* concluded that studying grammar has little or no effect on helping students think more clearly, and that formal study of grammar did not enhance or perhaps even affect grammatical competency in student writing. Repeatedly, rhetoricians and other scholars have concluded from empirical research that the teaching of grammar does not improve the quality of writing.

   Moreover, research into writers' revision habits has led to the following conclusions: writing teachers should not focus on grammatical problems in early drafts; and, when we identify and comment on grammatical problems, we should focus on patterns of error that appear in a student's work and emphasize how and why those errors impeded readers' understanding. You'll find in the annotated bibliography some articles that can help you reflect further on the issue of grammar and writing; some of these address specific teaching problems, such as assisting ESL writers with their fluency in English syntax.

JAMES BERLIN   *Rhetoric and Ideology in the Writing Class*

This classic essay provides an introduction to the theories that Berlin developed fully in Rhetoric and Reality: Writing Instruction in American Colleges, 1900–1985. *According to Berlin, an ideology addresses three questions: What exists? What is good? What is possible? Berlin suggests that there are three competing ideologies of writing instruction in our time: (1) cognitivist, (2) expressionist, and (3) social-epistemic. Each of these three ideologies carries its own notion of what writing is, what good writing and teaching are, and what we should aspire to accomplish with our students. Each of the three also represents a political stance, a take on the power relations that exist among author, audience, and text, as well as between teacher and student. This valuable essay can be used as a bibliography for further reading about these different approaches.*

The question of ideology has never been far from discussions of writing instruction in the modern American college. It is true that some rhetorics have denied their imbrication in ideology, doing so in the name of a disinterested scientism — as seen, for example, in various manifestations of current-traditional rhetoric. Most, however, have acknowledged the role of rhetoric in addressing competing discursive claims of value in the social, political, and cultural. This was particularly evident during the sixties and seventies, for example, as the writing classroom became one of the public areas for considering such strongly contested issues as Vietnam, civil rights, and economic equality. More recently the discussion of the relation between ideology and rhetoric has taken a new turn. Ideology is here foregrounded and problematized in a way that situates rhetoric within ideology, rather than ideology within rhetoric. In other words, instead of rhetoric acting as the transcendental recorder or arbiter of competing ideological claims, rhetoric is regarded as always already ideological. This position means that any examination of a rhetoric must first consider the ways its very discursive structure can be read so as to favor one version of economic, social, and political arrangements over other versions. A rhetoric then considers competing claims in these three realms from an ideological perspective made possible both by its constitution and by its application — the dialectical interaction between the rhetoric as text and the interpretive practices brought to it. A rhetoric can never be innocent, can never be a disinterested arbiter of the ideological claims of others because it is always already serving certain ideological claims. This perspective on ideology and rhetoric will be discussed in greater detail later. Here I merely wish to note that it has been forwarded most recently by such figures as Patricia Bizzell, David Bartholomae, Greg Myers, Victor Vitanza, and John Clifford and John Schilb. I have also called upon it in my monograph on writing instruction in twentieth-century American colleges. I would like to bring the discussion I began there up to date, focusing on ideology in the three rhetorics that have emerged as most conspicuous in classroom practices today: the rhetorics of cognitive psychology, of expressionism, and of a category I will call social-epistemic.

Each of these rhetorics occupies a distinct position in its relation to ideology. From the perspective offered here, the rhetoric of cognitive psychology refuses the ideological question altogether, claiming for itself the transcendent neutrality of science. This rhetoric is nonetheless easily preempted by a particular ideological position now in ascendancy because it encourages discursive practices that are compatible with dominant economic, social, and political formations. Expressionistic rhetoric, on the other hand, has always openly admitted its ideological predilections, opposing itself in no uncertain terms to the scientism of current-traditional rhetoric and the ideology it encourages. This rhetoric is, however, open to appropriation by the very forces it opposes in contradiction to its best intentions. Social-epistemic rhetoric is an alternative that is self-consciously aware of its ideological stand, making the very question of ideology the center of classroom activities, and in so doing providing itself a defense against preemption and a strategy for self-criticism and self-correction. This third rhetoric is the one I am forwarding here, and it provides the ground of my critique of its alternatives. In other words, I am arguing from ideology, contending that no other kind of argument is possible — a position that must first be explained.

Ideology is a term of great instability. This is true whether it is taken up by the Left or Right — as demonstrated, for example, by Raymond Williams in *Keywords* and *Marxism and Literature* and by Jorge Larrain in *The Concept of Ideology*. It is thus necessary to indicate at the outset the formulation that will be followed in a given discussion. Here I will rely on Göran Therborn's usage in *The Ideology of Power and the Power of Ideology*. Therborn, a Marxist sociologist at the University of Lund, Sweden, calls on the discussion of ideology found in Louis Althusser and on the discussion of power in Michel Foucault. I have chosen Therborn's adaptation of Althusser rather than Althusser himself because Therborn so effectively counters the ideology-science distinction of his source, a stance in which ideology is always false consciousness while a particular version of Marxism is defined as its scientific alternative in possession of objective truth. For Therborn, no position can lay claim to absolute, timeless truth, because finally all formulations are historically specific, arising out of the material conditions of a particular time and place. Choices in the economic, social, political, and cultural are thus always based on discursive practices that are interpretations, not mere transcriptions of some external, verifiable certainty. The choice for Therborn then is never between scientific truth and ideology, but between competing ideologies, competing discursive interpretations. Finally, Therborn calls upon Foucault's "micropolitics of power" (7) without placing subjects within a seamless web of inescapable, wholly determinative power relations. For Therborn, power can be identified and resisted in a meaningful way.

Therborn offers an especially valuable discussion for rhetoricians because of his emphasis on the discursive and dialogic nature of ideology. In other words, Therborn insists that ideology is transmitted through language practices that are always the center of conflict and contest:

> The operation of ideology in human life basically involves the constitution and patterning of how human beings live their lives as conscious, reflecting initiators of acts in a structured, meaningful world. Ideology operates as discourse, addressing or, as Althusser puts it, interpellating human beings as subjects. (15)

Conceived from the perspective of rhetoric, ideology provides the language to define the subject (the self), other subjects, the material world, and the relation of all of these to each other. Ideology is thus inscribed in language practices, entering all features of our experience.

Ideology for Therborn addresses three questions: "What exists? What is good? What is possible?" The first deals with epistemology, as Therborn explains: "what exists, and its corollary, what does not exist: that is, who we are, what the world is, what nature, society, men and women are like. In this way we acquire a sense of identity, becoming conscious of what is real and true; the visibility of the world is thereby structured by the distribution of spotlights, shadows, and darkness." Ideology thus interpellates the subject in a manner that determines what is real and what is illusory, and, most important, what is experienced and what remains outside the field of phenomenological experience, regardless of its actual material existence. Ideology also provides the subject with standards for making ethical and aesthetic decisions: "*what is good,* right, just, beautiful, attractive, enjoyable, and its opposites. In this way our desires become structured and normalized." Ideology provides the structure of desire, indicating what we will long for and pursue. Finally, ideology defines the limits of expectation: "*what is possible* and impossible; our sense of the mutability of our being-in-the-world and the consequences of change are hereby patterned, and our hopes, ambitions, and fears given shape" (18). This last is especially important since recognition of the existence of a condition (poverty, for example) and the desire for its change will go for nothing if ideology indicates that a change is simply not possible (the poor we have always with us). In other words, this last mode of interpellation is especially implicated in power relationships in a group or society, in deciding who has power and in determining what power can be expected to achieve.

Ideology always carries with it strong social endorsement, so that what we take to exist, to have value, and to be possible seems necessary, normal and inevitable — in the nature of things. Ideology also, as we have seen, always includes conceptions of how power should — again, in the nature of things — be distributed in a society. Power here means political force but covers as well social forces in everyday contacts. Power is an intrinsic part of ideology, defined and reinforced by it, determining, once again, who can act and what can be accomplished. These power relationships, furthermore, are inscribed in the discursive practices of daily experience — in the ways we use language and are used (interpellated) by it in ordinary parlance.

Finally, it should be noted that ideology is always pluralistic, a given historical moment displaying a variety of competing ideologies and a given individual reflecting one or another permutation of these conflicts, although the overall effect of these permutations tends to support the hegemony of the dominant class.

Cognitive Rhetoric

Cognitive rhetoric might be considered the heir apparent of current-traditional rhetoric, the rhetoric that appeared in conjunction with the new American university system during the final quarter of the last century. As Richard Ohmann has recently reminded us, this university was a response to the vagaries of competitive capitalism, the recurrent cycles of boom and bust that characterized the nineteenth-century economy. The university was an important part of the strategy to control this economic instability. Its role was to provide a center for experts engaging in "scientific" research designed to establish a body of knowledge that would rationalize all features of production, making it more efficient, more manageable, and, of course, more profitable. These experts were also charged with preparing the managers who were to take this new body of practical knowledge into the marketplace. The old nineteenth-century college had prepared an elite to assume its rightful place of leadership in church and state. The economic ideal outside the college was entirely separate, finding its fulfillment in the self-made, upwardly mobile entrepreneur who strikes it rich. The academic and the economic remained divided and discrete. In the new university, the two were joined as the path to success became a university degree in one of the new scientific specialities proven to be profitable in the world of industry and commerce. The new middle class of certified meritocrats had arrived. As I have indicated in my monograph on the nineteenth century, current-traditional rhetoric with its positivistic epistemology, its pretensions to scientific precision, and its managerial orientation was thoroughly compatible with the mission of this university.

Cognitive rhetoric has made similar claims to being scientific, although the method called upon is usually grounded in cognitive psychology. Janet Emig's *The Composing Process of Twelfth Graders* (1971), for example, attempted an empirical examination of the way students compose, calling on the developmental psychology of Jean Piaget in guiding her observations. In studying the cognitive skills observed in the composing behavior of twelve high school students, Emig was convinced that she could arrive at an understanding of the entire rhetorical context — the role of reality, audience, purpose, and even language in the composing act. Richard Larson was equally ambitious as throughout the seventies he called upon the developmental scheme of Jerome Bruner (as well as other psychologists) in proposing a problem-solving approach to writing, once again focusing on cognitive structures in arriving at an understanding of how college students compose. James Moffett and James Britton used a similar approach in dealing with the writing of students in grade school. For cognitive rhetoric, the structures of the mind correspond in perfect harmony with the structures of the material world, the minds of the audience, and the units of language (see my *Rhetoric and Reality* for a fuller discussion of this history). This school has been the strongest proponent of addressing the "process" rather than the "product" of writing in the classroom — although other theories have also supported this position even as they put forward a different process. Today the cognitivists continue to be a strong force in composition studies. The leading experimental research in this area is found in the work of Linda Flower and John Hayes, and I would like to focus the discussion of the relation of ideology and cognitive rhetoric on their contribution.

There is no question that Flower considers her work to fall within the domain of science, admitting her debt to cognitive psychology (Hayes' area of specialization), which she describes as "a young field — a reaction, in part, against assumptions of behaviorism" (vii). Her statements about the composing process of writing, furthermore, are based on empirical findings, on "data-based" study, specifically the analysis of protocols recording the writing choices of both experienced and inexperienced writers. This empirical study has revealed to Flower and Hayes — as reported in "A Cognitive Process Theory of Writing" — that there are three elements involved in composing: the task environment, including such external constraints as the rhetorical problem and the text so far produced; the writer's long-term memory, that is, the knowledge of the subject considered and the knowledge of how to write; and the writing processes that go on in the writer's mind. This last is, of course, of central importance to them, based as it is on the invariable structures of the mind that operate in a rational, although not totally predictable, way.

The mental processes of writing fall into three stages: the planning stage, further divided into generating, organizing, and goal setting; the translating stage, the point at which thoughts are put into words; and the reviewing stage, made up of evaluating and revising. This process is hierarchical, meaning that "components of the process [are] imbedded within other components" (Flower and Hayes 375), and it is recursive, the stages repeating themselves, although in no predetermined order. In other words, the elements of the process can be identified and their functions described, but the order of their operation will vary from task to task and from individual to individual, even though the practices of good writers will be very similar to each other (for a rich critique, see Bizzell). The "keystone" of the cognitive process theory, Flower and Hayes explain, is the discovery that writing is a goal-directed process: "In the act of composing, writers create a hierarchical network of goals and these in turn guide the writing process." Because of this goal directedness, the protocols of good writers examined consistently "reveal a coherent underlying structure" (377).

It is clear from this brief description that Flower and Hayes focus on the individual mind, finding in the protocol reports evidence of cognitive structures in operation. Writing becomes, as Flower's textbook indicates, just another instance of "problem-solving processes people use every day," most importantly the processes of experts, such as "master chess players, inventors, successful scientists, business managers, and artists" (Flower 2–3). Flower's textbook says little about artists, however, focusing instead on "real-world" writing. She has accordingly called upon the help of a colleague from the School of Industrial Management (vi), and she includes a concern for consulting reports and proposals as well as ordinary academic research reports — "the real world of college and work" (4). This focus on the professional activity of experts is always conceived in personal and managerial terms: "In brief, the goal of this book is to help you gain more control of your own composing process: to become more efficient as a writer and more effective with your readers" (2). And the emphasis is on self-made goals, "on your own goals as a writer, on what you want to do and say" (3).

As I said at the outset, the rhetoric of cognitive psychology refuses the ideological question, resting secure instead in its scientific examination of the composing process. It is possible, however, to see this rhetoric as being eminently suited to appropriation by the proponents of a particular ideological stance, a stance consistent with the modern college's commitment to preparing students for the world of corporate capitalism. And as we have seen above, the professional orientation of *Problem-Solving Strategies for Writing* — its preoccupation with "analytical writing" (4) in the "real world" of experts — renders it especially open to this appropriation.

For cognitive rhetoric, the real is the rational. As we observed above, for Flower and Hayes the most important features of composing are those which can be analyzed into discrete units and expressed in linear, hierarchical terms, however unpredictably recursive these terms may be. The mind is regarded as a set of structures that performs in a rational manner, adjusting and reordering functions in the service of the goals of the individual. The goals themselves are considered unexceptionally apparent in the very nature of things, immediately identifiable as worthy of pursuit. Nowhere, for example, do Flower and Hayes question the worth of the goals pursued by the manager, scientist, or writer. The business of cognitive psychology is to enable us to learn to think in a way that will realize goals, not deliberate about their value: "I have assumed that, whatever your goals, you are interested in discovering better ways to achieve them" (Flower and Hayes 1). The world is correspondingly structured to foreground goals inherently worth pursuing — whether these are private or professional, in writing or in work. And the mind is happily structured to perceive these goals and, thanks to the proper cognitive development of the observer — usually an expert — to attain them. Obstacles to achieving these goals are labelled "problems," disruptions in the natural order, impediments that must be removed. The strategies to resolve these problems are called "heuristics," discovery procedures that "are the heart of problem solving" (36). Significantly, these heuristics are not themselves rational, are not linear and predictable — "they do not come with a guarantee" (37). They appear normally as unconscious, intuitive processes that problem solvers use without realizing it, but even when formulated for conscious application they are never foolproof. Heuristics are only as good or bad as the person using them, so that problem solving is finally the act of an individual performing in isolation, solitary and alone (see Brodkey). As Flower explains: "Good writers not only have a large repertory of powerful strategies, but they have sufficient self-awareness of their own process to draw on these alternative techniques as they need them. In other words, they guide their own creative process" (37). The community addressed enters the process only after problems are analyzed and solved, at which time the concern is "adapting your writing to the needs of the reader" (1). Furthermore, although the heuristics used in problem solving are not themselves rational, the discoveries made through them always conform to the mensurable nature of reality, displaying "an underlying hierarchical organization" (10) that reflects the rationality of the world. Finally, language is regarded as a system of rational signs that is compatible with the mind and the external world, enabling the "translating" or "transforming" of the non-verbal intellectual operations into the verbal. There is thus a beneficent correspondence between the structures of the mind, the structures of the world, the structures of the minds of the audience, and the structures of language.

This entire scheme can be seen as analogous to the instrumental method of the modern corporation, the place where members of the meritocratic middle class, the 20 percent or so of the work force of certified college graduates, make a handsome living managing a capitalist economy (see Braverman ch. 18). Their work life is designed to turn goal-seeking and problem-solving behavior into profits. As we have seen in Flower, the rationalization of the writing process is specifically designated an extension of the rationalization of economic activity. The pursuit of self-evident and unquestioned goals in the composing process parallels the pursuit of self-evident and unquestioned profit-making goals in the corporate marketplace: "whatever your goals are, you are interested in achieving better ways to achieve them" (Flower 12). The purpose of writing is to create a commodified text (see Clines) that belongs to the individual and has exchange value — "problem solving turns composing into a goal-directed journey — writing my way to where I want to be" (4) — just as the end of corporate activity is to create a privately-owned profit. Furthermore, while all problem solvers use heuristic procedures — whether in solving hierarchically conceived writing problems or hierarchically conceived management problems — some are better at using them than are others. These individuals inevitably distinguish themselves, rise up the corporate ladder, and leave the less competent and less competitive behind. The class system is thus validated since it is clear that the rationality of the universe is more readily detected by a certain group of individuals. Cognitive psychologists specializing in childhood development can even isolate the environmental features of the children who will become excellent problem solvers, those destined to earn the highest grades in school, the highest college entrance scores, and, finally, the highest salaries. Middle-class parents are thus led to begin the cultivation of their children's cognitive skills as soon as possible — even in utero — and of course there are no shortage of expert-designed commodities that can be purchased to aid in the activity. That the cognitive skills leading to success may be the product of the experiences of a particular social class rather than the perfecting of inherent mental structures, skills encouraged because they serve the interests of a ruling economic elite, is never considered in the "scientific" investigation of the mind.

Cognitive rhetoric can be seen from this perspective as compatible with the ideology of the meritocratic university described in Bowles and Gintis' *Schooling in Capitalist America.* Power in this system is relegated to university-certified experts, those individuals who have the cognitive skills and the training for problem solving. Since social, political, and cultural problems are, like the economic, the result of failures in rational goal-seeking behavior, these same experts are the best prepared to address these matters as well. Furthermore, the agreement of experts in addressing commonly shared problems in the economic and political arenas is additional confirmation of their claim to power: all trained observers, after all, come to the same conclusions. Once again, the possibility that this consensus about what is good and possible is a product of class interest and class experience is never seriously entertained. Cognitive rhetoric, then, in its refusal of the ideological question leaves itself open to association with the reification of technocratic science characteristic of late capitalism, as discussed, for example, by Georg Lukács, Herbert Marcuse, and Jürgen Habermas (see Larrain ch. 6). Certain structures of the material world, the mind, and language, and their correspondence with certain goals, problem-solving heuristics, and solutions in the economic, social, and political are regarded as inherent features of the universe, existing apart from human social intervention. The existent, the good, and the possible are inscribed in the very nature of things as indisputable scientific facts, rather than being seen as humanly devised social constructions always remaining open to discussion.

Expressionistic Rhetoric

Expressionistic rhetoric developed during the first two decades of the twentieth century and was especially prominent after World War I. Its earliest predecessor was the elitist rhetoric of liberal culture, a scheme arguing for writing as a gift of genius, an art accessible only to a few, and then requiring years of literary study. In expressionistic rhetoric, this gift is democratized, writing becoming an art of which all are capable. This rhetoric has usually been closely allied with theories of psychology that argued for the inherent goodness of the individual, a goodness distorted by excessive contact with others in groups and institutions. In this it is the descendant of Rousseau on the one hand and of the romantic recoil from the urban horrors created by nineteenth-century capitalism on the other. Left to our own devices, this position maintains, each of us would grow and mature in harmony. Unfortunately, hardly anyone is allowed this uninhibited development, and so the fallen state of society is both the cause and the effect of its own distortion, as well as the corrupter of its individual members. In the twenties, a bowdlerized version of Freud was called upon in support of this conception of human nature. More recently — during the sixties and after — the theories of such figures as Carl Rogers, Abraham Maslow, Eric Fromm, and even Carl Jung have been invoked in its support. (For a fuller discussion of the history and character of expressionistic rhetoric offered here, see my "Contemporary Composition," and *Rhetoric and Reality* 43–46, 73–81, 159–65).

For this rhetoric, the existent is located within the individual subject. While the reality of the material, the social, and the linguistic are never denied, they are considered significant only insofar as they serve the needs of the individual. All fulfill their true function only when being exploited in the interests of locating the individual's authentic nature. Writing can be seen as a paradigmatic instance of this activity. It is an art, a creative act in which the process — the discovery of the true self — is as important as the product — the self discovered and expressed. The individual's use of the not-self in discovering the self takes place in a specific way. The material world provides sensory images that can be used in order to explore the self, the sensations leading to the apprehending-source of all experience. More important, these sense impressions can be coupled with language to provide metaphors to express the experience of the self, an experience which transcends ordinary non-metaphoric language but can be suggested through original figures and tropes. This original language in turn can be studied by others to understand the self and can even awaken in readers the experience of their selves. Authentic self-expression can thus lead to authentic self-experience for both the writer and the reader. The most important measure of authenticity, of genuine self-discovery and self-revelation, furthermore, is the presence of originality in expression; and this is the case whether the writer is creating poetry or writing a business report. Discovering the true self in writing will simultaneously enable the individual to discover the truth of the situation which evoked the writing, a situation that, needless to say, must always be compatible with the development of the self, and this leads to the ideological dimension of the scheme.

Most proponents of expressionistic rhetoric during the sixties and seventies were unsparingly critical of the dominant social, political, and cultural practices of the time. The most extreme of these critics demanded that the writing classroom work explicitly toward liberating students from the shackles of a corrupt society. This is seen most vividly in the effort known as "composition as happening." From this perspective, the alienating and fragmenting experience of the authoritarian institutional setting can be resisted by providing students with concrete experiences that alter political consciousness through challenging official versions of reality. Writing in response to such activities as making collages and sculptures, listening to the same piece of music in different settings, and engaging in random and irrational acts in the classroom was to enable students to experience "structure in unstructure; a random series of ordered events; order in chaos; the logical illogicality of dreams" (Lutz 35). The aim was to encourage students to resist the "interpretations of experience embodied in the language of others [so as] to order their own experience" (Paull and Kligerman 150). This more extreme form of political activism in the classroom was harshly criticized by the moderate wing of the expressionist camp, and it is this group that eventually became dominant. The names of Ken Macrorie, Walker Gibson, William Coles, Jr., Donald Murray, and Peter Elbow were the most visible in this counter effort. Significantly, these figures continued the ideological critique of the dominant culture while avoiding the overt politicizing of the classroom. In discussing the ideological position they encouraged, a position that continues to characterize them today, I will focus on the work of Murray and Elbow, both of whom explicitly address the political in their work.

From this perspective, power within society ought always to be vested in the individual. In Elbow, for example, power is an abiding concern — apparent in the title to his recent textbook *(Writing with Power)*, as well as in the opening pledge of his first to help students become "less helpless, both personally and politically" by enabling them to get "control over words" *(Writing without Teachers* vii). This power is consistently defined in personal terms: "power comes from the words somehow fitting the *writer* (not necessarily the reader) . . . power comes from the words somehow fitting *what they are about"* *(Writing with Power* 280). Power is a product of a configuration involving the individual and her encounter with the world, and for both Murray and Elbow this is a function of realizing one's unique voice. Murray's discussion of the place of politics in the classroom is appropriately titled "Finding Your Own Voice: Teaching Composition in an Age of Dissent," and Elbow emphasizes, "If I want power, I've got to use *my* voice" *(Embracing Contraries* 202). This focus on the individual does not mean that no community is to be encouraged, as expressionists repeatedly acknowledge that communal arrangements must be made, that, in Elbow's words, "the less acceptable hunger for participation and merging is met" (98). The community's right to exist, however, stands only insofar as it serves all of its members as individuals. It is, after all, only the individual, acting alone and apart from others, who can determine the existent, the good, and the possible. For Murray, the student "must hear the contradictory counsel of his readers, so that he learns when to ignore his teachers and his peers, listening to himself after evaluating what has been said about his writing and considering what he can do to make it work" ("Finding Your Own Voice" 144–45). For Elbow, the audience can be used to help improve our writing, but " the goal should be to move toward the condition where we don't necessarily need it in order to speak or write well." Since audiences can also inhibit us, Elbow continues, "we need to learn to write what is true and what needs saying even if the whole world is scandalized. We need to learn eventually to find in *ourselves* the support which — perhaps for a long time — we must seek openly from others" *(Writing with Power* 190).

Thus, political change can only be considered by individuals and in individual terms. Elbow, for example, praises Freire's focus on the individual in seeking the contradictions of experience in the classroom but refuses to take into account the social dimension of this pedagogy, finally using Freire's thought as an occasion for arriving at a personal realization of a "psychological contradiction, not an economic one or political one," at the core of our culture *(Embracing Contraries* 98). The underlying conviction of expressionists is that when individuals are spared the distorting effects of a repressive social order, their privately determined truths will correspond to the privately determined truths of all others: my best and deepest vision supports the same universal and eternal laws as everyone else's best and deepest vision. Thus, in *Writing without Teachers* Elbow admits that his knowledge about writing was gathered primarily from personal experience, and that he has no reservations about "making universal generalizations upon a sample of one" (16). Murray is even more explicit in his first edition of *A Writer Teaches Writing:* "the writer is on a search for himself. If he finds himself he will find an audience, because all of us have the same common core. And when he digs deeply into himself and is able to define himself, he will find others who will read with a shock of recognition what he has written" (4).

This rhetoric thus includes a denunciation of economic, political, and social pressures to conform — to engage in various forms of corporate-sponsored thought, feeling, and behavior. In indirectly but unmistakably decrying the dehumanizing effects of industrial capitalism, expressionistic rhetoric insists on defamiliarizing experience, on getting beyond the corruptions of the individual authorized by the language of commodified culture in order to re-experience the self and through it the external world, finding in this activity possibilities for a new order. For expressionistic rhetoric, the correct response to the imposition of current economic, political, and social arrangements is thus resistance, but a resistance that is always construed in individual terms. Collective retaliation poses as much of a threat to individual integrity as do the collective forces being resisted, and so is itself suspect. The only hope in a society working to destroy the uniqueness of the individual is for each of us to assert our individuality against the tyranny of the authoritarian corporation, state, and society. Strategies for doing so must of course be left to the individual, each lighting one small candle in order to create a brighter world.

Expressionistic rhetoric continues to thrive in high schools and at a number of colleges and universities. At first glance, this is surprising, unexpected of a rhetoric that is openly opposed to establishment practices. This subversiveness, however, is more apparent than real. In the first place, expressionistic rhetoric is inherently and debilitatingly divisive of political protest, suggesting that effective resistance can only be offered by individuals, each acting alone. Given the isolation and incoherence of such protest, gestures genuinely threatening to the establishment are difficult to accomplish. Beyond this, expressionistic rhetoric is easily co-opted by the very capitalist forces it opposes. After all, this rhetoric can be used to reinforce the entrepreneurial virtues capitalism most values: individualism, private initiative, the confidence for risk taking, the right to be contentious with authority (especially the state). It is indeed not too much to say that the ruling elites in business, industry, and government are those most likely to nod in assent to the ideology inscribed in expressionistic rhetoric. The members of this class see their lives as embodying the creative realization of the self, exploiting the material, social, and political conditions of the world in order to assert a private vision, a vision which, despite its uniqueness, finally represents humankind's best nature. (That this vision in fact represents the interests of a particular class, not all classes, is of course not acknowledged.) Those who have not attained the positions which enable them to exert this freedom have been prevented from doing so, this ideology argues, not by economic and class constraints, but by their own unwillingness to pursue a private vision, and this interpretation is often embraced by those excluded from the ruling elite as well as by the ruling elite itself. In other words, even those most constrained by their positions in the class structure may support the ideology found in expressionistic rhetoric in some form. This is most commonly done by divorcing the self from the alienation of work, separating work experience from other experience so that self-discovery and -fulfillment take place away from the job. For some this may lead to the pursuit of self-expression in intellectual or aesthetic pursuits. For most this quest results in a variety of forms of consumer behavior, identifying individual self-expression with the consumption of some commodity. This separation of work from authentic human activity is likewise reinforced in expressionistic rhetoric, as a glance at any of the textbooks it has inspired will reveal.

Social-Epistemic Rhetoric

The last rhetoric to be considered I will call social-epistemic rhetoric, in so doing distinguishing it from the psychological-epistemic rhetoric that I am convinced is a form of expressionism. (The latter is found in Kenneth Dowst and in Cyril Knoblauch and Lil Brannon, although Knoblauch's recent *College English* essay displays him moving into the social camp. I have discussed the notion of epistemic rhetoric and these two varieties of it in *Rhetoric and Reality* 145–55, 165–77, and 184–

85). There have been a number of spokespersons for social-epistemic rhetoric over the last twenty years: Kenneth Burke, Richard Ohmann, the team of Richard Young, Alton Becker and Kenneth Pike, Kenneth Bruffee, W. Ross Winterowd, Ann Berthoff, Janice Lauer, and, more recently, Karen Burke Lefever, Lester Faigley, David Bartholomae, Greg Myers, Patricia Bizzell, and others. In grouping these figures together I do not intend to deny their obvious disagreements with each other. For example, Myers, a Leftist, has offered a lengthy critique of Bruffee, who — along with Winterowd and Young, Becker and Pike — is certainly of the Center politically. There are indeed as many conflicts among the members of this group as there are harmonies. They are brought together here, however, because they share a notion of rhetoric as a political act involving a dialectical interaction engaging the material, the social, and the individual writer, with language as the agency of mediation. Their positions, furthermore, include an historicist orientation, the realization that a rhetoric is an historically specific social formation that must perforce change over time; and this feature in turn makes possible reflexiveness and revision as the inherently ideological nature of rhetoric is continually acknowledged. The most complete realization of this rhetoric for the classroom is to be found in Ira Shor's *Critical Teaching and Everyday Life*. Before considering it, I would like to discuss the distinguishing features of a fully articulated social-epistemic rhetoric.

For social-epistemic rhetoric, the real is located in a relationship that involves the dialectical interaction of the observer, the discourse community (social group) in which the observer is functioning, and the material conditions of existence. Knowledge is never found in any one of these but can only be posited as a product of the dialectic in which all three come together. (More of this in a moment.) Most important, this dialectic is grounded in language: the observer, the discourse community, and the material conditions of existence are all verbal constructs. This does not mean that the three do not exist apart from language: they do. This does mean that we cannot talk and write about them — indeed, we cannot know them — apart from language. Furthermore, since language is a social phenomenon that is a product of a particular historical moment, our notions of the observing self, the communities in which the self functions, and the very structures of the material world are social constructions — all specific to a particular time and culture. These social constructions are thus inscribed in the very language we are given to inhabit in responding to our experience. Language, as Raymond Williams explains in an application of Bakhtin (*Marxism and Literature* 21–44), is one of the material and social conditions involved in producing a culture. This means that in studying rhetoric — the ways discourse is generated — we are studying the ways in which knowledge comes into existence. Knowledge, after all, is an historically bound social fabrication rather than an eternal and invariable phenomenon located in some uncomplicated repository — in the material object or in the subject or in the social realm. This brings us back to the matter of the dialectic.

Understanding this dialectical notion of knowledge is the most difficult feature of social-epistemic rhetoric. Psychological-epistemic rhetoric grants that rhetoric arrives at knowledge, but this meaning-generating activity is always located in a transcendent self, a subject who directs the discovery and arrives through it finally only at a better understanding of the self and its operation — this self comprehension being the end of all knowledge. For social-epistemic rhetoric, the subject is itself a social construct that emerges through the linguistically circumscribed interaction of the individual, the community, and the material world. There is no universal, eternal, and authentic self that beneath all appearances is at one with all other selves. The self is always a creation of a particular historical and cultural moment. This is not to say that individuals do not ever act as individuals. It is to assert, however, that they never act with complete freedom. As Marx indicated, we make our own histories, but we do not make them just as we wish. Our consciousness is in large part a product of our material conditions. But our material conditions are also in part the products of our consciousness. Both consciousness and the material conditions influence each other, and they are both imbricated in social relations defined and worked out through language. In other words, the ways in which the subject understands and is affected by material conditions is circumscribed by socially devised definitions, by the community in which the subject lives. The community in turn is influenced by the subject and the material conditions of the moment. Thus, the perceiving subject, the discourse communities of which the subject is a part, and the material world itself are all the constructions of an historical discourse, of the ideological formulations inscribed in the language-mediated practical activity of a particular time and place. We are lodged within a hermeneutic circle, although not one that is impervious to change.

This scheme does not lead to an anarchistic relativism. It does, however, indicate that arguments based on the permanent rational structures of the universe or on the evidence of the deepest and most profound personal intuition should not be accepted without question. The material, the social, and the subjective are at once the producers and the products of ideology, and ideology must continually be challenged so as to reveal its economic and political consequences for individuals. In other words, what are the effects of our knowledge? Who benefits from a given version of truth? How are the material benefits of society distributed? What is the relation of this distribution to social relations? Do these relations encourage conflict? To whom does our knowledge designate power? In short, social-epistemic rhetoric views knowledge as an arena of ideological conflict: there are no arguments from transcendent truth since all arguments arise in ideology. It thus inevitably supports economic, social, political, and cultural democracy. Because there are no "natural laws" or "universal truths" that indicate what exists, what is good, what is possible, and how power is to be distributed, no class or group or individual has privileged access to decisions on these matters. They must be continually decided by all and for all in a way appropriate to our own historical moment. Finally, because of this historicist orientation, social-epistemic rhetoric contains within it the means for self-criticism and self-revision. Human responses to the material conditions of existence, the social relations they encourage, and the interpellations of subjects within them are always already ideological, are always already interpretations that must be constantly revised in the interests of the greater participation of all, for the greater good of all. And this of course implies an awareness of the ways in which rhetorics can privilege some at the expense of others, according the chosen few an unequal share of power, perquisites, and material benefits.

Social-epistemic rhetoric thus offers an explicit critique of economic, political, and social arrangements, the counterpart of the implicit critique found in expressionistic rhetoric. However, here the source and the solution of these arrangements are described quite differently. As Ira Shor explains, students must be taught to identify the ways in which control over their own lives has been denied them, and denied in such a way that they have blamed themselves for their powerlessness. Shor thus situates the individual within social processes, examining in detail the interferences to critical thought that would enable "students to be their own agents for social change, their own creators of democratic culture" (48). Among the most important forces preventing work toward a social order supporting the student's "full humanity" are forms of false consciousness — reification, pre-scientific thought, acceleration, mystification — and the absence of democratic practices in all areas of experience. Although Shor discusses these forms of false consciousness in their relation to working-class students, their application to all students is not hard to see, and I have selected for emphasis those features which clearly so apply.

In falling victim to reification, students begin to see the economic and social system that renders them powerless as an innate and unchangeable feature of the natural order. They become convinced that change is impossible, and they support the very practices that victimize them — complying in their alienation from their work, their peers, and their very selves. The most common form of reification has to do with the preoccupation with consumerism, playing the game of material acquisition and using it as a substitute for more self-fulfilling behavior. In pre-scientific thinking, the student is led to believe in a fixed human nature, always and everywhere the same. Behavior that is socially and self-destructive is then seen as inevitable, in the nature of things, or can be resisted only at the individual level, apart from communal activity. Another form of pre-scientific thinking is the belief in luck, in pure chance, as the source of social arrangements, such as the inequitable distribution of wealth. The loyalty to brand names, the faith in a "common sense" that supports the existing order, and the worship of heroes, such as actors and athletes, are other forms of this kind of thought, all of which prevent "the search for rational explanations to authentic problems" (66). Acceleration refers to the pace of everyday experience — the sensory bombardment of urban life and of popular forms of entertainment — which prevents critical reflection. Mystifications are responses to the problems of a capitalist society which obscure their real sources and solutions, responses based on racism, sexism, nationalism, and other forms of bigotry. Finally, students are constantly told they live in the most free, most democratic society in the world, yet they are at the same time systematically denied opportunities for "self-discipline, self-organization, collective work styles, or group deliberation" (70), instead being subjected at every turn to arbitrary authority in conducting everyday affairs.

Shor's recommendations for the classroom grow out of an awareness of these forces and are intended to counter them. The object of this pedagogy is to enable students to *"extraordinarily reexperience the ordinary"* (93), as they critically examine their quotidian experience in order to externalize false consciousness. (Shor's use of the term "critical" is meant to recall Freire as well as the practice of the Hegelian Marxists of the Frankfurt School.) The point is to "address self-in-society and social-relations-in-self" (95). The self then is regarded as the product of a dialectical relationship between the individual and the social, each given significance by the other. Self-autonomy and self-fulfillment are thus possible not through becoming detached from the social, but through resisting those social influences that alienate and disempower, doing so, moreover, in and through social activity. The liberatory classroom begins this resistance process with a dialogue that inspires "a democratic model of social relations, used to problematize the undemocratic quality of social life" (95). This dialogue — a model inspired by Paulo Freire — makes teacher and learner equals engaged in a joint practice that is "[l]oving, humble, hopeful, trusting, critical" (95). This is contrasted with the unequal power relations in the authoritarian classroom, a place where the teacher holds all power and knowledge and the student is the receptacle into which information is poured, a classroom that is "[l]oveless, arrogant, hopeless, mistrustful, acritical" (95). Teacher and student work together to shape the content of the liberatory classroom, and this includes creating the materials of study in the class — such as textbooks and media. Most important, the students are to undergo a conversion from "manipulated objects into active, critical subjects" (97), thereby empowering them to become agents of social change rather than victims. Shor sums up these elements: "social practice is studied in the name of freedom for critical consciousness; democracy and awareness develop through the form of dialogue; dialogue externalizes false consciousness, changing students from re-active objects into society-making subjects: the object-subject switch is a social psychology for empowerment; power through study creates the conditions for reconstructing social practice" (98).

This approach in the classroom requires interdisciplinary methods, and Shor gives an example from the study of the fast-food hamburger: "Concretely my class' study of hamburgers not only involved English and philosophy in our use of writing, reading, and conceptual analysis, but it also included economics in the study of the commodity relations which bring hamburgers to market, history and sociology in an assessment of what the everyday diet was like prior to the rise of the hamburger, and health science in terms of the nutritional value of the ruling burger" (114). This interdisciplinary approach to the study of the reproduction of social life can also lead to "the unveiling of hidden social history" (115), the discovery of past attempts to resist self-destructive experience. This in turn can lead to an examination of the roots of sexism and racism in our culture. Finally, Shor calls upon comedy to reunite pleasure and work, thought and feeling, and upon a resourceful use of the space of the classroom to encourage dialogue that provides students with information withheld elsewhere on campus — "informational, conceptual, personal, academic, financial" (120) — ranging from the location of free or inexpensive services to the location of political rallies.

This survey of the theory and practice of Ira Shor's classroom is necessarily brief and reductive. Still, it suggests the complexity of the behavior recommended in the classroom, behavior that is always open-ended, receptive to the unexpected, and subversive of the planned. Most important, success in this classroom can never by guaranteed. This is a place based on dialectical collaboration — the interaction of student, teacher, and shared experience within a social, interdisciplinary framework — and the outcome is always unpredictable. Yet, as Shor makes clear, the point of this classroom is that the liberated consciousness of students is the only educational objective worth considering, the only objective worth the risk of failure. To succeed at anything else is no success at all.

It should now be apparent that a way of teaching is never innocent. Every pedagogy is imbricated in ideology, in a set of tacit assumptions about what is real, what is good, what is possible, and how power ought to be distributed. The method of cognitive psychology is the most likely to ignore this contention, claiming that the rhetoric it recommends is based on an objective understanding of the unchanging structures of mind, matter, and language. Still, despite its commitment to the empirical and scientific, as we have seen, this rhetoric can easily be made to serve specific kinds of economic, social, and political behavior that works to the advantage of the members of one social class while disempowering others — doing so, moreover, in the name of objective truth. Expressionistic rhetoric is intended to serve as a critique of the ideology of corporate capitalism, proposing in its place an ideology based on a radical individualism. In the name of empowering the individual, however, its naivete about economic, social, and political arrangements can lead to the marginalizing of the individuals who would resist a dehumanizing society, rendering them ineffective through their isolation. This rhetoric also is easily co-opted by the agencies of corporate capitalism, appropriated and distorted in the service of the mystifications of bourgeois individualism. Social-epistemic rhetoric attempts to place the question of ideology at the center of the teaching of writing. It offers both a detailed analysis of dehumanizing social experience and a self-critical and overtly historicized alternative based on democratic practices in the economic, social, political, and cultural spheres. It is obvious that I find this alternative the most worthy of emulation in the classroom, all the while admitting that it is the least formulaic and the most difficult to carry out. I would also add that even those who are skeptical of the Marxian influence found in my description of this rhetoric have much to learn from it. As Kenneth Burke has shown, one does not have to accept the Marxian premise in order to realize the value of the Marxian diagnosis (109). It is likewise not necessary to accept the conclusions of Ira Shor about writing pedagogy in order to learn from his analysis of the ideological practices at work in the lives of our students and ourselves. A rhetoric cannot escape the ideological question, and to ignore this is to fail our responsibilities as teachers and as citizens.

Works Cited

Bartholomae, David. "Inventing the University." *When a Writer Can't Write: Research on Writer's Block and Other Writing Problems.* Ed. Mike Rose. New York: Guilford, 1986.

Berlin, James A. "Contemporary Composition: The Major Pedagogical Theories." *College Engish* 44 (1982): 765–77.

———. *Rhetoric and Reality: Writing Instruction in American Colleges, 1900–1985.* Carbondale: Southern Illinois UP, 1987.

———. *Writing Instruction in Nineteenth-Century American Colleges.* Carbondale: Southern Illinois UP, 1984.

Bizzell, Patricia. "Cognition, Convention, and Certainty: What We Need to Know about Writing." *PRETEXT* 3 (1982): 213–43.

Bowles, Samuel, and Herbert Gintis. *Schooling in Capitalist America.* New York: Basic, 1976.

Braverman, Harry. *Labor and Monopoly Capital: The Degradation of Work in the Twentieth Century.* New York: Monthly Review P, 1974.

Brodkey, Linda. "Modernism and the Scene of Writing." *College English* 49 (1987): 396–418.

Bruner, Jerome S. *The Process of Education.* Cambridge: Harvard UP, 1960.

Burke, Kenneth. *A Rhetoric of Motives.* Berkeley: U of California P, 1969.

Clifford, John, and John Schilb. "A Perspective on Eagleton's Revival of Rhetoric." *Rhetoric Review* 6 (1987): 22–31.

Clines, Ray. "Composition and Capitalism." *Progressive Composition* 14 (Mar. 1987): 4–5.

Dowst, Kenneth. "The Epistemic Approach: Writing, Knowing, and Learning." *Eight Approaches to Teaching Composition.* Ed. Timothy Donovan and Ben W. McClelland. Urbana: NCTE, 1980.

———. "An Epistemic View of Sentence Combining: A Rhetorical Perspective." *Sentence Combining: A Rhetorical Perspective.* Eds. Donald A. Daiker, Andrew Kerek, and Max Morenberg. Carbondale: Southern Illinois UP, 1986. 321–33.

Elbow, Peter. *Embracing Contraries: Explorations in Learning and Teaching.* New York: Oxford, 1981.

———. *Writing without Teachers.* New York: Oxford UP, 1973.

———. *Writing with Power: Techniques for Mastering the Writing Process.* New York: Oxford UP, 1981.

Emig, Janet. *The Composing Process of Twelfth Graders.* Research Report No. 13. Urbana: NCTE, 1971.

Flower, Linda. *Problem-Solving Strategies for Writing.* 2nd ed. San Diego: Harcourt, 1985.

Flower, Linda, and John R. Hayes. "A Cognitive Process Theory of Writing." *College Composition and Communication* 32 (1981): 365–87.

Knoblauch, C. H. "Rhetorical Constructions: Dialogue and Commitment." *College English* 50 (1988): 125–40.

Knoblauch, C. H., and Lil Brannon. *Rhetorical Traditions and the Teaching of Writing.* Upper Montclair: Boynton, 1984.

Larrain, Jorge. *The Concept of Ideology.* Athens: U of Georgia P, 1979.

Larson, Richard. "Discovery Through Questioning: A Plan for Teaching Rhetorical Invention." *College English* 30 (1968): 126–34.

———. "Invention Once More: A Role for Rhetorical Analysis." *College English* 32 (1971): 665–72.

———. "Problem-Solving, Composing, and Liberal Education." *College Composition and Communication* 23 (1972): 208–10.

Lutz, William D. "Making Freshman English a Happening." *College Composition and Communication* 22 (1971): 35–38.

Murray, Donald. "Finding Your Own Voice: Teaching Composition in an Age of Dissent." *College Composition and Communication* 20 (1969): 118–23.

———. *A Writer Teaches Writing.* Boston: Houghton, 1968.

Myers, Greg. "Reality, Consensus, and Reform in the Rhetoric of Composition Teaching." *College English* 48 (1986): 154–74.

Ohmann, Richard. "Literacy, Technology, and Monopoly Capital." *College English* 47 (1985): 675–89.

Paull, Michael, and Jack Kligerman. "Invention, Composition, and the Urban College." *College English* 33 (1972): 651–59.

Shor, Ira. *Critical Teaching and Everyday Life.* 1980. Chicago: U of Chicago P, 1987.

Therborn, Göran. *The Ideology of Power and the Power of Ideology.* London: Verso, 1980.

Vitanza, Victor. "'Notes' Towards Historiographies of Rhetorics; or, Rhetorics of the Histories of Rhetorics: Traditional, Revisionary, and Sub/Versive." *PRETEXT* 8 (1987): 63–125.

Williams, Raymond. *Keywords: A Vocabulary of Culture and Society.* Rev. ed. New York: Oxford UP, 1977.

———. *Marxism and Literature.* New York: Oxford UP, 1977.

Berlin's Insights as a Resource for Your Teaching

1. Make some notes on the ideology that dominates your own teaching. Which moments in your classroom practice most clearly illustrate your commitment to this ideology? What moments suggest that your classroom practice incorporates more than one ideology? While Berlin's tripartite model is a powerful tool for organizing our sense of what goes on in our classroom, actual practice is far too "messy" to be contained and fully delineated by such a simplistic model. Explore ways in which certain aspects of your teaching advance more than one ideology. Are some of your assignments driven by all three modes?

2. Which of Berlin's approaches to writing instruction do your students seem most inclined to accept? Do you have some budding expressionists in your classroom? Do you have any cognitivists on board? Consider ways of using ideological differences among your students as the basis for class discussion, even for writing.

Berlin's Insights as a Resource for the Writing Classroom

1. Classroom reality is always more complex than any clear-cut taxonomy or model. Monitor your teaching for a few weeks to see how the more successful moments in class discussion are grounded in ideology. If you find that you get the best results when you are an expressivist, then examine what within this approach causes the success. Can it be combined with the more appealing elements of other ideologies?

2. Have students write brief, informal accounts of how they see themselves as writers. Read through these accounts with Berlin's taxonomy in mind. Which ideologies rule your students' self-conceptions? Do ideological patterns emerge in the accounts of strong students as opposed to weak students? How might you use Berlin's thinking to address weaker students?

PETER ELBOW　　*Embracing Contraries in the Teaching Process*

This essay by Peter Elbow expresses clearly and eloquently what most writing teachers — whether novice or experienced — intuit and struggle to name. Elbow focuses on the dialectical process of teaching. He describes a "paradoxical coherence" that is necessary if we are to remain inspirited and effective as teachers. Elbow believes that we can use as a paradigm our conflicting loyalties of commitment to students and of commitment to standards. By taking a "contradictory stance" and by admitting that we will always be involved in the dialectic of students and standards, we will be less likely to confuse ourselves or our students. He anchors his philosophy in practical suggestions about using the dialectical process and argues that good teaching, like good writing, is a recursive process of "embracing contraries."

My argument is that good teaching seems a struggle because it calls on skills or mentalities that are actually contrary to each other and thus tend to interfere with each other. It was my exploration of writing that led me to look for contraries in difficult or complex processes. I concluded that good writing requires on the one hand the ability to conceive copiously of many possibilities, an ability which is enhanced by a spirit of open, accepting generativity; but on the other hand good writing also requires an ability to criticize and reject everything but the best, a very different ability which is enhanced by a tough-minded critical spirit. I end up seeing in good writers the ability somehow to be extremely creative and extremely critical, without letting one mentality prosper at the expense of the other or being halfhearted in both. (For more about this idea see my *Writing with Power* [New York: Oxford UP, 1981], especially chapter 1.)

In this frame of mind I began to see a paradoxical coherence in teaching where formerly I was perplexed. I think the two conflicting mentalities needed for good teaching stem from the two conflicting obligations inherent in the job: we have an obligation to students but we also have an obligation to knowledge and society. Surely we are incomplete as teachers if we are committed only to what we are teaching but not to our students, or only to our students but not to what we are teaching, or halfhearted in our commitment to both.

We like to think that these two commitments coincide, and often they do. It happens often enough, for example, that our commitment to standards leads us to give a low grade or tough comment, and it is just what the student needs to hear. But just as often we see that a student needs praise and support rather than a tough grade, even for her weak performance, if she is really to prosper as a student and a person — if we are really to nurture her fragile investment in her studies. Perhaps we can finesse this conflict between a "hard" and "soft" stance if it is early in the semester or we are only dealing with a rough draft; for the time being we can give the praise and support we sense is humanly appropriate and hold off strict judgment and standards till later. But what about when it is the end of the course or a final draft needs a grade? It is comforting to take as our paradigm that first situation where the tough grade was just right, and to consider the trickier situation as somehow anomalous, and thus to assume that we always serve students best by serving knowledge, and vice versa. But I now think I can throw more light on the nature of teaching by taking our conflicting loyalties as paradigmatic.

Our loyalty to students asks us to be their allies and hosts as we instruct and share: to invite all students to enter in and join us as members of a learning community — even if they have difficulty. Our commitment to students asks us to assume they are all capable of learning, to see things through their eyes, to help bring out their best rather than their worst when it comes to tests and grades. By taking this inviting stance we will help more of them learn.

But our commitment to knowledge and society asks us to be guardians or bouncers: we must discriminate, evaluate, test, grade, certify. We are invited to stay true to the inherent standards of what we teach, whether or not that stance fits the particular students before us. We have a responsibility to society — that is, to our discipline, our college or university, and to other learning communities of which we are members — to see that the students we certify really understand or can do what we teach, to see that the grades and credits and degrees we give really have the meaning or currency they are supposed to have.[1]

A pause for scruples. Can we give up so easily the paradigm of teaching as harmonious? Isn't there something misguided in the very idea that these loyalties are conflicting? After all, if we think we are being loyal to students by being extreme in our solicitude for them, won't we undermine the integrity of the subject matter or the currency of the credit and thereby drain value from the very thing we are supposedly giving them? And if we think we are being loyal to society by being extreme in our ferocity — keeping out *any* student with substantial misunderstanding — won't we deprive subject matter and society of the vitality and reconceptualizations they need to survive and grow? Knowledge and society only exist embodied — that is, flawed.

This sounds plausible. But even if we choose a middle course and go only so far as fairness toward subject matter and society, the very fact that we grade and certify at all — the very fact that we must sometimes flunk students — tempts many of them to behave defensively with us. Our mere fairness to subject matter and society tempts students to try to hide weaknesses from us, "psyche us out," or "con us." It is as though we are doctors trying to treat patients who hide their symptoms from us for fear we will put them in the hospital.

Student defensiveness makes our teaching harder. We say, "Don't be afraid to ask questions," or even, "It's a sign of intelligence to be willing to ask naive questions." But when we are testers and graders, students too often fear to ask. Toward examiners they must play it safe, drive defensively, not risk themselves. This stunts learning. When they trust the teacher to be wholly an ally, students are more willing to take risks, connect the self to the material, and experiment. Here is the source not just of learning but also of genuine development or growth.

Let me bring this conflict closer to home. A department chair or dean who talks with us about our teaching and who sits in on our classes is our ally insofar as she is trying to help us teach better; and we can get more help from her to the degree that we openly share with her our fears, difficulties, and failures. Yet insofar as she makes promotion or tenure decisions about us or even participates in those decisions, we will be tempted not to reveal our weaknesses and failures. If we want the best help for our shortcomings, someone who is merely fair is not enough. We need an ally, not a judge.

Thus we can take a merely judicious, compromised position toward our students only if we are willing to settle for being *sort of* committed to students and *sort of* committed to subject matter and society. This middling or fair stance, in fact, is characteristic of many teachers who lack investment in teaching or who have lost it. Most invested teachers, on the other hand, tend to be a bit passionate about supporting students or else passionate about serving and protecting the subject matter they love — and thus they tend to live more on one side or the other of some alleg-edly golden mean.

But supposing you reply, "Yes, I agree that a compromise is not right. Just mid-dling. Muddling. Not excellence or passion in either direction. But that's not what I'm after. My scruple had to do with your very notion of *two directions*. There is only one direction. Excellence. Quality. The very conception of conflict between loyalties is wrong. An inch of progress in one direction, whether toward knowledge or to-ward students, is always an inch in the direction of the other. The needs of students and of knowledge or society are in essential harmony."

To assert this harmony is, in a sense, to agree with what I am getting at in this paper. But it is no good just asserting it. It is like asserting, "Someday you'll thank me for this," or "This is going to hurt me worse than it hurts you." I may say to students, "My fierce grading and extreme loyalty to subject matter and society are really in your interests," but students will still tend to experience me as adversary and undermine much of my teaching. I may say to knowledge and society, "My extreme support and loyalty to all students is really in your interests," but society will tend to view me as a soft teacher who lets standards down.

It is the burden of this paper to say that a contradictory stance is possible — not just in theory but in practice — but not by pretending there is no tension or conflict. And certainly not by affirming only one version of the paradox, the "paternal" ver-sion, which is to stick up for standards and firmness by insisting that to do so is good for students in the long run, forgetting the "maternal" version, which is to stick up for students by insisting that to do so is good for knowledge and society in the long run. There is a genuine paradox here. The positions are conflicting and they are true.

Let me turn this structural analysis into a narrative about the two basic urges at the root of teaching. We often think best by telling stories. I am reading a novel and I interrupt my wife to say, "Listen to this, isn't this wonderful!" and I read a passage out loud. Or we are walking in the woods and I say to her, "Look at the tree!" I am enacting the pervasive human itch to share. It feels lonely, painful, or incomplete to appreciate something and not share it with others.[2]

But this urge can lead to its contrary. Suppose I say, "Listen to this passage," and my wife yawns or says, "Don't interrupt me." Suppose I say, "Look at that beau-tiful sunset on the lake," and she laughs at me for being so sentimental and reminds me that Detroit is right there just below the horizon — creating half the beauty with its pollution. Suppose I say, "Listen to this delicate irony," and she can't see it and thinks I am neurotic to enjoy such bloodless stuff. What happens then? I end up not wanting to share it with her. I hug it to myself. I become a lone connoisseur. Here is the equally deep human urge to protect what I appreciate from harm. Perhaps I share what I love with a few select others — but only after I find a way somehow to extract from them beforehand assurance that they will understand and appreciate what I appreciate. And with them I can even sneer at worldly ones who lack our taste or intelligence or sensibility.

Many of us went into teaching out of just such an urge to share things with others, but we find students turn us down or ignore us in our efforts to give gifts. Sometimes they even laugh at us for our very enthusiasm in sharing. We try to show them what we understand and love, but they yawn and turn away. They put their feet up on our delicate structures; they chew bubble gum during the slow move-ment; they listen to hard rock while reading *Lear* and say, "What's so great about Shakespeare?"

Sometimes even success in sharing can be a problem. We manage to share with students what we know and appreciate, and they love it and eagerly grasp it. But their hands are dirty or their fingers are rough. We overhear them saying, "Listen to this neat thing I learned," yet we cringe because they got it all wrong. Best not to share.

I think of the medieval doctrine of poetry that likens it to a nut with a tough husk protecting a sweet kernel. The function of the poem is not to disclose but rather to conceal the kernel from the many, the unworthy, and to disclose it only to the few worthy (D. W. Robertson, *A Preface to Chaucer* [Princeton: Princeton UP, 1963] 61ff.). I have caught myself more than a few times explaining something I know or love in this tricky double-edged way: encoding my meaning with a kind of complexity or irony such that only those who have the right sensibility will hear what I have to say — others will not understand at all. Surely this is the source of much obscurity in learned discourse. We would rather have readers miss entirely what we say or turn away in boredom or frustration than reply, "Oh, I see what you mean. How ridiculous!" or, "How naive!" It is marvelous, actually, that we can make one utterance do so many things: communicate with the right people, stymie the wrong people, and thereby help us decide who *are* the right and the wrong people.

I have drifted into an unflattering portrait of the urge to protect one's subject, a defensive urge that stems from hurt. Surely much bad teaching and academic foolishness derive from this immature reaction to students or colleagues who will not accept a gift we tried generously to give (generously, but sometimes ineffectually or condescendingly or autocratically). Surely I must learn not to pout just because I can't get a bunch of adolescents as excited as I am about late Henry James. Late Henry James may be pearls, but when students yawn, that doesn't make them swine.

But it is not immature to protect the integrity of my subject in a positive way, to uphold standards, to insist that students stretch themselves till they can do justice to the material. Surely these impulses are at the root of much good teaching. And there is nothing wrong with these impulses in themselves — only *by themselves.* That is, there is nothing wrong with the impulse to guard or protect the purity of what we cherish so long as that act is redeemed by the presence of the opposite impulse also to give it away.

In Piaget's terms learning involves both assimilation and accommodation. Part of the job is to get the subject matter to bend and deform so that it fits inside the learner (that is, so it can fit or relate to the learner's experiences). But that's only half the job. Just as important is the necessity for the learner to bend and deform himself so that he can fit himself around the subject without doing violence to it. Good learning is not a matter of finding a happy medium where both parties are transformed as little as possible. Rather both parties must be maximally transformed — in a sense deformed. There is violence in learning. We cannot learn something without eating it, yet we cannot really learn it either without letting it eat us.

Look at Socrates and Christ as archetypal good teachers — archetypal in being so paradoxical. They are extreme on the one hand in their impulse to share with everyone and to support all learners, in their sense that everyone can take and get what they are offering; but they are extreme on the other hand in their fierce high standards for what will pass muster. They did not teach gut courses, they flunked "gentleman C" performances, they insisted that only "too much" was sufficient in their protectiveness toward their "subject matter." I am struck also with how much they both relied on irony, parable, myth, and other forms of subtle utterance that hide while they communicate. These two teachers were willing in some respects to bend and disfigure and in the eyes of many to profane what they taught, yet on the other hand they were equally extreme in their insistence that learners bend or transform themselves in order to become fit receptacles.

It is as though Christ, by stressing the extreme of sharing and being an ally — saying "suffer the little children to come unto me" and praising the widow with her mite — could be more extreme in this sternness: "unless you sell all you have," and "I speak to them in parables, because seeing they do not see and hearing they do not hear, nor do they understand" (saying in effect, "I am making this a tough course *because* so many of you are poor students"). Christ embeds the two themes of giving away and guarding — commitment to "students" and to "subject matter" — in the one wedding feast story: the host invites the guests from the highways and byways, anybody, but then angrily ejects one into outer darkness because he lacks the proper garment.

Let me sum up the conflict in two lists of teaching skills. If on the one hand we want to help more students learn more, I submit we should behave in the following four ways:

1. We should see our students as smart and capable. We should assume that they can learn what we teach — all of them. We should look through their mistakes or ignorance to the intelligence that lies behind. There is ample documentation that this "teacher expectation" increases student learning (Robert Rosenthal, "Teacher Expectation and Pupil Learning," in R. D. Strom, ed., *Teachers and the Learning Process* [Englewood Cliffs: Prentice, 1971] 33–60).

2. We should show students that we are on their side. This means, for example, showing them that the perplexity or ignorance they reveal to us will not be used against them in tests, grading, or certifying. If they hide their questions or guard against us they undermine our efforts to teach them.

3. Indeed, so far from letting their revelations hurt them in reading, we should be as it were lawyers for the defense, explicitly trying to help students do better against the judge and prosecuting attorney when it comes to the "trial" of testing and grading. ("I may be able to get you off this charge but only if you tell me what you really were doing that night.") If we take this advocate stance students can learn more from us, even if they are guilty of the worst crimes in the book: not having done the homework, not having learned last semester, not *wanting* to learn. And by learning more — even if not learning perfectly — they will perform better, which in turn will usually lead to even better learning in the future.

4. Rather than try to be perfectly fair and perfectly in command of what we teach — as good examiners ought to be — we should reveal our own position, particularly our doubts, ambivalences, and biases. We should show we are still learning, still willing to look at things in new ways, still sometimes uncertain or even stuck, still willing to ask naive questions, still engaged in the interminable process of working out the relationship between what we teach and the rest of our lives. Even though we are not wholly peer with our students, we can still be peer in this crucial sense of also being engaged in learning, seeking, and being incomplete. Significant learning requires change, inner readjustments, willingness to let go. We can increase the chances of our students being willing to undergo the necessary anxiety involved in change if they see we are also willing to undergo it.

Yet if, on the other hand, we want to increase our chances of success in serving knowledge, culture, and institutions I submit that we need skill at behaving in four very different ways:

1. We should insist on standards that are high — in the sense of standards that are absolute. That is, we should take what is almost a kind of Platonic position that there exists a "real world" of truth, of good reasoning, of good writing, of knowledge of biology, whatever — and insist that anything less than the real thing is not good enough.

2. We should be critical-minded and look at students and student performances with a skeptical eye. We should assume that some students cannot learn and others will not, even if they can. This attitude will increase our chances of detecting baloney and surface skill masquerading as competence or understanding.

3. We should not get attached to students or take their part or share their view of things; otherwise we will find it hard to exercise the critical spirit needed to say, "No, you do not pass," "No, you cannot enter in with the rest of us," "Out you go into the weeping and gnashing of teeth."

4. Thus we should identify ourselves primarily with knowledge or subject matter and care more about the survival of culture and institutions than about individual students — even when that means students are rejected who are basically smart or who tried as hard as they could. We should keep our minds on the harm that can come to knowledge and society if standards break down or if someone is certified who is not competent, rather than on the harm that comes to individual students by hard treatment.

Because of this need for conflicting mentalities I think I see a distinctive distribution of success in teaching. At one extreme we see a few master or genius teachers, but they are striking for how differently they go about it and how variously and sometimes surprisingly they explain what they do. At the other extreme are people who teach very badly, or who have given up trying, or who quit teaching altogether: they are debilitated by the conflict between trying to be an ally as they teach and an adversary as they grade. Between these two extremes teachers find the three natural ways of making peace between contraries: there are "hard" teachers in whom loyalty to knowledge or society has won out; "soft" teachers in whom loyalty to students has won out; and middling, mostly dispirited teachers who are sort of loyal to students and sort of loyal to knowledge or society. (A few of this last group are not dispirited at all but live on a kind of knife edge of almost palpable tension as they insist on trying to be scrupulously fair both to students and to what they teach.)

This need for conflicting mentalities is also reflected in what is actually the most traditional and venerable structure in education: a complete separation between teaching and official assessment. We see it in the Oxford and Cambridge structure that makes the tutor wholly an ally to help the student prepare for exams set and graded by independent examiners. We see something of the same arrangement in many European university lecture-and-exam systems which are sometimes mimicked by American Ph.D. examinations. The separation of teaching and examining is found in many licensing systems and also in some new competence-based programs.

Even in conventional university curricula we see various attempts to strengthen assessment and improve the relationship between teacher and student by making the teacher more of an ally and coach. In large courses with many sections, teachers often give a common exam and grade each other's students. Occasionally, when two teachers teach different courses within each other's field of competence, they divide their roles and act as "outside examiner" for the other's students. (This approach, by the way, tends to help teachers clarify what they are trying to accomplish in a course since they must communicate their goals clearly to the examiner if there is to be any decent fit between the teaching and examining.) In writing centers, tutors commonly help students improve a piece of writing which another teacher will assess. We even see a hint of this separation of roles when teachers stress collaborative learning: they emphasize the students' role as mutual teachers and thereby emphasize their own pedagogic role as examiner and standard setter.

But though the complete separation of teacher and evaluator is hallowed and useful I am interested here in ways for teachers to take on both roles better. It is not just that most teachers are stuck with both; in addition I believe that opposite mentalities or processes can enhance each other rather than interfere with each other if we engage in them in the right spirit.

How can we manage to do contrary things? Christ said, "Be ye perfect," but I don't think it is good advice to try being immensely supportive and fierce in the same instant, as he and Socrates somehow managed to be. In writing, too, it doesn't usually help to try being immensely generative and critical-minded in the same instant as some great writers are — and as the rest of us sometimes are at moments of blessed inspiration. This is the way of transcendence and genius, but for most of us most of the time there is too much interference or paralysis when we try to do opposites at once.

But it is possible to make peace between opposites by alternating between them so that you are never trying to do contrary things at any one moment. One opposite leads naturally to the other; indeed, extremity in one enhances extremity in the other in a positive, reinforcing fashion. In the case of my own writing I find I can generate more and better when I consciously hold off critical-minded revising till later. Not only does it help to go whole hog with one mentality, but I am not afraid to make a fool of myself since I know I will soon be just as wholeheartedly critical. Similarly, I can be more fierce and discriminating in my critical revising because I have more and better material to work with through my earlier surrender to uncensored generating.

What would such an alternating approach look like in teaching? I will give a rough picture, but I do so hesitantly because if I am right about my theory of paradox, there will be widely different ways of putting it into practice.

In teaching we traditionally end with the critical or gatekeeper function: papers, exams, grades, or less institutionalized forms of looking back, taking stock, and evaluating. It is also traditional to start with the gatekeeper role: to begin a course by spelling out all the requirements and criteria as clearly as possible. We often begin a course by carefully explaining exactly what it will take to get an A, B, C, etc.

I used to be reluctant to start off on this foot. It felt so vulgar to start by emphasizing grades, and thus seemingly to reinforce a pragmatic preoccupation I want to squelch. But I have gradually changed my mind, and my present oppositional theory tells me I should exaggerate, or at least take more seriously than I often do, my gatekeeper functions rather than run away from them. The more I try to soft-pedal assessment, the more mysterious it will seem to students and the more likely they will be preoccupied and superstitious about it. The more I can make it clear to myself and to my students that I do have a commitment to knowledge and institutions, and the more I can make it specifically clear how I am going to fulfill that commitment, the easier it is for me to turn around and make a dialectical change of role into being an extreme ally to students.

Thus I start by trying to spell out requirements and criteria as clearly and concretely as possible. If I am going to use a midterm and final exam, it would help to pass out samples of these at the beginning of the course. Perhaps not a copy of precisely the test I will use but something close. And why not the real thing? If it feels as though I will ruin the effectiveness of my exam to "give it away" at the start, that means I must have a pretty poor exam — a simple-minded task that can be crammed for and that does not really test what is important. If the exam gets at the central substance of the course then surely it will help me if students see it right at the start. They will be more likely to learn what I want them to learn. It might be a matter of content: "Summarize the three main theories in this course and discuss their strengths and weaknesses by applying them to material we did not discuss." Or perhaps I am more interested in a process or skill: "Write an argumentative essay on this (new) topic." Or "Show how the formal characteristics of this (new) poem do and do not reinforce the theme." I might want to give room for lots of choice and initiative: "Write a dialogue between the three main people we have studied that illustrates what you think are the most important things about their work." Passing out the exam at the start — and perhaps even samples of strong and weak answers — is an invitation to make a tougher exam that goes more to the heart of what the course is trying to teach. If I don't use an exam, then it is even more crucial that I say how I will determine the grade — even if I base it heavily on slippery factors: e.g., "I will count half your grade on my impression of how well you motivate and invest yourself," or "how well you work collaboratively with your peers." Of course this kind of announcement makes for a tricky situation, but if these are my goals, surely I want my students to wrestle with them all term — in all their slipperiness and even if it means arguments about how unfair it is to grade on such matters — rather than just think about them at the end.

When I assign papers I should similarly start by advertising my gatekeeper role, by clearly communicating standards and criteria. That means not just talking theoretically about what I am looking for in an A paper and what drags a paper down to B or C or F, but rather passing out a couple of samples of each grade and talking concretely about what makes me give each one the grade I give it. Examples help because our actual grading sometimes reflects criteria we do not talk about, perhaps even that we are not aware of. (For example, I have finally come to admit that neatness counts.) Even if our practice fits our preaching, sometimes students do not really understand preaching without examples. Terms like "coherent" and even "specific" are notoriously hard for students to grasp because they do not read stacks of student writing. Students often learn more about well-connected and poorly connected paragraphs or specificity or the lack of it in examples from the writing of each other than they learn from instruction alone, or from examples of published writing.

I suspect there is something particularly valuable here about embodying our commitment to knowledge and society in the form of documents or handouts: words on palpable sheets of paper rather than just spoken words-in-the-air. Documents heighten the sense that I do indeed take responsibility for these standards; writing them forces me to try to make them as concrete, explicit, and objective as possible (if not necessarily fair). But most of all, having put all this on paper I can more easily go on to separate myself from them in some way — leave them standing — and turn around and schizophrenically start being a complete ally of students. I have been wholehearted and enthusiastic in making tough standards, but now I can say, "Those are the specific criteria I will use in grading; that's what you are up against, that's really me. But now we have most of the semester for me to help you attain those standards, do well on those tests and papers. They are high standards but I suspect all of you can attain them if you work hard. I will function as your ally. I'll be a kind of lawyer for the defense, helping you bring out your best in your battles with the other me, the prosecuting-attorney me when he emerges at the end. And if you really think you are too poorly prepared to do well in one semester, I can help you decide whether to trust that negative judgment and decide now whether to drop the course or stay and learn what you can."

What is pleasing about this alternating approach is the way it naturally leads a teacher to higher standards yet greater supportiveness. That is, I feel better about being really tough if I know I am going to turn around and be more on the student's side than usual. And contrarily I do not have to hold back from being an ally of students when I know I have set really high standards. Having done so, there is now no such thing as being "too soft," supportive, helpful, or sympathetic — no reason to hold back from seeing things entirely from their side, worrying about their problems. I can't be "cheated" or taken advantage of.

In addition, the more clearly I can say what I want them to know or be able to do, the better I can figure out what I must provide to help them attain those goals. As I make progress in this cycle, it means I can set my goals even higher — ask for the deep knowledge and skills that are really at the center of the enterprise.

But how, concretely, can we best function as allies? One of the best ways is to be a kind of coach. One has set up the hurdle for practice jumping, one has described the strengths and tactics of the enemy, one has warned them about what the prosecuting attorney will probably do: now the coach can prepare them for these rigors. Being an ally is probably more a matter of stance and relationship than of specific behaviors. Where a professor of jumping might say, in effect, "I will explain the principles of jumping," a jumping coach might say, in effect, "Let's work on learning to jump over those hurdles; in doing so I'll explain the principles of jumping." If we try to make these changes in stance, I sense we will discover some of the resistance, annoyances, and angers that make us indeed reluctant genuinely to be on the student's side. How can we be teachers for long without piling up resentment at having been misunderstood and taken advantage of? But the dialectical need to be in addition an extreme adversary of students will give us a legitimate medium for this hunger to dig in one's heels even in a kind of anger.

This stance provides a refreshingly blunt but supportive way to talk to students about weaknesses. "You're strong here, you're weak there, and over here you are really out of it. We've got to find ways to work on these things so you can succeed on these essays or exams." And this stance helps reward students for volunteering weaknesses. The teacher can ask, "What don't you understand? What skills are hard for you? I need to decide how to spend our time here and I want it to be the most useful for your learning."

One of the best ways to function as ally or coach is to role-play the enemy in a supportive setting. For example, one can give practice tests where the grade doesn't count, or give feedback on papers which the student can revise before they count for credit. This gets us out of the typically counterproductive situation where much of our commentary on papers and exams is really justification for the grade — or is seen that way. Our attempt to help is experienced by students as a slap on the wrist by an adversary for what they have done wrong. No wonder students so often fail to heed or learn from our commentary. But when we comment on practice tests or revisable papers we are not saying, "Here's why you got this grade." We are saying, "Here's how you can get a better grade." When later we read final versions as evaluator we can read faster and not bother with much commentary.[3]

It is the spirit or principle of serving contraries that I want to emphasize here, not any particular fleshing out in practice such as above. For one of the main attractions of this theory is that it helps explain why people are able to be terrific teachers in such diverse ways. If someone is managing to do two things that conflict with each other, he is probably doing something mysterious: it's altogether natural if his success involves slipperiness, irony, or paradox. For example, some good teachers look like they are nothing but fierce gatekeepers, cultural bouncers, and yet in some mysterious way — perhaps ironically or subliminally — they are supportive. I think of the ferocious Marine sergeant who is always cussing out the troops but who somehow shows them he is on their side and believes in their ability. Other good teachers look like creampuffs and yet in some equally subtle way they embody the highest standards of excellence and manage to make students exert and stretch themselves as never before.

For it is one's spirit or stance that is at issue here, not the mechanics of how to organize a course in semester units or how to deal in tests, grading, or credits. I do not mean to suggest that the best way to serve knowledge and society is by having tough exams or hard grading — or even by having exams or grades at all. Some teachers do it just by talking, whether in lectures or discussions or conversation. Even though there is no evaluation or grading, the teacher can still demonstrate her ability to be wholehearted in her commitment to what she teaches and wholehearted also in her commitment to her students. Thus her talk itself might in fact alternate between attention to the needs of students and flights where she forgets entirely about students and talks over their head, to truth, to her wisest colleagues, to herself.[4]

The teacher who is really in love with Yeats or with poetry will push harder, and yet be more tolerant of students' difficulties because his love provides the serenity he needs in teaching: he knows that students cannot hurt Yeats or his relationship with Yeats. It is a different story when we are ambivalent about Yeats or poetry. The piano teacher who mean-spiritedly raps the fingers of pupils who play wrong notes usually harbors some inner ambivalence in his love of music or some disappointment about his own talent.

In short, there is obviously no one right way to teach, yet I argue that in order to teach well we must find *some* way to be loyal both to students and to knowledge or society. Any way we can pull it off is fine. But if we are teaching less well than we should, we might be suffering from the natural tendency for these two loyalties to conflict with each other. In such a case we can usually improve matters by making what might seem an artificial separation of focus so as to give each loyalty and its attendant skills and mentality more room in which to flourish. That is, we can spend part of our teaching time saying in some fashion or other, "Now I'm being a tough-minded gatekeeper, standing up for high critical standards in my loyalty to what I teach"; and part of our time giving a contrary message: "Now my attention is wholeheartedly on trying to be your ally to try to help you learn, and I am not worrying about the purity of standards or grades or the need of society or institutions."

It is not that this approach makes things simple. It confuses students at first because they are accustomed to teachers being either "hard" or "soft" or in the middle — not both. The approach does not take away any of the conflict between trying to fulfill two conflicting functions. It merely gives a context and suggests a structure for doing so. Most of all it helps me understand better the demands on me and helps me stop feeling as though there is something wrong with me for feeling pulled in two directions at once.

I have more confidence that this conscious alternation or separation of mentalities makes sense because I think I see the same strategy to be effective with writing. Here too there is obviously no one right way to write, but it seems as though any good writer must find some way to be both abundantly inventive yet tough-mindedly critical. Again, any way we can pull it off is fine, but if we are not writing as well as we should — if our writing is weak in generativity or weak in tough-minded scrutiny (not to mention downright dismal or blocked) — it may well be that we are hampered by a conflict between the accepting mentality needed for abundant invention and the rejecting mentality needed for tough-minded criticism. In such a case too, it helps to move back and forth between sustained stretches of wholehearted, uncensored generating and wholehearted critical revising to allow each mentality and set of skills to flourish unimpeded.

Even though this theory encourages a separation that could be called artificial, it also points to models of the teaching and writing process that are traditional and reinforced by common sense: teaching that begins and ends with attention to standards and assessment and puts lots of student-directed supportive instruction in the middle; writing that begins with exploratory invention and ends with critical revising. But I hope that my train of thought rejuvenates these traditional models by emphasizing the underlying structure of contrasting mentalities which is central rather than merely a mechanical sequence of external stages which is not necessary at all.

In the end, I do not think I am just talking about how to serve students and serve knowledge or society. I am also talking about developing opposite and complementary sides of our character or personality: the supportive and nurturant side and the tough, demanding side. I submit that we all have instincts and needs of both sorts. The gentlest, softest, and most flexible among us really need a chance to stick up for our latent high standards, and the most hawk-eyed, critical-minded bouncers at the bar of civilization among us really need a chance to use our nurturant and supportive muscles instead of always being adversary.

Notes

[1]I lump "knowledge and society" together in one phrase but I acknowledge the importance of the potential conflict. For example, we may feel *society* asking us to adapt our students to it, while we feel *knowledge* — our vision of the truth — asking us to unfit our students for that society. Socrates was convicted of corrupting the youth. To take a more homely example, I may feel institutions asking me to teach students one kind of writing and yet feel impelled by my understanding of writing to teach them another kind. Thus where this paper paints a picture of teachers pulled in two directions, sometimes we may indeed be pulled in three.

[2]Late in life, I realize I must apologize and pay my respects to that form of literary criticism that I learned in college to scorn in callow fashion as the "Ah lovely!" school: criticism which tries frankly to share a perception and appreciation of the work rather than insist that there is some problem to solve or some complexity to analyze.

[3]Since it takes more time for us to read drafts and final versions too, no matter how quickly we read final versions, it is reasonable to conserve time in other ways — indeed I see independent merits. Don't require students to revise every draft. This permits you to grade students on their best work and thus again to have higher standards, and it is easier for students to invest themselves in revising if it is on a piece they care more about. And in giving feedback on drafts, wait till you have two drafts in hand and thus give feedback only half as often. When I have only one paper in hand I often feel, "Oh dear, everything is weak here; nothing works right; where can I start?" When I have two drafts in hand I can easily say, "This one is better for the following reasons; it's the one I'd choose to revise; see if you can fix the following problems." With two drafts it is easier to find genuine strengths and point to them and help students consolidate or gain control over them. Yet I can make a positive utterance out of talking about what *didn't* work in the better draft and how to improve it.

[4]Though my argument does not imply that we need to use grades at all, surely it implies that if we do use them we should learn to improve the way we do so. I used to think that conventional grading reflected too much concern with standards for knowledge and society,

but now I think it reflects too little. Conventional grading reflects such a single-minded hunger to *rank* people along a single scale or dimension that it is willing to forgo any communication of what the student really knows or can do. The competence-based movement, whatever its problems, represents a genuine attempt to make grades and credits do justice to knowledge and society. (See Gerald Grant et al., *On Competence: A Critical Analysis of Competence-Based Reform in Higher Education* [San Francisco: Jossey, 1979]. See also my "More Accurate Evaluation of Student Performance," *Journal of Higher Education* 40 [1969]: 219–30.)

Elbow's Insights as a Resource for Your Teaching

1. You may have been surprised by some of Elbow's statements because they either confirmed or challenged something you already believe about teaching. Reflect on your current beliefs to determine if some fall into "contraries." I encourage you to imitate Elbow's thinking and writing and engage in some "dialectical reasoning." Begin and maintain a double-entry journal. Use one side of the notebook for comments about your teaching that you would categorize as "loyalty to students." Use the other for comments about "loyalty to standards." Leave space in the entries so that you can come back to add anecdotes, insights, and questions.

   At the end of the semester, you can review entries and revise them to set the "contraries" — which are parallel in some way — side by side. If your word processing program has a split-screen feature, you can also keep this journal on disk.

2. Draft and redraft a "philosophy of teaching composition." You'll revise it as you teach and learn more from your students and from your colleagues as well as from your experiences in the classroom. Elbow is clearly offering his philosophy of teaching "mostly writing" and he tells us how he shaped his philosophy and what kind of rethinking informed it. (Elbow is equally specific in discussing his philosophy in *Writing without Teachers, Writing with Power, What Is English,* and the larger text *Embracing Contraries.*) Your responses to the concepts and philosophies in Chapter 1 might be good starting points for talking out your philosophy of teaching.

   If this drafting a philosophy seems too self-conscious to you, think about it pragmatically. A favorite and frequent interview question from members of writing faculties will be "So, what do you believe about teaching writing?" You'll be ready to respond confidently and eloquently because you will have been writing and reflecting through this philosophical essay.

3. Drafting an "attendance and grading policy statement" could be a way for you to embrace the contraries implicit in your teaching. In this statement, which should be shared with your students the first week of class, try to represent each of your important beliefs that you listed in exercise 1.

Elbow's Insights as a Resource for the Writing Classroom

1. First-year writers experience many conflicts of opposing ideas, values, lifestyles, and goals. They need assistance coping with the tension, frustration, anxiety, and even fear that those conflicts create. Being able to "embrace contraries" is a fairly mature activity and a sophisticated cognitive task. To aid your writers in transition as thinkers, writers, and members of the writing community, encourage them to use journal entries to list and describe the conflicts they experience. Initially, those entries might be mostly therapeutic, allowing the students to express perceptions and feelings that might be too risky to express in jam sessions or letters home. Eventually, the entries should allow the writers to begin to see patterns among the examples of "contraries." The journal can become a sourcebook of ideas for writing assignments that call for problem solving (see Chapter 15 of *The Bedford Guide for College Writers*).

2. Many first-year writers have difficulty moving from personal and expressive writing to the critical writing prompted by Part 2 of *The Bedford Guide for College Writers*. Teaching a writer to identify and then to analyze personal or campus-centered conflicts eases the transition. A demonstration of problem solving through dialectical statement taps personal experience and also leads to some objective evaluation. Show students how to write two basic paradigms — Hegelian and Marxist — for a dialectical situation.

   Hegelian dialectic describes a *thesis* and then an *antithesis*, a situation opposed to and creating conflict with the thesis. The *synthesis* is a recommendation about resolving the conflict. Often, "compromise" or "golden mean" solutions are created. Here's an example that many of your students will quickly identify from reading psychology. Freud defines the process of ego formation as a dialectical process.

   Thesis: The id, the unconscious, spontaneous, and individualistic energy of a person (the yea-saying child)

   Antithesis: The superego, the conscious, culturally influenced, and socially directed energy of a person (the nay-saying parent)

   Synthesis: The ego, the balancing of energies to accommodate the needs of self and society (the "let's consider this" adult)

   With the Marxist dialectic, the *thesis* describes a situation that inevitably gives rise to its *antithesis*. The *synthesis* describes a recommendation for resolving the conflict that is often not a compromise or a balancing of the tension between thesis and antithesis. Unlike the Hegelian synthesis, the Marxist synthesis provokes more dialectic. The synthesis becomes a thesis, which inevitably gives rise to an antithesis. Here are examples:

   Thesis: Feudalism met the human needs for stability and security roles.

   Antithesis: The human need for individual initiative and freedom came in conflict with the status quo of feudalism.

   Synthesis: An economic system developed allowing the individual to compete openly in a free market and to use the means of production and distribution to create capital.

   This historical dialectical process gives rise to

   Thesis: Capitalism allows the individual to compete freely and to use the means of production and distribution to create capital.

   Antithesis: Large numbers of workers are made the "means of production" and become oppressed and unable to prosper in capitalist society.

   Synthesis: In the Soviet Union, the revolution brought a "classless" society and communism. In the United States, the labor union movement brings "safety and protection of economic rights" to the rank and file.

   Students will jump in at this point of the demonstration to point out serious problems with Soviet (or Russian) communism and American labor unions; their observations can be described as "antitheses," and the thinking about "syntheses" will proceed.

   After the demonstration, ask students to work in small groups to generate a list of conflicts they are experiencing as first-year students. Tell them to select several of those conflicts and to frame them first as Hegelian and then as Marxist dialectics.

3. Follow up the class exercise in writing dialectical paradigms with an essay assignment that calls for use of the dialectical paradigm to generate thought and to structure an essay. Review with your students the discussions of the writing strategy of comparison and contrast (see Chapter 7; see also Chapter

18, "Strategies for Developing," and the techniques for generating ideas and shaping a draft in Chapter 11, "Evaluating"). Those treatments can help writers work with structuring an essay dialectically.

Have the class brainstorm transition terms and phrases, metaphors, and verbs that dramatize a conflict or a tension between opposites. During peer evaluation sessions, have editors restate the gist of the essay they are editing by abstracting its dialectical paradigm.

Expect the writers to surprise themselves with the new ideas they discover about their personal experiences and their ability to solve conflict. Recommend this process to students as one thinking strategy to use whenever they're asked to problem-solve in classes.

DAVID BARTHOLOMAE   # Writing with Teachers: A Conversation with Peter Elbow

Bartholomae sees English 101 — and other writing courses — as sites for critical inquiry where students "can learn to feel and see their position inside a text they did not invent and can never, at least, completely, control. Inside a practice: linguistic, rhetorical, cultural, historical." In his work with reading-writing connections (Ways of Reading, Boston: Bedford, 1996) and his reflection on discourse communities and multiple literacies, Bartholomae emphasizes the fact that all learners are situated in traditions, in cultural processes that create "busy, intertextual space." For Bartholomae, writing instructors assist students, through critical reading and the practice of questioning and critiquing their texts in the presence of others, to gain "authority" for their work.

His text is a talk he gave "in conversation with Peter Elbow" at the 1991 Conference on College Composition and Communication. The larger conversations — both talks, the replies of Elbow and Bartholomae to each other, and teachers' responses and "debate" about personal and academic reading — were published in the February issue of College Composition and Communication. *The nature and roles of personal and academic writing as the focus of English 101 have been set up as contraries; writing teachers are looking for ways to embrace or to reconcile the contraries.*

Where to Begin?

Most discussions like the one we are about to have begin or end by fretting over the central term, academic writing. It is clear that this is not just a contested term, but a difficult one to use with any precision. If, for example, it means the writing that is done by academics, or the writing that passes as currency in the academy, then it is a precise term only when it is loaded: academic writing — the unreadable created by the unspeakable; academic writing — stuffy, pedantic, the price of a career; academic writing — pure, muscular, lean, taut, the language of truth and reason; academic writing — language stripped of the false dressings of style and fashion, a tool for inquiry and critique.

And so on. I don't need to belabor this point. Academic writing is a single thing only in convenient arguments. If you collect samples of academic writing, within or across the disciplines, it has as many types and categories, peaks and valleys, as writing grouped under any other general category: magazine writing, business writing, political writing, sports writing. Or, I could put it this way: within the writing performed in 1990 under the rubric of English studies, writing by English professors, you can find writing that is elegant, experimental, sentimental, autobiographical, spare, dull, pretentious, abstract, boring, dull, whatever.

If I am here to argue for academic writing as part of an undergraduate's training, or as a form or motive to be taught / examined in the curriculum, I need to begin by saying that I am not here to argue for stuffy, lifeless prose or for mechanical (or dutiful) imitations of standard thoughts and forms. We need a different set of terms to frame the discussion. It is interesting, in fact, to consider how difficult it is to find positive terms for academic writing when talking to a group of academics, including those who could be said to do it for a living. It is much easier to find examples or phrases to indicate our sense of corporate shame or discomfort.

I don't have time to pursue this line of argument here, but I think it is part and parcel of the anti-professionalism Fish argues is a pose of both the academic right (for whom the prose in our journals is evidence of bad faith, of the pursuit of trends, an abandonment of the proper pursuit of humane values, great books), but also for the academic left (for whom professional practice is the busy work we do because we are co-opted). For both, academic writing is what you do when you are not doing your "real" work.

My Position, I Think

I want to argue that academic writing is the real work of the academy. I also want to argue for academic writing as a key term in the study of writing and the practice of instruction. In fact, I want to argue that if you are teaching courses in the university, courses where students write under your supervision, they can't not do it and you can't not stand for it (academic writing, that is) and, therefore, it is better that it be done out in the open, where questions can be asked and responsibilities assumed, than to be done in hiding or under another name.

To say this another way, there is no writing that is writing without teachers. I think I would state this as a general truth, but for today let me say that there is no writing done in the academy that is not academic writing. To hide the teacher is to hide the traces of power, tradition, and authority present at the scene of writing (present in allusions to previous work, in necessary work with sources, in collaboration with powerful theories and figures, in footnotes and quotations, and the messy business of doing your work in the shadow of others). Thinking of writing as academic writing makes us think of the page as crowded with others — or it says that this is what we learn in school, that our writing is not our own, nor are the stories we tell when we tell the stories of our lives — they belong to TV, to Books, to Culture and History.

To offer academic writing as something else is to keep this knowledge from our students, to keep them from confronting the power politics of discursive practice, or to keep them from confronting the particular representations of power, tradition, and authority reproduced whenever one writes.

Now — I say this as though it were obvious. Students write in a space defined by all the writing that has preceded them, writing the academy insistently draws together: in the library, in the reading list, in the curriculum. This is the busy, noisy, intertextual space — one usually hidden in our representations of the classroom; one that becomes a subject in the classroom when we ask young writers to think about, or better yet, confront, their situatedness.

And yet, it is also obvious that there are many classrooms where students are asked to imagine that they can clear out a space to write on their own, to express their own thoughts and ideas, not to reproduce those of others. As I think this argument through, I think of the pure and open space, the frontier classroom, as a figure central to composition as it is currently constructed. The open classroom; a free writing. This is the master trope. And, I would say, it is an expression of a desire for an institutional space free from institutional pressures, a cultural process free from the influence of culture, an historical moment outside of history, an academic setting free from academic writing.

Whose desire? That is a hard question to answer, and I will finesse it for the moment. I don't want to say that it is Peter's; I think it is expressed in Peter's work.

I can, however, phrase this question: "Whose desire is this, this desire for freedom, empowerment, an open field?" — I think I can phrase the question in terms of the larger debate in the academy about the nature of discourse and the humanities. The desire for a classroom free from the past is an expression of the desire for presence or transcendence, for a common language, free from jargon and bias, free from evasion and fear; for a language rooted in common sense rather than special sense, a language that renders (makes present) rather than explains (makes distant). It is a desire with a particularly American inflection and a particular resonance at a moment in the academy when it has become harder and harder to cast any story, let alone the story of education, in a setting that is free, Edenic, or Utopian.

"I have learned to relinquish authority in my classroom." How many times do we hear this now as the necessary conclusion in an argument about the goals of composition? "I want to empower my students." "I want to give my students ownership of their work." What could it mean — to have this power over language, history, and culture? to own it?

Unless it means stepping outside of the real time and place of our writing — heading down the river, heading out to the frontier, going nowhere. Unless it means stepping out of language and out of time. I am arguing for a class *in* time, one that historicizes the present, including the present evoked in students' writing. Inside this linguistic present, students (with instruction — more precisely, with lessons in critical reading) can learn to feel and see their position inside a text they did not invent and can never, at least completely, control. Inside a practice: linguistic, rhetorical, cultural, historical.

As I am thinking through this argument, I read Peter's work as part of a much larger project to preserve and reproduce the figure of the author, an independent, self-creative, self-expressive subjectivity. I see the argument against academic writing, and for another writing, sometimes called personal or expressive writing, as part of a general argument in favor of the author, a much beleaguered figure in modern American English departments. This is one way that the profession, English, has of arguing out the nature and role of writing as a subject of instruction — personal writing/academic writing — this opposition is the structural equivalent to other arguments, arguments about authorship and ownership, about culture and the individual, about single author courses, about the canon.

And these arguments are part of still other arguments, with different inflections, about production and consumption, about reading and writing, about presence and transcendence, culture and individualism — arguments working themselves out in particular ways at conferences and in papers in many settings connected to the modern academy. The desire for an open space, free from the past, is a powerful desire, deployed throughout the discourses of modern life, including the discourses of education.

The Contact Zone

When we talk about academic writing at CCCC, I don't think we are talking about discourse — at least, after Foucault, as discourse is a technical term. We are not, in other words, talking about particular discursive practices and how they are reproduced or policed within the academic disciplines.

I would say that we are talking about sites, possible scenes of writing, places, real and figurative, where writing is produced. This is why so much time is spent talking about the classroom and its literal or metaphorical arrangement of power and authority — where do we sit, who talks first, who reads the papers. Whether we rearrange the furniture in the classroom or rearrange the turns taken by speakers in a discussion, these actions have no immediate bearing on the affiliations of power brought into play in writing. At worst, the "democratic" classroom becomes the sleight of hand we perfect in order to divert attention for the unequal distribution of power that is inherent in our positions as teachers, as figures of institutional / disciplinary authority, and inherent in the practice of writing, where one is always second, derivative, positioned, etc.

I am trying to think about the scene of writing as a discursive space. So let me say that we shouldn't think of ourselves as frontier guides but as managers, people who manage substations in the cultural network, small shops in the general production of readers and writers. We don't choose this; it is the position we assume as teachers. If, from this position, we are going to do anything but preside over the reproduction of forms and idioms, we have to make the classroom available for critical inquiry, for a critique that is part of the lesson of practice. We have to do more, that is, than manage.

If our goal is to make a writer aware of the forces at play in the production of knowledge, we need to highlight the classroom as a substation — as a real space, not as an idealized utopian space. There is no better way to investigate the transmission of power, tradition, and authority than by asking students to do what academics do: work with the past, with key texts (we have been teaching Emerson, Rich, Simon Frith on rock and roll); working with other's terms (key terms from Rich, like "patriarchy," for example); struggling with the problems of quotation, citation, and paraphrase, where one version of a student's relationship to the past is represented by how and where he quotes Rich (does he follow the block quotation with commentary of his own? can Rich do more than "support" an argument, can a student argue with Rich's words, use them as a point to push off from?).

I want this issue to be precise as well as abstract. You can teach a lot about a writer's possible relations with the past by looking at how and why she uses a passage from an assigned text. This is not, in other words, simply a matter of reproducing standard texts, but as using them as points of deflection, appropriation, improvisation, or penetration (those are Mary Louise Pratt's terms). But you can't do this without making foremost the situatedness of writing, without outlining in red the network of affiliations that constitute writing in the academy.

Let me do this another way. There is a student in my class writing an essay on her family, on her parents' divorce. We've all read this essay. We've read it because the student cannot invent a way of talking about family, sex roles, separation. Her essay is determined by a variety of forces: the genre of the personal essay as it has shaped this student and this moment; attitudes about the family and divorce; the figures of "Father" and "Mother" and "Child" and so on. The moment of this essay is a moment of the general problematics of writing — who does what to whom; who does the writing, what can an individual do with the cultural field? Of course we can help the student to work on this essay by letting her believe it is hers — to think that the key problem is voice, not citation; to ask for realistic detail rather than to call attention to figuration. Almost two hundred years of sentimental realism prepares all of us for these lessons. We can teach students to be more effective producers of this product. We can also teach them its critique. Perhaps here is a way of talking about the real issues in the debate over academic writing? How can you not reproduce the master narrative of family life? How might a student writer negotiate with the professional literature? How and what might it mean to talk back to (or to talk with) Adrienne Rich about family life? What does it mean for a student to claim that her own experience holds equivalent status with Rich's memories as material to work on?

Teachers as Writers

We have several examples of academics announcing that they are now abandoning academic writing. I am thinking of Jane Tompkins' recent article, "Me and My Shadow." I am thinking of other similar moments of transcendence: Mina Shaughnessy's use of Hoggart and Baldwin as writers who could use autobiography to do intellectual work. I am thinking of Mike Rose's book, *Lives on the Boundary.* I am thinking of the recent issue of *PRE/TEXT* devoted to "expressive writing." I am thinking of the roles Gretel Ehrlich or Richard Selzer have played at this conference, or for scholars like Peter and Chuck Schuster. Or that wonderful session of CCCC where Nancy Sommers and Pat Hoy presented extended personal essays as conference papers. I am thinking of Don McQuade's chair's address at the 1989 CCCC. I am thinking of some of Peter's prose. And some of my own.

I seem to be saying that one cannot not write academic discourse, and yet here are examples of the academics pushing at the boundaries in decidedly academic settings. I don't see this as a contradiction. I would say that these are not examples of transcendence but of writers calling up, for a variety of purposes, different (but highly conventional) figures of the writer. These are writers taking pleasure in (or making capital of) what are often called "literary devices" — dialogue, description, the trope of the real, the figure of the writer at the center of sentimental realism. There is great pleasure in writing this way (making the world conform to one's image, exalting one's "point of view"), and there are strategic reasons for not doing academic writing when it is expected — I would say all great academic writers know this. I would call the writing I cited above examples of blurred genres, not free writing, and both genres represent cultural interests (in reproducing the distinct versions of experience and knowledge). In my department, this other form of narrative is often called "creative nonfiction" or "literary nonfiction" — it is a way to celebrate individual vision, the detail of particular worlds. There is an argument in this kind of prose too, an argument about what is real and what it means to inhabit the real. The danger is assuming that one genre is more real than the other (a detailed, loving account of the objects in my mother's kitchen is more "real" than a detailed loving account of the discourse on domesticity found in nineteenth-century American women's magazines) — in assuming that one is real writing and the other is only a kind of game academics play. The danger lies in letting these tendentious terms guide the choices we make in designing the curriculum.

A Brief History

Why, we might ask, do we have such a strong desire to talk about schooling as though it didn't have to be schooling, a disciplinary process? I have started one answer — it is part of a general desire to erase the past and its traces from the present.

I would also say that our current conversations are very much a product of an important moment in composition in the early 1970s — one in which Peter played a key role. At a time when the key questions facing composition could have been phrased as questions of linguistic difference — what is good writing and how is that question a question of race, class, or gender? — at a time when composition could have made the scene of instruction the object of scholarly inquiry, there was a general shift away from questions of value and the figure of the writer in a social context of writing to questions of process and the figure of the writer as an individual psychology. If you turn to work by figures who might otherwise be thought of as dissimilar — Britton, Moffett, Emig, Northrop Frye, Jerome Bruner — you will find a common displacement of the social and a celebration of the individual as fundamentally (or ideally) congruent with culture and history. Here is how it was phrased: there is no real difference between the child and the adult (that's Bruner); the curriculum is in the learner (that's Moffett and Britton); we find the universal mind of man in the work of individuals (that's Frye). All find ways of equating change with growth, locating both the process and the mechanism within an individual psychology, equating the learner with that which must be learned. And, as a consequence, schooling becomes secondary, not the primary scene of instruction, but a necessary evil in a world that is not well-regulated, where people would naturally mature into myth or prose or wisdom. School is secondary, instrumental, something to be overcome. And, in a similar transformation, writing becomes secondary, instrumental (to thinking or problem solving or deep feeling or unconscious imaginative forces).

I would say that the argument that produces archetypal criticism produces cognitive psychology, free writing, and new journalism: I've got Bruner, Linda Flower, Peter, Tom Wolfe, and John McPhee all lined up in this genealogy, this account of the modern curricular production of the independent author, the celebration of point-of-view as individual artifact, the promotion of sentimental realism (the true story of what I think, feel, know, and see).

Conclusion, or, So How Do I Get Out of This?

I am at the point where I should have a conclusion, but I don't. I could say this is strategic. Peter and I are having a conversation, and so it would be rude to conclude. Let me reimagine my position by rephrasing the questions that allow me access to it. Here is how I would now phrase the questions that I take to be the key questions in the debate on academic writing:

Should we teach new journalism or creative nonfiction as part of the required undergraduate curriculum? That is, should all students be required to participate in a first person, narrative or expressive genre whose goal it is to reproduce the ideology of sentimental realism — where a world is made in the image of a single, authorizing point of view? a narrative that celebrates a world made up of the details of private life and whose hero is sincere?

I don't have an easy answer to this question. It is like asking, should students be allowed to talk about their feelings after reading *The Color Purple*? Of course they should, but where and when? and under whose authority?

I think it is possible to say that many students will not feel the pleasure or power of authorship unless we make that role available. Without our classes, students will probably not have the pleasure or the power of believing they are the figure that they have seen in pieces they have read: the figure who is seeing the world for the first time, naming it, making their thoughts the center of the world, feeling the power of their own sensibilities. This has been true for teachers in the Writing Projects; it will be true in our classes. Unless we produce this effect in our classroom, students will not be Authors.

There is no question but that we can produce these effects. The real question is, should we?

In a sense, I feel compelled to argue that we should. We should teach students to write as though they were not the products of their time, politics, and culture, not our products, as though they could be free, elegant, smart, independent, the owners of all that they say. Why should they be denied this pleasure; or, why should it be reserved for some writers in our culture and not for others?

But I can also phrase the question this way: Why should I or a program I stand for be charged to tell this lie, even if it is a pleasant and, as they say, empowering one for certain writers or writers at a certain stage of their education? Why am I in charge of the reproduction of this myth of American life?

Or — is it a matter of stages in a writer's education? Should we phrase it this way: a nineteen-year-old has to learn to be a committed realist in order later to feel the potential for the critique of this position. People used to say something like this about traditional forms of order in the essay: you have to learn to write like E. B. White before you can learn to write like Gertrude Stein. Picasso couldn't have been a cubist if he hadn't learned to draw figures.

Learn to be logocentric? Learn to celebrate individualism? Learn to trust one's common sense point of view? Who needs to learn this at eighteen? Well, one might argue that students need to learn to do it well, so that it seems like an achievement. That is, students should master the figures and forms, learn to produce an elegant, convincing, even professional quality narrative before learning its critique and imagining its undoing.

I could phrase the question this way: Should composition programs self-consciously maintain a space for the "author" in a university curriculum that has traditionally denied students the category of author (by making students only summarizers or term paper writers)?

But it is too easy to say yes if I phrase the question like that. What if I put it this way? Should composition programs maintain a space for, reproduce the figure of, the author at a time when the figure of the author is under attack in all other departments of the academy? That is, should we be conservative when they are radical? Should we be retrograde in the face of an untested avante-garde?

Or — are we (should we be) a part of the critique, given our privileged role in the production of authors in the university curriculum, our positions in charge of substations in the culture's determined production of readers and writers?

When I phrase the question that way, the answers become easy. I don't think I need to teach students to be controlled by the controlling idea, even though I know my students could write more organized texts. I don't think I need to teach sentimental realism, even though I know my students could be better at it than they are. I don't think I need to because I don't think I should. I find it a corrupt, if extraordinarily tempting genre. I don't want my students to celebrate what would then become the natural and inevitable details of their lives. I think the composition course should be part of the general critique of traditional humanism. For all the talk of paradigm shifting, the composition course, as a cultural force, remains fundamentally unchanged from the nineteenth century. I would rather teach or preside over a critical writing, one where the critique is worked out in practice, and for lack of better terms I would call that writing, "academic writing."

Bartholomae's Insights as a Resource for Your Teaching

1. Bartholomae implies that we serve students more honestly when we acknowledge that discourse communities require novices to learn the ways of knowing and the "language" of the community. When writing instructors teach students to read texts actively and critically and to grapple in writing with the ideas, arguments, and words of the texts they read, then students will be better able to use writing as learning across the curriculum.

   If you share a short text with students and explain the process you use to read actively, you can model an identity as a writer and reader to students who need to practice such an identity. Some students will have a repertoire of reading strategies that they learned in high school, but may not have learned how to read texts — including their own texts — as writers. When you show students how to read nonfiction texts critically and how to use writing to practice discourse, you assist them both in writing courses and in other discourse communities. Don't be surprised if, when you pose questions that critique texts, students respond by exclaiming, "Now I know what my sociology teacher wants!" or "I never thought that the cultural context mattered."

2. Bartholomae states that "it is possible to say that many students will not feel the pleasure or power of authorship unless we make that role available." This may explain why student writers often select the personal narrative they wrote as the work they value most. Such an essay may be their first experience of feeling in control of the text and having authority, "making their thoughts the center of the world, feeling the power of their own sensibilities."

   Bartholomae implies that our instruction should produce this effect whether the writing be expressive or academic. Review your own intellectual history to see where and when you had the pleasure and belief Bartholomae describes. Collect those texts, if possible, and share them with your students along with a personal narrative that traces your processes of situating yourself among other texts with authority.

3. Use your dialectical journal to argue for and against personal writing and then academic writing as the focus of the course you teach. Talk with colleagues about their opinions. Draft a statement about your beliefs, and use it in your philosophy of teaching writing or as an entry in your teaching portfolio.

Bartholomae's Insights as a Resource for the Writing Classroom

1. Ask students who have written from recall to return to those narratives later in the semester and to connect them with professional texts. Look at the questions Bartholomae lists as he talks about teaching critique. If you structure such an assignment, present the prompt soon after evaluating and returning the writing from recall and allow plenty of time for research, reading, drafting, and revising. You may need to help the writers in individual conferences to brainstorm possible approaches and texts.

2. Organize small groups to critique one of the readings from *The Bedford Guide for College Writers,* using three perspectives they have learned in their core courses. Model for students how you approach a reading with multiple perspectives — using insights from sociology, political science, and cognitive psychology, for example. When groups report their findings, keep a list of the perspectives they applied. Ask students to come to the next class period prepared to repeat the exercise using three perspectives beyond reader's response to critique another reading from *The Bedford Guide for College Writers.*

3. Design a self-assessment protocol for students to identify and reflect on their critical reading processes. You might use questions such as these: (1) Describe as specifically as possible what you did to read this text. (2) What parts of the text did you find troublesome and why? (3) To what degree did you read this text in the way you habitually read texts? (4) How confident are you about your interpretation of the reading? (5) What goals do you have for becoming a stronger reader of texts?

You could also write a text-based set of questions that will let readers assess their command of the text. Ask them, after class discussion of the text, to reflect on their critical reading in their journal.

PATRICIA BIZZELL AND *Research as a Social Act*
BRUCE HERZBERG

Bizzell and Herzberg offer an alternative definition of research: "a social, collaborative act that draws on and contributes to the work of a community that cares about a given body of knowledge." They demonstrate that no researcher is solitary in a process of investigating. A sense of what can and should be researched develops from the "knowledge community" to which the researcher belongs. They explain that every researcher communicates with other researchers in a knowledge community and converses with them about preliminary results and directions of future research and writing. "Original" research extends the body of knowledge and also creates new channels for new knowing.

With this definition of research as a social act, the authors also provide a new definition of research-as-recovery. They report that this researcher "is interpreting and reinterpreting the community's knowledge in light of new needs and perspectives, and in so doing creating and disseminating new knowledge." (You can see in this discussion that Bizzell and Herzberg share many assumptions with Bartholomae [56]).

After defining research as a social and collaborative act, Bizzell and Herzberg suggest that we think about a writing classroom as one neighborhood in the larger academic community. The apprentice researchers in this small neighborhood are participating in the same processes of investigation as are the "experts" in the larger academic community.

With these definitions, the writers demystify research as an experience beyond the grasp of novice readers and writers. Notice how the discussion in A Writer's Research Manual *also shows student researchers interpreting and reinterpreting community knowledge and disseminating new knowledge.*

"Research" can be defined in several ways. First, it may mean discovery, as in the discovery of new information about the world by a researcher. We often call this work "original" research and think of the researcher as a solitary genius, alone in a study or, more likely, a laboratory. Second, "research" may mean the recovery from secondary sources of the information discovered by others. This is often the way we think of student research: students go to the library to extract information from books for a research paper. These two definitions call for some examination.

The first kind of research — discovery — seems more valuable than the second kind — recovery. Discovery adds to the world's knowledge, while recovery adds only to an individual's knowledge (some might add, "if we're lucky"). No matter how we protest that both kinds of research are valuable, there is a distinctly secondary quality to recovery. After all, recovery is dependent entirely upon discovery, original research, for its materials. Discovery actually creates new knowledge, while recovery merely reports on the results of the work of those solitary geniuses.

Common sense tells us that students, with rare exceptions, do not do original research until graduate school, if then. Students and teachers quite naturally share the feeling that research in school is, thus, mere recovery. Consequently, students and teachers often conclude that students are not likely to produce anything very good when they do this kind of research. Indeed, one cannot be doing anything very good while piling up the required number of facts discovered by others. Research-as-recovery seems to justify writing a paper by copying others' accounts of what they have discovered.

If we try, however, to remedy the defects of the research-as-recovery paper by calling for actual discovery, we run into more problems. Those who hope to do original research must know, before anything else, where gaps exist in current knowledge. And, of course, knowing where the holes are requires knowing where they are not. For most (perhaps all) students, this takes us back to research-as-recovery, that plodding effort to find out some of what others have already figured out.

Even research that evaluates sources of information, relates the accounts of information to one another, frames an argument that ties them together, and either reveals something important about the sources themselves or develops into a new contribution on the same topic requires, like discovery, a grasp of a field of knowledge that students cannot be expected to have.

The problem with both kinds of research, then, hinges on knowledge itself. The popular image of the solitary researcher in the lab or the library does not hint at the problem of knowledge — that these people are workers in knowledge who need knowledge as a prerequisite to their work. According to the popular image, they simply find facts. If that were all, presumably anyone could find them. But we know that is hardly the case.

What successful researchers possess that our students typically do not is knowledge, the shared body of knowledge that helps scholars define research projects and employ methods to pursue them. Invariably, researchers use the work of others in their field to develop such projects and consult others in the field to determine what projects will be of value. In short, all real research takes place and can only take place within a community of scholars. Research is a social act. Research is always collaborative, even if only one name appears on the final report.

This, then, is the third definition of research: a social, collaborative act that draws on and contributes to the work of a community that cares about a given body of knowledge. This definition is also a critique of the popular images that we have been examining. For, by the social definition of research, the solitary researcher is not at all solitary: the sense of what can and should be done is derived from the knowledge community. The researcher must be in constant, close communication with other researchers and will likely share preliminary results with colleagues and use their suggestions in further work. Her or his contributions will be extensions of work already done and will create new gaps that other researchers will try to close. Finally, his / her work of discovery is impossible without continuous recovery of the work of others in the community.

The social definition also allows us to revise the notion of research-as-recovery, for the recoverer in a community of knowledge is not merely rehashing old knowledge or informing himself / herself about a randomly chosen topic — he / she is interpreting and reinterpreting the community's knowledge in light of new needs and perspectives, and in so doing creating and disseminating new knowledge. The activity of interpretation reveals what the community values and where the gaps in knowledge reside. "Study knows that which yet it doth not know," as Shakespeare recognized long ago.

In many fields, the activities of synthesis and interpretation are primary forms of research. Think, for example, of the fields of history, philosophy, art and literary criticism, even sociology, economics, and psychology. But the important point is that no field of knowledge can do without such work. Clearly, the lab-science image of research is inaccurate, unrepresentative, and unhelpful. Research as a social act makes far more sense.

This new definition of research changes what it means for students to do research in school. In what ways do students participate in knowledge communities? One well-known and successful research assignment — the family history — suggests that in this very real community, student researchers find material to be interpreted, contradictions to be resolved, assertions to be supported, and gaps to be filled. They share the information and interpretations with the rest of the community, the family, who do not possess such a synthesis and are grateful to get it. But how do students fit into academic knowledge communities that are so much larger and colder than the family?

First, we must recognize that secondary- and middle-level students are novices, slowly learning the matter and method of school subjects. But they need not master the knowledge of the experts in order to participate in the sub-community of novices. They will need to know what other students know and do not know about a subject that they are all relatively uninformed about. In other words, they need to have a sense of what constitutes the shared body of knowledge of their community and a sense of the possible ways to increase that knowledge by useful increments. Imagine the classroom as a neighborhood in the larger academic community. Students contributing to the knowledge of the class are engaged in research in much the same way that expert researchers contribute to the larger community. They find out what is known — the first step in research — and identify what is unknown by sharing their knowledge amongst themselves. Then, by filling in the gaps and sharing what they find, they educate the whole community.

There are several practical implications for reimagining research in this way:

1. The whole class must work in the same area of inquiry — not the same topic, but different aspects of the same central issue. A well-defined historical period might do: by investigating work, play, social structure, literature, politics, clothing styles, food, and so on, students would become local experts contributing to a larger picture of the period. We will look at other examples later.

2. Students will need some common knowledge, a shared text or set of materials and, most of all, the opportunity to share with each other what they may already know about the subject. By collaborating on a questionnaire or interviewing each other, students learn valuable ways of doing primary research.

3. They will need to ask questions, critically examine the shared knowledge, and perhaps do some preliminary investigation to determine what the most tantalizing unknowns may be. Here again, some free exchange among class members will be helpful.

4. The exchange of ideas must continue through the process of discovery. Like expert researchers, students need to present working papers or colloquia to the research community, distribute drafts and respond to feedback, and contribute to the work of others when they are able. Finally, their work must be disseminated, published in some way, and made available to the group. The early framework of the research community ought not to be reduced to a way to introduce the regular old term paper.

A perfectly good way to choose the general area of research for a class is simply to choose it yourself. Teachers represent the larger community and can be expected to know something about the topic at hand and provide guidance, so if the topic interests the teacher, all the better. Of course, the teacher can lean toward topics that may interest the class. Students may be asked to choose from among several possibilities suggested by the teacher, but it is likely to be needlessly daunting to the students to leave the whole selection process to them. Among the possibilities for class topics: utopia, Shakespeare's England, Franklin's America, the jazz age, the death of the dinosaurs, the year you were born, images of childhood, the idea of school, work and play, wealth and poverty, country and city, quests and heroes, creativity — it's easy to go on and on.

Central texts can be books, photocopied selections, a film, or videotapes. More's *Utopia* might work for some classes, but a utopian science fiction book might be better for others, and the description of the Garden of Eden, a well-known utopia, is only three pages long. Shakespeare plays are easy to come by, as is Franklin's *Autobiography* or selections from it. Not every topic will require such materials, of course. For some topics, the students' interviews or other initial responses might be compiled into the central text.

The shared knowledge of the group might be elicited through alternate writing and discussion sessions, the students answering questions like "what do you know about X?" or "what would you like to know about X?" Interviews and questionnaires also work, as noted. All of this preliminary reading, writing, and discussion will help to create a sense of community and give students a jump-start on writing for the group, rather than for the teacher. Needless to say, the teacher ought not to grade and need not even read such preliminary work, beyond requiring that it be done.

Identifying a gap in the group's knowledge and choosing a topic for individual research may still be difficult, and it helps to be armed with suggestions if the students run out of ideas or need to be focused. Have a list of questions about utopias, a list of attempted utopian communities, the names of prominent figures in the period under discussion, some key ideas or events or issues to pursue, and so on. Students may not see, in the central text, problems like class differences in opportunities for schooling, or assumptions about the place of women, or attitudes linked to local or historical circumstances. If discussion and preliminary research do not turn them up, the teacher can reasonably help out. We need not pretend that we are inventing a new field of inquiry, but we must beware of the temptation to fall back on assigned topics.

Having students share drafts and give interim reports takes time, but it is usually time well spent. Students can learn to provide useful feedback to other students on drafts of papers — teachers should not read every draft. Students acting as draft-readers can respond to set questions (what did you find most interesting? what do you want to learn more about?) or work as temporary collaborators in attacking problem areas or listen to drafts read aloud and give oral responses. Other kinds of sharing may be worthwhile. Annotated bibliographies might be compiled and posted so that resources can be shared. Groups might lead panel discussions to take the edge off formal oral presentations. Reading aloud and oral reporting are good ways, too, of setting milestones for writing, and public presentation is important for maintaining the sense of community. Oral reports, by the way, tend to be better as drafts than as final presentations — the feedback is useful then, and anxiety about the performance is muted. Publishing the final results is the last step — copies of the papers might be compiled with a table of contents in a ring binder and put on reserve in the school library, for example.

These activities do not eliminate problems of footnote form and plagiarism, but in the setting of a research community, the issues of footnoting and plagiarism can be seen in a fresh light. Students should be able to articulate for themselves the reasons why members of a community would want to enforce among themselves (and their novices) a common and consistent method of citation. When knowledge exists to be exchanged, footnotes facilitate exchange. So too with plagiarism: members of the community would love to see themselves quoted and footnoted, but not robbed.

An excellent way to teach citation and reinforce community cohesion is to ask students to cite each other. How do you cite another student's paper, especially in draft form? How do you cite an oral report? How do you thank someone for putting you onto an idea? These citation forms may be used rarely, but they are good ways to stir up interest in the need for and uses of footnotes.

If the students are discovering the process of drafting, peer-review, and interim reports for the first time, the problems of discussing work-in-progress may come up in that context. Many students have learned that it is "wrong" to look at someone else's paper and will just be learning about the way professionals share and help each other with their work. A good place to see how collaboration works is to look at the pages of acknowledgments in books. Students will find, in all of their textbooks, long lists of people who are acknowledged for help in the process of writing. Writing their own acknowledgments will allow students to talk about how their ideas were shaped by others, especially by those who cannot reasonably be footnoted.

If the social act of research is successful, students have the opportunity to learn that knowledge is not just found, but created out of existing knowledge. And if people create knowledge, it is reasonable to expect knowledge to change. What people regard as true may be something other than absolute fact. Indeed, it may be only a temporary formulation in the search for better understanding. We can hope that our students will develop ways to evaluate knowledge as a social phenomenon and progress toward a critical consciousness of all claims to knowledge.

Bizzell and Herzberg's Insights as a Resource for Your Teaching

1. If you decide to conduct research in your writing classroom, keep in mind that your colleagues can assist you in defining a research question, in interpreting preliminary research, in determining the next steps to take in your research, and in preparing your essay for a scholarly journal or for presentation at a conference focused on composition studies. Notice how many of the writing theorists in this ancillary acknowledge collaboration in their research and writing.

Bizzell and Herzberg's Insights as a Resource for the Writing Classroom

1. Bizzell and Herzberg offer some very practical advice about designing research units or building a syllabus for a research writing course (a frequent second-semester requirement in American universities). If you are including a research unit in a writing course, invite the class members to brainstorm "central issues" that either the entire group or smaller research groups can use for inquiry. If you as the "expert" in the knowledge community decide on a central issue or theme, be prepared to assist students to generate topics from that central issue.

2. Particularly in the sciences and social sciences, students are required to work collaboratively and to conduct research that leads to a group essay. In Chap-

ter 29, "Writing the Research Paper," the authors of *The Bedford Guide* suggest that students team up to write a literary research paper. Be ready to facilitate the group process of research writing groups using the guidelines in Chapter 36 of *Practical Suggestions*; most first-year writers are unaccustomed to group research and group writing and will appreciate your guidance when they meet snags.

3. Bizzell and Herzberg emphasize that the instructor should not read every draft but should organize peer reading sessions. If you encourage students to use word processing for research writing, ask each writer to print several hard copies and distribute them for fellow writers to carry away and read and respond to.

4. Oral reports on research in process, as the authors suggest, provide additional opportunities for peer evaluation. In addition, you can hold conferences with writers about drafting a sustained essay from the research because your "preparation time" is freed up by students preparing for and presenting oral reports and / or syntheses.

5. Publication of completed researched essays is critical to defining a knowledge community. You'll find advice about publishing student writing in *Practical Suggestions*, Chapter 2.

PAULO FREIRE   *Excerpt from* **Pedagogy of the Oppressed**

Paolo Freire's Pedagogy of the Oppressed *ranks among this century's most important books about learning and teaching. In this excerpt, Freire delineates and sharply criticizes what he calls the "banking concept" of education, in which teachers narrate long blocks of material for students to memorize and then repeat on a test. Such an approach alienates the students from the teacher, from each other, from the material being taught, and from the world at large. It allows no space for dynamic interaction or critical engagement. Freire favors "problem-posing," an approach designed to sharpen the students' skills as critical thinkers and readers and to help them become active learners and citizens. Freire's work is grounded in deep phenomenological analysis, but it remains entirely accessible to those not familiar with these terms. Freire is committed to diminishing social injustice and oppression by recognizing the classroom as a potential scene of revolutionary struggle.*

A careful analysis of the teacher-student relationship at any level, inside or outside the school, reveals its fundamentally *narrative* character. This relationship involves a narrating Subject (the teacher) and patient, listening objects (the students). The contents, whether values or empirical dimensions of reality, tend in the process of being narrated to become lifeless and petrified. Education is suffering from narration sickness.

The teacher talks about reality as if it were motionless, static, compartmentalized, and predictable. Or else he expounds on a topic completely alien to the existential experience of the students. His task is to "fill" the students with the contents of his narration — contents which are detached from reality, disconnected from the totality that engendered them and could give them significance. Words are emptied of their concreteness and become a hollow, alienated, and alienating verbosity.

The outstanding characteristic of this narrative education, then, is the sonority of words, not their transforming power. "Four times four is sixteen; the capital of Pará is Belém." The student records, memorizes, and repeats these phrases without perceiving what four times four really means, or realizing the true significance of "capital" in the affirmation "the capital of Pará is Belém," that is, what Belém means for Pará and what Pará means for Brazil.

Narration (with the teacher as narrator) leads the students to memorize mechanically the narrated content. Worse yet, it turns them into "containers," into "receptacles" to be "filled" by the teacher. The more completely he fills the receptacles, the better a teacher he is. The more meekly the receptacles permit themselves to be filled, the better students they are.

Education thus becomes an act of depositing, in which the students are the depositories and the teacher is the depositor. Instead of communicating, the teacher issues communiqués and makes deposits which the students patiently receive, memorize, and repeat. This is the "banking" concept of education, in which the scope of action allowed to the students extends only as far as receiving, filing, and storing the deposits. They do, it is true, have the opportunity to become collectors or cataloguers of the things they store. But in the last analysis, it is men themselves who are filed away through the lack of creativity, transformation, and knowledge in this (at best) misguided system. For apart from inquiry, apart from the praxis, men cannot be truly human. Knowledge emerges only through invention and re-invention, through the restless, impatient, continuing, hopeful inquiry men pursue in the world, with the world, and with each other.

In the banking concept of education, knowledge is a gift bestowed by those who consider themselves knowledgeable upon those whom they consider to know nothing. Projecting an absolute ignorance onto others, a characteristic of the ideology of oppression, negates education and knowledge as processes of inquiry. The teacher presents himself to his students as their necessary opposite; by considering their ignorance absolute, he justifies his own existence. The students, alienated like the slave in the Hegelian dialectic, accept their ignorance as justifying the teacher's existence — but, unlike the slave, they never discover that they educate the teacher.

The *raison d'être* of libertarian education, on the other hand, lies in its drive towards reconciliation. Education must begin with the solution of the teacher-student contradiction, by reconciling the poles of the contradiction so that both are simultaneously teachers *and* students.

This solution is not (nor can it be) found in the banking concept. On the contrary, banking education maintains and even stimulates the contradiction through the following attitudes and practices, which mirror oppressive society as a whole:

(a) the teacher teaches and the students are taught;

(b) the teacher knows everything and the students know nothing;

(c) the teacher thinks and the students are thought about;

(d) the teacher talks and the students listen — meekly;

(e) the teacher disciplines and the students are disciplined;

(f) the teacher chooses and enforces his choice, and the students comply;

(g) the teacher acts and the students have the illusion of acting through the action of the teacher;

(h) the teacher chooses the program content, and the students (who were not consulted) adapt to it;

(i) the teacher confuses the authority of knowledge with his own professional authority, which he sets in opposition to the freedom of the students;

(j)   the teacher is the Subject of the learning process, while the pupils are mere objects.

It is not surprising that the banking concept of education regards men as adaptable, manageable beings. The more students work at storing the deposits entrusted to them, the less they develop the critical consciousness which would result from their intervention in the world as transformers of that world. The more completely they accept the passive role imposed on them, the more they tend simply to adapt to the world as it is and to the fragmented view of reality deposited in them.

The capability of banking education to minimize or annul the students' creative power and to stimulate their credulity serves the interests of the oppressors, who care neither to have the world revealed nor to see it transformed. The oppressors use their "humanitarianism" to preserve a profitable situation. Thus they react almost instinctively against any experiment in education which stimulates the critical faculties and is not content with a partial view of reality but always seeks out the ties which link one point to another and one problem to another.

Indeed, the interests of the oppressors lie in "changing the consciousness of the oppressed, not the situation which oppresses them";[1] for the more the oppressed can be led to adapt to that situation, the more easily they can be dominated. To achieve this end, the oppressors use the banking concept of education in conjunction with a paternalistic social action apparatus, within which the oppressed receive the euphemistic title of "welfare recipients." They are treated as individual cases, as marginal men who deviate from the general configuration of a "good, organized, and just" society. The oppressed are regarded as the pathology of the healthy society, which must therefore adjust these "incompetent and lazy" folk to its own patterns by changing their mentality. These marginals need to be "integrated," "incorporated" into the healthy society that they have "forsaken."

The truth is, however, that the oppressed are not "marginals," are not men living "outside" society. They have always been "inside" — inside the structure which made them "beings for others." The solution is not to "integrate" them into the structure of oppression, but to transform that structure so that they can become "beings for themselves." Such transformation, of course, would undermine the oppressors' purposes; hence their utilization of the banking concept of education to avoid the threat of student *conscientização*.

The banking approach to adult education, for example, will never propose to students that they critically consider reality. It will deal instead with such vital questions as whether Roger gave green grass to the goat, and insist upon the importance of learning that, on the contrary, Roger gave green grass to the rabbit. The "humanism" of the banking approach masks the effort to turn men into automatons — the very negation of their ontological vocation to be more fully human.

Those who use the banking approach, knowingly or unknowingly (for there are innumerable well-intentioned bank-clerk teachers who do not realize that they are serving only to dehumanize), fail to perceive that the deposits themselves contain contradictions about reality. But, sooner or later, these contradictions may lead formerly passive students to turn against their domestication and the attempt to domesticate reality. They may discover through existential experience that their present way of life is irreconcilable with their vocation to become fully human. They may perceive through their relations with reality that reality is really a *process*, undergoing constant transformation. If men are searchers and their ontological vocation is humanization, sooner or later they may perceive the contradiction in which banking education seeks to maintain them, and then engage themselves in the struggle for their liberation.

But the humanist, revolutionary educator cannot wait for this possibility to materialize. From the outset, his efforts must coincide with those of the students to engage in critical thinking and the quest for mutual humanization. His efforts must be imbued with a profound trust in men and their creative power. To achieve this, he must be a partner of the students in his relations with them.

The banking concept does not admit to such partnership — and necessarily so. To resolve the teacher-student contradiction, to exchange the role of depositor, prescriber, domesticator, for the role of student among students would be to undermine the power of oppression and serve the cause of liberation.

Implicit in the banking concept is the assumption of a dichotomy between man and the world: man is merely *in* the world, not *with* the world or with others; man is spectator, not re-creator. In this view, man is not a conscious being *(corpo consciente)*; he is rather the possessor of *a* consciousness: an empty "mind" passively open to the reception of deposits of reality from the world outside. For example, my desk, my books, my coffee cup, all the objects before me — as bits of the world which surrounds me — would be "inside" me, exactly as I am inside my study right now. This view makes no distinction between being accessible to consciousness and entering consciousness. The distinction, however, is essential: the objects which surround me are simply accessible to my consciousness, not located within it. I am aware of them, but they are not inside me.

It follows logically from the banking notion of consciousness that the educator's role is to regulate the way the world "enters into" the students. His task is to organize a process which already occurs spontaneously, to "fill" the students by making deposits of information which he considers to constitute true knowledge.[2] And since men "receive" the world as passive entities, education should make them more passive still, and adapt them to the world. The educated man is the adapted man, because he is better "fit" for the world. Translated into practice, this concept is well suited to the purposes of the oppressors, whose tranquility rests on how well men fit the world the oppressors have created, and how little they question it.

The more completely the majority adapt to the purposes which the dominant minority prescribe for them (thereby depriving them of the right to their own purposes), the more easily the minority can continue to prescribe. The theory and practice of banking education serve this end quite efficiently. Verbalistic lessons, reading requirements,[3] the methods for evaluating "knowledge," the distance between the teacher and the taught, the criteria for promotion: everything in this ready-to-wear approach serves to obviate thinking.

The bank-clerk educator does not realize that there is no true security in his hypertrophied role, that one must seek to live *with* others in solidarity. One cannot impose oneself, nor even merely co-exist with one's students. Solidarity requires true communication, and the concept by which such an educator is guided fears and proscribes communication.

Yet only through communication can human life hold meaning. The teacher's thinking is authenticated only by the authenticity of the students' thinking. The teacher cannot think for his students, nor can he impose his thought on them. Authentic thinking, thinking that is concerned about *reality,* does not take place in ivory tower isolation, but only in communication. If it is true that thought has meaning only when generated by action upon the world, the subordination of students to teachers becomes impossible.

Because banking education begins with a false understanding of men as objects, it cannot promote the development of what Fromm calls "biophily," but instead produces its opposite: "necrophily."

While life is characterized by growth in a structured, functional manner, the necrophilous person loves all that does not grow, all that is mechanical. The necrophilous person is driven by the desire to transform the organic into the inorganic, to approach life mechanically, as if all living persons were things. . . . Memory, rather than experience; having, rather than being, is what counts. The necrophilous person can relate to an object — a flower or a person — only if he possesses it; hence a threat to his possession is a threat to himself; if he loses possession he loses contact with the world. . . . He loves control, and in the act of controlling he kills life.[4]

Oppression — overwhelming control — is necrophilic; it is nourished by love of death, not life. The banking concept of education, which serves the interests of oppression, is also necrophilic. Based on a mechanistic, static, naturalistic, spatialized view of consciousness, it transforms students into receiving objects. It attempts to control thinking and action, leads men to adjust to the world, and inhibits their creative power.

When their efforts to act responsibly are frustrated, when they find themselves unable to use their faculties, men suffer. "This suffering due to impotence is rooted in the very fact that the human equilibrium has been disturbed."[5] But the inability to act which causes men's anguish also causes them to reject their impotence, by attempting

> to restore [their] capacity to act. But can [they], and how? One way is to submit to and identify with a person or group having power. By this symbolic participation in another person's life, [men have] the illusion of acting, when in reality [they] only submit to and become a part of those who act.[6]

Populist manifestations perhaps best exemplify this type of behavior by the oppressed, who, by identifying with charismatic leaders, come to feel that they themselves are active and effective. The rebellion they express as they emerge in the historical process is motivated by that desire to act effectively. The dominant elites consider the remedy to be more domination and repression, carried out in the name of freedom, order, and social peace (that is, the peace of the elites). Thus they can condemn — logically, from their point of view — "the violence of a strike by workers and [can] call upon the state in the same breath to use violence in putting down the strike."[7]

Education as the exercise of domination stimulates the credulity of students, with the ideological intent (often not perceived by educators) of indoctrinating them to adapt to the world of oppression. This accusation is not made in the naïve hope that the dominant elites will thereby simply abandon the practice. Its objective is to call the attention of true humanists to the fact that they cannot use banking educational methods in the pursuit of liberation, for they would only negate that very pursuit. Nor may a revolutionary society inherit these methods from an oppressor society. The revolutionary society which practices banking education is either misguided or mistrusting of men. In either event, it is threatened by the specter of reaction.

Unfortunately, those who espouse the cause of liberation are themselves surrounded and influenced by the climate which generates the banking concept, and often do not perceive its true significance or its dehumanizing power. Paradoxically, then, they utilize this same instrument of alienation in what they consider an effort to liberate. Indeed, some "revolutionaries" brand as "innocents," "dreamers," or even "reactionaries" those who would challenge this educational practice. But one does not liberate men by alienating them. Authentic liberation — the process of humanization — is not another deposit to be made in men. Liberation is a praxis:

the action and reflection of men upon their world in order to transform it. Those truly committed to the cause of liberation can accept neither the mechanistic concept of consciousness as an empty vessel to be filled, nor the use of banking methods of domination (propaganda, slogans — deposits) in the name of liberation.

Those truly committed to liberation must reject the banking concept in its entirety, adopting instead a concept of men as conscious beings, and consciousness as consciousness intent upon the world. They must abandon the educational goal of deposit-making and replace it with the posing of the problems of men in their relations with the world. "Problem-posing" education, responding to the essence of consciousness — *intentionality* — rejects communiqués and embodies communication. It epitomizes the special characteristic of consciousness: being *conscious of*, not only as intent on objects but as turned in upon itself in a Jasperian "split" — consciousness as consciousness *of* consciousness.

Liberating education consists in acts of cognition, not transferrals of information. It is a learning situation in which the cognizable object (far from being the end of the cognitive act) intermediates the cognitive actors — teacher on the one hand and students on the other. Accordingly, the practice of problem-posing education entails at the outset that the teacher-student contradiction be resolved. Dialogical relations — indispensable to the capacity of cognitive actors to cooperate in perceiving the same cognizable object — are otherwise impossible.

Indeed, problem-posing education, which breaks with the vertical patterns characteristic of banking education, can fulfill its function as the practice of freedom only if it can overcome the above contradiction. Through dialogue, the teacher-of-the-students and the students-of-the-teacher cease to exist and a new term emerges: teacher-student with students-teachers. The teacher is no longer merely the-one-who-teaches, but one who is himself taught in dialogue with the students, who in turn while being taught also teach. They become jointly responsible for a process in which all grow. In this process, arguments based on "authority" are no longer valid; in order to function, authority must be *on the side of* freedom, not *against* it. Here, no one teaches another, nor is anyone self-taught. Men teach each other, mediated by the world, by the cognizable objects which in banking education are "owned" by the teacher.

The banking concept (with its tendency to dichotomize everything) distinguishes two stages in the action of the educator. During the first, he cognizes a cognizable object while he prepares his lessons in his study or his laboratory; during the second, he expounds to his students about that object. The students are not called upon to know, but to memorize the contents narrated by the teacher. Nor do the students practice any act of cognition, since the object towards which that act should be directed is the property of the teacher rather than a medium evoking the critical reflection of both teacher and students. Hence in the name of the "preservation of culture and knowledge" we have a system which achieves neither true knowledge nor true culture.

The problem-posing method does not dichotomize the activity of the teacher-student: he is not "cognitive" at one point and "narrative" at another. He is always "cognitive," whether preparing a project or engaging in dialogue with the students. He does not regard cognizable objects as his private property, but as the object of reflection by himself and the students. In this way, the problem-posing educator constantly re-forms his reflections in the reflection of the students. The students — no longer docile listeners — are now critical co-investigators in dialogue with the teacher. The teacher presents the material to the students for their consideration, and re-considers his earlier considerations as the students express their own. The role of the problem-posing educator is to create, together with the students, the conditions under which knowledge at the level of the *doxa* is superseded by true knowledge, at the level of the *logos*.

Whereas banking education anesthetizes and inhibits creative power, problem-posing education involves a constant unveiling of reality. The former attempts to maintain the *submersion* of consciousness; the latter strives for the *emergence* of consciousness and *critical intervention* in reality.

Students, as they are increasingly posed with problems relating to themselves in the world and with the world, will feel increasingly challenged and obliged to respond to that challenge. Because they apprehend the challenge as interrelated to other problems within a total context, not as a theoretical question, the resulting comprehension tends to be increasingly critical and thus constantly less alienated. Their response to the challenge evokes new challenges, followed by new understandings; and gradually the students come to regard themselves as committed.

Education as the practice of freedom — as opposed to education as the practice of domination — denies that man is abstract, isolated, independent, and unattached to the world; it also denies that the world exists as a reality apart from men. Authentic reflection considers neither abstract man nor the world without men, but men in their relations with the world. In these relations consciousness and world are simultaneous: consciousness neither precedes the world nor follows it.

> La conscience et le monde sont dormés d'un même coup: extérieur par essence à la conscience, le monde est, par essence relatif à elle.[8]

In one of our culture circles in Chile, the group was discussing (based on a codification[9]) the anthropological concept of culture. In the midst of the discussion, a peasant who by banking standards was completely ignorant said: "Now I see that without man there is no world." When the educator responded: "Let's say, for the sake of argument, that all the men on earth were to die, but that the earth itself remained, together with trees, birds, animals, rivers, seas, the stars . . . wouldn't all this be a world?" "Oh no," the peasant replied emphatically. "There would be no one to say: 'this is a world'."

The peasant wished to express the idea that there would be lacking the consciousness of the world which necessarily implies the world of consciousness. *I* cannot exist without a *not-I*. In turn, the *not-I* depends on that existence. The world which brings consciousness into existence becomes the world *of* that consciousness. Hence, the previously cited affirmation of Sartre: *"La conscience et le monde sont dormés d'un même coup."*

As men, simultaneously reflecting on themselves and on the world, increase the scope of their perception, they begin to direct their observations towards previously inconspicuous phenomena:

> In perception properly so-called, as an explicit awareness [*Gewahren*], I am turned towards the object, to the paper, for instance. I apprehend it as being this here and now. The apprehension is a singling out, every object having a background in experience. Around and about the paper lie books, pencils, ink-well, and so forth, and these in a certain sense are also "perceived," perceptually there, in the "field of intuition"; but whilst I was turned towards the paper there was no turning in their direction, nor any apprehending of them, not even in a secondary sense. They appeared and yet were not singled out, were not posited on their own account. Every perception of a thing has such a zone of background intuitions or background awareness, if "intuiting" already includes the state of being turned towards, and this also is a "conscious experience," or more briefly

a "consciousness of" all indeed that in point of fact lies in the co-perceived objective background.[10]

That which had existed objectively but had not been perceived in its deeper implications (if indeed it was perceived at all) begins to "stand out," assuming the character of a problem and therefore of challenge. Thus, men begin to single out elements from their "background awarenesses" and to reflect upon them. These elements are now objects of men's consideration, and, as such, objects of their action and cognition.

In problem-posing education, men develop their power to perceive critically *the way they exist* in the world *with which* and *in which* they find themselves; they come to see the world not as a static reality, but as a reality in process, in transformation. Although the dialectical relations of men with the world exist independently of how these relations are perceived (or whether or not they are perceived at all), it is also true that the form of action men adopt is to a large extent a function of how they perceive themselves in the world. Hence, the teacher-student and the students-teachers reflect simultaneously on themselves and the world without dichotomizing this reflection from action, and thus establish an authentic form of thought and action.

Once again, the two educational concepts and practices under analysis come into conflict. Banking education (for obvious reasons) attempts, by mythicizing reality, to conceal certain facts which explain the way men exist in the world; problem-posing education sets itself the task of demythologizing. Banking education resists dialogue; problem-posing education regards dialogue as indispensable to the act of cognition which unveils reality. Banking education treats students as objects of assistance; problem-posing education makes them critical thinkers. Banking education inhibits creativity and domesticates (although it cannot completely destroy) the *intentionality* of consciousness by isolating consciousness from the world, thereby denying men their ontological and historical vocation of becoming more fully human. Problem-posing education bases itself on creativity and stimulates true reflection and action upon reality, thereby responding to the vocation of men as beings who are authentic only when engaged in inquiry and creative transformation. In sum: banking theory and practice, as immobilizing and fixating forces, fail to acknowledge men as historical beings; problem-posing theory and practice take man's historicity as their starting point.

Problem-posing education affirms men as beings in the process of *becoming* — as unfinished, uncompleted beings in and with a likewise unfinished reality. Indeed, in contrast to other animals who are unfinished, but not historical, men know themselves to be unfinished; they are aware of their incompletion. In this incompletion and this awareness lie the very roots of education as an exclusively human manifestation. The unfinished character of men and the transformational character of reality necessitate that education be an ongoing activity.

Education is thus constantly remade in the praxis. In order to *be*, it must *become*. Its "duration" (in the Bergsonian meaning of the word) is found in the interplay of the opposites *permanence* and *change*. The banking method emphasizes permanence and becomes reactionary; problem-posing education — which accepts neither a "well-be-haved" present nor a predetermined future — roots itself in the dynamic present and becomes revolutionary.

Problem-posing education is revolutionary futurity. Hence it is prophetic (and, as such, hopeful). Hence, it corresponds to the historical nature of man. Hence, it affirms men as beings who transcend themselves, who move forward and look ahead, for whom immobility represents a fatal threat, for whom looking at the past must only be a means of understanding more clearly what and who they are so that they can more wisely build the future. Hence, it identifies with the movement which engages men as beings aware of their incompletion — an historical movement which has its point of departure, its Subjects and its objective.

The point of departure of the movement lies in men themselves. But since men do not exist apart from the world, apart from reality, the movement must begin with the men-world relationship. Accordingly, the point of departure must always be with men in the "here and now," which constitutes the situation within which they are submerged, from which they emerge, and in which they intervene. Only by starting from this situation — which determines their perception of it — can they begin to move. To do this authentically they must perceive their state not as fated and unalterable, but merely as limiting — and therefore challenging.

Whereas the banking method directly or indirectly reinforces men's fatalistic perception of their situation, the problem-posing method presents this very situation to them as a problem. As the situation becomes the object of their cognition, the naïve or magical perception which produced their fatalism gives way to perception which is able to perceive itself even as it perceives reality, and can thus be critically objective about that reality.

A deepened consciousness of their situation leads men to apprehend that situation as an historical reality susceptible of transformation. Resignation gives way to the drive for transformation and inquiry, over which men feel themselves to be in control. If men, as historical beings necessarily engaged with other men in a movement of inquiry, did not control that movement, it would be (and is) a violation of men's humanity. Any situation in which some men prevent others from engaging in the process of inquiry is one of violence. The means used are not important; to alienate men from their own decision-making is to change them into objects.

This movement of inquiry must be directed towards humanization — man's historical vocation. The pursuit of full humanity, however, cannot be carried out in isolation or individualism, but only in fellowship and solidarity; therefore it cannot unfold in the antagonistic relations between oppressors and oppressed. No one can be authentically human while he prevents others from being so. Attempting *to be more* human, individualistically, leads to *having more,* egotistically: a form of dehumanization. Not that it is not fundamental *to have* in order *to be* human. Precisely because it *is* necessary, some men's *having* must not be allowed to constitute an obstacle to others' *having,* must not consolidate the power of the former to crush the latter.

Problem-posing education, as a humanist and liberating praxis, posits as fundamental that men subjected to domination must fight for their emancipation. To that end, it enables teachers and students to become Subjects of the educational process by overcoming authoritarianism and an alienating intellectualism; it also enables men to overcome their false perception of reality. The world — no longer something to be described with deceptive words — becomes the object of that transforming action by men which results in their humanization.

Problem-posing education does not and cannot serve the interests of the oppressor. No oppressive order could permit the oppressed to begin to question: Why? While only a revolutionary society can carry out this education in systematic terms, the revolutionary leaders need not take full power before they can employ the method. In the revolutionary process, the leaders cannot utilize the banking method as an interim measure, justified on grounds of expediency, with the intention of *later* behaving in a genuinely revolutionary fashion. They must be revolutionary — that is to say, dialogical — from the outset.

Notes

[1]Simone de Beauvoir, *La Pensée de Droite, Aujourd'hui* (Paris); ST, *El Pensamiento político de la Derecha* (Buenos Aires, 1963), 34.

[2]This concept corresponds to what Sartre calls the "digestive" or "nutritive" concept of education, in which knowledge is "fed" by the teacher to the students to "fill them out." See Jean-Paul Sartre, "Une idée fundamentale de la phénomenologie de Husserl: L'intentionalité," *Situations I* (Paris, 1947).

[3]For example, some professors specify in their reading lists that a book should be read from pages 10 to 15 — and do this to "help" their students!

[4]Fromm 41.

[5]Fromm 31.

[6]Fromm 31.

[7]Reinhold Niebuhr, *Moral Man and Immoral Society* (New York: Macmillan, 1960) 130.

[8]Sartre 32.

[9]See Chapter 3 [translator's note].

[10]Edmund Husserl, *Ideas: General Introduction to Pure Phenomenology* (London, 1969) 105–06.

Freire's Insights as a Resource for Your Teaching

1. Consider Freire's notion of "narration sickness." Nearly all of us give lectures to our students from time to time, but do all such lectures automatically succumb to "narration sickness"? Consider tailoring your own remarks in ways that maximize their efficacy as "problem posing." How would you gauge the difference, in your own terms, between classrooms that are based on "the banking concept" and those that strive to be "problem posing"?

2. Consider Freire's theory in light of Berlin's notions about ideology. Where does Freire's approach fit into Berlin's model? Which of Berlin's ideologies would most likely suffer from "narration sickness"?

Freire's Insights as a Resource for the Writing Classroom

1. Outline the basic structure of Freire's argument for your students, and then ask them to describe a memorable experience from their education that illustrates some of what Freire has theorized. Are there arguments to be made in favor of "banking" and "narration"? Have the students debate the issues that arise here.

2. Devote one week of class to a purely "problem-posing" model. Using Hillocks's six-step process, evaluate which dimensions of the experiment are successful and what sorts of unexpected results emerge. Are there gaps in the model you've implemented? Fine-tune your implementation, and see what happens during your second application of Freire's ideas.

KENNETH BRUFFEE   *Toward Reconstructing American Classrooms: Interdependent Students, Interdependent World*

Kenneth Bruffee researched and reflected on collaborative learning, writers, and writing in the 1970s and structured his book A Short Course in Writing *with peer tutoring and collaborative activities. The full title of the fourth edition shows the scope of his assumptions about the purpose of a writing course:* A Short Course in Writing: Composition, Collaborative Learning, and Constructive Reading. *Bruffee has written extensively about processes of collaboration and the social construction of knowledge in American classrooms; his extensive analysis and discussion in* Collaborative Learning *(Baltimore: Johns Hopkins UP, 1993) addresses the role of college and university teachers across the curriculum in helping "students converse with increasing facility in the language of the communities they want to join." The following article is Chapter 4 from this book.*

Bruffee, too, counsels instructors to identify and question their assumptions about the nature and authority of knowledge. Because collaborative learning contrasts markedly with the conventions of traditional teaching, Bruffee carefully defines terms and traces the philosophical history of collaborative learning. In particular, he emphasizes the distinctive role of assisting groups of students in classrooms or "transition communities"; all the students are leaving one community of knowledge to join a community that is new to them. Writing instructors can easily perceive connections among Bruffee's discussion of "translation" and "linguistic improvisation," their classrooms, and their reflective practice. They are likely to check out the volume to follow his references back to Chapter 3, where he specifically discusses teaching writing, or forward to Chapter 10, to eavesdrop on the translation groups William Perry reported in his study of sociocognitive development over college careers.

College and university teachers are likely to be successful in organizing collaborative learning to the degree that they understand the three kinds of negotiation that occur in the nonfoundational social construction of knowledge: negotiation among the members of a community of knowledgeable peers, negotiation at the boundaries among knowledge communities, and negotiation at the boundaries between knowledge communities and outsiders who want to join them.[1]

These three kinds of negotiation define both the practice of college and university teaching and the nature of college and university teaching as a profession. In Chapter 8 I will examine some of the professional implications of this distinguishing expertise. In the present chapter, after explaining the three kinds of negotiation in some detail, I will address some of their pedagogical and educational implications for colleges and universities and their teachers. In doing so, I will answer two questions: How does collaborative learning differ from foundational innovations in teaching? and, How does the thinking of college and university teachers about teaching have to change if change in college and university education is not to be superficial and ephemeral?

The first kind of negotiation that occurs in the nonfoundational social construction of knowledge is within a community of knowledgeable peers, among its members. Members of academic or professional knowledge communities such as law, medicine, and the academic disciplines negotiate with other members of the same community in order to establish and maintain the beliefs that constitute that community. Biochemists, for example (as we saw at the beginning of Chapter 3), review each other's work over the lab bench, and they read and respond to each other's published articles. This conversation within knowledge communities is what Thomas Kuhn calls *normal science* and, following Kuhn, what Richard Rorty calls *normal discourse.* As members of disciplinary and other kinds of knowledge communities, college and university teachers are fluent in the normal discourse of these communities.

The second kind of negotiation involved in constructing knowledge understood nonfoundationally occurs between different knowledge communities and is carried on at the boundaries where communities meet. Members of different academic and professional knowledge communities negotiate with one another in order to translate the language of one community into the language of another. They may do this so as to neutralize threats that one community seems to pose to the established beliefs of another, or they may do it to assimilate and normalize options that one knowledge community seems to offer to the other. Paleobotanists try to reconcile what they know with what the microbiologists are coming up with; New Critics defend themselves against what the deconstructionists have to say; physicists find themselves talking with historians, biologists with lawyers, ethnographers with literary critics. Kuhn and Rorty call this boundary negotiation *abnormal science* and *abnormal discourse*, respectively. Clifford Geertz calls it, somewhat less prejudicially if not necessarily more accurately, *nonstandard discourse*.

Nonstandard discourse is a demanding and uncertain kind of conversation. It is "nonstandard" because, in negotiation between two different knowledge communities, the language and ideas that one community accepts without resistance — for example, what they agree to count as a "real question" and an interesting answer to that question — is not likely to be accepted without resistance by another community. The standard that will prevail between two communities, if their boundary negotiation is successful, is a major part of what they have to negotiate. College and university teachers, as active members of their professional or academic communities, have to be able to engage in this nonstandard discourse of boundary negotiation between communities that they belong to and those that their colleagues belong to.

College and university teachers have to be especially adept at nonstandard, boundary discourse, because they have to engage in it professionally on two fronts. The third kind of negotiation involved in knowledge understood nonfoundationally occurs at community boundaries that may be even more difficult to negotiate than the boundaries that separate academic or professional communities. Teachers have to be able to translate at the community boundaries between the academic or professional knowledge communities that they belong to and uncountable numbers of nonacademic, nonprofessional communities that their students belong to. That is, they have to be able to translate the languages of academics and professionals into the languages of people who are not (yet) members of any academic or professional community, but who aspire to become members: from biologists to biology students, philosophers to philosophy students, literary critics to naive readers, and so on.

Mastering the linguistic improvisation involved in this third kind of nonstandard discourse — negotiation at the boundaries between knowledge communities and outsiders who want to join them — distinguishes a knowledge community's teachers from its ordinary members. More than anything else, this facility in negotiating what Mary Louise Pratt calls "contact zones . . . social spaces where cultures meet, clash, and grapple with each other, often in contexts of highly asymmetrical relations of power," defines the classroom authority of college and university teachers.[2] It also defines the cultural importance and cultural authority of college and university teachers outside the classroom and beyond the campus.

What makes boundary negotiation especially challenging is that people who are not yet members of the community of, say, chemists, philosophers, or literary critics are not simply members of no knowledge community at all. On the contrary, they are already stalwart, long-time, loyal members of an enormous array of other, mostly nonacademic, nonprofessional knowledge communities.

That is why negotiation between members of academic or professional communities and nonmembers is difficult. College and university students are decidedly not a *tabula rasa*. The language of caring, of counting to ten, of belligerence, or of baseball may be anybody's mother or father tongue, as the language of chemistry, say, can never be. So, although mere chemists have to be able to talk comprehensively as chemists with other chemists and, on occasion, perhaps, to a physicist, astronomer, biologist, or lawyer, college and university chemistry *teachers* have to be able to talk comprehensively as chemists also with all the Trekkies, romance-novel readers, canoers, computer hackers, fast-food restaurant assistant managers, and football players who aspire to become chemists or at least to learn something about chemistry.

Of these three kinds of negotiation, the most important to college and university teachers *as* teachers is of course the third. Skill in negotiating between knowledge communities of which the teacher is a member and those who aspire to join them — students — requires understanding first of all that every college and university classroom — indeed, every college and university — is a community that, like all communities, has its own set of rules, mores, values, and goals, all of them accepted, more or less, by everyone in the community. They regulate everyone's deportment, relationships, and expectations. They are appropriate to the assumptions, shared by everyone in the community, about human nature, the human mind, and the nature and authority of knowledge. The depth and persistence of these conventions and assumptions result in one of the quiet, nagging truths of college and university education: we tend to forget much of the subject matter of the courses we have taken shortly after we complete them, but we do not easily forget the conventions that govern those courses and the values implicit in them.

The foundational conventions that govern traditional college and university classrooms assume (as we shall see in Chapter 12) that the authority of teachers lies in their function as curators of acknowledged touchstones of value and truth above and beyond themselves, such as treasured artifacts of art, literature, science, mathematics, and the universals of sound reasoning. The authority of college and university teachers from this point of view rests on the understanding that knowledge is a kind of substance contained in and given form by the vessel we call the mind. Teachers transfer knowledge from their own fuller vessels to the less full vessels of their students. Teachers impart knowledge that was imparted to them, as it was imparted to them.

The classroom social structure and conventions implicit in these foundational assumptions — what Pratt aptly calls "pupiling" — are familiar to everyone who has attended an American college or university.[3] They prevail with few exceptions today the world over, from the two Cambridges to Tokyo, from first grade to Ph.D. They are so familiar that we take them for granted. Like the curatorial role of college and university teachers, they have an ancient and honorable history, they remain educationally valuable under certain local circumstances today, and they probably will always remain so.

The social structure and conventions of foundational college and university education assume a one-to-one relationship between student and teacher. Students talk to the teacher, write to the teacher, and determine their fate in relation to the teacher, individually. This is true no matter how many students there may be in a class: three, thirty, or three hundred. There is no recognized, validly institutionalized, productive relationship among students. More accurately, traditional teaching assumes and maintains a negative competitive relationship among students. They are officially anonymous to one another, and isolated. Classroom learning is an almost entirely individual process. It is not just that most foundational teaching does not encourage students to collaborate. Most foundational teaching does not recognize collaboration as educationally valid. In fact, in traditional teaching collaboration is highly suspect. In some forms it is the worst possible academic sin: plagiarism.

The conventions of traditional teaching can be classified under two headings, the Lecture Conventions and the Recitation Conventions. Lecture Convention teachers tend to talk and perform; their students listen and watch. Recitation Convention teachers tend to listen and watch; their students talk and perform. Most college and university teachers combine these conventions in some proportion or other. For example, Lecture-Recitation teachers may choose students who talk and perform particularly well to talk and perform in place of the teacher. Then the teacher listens and watches along with the rest of the class.

The normal goal of Lecture Convention teaching is to provide answers, promote the authority of those answers, and enhance the authority of the lecturer providing them. Since answers imply questions, it would seem that the role that questions play in Lecture Convention teaching must be particularly interesting and varied. In most cases, however, it is not. Most lecturers answer the questions that they are prepared and willing to answer. They may or may not accept questions raised by students, or they may answer some and finesse others.

The most common Lecture Convention in which questions do play a major role is Socratic Dialogue. The conventions of this form of teaching derive from Plato's *Meno,* in which Socrates teaches a slave. In Socratic Dialogue, students do not ask the questions. Teachers ask them, and the role that questions play in teaching is tightly controlled. Teachers approve or disapprove the answers students offer in response to questions. They try to lead students to say what teachers might as well have said themselves, had they chosen to. The line of reasoning taken during the dialogue is the teacher's own, leading to a point that the teacher has decided on beforehand.

Recitation Convention teaching differs from Lecture Convention teaching by shifting to students the burden of filling class time. In outlining the requirements of the course, the teacher makes it clear that students will do most of the talking and performing, specifies what they will perform and talk about, and explains what kind of talk it should be. The teacher retains the privilege of interrupting recitations at will in order to evaluate what students say, correct it, or elaborate on it.

Forms of Recitation Convention adapted to special circumstances include the Tutorial Convention, the Seminar Convention, the Writing Course Convention, and the Teamwork Convention. In each of these, students present their work individually, in written or oral form. Then they discuss their work with the teacher or answer questions that the teacher asks them about it. In turn, the teacher evaluates, corrects, or elaborates upon the student's work.

The Seminar Convention is a cost-efficient version of the Tutorial Convention. In tutorials, teachers meet students one at a time. In seminars, they meet them five to fifteen at a time. Tutorials and seminars both allow for considerable debate between students and the teacher and, in seminars under the teacher's direction and observation, among students. At issue is the quality of each student's live performance before the teacher in competition with other students. In a seminar a student sometimes replaces the teacher as the discussion moderator, but performance quality before the teacher is still the main criterion of judgment. Students who "take over the class" in this way become teacher surrogates. If they are wise and well adapted, they read a paper and field questions about their work in a way that is calculated to receive maximum approval from the teacher.

In the Writing Course Convention and its subgenre, the Creative Writing Course Convention, the teacher prompts students to comment on one another's essays, stories, poems, or plays. But in these classes, which are usually described publicly as being about writing, not about reading or criticism, teachers seldom instruct stu-

dents in how to engage helpfully in the intellectually demanding, aesthetically sophisticated, and socially delicate process of commenting helpfully on the work of
peers. As a result, students understand that their comments on one another's work
are made not primarily for the benefit of fellow students. They are a performance
before an audience of one, the teacher. In these comments students tend to become
(as we noticed in Chapter 1) alternately sharks and teddy bears, providing cutting
insult or effusive praise depending on their interpretation of "what the teacher
wants."

The Teamwork Convention is most often found in engineering and the sciences,
where it takes the form of research teams and in music, theater, and film in the form
of ensembles and production units. It is the most nearly collaborative of all traditional forms of teaching. Assigned to a team, students work together on a project
under the teacher's supervision. In some cases, all the members of the team are
equally responsible for the quality of the work they do together. In other cases, the
teacher evaluates a report written by each student on the team. At issue in most
cases is what students accomplish together, the product of their cooperative effort.
In educational teamwork at its best, the nature and quality of what students internalize and carry away from the experience is also at issue.

All four forms of the Recitation Convention allow teachers the prerogative of
lecturing when they choose, a prerogative that many teachers frequently exercise.
Science course laboratory work, for example, is a kind of recitation in which the
student's response takes the form of actively manipulating material and instruments
and then reporting that work in writing. But many labs are like the introductory
undergraduate astronomy lab described by one of Sheila Tobias's informants, in
which students saw no stars. The instructor spent every class hour working problems on the blackboard — in effect, lecturing. Some creative writing teachers fill
large portions of class time reading their own work to their students. Some seminar
teachers (the philosopher Edmund Husserl is reputed to have been a particularly
egregious example) lecture incessantly, believing all the while that they are "leading discussion."

A student's responsibility, according to these traditional classroom conventions,
is to "absorb" what the teacher, in one way or another, imparts. The teacher's responsibility is to impart knowledge to students and evaluate students' retention of
it. Teachers evaluate students in the same way their own teachers evaluated them,
and as the college or university in which they teach is likely to evaluate teachers, in
terms of their "product."

Dissatisfaction with the conventions of foundational teaching is hardly new. It
has grown throughout this century. John Dewey voiced it in the 1920s and 1930s. It
reached a peak in the late 1960s and early 1970s, when leading college and university teachers made well-known and widely discussed attempts to change the nature
of college and university teaching. Since that heyday of experimentation, widespread
interest in innovation has waned, except for scattered recent attempts to repackage
science education (discussed in Chapter 9); politically motivated efforts to change
or enlarge the literary "canon"; efforts to "personalize" teaching in the manner of
Roland Barthes; and a few largely speculative poststructuralist ventures (discussed
in Chapter 11).[4]

Most of these recent attempts are likely to fail for the same reason that similar
teaching innovations of the sixties failed, because their foundational assumptions
about the nature and authority of knowledge remain unquestioned. The innovations of the sixties tended to be of two types, corresponding to the inner-outer po-
larity of the foundational understanding of knowledge. Both hoped to improve stu-

dents' grasp of subject matter. One of the two alternatives was objectivist in approach, influenced by behaviorist notions of positive reinforcement, while the other was subjectivist, influenced by loosely thought-through notions borrowed from Rogerian group psychology.

One of the best known of the objectivist efforts to change the way college and university courses are traditionally taught was somewhat misleadingly called the personalized system of instruction, or PSI. In PSI, teachers determined procedures that students should follow and the results they should attain. Then they trained selected students to act as "proctors." Proctors reinforced both the procedures and the results achieved by those procedures. Thus, although PSI seemed to change the social relationship among students and between students and teachers by placing intermediaries between teachers and individual students, in fact it did not. It was a rigorously controlled "monitor" tutorial system of the sort described in Chapter 5. Proctors were, unequivocally for all involved, the teacher's agents — teachers writ small. Nor did PSI provide a vehicle for questioning the foundational assumptions that underlay it or in any way encourage such questions to be raised.

Taking the opposite tack from this objectivist approach, the motivating hope in subjectivist efforts to change college and university teaching was that students' emotional dependence on established authority could be overcome by giving them "complete freedom," defined as absence of direction from the teacher. These attempts at innovation equated freedom with individual enterprise. Their individualist emphasis reveals how deeply rooted these innovations were in traditional assumptions about the nature and authority of knowledge. The bottom line remained the individual student's "cognition." Lacking direction from the teacher and constructive relations with each other, a very few students — those who had already internalized the mores and practices favored by their teachers and who were comfortable in social isolation — showed themselves able to "handle" their "new-found freedom" by asserting their individuality. All the rest took one or another of the four alternatives that students typically have in traditional education: plodding acquiescence, cut-throat competition, self-destructive rebellion, or withdrawal.

The failure of these attempts to innovate without challenging the traditional understanding of knowledge tends to confirm John Dewey's observation that "the mere removal of external control" cannot guarantee "the production of self-control":

> It may be a loss rather than a gain to escape from the control of another person only to find one's conduct dictated by immediate whim and caprice; that is, at the mercy of impulses into whose formation intelligent judgment has not entered. A person whose conduct is controlled in this way has at most only the illusion of freedom. Actually he is directed by forces over which he has no command.[5]

Learning results, Dewey argues, when teachers exercise control indirectly through "work done as a social enterprise in which all individuals have an opportunity to contribute and to which all feel a responsibility." Productive community life of this sort, he insists, "does not organize itself in an enduring way spontaneously. It requires thought and planning ahead." Careful thought given to the social enterprise that controls the work is what the experimental teaching innovations of the sixties lacked. They rejected the tidy, reliable, well-understood, time-refined social conventions of traditional learning and the forms of schoolroom community life appropriate to the foundational understanding of knowledge. But they did not replace those conventions and forms with others appropriate to an alternative understanding of knowledge. Leaving the traditional understanding of knowledge implicitly in place and in many cases leaving students without guidance under stress, these honest efforts to innovate set themselves up to fail.[6]

Collaborative learning differs from these failed teaching innovations. It replaces the traditional social conventions of schoolroom community life with other conventions that students are, for the most part, already familiar with and can rely on for support under conditions of stress and that are appropriate to a clearly defined alternative understanding of knowledge. The social conventions of collaborative learning, which regulate deportment, relationships, and expectations, are of course not yet so time-refined as those of traditional teaching. Many college and university teachers are unfamiliar with them and with the understanding of knowledge appropriate to them. A good deal of conscious "thought and planning ahead" therefore still has to go into implementing them.

This thought and planning has to be directed toward organizing a classroom in which, as Dewey puts it, "all individuals have an opportunity to contribute something, and in which the activities in which all participate are the chief carrier of control."[7] In traditional classrooms, the teacher's intelligent judgment is exclusively in control. In collaborative learning, students, acting collaboratively, also exercise intelligent judgment, so their collaborative activities together with the teacher's become the chief carriers of control.

That is, the social structure and conventions of a collaborative classroom assume not a one-to-one relationship between student and teacher but, rather, a collaborative relationship among small groups of students and between the teacher and those groups functioning as classroom subunits. Students talk and write to the teacher and determine their fate in relation to the teacher. They do so, however, not as isolated individuals anonymous to one another, but organized in recognized, validly institutionalized, positive, productive relationships with other students.

Changing classroom social structure in this way changes not just how teachers exercise their authority but the very nature of the authority they exercise. It is therefore not the kind of change that teachers and students can merely acquiesce to. It has to be effected by thinking through and planning classroom social relationships in which authority is understood differently by teachers and students alike. It is classroom social relationships of this sort that collaborative learning establishes. In a collaborative learning classroom, no one's conduct is dictated by "impulses into whose formation intelligent judgment has not entered," and yet (as we saw in Chapters 2 and 3) a central issue is the locus of that intelligent judgment: the source of the prevailing authority of knowledge. By shifting the "activities" that are "the chief carrier of control" from those of a presiding individual to those of people working collaboratively, control is systematically reconstructed and relocated. It is located variously in student working groups of various sizes and complexity and in the knowledge communities that the teacher represents. The authority of the knowledge that each of these communities constructs varies according to the size and complexity of the community. That is, the authority of knowledge varies according to the intelligent judgment of the knowledge community that is at that moment in control in the classroom.

Collaborative learning therefore implies that teachers have to rethink what they have to do to get ready to teach and what they are doing when they are actually teaching. According to the traditional, foundational understanding of knowledge, teachers tend to think that the most important thing they have to do to prepare for teaching is to fill their own heads to overflowing with disciplinary knowledge and expertise so that they will have plenty in reserve with which to fill the heads of their students. Teachers stock up their own minds by reflecting reality as accurately as they can with their cognitive mental equipment, the mirror of nature we are all supposed to have built into our heads. Teachers read, do their research, and consult their notes. The mind's mirror collects images of the miscellaneous, unrelated elements that reality offers and presents those images to the other piece of mental equipment we are supposed to have in there, our inner eye. The teacher's inner eye discerns these images as coherently as it can, making sense of them by examining, interpreting, and synthesizing them according to some variety of mental structure, conceptual framework, or procedure of critical thinking and higher-order reasoning.

Once they have prepared themselves to teach, what teachers do when they actually set about teaching, understood foundationally, is reflect outward what their own inner eye has perceived, so that other people, their students, can reflect it in their mental mirrors and discern it with their inner eyes. Teachers reflect their knowledge outward by lecturing and leading students through their paces in recitation in ways outlined earlier in this chapter.

Throughout this process, the best teachers and the best students, we say, have insight. Theirs is "higher order" reasoning, because they have the clearest, most highly polished mental mirrors giving (when good teachers teach and when good students take tests) the most accurate, most all-encompassing reflection of reality, and they have the best trained, most sensitive, most discerning inner eyes to comprehend that reflection. In contrast, poor teachers, and students who learn slowly or inadequately are, as we say, "blind." Their mirrors don't reflect much reality, and the little bit they do reflect is inaccurate. Their inner eyes are insensitive and poorly trained. Theirs is "lower-order" reasoning. The reasoning of teachers must of course be of a "higher order," because their task is to "elevate" reasoning that we regard as being of a "lower order." Otherwise education would be a case, as we say, of "the blind leading the blind."

In contrast to this foundational view of what teachers do when they prepare and when they teach, the nonfoundational social constructionist understanding of knowledge implies that preparing to teach is not a process by which teachers stock up their own minds, and teaching is not a process by which they stock up others' in turn. Preparing to teach involves learning the languages of the relevant communities and creating social conditions in which students can become reacculturated into those communities by learning the languages that constitute them. That is, from this perspective, college and university teaching involves helping students converse with increasing facility in the language of the communities they want to join.

Thus, to teach mathematics, sociology, or classics is to create conditions in which students learn to converse as nearly as possible in the ways that, in their own communities, mathematicians converse with one another, sociologists converse with one another, and classicists converse with one another. To teach writing (as we saw in Chapter 3) is to create conditions in which students learn to converse with one another about writing as writers do, and it is also to create conditions in which students learn to write to each other as do the members of the community of literate people.

Setting out to teach this way leads teachers to ask themselves a set of questions that are quite different from the questions they ordinarily ask themselves. According to the foundational or cognitive understanding of knowledge, teachers ask themselves questions such as

- What's going on inside my students' heads?
- How can I get in there and change what's going on?
- What's the best way to impart to them what I know?

These questions arise when teachers believe that their job is to "reach" students and to empty into students' heads what teachers believe is filling their own. When teachers begin to think of their job instead as undertaking to reacculturate students into communities they are not yet members of, they tend to ask a wholly different set of questions. They no longer ask themselves subject-object questions about getting into other people's heads or teaching "how" *vs.* teaching "what." Instead, they ask themselves questions about what Thomas Kuhn calls "the special characteristics of the groups that create and use" the knowledge in question:

> How does one elect and how is one elected to membership in a particular community, scientific or not? What is the process and what are the stages of socialization to the group? What does the group collectively see as its goals; what deviations, individual or collective, will it tolerate; and how does it control the impermissible aberration?[8]

For college and university teachers, these questions have to be unpacked to reveal further questions about the social conditions in which students are most likely to gain fluency in the language of the disciplinary knowledge community that the teacher belongs to:

- What are those conditions and how can I best create them?

- How do the community languages my students already know reinforce or interfere with learning the language I am teaching?

- How can I help students renegotiate the terms of membership in the communities they already belong to?

- How can I make joining a new, unfamiliar community as unthreatening and fail-safe as possible?

In asking such questions as these, college and university teachers assume that learning is what Richard Rorty has called it. Learning, Rorty says, is not "a shift inside the person which now *suits* him to enter . . . new relationships" with "reality" and with other people. It is "a shift in a person's relations with others," period.[9] Teachers assume that their responsibility, as agents of educational reacculturation, is to help students make that shift. The best teachers, by this token, are those who mobilize students to work together in ways that make reacculturation possible. The best students are those who help effect constructive consensus by drawing both themselves and their peers into relevant conversation.

The most important tool that college and university teachers have at hand to help students reacculturate themselves into the knowledge communities they aspire to join is transition communities. Transition communities are small, new, temporary communities made up of people who want to make the same change. A teacher's role, besides helping students form transition communities, is (as we have seen in earlier chapters) to provide them with the tasks and occasions that will help them negotiate the transition they want to make.

Educational transition communities are sometimes misleadingly called support groups. This useful term was devised in the sixties by the women's liberation movement and the self-help mutual-aid movement to describe a basic reacculturative tool. Support groups are small autonomous or semiautonomous coalitions of people who recognize in each other similar needs and problems and learn to depend on one another to help fulfill those needs and solve those problems. Collaborative learning groups — for example, classroom consensus groups — are similar to support groups and in fact were first devised on the support-group model.[10]

Useful as it is, however, the term "support group" suggests that what is going on in the group is ancillary to something more important that those involved are doing somewhere else and which their work in the support group "supports." To call a "support group" a "transition community" has the advantage of suggesting that the most important thing going on — making a transition between established communities or constructing new communities yet to be established — is going on right there in that small local group, not somewhere else.

A close look at what goes on in transition communities suggests that what they really are is *translation* communities. They organize students into social relationships involving a "temporary fusion of interests" that allow them to relinquish dependence on their fluency in one community-constituting language (their "old" one) and acquire fluency in the language that constitutes the community of which they are now becoming members (their "new" one).[11] Enrolled in transition communities, students have a chance to learn and practice, relative to substantive issues, linguistic improvisation, that is, negotiation of the second kind listed at the beginning of this chapter. They carry on this nonstandard boundary discourse between the knowledge communities they belong to and one they do not belong to (the one in this case that they are trying to join), in order to reacculturate themselves to the standards — the language, mores, and goals — of that unfamiliar community.

The groups for learning medical judgment that Abercrombie reorganized students into were translation communities. In these groups, students translated the diverse languages they brought with them into the unfamiliar language of medical diagnosis that they were learning — the language of the new community that they aspired to join. The consensus groups that Harvard's New Pathways program plunges first-year medical students into and Uri Treisman's math and science study groups are translation communities in the same sense.

Many of the students William Perry interviewed had organized translation, or transition, communities in their residence houses (as we shall see in Chapter 10), but Perry thought it beneath the dignity of an instructor at Harvard College to help organize them.[12] Like Abercrombie's and Treisman's students but outside the institution's curricular framework, Perry's undergraduates negotiated among themselves the diverse languages they brought with them from their homes, and they negotiated between these languages and the new languages provided by the liberal education they were undertaking.

Such subcultural transitional social units as these maintain the coherence of students' lives in transit. They give their lives — and their language — a measure of stability as they loosen or give up their loyalties to the communities they are already members of, give up the comforts and sense of identity pertaining to those communities, form loyalties to communities that are new to them, and experience the comforts and sense of identity pertaining to those communities.

A transition community is therefore an odd, unstable, ephemeral social entity. Instability is of course entirely appropriate to communities of fence-sitters gathered on the boundary or "contact zone" between (probably) quite incompatible communities, engaged in what Thomas Kuhn correctly describes as the "threatening process" of translation.[13] The language and paralinguistic symbol systems that constitute transition communities — conversation across community boundaries — is nonstandard discourse in a number of respects. As we shall see in the next section, some of its language, some of its conventions, and some of the beliefs, values, traditions, interests, and goals that its members maintain are those of the communities its members are leaving. Some are those of the community they hope to join. Still others are common only to the conversation of transition communities. Furthermore, this unstable mix is itself undergoing constant change.

As a result, membership in a transition community may often be, as reacculturation always is, stressful and uncertain. The conversation of transition-community members is dominated by talk about these stresses and uncertainties of reacculturation. Much of it is in-the-same-boat talk. Members talk about what it was like to be a member of the old community, what it may be like to be a member of the new, unfamiliar community, and what a pain in the neck it is to change: nostalgia, anxious anticipation, and complaint.

Transition community members also talk a lot about coping. They trade hints and tips, some accurate, many apocryphal, about how a person is expected to behave and talk as a member of the community they hope to join. As Abercrombie noticed, they refute and cancel out each other's presuppositions and biases. They practice using the unfamiliar community's constituting language — sometimes accurately and appropriately, sometimes not, under as many different conditions, some relevant and some not, and in many different settings, some relevant and some not — so as gradually to become fluent in it.

To say that through collaborative learning nonfoundational teaching teaches the "languages" that constitute established knowledge communities, such as the academic disciplines and the professions, does not mean, however, that what it teaches is fluency in the jargon and methodological consensus of those communities. That is precisely the purpose of foundational teaching and jigsaw-puzzle tasks (described in Chapter 2). Foundational teaching inculcates students with disciplinary jargon and well established methods. As my wife, Anthea, once put it while she was in law school (and in most law schools legal study is a foundational exercise if there ever was one), what she was doing there was learning how to quack.

In contrast, the purpose of collaborative learning is not primarily to teach students how to quack. Collaborative learning tasks are designed to generate conversation in which students learn to "speak differently" (in Rorty's phrase), to speak in ways unlike their former habits of speaking. So students almost inevitably pick up a good deal of disciplinary jargon along the way. But in collaborative learning the route to fluency in the language of a new community is paved with ad hoc intermediary languages that students devise themselves to serve their own purposes as they work through the assigned task. Like foundational teaching, nonfoundational teaching will almost certainly teach students to quack. But on the way they will also learn to gobble, honk, peep, and squawk.

Some of this ad hoc language sticks. It is this measure of residual nondisciplinary vocabulary, however small, that helps distinguish the results of nonfoundational teaching from the results of foundational teaching. It represents a precious resource: the grain of newly constructed knowledge that collaboratively educated students take away from the course with them.

The process of ad hoc translation that goes on in a transition group was illustrated in detail for me once during a class in which I had asked students organized collaboratively to subdivide a paragraph and describe how the parts are related, in order to write a "descriptive outline" of it. This is a nonfoundational constructive tool-making task appropriate to collaborative learning for two reasons. First, there is no "right answer," although there may be some clear options, the merits of which can be negotiated. Second, students undertake the task at first without a prescribed, disciplinary vocabulary to work with. They have to root around in their own collective experience and make use of whatever language they find there.

During this particular class, I (unintentionally) overheard a student explaining something to the other members of his consensus group about the paragraph I had asked them to outline. It contained, he said, a "transition between the whoosie-whatsis and the other thing." No one would call these terms elegant or professional. But for the time being, the expression served this student's purposes and the pur-poses of the group he was working with. It negotiated the boundary between lan-guages that he and his fellow students knew and the one they were just beginning to learn, by cobbling together a variety of terms that every student in the group understood. To use a term of the Russian critic Bakhtin that has been fashionable recently among American literary academics, the expression was "heteroglossic." It drew on informal street-corner or beauty-parlor lingo ("whoosie-whatsis") and the plain, unvarnished speech of home, shop, and playground ("the other thing"), com-bining these with a new bit of classroom jargon ("transition").

Eventually, of course, these students replaced their rough-hewn, ad hoc linguistic tools with more efficient and appropriate terms as they explored further the nu-ances of the complex task they had been assigned. In fact, in any course taught collaboratively, adopting and culling linguistic tools to establish a transitional criti-cal language is implicitly as much the point of the assigned task as the point that the task explicitly targets. In collaborative learning, college and university students learn to lift themselves by their own verbal bootstraps, making new language by borrow-ing from, renovating, and reconstructing the old. Their transitional terms emerge from the conversational history they share with one another and with their teacher, as they identify the task before them, formulate it, and do it.

The kind of translation at community boundaries that students do in collabora-tive learning is translation of an especially "thick" and complex kind. Students trans-late the languages that they bring to the task into a composite working vocabulary common to the particular small group they are working in. That's where, for ex-ample, my students working on descriptive outlines got the phrases "whoosie-whatsis" and "the other thing." While students are translating among each other's languages in this way, furthermore, they are also translating into their own new composite vocabulary the language in which the teacher posed the task, which is the language of the community they aspire to join. That's where my writing stu-dents picked up the word "transition."

To turn classrooms into arenas in which students can negotiate their way into new knowledge communities in this way, college and university teachers have to discover points of access or ports of entry to the relevant community that are appro-priate to the varieties of nonmembers in their charge. They have to discover ways to help those nonmembers loosen their loyalty to some of the communities they are already members of — to "divorce" themselves from those communities, as Perry puts it — and marry instead into the knowledge community that the teacher repre-sents.[14]

What teachers teach in this way is how to establish and maintain intellectually productive rapport and ways to renegotiate that rapport when the task is done. They help students learn to negotiate boundaries between the communities they belong to and communities their fellow students may belong to. They allow students lati-tude to define their individuality not as a stark and lonesome independence, iso-lated or alienated from others, but as a function of interdependence among peers.

For college and university teachers to adapt themselves to teaching of this sort, however, may require (as Chapter 1 suggests) a depth of change that is difficult if not impossible for individuals to accomplish on their own. It is a process of reacculturation best undertaken, and perhaps only undertaken with success, collaboratively. In this chapter we found William Perry's confused undergraduates undertaking it by working together to construct new speech, lifting themselves by their own verbal bootstraps with a transitional language constructed for the purpose. In Chapter 7 we will find engaged in the same process Thomas Kuhn's scientists facing a theory crisis and Bruno Latour's example of a mother and child negotiating the name of birds.

Collaborative learning is most likely to fulfill its promise when faculty members of whole institutions, or of coherent subdivisions within them, build transitional conversational units similarly committed to this painful, painstaking collaborative talking-through. The next chapter will explore the most promising way to begin this process of institutionalizing collaborative learning. It uses leverage gained through a form of collaborative learning that I have alluded to but not discussed so far: peer tutoring.

Notes

[1]For a general discussion of negotiation see Fisher, Ury, and Patton, and Fisher and Brown. Although we know a lot about how negotiation works in political, legal, and economic situations, we are only beginning to learn (from studies such as those of Latour and Knorr-Cetina) how it works in epistemological or educational ones. Perhaps more to the point, as Fisher and Ury put it, we normally think of negotiation in any context as "positional bargaining." The craft of interdependence, involving what Fisher calls "principled negotiation," is a good deal more complex than that. It almost goes without saying that nothing like principled negotiation has yet been systematically applied to learning and to constructing knowledge.

Roger Fisher, William Ury, and Bruce Patton, *Getting to Yes: Negotiating Agreement without Giving In*, 2nd ed. (New York: Penguin, 1991).

Roger Fisher and Scott Brown, *Getting Together: Building a Relationship That Gets to Yes* (New York: Houghton, 1988).

[2]Mary Louise Pratt, "Arts of the Contact Zone," *Profession* 91 (New York: MLA, 1991) 33–40; 34, her emphasis.

[3]Pratt 38.

[4]On Roland Barthes, see Steve Ungar, "The Professor of Desire," *The Pedagogical Imperative: Teaching as a Literary Genre. Yale French Studies* 63, ed. Barbara Johnson (1982): 81–97.

[5]John Dewey, *Experience and Education* 1938; (New York: Collier, 1963) 64–65.

[6]Dewey 55–56.

[7]Dewey 56.

[8]Thomas S. Kuhn, "Second Thoughts on Paradigms," *The Structure of Scientific Theories*, ed. Frederick Suppe, 2nd ed. (Urbana: U of Illinois P, 1977) 209–10.

[9]Richard Rorty, *Contingency, Irony, and Solidarity*, (Cambridge: Cambridge UP, 1989) 187, his emphasis.

[10]On support groups see, for example, Glen Evans, *The Family Circle Guide to Self-Help* (New York: Ballantine, 1979).

[11]Karen D. Knorr-Cetina, *The Manufacture of Knowledge: An Essay on the Constructivist and Contextual Nature of Science* (Oxford: Pergamon, 1981) 131. In this passage Knorr-Cetina describes the process of enrollment in translation (or transition) communities, and the "process of conversion" involved, as it occurs in scientific research.

[12]William G. Perry, Jr., *Forms of Intellectual and Ethical Development in the College Years: A Scheme* (New York: Holt, 1968) 214.

[13]Kuhn 203.

[14]Perry 65.

Bruffee's Insights as a Resource for Your Teaching

1. Notice Bruffee's frequent references to "conscious thought and planning ahead" and the list of questions about the characteristics of groups of students who will construct and use the knowledge generated through collaboration. In your dialectical journal, it is useful to note what you think may be

true about the writer you will work with, based on your own experiences and your observations of others as students and writers in "transition." As you work with the "writing community," detail what you observe and learn about the students in large-class discussions, in small group projects, and in peer critique workshops. In a similar manner, write down your plans and processes for class activities; later jot down notes about what happened — by design or serendipity — and ways that students collaborated effectively. Use these data in your feedback to groups and individuals and in your planning for later activities and for later semesters.

2. If you are a new instructor, you may have recognized yourself in the descriptions of what learners do in their transition communities: conversing with others about such things as becoming a "real" writing teacher; coping with something new or different in the surrounding academic culture; and managing the stress of planning, responding, teaching, evaluating, facilitating collaborative learning, and "learning how to do it as you do it." Imitate those students who organized translation or transition communities to negotiate the languages you brought with you and the new languages you met — even in this set of readings — in the community of writing teachers. In addition, you can benefit from the exchange of what Stephen North in *The Making of Knowledge in Composition* defines as "practitioner's lore."

Bruffee's Insights as a Resource for the Classroom

1. Using Bruffee's distinctions, think about your course as a large transition community within which smaller groups often converse and advise each other about writing for their readers. In the large writing community, these early journal prompts are very useful to many students: the nature of the "old communities" writers left; how it feels to become a member of the college community or of the writing community; and shifts in perspectives and changes in identities.

   In a similar manner, many writers will respond to the "writing from recall" prompt with personal narratives about significant events from other knowledge communities. Encourage members of invention groups and critique workshops to ask and talk about the language and conventions specific to those communities; this will help the writer write specifically for readers who don't know his story.

2. Organize small groups to work collaboratively on a "glossary": the language of writing classes, of other disciplines, of the campus culture, and so on. Small groups will negotiate both contributions and meanings for what will become a class publication on "speaking differently" than they had before college.

3. When you become concerned about writers who restrict themselves to the "five-paragraph theme" or other writing strategies they mastered in earlier coursework, organize small groups to read and discuss alternative thinking and organizing patterns that are used successfully by class members. Bruffee explains why some students will accept the authority of peers more than that of an English teacher.

4. Bruffee indicates that the process of "adopting and culling linguistic tools to establish a transitional critical language is implicitly as much the point of the assigned task as the point that the task explicitly targets." Give students opportunities to talk and write about the collaborative skills and processes they are learning and refining: during class discussions, in journal entries, during one-on-one conferences, and in self-evaluations when the course concludes. Let groups practice evaluating their joint and individual participation in collaborative projects while you provide feedback from your observations as well.

5. If you have access to a networked classroom or can build an electronic conference, set up "chat topics" so class members can talk about coping, complain about difficulties with roommates, ask how others in the class interpret a reading, ask for reactions to ideas for essays, critique recent films, and so on. Cyberspace conversations frequently turn into collaborative inquiry; participants practice collaborative skills without thinking about being part of a group.

2. Thinking about the Writing Process

These readings all proceed from good teaching practice: carefully observing writers at work, reflecting on what was observed, posing research questions (whether for personal, classroom, or empirical research), and speculating from the data about the practices of developing, novice, and experienced writers. A habit of thinking about writers and their processes leads to creative design of prompts, syllabi, and collaborative learning activities; it also influences how writing teachers respond to and evaluate impromptu drafts, peer criticism, finished drafts, and portfolios. The following readings are organized under headings that describe issues writers face when they approach writing tasks. As with all the readings in this ancillary, the essays interconnect: they may modify, challenge, or confirm the insights of other essays. The series on audience particularly demonstrates such a "conversation" about what writers do when they consider the possible needs of their audiences.

GENERATING A DRAFT

As a result of the paradigm shift in composition studies from viewing writing as product to viewing writing as process, we now know much more about what writers do when they generate texts. *The Bedford Guide for College Writers* is designed to assist writers with the multiple and complex processes of getting started (prewriting, invention, discovery, planning, considering audience); drafting (composing by hand or on screen, planning, scanning, considering audience, invention, assessing, revising); and revising (rereading and goal-setting, re-visioning, considering audience, discovery, reorganizing, editing). Each writer's highly individualized and recursive processes of composing and constructing meaning cannot be easily or appropriately described as "the writing process." Composition research and theory centering on "sustained drafting" is helpful in focusing our thinking about writers in process, and it is extensive.

ANN E. BERTHOFF   *Dialectical Notebooks and the Audit of Meaning*

In all her writing, Ann E. Berthoff offers philosophical perspectives and practical teaching applications. Berthoff agrees with other teachers that journal writing helps students learn. In this essay, she argues that a "dialectical notebook" is a better method for generating a draft than other heuristics that are traditions in writing classrooms: freewriting, list making, brainstorming, or note taking. As she identifies the many purposes of dialectical notebooks, Berthoff explains her basic assumptions: language exists for making meaning; "necessary circularities" exist in the process of making meaning; and, the dialectical journal corresponds to the "inner dialogue" that generates and constitutes thinking.

I would claim that anybody concerned with working out ideas could, should, must be — willy-nilly — a writer, because writing provides the readiest means of carrying out what I. A. Richards calls an *audit of meaning*.[1] Writing as a way of knowing lets us represent ideas so that we can return to them and assess them.

Keeping a journal is the best habit any writer can have; indeed, most real writers probably couldn't function without their notebooks, whatever form they take or however they are kept. Notebooks can serve as cradles, which is the way Henry James characterized his jottings — scraps of conversations, speculations about one image or another, sketches of characters, plot ideas, etc.; notebooks can serve as shorthand records or as detailed accounts. Of what? Of observations — and observations of observations; recollections, remembrances, things to be remembered — memoranda; things to be returned to — *nota benes;* things to be looked up — ascertainable facts; notions to be puzzled over. Keeping a notebook is a way of keeping track of the development of ideas, as well as of their inception and origin, of monitoring a work in progress: what work? A writer's work is getting "it" down and the essential thing to realize is that "it" is an opinion, an observation, a recording, a formulation, a representation — there are no facts, "raw data" *given* to us. Thinking begins with perception: *all knowledge is mediated.*

Journals, diaries, monthlies, annuals, daybooks, almanacs, calendars, chronicles: we could say that these all constitute a class by reason of the fact that they all either record events chronologically or are organized as daily, monthly, or annual reports. It gets interesting when we begin to differentiate these kinds of records and representations, noting to what degree and in what respects they are public or private; speculative or factual; closer to history than to story. It gets very interesting, indeed, when we begin examining in what sense they are all fictions, in the sense that all representation is constructed. Records of all sorts provide the means of orienting ourselves in time. Orientation: Where do we start from? What directions are we to follow? What is a point of departure? Thinking about journals can bring us to the heart of current critical theory — and if we are to learn to use them to teach writing, we will need to be somewhat theoretical. It is the nexus of theory and practice which gives us method, and without freshly apprehended and considered method, pedagogy is enslaved to whatever implicit method comes with whatever practice we take up. Journals can be just as deadly as any other heuristic, if we don't think about what we are doing with them.

I will describe here a special kind of journal which I call a dialectical notebook. I like to remind myself (and others) that dialectic and dialogue are closely related; that thinking is a dialogue we have with ourselves; that dialectic is an audit of meaning — a continuing effort to review the meanings we are making in order to see further what they mean. The means we have of doing that are — meanings. The dialectical notebook keeps all our meanings handy. Here is how it works: the dialectical notebook is a double-entry journal with the two pages facing one another in dialogue. On one side are observations, sketches, noted impressions, passages copied out, jottings on reading or other responses; on the facing page are notes on these notes, responses to these responses — in current jargon, "meta-comment." The first thing the dialectical notebook can teach us is toleration of those necessary circularities. Everything about language, everything in composing, involves us in them: thinking about thinking; arranging our techniques for arranging; interpreting our interpretations.

For positivists — and therefore for most rhetoricians — these circularities are dizzying. They are abjured as *self*-consciousness. "Why tell people what they are doing when they are doing it normally, naturally? Why intervene with theory when they are creating without it?" The short answer is that *knowing how* to make meaning in one instance is facilitated by *knowing that* we have done so in other circumstances. Consciousness of consciousness makes that knowledge apprehendable.

All acts of symbolization take place in a social world framed by language; hence the importance of dialogue, pedagogically. We can't get under the net to reach "reality" directly. All knowledge is mediated: all knowledge is therefore partial. Making meaning is not very much like learning to ride a bicycle; nor is it "instinctual." Human beings are language animals: we are not controlled, limited, by a repertory of instincts. Language gives us the power of memory and envisagement, thus freeing us from the momentary, the eternal present of the beasts, and recreating us as historical creatures. The essential principle for a philosophy of rhetoric is what C. S. Peirce called Triadicity: interpreting interpretations is entailed in the way the mind works; interpretation is not added on the sign but is itself a constituent element of the sign.[2]

In an essay in *The Making of Meaning,* I explain this concept of mediation as follows:

> Let me suggest how we might keep in mind the nature of meaning as a means, a way to remember that meaning is dynamic and dialectical, that it depends on context and perspective, the setting and the angle. The model I'm thinking of is a triangle, but of a radically different sort from the familiar "triangle of discourse," which looks like this:

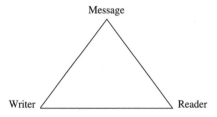

> Sometimes, *speaker/reality/audience* are at the three points, with language or text occupying the field enclosed. In this model there is no way of telling the relationship of message to either its sources or to the speaker or the form in which it is expressed. As we know, "messages" are continually sent in the real world without being understood, but there is nothing in this model to explain why, or what we, as teachers of reading and writing, might do about failures of "communication."
>
> The triangle I'm suggesting as a model helps on that score; it looks like this:

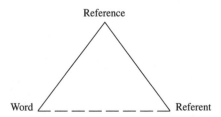

> This diagram represents the "sign," the "meaning relationship." What the word stands for — the referent — is known in terms of reference. The dotted line stands for the fact that there is no immediate, direct relationship between words and things (including other words); we interpret the word or symbol by means of the idea it represents to us. It takes an idea to find an idea. We know reality in terms of our ideas of reality. This curious triangle with the dotted line can help us remember that what we know, we know by means of mediating form. The triangle represents mediation, the interdependence of interpreter (what he already knows), the symbol (image or word), and the import or significance it has. Ironically, by not being quite a triangle, this triangle represents the triadicity of meaning relationships. It can help us keep in mind that we

must include the beholder, the interpreter, in our account of texts; that texts require contexts and that contexts depend on perspective.[3]

The dialectical notebook serves many purposes, both in the general sense of helping to develop habits of mind and in the practical sense of helping with academic work. I will list these, commenting briefly, before discussing procedures and actual academic uses of the notebook.

1. Looking and Looking Again

Learning to look carefully, to see what you're looking at, is perennially acclaimed as the essential skill for both artist and scientist, to say nothing of its being crucial for maturity in psychological terms. Looking is the *sine qua non* of inquiry; looking again is the method of inquiry. The willingness to entertain further questions, to return to assumptions, to re-assess what has been given or asserted is entailed in learning to think.

Ezra Pound first recounted the story of Agassiz and the fish — how the great naturalist sent a novice scientist back to look again — and again and again — at the specimen.[4] Paulo Freire freshly captures just what it is to teach oneself to look and look again:

> One focus of my efforts (in understanding the role of thinking about thinking) . . . is turning myself into a tramp of the obvious. . . . In playing the part of this vagrant, I have been learning how important the obvious becomes as the object of our critical reflection, and by looking deeply into it, I have discovered that the obvious is not always as obvious as it appears.[5]

Exercises in looking and looking again should properly include both the most careful observation of a natural object and what Freire calls "problematizing the existential situation." Such study becomes, then, a model for close reading: reading the Book of Nature has long provided the prolegomenon to critical inquiry, and if we add reading to the environment we have two very powerful models for composing.

2. Fostering Fluency: Gush vs. Dialectic

All writers dream of fluency, of having the words come, of not having to struggle towards accurate expression and substantial representation. But fluency can, of course, be gush: a competent writer — typically, say, the National Honor Society Freshman, miffed at not being exempted from English 101 — is capable of running off at the mouth precisely because he is capable of combining syntactical elements without really worrying about what weight they might bear. (Sentence combining is more likely to foster this kind of "competence" than it is to teach ways and means of subordination.) Fluency is something other than gush when the dialectic of feedback and feedforward is operating; how to get the dialectic going is the challenge.

"Free writing" can be very useful, but it is not always the best option for "getting started." The dialectical notebook can encourage list making and the development of a lexicon; it can accommodate phrases and fragmentary formulations — sketches which are not in the form of statements. What I have called "generating chaos" allows the writer to make use of looking again and thinking about what has been thought and is thus more likely to encourage a dialectical sort of fluency. Without this preparation, "free writing" is as likely as not to produce quantities of stuff, without necessarily producing points of departure. Once the dialectic of *feedback* and *feedforward* is in operation, the writer has a very powerful resource to call upon, namely the heuristic power of language itself. The tendency of words is to cluster, to form syntactic units. This tendency of words towards syntax is the *discursive* power of language: syntax brings thought along with it as it *runs along*. This is the kind of fluency the dialectical notebook can foster.

3. Tolerating Ambiguity

Learning the uses of chaos prepares the writer for tolerating ambiguity. I. A. Richards once remarked that "ambiguities are the very hinges of all thought"[6] — but they can't so function if they aren't recognized. The dialectical notebook offers the means of identifying ambiguities, of addressing them, of unsnarling contradictions and resolving paradoxes. The novice writer, if she does spot an ambiguity, may well decide that the best strategy is to disguise it by stretching words illegitimately, covertly. She may eliminate it by suppressing the element that has created it. Tolerating ambiguities, looking at them again as symptoms of faulty logic or of inadequate definition or as symptoms of unsorted plenitude is probably the best way of learning the strategies of argument. The dialectical notebook allows the writer to keep things tentative, to forestall "closure," in the jargon of psycholinguistics. The most important benefit is learning to make revision not a stage but a dimension of composing.[7] One of the hardest things about revision is how to keep from focusing too narrowly too soon. The dialectical notebook lets writers practice keeping the options open; it can toughen the resolve to change direction, to follow in new directions, if that's the way things seem to be going. The high cost of thesis statements and outlines and of the much vaunted "process" model of Prewriting, Writing, Rewriting is that they tend to cut down on the options, to hinder writers from learning to take risks by looking again at the meanings that are emerging.

4. Coming to Terms with Allatonceness

In composing, everything happens at once or it doesn't happen at all: we say and mean; we express and represent; we find words and words help us discover our meanings. If students can come to terms with this allatonceness, the problems and snarls which bedevil writing will more easily come under control. If teachers learn to come to terms with allatonceness, they will, in the process, revolutionize their practice. The chief virtue of the dialectical notebook is that it helps writers convert the allatonceness of composing from a formidable anxiety-producer to a resource for the making of meaning. Keeping a dialectical notebook is a way of making writing a mode of learning and a way of knowing, because its dialectical/dialogic form corresponds to the character of the inner dialogue which is thinking. In making meaning, complexity comes first: the dialectical notebook lets us begin with complexity — with looking again, with the chaos and ambiguity which are its consequence.

Because the dialectical notebook can serve as a medium for lecture notes and reading notes, as well as for notes towards the generation and development of ideas for assigned papers, it can help develop a sense of the interdependence of reading and writing, listening and speaking. All critical uses of language require the same habits of efficient apprehension, thoughtful expectation, and accurate representation. Thus, developing a skill in any one of them can help strengthen capacities in the others. The chief academic value of the dialectical notebook is that it helps a student to become a good reader, thereby learning to be a good writer. By helping students to take notes on their notes, it helps them learn to interpret their interpretations deliberately and cogently; it fosters the habit of questioning which is, of course, at the heart of inquiry and argumentation.

What writers need to learn is how to formulate questions which have heuristic value. They won't find out how from handbooks, rhetorics, or guides which generally urge students to *be clear*; to *think* of their audience; to *go over* their writing and *take out* unnecessary words and *put in* transitional phrases. Exhortation is not instruction. (Books which in one chapter mouth the slogan "Show, don't tell" are notably weak when it comes to showing how to do anything connected with actual writing.) Learning to question is not a matter of learning to convert Study Questions to ready-made thesis statements. The important challenge is to invent one's own study questions. One teacher who has been experimenting with dialectical notebooks in a rather traditional Freshman English course featuring the study of literature reported to me recently that the first thing to happen was that her students began asking if they could make up their own topics for the weekly paper. That seems to me symptomatic of an engagement with texts that is not entirely common these days. Inventing topics, recognizing points of departure, choosing perspectives — all of that flows from learning to question. Questioning is *problem-posing* and it engages the mind more radically than *problem-solving,* as generally conceived. Anything we can do to foster a student's capacity to pose questions in substantial terms will be helping to develop the inquiry procedures which are essential to all academic writing.

The logic most appropriate to inquiry is what C. S. Peirce called *abduction.* It is a matter of moving sideways, as it were — developing analogies, drawing inferences, hypothesizing, putting claims to the test, thereby making clear the conditions under which a statement might be said to be true, of laying bare assumptions and defining presuppositions. The best way to develop skill in abductive reasoning is to practice formulating "iffy" questions. For one thing, it keeps the *what* of the statement in dynamic dialectic with the *how.* To explain that changes in language are by no means all superficial — "just semantics" — I ask students to consider this question when they are working on their meta-comment: "How does it change my meaning if I put it *this* way?" A comparison, then, of two ways of saying allows for the exercise of choice and sets up a direction.

Inquiry proceeds with drawing out implications of the way the problem has been posed, a process Peirce called *ampliative inference.* The guiding question is "Does it follow, then, that X is a cause of / a source of / an analogue of / an instance of / etc. of Y?" Practice with double entries makes the task of handling further questions a way to foster fluency in writing.

The next phase is to represent inferences which have been drawn, to come to cases. In so doing, a writer learns to differentiate necessary and probable inferences and to see how they both differ from unwarranted claims. The best way I know to control this process is by developing opposite, borderline, and model cases.[8] It helps to organize an argument instead of putting off that problem until all the "examples" have been gathered. The absurd conception of research which informs the Term Paper only institutionalizes an irrational procedure of Gathering Data First. It is one more example of the positivist penchant for beginning with the allegedly particular and putting off generalization; whereas in the composing process dialectically conceived, there is no question of a linear progression.[9] The dialectical notebook develops the habit of moving continually from the general to the specific and back to the general, the movement of thought which Vygotsky saw as the essential characteristic of concept formation.

The topics of classical rhetoric — irrationally selected and only time-honored — are transmogrified, when students practice composing dialectically.[10] They become not slots to be filled or hoops to be aimed for but instruments of thought. We are no longer assigning a Compare-Contrast Paper, worrying about how it's related to Narrative and Description. We no longer save Definition for English 102. The interdependence of rhetorical modes, the dialectic of the "topics," is a discovery which can set students and teachers alike on the way to a pedagogy of knowing.

I have been claiming that the dialectical notebook is useful for students as they learn the procedures of critical inquiry, which is, in my view, neither psychologically nor logically antithetical to "creative" endeavor. The more we can see in common between science and poetry, the easier it will be, then, to value the peculiar strengths of each, as forms of knowledge. Those learning to write can learn a great deal from seeing how the scientist's work is related to the poet's and how what the historian does is close to both. As thinkers and formers, interpreters and creators — as composers and writers — they are all naming the world, bringing ideas to bear on what they are naming and imagining and hypothesizing and transforming.

The motive force that drives this process of interpreting interpretation in order to make meaning is analogy — or metaphor, if we name it in rhetorical terms. Analogy and metaphor are forms of comparison in which likeness is apprehended as being *in relation to, in terms of, with regard to:* these little connectors are emblematic of Triadicity. They remind us of the semiotic principle that just as we see or apprehend likeness only if we have a scale or context, so in all our judgments, we must know by some means. Analogy provides the chief and readiest means of knowing, of making meaning. J. Robert Oppenheimer's observation that analogy is an "indispensable instrument" for both exploration and analysis in science is a useful reminder that science is not to be reduced to measurement any more than writing is to outlining. And Walker Percy's disquisition in "Metaphor as Mistake" should dispel forever the notion that metaphor is cake frosting, something you add to your writing.[11]

Analogy is an idea we can think with; it is, in I. A. Richards' phrase, a "speculative instrument."[12] The habit of keeping a dialectical notebook makes the powerful instrument of analogy available to writers as a way of looking and looking again; of generating names and oppositions which create ambiguities which can serve as the hinges of thought. Analogies insist on being interpreted; no sooner do we create them than they yield further questions. Practice in double-entry journals is practice in analogizing and thus in critical and creative thought.

Notes

[1]I. A. Richards, *How to Read a Page* (1942; rprt., Boston: Beacon P, 1958) 240.

[2]In *The Making of Meaning: Metaphors, Models and Maxims for Writing Teachers* (Upper Montclair: Boynton, 1981), I have set forth the philosophical principles which I find essential for the development of what Paulo Freire calls a "pedagogy of knowing." See especially: "Forming Concepts and Conceptualizing Form"; "A Curious Triangle and the Double-Entry Notebook: or, How Theory Can Help Us Teach Reading and Writing"; "The Intelligent Eye and the Thinking Hand." In the comment introducing the four sections of *Reclaiming the Imagination: Philosophical Perspectives for Writers and Teachers of Writing* (Upper Montclair: Boynton, 1984), I have suggested how the arguments and speculations of the artists, scientists, and philosophers whose work I have gathered in this anthology can help us develop a philosophy of rhetoric. The sections are "Perception and the Apprehension of Form," "Language and the Making of Meaning," "Interpretation and the Making of Meaning," and "Artists at Work."

[3]33–34. See also my essay, "Is Teaching Still Possible?," *College English* 46 (1984): 743–55.

[4]*The ABC of Reading* (1934; rprt., New York: New Directions, 1960) 17.

[5]*The Politics of Education* (South Hadley, MA: Bergin, 1985) 171.

[6]*How to Read a Page* 24.

[7]I have tried to make this case in "Recognition, Representation, and Revision," *Journal of Basic Writing* 3 (Fall–Winter, 1981): 19–32; rprt. in *Rhetoric and Composition,* ed. Richard L. Graves (Upper Montclair: Boynton, 1984) 27–37.

[8]For explanations and demonstration, see John Wilson, *Thinking with Concepts* (Cambridge: Cambridge UP, 1963). It is very important to note that the sequence in which Wilson presents the cases — model, borderline, and opposite — is precisely the reverse of the one which is logically appropriate to the composing process: it is far easier to say what a concept is *not* than it is to define it at the start; that only encourages lexical definition, which cannot do the work of concept formation.

[9]In *Forming/Thinking/Writing: The Composing Imagination* (1978; Upper Montclair: Boynton, 1982), I have tried in all the exercises to keep the dialectic going. Only if complexity is recognized and accommodated from the first will there be a chance for writing to be a mode of learning.

[10]As Knoblauch and Brannon have pointed out, the topics we find perennially in the table of contents of each year's "rhetorics" represent only a fraction of, say, Aristotle's original list. See, *Rhetorical Traditions and the Teaching of Writing* (Upper Montclair: Boynton, 1984) chap. 2.

[11]Both Walker Percy's essay and Oppenheimer's "Analogy in Science" are reprinted in *Reclaiming the Imagination.*

[12]The idea of mediating ideas is recurrent in all of Richards' work, but see especially *Speculative Instruments* (New York: Harcourt, 1955).

Berthoff's Insights as a Resource for Your Teaching

1. Take the opportunity for "coming to terms with allatonceness" by keeping a dialectical journal as you begin your teaching career or when you teach a course that is new to you. Using one side of a journal to keep reading notes, classroom observations, impressions, and questions about writers' processes, and having the facing pages to review, reflect on, and respond to earlier entries is a useful and practical way to monitor your development as an effective teacher. If you prefer to keep the journal on disk, of course, it will be easy to open up spaces for your "writing about your writing and thinking about your thinking." To keep the visual feel of "dialectic," use a different font for these later, reflective entries than for daily journal entries. Berthoff asserts, "The most important benefit is learning to make revision not a stage but a dimension of composing." You can select materials from both sides of your notebook to model for students this concept of revision as a component of composing. Because some students will be confused by an assignment to maintain a "double-entry journal," show them how it works using a photocopy, an overhead transparency, or a computerized video presentation.

Berthoff's Insights as a Resource for the Writing Classroom

1. The dialectical notebook can be adapted to any classroom, including lecture courses. Organize a series of prompts directing students to keep a dialectical notebook for a two- or three-week period in a course that is new or challenging to them. Ask students to list and define key terms, keep notes from lectures, quote passages from course reading, record the instructor's interpretations of key events or data, and so forth. Using ten to fifteen minutes of class time periodically, direct writers to review a series of entries and to write some paragraphs responding to or reflecting on the earlier entries. Later in the semester, ask students to write a short narrative about "making meaning" in that course. Ask groups of students to read and respond to these narratives, looking for patterns or for learning strategies that could be transferred to other courses. Alternatively, you can devise a series of questions focused on the first-year college experience: students can record their experiences, and later reflect on them and conduct some self-assessment in order to set goals for maintaining or improving their "active learning."

2. The dialectical journal is particularly helpful for the "Writing from Reading" assignments, both to help writers generate topics and early drafts and to help students identify and reflect on the efficacy of their critical reading habits. Before you assign the "Writing from Reading" task, ask writers to use the double-entry format in their journals for one or two weeks while they sample readings or simply work with the reading in their other courses. Structure in-class time for nutshelling and paraphrasing a reading from *The Bedford Guide for College Writers*. Ask small groups to share their entries and discuss the common and unique perspectives on the main ideas of the reading. Assign a postdiscussion entry on what students observed about their own reading habits and approaches in comparison with those of their peers. Encourage students to "talk back" to issues or perspectives they find in the readings. Suggest they pose questions to the author of a selected reading about "ambiguities" in the reading, that they use one or two of the questions for "exploratory" entries, and that they let you read that sequence of entries to demonstrate their progress as active readers. This lets you emphasize the belief that as students become good readers, they learn to become good writers.

SONDRA PERL   *Understanding Composing*

Most writing teachers and theorists share Sondra Perl's belief that writing is a recursive process and that writers engage in "retrospective structuring" as they genrate drafts. This belief informs The Bedford Guide for College Writers. *Look particularly at the discussion of "recursiveness" in "Introduction: A Writing Process." Perl uses her own observations of the composing processes of a variety of writers to analyze the significance of those processes. She defines a "felt sense" that may be a very rich and necessary resource for the writer even as it may be one that the writer (and his or her audience) has difficulty describing and consciously triggering.*

Perl believes that "skilled writers" rely on a felt sense even when they don't know it. She implies that "unskilled writers" might come to use this felt sense and to engage in "retrospective structuring" more productively. She theorizes that writers who have internalized a model of writing as a recursive process rather than a linear process may have an easier time attending to their inner reflections.

I anticipate that you will find "new thoughts" about composing as you read Perl's conjectures about "felt sense." You'll be interested in the link of "felt sense" with "projective structuring," Perl's name for the process in which writers make what they intend to say intelligible to others.

> Any psychological process, whether the development of thought or voluntary behavior, is a process undergoing changes right before one's eyes. ... Under certain conditions it becomes possible to trace this development.[1]
> – L. S. Vygotsky

> It's hard to begin this case study of myself as a writer because even as I'm searching for a beginning, a pattern of organization, I'm watching myself, trying to understand my behavior. As I sit here in silence, I can see lots of things happening that never made it onto my tapes. My mind leaps from the task at hand to what I need at the vegetable stand for tonight's soup to the threatening rain outside to ideas voiced in my writing group this morning, but in between "distractions" I hear myself trying out words I might use. It's as if the extraneous thoughts are a counterpoint to the more steady attention I'm giving to composing. This is all to point out that the process is more complex than I'm aware of, but I think my tapes reveal certain basic patterns that I tend to follow.
> – Anne, New York City teacher

Anne is a teacher of writing. In 1979, she was among a group of twenty teachers who were taking a course in research and basic writing at New York University.[2] One of the assignments in the course was for the teachers to tape their thoughts while composing aloud on the topic "My Most Anxious Moment as a Writer." Everyone in the group was given the topic in the morning during class and told to compose later on that day in a place where they would be comfortable and relatively free from distractions. The result was a tape of composing aloud and a written product that formed the basis for class discussion over the next few days.

One of the purposes of this assignment was to provide teachers with an opportunity to see their own composing processes at work. From the start of the course, we recognized that we were controlling the situation by assigning a topic and that we might be altering the process by asking writers to compose aloud. Nonetheless we viewed the task as a way of capturing some of the flow of composing and, as Anne later observed in her analysis of her tape, she was able to detect certain basic patterns. This observation, made not only by Anne, then leads me to ask "What basic patterns seem to occur during composing?" and "What does this type of research have to tell us about the nature of the composing process?"

Perhaps the most challenging part of the answer is the recognition of recursiveness in writing. In recent years, many researchers including myself have questioned the traditional notion that writing is a linear process with a strict plan-write-revise sequence.[3] In its stead, we have advocated the idea that writing is a recursive process, that throughout the process of writing, writers return to substrands of the overall process, or subroutines (short successions of steps that yield results on which the writer draws in taking the next set of steps); writers use these to keep the process moving forward. In other words, recursiveness in writing implies that there is a forward-moving action that exists by virtue of a backward-moving action. The questions that then need to be answered are "To what do writers move back?" "What exactly is being repeated?" "What recurs?"

To answer these questions, it is important to look at what writers do while writing and what an analysis of their processes reveals. The descriptions that follow are based on my own observations of the composing processes of many types of writers including college students, graduate students, and English teachers like Anne.

Writing does appear to be recursive, yet the parts that recur seem to vary from writer to writer and from topic to topic. Furthermore, some recursive elements are easy to spot while others are not.

1. The most visible recurring feature or backward movement involves rereading little bits of discourse. Few writers I have seen write for long periods of time without returning briefly to what is already down on the page.

For some, like Anne, rereading occurs after every few phrases; for others, it occurs after every sentence; more frequently, it occurs after a "chunk" of information has been written. Thus, the unit that is reread is not necessarily a syntactic one, but rather a semantic one as defined by the writer.

2. The second recurring feature is some key word or item called up by the topic. Writers consistently return to their notion of the topic throughout the process of writing. Particularly when they are stuck, writers seem to use the topic or a key word in it as a way to get going again. Thus many times it is possible to see writers "going back," rereading the topic they were given, changing it to suit what they have been writing or changing what they have written to suit their notion of the topic.

3. There is also a third backward movement in writing, one that is not so easy to document. It is not easy because the move, itself, cannot immediately be identi-

fied with words. In fact, the move is not to any words on the page nor to the topic but to feelings or nonverbalized perceptions that *surround* the words, or to what the words already present evoke in the writer. The move draws on sense experience, and it can be observed if one pays close attention to what happens when writers pause and seem to listen or otherwise react to what is inside of them. The move occurs inside the writer, to what is physically felt. The term used to describe this focus of writers' attention is *felt sense*. The term "felt sense" has been coined and described by Eugene Gendlin, a philosopher at the University of Chicago. In his words, felt sense is

> the soft underbelly of thought . . . a kind of bodily awareness that . . . can be used as a tool . . . a bodily awareness that . . . encompasses everything you feel and know about a given subject at a given time. . . . It is felt in the body, yet it has meanings. It is body *and* mind before they are split apart.[4]

This felt sense is always there, within us. It is unifying, and yet, when we bring words to it, it can break apart, shift, unravel, and become something else. Gendlin has spent many years showing people how to work with their felt sense. Here I am making connections between what he has done and what I have seen happen as people write.

When writers are given a topic, the topic itself evokes a felt sense in them. This topic calls forth images, words, ideas, and vague fuzzy feelings that are anchored in the writer's body. What is elicited, then, is not solely the product of a mind but of a mind alive in a living, sensing body.

When writers pause, when they go back and repeat key words, what they seem to be doing is waiting, paying attention to what is still vague and unclear. They are looking to their felt experience, and waiting for an image, a word, or a phrase to emerge that captures the sense they embody.

Usually, when they make the decision to write, it is after they have a dawning awareness that something has clicked, that they have enough of a sense that if they begin with a few words heading in a certain direction, words will continue to come which will allow them to flesh out the sense they have.

The process of using what is sensed directly about a topic is a natural one. Many writers do it without any conscious awareness that that is what they are doing. For example, Anne repeats the words "anxious moments," using these key words as a way of allowing her sense of the topic to deepen. She asks herself, "Why are exams so anxiety provoking?" and waits until she has enough of a sense within her that she can go in a certain direction. She does not yet have the words, only the sense that she is able to begin. Once she writes, she stops to see what is there. She maintains a highly recursive composing style throughout and she seems unable to go forward without first going back to see and to listen to what she has already created. In her own words, she says:

> My disjointed style of composing is very striking to me. I almost never move from the writing of one sentence directly to the next. After each sentence I pause to read what I've written, assess, sometimes edit and think about what will come next. I often have to read the several preceding sentences a few times as if to gain momentum to carry me to the next sentence. I seem to depend a lot on the sound of my words and . . . while I'm hanging in the middle of this uncompleted thought, I may also start editing a previous sentence or get an inspiration for something which I want to include later in the paper.

What tells Anne that she is ready to write? What is the feeling of "momentum" like for her? What is she hearing as she listens to the "sound" of her words? When she experiences "inspiration," how does she recognize it?

In the approach I am presenting, the ability to recognize what one needs to do or where one needs to go is informed by calling on felt sense. This is the internal criterion writers seem to use to guide them when they are planning, drafting, and revising.

The recursive move, then, that is hardest to document but is probably the most important to be aware of is the move to felt sense, to what is not yet *in words* but out of which images, words, and concepts emerge.

The continuing presence of this felt sense, waiting for us to discover it and see where it leads, raises a number of questions.

Is "felt sense" another term for what professional writers call their "inner voice" or their feeling of "inspiration"?

Do skilled writers call on their capacity to sense more readily than unskilled writers?

Rather than merely reducing the complex act of writing to a neat formulation, can the term "felt sense" point us to an area of our experience from which we can evolve even richer and more accurate descriptions of composing?

Can learning how to work with felt sense teach us about creativity and release us from stultifyingly repetitive patterns?

My observations lead me to answer "yes" to all four questions. There seems to be a basic step in the process of composing that skilled writers rely on even when they are unaware of it and that less skilled writers can be taught. This process seems to rely on very careful attention to one's inner reflections and is often accompanied with bodily sensations.

When it's working, this process allows us to say or write what we've never said before, to create something new and fresh, and occasionally it provides us with the experience of "newness" or "freshness," even when "old words" or images are used.

The basic process begins with paying attention. If we are given a topic, it begins with taking the topic in and attending to what it evokes in us. There is less "figuring out" an answer and more "waiting" to see what forms. Even without a predetermined topic, the process remains the same. We can ask ourselves, "What's on my mind?" or "Of all the things I know about, what would I most like to write about now?" and wait to see what comes. What we pay attention to is the part of our bodies where we experience ourselves directly. For many people, it's the area of their stomachs; for others, there is a more generalized response and they maintain a hovering attention to what they experience throughout their bodies.

Once a felt sense forms, we match words to it. As we begin to describe it, we get to see what is there for us. We get to see what we think, what we know. If we are writing about something that truly interests us, the felt sense deepens. We know that we are writing out of a "centered" place.

If the process is working, we begin to move along, sometimes quickly. Other times, we need to return to the beginning, to reread, to see if we captured what we meant to say. Sometimes after rereading we move on again, picking up speed. Other times by rereading we realize we've gone off the track, that what we've written doesn't quite "say it," and we need to reassess. Sometimes the words are wrong and we need to change them. Other times we need to go back to the topic, to call up the sense it initially evoked to see where and how our words led us astray. Sometimes in rereading we discover that the topic is "wrong," that the direction we discovered in writing is where we really want to go. It is important here to clarify that the terms "right" and "wrong" are not necessarily meant to refer to grammatical structures or to correctness.

What is "right" or "wrong" corresponds to our sense of our intention. We intend to write something, words come, and now we assess if those words adequately capture our intended meaning. Thus, the first question we ask ourselves is "Are these words right for me?" "Do they capture what I'm trying to say?" "If not, what's missing?"

Once we ask "what's missing?" we need once again to wait, to let a felt sense of what is missing form, and then to write out of that sense.

I have labeled this process of attending, of calling up a felt sense, and of writing out of that place, the process of *retrospective structuring*. It is retrospective in that it begins with what is already there, inchoately, and brings whatever is there forward by using language in structured form.

It seems as though a felt sense has within it many possible structures or forms. As we shape what we intend to say, we are further structuring our sense while correspondingly shaping our piece of writing.

It is also important to note that what is there implicitly, without words, is not equivalent to what finally emerges. In the process of writing, we begin with what is inchoate and end with something that is tangible. In order to do so, we both discover and construct what we mean. Yet the term "discovery" ought not lead us to think that meaning exists fully formed inside of us and that all we need do is dig deep enough to release it. In writing, meaning cannot be discovered the way we discover an object on an archeological dig. In writing, meaning is crafted and constructed. It involves us in a process of coming-into-being. Once we have worked at shaping, through language, what is there inchoately, we can look at what we have written to see if it adequately captures what we intended. Often at this moment discovery occurs. We see something new in our writing that comes upon us as a surprise. We see in our words a further structuring of the sense we began with and we recognize that in those words we have discovered something new about ourselves and our topic. Thus when we are successful at this process, we end up with a product that teaches us something, that clarifies what we know (or what we knew at one point only implicitly), and that lifts out or explicates or enlarges our experience. In this way, writing leads to discovery.

All the writers I have observed, skilled and unskilled alike, use the process of retrospective structuring while writing. Yet the degree to which they do so varies and seems, in fact, to depend upon the model of the writing process that they have internalized. Those who realize that writing can be a recursive process have an easier time with waiting, looking, and discovering. Those who subscribe to the linear model find themselves easily frustrated when what they write does not immediately correspond to what they planned or when what they produce leaves them with little sense of accomplishment. Since they have relied on a formulaic approach, they often produce writing that is formulaic as well, thereby cutting themselves off from the possibility of discovering something new.

Such a result seems linked to another feature of the composing process, to what I call *projective structuring*, or the ability to craft what one intends to say so that it is intelligible to others.

A number of concerns arise in regard to projective structuring; I will mention only a few that have been raised for me as I have watched different writers at work.

1. Although projective structuring is only one important part of the composing process, many writers act as if it is the whole process. These writers focus on what

they think others want them to write rather than looking to see what it is they want to write. As a result, they often ignore their felt sense and they do not establish a living connection between themselves and their topic.

2. Many writers reduce projective structuring to a series of rules or criteria for evaluating finished discourse. These writers ask, "Is what I'm writing correct?" and "Does it conform to the rules I've been taught?" While these concerns are important, they often overshadow all others and lock the writer in the position of writing solely or primarily for the approval of readers.

Projective structuring, as I see it, involves much more than imagining a strict audience and maintaining a strict focus on correctness. It is true that to handle this part of the process well, writers need to know certain grammatical rules and evaluative criteria, but they also need to know how to call up a sense of their reader's needs and expectations.

For projective structuring to function fully, writers need to draw on their capacity to move away from their own words, to decenter from the page, and to project themselves into the role of the reader. In other words, projective structuring asks writers to attempt to become readers and to imagine what someone other than themselves will need before the writer's particular piece of writing can become intelligible and compelling. To do so, writers must have the experience of being readers. They cannot call up a felt sense of a reader unless they themselves have experienced what it means to be lost in a piece of writing or to be excited by it. When writers do not have such experiences, it is easy for them to accept that readers merely require correctness.

In closing, I would like to suggest that retrospective and projective structuring are two parts of the same basic process. Together they form the alternating mental postures writers assume as they move through the act of composing. The former relies on the ability to go inside, to attend to what is there, from that attending to place words upon a page, and then to assess if those words adequately capture one's meaning. The latter relies on the ability to assess how the words on that page will affect someone other than the writer, the reader. We rarely do one without the other entering in; in fact, again in these postures we can see the shuttling back-and-forth movements of the composing process, the move from sense to words and from words to sense, from inner experience to outer judgment and from judgment back to experience. As we move through this cycle, we are continually composing and recomposing our meanings and what we mean. And in doing so, we display some of the basic recursive patterns that writers who observe themselves closely seem to see in their own work. After observing the process for a long time we may, like Anne, conclude that at any given moment the process is more complex than anything we are aware of; yet such insights, I believe, are important. They show us the fallacy of reducing the composing process to a simple linear scheme and they leave us with the potential for creating even more powerful ways of understanding composing.

Notes

[1]L. S. Vygotsky, *Mind in Society*, trans. M. Cole, V. John-Steiner, S. Scribner, and E. Souberman (Cambridge: Harvard UP, 1978) 61.

[2]This course was team-taught by myself and Gordon Pradl, Associate Professor of English Education at New York University.

[3]See Janet Emig, *The Composing Processes of Twelfth-Graders*, NCTE Research Report No. 13 (Urbana: NCTE, 1971); Linda Flower and J. R. Hayes, "The Cognition of Discovery," CCC 31 (Feb. 1980): 21–32; Nancy Sommers, "The Need for Theory in Composition Research," CCC 30 (Feb. 1979): 46–49.

[4]Eugene Gendlin, *Focusing* (New York: Everest, 1978) 35, 165.

Perl's Insights as a Resource for Your Teaching

1. Perl models a "holistic perspective" on the composing process and pays careful attention to the composing processes of the students she teaches. As you read this article and reflect on it, jot down your own memories of this experience of a "felt sense" as well as statements your students have made about such experiences. Save those notes for use in your discussions of getting started with a writing task.

2. Many of the "generating" strategies described in Chapter 15 — those used by individual writers as well as the more formally described heuristics like freewriting, brainstorming, and the reporter's questions — help students start paying attention to inner reflections and to accompanying physical sensations. After they have practiced with several formal heuristics, ask your students to tell you, either in journal entries or in fifteen-minute writing sessions, about what they can notice about their "getting started" and their "beginning again."

3. Journal entries that ask writers simply to list "what I'm thinking now about this assignment" or "things I feel I need to say sometime this year" often provoke students to "listen in" on their inner reflections. The double-entry journal format assists writers, as they are retrospective in second entries, to become more aware of the "felt sense" Perl describes. The writing assignment for Chapter 4, "Writing from Imagination," gives students license to work from "retrospective structuring"; some students will surprise themselves with their composing for this assignment.

4. Be sure to ask students periodically, particularly at the end of the term, to tell you about times they surprised themselves by composing from "inspiration." Let students know, because you discuss it, that composing often has this basic process of calling on "felt sense." Be careful to respect the comments writers make in conferences (such as "It isn't right yet") and not to appropriate their texts with your judgment about their drafts.

Perl's Insights as a Resource for the Writing Classroom

1. Perl insists that to craft a writing to be accessible and intelligible to others, writers have to project themselves as readers of the work. They must anticipate the needs of readers even before and while the writing is in process. This sort of "decentering" is difficult for many students. Perl recommends reading as a major resource for such projective structuring. To assist students to call up a felt sense of their readers, ask them to discuss, in journals or in small groups, experiences they have had of being excited by something they read.

    Organize a class discussion of a "difficult" reading in *The Bedford Guide* (see *The Bedford Guide* Readings at a Glance on p. 383 of *Practical Suggestions*). Ask students to discuss any experiences of feeling lost or overwhelmed or puzzled by the reading or parts of it. Ask them to use sensory description, if appropriate to their experience.

    This discussion assists students in improving as critical readers and in thinking about readers' needs that they may have anticipated in the essays they are currently drafting.

2. Ask students to write for five minutes listing moments when they felt exhilarated by "inspiration" while reading, writing, or participating in class discussion. Then ask each student to choose one event and to describe it to the class, ending the description with some explanation of "effect." If students say they can't recall such events, tell them to listen carefully to other class members; someone will describe an event that will jar their memories. This exercise could prompt responses to the writing assignment in Chapter 1 that might surprise the students who had never considered their creative lives or learning experiences as topics for discussion, writing, and reading.

CONSIDERING AUDIENCE

From Aristotle on, teachers have questioned how best they might assist apprentice writers to recognize audience as a critical part of any communication process. The authors of *The Bedford Guide* have defined "the reader" in "Introduction: A Writing Process" as "yourself," "your instructors," "your classmates," and "your own first reader." They indicate that some of the assignments in the text, particularly those in Chapters 9 and 10, and "assignments" in the academic community and the professional world will require the writer to pay close attention to the needs and discourse expectations of his or her audience.

The decision to identify the audience, beginning with the self, is pragmatic; writers must write to and from the self to be authentic, whether in public or private discourse. Fellow writers can provide immediate response to the success of a draft and can tell a writer what needs they still have as readers and "decoders" of the communication. The writing instructor can role-play other kinds of readers in addition to clearly describing his or her reader's response to a draft. Through the support of this writing community, individual writers increase their awareness of the reader-writer relationship. They become more confident about considering the nature and needs of the reader in writing situations that are new to them.

Throughout *The Bedford Guide for College Writers*, the authors ask questions to help focus the writers' attention — most often during revision — on anticipating and meeting the needs of the audience. The literature on audience is extensive. The readings here provide an overview of the discussion of audience in contemporary composition theory and pedagogy along with practical recommendations for how and when to assist student writers to consider the reader.

WAYNE C. BOOTH   *The Rhetorical Stance*

Although this essay was written nearly thirty-five years ago, it continues to enjoy frequent reprinting and much discussion among those who teach writing. Booth mixes casual anecdote about his classroom practice with a sophisticated study of traditional rhetoric. Booth's central insight is that the success or failure of a piece of writing hinges on how the writer stages the author-audience relationship within the text. He suggests that the best writing alternates between utter disregard for the audience and a regard for the audience that is overbearing. The former stance he calls the pedant's stance, for such writers are more interested in the information they're presenting than in the audience's need to process this information. He defines the latter as the advertiser's stance: writers who take this stance offer little by way of substantial content and try to woo the audience through flashy, and sometimes vapid, devices. The ideal stance is one that floats half-way between these two, which Booth calls the rhetorical stance.

Last fall I had an advanced graduate student, bright, energetic, well-informed, whose papers were almost unreadable. He managed to be pretentious, dull, and disorganized in his paper on *Emma,* and pretentious, dull, and disorganized on *Madame Bovary.* On *The Golden Bowl* he was all these and obscure as well. Then one day, toward the end of term, he cornered me after class and said, "You know, I think you were all wrong about Robbe-Grillet's *Jealousy* today." We didn't have time to discuss it, so I suggested that he write me a note about it. Five hours later I found in my faculty box a four-page polemic, unpretentious, stimulating, organized, convincing. Here was a man who had taught freshman composition for several years and who was incapable of committing any of the more obvious errors that we think of as characteristic of bad writing. Yet he could not write a decent sentence, paragraph, or paper until his rhetorical problem was solved — until, that is, he had found a definition of his audience, his argument, and his own proper tone of voice.

The word *rhetoric* is one of those catch-all terms that can easily raise trouble when our backs are turned. As it regains a popularity that it once seemed permanently to have lost, its meanings seem to range all the way from something like "the whole art of writing on any subject," as in Kenneth Burke's *The Rhetoric of Religion*, through "the special arts of persuasion," on down to fairly narrow notions about rhetorical figures and devices. And of course we still have with us the meaning of "empty bombast," as in the phrase "merely rhetorical."

I suppose that the question of the role of rhetoric in the English course is meaningless if we think of rhetoric in either its broadest or its narrowest meanings. No English course could avoid dealing with rhetoric in Burke's sense, under whatever name, and on the other hand nobody would ever advocate anything so questionable as teaching "mere rhetoric." But if we settle on the following, traditional, definition, some real questions are raised: "Rhetoric is the art of finding and employing the most effective means of persuasion on any subject, considered independently of intellectual mastery of that subject." As the students say, "Prof. X knows his stuff but he doesn't know how to put it across." If rhetoric is thought of as the art of "putting it across," considered as quite distinct from mastering an "it" in the first place, we are immediately landed in a bramble bush of controversy. Is there such an art? If so, what does it consist of? Does it have a content of its own? Can it be taught? Should it be taught? If it should, how do we go about it, head on or obliquely?

Obviously it would be foolish to try to deal with many of these issues in twenty minutes. But I wish that there were more signs of our taking all of them seriously. I wish that along with our new passion for structural linguistics, for example, we could point to the development of a rhetorical theory that would show just how knowledge of structural linguistics can be useful to anyone interested in the art of persuasion. I wish there were more freshman texts that related every principle and every rule to functional principles of rhetoric, or, where this proves impossible, I wish one found more systematic discussion of why it is impossible. But for today, I must content myself with a brief look at the charge that there is nothing distinctive and teachable about the art of rhetoric.

The case against the isolability and teachability of rhetoric may look at first like a good one. Nobody writes rhetoric, just as nobody ever writes writing. What we write and speak is always *this* discussion of the decline of railroading and *that* discussion of Pope's couplets and the other argument for abolishing the poll-tax or for getting rhetoric back into English studies.

We can also admit that like all the arts, the art of rhetoric is at best very chancy, only partly amenable to systematic teaching; as we are all painfully aware when our 1:00 section goes miserably and our 2:00 section of the same course is a delight, our own rhetoric is not entirely under control. Successful rhetoricians are to some extent like poets, born, not made. They are also dependent on years of practice and experience. And we can finally admit that even the firmest of principles about writing cannot be taught in the same sense that elementary logic or arithmetic or French can be taught. In my first year of teaching, I had a student who started his first two essays with a swear word. When I suggested that perhaps the third paper ought to start with something else, he protested that his high school teacher had taught him always to catch the reader's attention. Now the teacher was right, but the application of even such a firm principle requires reserves of tact that were somewhat beyond my freshman.

But with all of the reservations made, surely the charge that the art of persuasion cannot in any sense be taught is baseless. I cannot think that anyone who has ever read Aristotle's *Rhetoric* or, say, Whateley's *Elements of Rhetoric* could seriously make the charge. There is more than enough in these and the other traditional rhetorics to provide structure and content for a year-long course. I believe that such a course, when planned and carried through with intelligence and flexibility, can be one of the most important of all educational experiences. But it seems obvious that the arts of persuasion cannot be learned in one year, that a good teacher will continue to teach them regardless of his subject matter, and that we as English teachers have a special responsibility at all levels to get certain basic rhetorical principles into all of our writing assignments. When I think back over the experiences which have had any actual effect on my writing, I find the great good fortune of a splendid freshman course, taught by a man who believed in what he was doing, but I also find a collection of other experiences quite unconnected with a specific writing course. I remember the instructor in psychology who pencilled one word after a peculiarly pretentious paper of mine: *bull.* I remember the day when P. A. Christensen talked with me about my Chaucer paper, and made me understand that my failure to use effective transitions was not simply a technical fault but a fundamental block in my effort to get him to see my meaning. His off-the-cuff pronouncement that I should never let myself write a sentence that was not in some way explicitly attached to preceding and following sentences meant far more to me at that moment, when I had something I wanted to say, than it could have meant as part of a pattern of such rules offered in a writing course. Similarly, I can remember the devastating lessons about my bad writing that Ronald Crane could teach with a simple question mark on a graduate seminar paper, or a pencilled "Evidence for this?" or "Why this section here?" or "Everybody says so. Is it true?"

Such experiences are not, I like to think, simply the result of my being a late bloomer. At least I find my colleagues saying such things as "I didn't learn to write until I became a newspaper reporter," or "The most important training in writing I had was doing a dissertation under old *Blank.*" Sometimes they go on to say that the freshman course was useless; sometimes they say that it was an indispensable preparation for the later experience. The diversity of such replies is so great as to suggest that before we try to reorganize the freshman course, with or without explicit confrontations with rhetorical categories, we ought to look for whatever there is in common among our experiences, both of good writing and of good writing instruction. Whatever we discover in such an enterprise ought to be useful to us at any level of our teaching. It will not, presumably, decide once and for all what should be the content of the freshman course, if there should be such a course. But it might serve as a guideline for the development of widely different programs in the widely differing institutional circumstances in which we must work.

The common ingredient that I find in all of the writing I admire — excluding for now novels, plays and poems — is something that I shall reluctantly call the rhetorical stance, a stance which depends on discovering and maintaining in any writing situation a proper balance among the three elements that are at work in any communicative effort: the available arguments about the subject itself, the interests and peculiarities of the audience, and the voice, the implied character, of the speaker. I should like to suggest that it is this balance, this rhetorical stance, difficult as it is to describe, that is our main goal as teachers of rhetoric. Our ideal graduate will strike this balance automatically in any writing that he considers finished. Though he may never come to the point of finding the balance easily, he will know that it is what makes the difference between effective communication and mere wasted effort.

What I mean by the true rhetorician's stance can perhaps best be seen by contrasting it with two or three corruptions, unbalanced stances often assumed by people who think they are practicing the arts of persuasion.

The first I'll call the pedant's stance; it consists of ignoring or underplaying the personal relationship of speaker and audience and depending entirely on statements about a subject — that is, the notion of a job to be done for a particular audience is left out. It is a virtue, of course, to respect the bare truth of one's subject, and there may even be some subjects which in their very nature define an audience and a rhetorical purpose so that adequacy to the subject can be the whole art of presentation. For example, an article on "The relation of the ontological and teleological proofs," in a recent *Journal of Religion*, requires a minimum of adaptation of argument to audience. But most subjects do not in themselves imply in any necessary way a purpose and an audience and hence a speaker's tone. The writer who assumes that it is enough merely to write an exposition of what he happens to know on the subject will produce the kind of essay that soils our scholarly journals, written not for readers but for bibliographies.

In my first year of teaching I taught a whole unit on "exposition" without ever suggesting, so far as I can remember, that the students ask themselves what their expositions were *for*. So they wrote expositions like this one — I've saved it, to teach me toleration of my colleagues: the title is "Family Relations in More's *Utopia*." "In this theme I would like to discuss some of the relationships with the family which Thomas More elaborates and sets forth in his book, *Utopia*. The first thing that I would like to discuss about family relations is that overpopulation, according to More, is a just cause of war." And so on. Can you hear that student sneering at me, in this opening? What he is saying is something like "you ask for a meaningless paper, I give you a meaningless paper." He knows that he has no audience except me. He knows that I don't want to read his summary of family relations in *Utopia*, and he knows that I know that he therefore has no rhetorical purpose. Because he has not been led to see a question which he considers worth answering, or an audience that could possibly care one way or the other, the paper is worse than no paper at all, even though it has no grammatical or spelling errors and is organized right down the line, one, two, three.

An extreme case, you may say. Most of us would never allow ourselves that kind of empty fencing? Perhaps. But if some carefree foundation is willing to finance a statistical study, I'm willing to wager a month's salary that we'd find at least half of the suggested topics in our freshman texts as pointless as mine was. And we'd find a good deal more than half of the discussions of grammar, punctuation, spelling, and style totally divorced from any notion that rhetorical purpose to some degree controls all such matters. We can offer objective descriptions of levels of usage from now until graduation, but unless the student discovers a desire to say something to somebody and learns to control his diction for a purpose, we've gained very little. I once gave an assignment asking students to describe the same classroom in three different statements, one for each level of usage. They were obedient, but the only ones who got anything from the assignment were those who intuitively imported the rhetorical instructions I had overlooked — such purposes as "Make fun of your scholarly surroundings by describing this classroom in extremely elevated style," or "Imagine a kid from the slums accidentally trapped in these surroundings and forced to write a description of this room." A little thought might have shown me how to give the whole assignment some human point, and therefore some educative value.

Just how confused we can allow ourselves to be about such matters is shown in a recent publication of the Educational Testing Service, called "Factors in Judgments of Writing Ability." In order to isolate those factors which affect differences in grading standards, ETS set six groups of readers — business men, writers and editors, lawyers, and teachers of English, social science and natural science — to reading the same batch of papers. Then ETS did a hundred-page "factor analysis" of the amount of agreement and disagreement, and of the elements which different kinds of graders emphasized. The authors of the report express a certain amount of shock at the discovery that the median correlation was only .31 and that 94 percent of the papers received either seven, eight, or nine of the nine possible grades.

But what *could* they have expected? In the first place, the students were given no purpose and no audience when the essays were assigned. And then all these editors and business men and academics were asked to judge the papers in a complete vacuum, using only whatever intuitive standards they cared to use. I'm surprised that there was any correlation at all. Lacking instructions, some of the students undoubtedly wrote polemical essays, suitable for the popular press; others no doubt imagined an audience, say, of *Reader's Digest* readers, and others wrote with the English teachers as implied audience; an occasional student with real philosophical bent would no doubt do a careful analysis of the pros and cons of the case. This would be graded low, of course, by the magazine editors, even though they would have graded it high if asked to judge it as a speculative contribution to the analysis of the problem. Similarly, a creative student who has been getting A's for his personal essays will write an amusing colorful piece, failed by all the social scientists present, though they would have graded it high if asked to judge it for what it was. I find it shocking than tens of thousands of dollars and endless hours should have been spent by students, graders, and professional testers analyzing essays and grading results totally abstracted from any notion of purposeful human communication. Did nobody protest? One might as well assemble a group of citizens to judge students' capacity to throw balls, say, without telling the students or the graders whether altitude, speed, accuracy or form was to be judged. The judges would be drawn from football coaches, jai-lai experts, lawyers, and English teachers, and asked to apply whatever standards they intuitively apply to ball throwing. Then we could express astonishment that the judgments did not correlate very well, and we could do a factor analysis to discover, lo and behold, that some readers concentrated on altitude, some on speed, some on accuracy, some on form — and the English teachers were simply confused.

One effective way to combat the pedantic stance is to arrange for weekly confrontations of groups of students over their own papers. We have done far too little experimenting with arrangements for providing a genuine audience in this way. Short of such developments, it remains true that a good teacher can convince his students that he is a true audience, if his comments on the papers show that some sort of dialogue is taking place. As Jacques Barzun says in *Teacher in America*, students should be made to feel that unless they have said something to someone, they have failed; to bore the teacher is a worse form of failure than to anger him. From this point of view we can see that the charts of grading symbols that mar even the best freshman texts are not the innocent time savers that we pretend. Plausible as it may seem to arrange for more corrections with less time, they inevitably reduce the student's sense of purpose in writing. When he sees innumerable W13s and P19s in the margin, he cannot possibly feel that the art of persuasion is as important to his instructor as when he reads personal comments, however few.

This first perversion, then, springs from ignoring the audience or overreliance on the pure subject. The second, which might be called the advertiser's stance, comes from *under*valuing the subject and overvaluing pure effect: how to win friends and influence people.

Some of our best freshman texts — Sheridan Baker's *The Practical Stylist*, for example — allow themselves on occasion to suggest that to be controversial or argumentative, to stir up an audience is an end in itself. Sharpen the controversial edge, one of them says, and the clear implication is that one should do so even if the truth of the subject is honed off in the process. This perversion is probably in the long run a more serious threat in our society than the danger of ignoring the audience. In the time of audience-reaction meters and pre-tested plays and novels, it is not easy to convince students of the old Platonic truth that good persuasion is honest persuasion, or even of the old Aristotelian truth that the good rhetorician must be master of his subject, no matter how dishonest he may decide ultimately to be. Having told them that good writers always to some degree accommodate their arguments to the audience, it is hard to explain the difference between justified accommodation — say changing *point one* to the final position — and the kind of accommodation that fills our popular magazines, in which the very substance of what is said is accommodated to some preconception of what will sell. "The publication of *Eros* [magazine] represents a major breakthrough in the battle for the liberation of the human spirit."

At a dinner about a month ago I sat between the wife of a famous civil rights lawyer and an advertising consultant. "I saw the article on your book yesterday in the *Daily News*," she said, "but I didn't even finish it. The title of your book scared me off. Why did you ever choose such a terrible title? Nobody would buy a book with a title like that." The man on my right, whom I'll call Mr. Kinches, overhearing my feeble reply, plunged into a conversation with her, over my torn and bleeding corpse. "Now with my *last* book," he said, "I listed twenty possible titles and then tested them out on four hundred businessmen. The one I chose was voted for by 90 percent of the businessmen." "That's what I was just saying to Mr. Booth," she said. "A book title ought to grab you, and *rhetoric* is not going to grab anybody." "Right," he said. "My *last* book sold fifty thousand copies already; I don't know how this one will do, but I polled two hundred businessmen on the table of contents, and. . . ."

At one point I did manage to ask him whether the title he chose really fit the book. "Not quite as well as one or two of the others," he admitted, "but that doesn't matter, you know. If the book is designed right, so that the first chapter pulls them in, and you *keep* 'em in, who's going to gripe about a little inaccuracy in the title?"

Well, rhetoric is the art of persuading, not the art seeming to persuade by giving everything away at the start. It presupposes that one has a purpose concerning a subject which itself cannot be fundamentally modified by the desire to persuade. If Edmund Burke had decided that he could win more votes in Parliament by choosing the other side — as he most certainly could have done — we would hardly hail this party-switch as a master stroke of rhetoric. If Churchill had offered the British "peace in our time," with some laughs thrown in, because opinion polls had shown that more Britishers were "grabbed" by these than by blood, sweat, and tears, we could hardly call his decision a sign of rhetorical skill.

One could easily discover other perversions of the rhetorician's balance — most obviously what might be called the entertainer's stance — the willingness to sacrifice substance to personality and charm. I admire Walker Gibson's efforts to startle us out of dry pedantry, but I know from experience that his exhortations to find and develop the speaker's voice can lead to empty colorfulness. A student once said to me, complaining about a colleague, "I soon learned that all I had to do to get an A was imitate Thurber."

But perhaps this is more than enough about the perversions of the rhetorical stance. Balance itself is always harder to describe than the clumsy poses that result when it is destroyed. But we all experience the balance whenever we find an author who succeeds in changing our minds. He can do so only if he knows more about the subject than we do, and if he then engages us in the process of thinking — and feeling — it through. What makes the rhetoric of Milton and Burke and Churchill great is that each presents us with the spectacle of a man passionately involved in thinking an important question through, in the company of an audience. Though each of them did everything in his power to make his point persuasive, including a pervasive use of the many emotional appeals that have been falsely scorned by many a freshman composition text, none would have allowed himself the advertiser's stance; none would have polled the audience in advance to discover which position would get the votes. Nor is the highly individual personality that springs out at us from their speeches and essays present for the sake of selling itself. The rhetorical balance among speakers, audience, and argument is with all three men habitual, as we see if we look at their non-political writings. Burke's work on the Sublime and Beautiful is a relatively unimpassioned philosophical treatise, but one finds there again a delicate balance: though the implied author of this work is a far different person, far less obtrusive, far more objective, than the man who later cried *sursum corda* to the British Parliament, he permeates with his philosophical personality his philosophical work. And though the signs of his awareness of his audience are far more subdued, they are still here: every effort is made to involve the *proper* audience, the audience of philosophical minds, in a fundamentally interesting inquiry, and to lead them through to the end. In short, because he was a man engaged with men in the effort to solve a human problem, one could never call what he wrote dull, however difficult or abstruse.

Now obviously the habit of seeking this balance is not the only thing we have to teach under the heading of rhetoric. But I think that everything worth teaching under that heading finds its justification finally in that balance. Much of what is now considered irrelevant or dull can, in fact, be brought to life when teachers and students know what they are seeking. Churchill reports that the most valuable training he ever received in rhetoric was in the diagramming of sentences. Think of it! Yet the diagramming of a sentence, regardless of the grammatical system, can be a live subject as soon as one asks not simply "How is this sentence put together," but rather "Why is it put together in this way?" or "Could the rhetorical balance and hence the desired persuasion be better achieved by writing it differently?"

As a nation we are reputed to write very badly. As a nation, I would say, we are more inclined to the perversions of rhetoric than to the rhetorical balance. Regardless of what we do about this or that course in the curriculum, our mandate would seem to be, then, to lead more of our students than we now do to care about and practice the true arts of persuasion.

Booth's Insights as a Resource for Your Teaching

1. Read any piece of writing by a student, and track the ways the author appeals to you as a reader. Where does the author adopt the pedant's stance? The advertiser's stance? How might these terms help you to comment on student work that needs improvement?

2. Consider the stance that you "model" for your students. Do you alternate between pedant and advertiser, or do you strike a rhetorical stance most of the time? How do the students respond to the various stances we model for them?

Booth's Insights as a Resource for the Writing Classroom

1. Assign Booth's essay to your students. Once they've read it, have them explore it according to the terms Booth himself presents. Is Booth's essay characterized by a subtle balance between the pedant and the advertiser? If so, how and where does he manage to strike this balance? Are there any places where the stance seems imbalanced and starts to lean in one direction or another?

2. Ask students to examine their own work or each other's in light of Booth's essay. Have them focus on passages in their own writing that were less than successful. Can they use Booth's terms to diagnose and fix problems?

LISA EDE AND
ANDREA LUNSFORD

Audience Addressed/ Audience Invoked: The Role of Audience in Composition Theory and Pedagogy

Lisa Ede and Andrea Lunsford skillfully demonstrate two major, and seemingly opposed, perspectives on whether and how to emphasize audience in writing courses. They characterize as "audience addressed" the assumptions of many writing teachers and theorists that writers must know — or learn about — the attitudes, beliefs, and expectations of their readers. The authors focus on the theory of Ruth Mitchell and Mary Taylor, who base a writing pedagogy on the concept of addressing the "real" reader. The classification could also include other theorists like Linda Flower, who discusses "reader-based prose" and presents planning strategies for deciding how to address the reader.

Ede and Lunsford contrast the concept of audience addressed with that of "audience invoked." This theory states that the writer invokes an audience by providing "cues" that tell the reader what role the writer wants the reader to play. The authors discuss Walter Ong's "The Writer's Audience Is Always a Fiction," but your students may invoke their audience most clearly in papers they write in response to Chapter 9, "Taking a Stand," and Chapter 10, "Proposing a Solution." In each type of persuasive writing, the successful student not only shapes a persona that readers will trust or respect but also creates a character or role for the reader — perhaps that of being altruistic and humane or of being rational yet cautiously sympathetic.

Through their analysis of the two perspectives on audience, Ede and Lunsford demonstrate that writers need to have skills both to invoke readers and to anticipate and address readers, depending on the rhetorical situation. They remind us how writers redefine audience during revision and cite their own processes of writing the article. They conclude that a "fully elaborated view of audience . . . must balance the creativity of the writer with the different, but equally important, creativity of the reader."

One important controversy currently engaging scholars and teachers of writing involves the role of audience in composition theory and pedagogy. How can we best define the audience of a written discourse? What does it mean to address an audience? To what degree should teachers stress audience in their assignments and discussions? What is the best way to help students recognize the significance of this critical element in any rhetorical situation?

Teachers of writing may find recent efforts to answer these questions more confusing than illuminating. Should they agree with Ruth Mitchell and Mary Taylor, who so emphasize the significance of the audience that they argue for abandoning conventional composition courses and instituting a "cooperative effort by writing and subject instructors in adjunct courses? The cooperation and courses take two main forms. Either writing instructors can be attached to subject courses where writing is required, an organization which disperses the instructors throughout the departments participating; or the composition courses can teach students how to write the papers assigned in other concurrent courses, thus centralizing instruction but diversifying topics."[1] Or should teachers side with Russell Long, who asserts that those advocating greater attention to audience overemphasize the role of "observable physical or occupational characteristics" while ignoring the fact that most writers actually create their audiences? Long argues against the usefulness of such methods as developing hypothetical rhetorical situations as writing assignments, urging instead a more traditional emphasis on "the analysis of texts in the classroom with a very detailed examination given to the signals provided by the writer for his audience."[2]

To many teachers, the choice seems limited to a single option — to be for or against an emphasis on audience in composition courses. In the following essay, we wish to expand our understanding of the role audience plays in composition theory and pedagogy by demonstrating that the arguments advocated by each side of the current debate oversimplify the act of making meaning through written discourse. Each side, we will argue, has failed adequately to recognize (1) the fluid, dynamic character of rhetorical situations and (2) the integrated, interdependent nature of reading and writing. After discussing the strengths and weaknesses of the two central perspectives on audience in composition — which we group under the rubrics of *audience addressed* and *audience invoked*[3] — we will propose an alternative formulation, one which we believe more accurately reflects the richness of "audience" as a concept.[4]

Audience Addressed

Those who envision audience as addressed emphasize the concrete reality of the writer's audience; they also share the assumption that knowledge of this audience's attitudes, beliefs, and expectations is not only possible (via observation and analysis) but essential. Questions concerning the degree to which this audience is "real" or imagined, and the ways it differs from the speaker's audience, are generally either ignored or subordinated to a sense of the audience's powerfulness. In their discussion of "A Heuristic Model for Creating a Writer's Audience," for example, Fred Pfister and Joanne Petrik attempt to recognize the ontological complexity of the writer-audience relationship by noting that "students, like all writers, must fictionalize their audience."[5] Even so, by encouraging students to "construct in their imagination an audience that is as nearly a replica as is possible of *those many readers who actually exist in the world of reality*," Pfister and Petrik implicitly privilege the concept of audience as addressed.[6]

Many of those who envision audience as addressed have been influenced by the strong tradition of audience analysis in speech communication and by current research in cognitive psychology on the composing process.[7] They often see themselves as reacting against the current-traditional paradigm of composition, with its arhetorical, product-oriented emphasis.[8] And they also frequently encourage what is called "real-world" writing.[9]

Our purpose here is not to draw up a list of those who share this view of audience but to suggest the general outline of what most readers will recognize as a central tendency in the teaching of writing today. We would, however, like to focus on one particularly ambitious attempt to formulate a theory and pedagogy for composition based on the concept of audience as addressed: Ruth Mitchell and Mary Taylor's "The Integrating Perspective: An Audience-Response Model for Writing." We choose Mitchell and Taylor's work because of its theoretical richness and practical specificity. Despite these strengths, we wish to note several potentially significant limitations in their approach, limitations which obtain to varying degrees in much of the current work of those who envision audience as addressed.

In their article, Mitchell and Taylor analyze what they consider to be the two major existing composition models: one focusing on the writer and the other on the written product. Their evaluation of these two models seems essentially accurate. The "writer" model is limited because it defines writing as either self-expression or "fidelity to fact" (255) — epistemologically naive assumptions which result in troubling pedagogical inconsistencies. And the "written product" model, which is characterized by an emphasis on "certain intrinsic features [such as a] lack of comma splices and fragments" (258), is challenged by the continued inability of teachers of writing (not to mention those in other professions) to agree upon the precise intrinsic features which characterize "good" writing.

Most interesting, however, is what Mitchell and Taylor *omit* in their criticism of these models. Neither the writer model nor the written product model pays serious attention to invention, the term used to describe those "methods designed to aid in retrieving information, forming concepts, analyzing complex events, and solving certain kinds of problems."[10] Mitchell and Taylor's lapse in not noting this omission is understandable, however, for the same can be said of their own model. When these authors discuss the writing process, they stress that "our first priority for writing instruction at every level ought to be certain major tactics for structuring material because these structures are the most important in guiding the reader's comprehension and memory" (271). They do not concern themselves with where "the material" comes from — its sophistication, complexity, accuracy, or rigor.

Mitchell and Taylor also fail to note another omission, one which might be best described in reference to their own model (Figure 1). This model has four components. Mitchell and Taylor use two of these, "writer" and "written product," as labels for the models they condemn. The third and fourth components, "audience" and "response," provide the title for their own "audience-response model for writing" (249).

Mitchell and Taylor stress that the components in their model interact. Yet, despite their emphasis on interaction, it never seems to occur to them to note that the two other models may fail in large part because they overemphasize and isolate one of the four elements — wrenching it too greatly from its context and thus inevitably distorting the composing process. Mitchell and Taylor do not consider this possibility, we suggest, because their own model has the same weakness.

Mitchell and Taylor argue that a major limitation of the "writer" model is its emphasis on the self, the person writing, as the only potential judge of effective discourse. Ironically, however, their own emphasis on audience leads to a similar distortion. In their model, the audience has the sole power of evaluating writing, the success of which "will be judged by the audience's reaction: 'good' translates into 'effective,' 'bad' into 'ineffective.' " Mitchell and Taylor go on to note that "the audience not only judges writing; it also motivates it" (250),[11] thus suggesting that the writer has less control than the audience over both evaluation and motivation.

Despite the fact that Mitchell and Taylor describe writing as "an interaction, a dynamic relationship" (250), their model puts far more emphasis on the role of the audience than on that of the writer. One way to pinpoint the source of imbalance in

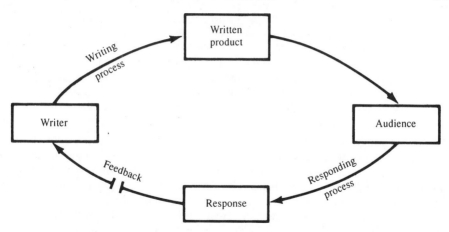

Figure 1. Mitchell and Taylor's "general model of writing" (250)

Mitchell and Taylor's formulation is to note that they are right in emphasizing the creative role of readers who, they observe, "actively contribute to the meaning of what they read and will respond according to a complex set of expectations, preconceptions, and provocations" (251), but wrong in failing to recognize the equally essential role writers play throughout the composing process not only as creators but also as *readers* of their own writing.

As Susan Wall observes in "In the Writer's Eye: Learning to Teach the Rereading/Revising Process," when writers read their own writing, as they do continuously while they compose, "there are really not one but two contexts for rereading: there is the writer-as-reader's sense of what the established text is actually saying, as of this reading; and there is the reader-as-writer's judgment of what the text might say or should say. . . ."[12] What is missing from Mitchell and Taylor's model, and from much work done from the perspective of audience as addressed, is a recognition of the crucial importance of this internal dialogue, through which writers analyze inventional problems and conceptualize patterns of discourse. Also missing is an adequate awareness that, no matter how much feedback writers may receive after they have written something (or in breaks while they write), as they compose writers must rely in large part upon their own vision of the reader, which they create, as readers do their vision of writers, according to their own experiences and expectations.

Another major problem with Mitchell and Taylor's analysis is their apparent lack of concern for the ethics of language use. At one point, the authors ask the following important question: "Have we painted ourselves into a corner, so that the audience-response model must defend sociologese and its related styles?" (265). Note first the ambiguity of their answer, which seems to us to say no and yes at the same time, and the way they try to deflect its impact:

> No. We defend only the right of audiences to set their own standards and we repudiate the ambitions of English departments to monopolize that standard-setting. If bureaucrats and scientists are happy with the way they write, then no one should interfere.
> But evidence is accumulating that they are not happy. (265)

Here Mitchell and Taylor surely underestimate the relationship between style and substance. As those concerned with Doublespeak can attest, for example, the problem with sociologese is not simply its (to our ears) awkward, convoluted, highly nominalized style, but the way writers have in certain instances used this style to make statements otherwise unacceptable to lay persons, to "gloss over" potentially controversial facts about programs and their consequences, and thus violate the ethics of language use. Hence, although we support Mitchell and Taylor when they insist that we must better understand and respect the linguistic traditions of other disciplines and professions, we object to their assumption that style is somehow value free.

As we noted earlier, an analysis of Mitchell and Taylor's discussion clarifies weaknesses inherent in much of the theoretical and pedagogical research based on the concept of audience as addressed. One major weakness of this research lies in its narrow focus on helping students learn how to "continually modify their work with reference to their audience" (251). Such a focus, which in its extreme form becomes pandering to the crowd, tends to undervalue the responsibility a writer has to a subject and to what Wayne Booth in *Modern Dogma and the Rhetoric of Assent* calls "the art of discovering good reasons." [13] The resulting imbalance has clear ethical consequences, for rhetoric has traditionally been concerned not only with the effectiveness of a discourse, but with truthfulness as well. Much of our difficulty with the language of advertising, for example, arises out of the ad writer's powerful concept of audience as addressed divorced from a corollary ethical concept. The toothpaste ad that promises improved personality, for instance, knows too well how to address the audience. But such ads ignore ethical questions completely.

Another weakness in research done by those who envision audience as addressed suggests an oversimplified view of language. As Paul Kameen observes in "Rewording the Rhetoric of Composition," "discourse is not grounded in forms or experience or audience; it engages all of these elements simultaneously." [14] Ann Berthoff has persistently criticized our obsession with one or another of the elements of discourse, insisting that meaning arises out of their synthesis. Writing is more, then, than "a means of acting upon a receiver" (Mitchell and Taylor 250); it is a means of making meaning for writer *and* reader. [15] Without such a unifying, balanced understanding of language use, it is easy to overemphasize one aspect of discourse, such as audience. It is also easy to forget, as Anthony Petrosky cautions us, that "reading, responding, and composing are aspects of understanding, and theories that attempt to account for them outside of their interaction with each other run the serious risk of building reductive models of human understanding." [16]

Audience Invoked

Those who envision audience as invoked stress that the audience of a written discourse is a construction of the writer, a "created fiction" (Long 225). They do not, of course, deny the physical reality of readers, but they argue that writers simply cannot know this reality in the way that speakers can. The central task of the writer, then, is not to analyze an audience and adapt discourse to meet its needs. Rather, the writer uses the semantic and syntactic resources of language to provide cues for the reader — cues which help to define the role or roles the writer wishes the reader to adopt in responding to the text. Little scholarship in composition takes this perspective; only Russell Long's article and Walter Ong's "The Writer's Audience Is Always a Fiction" focus centrally on this issue. [17] If recent conferences are any indication, however, a growing number of teachers and scholars are becoming concerned with what they see as the possible distortions and oversimplifications of the approach typified by Mitchell and Taylor's model. [18]

Russell Long's response to current efforts to teach students analysis of audience and adaptation of text to audience is typical: "I have become increasingly disturbed not only about the superficiality of the advice itself, but about the philosophy which seems to lie beneath it" (221). Rather than detailing Long's argument, we wish to turn to Walter Ong's well-known study. Published in *PMLA* in 1975, "The Writer's Audience Is Always a Fiction" has had a significant impact on composition studies, despite the fact that its major emphasis is on fictional narrative rather than expository writing. An analysis of Ong's argument suggests that teachers of writing may err if they uncritically accept Ong's statement that "what has been said about fictional narrative applies ceteris paribus to all writing" (17).

Ong's thesis includes two central assertions: "What do we mean by saying the audience is a fiction? Two things at least. First, that the writer must construct in his imagination, clearly or vaguely, an audience cast in some sort of role. . . . Second, we mean that the audience must correspondingly fictionalize itself" (12). Ong emphasizes the creative power of the adept writer, who can both project and alter audiences, as well as the complexity of the reader's role. Readers, Ong observes, must learn or "know how to play the game of being a member of an audience that 'really' does not exist" (12).

On the most abstract and general level, Ong is accurate. For a writer, the audience is not *there* in the sense that the speaker's audience, whether a single person or a large group, is present. But Ong's representative situations — the orator addressing a mass audience versus a writer alone in a room — oversimplify the potential range and diversity of both oral and written communication situations.

Ong's model of the paradigmatic act of speech communication derives from traditional rhetoric. In distinguishing the terms audience and reader, he notes that "the orator has before him an audience which is a true audience, a collectivity. . . . Readers do not form a collectivity, acting here and now on one another and on the speaker as members of an audience do" (11). As this quotation indicates, Ong also stresses the potential for interaction among members of an audience, and between an audience and a speaker.

But how many audiences are actually collectives, with ample opportunity for interaction? In *Persuasion: Understanding, Practice, and Analysis*, Herbert Simons establishes a continuum of audiences based on opportunities for interaction.[19] Simons contrasts commercial mass media publics, which "have little or no contact with each other and certainly have no reciprocal awareness of each other as members of the same audience" with "face-to-face work groups that meet and interact continuously over an extended period of time." He goes on to note that: "Between these two extremes are such groups as the following: (1) the *pedestrian audience*, persons who happen to pass a soap box orator . . . ; (2) the *passive, occasional audience*, persons who come to hear a noted lecturer in a large auditorium . . . ; (3) the *active, occasional audience*, persons who meet only on specific occasions but actively interact when they do meet" (97–98).

Simons's discussion, in effect, questions the rigidity of Ong's distinctions between a speaker's and a writer's audience. Indeed, when one surveys a broad range of situations inviting oral communication, Ong's paradigmatic situation, in which the speaker's audience constitutes a "collectivity, acting here and now on one another and on the speaker" (11), seems somewhat atypical. It is certainly possible, at any rate, to think of a number of instances where speakers confront a problem very similar to that of writers: lacking intimate knowledge of their audience, which comprises not a collectivity but a disparate, and possibly even divided, group of individuals, speakers, like writers, must construct in their imaginations "an audience cast in some sort of role."[20] When President Carter announced to Americans during a speech broadcast on television, for instance, that his program against inflation was "the moral equivalent of warfare," he was doing more than merely characterizing his economic policies. He was providing an important cue to his audience concerning the role he wished them to adopt as listeners — that of a people braced for a painful but necessary and justifiable battle. Were we to examine his speech in detail, we would find other more subtle, but equally important, semantic and syntactic signals to the audience.

We do not wish here to collapse all distinctions between oral and written communication, but rather to emphasize that speaking and writing are, after all, both rhetorical acts. There are important differences between speech and writing. And the broad distinction between speech and writing that Ong makes is both commonsensical and particularly relevant to his subject, fictional narrative. As our illustration demonstrates, however, when one turns to precise, concrete situations, the relationship between speech and writing can become far more complex than even Ong represents.

Just as Ong's distinction between speech and writing is accurate on a highly general level but breaks down (or at least becomes less clear-cut) when examined closely, so too does his dictum about writers and their audiences. Every writer must indeed create a role for the reader, but the constraints on the writer and the potential sources of and possibilities for the reader's role are both more complex and diverse than Ong suggests. Ong stresses the importance of literary tradition in the creation of audience: "If the writer succeeds in writing, it is generally because he can fictionalize in his imagination an audience he has learned to know not from daily life but from earlier writers who were fictionalizing in their imagination audiences they had learned to know in still earlier writers, and so on back to the dawn of written narrative" (11). And he cites a particularly (for us) germane example, a student "asked to write on the subject to which schoolteachers, jaded by summer, return compulsively every autumn: 'How I Spent My Summer Vacation'" (11). In order to negotiate such an assignment successfully, the student must turn his real audience, the teacher, into someone else. He or she must, for instance, "make like Samuel Clemens and write for whomever Samuel Clemens was writing for" (11).

Ong's example is, for his purposes, well chosen. For such an assignment does indeed require the successful student to "fictionalize" his or her audience. But why is the student's decision to turn to a literary model in this instance particularly appropriate? Could one reason be that the student knows (consciously or unconsciously) that his English teacher, who is still the literal audience of his essay, appreciates literature and hence would be entertained (and here the student may intuit the assignment's actual aim as well) by such a strategy? In Ong's example the audience — the "jaded" schoolteacher — is not only willing to accept another role but, perhaps, actually yearns for it. How else to escape the tedium of reading twenty-five, fifty, seventy-five student papers on the same topic? As Walter Minot notes, however, not all readers are so malleable:

> In reading a work of fiction or poetry, a reader is far more willing to suspend his beliefs and values than in a rhetorical work dealing with some current social, moral, or economic issue. The effectiveness of the created audience in a rhetorical situation is likely to depend on such constraints as the actual identity of the reader, the subject of the discourse, the identity and purpose of the writer, and many other factors in the real world.[21]

An example might help make Minot's point concrete.

Imagine another composition student faced, like Ong's, with an assignment. This student, who has been given considerably more latitude in her choice of topic, has decided to write on an issue of concern to her at the moment, the possibility that a home for mentally retarded adults will be built in her neighborhood. She is alarmed by the strongly negative, highly emotional reaction of most of her neighbors and wishes in her essay to persuade them that such a residence might not be the disaster they anticipate.

This student faces a different task from that described by Ong. If she is to succeed, she must think seriously about her actual readers, the neighbors to whom she wishes to send her letter. She knows the obvious demographic factors — age, race, class — so well that she probably hardly needs to consider them consciously. But other issues are more complex. How much do her neighbors know about mental retardation, intellectually or experientially? What is their image of a retarded adult? What fears does this project raise in them? What civic and religious values do they most respect? Based on this analysis — and the process may be much less sequential than we describe here — she must, of course, define a role for her audience, one congruent with her persona, arguments, the facts as she knows them, etc. She must, as Minot argues, *both* analyze and invent an audience.[22] In this instance, after detailed analysis of her audience and her arguments, the student decided to begin her essay by emphasizing what she felt to be the genuinely admirable qualities of her neighbors, particularly their kindness, understanding, and concern for others. In so doing, she invited her audience to see themselves as she saw them: as thoughtful, intelligent people who, if they were adequately informed, would certainly not act in a harsh manner to those less fortunate than they. In accepting this role, her readers did not have to "play the game of being a member of an audience that 'really' does not exist" (Ong 12). But they did have to recognize in themselves the strengths the student described and to accept her implicit linking of these strengths to what she hoped would be their response to the proposed "home."

When this student enters her history class to write an examination she faces a different set of constraints. Unlike the historian who does indeed have a broad range of options in establishing the reader's role, our student has much less freedom. This is because her reader's role has already been established and formalized in a series of related academic conventions. If she is a successful student, she has so effectively internalized these conventions that she can subordinate a concern for her complex and multiple audiences to focus on the material on which she is being tested and on the single audience, the teacher, who will respond to her performance on the test.[23]

We could multiply examples. In each instance the student writing — to friend, employer, neighbor, teacher, fellow readers of her daily newspaper — would need, as one of the many conscious and unconscious decisions required in composing, to envision and define a role for the reader. But *how* she defines that role — whether she relies mainly upon academic or technical writing conventions, literary models, intimate knowledge of friends or neighbors, analysis of a particular group, or some combination thereof — will vary tremendously. At times the writer may establish a role for the reader which indeed does not "coincide with his role in the rest of actual life" (Ong 12). At other times, however, one of the writer's primary tasks may be that of analyzing the "real life" audience and adapting the discourse to it. One of the factors that makes writing so difficult, as we know, is that we have no recipes: each rhetorical situation is unique and thus requires the writer, catalyzed and guided by a strong sense of purpose, to reanalyze and reinvent solutions.

Despite their helpful corrective approach, then, theories which assert that the audience of a written discourse is a construction of the writer present their own dangers.[24] One of these is the tendency to overemphasize the distinction between speech and writing while undervaluing the insights of discourse theorists, such as James Moffett and James Britton, who remind us of the importance of such additional factors as distance between speaker or writer and audience and levels of abstraction in the subject. In *Teaching the Universe of Discourse*, Moffett establishes the following spectrum of discourse: recording ("the drama of what is happening"), reporting ("the narrative of what happened"), generalizing ("the exposition of what happens"), and theorizing ("the argumentation of what will, may happen").[25] In an extended example, Moffett demonstrates the important points of connection between communication acts at any one level of the spectrum, whether oral or written:

> Suppose next that I tell the cafeteria experience to a friend some time later in conversation. . . . Of course, instead of recounting the cafeteria scene to my friend in person I could write it in a letter to an audience more removed in time and space. Informal writing is usually still rather spontaneous, directed at an audience known to the writer, and reflects the transient mood and circumstances in which the writing occurs. Feedback and audience influence, however, are delayed and weakened. . . . *Compare in turn now the changes that must occur all down the line when I write about this cafeteria experience in a discourse destined for publication and distribution to a mass, anonymous audience of present and perhaps unborn people.* I cannot allude to things and ideas that only my friends know about. I must use a vocabulary, style, logic, and rhetoric that anybody in that mass audience can understand and respond to. I must name and organize what happened during those moments in the cafeteria that day in such a way that this mythical average reader can relate what I say to some primary moments of experience of his own. (37–38; our emphasis)

Though Moffett does not say so, many of these same constraints would obtain if he decided to describe his experience in a speech to a mass audience — the viewers of a television show, for example, or the members of a graduating class. As Moffett's example illustrates, the distinction between speech and writing is important; it is, however, only one of several constraints influencing any particular discourse.

Another weakness of research based on the concept of audience as invoked is that it distorts the processes of writing and reading by overemphasizing the power of the writer and undervaluing that of the reader. Unlike Mitchell and Taylor, Ong recognizes the creative role the writer plays as reader of his or her own writing, the way the writer uses language to provide cues for the reader and tests the effectiveness of these cues during his or her own rereading of the text. But Ong fails adequately to recognize the constraints placed on the writer, in certain situations, by the audience. He fails, in other words, to acknowledge that readers' own experiences, expectations, and beliefs do play a central role in their reading of a text, and that the writer who does not consider the needs and interests of his audience risks losing that audience. To argue that the audience is a "created fiction" (Long 225), to stress that the reader's role "seldom coincides with his role in the rest of actual life" (Ong 12), is just as much an oversimplification, then, as to insist, as Mitchell and Taylor do, that "the audience not only judges writing, it also motivates it" (250). The former view overemphasizes the writer's independence and power; the latter, that of the reader.

Rhetoric and Its Situations [26]

If the perspectives we have described as audience addressed and audience invoked represent incomplete conceptions of the role of audience in written discourse, do we have an alternative? How can we most accurately conceive of this essential rhetorical element? In what follows we will sketch a tentative model and present several defining or constraining statements about this apparently slippery concept, "audience." The result will, we hope, move us closer to a full understanding of the role audience plays in written discourse.

Figure 2 represents our attempt to indicate the complex series of obligations, resources, needs, and constraints embodied in the writer's concept of audience. (We emphasize that our goal here is *not* to depict the writing process as a whole — a much more complex task — but to focus on the writer's relation to audience.) As our model indicates, we do not see the two perspectives on audience described earlier as necessarily dichotomous or contradictory. Except for past and anomalous audiences, special cases which we describe paragraphs hence, all of the audience roles we specify — self, friend, colleague, critic, mass audience, and future audience — may be invoked or addressed.[27] It is the writer who, as writer and reader of his or her own text, one guided by a sense of purpose and by the particularities of a specific rhetorical situation, establishes the range of potential roles an audience may play. (Readers may, of course, accept or reject the role or roles the writer wishes them to adopt in responding to a text.)

Writers who wish to be read must often adapt their discourse to meet the needs and expectations of an addressed audience. They may rely on past experience in addressing audiences to guide their writing, or they may engage a representative of that audience in the writing process. The latter occurs, for instance, when we ask a colleague to read an article intended for scholarly publication. Writers may also be required to respond to the intervention of others — a teacher's comments on an essay, a supervisor's suggestions for improving a report, or the insistent, catalyzing questions of an editor. Such intervention may in certain cases represent a powerful stimulus to the writer, but it is the writer who interprets the suggestions — or even

Figure 2. The concept of audience

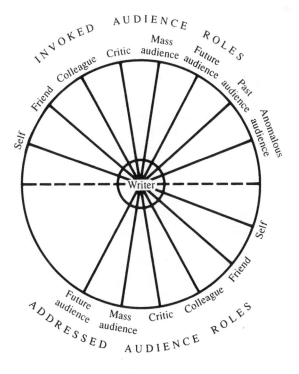

commands — of others, choosing what to accept or reject. Even the conscious decision to accede to the expectations of a particular addressed audience may not always be carried out; unconscious psychological resistance, incomplete understanding, or inadequately developed ability may prevent the writer from following through with the decision — a reality confirmed by composition teachers with each new set of essays.

The addressed audience, the actual or intended readers of a discourse, exists outside of the text. Writers may analyze these readers' needs, anticipate their biases, even defer to their wishes. But it is only through the text, through language, that writers embody or give life to their conception of the reader. In so doing, they do not so much create a role for the reader — a phrase which implies that the writer somehow creates a mold to which the reader adapts — as invoke it. Rather than relying on incantations, however, writers conjure their vision — a vision which they hope readers will actively come to share as they read the text — by using all the resources of language available to them to establish a broad, and ideally coherent, range of cues for the reader. Technical writing conventions, for instance, quickly formalize any of several writer-reader relationships, such as colleague to colleague or expert to lay reader. But even comparatively local semantic decisions may play an equally essential role. In "The Writer's Audience Is Always a Fiction," Ong demonstrates how Hemingway's use of definite articles in *A Farewell to Arms* subtly cues readers that their role is to be that of a "companion in arms . . . a confidant" (13).

Any of the roles of the addressed audience cited in our model may be invoked via the text. Writers may also invoke a past audience, as did, for instance, Ong's student writing to those Mark Twain would have been writing for. And writers can also invoke anomalous audiences, such as a fictional character — Hercule Poirot perhaps. Our model, then, confirms Douglas Park's observation that the meanings of audience, though multiple and complex, "tend to diverge in two general directions: one toward actual people external to the text, the audience whom the writer must accommodate; the other toward the text itself and the audience implied there: a set of suggested or evoked attitudes, interests, reactions, conditions of knowledge which may or may not fit with the qualities of actual readers or listeners."[28] The most complete understanding of audience thus involves a synthesis of the perspectives we have termed audience addressed, with its focus on the reader, and audience invoked, with its focus on the writer.

One illustration of this constantly shifting complex of meanings for "audience" lies in our own experiences writing this essay. One of us became interested in the concept of audience during an NEH Seminar, and her first audience was a small, close-knit seminar group to whom she addressed her work. The other came to contemplate a multiplicity of audiences while working on a textbook; the first audience in this case was herself, as she debated the ideas she was struggling to present to a group of invoked students. Following a lengthy series of conversations, our interests began to merge: we shared notes and discussed articles written by others on audience, and eventually one of us began a draft. Our long distance telephone bills and the miles we travelled up and down I-5 from Oregon to British Columbia attest most concretely to the power of a co-author's expectations and criticisms and also illustrate that one person can take on the role of several different audiences: friend, colleague, and critic.

As we began to write and rewrite the essay, now for a particular scholarly journal, the change in purpose and medium (no longer a seminar paper or a textbook) led us to new audiences. For us, the major "invoked audience" during this period was Richard Larson, editor of this journal, whose questions and criticisms we imagined and tried to anticipate. (Once this essay was accepted by *CCC*, Richard Larson became for us an addressed audience: he responded in writing with questions, criticisms, and suggestions, some of which we had, of course, failed to anticipate.) We also thought of the readers of *CCC* and those who attend the annual CCCC, most often picturing you as members of our own departments, a diverse group of individuals with widely varying degrees of interest in and knowledge of composition. Because of the generic constraints of academic writing, which limit the range of roles we may define for our readers, the audience represented by the readers of *CCC* seemed most vivid to us in two situations: (1) when we were concerned about the degree to which we needed to explain concepts or terms and (2) when we considered central organizational decisions, such as the most effective way to introduce a discussion. Another, and for us extremely potent, audience was the authors — Mitchell and Taylor, Long, Ong, Park, and others — with whom we have seen ourselves in silent dialogue. As we read and reread their analyses and developed our responses to them, we felt a responsibility to try to understand their formulations as fully as possible, to play fair with their ideas, to make our own efforts continue to meet their high standards.

Our experience provides just one example, and even it is far from complete. (Once we finished a rough draft one particular colleague became a potent but demanding addressed audience, listening to revision upon revision and challenging us with harder and harder questions. And after this essay is published, we may revise our understanding of audiences we thought we knew or recognize the existence of an entirely new audience. The latter would happen, for instance, if teachers of speech communication for some reason found our discussion useful.) But even this single case demonstrates that the term *audience* refers not just to the intended, actual, or eventual readers of a discourse, but to *all* those whose image, ideas, or actions influence a writer during the process of composition. One way to conceive of "audience," then, is as an overdetermined or unusually rich concept, one which may perhaps be best specified through the analysis of precise, concrete situations.

We hope that this partial example of our own experience will illustrate how the elements represented in Figure 2 will shift and merge, depending on the particular rhetorical situation, the writer's aim, and the genre chosen. Such an understanding is critical: because of the complex reality to which the term audience refers and because of its fluid, shifting role in the composing process, any discussion of audience which isolates it from the rest of the rhetorical situation or which radically overemphasizes or underemphasizes its function in relation to other rhetorical constraints is likely to oversimplify. Note the unilateral direction of Mitchell and Taylor's model (5), which is unable to represent the diverse and complex role(s) audience(s) can play in the actual writing process — in the creation of meaning. In contrast, consider the model used by Edward P. J. Corbett in his *Little Rhetoric and Handbook* [see Figure 3].[29] This representation, which allows for interaction among all the elements of rhetoric, may at first appear less elegant and predictive than Mitchell and Taylor's. But it is finally more useful since it accurately represents the diverse range of potential interrelationships in any written discourse.

We hope that our model also suggests the integrated, interdependent nature of reading and writing. Two assertions emerge from this relationship. One involves the writer as reader of his or her own work. As Donald Murray notes in "Teaching the Other Self: The Writer's First Reader," this role is critical, for "the reading writer — the map-maker and map-reader — reads the word, the line, the sentence, the paragraph, the page, the entire text. This constant back-and-forth reading monitors the multiple complex relationships between all the elements in writing."[30] To ignore or devalue such a central function is to risk distorting the writing process as

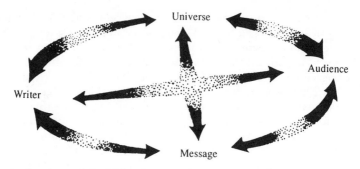

Figure 3. Corbett's model of "the rhetorical interrelationships" (5)

a whole. But unless the writer is composing a diary or journal entry, intended only for the writer's own eyes, the writing process is not complete unless another person, someone other than the writer, reads the text also. The second assertion thus emphasizes the creative, dynamic duality of the process of reading and writing, whereby writers create readers and readers create writers. In the meeting of these two lies meaning, lies communication.

A fully elaborated view of audience, then, must balance the creativity of the writer with the different, but equally important, creativity of the reader. It must account for a wide and shifting range of roles for both addressed and invoked audiences. And, finally, it must relate the matrix created by the intricate relationship of writer and audience to all elements in the rhetorical situation. Such an enriched conception of audience can help us better understand the complex act we call composing.

Notes

[1]Ruth Mitchell and Mary Taylor, "The Integrating Perspective: An Audience-Response Model for Writing," *CE* 41 (Nov. 1979): 267. Subsequent references to this article will be cited in the text.

[2]Russell C. Long, "Writer-Audience Relationships: Analysis or Invention," *CCC* 31 (May 1980): 223, 225. Subsequent references to this article will be cited in the text.

[3]For these terms we are indebted to Henry W. Johnstone, Jr., who refers to them in his analysis of Chaim Perelman's universal audience in *Validity and Rhetoric in Philosophical Argument: An Outlook in Transition* (University Park, PA: Dialogue of Man and World, 1978) 105.

[4]A number of terms might be used to characterize the two approaches to audience which dominate current theory and practice. Such pairs as identified/envisaged, "real"/fictional, or analyzed/created all point to the same general distinction as do our terms. We chose "addressed/invoked" because the terms most precisely represent our intended meaning. Our discussion will, we hope, clarify their significance; for the present, the following definitions must serve. The "addressed" audience refers to those actual or real-life people who read a discourse, while the "invoked" audience refers to the audience called up or imagined by the writer.

[5]Fred R. Pfister and Joanne F. Petrik, "A Heuristic Model for Creating a Writer's Audience," *CCC* 31 (May 1980): 213.

[6]Pfister and Petrik 214; our emphasis.

[7]See, for example, Lisa S. Ede, "On Audience and Composition," *CCC* 30 (Oct. 1979): 291–95.

[8]See, for example, David Tedlock, "The Case Approach to Composition," *CCC* 32 (Oct. 1981): 253–61.

[9]See, for example, Linda Flower's *Problem-Solving Strategies for Writers* (New York: Harcourt, 1981) and John P. Field and Robert H. Weiss's *Cases for Composition* (Boston: Little, 1979).

[10]Richard E. Young, "Paradigms and Problems: Needed Research in Rhetorical Invention," *Research on Composing: Points of Departure,* ed. Charles R. Cooper and Lee Odell (Urbana: NCTE, 1978) 32n3.

[11]Mitchell and Taylor do recognize that internal psychological needs ("unconscious challenges") may play a role in the writing process, but they cite such instances as an "extreme case (often that of the creative writer)" (251). For a discussion of the importance of self-evaluation in the composing process see Susan Miller, "How Writers Evaluate Their Own Writing," *CCC* 33 (May 1982): 176–83.

[12]Susan Wall, "In the Writer's Eye: Learning to Teach the Rereading/Revising Process," *English Education* 14 (Feb. 1982): 12.

[13]Wayne Booth, *Modern Dogma and the Rhetoric of Assent* (Chicago: U of Chicago P, 1974) xiv.

[14]Paul Kameen, "Rewording the Rhetoric of Composition," *Pre/Text* 1 (Spring–Fall 1980): 82.

[15]Mitchell and Taylor's arguments in favor of adjunct classes seem to indicate that they see writing instruction, wherever it occurs, as a skills course, one instructing students in the proper use of a tool.

[16]Anthony R. Petrosky, "From Story to Essay: Reading and Writing," *CCC* 33 (Feb. 1982): 20.

[17]Walter J. Ong, S.J., "The Writer's Audience Is Always a Fiction," *PMLA* 90 (Jan. 1975): 9–21. Subsequent references to this article will be cited in the text.

[18]See, for example, William Irmscher, "Sense of Audience: An Intuitive Concept," paper delivered at the CCCC in 1981; Douglas B. Park, "The Meanings of Audience: Pedagogical Implications," paper delivered at the CCCC in 1981; and Luke M. Reinsma, "Writing to an Audience: Scheme or Strategy?" paper delivered at the CCCC in 1982.

[19]Herbert W. Simons, *Persuasion: Understanding, Practice, and Analysis* (Reading: Addison, 1976).

[20]Ong 12. Ong recognizes that oral communication also involves role-playing, but he stresses that it "has within it a momentum that works for the removal of masks" (20). This may be true in certain instances, such as dialogue, but does not, we believe, obtain broadly.

[21]Walter S. Minot, "Response to Russell C. Long," *CCC* 32 (Oct. 1981): 337.

[22]We are aware that the student actually has two audiences, her neighbors and her teacher, and that this situation poses an extra constraint for the writer. Not all students can manage such a complex series of audience constraints, but it is important to note that writers in a variety of situations often write for more than a single audience.

[23]In their paper on "Student and Professional Syntax in Four Disciplines" (paper delivered at the CCCC in 1981), Ian Pringle and Aviva Freedman provide a good example of what can happen when a student creates an aberrant role for an academic reader. They cite an excerpt from a third-year history assignment, the tone of which "is essentially the tone of the opening of a television travelogue commentary" and which thus asks the reader, a history professor, to assume the role of the viewer of such a show. The result is as might be expected: "Although the content of the paper does not seem significantly more abysmal than other papers in the same set, this one was awarded a disproportionately low grade" (2).

[24]One danger which should be noted is a tendency to foster a questionable image of classical rhetoric. The agnostic speaker-audience relationship which Long cites as an essential characteristic of classical rhetoric is actually a central point of debate among those involved in historical and theoretical research in rhetoric. For further discussion, see Lisa Ede and Andrea Lunsford, "On Distinctions between Classical and Modern Rhetoric," *Classical Rhetoric and Modern Discourse: Essays in Honor of Edward P. J. Corbett,* ed. Robert Connors, Lisa Ede, and Andrea Lunsford (Carbondale: Southern Illinois UP, 1984).

[25]James Moffett, *Teaching the Universe of Discourse* (Boston: Houghton, 1968) 47. Subsequent references will be mentioned in the text.

[26]We have taken the title of this section from Scott Consigny's article of the same title, *Philosophy and Rhetoric* 7 (Summer 1974): 175–86. Consigny's effort to mediate between two opposing views of rhetoric provided a stimulating model for our own efforts.

[27]Although we believe that the range of audience roles cited in our model covers the general spectrum of options, we do not claim to have specified all possibilities. This is particularly the case since, in certain instances, these roles may merge and blend — shifting sub-

tly in character. We might also note that other terms for the same roles might be used. In a business setting, for instance, colleague might be better termed co-worker, critic, supervisor.

[28]Douglas B. Park, "The Meanings of 'Audience,' " *CE* 44 (Mar. 1982): 249.

[29]Edward P. J. Corbett, *The Little Rhetoric and Handbook,* 2nd ed. (Glenview: Scott, 1982) 5.

[30]Donald M. Murray, "Teaching the Other Self: The Writer's First Reader," *CCC* 33 (May 1982): 142.

Ede and Lunsford's Insights as a Resource for Your Teaching

1. Review the introductory handouts and assignment sheets that you gave your students. To what extent do your materials influence student writers to shape a draft for "audience addressed" or "audience invoked"? Prompt a class discussion about responses to an assignment; ask writers to explain how they decided who would be the audience. If you find all the writers focused on only one concept of audience, you might want to analyze your materials to determine whether you might be unconsciously limiting their understanding of audience.

2. If you have access to a video camera, arrange to have several of your classes taped. Watch them until you get past "ego shock" and can see patterns in the way that you speak to your audience of students. List the assumptions that you have about your students as evidenced by your speaking and nonverbal performance. Then go back to your early handouts and assignments and list the assumptions you have about your students as evidenced by your writing. Use the insights from this exercise to analyze how effectively you "model" attention to the needs of your audience, whether addressed or invoked.

Ede and Lunsford's Insights as a Resource for the Writing Classroom

1. When students keep a reading journal to generate topics for the writing assignment in Chapter 5, "Reading Critically," ask them to record their responses to "how the writer talked to me." Have them read a short essay in class and record their responses to "how the writer considered me as the reader." Use the entries to initiate a discussion of audience from their understanding as readers of ways that writers consider audience. Ask them to "imitate" in a twenty-minute writing session one of the writers they read and to focus on "writing to the reader" in the same way that the original writer chose to write. In this exercise, content is less important than rhetorical flexibility with audience.

2. Writing instructors often ask students to write at the top of the manuscript the "audience" whom they were conscious they wrote for. Ask your students to go one step further and analyze in a short self-assessment whether they were addressing or invoking an audience. In your comments on the draft, describe your reader's response as a member of the audience addressed, as a member of the audience invoked, and as the guide in the writing classroom. Ask peer editors who respond to the writings in response to Chapters 9 and 10 to also write comments from the roles of audience addressed, audience invoked, and fellow writer.

PETER ELBOW *Closing My Eyes as I Speak: An Argument for Ignoring Audience*

Peter Elbow argues that writers often need simply to ignore audience. Even though he credits several arguments for audience awareness and agrees that some audiences invite and enable the writer to generate thought and feeling, he cautions that some audiences inhibit and even block writing. In particular, audience awareness in the earliest stages of writing may confuse and inhibit the writer while audience awareness during revision may enlighten and liberate the writer. (Notice how the authors of The Bedford Guide for College Writers *prompt more awareness of the reader through the revision checklists and peer editing checklists than during the "getting started" discussion of each chapter.)*

Elbow asserts that when attention to audience complicates thinking so much that writers short out, we should suggest that the writers ignore the audience and pay attention to their own thinking. Once the writers work out through drafts and "internal conversation" what they think, they can turn their attention back to audience. Elbow insists that "ignoring audience can lead to worse drafts but better revisions."

Elbow disagrees with an interpretation of Piaget's model of cognitive development that leads some writing theorists to look at "writer-based prose," writing that ignores audience, as an indication that the writer is necessarily immature. He disagrees that writers who shape "reader-based prose" are ipso facto more cognitively mature. He insists that the ability to turn off audience awareness when it is distracting or confusing is a higher skill. Writers who can switch off audience awareness and sustain quiet, thoughtful reflection, who can in private reflection make meaning for themselves and shape a discourse from such thinking alone, are independent and mature thinkers. Elbow offers Vygotsky's cognitive model that "development in thinking is not from the individual to the socialized, but from the social to the individual" as support for his assertion that ignoring audience can lead to dialogue with self.

Elbow insists that "private writing" that turns off and away from audience is as important to humans as public writing that addresses and invokes the audience. Writing instructors need to assist their students to discover public writing as a way of "taking part in a community of discourse" and private writing as a means for writing better reflectively. Elbow shows a symbiosis of the two kinds of discourse; each sustains the other.

Elbow concludes with very sound and practical suggestions for how teachers can help students discover the values of both kinds of discourse. He suggests that we must counteract the reality that most schools offer little privacy for writing and little social dimension for writing by heightening both the public and private dimensions of writing. I recommend the discussion of freewriting and of keeping a journal in Chapter 15, "Strategies for Generating Ideas," and the discussion of the personal strategies of a variety of writers for getting started in Chapter 17, "Strategies for Drafting." They show students how critical personal discourse is for developing the private dimension of their mental and emotional lives. Chapter 20, "Strategies for Working with Other Writers: Collaborative Learning," and the many exercises for group learning throughout the text emphasize how critical public discourse is to our growth as thoughtful and creative persons.

> Very often people don't listen to you when you speak to them. It's only when you talk to yourself that they prick up their ears.
>
> – John Ashbery

When I am talking to a person or a group and struggling to find words or thoughts, I often find myself involuntarily closing my eyes as I speak. I realize now that this behavior is an instinctive attempt to blot out awareness of audience when I need all my concentration for just trying to figure out or express what I want to say. Because the audience is so imperiously present in a speaking situation, my instinct reacts with this active attempt to avoid audience awareness. This behavior — in a sense impolite or antisocial — is not so uncommon. Even when we write, alone in a room to an absent audience, there are occasions when we are struggling to figure something out and need to push aside awareness of those absent readers. As Donald Murray puts it, "My sense of audience is so strong that I have to suppress my conscious awareness of audience to hear what the text demands" (Berkenkotter and

Murray 171). In recognition of how pervasive the role of audience is in writing, I write to celebrate the benefits of ignoring audience.[1]

It will be clear that my argument for writing without audience awareness is not meant to undermine the many good reasons for writing *with* audience awareness some of the time. (For example, that we are liable to neglect audience because we write in solitude; that young people often need more practice in taking into account points of view different from their own; and that students often have an impoverished sense of writing as communication because they have only written in a school setting to teachers.) Indeed I would claim some part in these arguments for audience awareness — which now seem to be getting out of hand.

I start with a limited claim: even though ignoring audience will usually lead to weak writing at first — to what Linda Flower calls "writer-based prose," this weak writing can help us in the end to better writing than we would have written if we'd kept readers in mind from the start. Then I will make a more ambitious claim: writer-based prose is sometimes better than reader-based prose. Finally I will explore some of the theory underlying these issues of audience.

A Limited Claim

It's not that writers should never think about their audience. It's a question of when. An audience is a field of force. The closer we come — the more we think about these readers — the stronger the pull they exert on the contents of our minds. The practical question, then, is always whether a particular audience functions as a helpful field of force or one that confuses or inhibits us.

Some audiences, for example, are *inviting* or *enabling*. When we think about them as we write, we think of more and better things to say — and what we think somehow arrives more coherently structured than usual. It's like talking to the perfect listener: we feel smart and come up with ideas we didn't know we had. Such audiences are helpful to keep in mind right from the start.

Other audiences, however, are powerfully *inhibiting* — so much so, in certain cases, that awareness of them as we write blocks writing altogether. There are certain people who always make us feel dumb when we try to speak to them: we can't find words or thoughts. As soon as we get out of their presence, all the things we want to say pop back into our minds. Here is a student telling what happens when she tries to follow the traditional advice about audience:

> You know _____ [author of a text] tells us to pay attention to the audience that will be reading our papers, and I gave that a try. I ended up without putting a word on paper until I decided the hell with _____; I'm going to write to who I damn well want to; otherwise I can hardly write at all.

Admittedly, there are some occasions when we benefit from keeping a threatening audience in mind from the start. We've been putting off writing that letter to that person who intimidates us. When we finally sit down and write *to* them — walk right up to them, as it were, and look them in the eye — we may manage to stand up to the threat and grasp the nettle and thereby find just what we need to write.

Most commonly, however, the effect of audience awareness is somewhere between the two extremes: the awareness disturbs or disrupts our writing and thinking without completely blocking it. For example, when we have to write to someone we find intimidating (and of course students often perceive teachers as intimidating), we often start thinking wholly defensively. As we write down each thought or sentence, our mind fills with thoughts of how the intended reader will criticize or object to it. So we try to qualify or soften what we've just written — or write out some answer to a possible objection. Our writing becomes tangled. Sometimes we get so tied in knots that we cannot even figure out what we *think*. We may not realize how often audience awareness has this effect on our students when we don't see the writing process behind their papers: we just see texts that are either tangled or empty.

Another example. When we have to write to readers with whom we have an awkward relationship, we often start beating around the bush and feeling shy or scared, or start to write in a stilted, overly careful style or voice. (Think about the cute, too-clever style of many memos we get in our departmental mailboxes — the awkward self-consciousness academics experience when writing to other academics.) When students are asked to write to readers they have not met or cannot imagine, such as "the general reader" or "the educated public," they often find nothing to say except clichés they know *they* don't even quite believe.

When we realize that an audience is somehow confusing or inhibiting us, the solution is fairly obvious. We can ignore that audience altogether during the *early* stages of writing and direct our words only to ourselves or to no one in particular — or even to the "wrong" audience, that is, to an *inviting* audience of trusted friends or allies. This strategy often dissipates the confusion; the clenched, defensive discourse starts to run clear. Putting audience out of mind is of course a traditional practice: serious writers have long used private journals for early explorations of feeling, thinking, or language. But many writing teachers seem to think that students can get along without the private writing serious writers find so crucial — or even that students will *benefit* from keeping their audience in mind for the whole time. Things often don't work out that way.

After we have figured out our thinking in copious exploratory or draft writing — perhaps finding the right voice or stance as well — *then* we can follow the traditional rhetorical advice: think about readers and revise carefully to adjust our words and thoughts to our intended audience. For a particular audience it may even turn out that we need to *disguise* our point of view. But it's hard to disguise something while engaged in trying to figure it out. As writers, then, we need to learn when to think about audience and when to put readers out of mind.

Many people are too quick to see Flower's "writer-based prose" as an analysis of what's wrong with this type of writing and miss the substantial degree to which she was celebrating a natural, and indeed developmentally enabling, response to cognitive overload. What she doesn't say, however, despite her emphasis on planning and conscious control in the writing process, is that we can *teach* students to notice when audience awareness is getting in their way — and when this happens, consciously to put aside the needs of readers for a while. She seems to assume that when an overload occurs, the writer-based gear will, as it were, automatically kick into action to relieve it. In truth, of course, writers often persist in using a malfunctioning *reader*-based gear despite the overload — thereby mangling their language or thinking. Though Flower likes to rap the knuckles of people who suggest a "correct" or "natural" order for steps in the writing process, she implies such an order here: when attention to audience causes an overload, start out by ignoring them while you attend to your thinking; after you work out your thinking, turn your attention to audience.

Thus if we ignore audience while writing on a topic about which we are not expert or about which our thinking is still evolving, we are likely to produce exploratory writing that is unclear to anyone else — perhaps even inconsistent or a complete mess. Yet by doing this exploratory "swamp work" in conditions of safety, we can often coax our thinking through a process of new discovery and development. In this way we can end up with something better than we could have produced if we'd tried to write to our audience all along. In short, ignoring audience can lead to worse drafts but better revisions. (Because we are professionals and adults, we often write in the role of expert: we may know what we think without new exploratory writing; we may even be able to speak confidently to critical readers. But students seldom experience this confident professional stance in their writing. And think how much richer *our* writing would be if we defined ourselves as *in*expert and allowed ourselves private writing for new explorations of those views we are allegedly sure of.)

Notice then that two pieties of composition theory are often in conflict:

1. Think about audience as you write (this stemming from the classical rhetorical tradition).

2. Use writing for *making new meaning*, not just transmitting old meanings already worked out (this stemming from the newer epistemic tradition I associate with Ann Berthoff's classic explorations).

It's often difficult to work out new meaning while thinking about readers.

A More Ambitious Claim

I go further now and argue that ignoring audience can lead to better writing — immediately. In effect, writer-based prose can be *better* than reader-based prose. This might seem a more controversial claim, but is there a teacher who has not had the experience of struggling and struggling to no avail to help a student untangle his writing, only to discover that the student's casual journal writing or freewriting is untangled and strong? Sometimes freewriting is stronger than the essays we get only because it is expressive, narrative, or descriptive writing and the student was not constrained by a topic. But teachers who collect drafts with completed assignments often see passages of freewriting that are strikingly stronger *even* when they are expository and constrained by the assigned topic. In some of these passages we can sense that the strength derives from the student's unawareness of readers.

It's not just unskilled, tangled writers, though, who sometimes write better by forgetting about readers. Many competent and even professional writers produce mediocre pieces *because* they are thinking too much about how their readers will receive their words. They are acting too much like a salesman trained to look the customer in the eye and to think at all times about the characteristics of the "target audience." There is something too staged or planned or self-aware about such writing. We see this quality in much second-rate newspaper or magazine or business writing: "good-student writing" in the awful sense of the term. Writing produced this way reminds us of the ineffective actor whose consciousness of self distracts us: he makes us too aware of his own awareness of us. When we read such prose, we wish the writer would stop thinking about us — would stop trying to "adjust" or "fit" what he is saying to our frame of reference. "Damn it, put all your attention on what you are saying," we want to say, "and forget about us and how we are reacting."

When we examine really good student or professional writing, we can often see that its goodness comes from the writer's having gotten sufficiently wrapped up in her meaning and her language as to forget all about audience needs: the writer manages to "break through." The Earl of Shaftesbury talked about writers needing to escape their audience in order to find their own ideas (Cooper 1:109; see also Griffin). It is characteristic of much truly good writing to be, as it were, on fire with its meaning. Consciousness of readers is burned away; involvement in subject determines all. Such writing is analogous to the performance of the actor who has managed to stop attracting attention to her awareness of the audience watching her.

The arresting power in some writing by small children comes from their obliviousness to audience. As readers, we are somehow sucked into a more-than-usual connection with the meaning itself because of the child's gift for more-than-usual concentration on what she is saying. In short, we can feel some pieces of children's writing as being very writer-based. Yet it's precisely that quality which makes it powerful for us as readers. After all, why should we settle for a writer's entering our point of view, if we can have the more powerful experience of being sucked out of our point of view and into her world? This is just the experience that children are peculiarly capable of giving because they are so expert at total absorption in their world as they are writing. It's not just a matter of whether the writer "decenters," but of whether the writer has a sufficiently strong focus of attention to make the *reader* decenter. This quality of concentration is what D. H. Lawrence so admires in Melville:

> [Melville] was a real American in that he always felt his audience in front of him. But when he ceases to be American, when he forgets all audience, and gives us his sheer apprehension of the world, then he is wonderful, his book [*Moby Dick*] commands a stillness in the soul, an awe. (158)

What most readers value in really excellent writing is not prose that is right for readers but prose that is right for thinking, right for language, or right for the subject being written about. If, in addition, it is clear and well suited to readers, we appreciate that. Indeed we feel insulted if the writer did not somehow try to make the writing *available* to us before delivering it. But if it succeeds at being really true to language and thinking and "things," we are willing to put up with much difficulty as readers:

> Good writing is not always or necessarily an adaptation to communal norms (in the Fish/Bruffee sense) but may be an attempt to construct (and instruct) a reader capable of reading the text in question. The literary history of the "difficult" work — from Mallarmé to Pound, Zukofsky, Olson, etc. — seems to say that much of what we value in writing we've had to learn to value by learning how to read it. (Trimbur)

The effect of audience awareness on voice is particularly striking — if paradoxical. Even though we often develop our voice by finally "speaking up" to an audience or "speaking out" to others, and even though much dead student writing comes from students not really treating their writing as a communication with real readers, nevertheless, the opposite effect is also common: we often do not really develop a strong, authentic voice in our writing till we find important occasions for *ignoring* audience — saying, in effect, "To hell with whether they like it or not. I've got to say this the way I want to say it." Admittedly, the voice that emerges when we ignore audience is sometimes odd or idiosyncratic in some way, but usually it is stronger. Indeed, teachers sometimes complain that student writing is "writer-based" when the problem is simply the idiosyncrasy — and sometimes in fact the *power* — of the voice. They would value this odd but resonant voice if they found it in a published writer (see Elbow, "Real Voice," *Writing with Power*). Usually we cannot *trust* a voice unless it is unaware of us and our needs and speaks out in its own terms (see the Ashbery epigraph). To celebrate writer-based prose is to risk the charge of *romanticism:* just warbling one's woodnotes wild. But my position also contains the austere *classic* view that we must nevertheless *revise* with conscious awareness of audience in order to figure out which pieces of writer-based prose are good as they are — and how to discard or revise the rest.

To point out that writer-based prose can be *better* for readers than reader-based prose is to reveal problems in these two terms. Does *writer-based* mean:

1. That the text doesn't work for readers because it is too much oriented to the writer's point of view?
2. Or that the writer was not thinking about readers as she wrote, although the text *may* work for readers?

Does *reader-based* mean:

3. That the text works for readers — meets their needs?
4. Or that the writer was attending to readers as she wrote although her text *may* not work for readers?

In order to do justice to the reality and complexity of what actually happens in both writers and readers, I was going to suggest four terms for the four conditions listed above, but I gradually realized that things are even too complex for that. We really need to ask about what's going on in three dimensions — in the *writer*, in the *reader*, and in the *text* — and realize that the answers can occur in virtually any combination:

Was the writer thinking about readers or oblivious to them?

Is the *text* oriented toward the writer's frame of reference or point of view, or oriented toward that of readers? (A writer may be thinking about readers and still write a text that is largely oriented toward her own frame of reference.)

Are the readers' needs being met? (The text may meet the needs of readers whether the writer was thinking about them or not, and whether the text is oriented toward them or not.)

Two Models of Cognitive Development

Some of the current emphasis on audience awareness probably derives from a model of cognitive development that needs to be questioned. According to this model, if you keep your readers in mind as you write, you are operating at a higher level of psychological development than if you ignore readers. Directing words to readers is "more mature" than directing them to no one in particular or to yourself. Flower relates writer-based prose to the inability to "decenter" which is characteristic of Piaget's early stages of development, and she relates reader-based prose to later more mature stages of development.

On the one hand, of course this view must be right. Children do decenter as they develop. As they mature they get better at suiting their discourse to the needs of listeners, particularly to listeners very different from themselves. Especially, they get better at doing so *consciously* — thinking *awarely* about how things appear to people with different viewpoints. Thus much unskilled writing is unclear or awkward *because* the writer was doing what it is so easy to do — unthinkingly taking her own frame of reference for granted and not attending to the needs of readers who might have a different frame of reference. And of course this failure is more common in younger, immature, "egocentric" students (and also more common in writing than in speaking since we have no audience present when we write).

But on the other hand, we need the contrary model that affirms what is also obvious once we reflect on it, namely that the ability to *turn off* audience awareness — especially when it confuses thinking or blocks discourse — is also a "higher" skill. I am talking about an ability to use language in "the desert island mode," an ability that tends to require learning, growth, and psychological development. Children, and even adults who have not learned the art of quiet, thoughtful, inner reflection, are often unable to get much cognitive action going in their heads unless there are other people present to have action *with*. They are dependent on live audience and the social dimension to get their discourse rolling or to get their thinking off the ground.

For in contrast to a roughly Piagetian model of cognitive development that says we start out as private, egocentric little monads and grow up to be public and social, it is important to invoke the opposite model that derives variously from Vygotsky, Bakhtin, and Meade. According to this model, we *start out* social and plugged into others and only gradually, through learning and development, come to "unplug" to any significant degree so as to function in a more private, individual and differentiated fashion: "Development in thinking is not from the individual to the socialized, but from the social to the individual" (Vygotsky 20). The important general principle in this model is that we tend to *develop* our important cognitive capacities by means of social interaction with others, and having done so we gradually learn to perform them alone. We fold the "simple" back-and-forth of dialogue into the "complexity" (literally, "foldedness") of individual, private reflection.

Where the Piagetian (individual psychology) model calls our attention to the obvious need to learn to enter into viewpoints other than our own, the Vygotskian (social psychology) model calls our attention to the equally important need to learn to produce good thinking and discourse *while alone*. A rich and enfolded mental life is something that people achieve only gradually through growth, learning, and practice. We tend to associate this achievement with the fruits of higher education.

Thus we see plenty of students who lack this skill, who have nothing to say when asked to freewrite or to write in a journal. They can dutifully "reply" to a question or a topic, but they cannot seem to *initiate* or *sustain* a train of thought on their own. Because so many adolescent students have this difficulty, many teachers chime in: "Adolescents have nothing to write about. They are too young. They haven't had significant experience." In truth, adolescents don't lack experience or material, no matter how "sheltered" their lives. What they lack is practice and help. Desert island discourse is a learned cognitive process. It's a mistake to think of private writing (journal writing and freewriting) as merely "easy" — merely a relief from trying to write right. It's also hard. Some exercises and strategies that help are Ira Progoff's "Intensive Journal" process, Sondra Perl's "Composing Guidelines," or Elbow's "Loop Writing" and "Open Ended Writing" processes (*Writing with Power* 50–77).

The Piagetian and Vygotskian developmental models (language-begins-as-private vs. language-begins-as-social) give us two different lenses through which to look at a common weakness in student writing, a certain kind of "thin" writing where the thought is insufficiently developed or where the language doesn't really explain what the writing implies or gestures toward. Using the Piagetian model, as Flower does, one can specify the problem as a weakness in audience orientation. Perhaps the writer has immaturely taken too much for granted and unthinkingly assumed that her limited explanations carry as much meaning for readers as they do for herself. The cure or treatment is for the writer to think more about readers.

Through the Vygotskian lens, however, the problem and the "immaturity" look altogether different. Yes, the writing isn't particularly clear or satisfying for readers, but this alternative diagnosis suggests a failure of the private desert island dimension: the writer's explanation is too thin because she didn't work out her train of thought fully enough *for herself.* The suggested cure or treatment is *not* to think more about readers but to think more for herself, to practice exploratory writing in order to learn to engage in that reflective discourse so central to mastery of the writing process. How can she engage readers more till she has engaged herself more?

The current emphasis on audience awareness may be particularly strong now for being fueled by *both* psychological models. From one side, the Piagetians say, in effect, "The egocentric little critters, we've got to *socialize* 'em! Ergo, make them think about audience when they write!" From the other side, the Vygotskians say, in effect, "No wonder they're having trouble writing. They've been bamboozled by the Piagetian heresy. They think they're solitary individuals with private selves when really they're just congeries of voices that derive from their discourse community. Ergo, let's intensify the social context — use peer groups and publication: make them think about audience when they write! (And while we're at it, let's hook them up with a better class of discourse community.)" To advocate ignoring audience is to risk getting caught in the crossfire from two opposed camps.

Two Models of Discourse: Discourse as Communication and Discourse as Poesis or Play

We cannot talk about writing without at least implying a psychological or developmental model. But we'd better make sure it's a complex, paradoxical, or spiral model. Better yet, we should be deft enough to use two contrary models or lenses. (Bruner pictures the developmental process as a complex movement in an upward reiterative spiral — not a simple movement in one direction.)

According to one model, it is characteristic of the youngest children to direct their discourse to an audience. They learn discourse *because* they have an audience; without an audience they remain mute, like "the wild child." Language is social from the start. But we need the other model to show us what is also true, namely that it is characteristic of the youngest children to use language in a *nonsocial* way. They use language not only because people talk to them but also because they have such a strong propensity to play and to build — often in a *nonsocial* or non-audience-oriented fashion. Thus although one paradigm for discourse is social communication, another is private exploration or solitary play. Babies and toddlers tend to babble in an exploratory and reflective way — to themselves and not to an audience — often even with no one else near. This archetypally private use of discourse is strikingly illustrated when we see a pair of toddlers in "parallel play" alongside each other — each busily talking but not at all trying to communicate with the other.

Therefore, when we choose paradigms for discourse, we should think not only about children using language to communicate, but also about children building sandcastles or drawing pictures. Though children characteristically show their castles or pictures to others, they just as characteristically trample or crumple them before anyone else can see them. Of course sculptures and pictures are different from words. Yet discourse implies more media than words; and even if you restrict discourse to words, one of our most mature uses of language is for building verbal pictures and structures for their own sake — not just for communicating with others.

Consider this same kind of behavior at the other end of the life cycle: Brahms staggering from his deathbed to his study to rip up a dozen or more completed but unpublished and unheard string quartets that dissatisfied him. How was he relating to audience here — worrying too much about audience or not giving a damn? It's not easy to say. Consider Glenn Gould deciding to renounce performances before an audience. He used his private studio to produce recorded performances for an audience, but to produce ones that satisfied *himself* he clearly needed to suppress audience awareness. Consider the more extreme example of Kerouac typing page after page — burning each as soon as he completed it. The language behavior of humans is slippery. Surely we are well advised to avoid positions that say it is "always X" or "essentially Y."

James Britton makes a powerful argument that the "making" or poesis function of language grows out of the expressive function. Expressive language is often for the sake of communication with an audience, but just as often it is only for the sake of the speaker — working something out for herself (66–67, 74ff). Note also that "writing to learn," which writing-across-the-curriculum programs are discovering to be so important, tends to be writing for the self or even for no one at all rather than for an outside reader. You throw away the writing, often unread, and keep the mental changes it has engendered.

I hope this emphasis on the complexity of the developmental process — the limits of our models and of our understanding of it — will serve as a rebuke to the tendency to label students as being at a lower stage of cognitive development just because they don't yet write well. (Occasionally they *do* write well — in a way — but not in the way that the labeler finds appropriate.) Obviously the psychologistic labeling impulse started out charitably. Shaughnessy was fighting those who called basic writers *stupid* by saying they weren't dumb, just at an earlier developmental stage. Flower was arguing that writer-based prose is a natural response to a cognitive overload and indeed developmentally enabling. But this kind of talk can be dangerous since it labels students as literally "retarded" and makes teachers and administrators start to think of them as such. Instead of calling poor writers *either* dumb or slow (two forms of blaming the victim), why not simply call them poor writers? If years of schooling haven't yet made them good writers, perhaps they haven't gotten the kind of teaching and support they need. Poor students are often deprived of the very thing they need most to write well (which is given to good students): lots of extended and adventuresome writing for self and for audience. Poor students are often asked to write only answers to fill-in exercises.

As children get older, the developmental story remains complex or spiral. Though the first model makes us notice that babies start out with a natural gift for using language in a social and communicative fashion, the second model makes us notice that children and adolescents must continually learn to relate their discourse better to an audience — must struggle to decenter better. And though the second model makes us notice that babies also start out with a natural gift for using language in a *private*, exploratory and playful way, the first model makes us notice that children and adolescents must continually learn to master this solitary, desert island, poesis mode better. Thus we mustn't think of language only as communication — nor allow communication to claim dominance either as the earliest or as the most "mature" form of discourse. It's true that language is inherently communicative (and without communication we don't develop language), yet language is just as inherently the stringing together of exploratory discourse for the self — or for the creation of objects (play, poesis, making) for their own sake.

In considering this important poesis function of language, we need not discount (as Berkenkotter does) the striking testimony of so many witnesses who think and care most about language: professional poets, writers, and philosophers. Many of them maintain that their most serious work is *making*, not *communicating*, and that their commitment is to language, reality, logic, experience, not to readers. Only in their willingness to cut loose from the demands or needs of readers, they insist, can they do their best work. Here is William Stafford on this matter:

I don't want to overstate this . . . but . . . my impulse is to say I don't think of an audience at all. When I'm writing, the satisfactions in the process of writing are my satisfactions in dealing with the language, in being surprised by phrasings that occur to me, in finding that this miraculous kind of convergent focus begins to happen. That's my satisfaction, and to think about an audience would be a distraction. I try to keep from thinking about an audience. (Cicotello 176)

And Chomsky:

I can be using language in the strictest sense with no intention of communicating. . . . As a graduate student, I spent two years writing a lengthy manuscript, assuming throughout that it would never be published or read by anyone. I meant everything I wrote, intending nothing as to what anyone would [understand], in fact taking it for granted that there would be no audience. . . . Communication is only one function of language, and by no means an essential one. (Qtd. in Feldman 5–6)

It's interesting to see how poets come together with philosophers on this point — and even with mathematicians. All are emphasizing the "poetic" function of language in its literal sense — "poesis" as "making." They describe their writing process as more like "getting something right" or even "solving a problem" for its own sake than as communicating with readers or addressing an audience. The task is not to satisfy readers but to satisfy the rules of the system: "[T]he writer is not thinking of a reader at all; he makes it 'clear' as a contract with *language*" (Goodman 164).

Shall we conclude, then, that solving an equation or working out a piece of symbolic logic is at the opposite end of the spectrum from communicating with readers or addressing an audience? No. To draw that conclusion would be a fall again into a one-sided position. Sometimes people write mathematics *for* an audience, sometimes not. The central point in this essay is that we cannot answer audience questions in an *a priori* fashion based on the "nature" of discourse or of language or of cognition — only in terms of the different *uses* or *purposes* to which humans put discourse, language, or cognition on different occasions. If most people have a restricted repertoire of uses for writing — if most people use writing only to send messages to readers, that's no argument for constricting the *definition* of writing. It's an argument for helping people expand their repertoire of uses.

The value of learning to ignore audience while writing, then, is the value of learning to cultivate the private dimension: the value of writing in order to make meaning to oneself, not just to others. This involves learning to free oneself (to some extent, anyway) from the enormous power exerted by society and others, to unhook oneself from external prompts and social stimuli. We've grown accustomed to theorists and writing teachers puritanically stressing the *problem* of writing: the tendency to neglect the needs of readers because we usually write in solitude. But let's also celebrate this same feature of writing as one of its glories: writing *invites* disengagement too, the inward turn of mind, and the dialogue with self. Though writing is deeply social and though we usually help things by enhancing its social dimension, writing is also the mode of discourse best suited to helping us develop the reflective and private dimension of our mental lives.

"But Wait a Minute, ALL Discourse Is Social"

Some readers who see *all* discourse as social will object to my opposition between public and private writing (the "trap of oppositional thinking") and insist that *there is no such thing as private discourse*. What looks like private, solitary mental work, they would say, is really social. Even on the desert island I am in a crowd.

> By ignoring audience in the conventional sense, we return to it in another sense. What I get from Vygotsky and Bakhtin is the notion that audience is not really out there at all but is in fact "always already" (to use that poststructuralist mannerism . . .) inside, interiorized in the conflicting languages of others — parents, former teachers, peers, prospective readers, whomever — that writers have to negotiate to write, and that we do negotiate when we write whether we're aware of it or not. The audience we've got to satisfy in order to feel good about our writing is as much in the past as in the present or future. But we experience it (it's so internalized) as *ourselves.* (Trimbur)

(Ken Bruffee likes to quote from Frost: " 'Men work together, . . . / Whether they work together or apart' " ["The Tuft of Flowers"]). Or — putting it slightly differently — when I engage in what seems like private non-audience-directed writing, I am really engaged in communication with the "audience of self." For the self is multiple, not single, and discourse to self is communication from one entity to another. As Feldman argues, "The self functions as audience in much the same way that others do" (290).

Suppose I accept this theory that all discourse is really social — including what I've been calling "private writing" or writing I don't intend to show to any reader. Suppose I agree that all language is essentially communication directed toward an audience — whether some past internalized voice or (what may be the same thing) some aspect of the self. What would this theory say to my interest in "private writing"?

The theory would seem to destroy my main argument. It would tell me that there's no such thing as "private writing"; it's impossible *not* to address audience; there are no vacations from audience. But the theory might try to console me by saying not to worry, because we don't *need* vacations from audience. Addressing audience is as easy, natural, and unaware as breathing — and we've been at it since the cradle. Even young, unskilled writers are already expert at addressing audiences.

But if we look closely we can see that in fact this theory doesn't touch my central practical argument. For even if all discourse is naturally addressed to *some* audience, it's not naturally addressed to the *right* audience — the living readers we are actually trying to reach. Indeed the pervasiveness of past audiences in our heads is one more reason for the difficulty of reaching present audiences with our texts. Thus even if I concede the theoretical point, there still remains an enormous practical and phenomenological difference between writing "public" words for others to read and writing "private" words for no one to read.

Even if "private writing" is "deep down" social, the fact remains that, as we engage in it, we don't have to worry about whether it works on readers or even makes sense. We can refrain from doing all the things that audience-awareness advocates advise us to do ("keeping our audience in mind as we write" and trying to "decenter"). Therefore this social-discourse theory doesn't undermine the benefits of "private writing" and thus provides no support at all for the traditional rhetorical advice that we should "always try to think about (intended) audience as we write."

In fact this social-discourse theory reinforces two subsidiary arguments I have been making. First, even if there is no getting away from *some* audience, we can get relief from an inhibiting audience by writing to a more inviting one. Second, audience problems don't come only from *actual* audiences but also from phantom "audiences in the head" (Elbow, *Writing with Power* 186ff). Once we learn how to be more aware of the effects of both external and internal readers and how to direct our words elsewhere, we can get out of the shadow even of a troublesome phantom reader.

And even if all our discourse is *directed to* or *shaped by* past audiences or voices, it doesn't follow that our discourse is *well directed to* or *successfully shaped for* those audiences or voices. Small children *direct* much talk to others, but that doesn't mean they always *suit* their talk to others. They often fail. When adults discover that a piece of their writing has been "heavily shaped" by some audience, this is bad news as much as good: often the writing is crippled by defensive moves that try to fend off criticism from this reader.

As teachers, particularly, we need to distinguish and emphasize "private writing" in order to teach it, to teach that crucial cognitive capacity to engage in extended and productive thinking that doesn't depend on audience prompts or social stimuli. It's sad to see so many students who can reply to live voices but cannot engage in productive dialogue with voices in their heads. Such students often lose interest in an issue that had intrigued them — just because they don't find other people who are interested in talking about it and haven't learned to talk reflectively to *themselves* about it.

For these reasons, then, I believe my main argument holds force even if I accept the theory that all discourse is social. But, perhaps more tentatively, I resist this theory. I don't know all the data from developmental linguistics, but I cannot help suspecting that babies engage in *some* private poesis — or "play-language" — some private babbling in addition to social babbling. Of course Vygotsky must be right when he points to so much social language in children, but can we really trust him when he denies *all* private or nonsocial language (which Piaget and Chomsky see)? I am always suspicious when someone argues for the total nonexistence of a certain kind of behavior or event. Such an argument is almost invariably an act of definitional aggrandizement, not empirical searching. To say that *all* language is social is to flop over into the opposite one-sidedness that we need Vygotsky's model to save us from.

And even if all language is *originally* social, Vygotsky himself emphasizes how "inner speech" becomes more individuated and private as the child matures. "Egocentric speech is relatively accessible in three-year-olds but quite inscrutable in seven-year-olds: the older the child, the more thoroughly has his thought become inner speech" (Emerson 254; see also Vygotsky 134). "The inner speech of the adult represents his 'thinking for himself' rather than social adaptation. . . . Out of context, it would be incomprehensible to others because it omits to mention what is obvious to the 'speaker' " (Vygotsky 18).

I also resist the theory that all private writing is really communication with the *"audience of self."* ("When we represent the objects of our thought in language, we intend to make use of these representations at a later time. . . . [T]he speaker-self must have audience directed intentions toward a listener-self" [Feldman 289].) Of course private language often is a communication with the audience of self:

- When we make a shopping list. (It's obvious when we can't decipher that third item that we're confronting *failed* communication with the self.)

- When we make a rough draft for ourselves but not for others' eyes. Here we are seeking to clarify our thinking with the leverage that comes from standing outside and reading our own utterance as audience — experiencing our discourse as receiver instead of as sender.

- When we experience ourselves as slightly split. Sometimes we experience ourselves as witness to ourselves and hear our own words from the outside — sometimes with great detachment, as on some occasions of pressure or stress.

But there are other times when private language is not communication with audience of self:

- Freewriting to no one: for the *sake* of self but not *to* the self. The goal is not to communicate but to follow a train of thinking or feeling to see where it leads. In doing this kind of freewriting (and many people have not learned it), you don't particularly plan to come back and read what you've written. You just write along and the written product falls away to be ignored, while only the "real product" — any new perceptions, thoughts, or feelings produced in the mind by the freewriting — is saved and looked at again. (It's not that you don't experience your words *at all* but you experience them only as speaker, sender, or emitter — not as receiver or audience. To say that's the same as being audience is denying the very distinction between "speaker" and "audience.")

As this kind of freewriting actually works, it often *leads* to writing we look at. That is, we freewrite along to no one, following discourse in hopes of getting somewhere, and then at a certain point we often sense that we have *gotten* somewhere: we can tell (but not because we stop and read) that what we are now writing seems new or intriguing or important. At this point we may stop writing; or we may keep on writing, but in a new audience-relationship, realizing that we *will* come back to this passage and read it as audience. Or we may take a new sheet (symbolizing the new audience-relationship) and try to write out for ourselves what's interesting.

- Writing as exorcism is a more extreme example of private writing *not* for the audience of self. Some people have learned to write in order to get rid of thoughts or feelings. By freewriting what's obsessively going round and round in our head we can finally let it go and move on.

I am suggesting that some people (and especially poets and freewriters) engage in a kind of discourse that Feldman, defending what she calls a "communication-intention" view, has never learned and thus has a hard time imagining and understanding. Instead of always using language in an audience-directed fashion for the sake of communication, these writers unleash language for its own sake and let it function a bit on its own, without much *intention* and without much need for *communication*, to see where it leads — and thereby end up with some intentions and potential communications they didn't have before.

It's hard to turn off the audience-of-self in writing — and thus hard to imagine writing to no one (just as it's hard to turn off the audience of *outside* readers when writing an audience-directed piece). Consider "invisible writing" as an intriguing technique that helps you become less of an audience-of-self for your writing. Invisible writing prevents you from seeing what you have written: you write on a computer with the screen turned down, or you write with a spent ballpoint pen on paper with carbon paper and another sheet underneath. Invisible writing tends to get people not only to write faster than they normally do, but often better (see Blau). I mean to be tentative about this slippery issue of whether we can really stop being audience to our own discourse, but I cannot help drawing the following conclusion: just as in freewriting, suppressing the *other* as audience tends to enhance quantity and sometimes even quality of writing; so in invisible writing, suppressing the *self* as audience tends to enhance quantity and sometimes even quality.

Contraries in Teaching

So what does all this mean for teaching? It means that we are stuck with two contrary tasks. On the one hand, we need to help our students enhance the social dimension of writing: to learn to be *more* aware of audience, to decenter better and learn to fit their discourse better to the needs of readers. Yet it is every bit as important to help them learn the private dimension of writing: to learn to be *less* aware of audience, to put audience needs aside, to use discourse in the desert island mode. And if we are trying to advance contraries, we must be prepared for paradoxes.

For instance if we emphasize the social dimension in our teaching (for example, by getting students to write to each other, to read and comment on each other's writing in pairs and groups, and by staging public discussions and even debates on the topics they are to write about), we will obviously help the social, public, communicative dimension of writing — help students experience writing not just as jumping through hoops for a grade but rather as taking part in the life of a community of discourse. But "social discourse" can also help private writing by getting students sufficiently involved or invested in an issue so that they finally want to carry on producing discourse alone and in private — and for themselves.

Correlatively, if we emphasize the private dimension in our teaching (for example, by using lots of private exploratory writing, freewriting, and journal writing and by helping students realize that of course they may need practice with this "easy" mode of discourse before they can use it fruitfully), we will obviously help students learn to write better reflectively for themselves without the need for others to interact with. Yet this private discourse can also help public, social writing — help students finally feel full enough of their *own* thoughts to have some genuine desire to *tell* them to others. Students often feel they "don't have anything to say" until they finally succeed in engaging themselves in private desert island writing for themselves alone.

Another paradox: whether we want to teach greater audience awareness or the ability to ignore audience, we must help students learn not only to "try harder" but also to "just relax." That is, sometimes students fail to produce reader-based prose because they don't *try* hard enough to think about audience needs. But sometimes the problem is cured if they just relax and write *to* people — as though in a letter or in talking to a trusted adult. By unclenching, they effortlessly call on social discourse skills of immense sophistication. Sometimes, indeed, the problem is cured if the student simply writes in a more social *setting* — in a classroom where it is habitual to share lots of writing. Similarly, sometimes students can't produce sustained private discourse because they don't try hard enough to keep the pen moving and forget about readers. They must persist and doggedly push aside those feelings of, "My head is empty, I have run out of anything to say." But sometimes what they need to learn through all that persistence is how to relax and let go — to unclench.

As teachers, we need to think about what it means to *be an audience* rather than just be a teacher, critic, assessor, or editor. If our only response is to tell students what's strong, what's weak, and how to improve it (diagnosis, assessment, and advice), we actually *undermine* their sense of writing as a social act. We reinforce their sense that writing means doing school exercises, producing for authorities what they already know — *not* actually trying to say things to readers. To help students experience us as *audience* rather than as assessment machines, it helps to respond by "replying" (as in a letter) rather than always "giving feedback."

Paradoxically enough, one of the best ways teachers can help students learn to turn off audience awareness and write in the desert island mode — to turn off the babble of outside voices in the head and listen better to quiet inner voices — is to be a special kind of private audience to them, to be a reader who nurtures by trusting and believing in the writer. Britton has drawn attention to the importance of teacher as "trusted adult" for school children (67–68). No one can be good at private, reflective writing without some *confidence and trust in self.* A nurturing reader can give a writer a kind of permission to forget about other readers or to be one's own reader. I have benefited from this special kind of audience and have seen it prove useful to others. When I had a teacher who believed in me, who was interested in me and interested in what I had to say, I wrote well. When I had a teacher who thought I was naive, dumb, silly, and in need of being "straightened out," I wrote badly and sometimes couldn't write at all. Here is an interestingly paradoxical instance of the social-to-private principle from Vygotsky and Meade: we learn to listen better and more trustingly to *ourselves* through interaction with trusting *others.*

Look for a moment at lyric poets as paradigm writers (instead of seeing them as aberrant), and see how they heighten *both* the public and private dimensions of writing. Bakhtin says that lyric poetry implies "the absolute certainty of the listener's sympathy" (113). I think it's more helpful to say that lyric poets learn to create more than usual privacy in which to write *for themselves* — and then they turn around and let *others overhear.* Notice how poets tend to argue for the importance of no-audience writing, yet they are especially gifted at being public about what they produce in private. Poets are revealers — sometimes even grandstanders or showoffs. Poets illustrate the need for opposite or paradoxical or double audience skills: on the one hand, the ability to be private and solitary and tune out others — to write only for oneself and not give a damn about readers, yet on the other hand, the ability to be more than usually interested in audience and even to be a ham.

If writers really need these two audience skills, notice how bad most conventional schooling is on both counts. Schools offer virtually no privacy for writing: everything students write is collected and read by a teacher, a situation so ingrained students will tend to complain if you don't collect and read every word they write. Yet on the other hand, schools characteristically offer little or no social dimension for writing. It is *only* the teacher who reads, and students seldom feel that in giving their writing to a teacher they are actually communicating something they really want to say to a real person. Notice how often they are happy to turn in to teachers something perfunctory and fake that they would be embarrassed to show to classmates. Often they feel shocked and insulted if we want to distribute to classmates the assigned writing they hand in to us. (I think of Richard Wright's realization that the naked white prostitutes didn't bother to cover themselves when he brought them coffee as a black bellboy because they didn't really think of him as a man or even a person.) Thus the conventional school setting for writing tends to be the least private and the least public — when what students need, like all of us, is practice in writing that is the most private and also the most public.

Practical Guidelines about Audience

The theoretical relationships between discourse and audience are complex and paradoxical, but the practical morals are simple:

1. Seek ways to heighten both the *public* and *private* dimensions of writing. (For activities, see the previous section.)

2. When working on important audience-directed writing, we must try to emphasize audience awareness *sometimes.* A useful rule of thumb is to start by putting the readers in mind and carry on as long as things go well. If difficulties arise, try putting readers out of mind and write either to no audience, to self, or to an inviting audience. Finally, always *revise* with readers in mind. (Here's another occasion when orthodox advice about writing is wrong — but turns out right if applied to revising.)

3. Seek ways to heighten awareness of one's writing process (through process writing and discussion) to get better at taking control and deciding when to keep readers in mind and when to ignore them. Learn to discriminate factors like these:

a. The writing task. Is this piece of writing *really* for an audience? More often than we realize, it is not. It is a draft that only we will see, though the final version will be for an audience; or exploratory writing for figuring something out; or some kind of personal private writing meant only for ourselves.

b. Actual readers. When we put them in mind, are we helped or hindered?

c. One's own temperament. Am I the sort of person who tends to think of what to say and how to say it when I keep readers in mind? Or someone (as I am) who needs long stretches of forgetting all about readers?

d. Has some powerful "audience-in-the-head" tricked me into talking to it when I'm really trying to talk to someone else — distorting new business into old business? (I may be an inviting teacher-audience to my students, but they may not be able to pick up a pen without falling under the spell of a former, intimidating teacher.)

e. Is *double audience* getting in my way? When I write a memo or report, I probably have to suit it not only to my "target audience" but also to some colleagues or supervisor. When I write something for publication, it must be right for readers, but it won't be published unless it is also right for the editors — and if it's a book it won't be much read unless it's right for reviewers. Children's stories won't be bought unless they are right for editors and reviewers *and* parents. We often tell students to write to a particular "real-life" audience — or to peers in the class — but of course they are also writing for us as graders. (This problem is more common as more teachers get interested in audience and suggest "second" audiences.)

f. Is *teacher-audience* getting in the way of my students' writing? As teachers we must often read in an odd fashion: in stacks of twenty-five or fifty pieces all on the same topic; on topics we know better than the writer; not for pleasure or learning but to grade or find problems (see Elbow, *Writing with Power* 216–36).

To list all these audience pitfalls is to show again the need for thinking about audience needs — yet also the need for vacations from readers to think in peace.

Notes

I benefited from much help from audiences in writing various drafts of this piece. I am grateful to Jennifer Clarke, with whom I wrote a collaborative piece containing a case study on this subject. I am also grateful for extensive feedback from Pat Belanoff, Paul Connolly, Sheryl Fontaine, John Trimbur, and members of the Martha's Vineyard Summer Writing Seminar.

[1]There are many different entities called audience: (a) The actual readers to whom the text will be given; (b) the writer's conception of those readers — which may be mistaken (see Ong; Park; Ede and Lunsford); (c) the audience that the text implies — which may be different still (see Booth); (d) the discourse community or even genre addressed or implied by the text (see Walzer); (e) ghost or phantom "readers in the head" that the writer may unconsciously address or try to please (see Elbow, *Writing with Power* 186ff. Classically, this is a powerful former teacher. Often such an audience is so ghostly as not to show up as actually "implied" by the text). For the essay I am writing here, these differences don't much matter: I'm celebrating the ability to put aside the needs or demands of *any* or all of these audiences. I recognize, however, that we sometimes cannot fight our way free of unconscious or tacit audiences (as in b or e above) unless we bring them to greater conscious awareness.

Works Cited

Bakhtin, Mikhail. "Discourse in Life and Discourse in Poetry." Appendix. *Freudianism: A Marxist Critique.* By F. N. Volosinov. Trans. I. R. Titunik. Ed. Neal H. Bruss. New York: Academic, 1976. (Holquist's attribution of this work to Bakhtin is generally accepted.)

Berkenkotter, Carol, and Donald Murray. "Decisions and Revisions: The Planning Strategies of a Publishing Writer and the Response of Being a Rat — or Being Protocoled." *College Composition and Communication* 34 (1983): 156–72.

Blau, Sheridan. "Invisible Writing." *College Composition and Communication* 34 (1983): 297–312.

Booth, Wayne. *The Rhetoric of Fiction.* Chicago: U Chicago P, 1961.

Britton, James. *The Development of Writing Abilities, 11–18.* Urbana: NCTE, 1977.

Bruffee, Kenneth A. "Liberal Education and the Social Justification of Belief." *Liberal Education* 68 (1982): 95–114.

Bruner, Jerome. *Beyond the Information Given: Studies in the Psychology of Knowing.* Ed. Jeremy Anglin. New York: Norton, 1973.

———. *On Knowing: Essays for the Left Hand.* Expanded ed. Cambridge: Harvard UP, 1979.

Chomsky, Noam. *Reflections on Language.* New York: Random, 1975.

Cicotello, David M. "The Art of Writing: An Interview with William Stafford." *College Composition and Communication* 34 (1983): 173–77.

Clarke, Jennifer, and Peter Elbow. "Desert Island Discourse: On the Benefits of Ignoring Audience." *The Journal Book.* Ed. Toby Fulwiler. Montclair: Boynton, 1987.

Cooper, Anthony Ashley, 3rd Earl of Shaftesbury. *Characteristics of Men, Manners, Opinions, Times, Etc.* Ed. John M. Robertson. 2 vols. Gloucester, MA: Smith, 1963.

Ede, Lisa, and Andrea Lunsford. "Audience Addressed / Audience Invoked: The Role of Audience in Composition Theory and Pedagogy." *College Composition and Communication* 35 (1984): 140–54.

Elbow, Peter. *Writing with Power.* New York: Oxford UP, 1981.

———. *Writing without Teachers.* New York: Oxford UP, 1973.

Emerson, Caryl. "The Outer Word and Inner Speech: Bakhtin, Vygotsky, and the Internalization of Language." *Critical Inquiry* 10 (1983): 245–64.

Feldman, Carol Fleisher. "Two Functions of Language." *Harvard Education Review* 47 (1977): 282–93.

Flower, Linda. "Writer-Based Prose: A Cognitive Basis for Problems in Writing." *College English* 41 (1979): 19–37.

Goodman, Paul. *Speaking and Language: Defense of Poetry.* New York: Random, 1972.

Griffin, Susan. "The Internal Voices of Invention: Shaftesbury's Soliloquy." Unpublished. 1986.

Lawrence, D. H. *Studies in Classic American Literature.* Garden City: Doubleday, 1951.

Ong, Walter. "The Writer's Audience Is Always a Fiction." *PMLA* 90 (1975): 9–21.

Park, Douglas B. "The Meanings of 'Audience.' " *College English* 44 (1982): 247–57.

Perl, Sondra. "Guidelines for Composing." Appendix A. *Through Teachers' Eyes: Portraits of Writing Teachers at Work.* By Sondra Perl and Nancy Wilson. Portsmouth: Heinemann, 1986.

Progoff, Ira. *At a Journal Workshop.* New York: Dialogue, 1975.

Shaughnessy, Mina. *Errors and Expectations: A Guide for the Teacher of Basic Writing.* New York: Oxford UP, 1977.

Trimbur, John. "Beyond Cognition: Voices in Inner Speech." Forthcoming in *Rhetoric Review.*

———. Letter to the author. September 1985.

Vygotsky, L. S. *Thought and Language.* Trans. and ed. E. Hanfmann and G. Vakar. 1934. Cambridge: MIT P, 1962.

Walzer, Arthur E. "Articles from the 'California Divorce Project': A Case Study of the Concept of Audience." *College Composition and Communication* 36 (1985): 150–59.

Wright, Richard. *Black Boy.* New York: Harper, 1945.

Elbow's Insights as a Resource for Your Teaching

1. Consider the "desert island mode" that Elbow discusses. Demonstrate to your students how valuable such private writing is to you by discussing how you have kept a journal or notebook and when you used it as a resource. Encourage your students to write a journal entry on any experience they had with

writing entirely for themselves and without the distraction of a reader. A standard technique writing instructors use both to respect the "personal" in personal writing and to encourage private reflection is to require that students write daily but to give students the option of stapling together any entries that were not written with an outside reader in mind.

2. Try Elbow's recommendation to turn off the screen while writing with a computer, and report to your class what happened to you when you ignored audience as you generated some writing. The authors of *The Bedford Guide for College Writers* recommend this exercise in "Strategies for Writing with a Computer" in Chapter 21 to help writers from becoming too self-conscious about tapping the resource of imagination and thus triggering a "writing block." Their concern there is clearly parallel to Elbow's concern about premature self-consciousness about audience.

Elbow's Insights as a Resource for the Writing Classroom

1. Elbow's "ghost reader" — a student's sense of an inflexible teacher-as-evaluator — surfaces frequently in early essays from first-year writers and most often in "diagnostic" essays written the first week. Photocopy a few samples of writing where the ghost reader clearly frightened the writer into dense or unclear or stuffy or inauthentic prose. Ask the class to decide where "thinking too much about the 'ghost teacher as reader' got in the way" and to suggest ways to exorcise the ghost reader.

2. Encourage the "desert island mode" by asking students to close their eyes and open their ears while you play something calming like Pachelbel's Canon in D Major or Albinoni's Adagio or some recent new age music. After five minutes, ask them to freewrite for twenty minutes. Repeat this technique several times during the semester; tell the writers that this sequence is for their private writing. Observe whether all writers are freewriting, but don't collect or read the writing. Will some students bluff you? Inevitably a few will waste the opportunity, but worry more about the writers who need some modeling of ways to move into self-discourse.

3. Ask students to supplement the discussion of "Setting Up Circumstances" in Chapter 15, "Strategies for Generating Ideas," by describing, either in journal entries or a brainstorming session, ways they have set up their own circumstances for writing from imagination and for self-reflection.

REVISING A DRAFT

We know that the strongest writing comes from the process of multiple drafting and serious rethinking, reordering, and rewriting. Many students have difficulty looking critically at their writing and beginning again to generate ideas, to shape a draft, and to edit. Learning to revise and to rewrite a draft may be the most dramatic experience some of your students have this semester.

NANCY SOMMERS   *Revision Strategies of Student Writers and Experienced Adult Writers*

In this landmark study of the revision strategies used by students and by "adult" writers, Sommers concludes that student writers do not work from a holistic perspective on writing or perceive revision as a recursive process. Her categories of "student" and "experienced adult" writers can be borrowed and applied to members of a first-year composition course. Many class members already understand revising as "discovery — a repeated process of beginning over again, starting out new." They are ready to work with the rewriting strategies, the discovery checklists, and the peer editing checklists of The Bedford Guide for College Writers. *Some writers need to acquire this "new" perspective on revision.*

Sommers cites or implies several reasons that students see revision only as a linear process attending to surface features of a manuscript: previous writing experiences, infrequent practice, traditional dicta about the nature of revising, and cognitive readiness. She asserts that writing teachers can assist student writers to mature and to acquire a perspective on writing as discovery and development. She indicates that writing teachers can assist student writers to become comfortable with the same insight she gleaned from her own experience and from her research with adult, experienced writers: "Good writing disturbs; it creates dissonance."

Sommers's discussion in "Responding to Student Writing" (Part Three) shows us the practical effects on student writers of our written responses to their texts. She makes it clear that teacher commentary can directly affect and improve the revision strategies of writers.

Although various aspects of the writing process have been studied extensively of late, research on revision has been notably absent. The reason for this, I suspect, is that current models of the writing process have directed attention away from revision. With few exceptions, these models are linear; they separate the writing process into discrete stages. Two representative models are Gordon Rohman's suggestion that the composing process moves from prewriting to writing to rewriting and James Britton's model of the writing process as a series of stages described in metaphors of linear growth, conception — incubation — production.[1] What is striking about these theories of writing is that they model themselves on speech: Rohman defines the writer in a way that cannot distinguish him from a speaker ("A writer is a man who . . . puts [his] experience into words in his own mind" [15]); and Britton backs his theory of writing on what he calls (following Jakobson) the "expressiveness" of speech.[2] Moreover, Britton's study itself follows the "linear model" of the relation of thought and language in speech proposed by Vygotsky, a relationship embodied in the linear movement "from the motive which engenders a thought to the shaping of the thought, *first* in inner speech, *then* in meanings of words, and *finally* in words" (qtd. in Britton 40). What this movement fails to take into account in its linear structure — "first . . . then . . . finally" — is the recursive shaping of thought by language; what it fails to take into account is *revision*. In these linear conceptions of the writing process revision is understood as a separate stage at the end of the process — a stage that comes after the completion of a first or second draft and one that is temporally distinct from the prewriting and writing stages of the process.[3]

The linear model bases itself on speech in two specific ways. First of all, it is based on traditional rhetorical models, models that were created to serve the spoken art of oratory. In whatever ways the parts of classical rhetoric are described, they offer "stages" of composition that are repeated in contemporary models of the writing process. Edward Corbett, for instance, describes the "five parts of a discourse" — *inventio, dispositio, elocutio, memoria, pronuntiatio* — and, disregarding the last two parts since "after rhetoric came to be concerned mainly with written discourse, there was no further need to deal with them,"[4] he produces a model very close to Britton's conception [*inventio*], incubation [*dispositio*], production [*elocutio*]. Other rhetorics also follow this procedure, and they do so not simply because of historical accident. Rather, the process represented in the linear model is based on the irreversibility of speech. Speech, Roland Barthes says, "is irreversible":

A word cannot be retracted, except precisely by saying that one retracts it. To cross out here is to add: if I want to erase what I have just said, I cannot do it without showing the eraser itself (I must say: "*or rather . . .*" "*I expressed myself badly . . .*"); paradoxically, it is ephemeral speech which is indelible, not monumental writing. All that one can do in the case of a spoken utterance is to tack on another utterance.[5]

a luxury of writers

What is impossible in speech is *revision:* like the example Barthes gives, revision in speech is an afterthought. In the same way, each stage of the linear model must be exclusive (distinct from the other stages) or else it becomes trivial and counterproductive to refer to these junctures as "stages."

By staging revision after enunciation, the linear models reduce revision in writing, as in speech, to no more than an afterthought. In this way such models make the study of revision impossible. Revision, in Rohman's model, is simply the repetition of writing; or to pursue Britton's organic metaphor, revision is simply the further growth of what is already there, the "preconceived" product. The absence of research on revision, then, is a function of a theory of writing which makes revision both superfluous and redundant, a theory which does not distinguish between writing and speech.

What the linear models do produce is a parody of writing. Isolating revision and then disregarding it plays havoc with the experiences composition teachers have of the actual writing and rewriting of experienced writers. Why should the linear model be preferred? Why should revision be forgotten, superfluous? Why do teachers offer the linear model and students accept it? One reason, Barthes suggests, is that "there is a fundamental tie between teaching and speech," while "writing begins at the point where speech becomes *impossible.*"[6] The spoken word cannot be revised. The possibility of revision distinguishes the written text from speech. In fact, according to Barthes, this is the essential difference between writing and speaking. When we must revise, when the very idea is subject to recursive shaping by language, then speech becomes inadequate. This is a matter to which I will return, but first we should examine, theoretically, a detailed exploration of what student writers as distinguished from experienced adult writers *do* when they write and rewrite their work. Dissatisfied with both the linear model of writing and the lack of attention to the process of revision, I conducted a series of studies over the past three years which examined the revision processes of student writers and experienced writers to see what role revision played in their writing processes. In the course of my work the revision process was redefined as *a sequence of changes in a composition — changes which are initiated by cues and occur continually throughout the writing of a work.*

Methodology

I used a case study approach. The student writers were twenty freshmen at Boston University and the University of Oklahoma with SAT verbal scores ranging from 450–600 in their first semester of composition. The twenty experienced adult writers from Boston and Oklahoma City included journalists, editors, and academics. To refer to the two groups, I use the terms *student writers* and *experienced writers* because the principal difference between these two groups is the amount of experience they have had in writing.

Each writer wrote three essays, expressive, explanatory, and persuasive, and rewrote each essay twice, producing nine written products in draft and final form. Each writer was interviewed three times after the final revision of each essay. And each writer suggested revisions for a composition written by an anonymous author. Thus extensive written and spoken documents were obtained from each writer.

The essays were analyzed by counting and categorizing the changes made. Four revision operations were identified: deletion, substitution, addition, and reordering. And four levels of changes were identified: word, phrase, sentence, theme (the extended statement of one idea). A coding system was developed for identifying the frequency of revision by level and operation. In addition, transcripts of the interviews in which the writers interpreted their revisions were used to develop what was called a *scale of concerns* for each writer. This scale enabled me to codify what were the writer's primary concerns, secondary concerns, tertiary concerns, and whether the writers used the same scale of concerns when revising the second or third drafts as they used in revising the first draft.

Revision Strategies of Student Writers

Most of the students I studied did not use the terms *revision* or *rewriting*. In fact, they did not seem comfortable using the word *revision* and explained that revision was not a word they used, but the word their teachers used. Instead, most of the students had developed various functional terms to describe the type of changes they made. The following are samples of these definitions:

Scratch Out and Do Over Again: "I say scratch out and do over, and that means what it says. Scratching out and cutting out. I read what I have written and I cross out a word and put another word in; a more decent word or a better word. Then if there is somewhere to use a sentence that I have crossed out, I will put it there."

Reviewing: "Reviewing means just using better words and eliminating words that are not needed. I go over and change words around."

Reviewing: "I just review every word and make sure that everything is worded right. I see if I am rambling; I see if I can put a better word in or leave one out. Usually when I read what I have written, I say to myself, 'that word is so bland or so trite,' and then I go and get my thesaurus."

Redoing: "Redoing means cleaning up the paper and crossing out. It is looking at something and saying, no that has to go, or no, that is not right."

Marking Out: "I don't use the word rewriting because I only write one draft and the changes that I make are made on top of the draft. The changes that I make are usually just marking out words and putting different ones in."

Slashing and Throwing Out: "I throw things out and say they are not good. I like to write like Fitzgerald did by inspiration, and if I feel inspired then I don't need to slash and throw much out."

The predominant concern in these definitions is vocabulary. The students understand the revision process as a rewording activity. They do so because they perceive words as the unit of written discourse. That is, they concentrate on particular words apart from their role in the text. Thus one student quoted above thinks in terms of dictionaries, and, following the eighteenth-century theory of words parodied in *Gulliver's Travels,* he imagines a load of things carried about to be exchanged. Lexical changes are the major revision activities of the students because economy is their goal. They are governed, like the linear model itself, by the Law of Occam's razor that prohibits logically needless repetition: redundancy and superfluity. Nothing governs speech more than such superfluities; speech constantly repeats itself precisely because spoken words, as Barthes writes, are expendable in the cause of communication. The aim of revision according to the students' own description is therefore to clean up speech; the redundancy of speech is unnecessary in writing, their logic suggests, because writing, unlike speech, can be reread. Thus one student said, "Redoing means cleaning up the paper and crossing out." The remarkable contradiction of cleaning by marking might, indeed, stand for student revision as I have encountered it.

at the word level

The students place a symbolic importance on their selection and rejection of words as the determiners of success or failure for their compositions. When revising, they primarily ask themselves: can I find a better word or phrase? A more impressive, not so clichéd, or less humdrum word? Am I repeating the same word or phrase too often? They approach the revision process with what could be labeled as a "thesaurus philosophy of writing"; the students consider the thesaurus a harvest of lexical substitutions and believe that most problems in their essays can be solved by rewording. What is revealed in the students' use of the thesaurus is a governing attitude toward their writing: that the meaning to be communicated is already there, already finished, already produced, ready to be communicated, and all that is necessary is a better word "rightly worded." One student defined *revision* as "redoing"; *redoing* meant "just using better words and eliminating words that are not needed." For the students, writing is translating: the thought to the page, the language of speech to the more formal language of prose, the word to its synonym. Whatever is translated, an original text already exists for students, one which need not be discovered or acted upon, but simply communicated.[7]

The students list repetition as one of the elements they most worry about. This cue signals to them that they need to eliminate the repetition either by substituting or deleting words or phrases. Repetition occurs, in large part, because student writing imitates — transcribes — speech: attention to repetitious words is a manner of cleaning speech. Without a sense of the developmental possibilities of revision (and writing in general) students seek, on the authority of many textbooks, simply to clean up their language and prepare to type. What is curious, however, is that students are aware of lexical repetition, but not conceptual repetition. They only notice the repetition if they can "hear" it; they do not diagnose lexical repetition as symptomatic of problems on a deeper level. By rewording their sentences to avoid the lexical repetition, the students solve the immediate problem, but blind themselves to problems on a textual level; although they are using different words, they are sometimes merely restating the same idea with different words. Such blindness, as I discovered with student writers, is the inability to "see" revision as a process: the inability to "re-view" their work again, as it were, with different eyes, and to start over.

The revision strategies described above are consistent with the students' understanding of the revision process as requiring lexical changes but not semantic changes. For the students, the extent to which they revise is a function of their level of inspiration. In fact, they use the word *inspiration* to describe the ease or difficulty with which their essay is written, and the extent to which the essay needs to be revised. If students feel inspired, if the writing comes easily, and if they don't get stuck on individual words or phrases, then they say that they cannot see any reason to revise. Because students do not see revision as an activity in which they modify and develop perspectives and ideas, they feel that if they know what they want to say, then there is little reason for making revisions.

The only modification of ideas in the students' essays occurred when they tried out two or three introductory paragraphs. This results, in part, because the students have been taught in another version of the linear model of composing to use a thesis statement as a controlling device in their introductory paragraphs. Since they write their introductions and their thesis statements even before they have really discovered what they want to say, their early close attention to the thesis statement, and more generally the linear model, function to restrict and circumscribe not only the development of their ideas, but also their ability to change the direction of these ideas.

Too often as composition teachers we conclude that students do not willingly revise. The evidence from my research suggests that it is not that students are unwilling to revise, but rather that they do what they have been taught to do in a consistently narrow and predictable way. On every occasion when I asked students why they hadn't made any more changes, they essentially replied, "I knew something larger was wrong, but I didn't think it would help to move words around." The students have strategies for handling words and phrases and their strategies helped them on a word or sentence level. What they lack, however, is a set of strategies to help them identify the "something larger" that they sensed was wrong and work from there. The students do not have strategies for handling the whole essay. They lack procedures or heuristics to help them reorder lines of reasoning or ask questions about their purposes and readers. The students view their compositions in a linear way as a series of parts. Even such potentially useful concepts as "unity" or "form" are reduced to the rule that a composition, if it is to have form, must have an introduction, a body, and a conclusion, or the sum total of the necessary parts.

The students decide to stop revising when they decide that they have not violated any of the rules for revising. These rules, such as "Never begin a sentence with a conjunction" or "Never end a sentence with a preposition," are lexically cued and rigidly applied. In general, students will subordinate the demands of the specific problems of their text to the demands of the rules. Changes are made in compliance with abstract rules about the product, rules that quite often do not apply to the specific problems in the text. These revision strategies are teacher-based, directed towards a teacher-reader who expects compliance with rules — with pre-existing "conceptions" — and who will only examine parts of the composition (writing comments about those parts in the margins of their essays) and will cite any violations of rules in those parts. At best the students see their writing altogether passively through the eyes of former teachers or their surrogates, the textbooks, and are bound to the rules which they have been taught.

Revision Strategies of Experienced Writers

One aim of my research has been to contrast how student writers define revision with how a group of experienced writers define their revision processes. Here is a sampling of the definitions from the experienced writers:

Rewriting: "It is a matter of looking at the kernel of what I have written, the content, and then thinking about it, responding to it, making decisions, and actually restructuring it."

Rewriting: "I rewrite as I write. It is hard to tell what is a first draft because it is not determined by time. In one draft, I might cross out three pages, write two, cross out a fourth, rewrite it, and call it a draft. I am constantly writing and rewriting. I can only conceptualize so much in my first draft — only so much information can be held in my head at one time; my rewriting efforts are a reflection of how much information I can encompass at one time. There are levels and agenda which I have to attend to in each draft."

Rewriting: "Rewriting means on one level, finding the argument, and on another level, language changes to make the argument more effective. Most of the time I feel as if I can go on rewriting forever. There is always one part of a piece that I could keep working on. It is always difficult to know at what point to abandon a piece of writing. I like this idea that a piece of writing is never finished, just abandoned."

Rewriting: "My first draft is usually very scattered. In rewriting, I find the line of argument. After the argument is resolved, I am much more interested in word choice and phrasing."

Revising: "My cardinal rule in revising is never to fall in love with what I have written in a first or second draft. An idea, sentence, or even a phrase that looks catchy, I don't trust. Part of this idea is to wait a while. I am much more in love with something after I have written it than I am a day or two later. It is much easier to change anything with time."

Revising: "It means taking apart what I have written and putting it back together again. I ask major theoretical questions of my ideas, respond to those questions, and think of proportion and structure, and try to find a controlling metaphor. I find out which ideas can be developed and which should be dropped. I am constantly chiseling and changing as I revise."

The experienced writers describe their primary objective when revising as finding the form or shape of their argument. Although the metaphors vary, the experienced writers often use structural expressions such as "finding a framework," "a pattern," or "a design" for their argument. When questioned about this emphasis, the experienced writers responded that since their first drafts are usually scattered attempts to define their territory, their objective in the second draft is to begin observing general patterns of development and deciding what should be included and what excluded. One writer explained, "I have learned from experience that I need to keep writing a first draft until I figure out what I want to say. Then in a second draft, I begin to see the structure of an argument and how all the various sub-arguments which are buried beneath the surface of all those sentences are related." What is described here is a process in which the writer is both agent and vehicle. "Writing," says Barthes, unlike speech, "develops like a seed, not a line,"[8] and like a seed it confuses beginning and end, conception and production. Thus, the experienced writers say their drafts are "not determined by time," that rewriting is a "constant process," that they feel as if they "can go on forever." Revising confuses the beginning and end, the agent and vehicle; it confuses, *in order to find*, the line of argument.

After a concern for form, the experienced writers have a second objective: a concern for their readership. In this way, "production" precedes "conception." The experienced writers imagine a reader (reading their product) whose existence and whose expectations influence their revision process. They have abstracted the standards of a reader and this reader seems to be partially a reflection of themselves and functions as a critical and productive collaborator — a collaborator who has yet to love their work. The anticipation of a reader's judgment causes a feeling of dissonance when the writer recognizes incongruities between intention and execution, and requires these writers to make revisions on all levels. Such a reader gives them just what the students lacked: new eyes to "re-view" their work. The experienced writers believe that they have learned the causes and conditions, the product, which will influence their reader, and their revision strategies are geared towards creating these causes and conditions. They demonstrate a complex understanding of which examples, sentences, or phrases should be included or excluded. For example, one experienced writer decided to delete public examples and add private examples when writing about the energy crisis because "private examples would be less controversial and thus more persuasive." Another writer revised his transitional sentences because "some kinds of transitions are more easily recognized as transitions than others." These examples represent the type of strategic attempts these experienced writers use to manipulate the conventions of discourse in order to communicate to their reader.

But these revision strategies are a process of more than communication; they are part of the process of *discovering meaning* altogether. Here we can see the importance of dissonance; at the heart of revision is the process by which writers recognize and resolve the dissonance they sense in their writing. Ferdinand de Saussure has argued that meaning is differential or "diacritical," based on differences between terms rather than "essential" or inherent qualities of terms. "Phonemes," he said, "are characterized not, as one might think, by their own positive quality but simply by the fact that they are distinct."[9] In fact, Saussure bases his entire *Course in General Linguistics* on these differences, and such differences are dissonant; like musical dissonances which gain their significance from their relationship to the "key" of the composition which itself is determined by the whole language, specific language (parole) gains its meaning from the system of language (langue) of which it is a manifestation and part. The musical composition — a "composition" of parts — creates its "key" as in an overall structure which determines the value (meaning) of its parts. The analogy with music is readily seen in the compositions of experienced writers: both sorts of composition are based precisely on those structures experienced writers seek in their writing. It is this complicated relationship between the parts and the whole in the work of experienced writers which destroys the linear model; writing cannot develop "like a line" because each addition or deletion is a reordering of the whole. Explicating Saussure, Jonathan Culler asserts that "meaning depends on difference of meaning."[10] But student writers constantly struggle to bring their essays into congruence with a predefined meaning. The experienced writers do the opposite: they seek to discover (to create) meaning in the engagement with their writing, in revision. They seek to emphasize and exploit the lack of clarity, the differences of meaning, the dissonance, that writing as opposed to speech allows in the possibility of revision. Writing has spatial and temporal features not apparent in speech — words are recorded in space and fixed in time — which is why writing is susceptible to reordering and later addition. Such features make possible the dissonance that both provokes revision and promises, from itself, new meaning.

For the experienced writers the heaviest concentration of changes is on the sentence level, and the changes are predominantly by addition and deletion. But, unlike the students, experienced writers make changes on all levels and use all revision operations. Moreover, the operations the students fail to use — reordering and addition — seem to require a theory of the revision process as a totality — a theory which, in fact, encompasses the *whole* of the composition. Unlike the students, the experienced writers possess a nonlinear theory in which a sense of the whole writing both precedes and grows out of an examination of the parts. As we saw, one writer said he needed "a first draft to figure out what to say," and "a second draft to see the structure of an argument buried beneath the surface." Such a "theory" is both theoretical and strategical; once again, strategy and theory are conflated in ways that are literally impossible for the linear model. Writing appears to be more like a seed than a line.

Two elements of the experienced writers' theory of the revision process are the adoption of a holistic perspective and the perception that revision is a recursive process. The writers ask: what does my essay as a *whole* need for form, balance, rhythm, or communication. Details are added, dropped, substituted, or reordered according to their sense of what the essay needs for emphasis and proportion. This sense, however, is constantly in flux as ideas are developed and modified; it is constantly "re-viewed" in relation to the parts. As their ideas change, revision becomes an attempt to make their writing consonant with that changing vision.

The experienced writers see their revision process as a recursive process — a process with significant recurring activities — with different levels of attention and different agenda for each cycle. During the first revision cycle their attention is primarily directed towards narrowing the topic and delimiting their ideas. At this point, they are not as concerned as they are later about vocabulary and style. The experienced writers explained that they get closer to their meaning by not limiting themselves too early to lexical concerns. As one writer commented to explain her revision process, a comment inspired by the summer 1977 New York power failure: "I feel like Con Edison cutting off certain states to keep the generators going. In first and second drafts, I try to cut off as much as I can of my editing generator, and in a third draft, I try to cut off some of my idea generators, so I can make sure that I will actually finish the essay." Although the experienced writers describe their revision process as a series of different levels or cycles, it is inaccurate to assume that they have only one objective. The same objectives and sub-processes are present in each cycle, but in different proportions. Even though these experienced writers place the predominant weight upon finding the form of their argument during the first cycle, other concerns exist as well. Conversely, during the later cycles, when the experienced writers' primary attention is focused upon stylistic concerns, they are still attuned, although in a reduced way, to the form of the argument. Since writers are limited in what they can attend to during each cycle (understandings are temporal), revision strategies help balance competing demands on attention. Thus, writers can concentrate on more than one objective at a time by developing strategies to sort out and organize their different concerns in successive cycles of revision.

It is a sense of writing as discovery — a repeated process of beginning over again, starting out new — that the students failed to have. I have used the notion of dissonance because such dissonance, the incongruities between intention and execution, governs both writing and meaning. Students do not see the incongruities. They need to rely on their own internalized sense of good writing and to see their writing with their "own" eyes. Seeing in revision — seeing beyond hearing — is at the root of the word *revision* and the process itself; current dicta on revising blind our students to what is actually involved in revision. In fact, they blind them to what constitutes good writing altogether. Good writing disturbs: it creates dissonance. Students need to seek the dissonance of discovery, utilizing in their writing, as the experienced writers do, the very difference between writing and speech — the possibility of revision.

Notes

The author wishes to express her gratitude to Professor William Smith, University of Pittsburgh, for his vital assistance with the research reported in this article and to Patrick Hays, her husband, for extensive discussions and critical help.

[1]D. Gordon Rohman and Albert O. Wlecke, "Pre-writing: The Construction and Application of Models for Concept Formation in Writing," Cooperative Research Project No. 2174, U.S. Office of Education, Department of Health, Education, and Welfare; James Britton, Anthony Burgess, Nancy Martin, Alex McLeod, Harold Rosen, *The Development of Writing Abilities* (11–18) (London: Macmillan, 1975).

[2]Britton is following Roman Jakobson, "Linguistics and Poetics," *Style in Language*, ed. T. A. Sebeok (Cambridge: MIT P, 1960).

[3]For an extended discussion of this issue see Nancy Sommers, "The Need for Theory in Composition Research," *College Composition and Communication* 30 (Feb. 1979): 46–49.

[4]*Classical Rhetoric for the Modern Student* (New York: Oxford UP, 1965) 27.

[5]Roland Barthes, "Writers, Intellectuals, Teachers," *Image-Music-Text,* trans. Stephen Heath (New York: Hill, 1977) 190–91.

[6]Barthes 190.

[7]Nancy Sommers and Ronald Schleifer, "Means and Ends: Some Assumptions of Student Writers," *Composition and Teaching* 2 (1980): 69–76.

[8]*Writing Degree Zero, in Writing Degree Zero and Elements of Semiology,* trans. Annette Lavers and Colin Smith (New York: Hill, 1968) 20.

[9]*Course in General Linguistics,* trans. Wade Baskin (New York, 1966) 119.

[10]Jonathan Culler, Saussure, Penguin Modern Masters Series (London: Penguin, 1976) 70.

Sommers's Insights as a Resource for Your Teaching

1. In your dialectical journal, reflect on the experiences that influenced you to think about revising your own texts.

2. When you work with a writer who engages in "deep revision," ask whether that writer will give you permission to use excerpts from his or her multiple drafts. With these drafts, you can demonstrate to future students what can happen when a writer moves beyond surface revision. (Any time you want to use student writing — for teaching or research or published writing — you must receive permission.)

3. Computer drafting has profoundly changed the revision process for writers by eliminating the need to start over for each change. Some writers have a stronger sense of "retrospective structuring" and of composing from the "felt sense" Perl describes. Some writers are less conscious of revisions, major and minor, that they make on disk (rather than by hand). Encourage students to keep hard copies of drafts so they can review and reflect on their revision strategies and share the strategies with you in conferences.

Sommers's Insights as a Resource for the Writing Classroom

1. Ask your students to reflect — in journal entries or in fifteen-minute writing sessions — on their definitions of "revision." Have them write before their first experience with peer evaluation in the course and before you hand back their first writing with your comments about revision. Ask them to reflect again on their definitions of "revision" midway through the term and as they near completion of the course. (If this is your students' first assignment involving journal writing, suggest that they consult "Keeping a Journal" in Chapter 15, "Strategies for Generating Ideas.")

2. Use the categories Sommers sets up to prompt small-group discussion about revision. Ask the groups to list what they view as characteristics of good revising. Then introduce the concept of "student" and "mature or experienced student" and ask them to classify the characteristics they described as representative of one or the other. Often students will volunteer descriptions that echo those that Sommers lists. If they don't, you should feel free to cite the "research" you read and ask the students to consider Sommers's list as categories by which they can look at their own revising strategies. If you establish with your students that a "mature" college writer views revision as a recursive process, you give them one criterion by which to assess their growth as writers.

3. Prepare a sampler of revision suggestions from completed peer editing checklists or from transcripts of workshop sessions. (Borrow such materials from a teaching colleague if you are teaching for the first time or find your students apprehensive about seeing their comments used anonymously.) Organize small groups to evaluate peer crticism, deciding which comments encourage revisions to improve the form and substance of the writer's argument; which comments focus the writer's attention on the needs of multiple readers; and which comments address lexical concerns. Ask each group to list the

comments they would welcome on working drafts, and to define or describe what makes those comments useful. Have them explain what makes the other comments less useful or less accessible to them. When each group reports to the class, ask for other examples of excellent peer criticism that students have encountered in the past. Don't be surprised if some class members find the exercise challenging: many have never been asked to reflect on their critical thinking or encouraged to regard peer criticism as a significant writing experience, as Mara Holt reminds us in the following essay.

MARA HOLT   *The Value of Written Peer Criticism*

When Mara Holt experimented with and reflected on her classroom practices with regard to written peer criticism, she arrived at a collaborative editing approach that directs both the instructor and the student writer into "taking peer criticism seriously as a writing exercise." Holt explains that it is important for peer critics to write about their responses, expectations, and needs as readers, thus providing an audience for writers to consider. She emphasizes that it is equally important that they respond to the substantive issues and ideas, helping the writer to "negotiate the assignment" and meet the demands or expectations of the teacher. Holt explains that an "interplay" of these two kinds of peer criticism challenges students to "engage in intellectual discourse in writing." She anchors her insights to an extended discussion of the peer critique experiences of one writer. Holt's discussion of the strengths and weaknesses of both approaches to peer criticism seem to mediate Elbow and Bartholomae's debate — or public conversation — about personal writing/academic writing in English 101.

When I talk to graduate students and colleagues about their use of collaborative learning, I often hear stories about when it doesn't work. No one's version of collaborative pedagogy is universally rewarding, of course, but I have found some approaches consistently more successful than others. Often, peer criticism consists of oral or hastily written comments by students in a classroom group; sometimes students fill out a checklist or a form that resembles a short-answer test (for example Huff and Kline 122–23). In these cases, neither teacher nor student is taking peer criticism seriously as a writing exercise. Furthermore, much oral or checklist peer criticism is limited to students' evaluations of their peers' writing techniques, thus neglecting discussion of the substantive issues in the paper. Finally, much peer criticism focuses either on the subjective experience of the critic, such as Peter Elbow's "movies of people's minds while they read your words" (*Writing without Teachers* 77), or objectified standard criteria, such as his "criterion-based feedback" (*Writing with Power* 240–45). I would like to propose a melding of exercises from Peter Elbow and Pat Belanoff's book *Sharing and Responding* with the series of written peer critiques Kenneth Bruffee describes in his text *A Short Course in Writing*. These two kinds of peer criticism work best in tandem in the collaborative classroom because together they capture the struggle between individual expression and social constraint that most of us experience as writers.

Sharing and Responding can function on its own or as a companion piece to Elbow and Belanoff's *A Community of Writers* . . . with which it was published. (In the second edition, *Sharing and Responding* is part of *A Community of Writers*.) The exercises continue the tradition of reader-based responding that Elbow began in *Writing without Teachers* and *Writing with Power*, but with a twist. The exercises in *Sharing and Responding* have a more developed social framework than their earlier manifestations. Although the emphasis is still on the writer's making individual choices, the structure of group interaction is more clearly developed than in Elbow's earlier work. For instance, each exercise has sample reader responses followed by a section called "What a Writer Might Think about This Feedback." These exercises (as well as other subjective or comment-based — rather than essay-length — peer criticism) work well to get students started in peer criticism and to prod them to think more about a piece of writing when they run out of ideas. A sample of such exercises, several of which will be discussed in this paper, is listed in Table 1.

Elbow and Belanoff's exercises are generally used by students in small groups in class. Teachers and students can pick and choose exercises from *Sharing and Responding*. There is no set structure or sequence to the approach, although the focus is clearly on writing as a process of revision, and the method works well with portfolio grading. The writer is top priority in Elbow and Belanoff's approach. The writer chooses what responses she wants and in what form. Students can write their responses to fellow students' papers and read them in the group or hand them to the writer; students can also respond to other students' writing orally. Student writers gain a sense of play and inventiveness about their writing, and student responders learn that they have useful and creative things to say about their peers' work.

Bruffee's *A Short Course in Writing*, published first in 1972, has served as the primary college textbook for teaching writing using collaborative learning. Bruffee's approach to peer criticism is a modification of the peer-review process of professional journals; it is dialogic in structure. Bruffee's approach, which empha-

Table 1
Sample of Elbow and Belanoff's Peer-Response Exercises

1. *Sayback:* Ask readers: "Say back to me in your own words what you hear me getting at in my writing."[a]

2. *Movies of the Reader's Mind:* Get readers to tell you frankly *what happens inside their heads* as they read your words.

3. *Pointing:* Ask readers: "Which words or phrases stick in mind? Which passages or features did you like best? Don't explain why."

4. *What's Almost Said or Implied:* Ask readers: "What's *almost* said, implied, hovering around the edges? What would you like to hear more about?"

5. *Voice, Point of View, Attitude toward the Reader, Language, Diction, Syntax:* Ask readers to describe each of these features or dimensions of your writing.

6. *Center of Gravity:* Ask readers: "What do you sense as the source of energy, the focal point, the seedbed, the generative center for this piece (not necessarily the main point)?"[b]

7. *Believing and Doubting:* Ask readers: "Believe (or pretend to believe) everything I have written. Be my ally and tell me what you see. Give me more ideas and perceptions to help my case. Then doubt everything and tell me what you see. What arguments can be made against what I say?"[c]

Source: Elbow and Belanoff, *Sharing and Responding* 64–67.
[a]Elbow and Belanoff attribute "sayback" to Elaine Avidon and Sondra Perl of the New York City Writing Project. Exercises 1–5 can also be found in Elbow's *Writing without Teachers* (76–116) and/or *Writing with Power* (255–63).
[b]This exercise first appeared in *Writing without Teachers* (35).
[c]Articles from which this exercise comes can be found in the appendix of *Writing without Teachers* (147–91) and the more recent *Embracing Contraries* (253–300).

sizes the process of negotiation, complements Elbow's focus on invention. Table 2 outlines the stages of Bruffee's peer-review process.

Bruffee's ideal class for the peer-critique sequence is a semester-long course in which students have time to practice the steps of the peer critique cumulatively, as shown in Table 2. For Paper 1, the teacher assigns a persuasive essay of three to four paragraphs focused on the support of a strong thesis (53–84). The student writer composes her paper, then writes for her own paper a descriptive outline, describing what each paragraph says, as well as how each paragraph functions in the essay as a whole (97–107). At this point she gives her paper (without the descriptive outline) to another student, who writes a descriptive outline of her paper (generally outside of class). The two students then have an opportunity in class to compare descriptive outlines and discuss the reasons for the differences before the writer revises her paper in preparation for handing it in to the teacher. The teacher grades the writer's paper (writer's descriptive outline included) and the critic's descriptive outline and then hands the graded assignments back to their proper owners. As Table 2 indicates, another stage in the peer-critique process is added for each of Papers 2 through 5. This cumulative approach gives students a chance to learn the various stages of the peer-critique process slowly enough both to understand it and to adjust emotionally to its increasing complexity.

Elbow and Belanoff's approach to peer response and Bruffee's peer-critique sequence have strengths and weaknesses that complement each other. *Sharing and Responding* offers creative and provocative invention techniques that are crucial for students whose only previous model for peer review may have been a teacher's grade. *Sharing and Responding* also includes good analytical exercises, but these are

Table 2
Bruffee's Cumulative Peer-Critique Process

	Writer's Tasks	*Critic's Tasks*
Paper 1	(1) short persuasive essay with descriptive outline (3) optional revision	(2) descriptive outline
Paper 2	(1) short persuasive essay with descriptive outline (3) optional revision	(2) descriptive outline with evaluative and substantive peer critique
Paper 3	(1) short persuasive essay with descriptive outline (3) writer's response (4) optional revision	(2) descriptive outline with evaluative and substantive peer critique
Paper 4	(1) short persuasive essay with descriptive outline (3) writer's response (5) optional revision	(2) descriptive outline with evaluative and substantive peer critique (4) second critique (mediation)
Paper 5	(1) short persuasive essay with descriptive outline (3) writer's response (5) final writer's response (6) optional revision	(2) descriptive outline with evaluative and substantive peer critique (4) second critique (mediation)

Source: Bruffee, *A Short Course in Writing* 140–52.

less thorough than Bruffee's fuller analytical writing assignments, which ask a student to write the equivalent of a professional peer review of another student's paper. Bruffee's series of peer critiques is very useful for analytical skills and for making arguments, but not as helpful for eliciting responses from students about writing in the first place. Used together, the peer-response exercises of Elbow/Belanoff and Bruffee give students something to say and then push them toward a more complicated cognitive perspective in writing a peer review — supporting what they say and being evaluated themselves for their writing skills as reflected by the critique. The result is a fuller, more meaningful peer review process which I elaborate upon using Bruffee's "Paper 5" sequence (see Table 3) as an example inclusive of the entire process.

While very early drafts of the persuasive essay are being composed, Elbow and Belanoff's exercises from *Sharing and Responding* provide a variety of ways to initiate students' interaction with one another on the subject of writing (Table 3, Stage 1). "Sayback," for instance, is an exercise in which a student listens to another student read a passage; then the listener "says back" what she has heard. "Pointing," in which a student merely underlines words or phrases or passages that appeal to her, is a wonderful way for students simply to enjoy classmates' writing before having to explain why. Others include "what's almost said or implied," in which the reader or listener notes implications of the writer's words which may not be explicitly stated; "believing and doubting," which asks the reader to both accept and reject (in turn) what the writer is saying; and finally, "movies of the reader's mind," in which the reader is asked to say what was on her mind while she was reading the paper. These exercises are user-friendly response tools that help students break

Table 3
Elbow/Belanoff's Exercises Incorporated into
Bruffee's Paper 5 Sequence*

	Bruffee Task	*Elbow/Belanoff Exercises*
Stage 1	3–4 paragraph essay with descriptive outline (writer)	"sayback," "pointing," "what's almost said or implied," "believing and doubting," "movies of the reader's mind" (critics)
Stage 2	first critique, including descriptive, evaluative and substantive response (first critic)	exercises from Stage 1 (first critic)
Stage 3	writer's response (writer)	"voice," "point of view" "attitude toward the reader," "believing and doubting" (writer)
Stage 4	second critique or mediation (second critic)	exercises from Stage 1 and/or Stage 3 (second critic)
Stage 5	final writer's response (writer)	exercises from Stage 3 (writer)
Stage 6	optional revision (writer)	

Sources: Bruffee, *A Short Course in Writing* 140–52; Elbow and Belanoff, *Sharing and Responding* 64–67.

*These exercises from Elbow and Belanoff's text are a sample of many possible exercises from their text that would be useful in the various stages of Bruffee's sequence with Paper 5.

through emotional barriers they may have erected against the idea of talking about anybody else's writing. Used with early drafts of the persuasive paper, these exercises can fill a gap in Bruffee's system students sometimes have trouble with, invention.

When the persuasive papers are scheduled to be given to the peer critics, writers read them aloud in class and exchange them with class members chosen by the writers (Table 3, Stage 2). I do not call the paper given to the critic at Stage 2 a "draft" (although technically it is), because I want students to have taken the paper as far as they can without formal feedback and then to present it to their peers in "final draft" form. The student critic at Stage 2 writes a three-part critique which consists of a descriptive outline, an evaluation, and a substantive response to the issues in the paper. The descriptive outline proves that the critic has closely read the paper and that she understands its form and content. The evaluative and substantive parts of the critique can be written in the form of an essay modeled after the ideal professional peer review or in the form of a letter (for specific assignments, see Bruffee 148–52). The vocabulary of response gleaned from the earlier subjective exercises in Elbow and Belanoff's *Sharing and Responding* provides a basis for student critics to go beyond the simple response level toward making suggestions for improvement. At this point the student is responding not only to the writing in terms of her own expectations (the thrust of the Elbow and Belanoff exercises), but also to the assignment — to the teacher's demands. The critic's job is to help her fellow student negotiate the assignment, which represents the social constraints of the writing situation.

In addition to an analysis of strengths and weaknesses, the Stage 2 critique involves an engagement with substantive issues in the paper. This can take the critic beyond the micropolitics of the classroom into a discussion of broader social concerns. For example, a student whom I will call Thomas, a Hispanic engineering student, wrote a paper in which he argued in support of affirmative action, even though it would mean that white male students might be discriminated against. His first critic, "John" (a white male), gave him good suggestions for making his argument stronger, then proceeded to disagree strongly with his thesis, saying, "It goes against the principles of this country. . . . There are many minorities who began poor and later on became successful without the aid of affirmative action (not just basketball players). . . . I believe this country is the land of *equal* opportunity."

This comment provoked Thomas into making a stronger argument for affirmative action in his writer's response, the next stage of the critique process (Table 3, Stage 3). The first part of Bruffee's assignment for the writer's response is to "explain how each aspect of the evaluation affects you as a writer" (151–52). Thomas complimented John on the usefulness of his critique and made suggestions for improving it. Elbow and Belanoff's subjective response exercises come in handy at this point, giving the student tools to try to articulate reactions that may help the critic learn to do his job better. Elbow and Belanoff's structured responses to the "voice" of the critique, to its "point of view," and to its "attitude toward the reader," as well as "believing and doubting" exercises, can be useful to the writer at Stage 3 (Table 3, Stage 3). The second task of the writer in Stage 3 is to continue the discussion of issues. In an eloquent defense of affirmative action and re-vision of "equal opportunity," Thomas took on John's assertion that affirmative action precludes the American ideal of democracy:

> The only equal opportunities minorities have along with white people are for low-paying jobs. I too believe that it's morally impermissible to discriminate, but I believe that it's even more impermissible to continue to hold one class in

poverty when a more equitable distribution of wealth should emerge in a truly "democratic" society. In a democratic society, the proportion of people living in poverty for all types of people should be equal. Similarly, the proportion living above the poverty line should be equal if everyone is presented with "equal opportunity."

The writer's growing social perspective is expanded even further when he entrusts his paper, his critic's response, and his response to his critic to a second critic (or mediator) who reads the discussion that has occurred on paper between the writer and the critic and then writes a critique of the original paper and the responses (Table 3, Stage 4). The mediator has three tasks. First, he may mediate between the writer and the first critic. Second, he responds to and evaluates the writing skills of both the writer and the first critic. Finally, he becomes another voice in the conversation about the issues (Bruffee 151–52). Adding a third person to this conversation complicates the set of social constraints similar to the way professional writing may be scrutinized. This mediation stage represents students working together to deal collectively with the social constraints of the writing task and the power of institutional evaluation represented by the teacher. The task of the student critics is to help the writer say what he wants to say in such a way that it will be heard by his audience. The critics both serve as his audience (this is where Elbow and Belanoff's diverse and provocative exercises are helpful) and help him strategize ways to reach his ultimate audience: the teacher (this is where Bruffee's clearly structured essay assignments are helpful). In working together in this way, students become freer from dependence upon the teacher. Students gain "the ability to reinterpret (institutional) power by defining the authority of knowledge as a relationship among people . . . " (Kail and Trimbur 12). They can develop political skills as a result of learning to work collectively to accomplish goals in an environment of unequal power relations and learning to argue fruitfully with peers.

To continue with my extended example, the second critic, let's call him Craig, read Thomas's paper, John's critique, and Thomas's writer's response. He then gave Thomas some good advice for making his argument stronger. "Your third paragraph is good up to sentence five," Craig noted. "Say something then to the effect that when white males dominate society, they utilize a poor work force (of mostly minorities), and by not promoting them, minorities stay in the work force; they don't compete for higher level jobs (the white males' own) and they stay poor. Then say affirmative action requires white males to promote minorities, reversing this inequity." After giving Thomas suggestions to strengthen his argument in support of affirmative action in order to help him negotiate the teacher's assignment, Craig switched gears to argue against affirmative action in his substantive discussion, drawing upon his own experience as a white male bartender and restaurant manager:

> Why change things? From my standpoint, everything works fine. I have two good jobs won through skill and determination; no one gave me a job because I am white. In fact, my major employer is almost entirely Hispanic. I started out flipping burgers and have worked my way up . . . because I tried. I was (and am) determined to better my financial and employment status. . . . I think the poor remain poor because they resign themselves to it.

In switching the argument from an "objective" to a "subjective" realm, Craig provided an opportunity for Thomas to reframe his own argument in terms of his experience. Because this was all done in writing and evaluated by the teacher as a series of essays, the students were constrained to participate articulately in both evaluative and substantive discussions, supporting what they said more fully than they might have done in a spoken conversation.

A final writer's response ends the sequence of peer critiques (Table 3, Stage 5). The writer has the last word; he can comment upon what he chooses — ranging from form to content, from style to substance. Bruffee urges students to "reevaluate the essay in light of the peer criticism" and to "reevaluate the peer criticism." Additionally, he suggests that students "review the whole peer critique process, from the points of view of both a peer critic and a writer" (152). The student can choose to revise his paper (Table 3, Stage 6) before handing it in to the teacher. In his final writer's response, Thomas thanks "all the white guys in class for jumping all over me and showing me that I needed to strengthen my arguments." His very successful final revision, titled "Justice and Injustice," begins with a description of his experience as someone who had had no chance of attending college without affirmative action scholarships. Thomas's talent and intelligence are apparent to everyone; his example is more persuasive and his arguments stronger than the more formulaic stance he had taken in his first draft — before being prodded by the arguments of his peers.

After Stage 6, the writers hand in to the teacher their original essays, the critiques that their peers have written for them, their responses to those critiques, and their revisions of the original essay. The teacher can read these separate pieces as a set of narratives of the students' writing processes. She grades each essay and its corresponding responses (Bruffee 147–48). The teacher then returns each paper with its critiques to the writers, who keep their persuasive essays and writers' responses and return the critiques to the critics who wrote them. It is beneficial for the teacher to give writers and critics class time to read and possibly discuss the teacher's comments on the papers and critiques so they can get a better sense of how the group of students and the teacher responded to and influenced one another.

The five-step procedure I have described should be modified to fit various situations. I have used it most successfully as a cumulative process in advanced writing courses on a semester schedule (as in Table 2). Sometimes in first-year English classes I have asked students to do only the first peer critique each time a paper is due (Table 3, Stages 1 and 2). For other classes, I have structured the tasks more explicitly, making the peer critique more like an essay exam than an essay or letter. As I am teaching under a quarter system now and would like to try the whole process, I am considering extending the one persuasive essay and four peer critiques ("Paper 5") over an entire quarter. I have used Bruffee's *Short Course* model without Elbow's subjective inventive responses, and I have at various times used either Elbow's *Writing with Power* or Elbow and Belanoff's *A Community of Writers* without Bruffee's written critiques, but I have seldom had a completely successful class employing either method by itself. It is the conjunction of the two that has made the difference.

In recent years many writing instructors have argued that peer critiques can help students learn firsthand the communal nature and intellectual excitement of writing. But less attention has been given to distinguishing among the kinds of peer criticism that students can fruitfully engage in. The interplay of the subjective and the socially mediated exercises insures that students write imaginatively and creatively as well as conventionally and analytically. Both approaches to academic writing are validated, and students begin to see how the use of each kind of discourse can enable the other. Furthermore, the use of both kinds of peer critique is politically important in that it challenges students to engage in intellectual discourse in writing. This is an excellent pedagogy in a course in which gender, race, and class are the focus; such courses sometimes focus on political content without teaching students political skills. With cumulative peer response, social negotiation becomes part of the political content of the course. In part through the peer-review process the student in a collaborative classroom finds her identity as a writer not just in imitating models, but in the way we who publish in the disciplines do — by negotiating with peers.

Works Cited

Bruffee, Kenneth A. *A Short Course in Writing: Practical Rhetoric for Teaching Composition through Collaborative Learning.* 3rd ed. Boston: Little, 1985.

Elbow, Peter. *Embracing Contraries.* New York: Oxford UP, 1986.

———. *Writing without Teachers.* New York: Oxford UP, 1973.

———. *Writing with Power.* New York: Oxford UP, 1981.

Elbow, Peter, and Pat Belanoff. *A Community of Writers: A Workshop Course in Writing.* New York: Random, 1989.

———. *Sharing and Responding.* New York: Random, 1989.

Huff, Roland, and Charles R. Kline, Jr. *The Contemporary Writing Curriculum: Rehearsing, Composing, and Valuing.* New York: Teachers College P, 1987.

Kail, Harvey, and John Trimbur. "The Politics of Peer Tutoring." *Writing Program Administration* 11.1–2 (Fall 1987): 5–12.

Holt's Insights as a Resource for Your Teaching

1. Consider Holt's practice when she refuses to call the paper given to the critic a "draft." Students inexperienced at peer editing, apprehensive about writing, or overconfident about the quality of works they produce at 6:00 A.M. for a 7:30 A.M. peer evaluation should be encouraged to draft and revise before they receive formal feedback from peers. The further developed and refined the draft they share with peers, the more they — and their readers — can profit from peer critique.

2. Holt emphasizes that both teachers and learners should take peer criticism seriously as a writing exercise that "challenges students to engage in intellectual discourse in writing." To facilitate intellectual discourse, you need to monitor initial peer review sessions, evaluate the quality of peer critique, and assess (along with the writers) peer readers' growth. When you monitor initial peer review sessions, indicate why you are reading (or listening to) peer response: to observe whether the critic has been helpfully specific. (Often, critics slip into "writer-based prose" when they need to be as detailed in their discussion as professional reviewers are.) You can also evaluate the effect of the critics' voice, and whether they apply sound reasoning, offer supportive advice, and discuss candidly what they as readers think about the issues. Finally, you can monitor students' improvement over time as peer critics. Indicate that you expect students to become effective peer critics, and reward improvement: good peer criticism also trains critics to more thoroughly attend to audience(s) and more carefully consider multiple perspectives when they write. Design journal prompts and self-assessment protocols that focus the critics' attention on their practice, on what they have learned through serving as peer critics, and on how their critique and communication has changed. During a midterm conference ask each student about the experiences of giving and receiving peer criticism.

3. Try Holt's method of merging the two peer review approaches. Solicit feedback in journal entries or course evaluations about the benefits and drawbacks with each approach and use that feedback in designing your syllabus for second semester.

Holt's Insights as a Resource for the Writing Classroom

1. Intellectual discourse about writing can include student critique of the peer criticism methods the class employs. Ask for journal entries analyzing and

evaluating the benefits and drawbacks of each method you use. After mid-term, prompt the class to negotiate methods and review questions.

2. Students appreciate knowing the questions they will use for peer critique. Some students use those items as heuristics while they draft; others use them during their final revision before peer critique. When you design or supply those questions, give them to students when you introduce the writing assignment to show them the outcomes you anticipate.

TEACHING WRITING WITH COMPUTERS

Computer literacy is no longer optional; writers need computer literacy to succeed at the university and beyond. As the conferences on computers and writing indicate, teacher expertise in working with computer-assisted or computer-mediated writing varies greatly. Because classrooms may also vary greatly, writing instructors must try to keep up to date by interacting with colleagues — whether at work, at conferences, or online — and by reading professional journals (see the Annotated Bibliography). For more about using computer technology in your course, see *Teaching with* THE BEDFORD GUIDE FOR COLLEGE WRITERS. *3. Online* and Chapter 5 in *Practical Suggestions*.

CHARLES MORAN *Computers and the Writing Classroom: A Look to the Future*

Charles Moran, in this first chapter from Reimagining Computers and Composition, *writes from his extensive experience teaching writing and working with computers in writing classrooms. Answering the question, "What if a writing classroom in 2050 . . . ?," he writes about the necessity for writing teachers to think seriously about present and potential uses of computer-mediated communication and to "begin to build, at least in our imaginations, the writing class of the coming virtual age."*

Moran cites three forces — "national dissatisfaction with schools as they are, the rising energy-cost of such schools, and the decreasing cost of computer and communications technology" — that make it imperative for writing teachers to rethink the experiences possible in the writing classroom of the future. He describes two existing classrooms: "the computer-equipped, brick-and-mortar classroom and the computer-mediated, on-line classroom." From his perspective ("not as a techno-groupie but as a moderately rational writing teacher"), Moran believes that computer technology creates unique opportunitiess for writing teachers to create, fine-tune, or maintain real interactive writing classrooms.

The real impact in computers is not the silicon. It's not even the current software. It's the re-thinking.

– Robert Frankston

The college writing classroom of the year 2050 will not be what it is today. But what will this writing classroom look like? What shapes and characteristics will it have? How will it be equipped? As Robert Frankston suggests in the epigraph, the future design of the writing classroom will be less the result of the new technology than it will be the result of the deep, merciless re-thinking that this new technology compels us to undertake. So let us begin the re-thinking here by looking at the conventional writing classroom and asking ourselves, "What do these college writing classrooms look like now? Are they now what we want? And what, given the advent of computer technology, are the alternatives?"

The "Real" Writing Classroom

Suddenly the conventional college writing classroom seems an odd place, a "virtual reality" of its own, frozen in time, remarkably similar to the turn-of-the-century urban school classrooms pictured in histories of American education (e.g., Tyack 46, 56). This writing classroom is an expensive, impersonal structure serially inhabited by different classes, none of which leaves any trace in the room. The room serves as a "writing" classroom only when the writers and their teacher appear; at other times, it serves as a classroom for History 102, Economics 312, German 103, Philosophy 201, Management 207. There are no books in the room, except for those that students and teachers bring with them. There is a teacher's desk at the head of the room, a symbol of authority that has in it only the fugitive piece of chalk and perhaps an old blue-book or two. Otherwise, there are no writing materials in this desk, which is a stage device, a prop, and not a workspace. The teacher works at another, "real" desk, at home or in a college office, where there are pencils, pens, staplers, paper, stamps, paper-clips, a typewriter and/or a PC, an address-book; and, somewhere near the desk, there are bookshelves, a bulletin-board with reminders and mementos on it, pictures, a telephone, a file cabinet.

Facing the classroom teacher-desk, there are student desks, not often, these days, bolted to the floor, but still set in rows. These desks, like the teacher's classroom desk, are "unreal" work-spaces. They are also poor writing places. The writing surface is often irregular, often small, and, for those who are left-handed, awkwardly placed. And if one wants to set up small groups, these pieces of furniture suddenly become awkward and heavy, for they have been built of metal and laminated, wood-grained plastic — to last.

There are other pieces of equipment in this conventional classroom that, given our deconstructive move, now seem as unreal as the unreal desk. Behind the desk is a chalkboard that, in colleges and university classrooms, is usually empty at the beginning of class; a given class meets there so seldom that any messages "saved" on the chalkboard will likely not survive the two-to-four-day interval between classes. On the walls of the classroom there are bulletin boards which, by default, have been taken over by those paid to staple advertising — for vacation travel or magazine subscriptions — on every available open wall-space. These materials have a somewhat hallucinatory connection with the business of the writing class. In an elementary school, where students and teachers spend the full day in one room, the class can post its writing on bulletin boards and thus "publish" on the classroom walls. But here the walls, the furniture, belong to everyone and to no one — as impersonal as a room in a motel.

Reasons for Change

From this perspective, we begin to see that this classroom we inhabit is not an inevitable structure, or even a good one, *for* our purposes. Indeed, to argue *for* the conventional writing classroom is not going to be easy. We would, if we could, re-design these writing rooms, even without the impetus of technological change. We would go to our administrators and schedule writing classes in particular rooms for the entire school day, and we would turn these rooms into writing rooms: equip them with dictionaries, paper, staplers, file cabinets, envelopes, stamps, paper clips, typewriters, copy machines, handbooks, thesauri — anything that a writer might want or need. We might ask for a mix of furniture: some writing desks where a writer could write alone, and some small round tables where writers could read and discuss one another's projects. There might be something like the "author's chair" of some elementary classrooms, a place where, by custom, writers read their work to others, for response and comment.

So we should re-think the writing classroom in any case. But today there are forces that would drive us to re-think the writing classroom in its present form, even if it were now acceptable to us. The first of these forces is the widespread perception that we are not now doing our job very well. We can assign some, and perhaps most, of this public dissatisfaction with higher education to demographic and economic factors, but we are left with an uncomfortable residue — a feeling that we might, somehow, do better. We cannot be long satisfied with the outcome of our teaching if so many others are dissatisfied.

A second force is the cost of the brick-and-mortar classroom. This conventional classroom must be heated and cooled, lighted and swept, secured and re-painted and maintained — and it will be used for two thirteen-week periods during the year — half of the year! — and only for five days/week — 130 days! — and at most fourteen hours/day. There may be occasional, or even systematic, use of the facility in the off-season, and colleges on trimester or quarter systems may make better use of their facilities, but even with a summer-school and a conscientious division of continuing education, it would be hard to imagine a classroom that was used for more than 50 percent of the hours in a given year. The cost of constructing, maintaining, securing, lighting, heating, and cooling this largely-unused classroom will, given the inevitable rise in energy cost, force us to consider alternatives.

The third force that will drive change in our classrooms is the precipitous drop in the price of computer technology. Though higher education is not now spending widely, or even wisely, on the acquisition of computer technology (Flynn), it won't be too long before the cost of computer and communications equipment will look like a pleasant alternative to the rising, energy-driven cost of the brick-and-mortar classroom. And we writing teachers are well placed to utilize this technology, because we don't need tremendously expensive systems. One can write now, and perhaps forever, on a simple PC, and one can connect, with this same PC, to other writers on other PC's. Despite the advent of multi-media environments, as writing teachers all we really need to work with is a PC and a wire.

Given these I-think-unarguable facts, I look ahead to the "new" writing classroom not as a techno-groupie but as a moderately rational writing teacher, one who is attempting to see the outlines of a future that is sure to arrive. If we were now, as a nation, satisfied with the products of our existing writing classrooms; if our present system of higher education were not rapidly pricing itself out of the American marketplace; and if the cost of computer technology were not dropping exponentially; then the following sections would be, even in my own eyes, self-indulgent. But it seems clear to me and to others (e.g., Tiffin) that the writing classroom of the next millennium will be radically different from the writing classroom of today. In the sections that follow, I will look at two different but related models: the computer-equipped, brick-and-mortar writing classroom, and the "virtual," on-line classroom.

The Computer-Equipped Writing Classroom

It is certain that the new will first inhabit the forms of the old. Indeed, much of the old may persist within the new. We still "drive" automobiles, and we speak of their "horsepower." And the fact that neither of the two books emanating from the recent English Coalition (Lloyd-Jones and Lunsford; Elbow) considers our subject suggests that most of us are not eager to contemplate the changes in school design that lie ahead. We will begin therefore by considering the computer-equipped writing classroom — a brick-and-mortar classroom, with all its attendant energy costs, but one with computers in it — a room that students are scheduled into just as they are into conventional classrooms. This facility will not be more cost-effective than the conventional classroom, but we'll assume that for the near-term we will be reluctant to abandon the ways in which our colleges presently operate in space and time. Students will continue to come to brick-and-mortar classrooms, physical spaces within which teaching and learning occur. Given this assumption, we can ask, "What will these new writing-rooms look like? What will their equipment be? And how will it seem to learn, and to teach, in these rooms?"

I describe here my own college-level, computer-equipped classroom, one that operates on a "MWF" and "TuTh" schedule and serves 16–20 different teachers and classes each semester. The room has a few more workstations than students — to minimize the disruption caused by inevitable hardware failure. The workstations are networked. Each class has its own "area" or section of the subdirectory structure on the file-server's hard disk. Each teacher has, as well, his or her own subdirectory — his or her "desk." Given the ability of LAN-software to "map" and to assign "rights," each class "sees" only its own subdirectory structure, one that can be customized according to its needs but which will remain constant throughout the semester — a "virtual" workplace, where assignments, syllabi, prompts, and peer-responding instructions are kept in read-only form; where work-in-progress is saved in read/write form; and where final products are sent to a "turn-in" subdirectory. In a writing classroom that was not computer-equipped, even one as marvelous as the ideal writing classroom we imagined above, we would not have storage space for all of this paper: we would need twenty file drawers for the writing of all the students in the twenty classes that write in this room; we would need bookshelves for multiple copies of hard-bound dictionaries, handbooks, and thesauri; we would need wall space sufficient for multiple, proprietary blackboards and bulletin boards; and we would need a secure place for teachers to store attendance and grade records. In the computer-equipped classroom, all of this material resides in the system's file-server, which is the size of one instructor's briefcase, or, more accurately, it resides on the file-server's hard disk, which is, at the moment of this writing, the size of a pocket-dictionary.

The materials accessible on the classroom's hard disk become a "virtual space," designed and furnished by the teacher and the students together. We live and work in this virtual classroom through an act of imagining, just as we construct the "virtual" worlds created by novels, plays, poems, and computer-games. Through the screen each class accesses its own bulletin-board, mail-system, virtual filing-and-storage system for student writing, and store of syllabi, schedules, writing prompts, teachers' comments, peer-readers' comments, and attendance records. Teachers may access through the screen their own private files: a "virtual" grade-book, class roster, annotated syllabus, and notes on, let's say, particular students' progress toward particular goals. Given the compression that occurs when you convert print-text into magnetically charged bits of iron oxide, and given a network with a file server with a 300 MB hard disk — trailing-edge technology, as of this writing — there is room in this system for roughly 150,000 pages of double-spaced student writing, or, assuming that we need 60 MB for software and that in a given semester the system will be used by twenty sections of twenty students, the system has the capacity to store some three hundred pages of text per student. Further, students have their own disks, private spaces where they can store hundreds of "pages" of their own material. And all of this electronic text can be made shareable or, to put the matter more accurately, can be copied and re-copied without cost or increase in physical dimension.

In a typical class in this typical computer-equipped writing room, students log in, using their instructor's name and password, and a log-in script invisibly and silently routes them to their class subdirectory structure — their own working environment. What first appears on their screen is a greeting from their instructor, and, let us say, instructions to pick up the day's writing prompt from the Prompt box. Or the instructions may be to read through the final drafts submitted in the Turn-in box, and, opening a second window, to write a response to the author of their, or the teacher's, choice. In one of these "boxes" may also be "magazines" edited by groups of students from work submitted to them in yet another "box." The writers, as they work on their screens, are in their "home room" — a digitized space, a literate environment, filled with writing tools and their own writing.

Where does the teacher fit into this structure? It depends to a considerable degree on the design of the physical and virtual spaces. We could design a computer-equipped classroom that replicated the structure of the conventional classroom — not *my* choice, but a choice nevertheless. To do so, we'd mark a workstation, by position or custom, as the "teacher's place." This workstation could stand at the "head" of the class, facing the students' workstations, in the same layout as that of a conventional classroom, where the teacher's desk faces the students' desks. Or the teacher's workstation could be electronically exalted: through software now available, such as *Real-Time Writer* or *Timbuktu,* the teacher would be given the right to take over student screens, write on them, broadcast to them, or observe them. And the teacher's workstation could have near it an overhead projector, one that permits the teacher's screen to become an electronic chalkboard for purposes of demonstration.

Why would we design a computer-equipped writing classroom in this way? As a small and therefore inefficient lecture hall? Samuel Johnson argued in 1781 that, given the availability of books and the ability to read, lectures were no longer a necessary mode of education (Boswell 1136). Yet in 1987, more than two centuries later, the English Coalition felt the need to argue that the freshman writing course should not be teacher-centered, but should "stress an *active, interactive theory of learning* (rather than a theory of teaching), one that assumes students do not learn by being passive eavesdroppers on an academic conversation or vessels into which knowledge is being poured" (Lloyd-Jones and Lunsford 27; see also Elbow 32). Apparently a change in available media does not significantly change the ways in which teaching and learning are conducted. All I can say, therefore, is that computer technology *presents us with the opportunity* to break with the past and to create interactive writing classrooms.

Let us therefore re-imagine the classroom and the software in such a way that the teacher becomes a member of an interactive community of writers — distinguished from the student writers by degree of writing experience and training, so still clearly the writing teacher, but otherwise inhabiting the same world as the students. With such a goal we would not distinguish a "teacher's workstation" but would set our workstations in sets of six or eight, in "pods" or islands extending from one of the room's walls. The workstations would be identical, but the teacher, given a log-in and password procedure, could be assigned "rights" that students do not have. For instance, the students could be given full read/write rights to several subdirectories, but read-only rights to others.

I am assuming that the teacher and class have the autonomy to build their own "virtual classrooms" — and I need to note here that this is an assumption and a hope, not an inevitable consequence of the character of computer technology. Indeed, network management is difficult, and once you give the users a measure of autonomy, you multiply network management problems exponentially. System managers' need to standardize applications is in sharp conflict with users' need to choose their own applications. At issue here is the teacher's authority within the larger educational system. In America we have been moving to grant teachers more power in their schools. Electronic classrooms will run easier and cheaper from "dumb" terminals which grant access to a single, managed curriculum. Teacher autonomy will be expensive and will make running the system harder — and schools will be tempted to move, as businesses have, toward the "dumb" terminal and the centralized control which this equipment makes easy. What businesses see as an evil — "hanky-panky on the network" (Lewis, sec. 3:4) — may be, for teachers and for students, the lifeblood of creative teaching and learning.

This computer-equipped classroom will have in it, in addition to networked workstations, a range of on-line writer's aids: a beginning, simplified word-processing program and a more powerful word-processing program for those who feel the need for such features as complex formatting, sorting, searching, indexing, and the inclusion of graphics with text. There will be an on-line thesaurus, an on-line dictionary, and an on-line spell-checker. There can be on-line as well style-checkers and a range of programs that function as heuristics, asking the writer questions that are intended to stimulate invention, the generation of ideas. The limit to the number and range of these writers' aids is the teacher's judgment about the extent to which these programs can be helpful to writers.

To the extent that the teacher wants to have students "discuss" on-line, perhaps as a pre-writing activity, a "chat" program like the Daedalus *Interchange* will permit on-line, real-time, written exchange of views: a quick e-mail exchange, in effect, or a rapid epistolary exchange, with instantaneous electronic copies for all participants. Such a program will permit group interaction but with the written language as the medium through which the self is presented. The teacher will have to decide on the degree of autonomy students will have in these on-line, written discussions. Will the teacher begin the session with a prompt? Will the teacher join in the discussion and control "flaming" or discourse that is potentially hurtful to members of the group? Will the teacher direct the formation of sub-conferences or permit students to set up their own? Will the teacher permit students to adopt pseudonyms and thus change their relationship to their written texts? As I have indicated above, the computer-equipped classroom presents us with choices.

A final choice we will have to make in the design of our computer-equipped classroom is the relative value we give to print-text and on-line text. The computer-equipped writing classroom should have printing facilities in it: ideally quiet, laser- or ink-jet printers. The printers will be available to all workstations, through the network. But what uses should teachers make of these printers? On-line text is essentially "free": once the equipment is available, the cost of "printing" a text on-line is zero. Printers, toner, and paper are expensive. For cost effectiveness, both locally and globally, our classes should operate entirely on-line: students submit their writing on-line, and teachers read this writing on-line.

Yet we now live, and will likely continue to live for some time, in an amphibious condition, one where we function both in the "elements" of print-text and on-line text. College curricula are still print-based: there are bookstores, printed lecture-note services, written and proctored examinations, and libraries with huge investments in printed books. Our students will, outside our writing classes, be writing for teachers who will read their work in print-text form. To the extent to which this is true, we'll not want to force our writing students to work exclusively in an environment of electronic text. We will, instead, want to help our students manage the transition between electronic text and print in ways that take advantage of the special characteristics of the two media.

For this reason, our computer-equipped classrooms will have graphics programs and desk-top publishing programs that will permit student writers to format and to publish their work. In some classrooms, document design will become part of the curriculum. In these classrooms, editing "teams" will work collaboratively, through the network, in assembling documents: flyers, brochures, volumes of essays, all published in printed form through xerography. And, so long as the print-culture of higher education requires students to submit "papers" to their teachers, we will need to have in our classroom at least one workstation with a large-screen, 8 1/2 x 11 black-on-white monitor. With this equipment, we can help our students manage both the rhetorical and formal processes involved in effecting the transition from electronic author to print-text reader.

Beyond Time and Place in the
Computer-Equipped Classroom

So far we have been thinking of this computer-equipped classroom as existing in space and time, a function of cinder-blocks, glass, hardware, and wire. We have also, however, considered the extent to which this classroom is a site for the construction of many "virtual" classrooms. The student working in one of these computer-equipped classrooms is physically present but related to a digitized world that is accessed through the class log-in script. In such a networked system that serves many classes, the "reality" that one enters is a function of bricks and mortar, yes, and of the teacher's "live" presence, but this reality is as well a function of one's password, which permits one to enter the virtual world of Prof. Moran's writing class. With another password, you'd enter someone else's class-world, with different software options and a different subdirectory structure, let alone different prompts, messages, journal entries, and files of student writing. In our computer-equipped classrooms at the University of Massachusetts, we see that the computer-equipped classroom begins to break down the physical sense of "the class." When I and my class are scheduled into Bartlett 105, the computer-equipped classroom, I work with my own students, to be sure, but it is likely that there will be in the room also a few students from other sections, logged into their own digitized class environments, and even the occasional teacher, doing class preparation, logged into his or her own subdirectory structure. Our teachers report that on occasion these "visitors" choose to join in, finding the work of the class to their taste. So even in this somewhat retrograde brick-and-mortar computer-equipped classroom, the boundaries of the "class" begin to become permeable, and we begin to see that the "class," defined as a packet of students delivered to a particular place at a particular time, is not a given, unless one accepts the inevitability of the industrial model.

The next step in this deconstruction of the "class" will be to connect our computer-equipped classroom, through bulletin-board or e-mail soft-ware, to information sources outside the room. Through telephone lines we can access data bases such as on-line library catalogues. Through these same telephone lines we can connect with resource persons outside the classroom, bringing their expertise and perspective into our rapidly expanding virtual world. At the 1990 Conference on Computers and Writing in Austin, Texas, we heard of a class that had in this way made contact with a District Attorney and had used this contact to gain direct access to both information and professional opinion relative to a topic the group was writing about. The virtues of this system, as explained by the speaker, were those of an e-mail system: the District Attorney could, on his own schedule, read the communications from the students and write his responses. For him, this situation was feasible. A "live" class visit would not have been possible (Hughes). Or we could connect our writing class with another writing class, as has been happening through networks such as BreadNet, which operates out of Middlebury College in Vermont. We could bring together in an on-line conference writing classes that were from different cultures — say a northern urban school with a school in the mountains of Kentucky.

But now I begin to anticipate our next move, a move into the writing classroom that exists entirely and solely on-line. Oh for hypertext!

The On-Line Classroom

The on-line class now exists. Indeed, on page 30 of the November 1990 *Education Life* section of the *New York Times,* there is an advertisement for the "American Open University of NYIT," or New York Institute of Technology. The advertisement reads as follows: "The modern way for adults to pursue an undergraduate degree without having to attend traditional classes. Obtain a baccalaureate degree in such areas as business, behavioral sciences, and general studies through computer teleconferencing anywhere in the world." The phrase *open university* connects the NYIT program with a similar program at the Open University in Great Britain, described in the work of Kaye, Mason, and Rumble. Other academic programs delivered solely through computer conferencing are described by Naidu, Mason, Roberts, and McCreary. And in a recent article Romiszowski writes, "In the state of New York alone, more than 100 educational establishments use some form of teleconferencing to supplement, or supplant, face-to-face education" (234). Research into this area brings us into contact with such established conventions as the abbreviations CC (Computer Conferencing) and CMC (Computer-mediated Communication) and such established journals as *Distance Education* and the *American Journal of Distance Education.*

So in imagining an on-line writing classroom we are not engaging in ungrounded fantasy. There are many on-line courses now being taught. In England, Canada, and the United States, these courses are generally offered, as the NYIT advertisement suggests, to adults who for one reason or another can not be in our conventional classrooms M-W-F 10:05 A.M. and who, because of work and parenting schedules, need to work and learn when they can. In other areas, such as Micronesia and northern Canada, where a physical meeting of a class is not economically feasible, "distance learning" is the only alternative, and, with satellite uplinks, computer conferencing "may well be the fastest growing area of applications of technology to communication and education" (Romiszowski 236).

What would an on-line writing classroom "look" like? It would have three elements, both separable and potentially interactive: (1) a "mail" system; (2) a "filing," or storage-and-retrieval system; and (3) a computer-mediated conferencing system. For the sake of clarity, I will look at these three subsystems separately.

The on-line mail system makes possible a writing course that is much like the learn-to-write-by-mail services that are advertised in such publications as *Writer's Market* or *Writer's Digest,* or the conference-based writing class envisioned by Lester Fisher and Donald Murray. The essential transaction in this model is that between the writer and the editor. Writers send their writing via a "mail" system; the writing is read, and the editor sends a response by return mail. The editor could be the teacher, or could be students, or both in some mixture and alternation, depending upon the teacher's and students' values and goals.

The virtues of editing on-line are several: the editors can edit at their convenience, picking up the manuscript at any time of day; the editor will comment in writing and, in so doing, practice both writing and editing skills; and the editor can take the time to reflect and even return to and modify the first response with a subsequent re-vision or re-mailing of the second thoughts. Important here is the fast turn-around made possible by CMC; Kaye notes that in a correspondence course the typical turn-around time is three weeks (Mason and Kaye, 12). During this interval, Kaye notes, the student has most often proceeded to a new piece of the course, so the feedback comes too late to be useful. On-line, the turn-around can be rapid and therefore more effective.

The disadvantages of on-line editing are clear: the difficulty of making comments in a "margin" and the difficulty of drawing arrows and lines — the kinds of editing that we have become so used to on paper do not yet have their equivalent on-line. Red-lining programs are mildly useful, but they tend to be unwieldly and they produce a text that, with its embedded deletions and additions, is difficult to read. Yet the speed of response may more than compensate for the difficulties we now have in commenting flexibly and economically on-line on an extended piece of writing. And hypertext holds the promise of an environment where comments-on-text can be more easily made and received.

In addition to the "mail" system, the on-line classroom would include a virtual storage-and-retrieval system. In this electronic filing cabinet would be all texts produced by the group — more-or-less formal pieces of writing, editors' comments, all mail-messages sent during the semester, texts brought in by members of the group as references, examples, authority. Available also would be transcripts of the on-line conferences, retrievable by author or topic. Our class storage area would be connected to on-line, public data bases that students could search as they needed to for their own or their group's writing. We would need to establish protocols that would permit privacy, where appropriate, and access, where appropriate. We can imagine that access to our "classroom's" storage area would be limited to the members of the class itself. It might be important for each member of the class, and here I include the teacher, to have his or her own virtual desk — either housed in memory in the host computer or in the memory of the participant's own workstation — in either case a part of the virtual classroom. The student and teacher would be at their "desks," at school, at home, or wherever, and could log into the "class" at any time.

A third element in our on-line writing course would be the computer-mediated conference (CMC), a process that may, as some predict, "ultimately emerge as a new educational paradigm, taking its place alongside both face-to-face and distance education" (Kaye, "Computer-Mediated" 3). CMC is seen by some (e.g., Feenberg 26) to hold the "promise that writing will once again become a universal form of expression," as "written," on-line conferences and e-mail exchanges begin to be used instead of voice communication by telephone.

The computer-mediated conference is a much more flexible medium than the two-way epistolary correspondence. And, whereas the "mail" and "filing" functions are individual in their orientation, CMC is potentially — some would say inevitably — social and interactive. Through the conference, the teacher and students together can design an on-line classroom that is as full and functional as is the digitized environment stored in the file-server of our computer-equipped writing classroom, described above. That the students are connected to the system by telephone lines, rather than by an Ethernet wire, might seem for most purposes irrelevant. In such a classroom the teacher and students can orchestrate reading-and-writing groups, on-line, written discussions, brain storming bulletin-board sessions, and on-line publication. The response-time in this on-line classroom would on occasion be slower than it is in a classroom where readers and writers are physically present, but it is not clear that a somewhat relaxed and deliberate cycle of writing-and-response is a disadvantage. And quasi-synchronous conferencing sessions, such as those made possible by Interchange in the computer-equipped classroom, are possible to arrange on-line, though for these sessions the class would have to agree to be on-line simultaneously.

Researchers and practitioners have found, too, that CMC is a new and not unproblematic communication medium. Face-to-face communication occurs in a rich context of cues: tone of voice, gesture, facial expression. Andrew Feenberg asserts that "In computer conferencing the only tacit sign we can transmit is our silence, a message that is both brutal and ambiguous" (34). CMC, using as it does just the written word, requires that we pay attention to context-building. This context-building can be the work of the teacher-moderator, whose work, according to Feenberg (35–36), consists of creating an initial context for the discussion, setting norms, setting agenda, recognizing and prompting the participants, "meta-commenting," or dealing with "problems in context, norms, or agenda, clarity, irrelevance, and information overload" (35), and "Weaving," which is "to summarise the state of the discussion and to find unifying threads in participants' comments" (35). Part of the context-building may be one or more face-to-face meetings. All this, Feenberg states, is "an admission of defeat" (37) — the medium is not yet good enough to do what we'd like it to do. Feenberg's teacher-moderator sounds, however, suspiciously like the present classroom teacher who leads and facilitates a classroom discussion. Perhaps Feenberg is right: computer-mediated conferences may require a leader/facilitator. But it is just as likely that we will develop new conventions — such as the "emoticons" of e-mail correspondence — once we have learned to live and work in our virtual classrooms.

The structures of the on-line classroom can help the participants imagine not just a "virtual classroom" but a "virtual college," a complete educational environment. Lynn Davie carefully constructs a range of "sites" in her computer-mediated conferences: "I may call the main discussion the seminar room; provide a faculty office for advising; provide a small meeting room for informal interactions or help; provide an in-basket for student assignments; or provide workspaces for small group projects, subjects, etc" (79). Davie goes on to say that these metaphors can "help the student learn to navigate" the conference but notes as well that "we need to examine closely the advantages and disadvantages of different metaphors" (79). The context-setting metaphors can be visual and iconic as well as verbal. Alexander and Lincoln have described a graphical-user interface for their Thought Box project, one that permits students to choose from among boxes in the "Courses Building" which consist of "T101 News," "T101 Activities," "T101 Assignments," and "T101 Forum"; from boxes in the "Student Union" which consist of "Book Exchange," "Forum," "Help and Advice," and "Classified Ads": and from icons such as "The Library," in- and out-baskets, newspapers, calendars, calculators, and class notes (90–91). With the graphical interface used by the Open University, we make a full move from the "virtual classroom" to a "virtual university." The "Electronic Campus Map" of the Open University presents the user with a graphic "map," with paths connecting six "buildings" — the Mail Building, the Staff Building, the Courses Building, the Student Union, the Tutorial Building, and the Resource and Information Center (Mason 117). Each building is faced with panels that represent choices that you'd make by "clicking" on the panel with a mouse: the Mail Building, for example, has panels labelled "in tray," "out tray," "your mail," "tutor A's mail," and so on. To the north of the Mail Building is a park-like space, with strolling people in it, labelled "Conversation area."

The "context" of the on-line classroom can include virtual spaces that stretch or exceed the academic metaphor that seems now to be the norm. Connections to non-academic settings, where students can participate in writing tasks that are being undertaken in worlds outside the college and the university, make possible a virtual "office" space where writers from workplaces join writers from the academy in collaborative writing tasks. In the conventional classroom, the logistics of such an undertaking make it extremely difficult. The working writer does not have time to come to class to explain the context; interaction-at-a-distance is too slow for both sides of this transaction. On-line, we can construct a virtual space where the student writers and writers at worksites meet to discuss the writing task in progress.

What Do We Gain? Lose?

But what is lost in this new classroom? I think of Walt Whitman here, who saw the end of writing in the invention of the typewriter (Traubel 314). Will the on-line classroom be the end of our teaching? Certainly we lose face-to-face contact. But might we not generate another relationship, a different intimacy that might have its own virtues? Might the virtual classroom foster new relationships and new kinds of learning?

Researchers in this field have found that distance learning is often as effective as face-to-face instruction (Chute; George). Barbara Grabowski et al. have summarized the research in the field, conspicuously citing the work of Linda Harasim, who found that students in an on-line, computer-mediated conference experienced and demonstrated increased initiative and increased responsibility for their own learning, and of Downing et al., who found that in an on-line engineering course, students "asked more challenging questions, and that students reported high-quality instructor responses to their inquiries" (Grabowski, Pusch, and Pusch). And Starr Hiltz finds that for some learners, CMC is a better learning environment than the brick-and-mortar classroom. In her study, Hiltz finds also that students reacted more favorably to the on-line environment when the courses were constructed in such a way as to foster collaborative learning. She notes as well that one computer-mediated conference was still going strong a month after the end of the semester, "with over a hundred new entries which continued to discuss the issues raised in the course" (7). Hiltz's findings are supported by Linda Harasim, who argues that "as a medium, it [CMC] is particularly conducive to information-sharing, brain-storming, networking, and group synergy" (61), and by McCreary, who finds that CMC has enriched the entire academic culture at her university, the University of Guelph, Ontario.

Given the research now extant, the proposition that on-line classrooms are somehow cold and impersonal and therefore in some way dangerous is arguable. Is an epistolary relationship less warm, less personal, less intimate than a "live" relationship? Is a class conducted through a computer-mediated conference less warm, less personal, less intimate than a face-to-face classroom experience? Given the powers of the human imagination, are human warmth and a sense of intimacy necessarily dependent upon physical presence? There is some doubt.

The on-line writing classroom has much to offer. It has all the virtues of distance education, in that it opens the class to people who cannot, for one reason or another, travel to a particular place at a particular time. The on-line classroom does not require the heating, cooling, and maintenance of the conventional classroom. And the on-line classroom does not require travel to a physical place, a factor that is now crucial in areas of low population density, but given that the cost of travel increases at double the rate of inflation (Chute 265), it will become increasingly important in all institutions of higher education. But perhaps more important, because the on-line classroom offers such wide access, it creates the possibility that classes could be more diverse than they now are: on-line writing classes could be deliberately composed of writers from different backgrounds, of different ages, and of different cultures. Such classes could become forums for our emerging cultural democracy. Further, the on-line, computer-mediated conference may be a site that will encourage the emancipating discourse envisioned by Boyd, Cooper, and Selfe, and Flores — discourse in which status is less than it now is a function of race, gender, and class.

Clearly there are differences between on-line and "live" teaching and learning. These differences may seem to some to be losses. To the extent that students and teachers have experienced agency in "live" teaching situations, both will experience the virtual classroom as change and perhaps discomfort. Shoshana Zuboff has described the dislocation felt by workers at industrial sites as they moved from the foundry floor to the air-conditioned, information-processing booths above the floor. It would be extraordinary to imagine that students and teachers would not feel the sense of loss that attends the change in the nature of their work. To the extent that students and teachers have learned to be "good on their feet" in oral, face-to-face discussion, we'd expect the on-line environment to seem to them restrictive: impersonal, cold, devoid of human contact. And, so long as the on-line environment is created by the written language, students with learning disabilities that affect the production and reception of the written language will be at a disadvantage.

But, despite the fact that for some this will be a difficult transition and despite the fact that questions of access and equity remain to be addressed, for the reasons I have laid out above — our national dissatisfaction with schools as they are, the rising energy-cost of such schools, and the decreasing cost of computer and communications technology — we need to begin now to consider the shape that our writing classrooms may take in the second millennium. The two writing rooms I have described — the computer-equipped, brick-and-mortar classroom and the computer-mediated, on-line classroom — both now exist. From my perspective, writing now in 1991, they will soon, perhaps by the year 2050, seem entirely normal. John Tiffin argues that "the fibre optic telecommunication system will be to the current copper-based telephone system what the railway lines were to a donkey-track." Given the emerging capacity for electronic communication, he argues, "It seems highly unlikely that schools will survive in anything like their present form" (240). I think that Tiffin is right. It is time to begin to build, at least in our imaginations, the writing class of the coming virtual age.

Works Cited

Alexander, Gary, and Ches Lincoln. "The Thought Box: A Computer-Based Communication System to Support Distance Learning." Mason and Kaye 86–100.

Boswell, James. *The Life of Samuel Johnson, LL.D.* Ed. R.W. Chapman. London: Oxford UP, 1960.

Boyd, Gary. "Emancipative Educational Technology." *Canadian Journal of Educational Technology* 16.2 (1987): 167–72.

Chute, Alan G. "Strategies for Implementing Teletraining Systems." *Educational and Training Technology International* 27.3 (1990): 264–70.

Cooper, Marilyn M. and Cynthia L. Selfe. "Computer Conferences and Learning: Authority, Resistance, and Internally Persuasive Discourse." *College English* 52.8 (1990): 847–69.

Davie, Lynn. "Facilitation Techniques for the On-Line Tutor." Mason and Kaye 74–85.

Elbow, Peter. *What Is English?* New York: MLA, 1990.

Feenberg, Andrew. "The Written World: On the Theory and Practice of Computer Conferencing." Mason and Kaye 22–39.

Fisher, Lester, and Donald Murray. "Perhaps the Professor Should Cut Class." *College English* 35 (1973): 169–73.

Flores, Mary J. "Computer Conferencing: Composing a Feminist Community of Writers." *Computers and Community*. Ed. Carolyn Handa. Portsmouth: Boynton, 1990. 106–17.

Flynn, Laurie. "Funding PC Purchases Is Low Priority on Campus." *InfoWorld* 12.42 (1990): 5.

Frangston, Robert. Interview "Welcome to the *Byte* Summit." *Byte* 15.9 (1990): 271.

George, Judith. "Audioconferencing — just another Small Group Activity." *Educational and Training Technology International* 27.3 (1990): 244–48.

Grabowski, Barbara, and Suciati and Wende Pusch. "Social and Intellectual Value of Computer-Mediated Communications in a Graduate Community." *Educational and Training Technology International* 27.3 (1990): 276–83.

Harasim, Linda. "On-Line Education: A New Domain." Mason and Kaye 50–73.

Hiltz, Starr R. "Collaborative Learning in a Virtual Classroom: Highlights of Findings." Paper presented at the Computer Supported Cooperative Work Conference, June 1988. Revision for CSCW Proceedings. ED 305–895.

Hughes, Bradley. "The Police Chief, The Judge, The District Attorney, and The Defender: Using Networked Writing to Bring Professionals into an Undergraduate Course on Criminal Justice." Paper given at the Sixth Conference on Computers and Writing, Austin, TX, 17–20 May 1990.

Kaye, Anthony. "Computer-Mediated Communication and Distance Education." Mason and Kaye 3–21.

———. "Computer Conferencing for Education and Training: Project Description." Project Report CCET/1. Open University, Walton, Bletchley, Bucks (England). Institute of Technology. 1985. ED 273–60.

Lewis, Peter H. "The Executive Computer," *New York Times* 6 June 1990, sec. 3:4.

Lloyd-Jones, Richard, and Andrea Lunsford. *The English Coalition Conference: Democracy through Language*. Urbana, Ill: NCTE, 1989.

Mason, Robin and Anthony Kaye, eds. *Mindweave*. New York: Pergamon P, 1989.

Mason, Robin. "An Evaluation of CoSy on an Open University Course." Mason and Kaye 115–45.

———. "Computer Conferencing: A Contribution to Self-Directed Learning." *British Journal of Educational Technology* 19.1 (1988): 28–41.

McCreary, Elaine. "Computer-Mediated Communication and Organisational Culture." Mason and Kaye 101–12.

Moran, Charles. "The Computer-Writing Room: Authority and Control." *Computers and Composition* 7.2 (1990): 61–70.

Naidu, Som. "Computer Conferencing in Distance Education." 1988. ED 310–74.

Roberts, Lowell. "The Electronic Seminar: Distance Education by Computer Conferencing." Paper presented at the Fifth Annual Conference on Non-Traditional and Interdisciplinary Programs, Fairfax, VA, May 1987. ED 291–358.

Romiszowski, Alexander. "Shifting Paradigms in Education and Training: What Is the Connection with Telecommunications?" *Educational and Training Technology International* 27.3 (1990): 233–36.

Rumble, Greville. "The Use of Microcomputers in Distance Teaching Systems." ZIFF Papiere 70, Fernuniversitat, Hagen (West Germany), 1988.

Selfe, Cynthia L. "Technology in the English Classroom: Computers through the Lens of Feminist Theory. *Computers and Community*. Ed. Carolyn Handa. Portsmouth: Boynton, 1990. 118–39.

Tiffin, John. "Telecommunications and the Trade in Teaching." *Educational and Training Technology International* 27.3 (1990): 240–44.

Traubel, Horace. *With Walt Whitman in Camden*. New York: Rowman, 1961.

Tyack, David B. *The One Best System*. Cambridge: Harvard UP, 1974.

Zuboff, Shoshana. *In the Age of the Smart Machine: The Future of Work and Power*. New York: Basic, 1988.

Moran's Insights as a Resource for Your Teaching

1. You may be a novice or you may already have designed your writing class-room to take advantage of computer technology. Look at your experiences, as a student or a writer, with computers and writing and reflect on your prac-tices as you wrote by hand, by computer, or by some mix. In your double-entry journal, write entries prompted by these questions: What can I do with my computer-equipped, brick and mortar classroom? What if I shifted to a computer-mediated, online classroom? Use that speculation as you design your course syllabus and when you visit with the support staff on your cam-pus who help faculty use academic computing resources.

2. Moran provides a clear overview of "computer-equipped" and "computer-mediated" writing sites and describes some practices in specific detail. He also provides a useful bibliography containing theoretical perspectives and practical advice that can broaden your understanding of computers and class-rooms. You can also use online resources, both local and national. Many public discussions about writing, pedagogy, composition theory, rhetorical theory, and cultural-studies theory foster conversation among teachers and research-ers.

   If you haven't listened in yet, try one of the following lists. To subscribe to any that pique your interest, send a note. For example, subscribe to a list for writing program administrators by sending a note to listserv@asuvm.inre .asu.edu.

   LISTPROC@LISTSERV.TTU.EDU   The Alliance for Computers and Writing is open to anyone interested in using computing technologies in their writ-ing classrooms. This professionional organization is dominated by young writing instructors and researchers, but you will also find many veteran teach-ers and researchers like Moran participating in the on-line conversations.

   PRETEXT@ONRAMP.NET   On this list sponsored by Victor Vitanza, you'll find conversations tending more toward rhetorical and cultural-studies theory, and ranging from substantive, structured scholarly discussions of theory to open conversation lists.

Moran's Insights as a Resource for the Writing Classroom

1. Moran encourages us to reimagine the classroom and software so that the writing instructor is a member of an interactive writing community. Like the pedagogy of Paolo Freire indicates, the instructor would be a "master learner" working collaboratively with "learners" (as opposed to "students," who are acted on rather than agents). However, with computers and writing, some learners would be the "master learners" for the teacher and their peers. This is particularly the case when you equip or mediate a writing classroom with computers. Write a questionnaire or journal prompt to survey the expertise with computers and writing that students bring to your classroom. It's likely that several of your students have gone further in cyberspace than others, and they can be helpful guides and troubleshooters.

2. If you don't have access to a networked classroom or lab, improvise and set up an "electronic conference" on e-mail to facilitate online written discus-sions. The electronic conference can enhance invention strategies: it provides a "safe" space for writers to ask whether a topic or thesis or organization or persona sounds "okay" to peers; writers can also eavesdrop on discussions of writing and learn how peers might respond to a prompt. The conversation is "linear" (as opposed to real-time, with instantaneous electronic copies to all class members), but it is leagues beyond the classtime-bound conversa-tions of the traditional classroom.

   If you haven't set up such a conference before, you can learn how by following the tutorial that accompanies your e-mail software. Moran's questions will be helpful as you work with an electronic conference. He doesn't pose a question about how writers might "contextualize" their contribution and write for online readers.

When participating in e-conferences peers use direct address to a specific "speaker" online, restate themes or passages to bring the conversation back to the strand they want to follow, and cite specific "speakers" and statements, including and acknowledging other participants in the discussion. They follow the oral conventions of conversation or jam sessions when they can't see their audience and seem, so far, to be writing to their online listeners more consciously than they write to readers of their print texts.

PATRICIA R. WEBB   *Narratives of Self in Networked Communications*

According to the Daedalus Web site, the InterChange *interactive writing program*

> *facilitates synchronous, or 'real-time,' discussions for whole classes, small groups, or both simultaneously. Students compose private messages and send them to all the members of a discussion group for immediate viewing. Transcripts of these discussions are automatically saved to your fileserver, and can be saved to disk or printed and reviewed at any time.*

Some theorists argue that Daedalus InterChange *and similar programs herald the birth of a new writing genre. They claim that online discussion radically transforms the writing process and liberates both student and teacher from traditional rules and assumptions. In the following essay, Patricia Webb refutes this theory, suggesting that* InterChange *and other networked programs can "easily coexist with . . . humanist conceptions of the author as a unitary genius writing alone in his garret" (p. 181). Webb believes that students and teachers have much to gain from working with* InterChange *and related technologies, but she does not propose that technology alone can revolutionize the way students think, write, and revise. Webb takes a more cautious approach to online learning, recommending that teachers challenge students' assumptions about online discussion and authorship, and suggests ways to use dialogic technologies to their advantage.*

> While electronic discourse explodes the belief in a stable unified self, it offers a means of exploring how identity is multiply constructed and how agency resides in the power of connecting with others and building alliances.
> – Lester Faigley (199), discussing his experience with *InterChange*

> I usually don't use other people's writing to write my own piece. I may get a few ideas from other sources but I don't think that only using a few of your own sentences in a piece is a good idea.
> – Paula[1] in an *InterChange* discussion about writing processes

The contradictions between Faigley's assertion that authorship is radically changed by Daedalus *InterChange* discussions and Paula's individualistic and traditional description of her writing offered during an actual *InterChange* session in one of my composition courses are striking. They highlight the problematic claims surrounding networked communications used in the classroom. Although it has been argued that the unified stable self is challenged by the inclusion of networked technologies in our classrooms (Barker and Kemp; Batson; Bolter; Faigley; Joyce; Landow; Spender; Turkle), students' own usage of these technologies and their reflective accounts of their interactions in those spaces suggest that, far from being radical, technologies such as *InterChange* easily coexist with and are supportive of humanist conceptions of the author as a unitary genius writing alone in his garret. Unless we emphasize critical use (Hawisher and Selfe) of networked technologies, we will perpetuate the ideas of self and author we are supposedly challenging by including these new technologies in our classrooms.

My experience with using networked technologies in composition courses was that our *InterChange* discussions allowed students to explicitly describe their perceptions of themselves as writers, perceptions that were grounded in humanist notions of the unitary, rational self. Soliciting our students' perceptions and making them a focal point of discussion is an important first step; however, once these ideas are clearly laid out, it is then crucial that we explicitly and concretely illustrate the ways networked technologies can alter these traditional conceptions. This second component is difficult to implement in a climate shaped by technological enthusiasm untempered by theoretical reflection about technologies' implications. This paper highlights ways the unitary self was reasserted throughout the *InterChange* discussions in my two composition courses during the Fall of 1995, explores the necessity of critically using network technologies to question students' assumptions about writing, and points to practical ways of critically integrating technologies into our composition classrooms.

Current Research on Network Technologies' Influences on Student Writers

Since the introduction of computer networking into composition classrooms across the country, instructors who have included networked conversations in their classrooms have acknowledged the changes that occur in students' writing as a result. Not only do these technologies change what students are writing, theorists claim, but they radically change what it means to write. Asserting that real-time conferencing programs allow a heteroglossia of voices, Paul Taylor suggested that "computer conferencing is evolving into a new genre, a new form of communication that has not been possible before now" (145). Echoing this idea of a new genre of communication, M. Diane Langston and Trent Batson found in their research that networks used in composition classrooms help students develop a sense of a "real" audience and interact more with their peers. On the basis of these findings, they argued that network technologies can create a sense of community in the classroom that would otherwise be impossible. Expanding on this notion of community, Thomas Barker and Fred Kemp stated that although "the usual complaint against using computers pedagogically in the classroom is that they isolate students. . . . Actually the opposite occurs when computers are networked and programmed to manage text transactions between class members" (16). And, in their research, Kathleen Skubikowski and John Elder noted that "what surprised us was the degree to which networked corresponding enhanced our creation of a writing community" (104). At the heart of these theorists' arguments and findings, then, is the assertion that networked technologies such as *InterChange* allowed instructors to implement social constructionist ways of thinking in their classrooms, thus challenging traditional notions of what it means to write.

Even students in my composition course touted the great possibilities of networked communication. When asked to reflect on how *InterChange* discussions differed from traditional interactions in a classroom, Lucas wrote that

> in class discussions a person's ideas may be lost because they did not have the chance to respond before the topic was changed. In the *InterChange* everyone

got to respond. Whether or not a person wanted to "hear" them was their choice. (journal entry)

To the same question, Erin responded that

the *InterChange* discussion seems very different from regular classroom discussion. It seems as though everybody offers more ideas on the computer. There is a lot more interaction among students on the *InterChange*. . . . I enjoyed giving my opinions and receiving feedback specifically directed back to me. (journal entry)

These student comments echo Trent Batson's claim that "networks create an unusual opportunity to shift away from the traditional writing classroom because they create entirely new pedagogical dynamics" (32). And, like some students who did not like the *InterChange* discussions at first but came to find the discussions useful as the semester progressed, many composition theorists too note the drawbacks of networked technologies only to reach the conclusion that even with the drawbacks, they will still use the technologies because of the overwhelming benefits. Geoffrey Sirc and Thomas Reynolds claimed that after two years of using networked technologies in their classrooms, they were

happy with the results we see in the transcripts. Students may not always enjoy the reading and writing assignments we give them, but they see the logic of them and, more importantly, they are always willing to discuss ideas and concepts. . . . You can found a course on network interaction, we feel, but you must let it all ride on the *InterChange*, lift off the lid and see for yourself, and let students see for themselves, what sort of exotic things are under there. (156)

Despite the problems they encountered while using computer-mediated communications (CMC) technologies, these theorists clearly still emphasized the benefits over the drawbacks, suggesting that the changes in the concept of authorship created by the technologies were worth the hassles they may have faced.

One of the most persuasive proponents of the claim that networked technologies change traditional notions of writer and writing is Dale Spender. She contended that because we are entering a new phase, one in which print technology and computer technology are beginning to combine, what it means to be an author is radically changing. In *Nattering on the Net*, Spender argued that computer technologies, especially network technologies, allow more people to author texts online. The usual gatekeeping systems of print technology (publishers, editors, and reviewers) seem to have little place in this new online conversation, and thus, Spender contended, authorship is being democratized. The self that produces text online is allowed and even encouraged to be multiple, contradictory, and unstable. As a result, she argued that "we are now on course to see composition as a human skill, the production of information as a human right, within the range of all individuals and not just limited as a privilege of a professional few" (86).

But how different are electronic classrooms? How do they challenge the usual ways of thinking about our students' relationship to writing? The previously described claims seem to suggest that all that is needed to change the traditional view of authorship is to have students write together online or talk to one another about writing online. We all know by now that this is an overly simplistic solution to complex problems writing instructors face today. And, although I admire Spender's (and others') enthusiasm and want to believe her predictions, I am hesitant to accept that network technologies are democratizing or that they change our conception of what it means to be a self writing.

For some composition theorists, the euphoria produced by computer technologies has begun to wear off, and they are now moving toward a more moderate view, arguing for critical and reflective use of these technologies. These voices from within the academy argue that there is nothing inherent in network technologies that assures communication occurring there will challenge the humanist rational self; rather, it is how the technology is used and presented that counts — the pedagogy. Supporting this point, Gail Hawisher and Cynthia Selfe wrote that "if electronic technology is to help us bring about positive changes in writing classes, we must identify and confront the potential problems that computers pose and redirect our efforts" (56). They do not claim that technology is inherently bad, so therefore we should not use it; rather, they caution us to think critically about our use and to pay close attention to the problems that arise as we use network technologies. Their "objections lie not in the use of computer technology and on-line conferences but rather in the uncritical enthusiasm that frequently characterizes the reports of those of us who advocate and support electronic writing classes" (56). They thus critiqued those who uncritically embrace technologies as the automatic answer to problems of authorship and authority in the classroom. Network technologies *can* help us challenge traditional notion of authorship and authority, they contended, but only if used critically and reflexively.

Because of the enthusiasm for new technologies and because of theorists' promises of change, I chose to include several *InterChange* discussions throughout the semester in my composition class. I integrated the *InterChange* discussions into our other class work even while I made them the basis for discussion. For example, before the first discussion, students read a piece in which an author described his writing process. We then used *InterChange* to discuss the students' responses to the author's unorthodox approach to writing. I then made our *InterChange* discussion the "text" for analysis in the next class period, asking students for responses to the medium. In this way, I attempted to change the shape of my classroom by giving students more of a voice in the initial discussion and then asking them to reflect on how that space felt to them. My goal was to use the technology critically and reflexively. But as I analyzed the transcripts of our many *InterChange* discussions throughout the semester, I realized that though students were using a new medium, they still clung to many of the same rules and expectations of traditional classroom discussion: Students still conceived of themselves as unitary and stable selves who had to come up with their own ideas in order for them to count. If they relied on their discussions with others to generate their essays and if others helped them write their papers, their work did not count — it was not a rightful text unless they had produced it in isolation and could then claim their ideas exclusively as their own. The comments students made during *InterChange* discussions and in journal reflections about *InterChange* discussions suggest that the discussions did not reveal the social nature of writing. Although Langston and Batson contended that "in an electronic, conversational writing environment, the position of individuals in ongoing social dialectics is more obvious and concrete. . . . Collaboration and social context attain a practical reality" (151), my students' comments and reflections seemed to present the opposite view.

Furthermore, *InterChange* discussions were viewed as an extension of class discussions rather than as a text that could be integrated into students' own writing or could help them generate their own writing. They did not see that they were collectively producing a text based on group knowledge, as Barker and Kemp have claimed;[2] instead, they thought they were "talking." And in a composition class, "talking" supposedly does not count.[3] Although Langston and Batson suggested that real-time conversations online effectively help students merge the conversation and the composing process, students in my classes did not make the connection between what they were doing in *InterChange* discussions and what they did when they were composing their papers. What I found, then, is that even though I had incorporated this supposedly "radical" technology into my classroom, students' conceptions of what it meant to write and to be an author were not in the least changed by their experiences with *InterChange*. The narrative of author as singular self is strongly held indeed. These narratives prevailed in my students' reflections about writing (or speaking) in *InterChange* discussions. Although network technologies can offer us opportunities to challenge traditional notions of self, we must first understand how strongly entrenched those narratives are and what shape they take before we can begin to consider disrupting them. Merely introducing technology into the classroom is not, as I found, a guarantee that these narratives will be disrupted.

My experiences with using *InterChange* in my composition classes, then, complicated my notions of what it means to be an online writer and writing teacher in college classrooms. Unabashed enthusiasm or hype about technology in the classroom leads to a further propagation of the humanist view of the writer as single, autonomous individual who must create his work in isolation for it to be considered important work. If we introduce technology without explaining to students the ways it can be used, we are encouraging them to place traditional narratives of self onto new technology. If we do not bring their perceptions of technologies and writing to the foreground and make these perceptions part of class discussion, we make no headway. Once we engage their perceptions and assumptions, we can teach students to use the technology to collaborate with one another, to question their assumptions about writing, and to expand their concept of audience. Relying upon the hype without critiquing it will reproduce the classroom we claim network technologies challenge.

The Self Reiterated: *InterChange* Discussions on Writing

My experience using Daedalus *InterChange* in writing classes suggests that students can adapt to new technologies without challenging their notions of self. Having extensively read the many sides of the debate concerning computer technologies, during the Fall of 1995, I again decided to include *InterChange* discussions in both my writing classes, this time in two sections of the university's introductory first-year composition course. The first session took place in the second week of the semester. It centered on a piece of writing I had asked the students to read for that class period. The piece, written by Michael Greer, a production editor with the National Council of Teachers of English in Urbana, Illinois, explained the process he used to write a book "annotation" that would be printed on the back cover of a book:

> I'll describe here the process I used to produce a single piece of copy, a two hundred-word annotation that would be used as a jacket blurb and marketing copy, in promotional fliers, and on-line advertising. The book I had to write this copy for was *Critical Theory and the Teaching of Literature,* edited by James F. Slevin and Art Young; it's a college-level collection of essays by twenty-one different contributors. Given that the book would occupy a crowded field, I had to write marketing copy that would make the book sound new, different, exciting. I had to write a description that would make people want to buy the book. I had a relatively set format and voice in which to write the piece; in other words, the conventions were more or less set for me: I had to work within the parameters defined by "annotation" and "marketing copy." (1)

As part of a unit that focused on writing processes, I asked students to respond to his writing process and to compare it to their own.

My first class was composed of fifteen students, nine women and six men. From the beginning of the semester, they, as a group, were talkative in face-to-face interactions. It was not surprising, then, that the group actively responded to one another during the first *InterChange* session, even though they did not know each other well. In her reflections about her first *InterChange* experience, Ava explained that

> at the beginning many of us did not know each other so it was even less difficult to say what we wanted to say. But we all could get an idea of how the class as a whole felt on a particular subject. . . . Some people decided to have their own conversations, while others remained on the main topic of concern. Others started their own topics by asking their own questions or expressing their opinions. Regardless, every ones "voice" was heard. (journal comments)

Students quickly adapted to the mechanics of the program: they learned that text scrolled by quickly and that they would have to scroll back up to read it; as Ava pointed out, they realized that several conversations could be held concurrently and that maneuvering in this space required different skills than were required in traditional classroom discussions; they learned that they could respond directly to others and ask questions of others without first going through me, the instructor. The first *InterChange* session was different from traditional classroom discussions in that it disrupted the usual initiation, response, evaluation pattern (Mehan). In a journal response, Amy summed the experience up, saying

> *InterChange* discussions are different from in class discussions for many reasons. I can respond whenever I want to and do not have to "wait my turn," I can take my time and think about what others have written before responding, I can talk specifically to one person, I can change the topic if I so desire, I can ignore comments, I can see direct feedback from others about my own ideas and thoughts.

Clarence, the first to post a comment, writes "Hi everyone!" This prompt elicits several responses, all of a chatty, getting-to-know-one-another nature. Just as the students greeted each other when they entered the traditional classroom space, on *InterChange* they also chatted briefly before getting down to business. One student, who was particularly eager in class and who appeared always to be prepared and enthusiastic about class, was the first to compare her writing process with the editor's. In message #6 of this first *InterChange* discussion, Catherine writes: "Thank goodness we don't have as many critics of our writing as this person did!" This response reflects the pattern of the first wave of responses to the editor's writing process. Another student commented that he had never revised that much before; another commented that "this guy's writing process is absolutely nothing like mine. He's way too technical." In addition to responding on the basis of their own experiences, students also began to critique the writer's process. These critiques ranged from accusing the author of plagiarism because he pulled from a variety of sources to write the annotation to the charge that he revised far too much and got advice from too many people. Clearly, the modernist assumption about author as isolated genius was guiding student responses to the editor's writing process.

The student critiques expressed traditional beliefs about writing, which I found both commonplace and odd — commonplace in the sense that they had been taught certain standards of writing and it was not surprising that they used those criteria to judge this person's writing; odd in that they were using what some have called "revolutionary technology" to put forth traditional beliefs about writing. Hawisher and Selfe pointed to this occurrence also, arguing that "given the considerable corporate and community investment accompanying this technology as its use expands within our educational system" (55), we need to closely scrutinize the ways we are using these technologies. Many times, however, new technologies are used to propagate traditional beliefs. Hawisher and Selfe contended that writing instructors "have not always recognized the natural tendency when using such machines, as cultural artifacts embodying society's values, to perpetuate those values currently dominant within our culture and our educational system" (55). The physical setting in which my students posted their responses during the *InterChange* discussion added to this natural tendency. Sitting by themselves at computer terminals posting individual responses to their peers feeds into student perceptions of author as singular entity. Clearly, the material conditions in which we deploy these technologies and the framework of the technologies themselves can counteract our intentions for them to highlight the dialogic nature of writing. As our use of these network technologies increases, so too should our awareness of the ways we are situated in relation to technologies and how these technologies position us in relation to themselves. This awareness must include a consideration of not only the effects that we think technology is having on students, but also student accounts of their use of the technology.

Of the critiques students posed during the *InterChange* discussion, I find the charge of plagiarism most interesting. Brice, who was unafraid to state his position in class and on *InterChange,* was the first to make this accusation: "I really cannot identify with experience. To me it almost sound like the entire piece was a compilation of someone else's words. Can you say PLAGIARISM?" The all caps presentation of the word *plagiarism* not only stresses his disdain in his critique, but also makes his comment stand out from the others. In a visual arena, Brice is the first to explore the possibilities of creating a sense of tone and voice even in the space of a narrow bandwidth technology. Matthew quickly agrees with Brice's accusation of plagiarism, but, interestingly enough, he doesn't remember the name of the person who made the charge: "I agree with whoever accused the author of plagiarism. It seems that he used very little of his own writing." Thus, even as he argues for the importance of individual authorship, Matthew himself does not cite the author of the comment to which he is responding.

Other composition theorists who have studied network communication also discovered this tension. In their study of woman@waytoofast, an online discussion group for the academic women in their study, Gail Hawisher and Patricia Sullivan (in press) noticed that discussion members forgot who had made a comment but still remembered the comment (Gail Hawisher, personal communication, July 15, 1995). For my class, this discrepancy could be explained by the fact that students did not know each other well and could not connect an in-real-life (IRL) face to the name on the screen. Also, though, this seems to support Lee Sproull and Sara Kiesler's assertion that who says the comment is not necessarily as important as what the comment is. To support their point, they cited Shoshana Zuboff, who argued that

> all messages have an equal chance because they all look alike. The only thing that sets them apart is their content. If you are a hunchback, a paraplegic, a woman, a black, fat, old, have two hundred warts on your face, or never take a bath, you still have the same chance. It strips away the halo effects from age, sex, or appearance. (370)

In the beginning of the semester this argument seemed to be true. Once the students got to know each other face to face, however, the situation changed. They responded directly to each other by name and carried on sustained conversations with others in the classroom. When calling people on their arguments, they hailed them by name. In his journal reflections about his experiences with *InterChange,* Brice wrote over the course of the class, our *InterChange* discussion took a lighter tone. As we began to know each other we were freer in our comments and opinions. We also knew the instructor better and we were less fearful of repercussions for comedic remarks. I also think that as time went on I learned to focus better on the people that I thought were going to contribute something useful to the discussion. (journal comments)

Likewise, Clarence noted that "at first we didn't know each other. We . . . were responding to names . . . without actually knowing who that person was. As time went on, however, and the students began to know each other, *InterChange* was more productive" (journal comments). Thus, students noted that when they did not know each other, the self who said the comment was less important. When they were familiar with each other's IRL personalities, the IRL self began to matter. By pointing to the ways that external cues have a direct effect on networked communications, these findings complicate assertions such as Sproull and Kiesler's.

During the first *InterChange* discussion in class, the argument for belief in the authority of the author (and that texts can be and should be owned by individuals) is first introduced with this accusation of plagiarism, but the theme is continued through much of the discussion. One example of this occurred in the discussion that arose around the word *montage*. In his description of his writing process, the editor labeled the finished product a montage. Greer described his work in this way:

> The text that I wrote was thus a montage or a collection of other people's writing more than my own. I picked sentences I found effective and began to order them on my own page, and a shape began to emerge. This activity was more like building or sculpting than like 'writing' in our traditional sense. (1)

A discussion ensues about the word *montage* and the view of writing that it embodies. Elizabeth introduces the topic: "I've never heard or read the word montage before." Picking up on her message, Brice expresses his frustration with the way the editor presented *montage,* writing "I don't appreciate the fact that it seemed like he thought we wouldn't understand the meaning of a montage, so he had to give us another word to define it." Interestingly, Brice was upset because the author chose to define the term for his audience, while Elizabeth expressed a lack of knowledge about the term. Two different receptions of this one word, then, illustrate the different ways readers approach the text; however, Brice is quick to assume that he speaks for a universal reader, whereas Elizabeth merely expresses her personal confusion. Many messages later, another student, Rachel, re-introduces the topic. "Actually, I heard 'montage' before in art class," she writes. No one responds to her comment, yet she pursues this train of thought, later writing "Isn't 'montage' like 'patchwork'?" No one responds to her, and she herself moves on to other topics.

Even though this discussion of *montage* was brief, it indexes some interesting questions. First, the word *montage,* which means "a single pictorial composition made by juxtaposing or superimposing many pictures or designs" (*American Heritage Dictionary,* 1170) seems to highlight the ways computers are supposed to be changing our writing, but some students didn't know what the term meant. Second, some responded negatively to the editor's use of it. Rachel attempted to define it from the context of her art class, but by that time the class had moved on to another discussion. The editor's writing process — pasting together a variety of sources to construct a coherent annotation — relied on montage. The computer makes this sort of cutting and pasting easier, but it has also been argued that the computer reflects postmodern fragmentation in that it changes our view of text.[4] Instead of seeing the whole product, we now think of the text in terms of the scrolling of screens. We are unable to view all the text at one time, so this has supposedly affected writing methods and argumentation patterns: the traditional essay form with its beginning, middle, and end does not hold up well when we can jump back and forth between screens. In Brice's response to the use of the word *montage,* then, I would contend that he is responding negatively not only to the author's use of another word to define *montage,* but also to the very premise on which montages are based — a piecing together of a variety of things to construct a new "whole." Clearly, Brice perceives texts as constructed and presented in certain ways, and the editor's construction of the annotation does not fit into that pre-existing definition of *text* and *author.* Brice's initial hostility toward the editor continues throughout the discussion. In his eyes, the editor is breaking some cardinal rules of writing, and Brice continually critiques him for that. Underlying Brice's assertions are the assumptions that texts are supposed to be individually produced, that the author of the text is clearly delineated and given credit, and that the author owns the text.

At the heart of this assertion is a narrative of a coherent, stable self grounded in a body. Allucquere Rosanne Stone contended that it is the combination of the psychic self and the body upon which humanist notions of self-determination are based. This notion of a self grounded in a body in turn shapes our view of community. Stone wrote:

> Our commonsense notions of community and of the bodies from which communities are formed take as starting points, among others, that communities are made up of aggregations of individual "selves" and that each self is equipped with a single physical body. I tell inquiring scholars that at the Department of Radio-TV-Film here at the University of Texas at Austin, we refer to these principles as BUGS — a body unit grounded in a self. The notion of the self as we know it, called in various studies the "I" and in others the "subject," that tenacious just-so story that goes on to assure us that there exists an "I" for each body and that while there can be more than one "I" on tap there can only be one present at any time, seems a natural and inevitable part of life. (84–85)

If the basic unit of reality is the self and this self is supposed to be contained within a body, then multiple positions within one body at any one time are not allowed. This rule supposedly applies to writing also. The author who writes a text is supposedly a self grounded in a body. This self may have different roles to play, but at any one time, the author must be firmly grounded in one role. This requirement makes the self appear coherent and stable, rather than recognizing the ways selves are always already multiple, contradictory, and fragmentary. Thus, one way of constructing the self in this way involves the narrative of writing as a solitary, self-based act. My students' assertions about what an author is and is not are based in this narrative.

The narrative of the author as a coherent, stable self grounded in a body was reiterated in my other class' *InterChange* discussion. The other writing class was composed of thirteen students, six men and seven women. From the beginning of the semester, it was clear that this group did not coalesce well. Throughout much of the semester, they did not like to talk in class, they did not actively participate in class discussions, and they did not freely respond to each other's comments or questions. In their first *InterChange* discussion, students were responding to the same assignment — the NCTE editor's discussion of his writing process. They, like my first class, began by addressing the issue of plagiarism. They commented that their writing was different from his because they included original material, rather than just using other people's words. This observation led to an interesting discussion about originality and creativity. As they struggled to define what creativity was, they defined their perception of the writer's role. Even though they were doing so in an online discussion using innovative technology, their definition of an author, like that of the other class, was based on a traditional narrative of author. Using the technology did not radically change their conceptions of themselves and others. The following is a partial transcript of the discussion that ensued around the topic of creativity:

Brandy (Message #10): I use more of my own ideas when I write instead of copying others' ideas

Mark (Message #11): I don't usually get myself involved in compilations. I just write whatever comes into my head.

Dan (Message #12): most of the material in my papers is original that's called plagiarism

Regina (Message #13): I feel that if you pull things from other peoples work, then it's not writing, it merely copying.

Shelly (Message #14): Whatever works for him. He had a deadline he wasn't ready for and had to write something.

Dan (Message #16): it's called creative copying

Paula (Message #17): I don't usually use other people's writing to write my own piece, i may get a few ideas from other sources but i don't think that only using a few of your own sentences in a piece is a good idea.

Eliza (Message #18): TRUE

Bernie (Message #19): I think that good because he gets support from other people, as long as he quotes them.

Jessica (Message #20): My writing process is different because I don't draw sentences and phrases from other works. I use my own sentences. I also don't have that many people revise my work.

Jane (Message #22): Whenever I write a paper I may ask one or two people to read it, but never any more. My friends write totally different and I would literally have to re-write my paper to please all of them.

Mark (Message #24): Copying is boring. You have to just let your ideas flow freely or else you're not going to come out with a product that is satisfying to you.

Regina (Message #29): I agree Jessica: everyone writes different. All papers should include originality.

In this discussion, the students all agree that the editor's work is not original or creative because he merely pieced together sentences from other sources, thus highlighting their perceptions of what it means to be an author. The narrative about writing the editor provides for the students contradicts the dominant narrative of writer as self-contained and writing as owned. Because of this discrepancy, they argue that the annotation is not original and should not be attributed to the author — i.e., the author doesn't own the work because he used other people's ideas. This discussion overlooks the context of the editor's task, however. Students were responding to his writing based upon their own educational experiences — what they've learned, what writing situations they have been in, and what they have been rewarded for. When they argue against using other people's writing in their own texts, they reinforce humanist notions of the individual as coherent, rational, and singular. The students claimed that they may consult other works to help them generate ideas, but the texts they write are reflections of their own thinking. Although theorists such as Landow and Bolter often argue that computers are changing the way we view texts by highlighting the intertextual nature of writing, these students clearly argued against intertextuality in favor of a traditional sense of creativity. They viewed intertextuality and creativity as antithetical to one another. By privileging ahistorical creativity, the students overlooked the fact that all writing, including the NCTE editor's project, is context bound. The situation in which the editor wrote — as the *production editor,* not the *author,* of the book — and the text he was writing — "an annotation that would be used as a jacket blurb and marketing copy," a text, after all, that is not owned or claimed by one single author — were not addressed by the students. The editor relied on other people's works because his situation called for it. The students did not consider that the dynamics of his working space were different from the dynamics under which they operated. Instead of taking these different contextual issues into account, they relied purely on their own experience and condemned the editor for not adhering to those traditional boundaries.

The editor clearly explained that his writing process is different from traditional conceptions of writing. The editor's description of his writing process challenges the students' traditional assumptions, but instead of rethinking their own processes (and realizing how multivocal texts really are, after all, because we are always processing other people's ideas in our writing, no matter who gets to claim the status of author), they judged the editor and decided that what he had done was merely copying. They did not recognize that organizing and selecting the sentences and sculpting them to appear as a coherent text could be considered an original act — a kind of collaboration. This response is in large part dictated by their previous schooling experiences. Grades are given to individuals for their original work. Writing is taught as a process that requires a single individual at the center. Even the texts assigned as writing models emphasize the singularity of the author and the importance of one person's contributions. To assert, as some have, that network technologies provide a space for students to learn about the multivocality of texts is overly simplified. Networks can provide that space, but unless we, as instructors, provide our students with direct instruction about multivocality and the potentials for collaboration that networks offer, they will use new technologies to support old, limiting ideas of author and self.

My experience in using *InterChange* points to a key flaw in the writing class itself: In its current configuration, the writing class is a separate, self-contained entity. Students do not write for any sort of "real world" context other than to get a grade. Lynn Veach Sadler also addressed this point, arguing

> the composition classroom is an artificial construct. English professors will not be one's audience in the after-life of college (except in the few instances in which people become college professors), and we English teachers probably do not spend enough of our precious teaching time on this topic. (158)

Sadler contended that we need to teach students to see the bigger picture — to place their writing situation in the context of their audience's expectations and their own goals as writers. Writers always write in certain contexts and, therefore, they must understand how a piece of writing fits into the history of other writing done in particular contexts. We need to teach our students to assess the context of their writing situations. Networked technologies such as *InterChange* can help this assessment by allowing writers to converse with their audience (other students in this case), but we must teach students to use the technologies in this way. If we assume that they will automatically see the revolutionary potentials *InterChange* has for providing them contact with their audience, we will be disappointed again and again as students use technology to support their usual perceptions of self and of writing.

If we ask our students to write for an ambiguously defined "educated" audience, we are most likely encouraging them to write to us, their teachers. To solve this difficulty, we could ask our students to write for specifically described audiences other than the usual academic, "educated" other. Network technologies can assist us with this goal, but we must be sure that students receive actual feedback from that audience. Often, students are given other, business-oriented audiences to write for, but they rarely receive feedback from their intended audience. In such situations, students still write for the teacher, because the only person reading their work is their teacher. Thus, even though this environment appears to be providing students with concrete audiences, we are still asking them to write in an academic void. Arguing for this point, Susan Miller asserted that

> to date, it is uncommon for either freshmen or advanced students to be asked to discover how much, what kind, and what quality of writing they are responsible for, either as students or as later professionals. It is equally uncommon to ask them to imagine the results they wish from a piece or writing, or to give attention to the realities of deadlines and collaboration that writing situations impose on their individual processes. For instance, few people who write effectively are responsible alone for every element of a text's production. But the roles of the person or situation that creates an actual writing "assignment" or of the person or organization responsible for the text's publishable form are rarely enacted in compositions, even in those that depend heavily on peer group and collaborative processes. (199)

When we add network technologies to our classroom, we do not automatically alleviate the problem students face when asked to write for an abstract "educated" audience with whom they have no contact. Often, assignments are written in ways that encourage the students to place the teacher in the position of "reader" and, therefore, they do not see their peers as part of their audience. Thus, using *InterChange*, students can receive feedback from peers about their writing, but if these discussions are treated as informal conversations with people who are not part of their paper's audience, students will not likely regard very highly the response they get there. Such a structure furthers the modernist notion of the writer as individual whose work is not shaped by interaction with others: Students write papers to get grades and do not really see how their peers, who are after all in the same position as themselves, can help them. If we set up our assignments this way, we are actually hiding the political and social implications of what occurs in our classrooms and the effects our assignments have; again, we are emphasizing the individual writer who places ingenuity first and audience considerations second. When we require students to write in a void, we're actually asking them to replicate the standards of the academy, but instead of foregrounding this goal, we package it as if we are teaching them the essentials, the basics of writing. As David Bartholomae suggested, we often keep secrets from students and fail to adequately explain why their writing will succeed or fail in the academy. The academy, like society at large, is heavily invested in the notion of the single, coherent, rational self and the discourse that sustains it.

The belief in durable, stable boundaries between self and other is demonstrated in my students' definitions of *author*. The narrative of the humanist self is embodied in many classroom practices — grading procedures, classroom designs, process approaches to writing. It is not surprising, then, that this humanist self can also be found when we use new technologies in our classroom because, as Michel Foucault argued in *Discipline and Punish*, the humanist self is at the core of Western identity. Stone extended Foucault's argument when she stated the coupling between our bodies and our selves is a powerfully contested site, densely structured, at which governments, industries, scientists, technologists, religious fanatics, religious moderates, media practitioners, and scholars fight for the right to speech, for a profoundly moral high ground, and not incidentally for the right to control the epistemic structures by which our bodies mean. (84)

The struggle to define self is, then, central to all facets of life. What it means to have a self is at the core of power-knowledge relations. It is no wonder, then, that traditional narratives are so pervasive. After all, many people benefit from the status quo. It is also no wonder that so many challenges have been waged against these traditional narratives. The composition classroom is just one site of this struggle, but it is a crucial site; because the acts of writing and reading construct powerful narratives of identity, who gets to control the shape of those endeavors is an important question.

Conclusion

What stories were told during my classes' *InterChange* discussions? The narrative of the stable, coherent, rational self as embodied in the individual author was a narrative told again and again by my students. The narrative my students told does not necessarily contradict the dominant narratives shaping technology; rather, my students' interactions with the technologies seem to be on a completely different but recognizable plane. At the heart of both sides of the argument concerning technology is a belief that network technologies are new and will thus have unpredictable effects. To the young adults in my class, though, computer technologies are not new. They've grown up in a world directly shaped by technology. They've played video games, have home computers, are familiar with the Net. Even if they aren't technocrats, their view of life has been shaped by a certain laissez-faire view of technology. For them technology does not challenge the traditional narrative of self; it merely enacts it more pervasively by situating lone writers at terminals. The claims theorists make, or the uncritical enthusiasm about technology, and the realities that students live in are, thus, very different. To understand what is going on here, we must acknowledge that difference, understand the nature of it, and analyze how it is played out in composition classrooms.

Notes

I thank Gail Hawisher, Paul Prior, and Michael Greer for their insightful comments on various drafts of this article. Gail's encouragement and vision have directly influenced this work. Paul's wonderful suggestions about the shaping of my ideas were offered at just the right time. And Michael's lively conversations and suggestions and his patient editing were extremely helpful.

[1]All student names have been changed to pseudonyms, and permission has been granted to the author to use student comments in this paper.

[2]Barker and Kemp argued that

the essential activity in writing instruction is the textual transactions between students. These transactions should be so managed by the network as to encourage a sense of *group knowledge*, a sense that every *transactor* influences and is influenced by such group knowledge, and a sense that such group knowledge is properly *malleable* (responsive to the influences of each transactor). (15)

I did not find that my students developed this sense of group knowledge when they used *InterChange*.

[3]Janet Eldred and Ron Fortune argued that analyzing the metaphors we use to describe computer interactions is important because metaphors powerfully shape the way we view our relationship within the world. "Metaphors . . . work from a known or familiar frame of

reference to explain something whose attraction is based in part on its departure and difference from that frame" (59). They contended that often the ways we use metaphors repeat the traditional oral/literacy dichotomy in which oral conversation is devalued over formal writing practices. Oral conversations are used to generate topics, but the actual work of writing takes place alone — between the student and her text. These divisions are played out in online synchronous conferencing as well.

[4]In *Writing Space: The Computer, Hypertext, and the History of Writing,* Jay David Bolter argued that hypertext changes the ways we engage with texts — both as readers and as writers. He wrote:

> Writing is the creative play of signs, and the computer offers us a new field for that play. It offers a new surface for recording and presenting text together with new techniques for organizing our writing. In other words, it offers us a new writing space. (11)

References

The American Heritage Dictionary of the English Language. 3rd ed. Boston: Houghton, 1992.

Barker, Thomas, and Fred O. Kemp. Network Theory: A Postmodern Pedagogy for the Writing Classroom. *Computers and Community: Teaching Composition in the Twenty-First Century.* Ed. Carolyn Handa. Portsmouth: Boynton, 1–27.

Barrett, Edward, *The Society of Text: Hypertext, Hypermedia, and the Social Construction of Information.* Cambridge: MIT P, 1989.

Bartholomae, David. "Inventing the University." In *When a Writer Can't Write.* Ed. Mike Rose. New York: Guilford, 1985, 134–65.

Batson, Trent. "The ENFI Project: A Networked Classroom Approach to Writing Instruction." *Academic Computing* 1 (1988): 32–33.

Bolter, Jay David. *Writing Space: The Computer, Hypertext, and the History of Writing.* Hillsdale: Erlbaum, 1991.

Eldred, Janet, and Ron Fortune. "Exploring the Implications of Metaphors for Computer Networks and Hypermedia." *Re-imagining Computers and Composition: Research and Teaching in the Virtual Age.* Ed. Gail E. Hawisher and Paul LeBlanc. Portsmouth: Boynton, 1992. 58–73.

Faigley, Lester. *Fragments of Rationality: Postmodernity and the Subject of Composition.* Pittsburgh: U Pittsburgh P, 1992.

Foucault, Michel. *Discipline and Punish: The Birth of the Prison.* New York: Vintage, 1979.

Greer, Michael S. "The Writing Process at Work." Manuscript. 1995.

Hawisher, Gail E., and Cynthia L. Selfe. "The Rhetoric of Technology and the Electronic Writing Class." *College Composition and Communication,* 42.1 (1991): 55–67.

Hawisher, Gail E., and Patricia Sullivan. *Women on the Networks: Searching for e-Spaces of Their Own.* New York: MLA, in press.

Joyce, Michael. *Of Two Minds: Hypertext, Pedagogy, and Poetics.* Ann Arbor: U of Michigan P, 1995.

Landow, George P. *Hypertext: The Convergence of Contemporary Critical Theory and Technology.* Baltimore: Johns Hopkins UP, 1992.

Langston, M. Diane, and Trent W. Batson. "The Social Shifts Invited by Working Collaboratively on Computer Networks: The ENFI Project." *Computers and Community: Teaching Composition in the Twenty-First Century.* Ed. Carolyn Handa. Portsmouth: Boynton, 1990.

Mehan, Hugh. *Learning Lessons: Social Organization in the Classroom.* Cambridge: Harvard UP, 1979.

Miller, Susan. *Textual Carnivals: The Politics of Composition.* Carbondale: Southern Illinois UP, 1991.

Peek, Robin P., and Gregory B. Newby, eds. *Scholarly Publishing: The Electronic Frontier.* Cambridge: MIT P, 1996.

Rheingold, Howard. *The Virtual Community: Homesteading on the Electronic Frontier.* New York: Harper, 1993.

Sadler, Lynn Veach. "Preparing for the White Rabbit and Taking it on the Neck: Tales of the Workplace and Writingplace." *Professional Writing in Context: Lessons from Teaching and Consulting in Worlds of Work.* Ed. John Frederick Reynolds, Carolyn B. Matalene, Joyce Neff Magnotto, Donald C. Samson, Jr., and Lynn Veach Sadler. Hillsdale: Erlbaum, 1995. 129–78.

Sirc, Geoffrey, and Thomas Reynolds. "Seeing Students as Writers." *Network-Based Classrooms: Promises and Realities.* Ed. Bertram Bruce, Joy Kreeft Peyton, and Trent Batson. Cambridge: Cambridge UP, 1993. 138–60.

Skubikowski, Kathleen, and John Elder. "Computers and the Social Contexts of Writing." *Computers and Community: Teaching Composition in the Twenty-First Century.* Ed. Carolyn Handa. Portsmouth: Boynton, 1990. 89–105.

Spender, Dale. *Nattering on the Net: Women, Power, and Cyberspace.* North Melbourne, Aust.: Spinifex, 1995.

Sproull, Lee, and Sara Kiesler. *Connections: New Ways of Working in the Networked Organization.* Cambridge: MIT P, 1991.

Stone, Allucquere Rosanne. *The War of Desire and Technology at the Close of the Mechanical Age.* Cambridge: MIT P, 1995.

Taylor, Paul. "Social Epistemic Rhetoric and Chaotic Discourse." *Re-imagining Computers and Composition: Teaching and Research in the Virtual Age.* Ed. Gail Hawisher and Paul LeBlanc. Portsmouth: Boynton, 1992.

Turkle, Sherry. *Life on the Screen: Identity in the Age of the Internet.* New York: Simon, 1995.

Zuboff, Shoshana. *In the Age of the Smart Machine: The Future of Work and Power.* New York: Basic, 1988.

Webb's Insights as a Resource for Your Teaching

1. In your journal, reflect on the ways that students used the *InterChange* discussions in their writing processes. In what ways did using *InterChange* as a part of the writing process help your students to see writing as a collaborative, social activity?

2. Reflect on your own writing practices — both online and off. In what ways do you collaborate? How has your writing changed as a result of using networked computers? Share these reflections with your students and use them to guide your teaching strategies.

Webb's Insights as a Resource for the Writing Classroom

The following are Patricia Webb's suggestions for using networking programs such as *InterChange* in the classroom:

1. Encourage students to question their traditional definitions of *original* and *creative.* The image of the singular author writing in his garret alone scarcely resembles the ways writers in real world contexts actually write. Encourage students to adapt such metaphors as *montage* to describe the process of writing.

2. Have students read "real-world" authors' descriptions of their writing processes.[1] Or, if possible, set up real-time conferences with writers in various fields. In these conferences, guest speakers could explain how they write,

---

[1] In *The Virtual Community: Homesteading on the Electronic Frontier,* Rheingold (1993) defined cyberspace as a "place" with all the qualities of other important spaces in our life. Because of its ability to link people across time and space, cyberspace, according to Rheingold, is perhaps

> one of the informal public places where people can rebuild aspects of community that were lost when the malt shop became a mall. Or perhaps cyberspace is precisely the wrong place to look for the rebirth of community, offering not a tool for conviviality but a life-denying simulacrum of real passion and true commitment to one another. In either case, we need to find out soon. (26)

He then goes on to show clearly that he supports and favors the first of those two options and fears the second option, which, he claimed, will happen if corporations take control of the Web.

what writing situations they face, and with whom they write. Students could then ask them questions to get a better sense of real world writing situations and the types of collaboration that occur there.

3. Create assignments that require students to work together to gather and present information. If students have access to the Internet, require that they use those resources together to track down the information they seek. (Again, make sure their use of the technology is integrated into class goals.) . . .

4. Have students subscribe to listservs and other online conversations so that their writing has a real world context. Listservs call for a different sort of writing than most students will expect to do in a writing class. Furthermore, other members of the listserv may respond to them, highlighting the ways their writing has real effects.

3. Responding to and Evaluating Student Writing

Careful reflection on classroom practice prompted the articles in Chapter 3 of this volume. Each essay is, of course, informed by philosophical perspectives, but all these readings focus very specifically on practical strategies for working with students at different skill levels in a variety of writing sites. You'll find many connections among the readings and a high degree of "intertextuality." Although you may be tempted to turn to just one of these readings only as a strong need arises, we recommend that you read them all and that you read them against the other pieces in this collection. These articles all resonate with a strong concern for student growth and empowerment.

Teachers' responses to student texts are continuously cited as the most significant influence — positive or negative — on students' concepts of themselves as writers. Although to many students "teacher response" signifies grades and summary comments, teachers may respond to student writing in several other ways: inside and outside the classroom, through structured feedback and spontaneously, and as both ally and gatekeeper. From the essays in this section, you can carry away caveats about ways of responding and strategies to try.

NANCY SOMMERS *Responding to Student Writing*

In the conclusion of this landmark essay, Nancy Sommers describes what continues to be a major responsibility for writing teachers: "The challenge we face as teachers is to develop comments which will provide an inherent reason for students to revise; it is a sense of revision as discovery, as a repeated process of beginning again, as starting out new, that our students have not learned. We need to show our students how to seek, in the possibility of revision, the dissonances of discovery — to show them through our comments why new choices would positively change their texts, and thus to show them the potential for development implicit in their own writing."

Sommers's article reports the findings and the significance to teaching practice of collaborative research on the nature and effects of teachers' comments on first and second drafts. Lil Brannon, Cyril Knoblach, and Sommers learned that instructor commentary can "appropriate" student texts — that is, distract writers from their own purposes in writing texts and focus them instead on responding to what they perceive the instructor wants in future drafts. They also found that instructor commentary was rarely text-based but rather exemplified the abstract, vague, and generic writing that we ask our students to avoid.

The article prompts writing teachers to analyze how they respond to student writing in all its stages, to adapt their comments on each draft to the needs and purpose of the writer, and to demonstrate through text-based comments the "thoughtful commentary" of attentive readers.

More than any other enterprise in the teaching of writing, responding to and commenting on student writing consumes the largest proportion of our time. Most teachers estimate that it takes them at least twenty to forty minutes to comment on an individual student paper, and those twenty to forty minutes times twenty students per class, times eight papers, more or less, during the course of a semester add up to an enormous amount of time. With so much time and energy directed to a single activity, it is important for us to understand the nature of the enterprise. For it seems, paradoxically enough, that although commenting on student writing is the most widely used method for responding to student writing, it is the least understood. We do not know in any definitive way what constitutes thoughtful commentary or what effect, if any, our comments have on helping our students become more effective writers.

Theoretically, at least, we know that we comment on our students' writing for the same reasons professional editors comment on the work of professional writers or for the same reasons we ask our colleagues to read and respond to our own writing. As writers we need and want thoughtful commentary to show us when we have communicated our ideas and when not, raising questions from a reader's point of view that may not have occurred to us as writers. We want to know if our writing has communicated our intended meaning and, if not, what questions or discrepancies our reader sees that we, as writers, are blind to.

In commenting on our students' writing, however, we have an additional pedagogical purpose. As teachers, we know that most students find it difficult to imagine a reader's response in advance, and to use such responses as a guide in composing. Thus, we comment on student writing to dramatize the presence of a reader, to help our students to become that questioning reader themselves, because, ultimately, we believe that becoming such a reader will help them to evaluate what they have written and develop control over their writing.[1]

Even more specifically, however, we comment on student writing because we believe that it is necessary for us to offer assistance to student writers when they are in the process of composing a text, rather than after the text has been completed. Comments create the motive for revising. Without comments from their teachers or from their peers, student writers will revise in a consistently narrow and predictable way. Without comments from readers, students assume that their writing has communicated their meaning and perceive no need for revising the substance of their text.[2]

Yes as much as we as informed professionals believe in the soundness of this approach to responding to student writing, we also realize that we don't know how our theory squares with teachers' actual practice — do teachers comment and students revise as the theory predicts they should? For the past year my colleagues, Lil Brannon, Cyril Knoblach, and I have been researching this problem, attempting to discover not only what messages teachers give their students through their comments, but also what determines which of these comments the students choose to use or to ignore when revising. Our research has been entirely focused on comments teachers write to motivate revisions. We have studied the commenting styles of thirty-five teachers at New York University and the University of Oklahoma, studying the comments these teachers wrote on first and second drafts, and interviewing a representative number of these teachers and their students. All teachers also commented on the same set of three student essays. As an additional reference point, one of the student essays was typed into the computer that had been programmed with the "Writer's Workbench," a package of twenty-three programs developed by Bell Laboratories to help computers and writers work together to improve a text rapidly. Within a few minutes, the computer delivered editorial comments on the student's text, identifying all spelling and punctuation errors, isolating problems with wordy or misused phrases, and suggesting alternatives, offering a stylistic analysis of sentence types, sentence beginnings, and sentence lengths, and finally, giving our freshman essay a Kincaid readability score of eighth grade which, as the computer program informed us, "is a low score for this type of document." The sharp contrast between the teachers' comments and those of the computer highlighted how arbitrary and idiosyncratic most of our teachers' comments are. Besides, the calm, reasonable language of the computer provided quite a contrast to the hostility and mean-spiritedness of most of the teachers' comments.

The first finding from our research on styles of commenting is that *teachers' comments can take students' attention away from their own purposes in writing a particular text and focus that attention on the teachers' purpose in commenting.* The teacher appropriates the text from the student by confusing the student's purpose in writing the text with her own purpose in commenting. Students make the changes the teacher wants rather than those that the student perceives are necessary, since the teachers' concerns imposed on the text create the reasons for the subsequent changes. We have all heard our perplexed students say to us when confused by our comments: "I don't understand how you want me to change this" or "Tell me what *you* want me to do." In the beginning of the process there was the writer, her words, and her desire to communicate her ideas. But after the comments of the teacher are imposed on the first or second draft, the student's attention dramatically shifts from "This is what I want to say," to "This is what *you* the teacher are asking me to do."

This appropriation of the text by the teacher happens particularly when teachers identify errors in usage, diction, and style in a first draft and ask students to correct these errors when they revise; such comments give the student an impression of the importance of these errors that is all out of proportion to how they should view these errors at this point in the process. The comments create the concern that these "accidents of discourse" need to be attended to before the meaning of the text is attended to.

It would not be so bad if students were only commanded to correct errors, but, more often than not, students are given contradictory messages; they are commanded to edit a sentence to avoid an error or to condense a sentence to achieve greater brevity of style, and then told in the margins that the particular paragraph needs to be more specific or to be developed more. An example of this problem can be seen in the following student paragraph:

In commenting on this draft, the teacher has shown the student how to edit the sentences, but then commands the student to expand the paragraph in order to make it more interesting to a reader. The interlinear comments and the marginal comments represent two separate tasks for this student; the interlinear comments encourage the student to see the text as a fixed piece, frozen in time, that just needs some editing. The marginal comments, however, suggest that the meaning of the text is not fixed, but rather that the student still needs to develop the meaning by doing some more research. Students are commanded to edit and develop at the same time; the remarkable contradiction of developing a paragraph after editing the sentences in it represents the confusion we encountered in our teachers' commenting styles. These different signals given to students, to edit and develop, to condense and elaborate, represent also the failure of teachers' comments to direct genuine revision of the text as a whole.

Moreover, the comments are worded in such a way that it is difficult for students to know what is the most important problem in the text and what problems are of lesser importance. No scale of concerns is offered to a student, with the result that a comment about spelling or a comment about an awkward sentence is given weight equal to a comment about organization or logic. The comment that seemed to represent this problem best was one teacher's command to his student: "Check your commas and semicolons and think more about what you are thinking about." The language of the comments makes it difficult for a student to sort out and decide what is most important and what is least important.

When the teacher appropriates the text for the student in this way, students are encouraged to see their writing as a series of parts — words, sentences, paragraphs — and not as a whole discourse. The comments encourage students to believe that their first drafts are finished drafts, not invention drafts, and that all they need to do is patch and polish their writing. That is, teachers' comments do not provide their students with an inherent reason for revising the structure and meaning of their texts, since the comments suggest to students that the meaning of their text is already there, finished, produced, and all that is necessary is a better word or phrase. The processes of revising, editing, and proofreading are collapsed and reduced to a single trivial activity, and the students' misunderstanding of the revision process as a rewording activity is reinforced by their teachers' comments.

It is possible, and it quite often happens, that students follow every comment and fix their texts appropriately as requested, but their texts are not improved substantially, or, even worse, their revised drafts are inferior to their previous drafts. Since the teachers' comments take the students' attention away from their own original purposes, students concentrate more, as I have noted, on what the teachers commanded them to do than on what they are trying to say. Sometimes students do not understand the purpose behind their teachers' comments and take these comments very literally. At other times students understand the comments, but the teacher has misread the text and the comments, unfortunately, are not applicable. For instance, we repeatedly saw comments in which teachers commanded students to reduce and condense what was written, when in fact what the text really needed at this stage was to be expanded in conception and scope.

The process of revising always involves a risk. But, too often revision becomes a balancing act for students in which they make the changes that are requested but do not take the risk of changing anything that was not commented on, even if the students sense that other changes are needed. A more effective text does not often evolve from such changes alone, yet the student does not want to take the chance of reducing a finished, albeit inadequate, paragraph to chaos — to fragments — in order to rebuild it, if such changes have not been requested by the teacher.

The second finding from our study is that *most teachers' comments are not text-specific and could be interchanged, rubber-stamped, from text to text.* The comments are not anchored in the particulars of the students' texts, but rather are a series of vague directives that are not text-specific. Students are commanded to "Think more about [their] audience, avoid colloquial language, avoid the passive, avoid prepositions at the end of sentences or conjunctions at the beginning of sentences, be clear, be specific, be precise, but above all, think more about what [they] are thinking about." The comments on the following student paragraph illustrate this problem:

*Begin by telling your reader
what you are going to write about.*

In the sixties it was drugs, in the seventies it was rock and roll. Now
avoid "one of the"
in the eighties, <u>one of the</u> most controversial subjects is nuclear power.
elaborate
The United States <u>is in great need of its own</u> source of power. Because

of environmentalists, coal is not an acceptable source of energy.
be specific
[Solar and wind power have not yet received the technology neces-
avoid "it seems"
sary to use them.] <u>It seems</u> that nuclear power is the only feasible

means right now for obtaining self-sufficient power. However, too

large a percentage of the population are against nuclear power claim-
be precise
ing it is unsafe. <u>With as many problems</u> as the United States is having

concerning energy, it seems a shame that the public is so quick to "can"

a very feasible means of power. Nuclear energy should not be given

up on, but rather, more nuclear plants should be built.

Think more about your reader.

Thesis sentence needed.

One could easily remove all the comments from this paragraph and rubber-stamp them on another student text, and they would make as much or as little sense on the second text as they do here.

We have observed an overwhelming similarity in the generalities and abstract commands given to students. There seems to be among teachers an accepted, albeit unwritten canon for commenting on student texts. This uniform code of commands, requests, and pleadings demonstrates that the teacher holds license for vagueness while the student is commanded to be specific. The students we interviewed admitted to having great difficulty with these vague directives. The students stated that when a teacher writes in the margins or as an end comment, "choose precise language," or "think more about your audience," revising becomes a guessing game. In effect, the teacher is saying to the student, "Somewhere in this paper is imprecise language or lack of awareness of an audience and you must find it." The problem presented by these vague commands is compounded for the students when they are not offered any strategies for carrying out these commands. Students are told that they have done something wrong and that there is something in their text that needs to be fixed before the text is acceptable. But to tell students that they have done something wrong is not to tell them what to do about it. In order to offer a useful revision strategy to a student, the teacher must anchor that strategy in the specifics of the student's text. For instance, to tell our student, the author of the above paragraph, "to be specific," or "to elaborate," does not show our student what questions the reader has about the meaning of the text, or what breaks in logic exist, that could be resolved if the writer supplied specific information; nor is the student shown how to achieve the desired specificity.

Instead of offering strategies, the teachers offer what is interpreted by students as rules for composing; the comments suggest to students that writing is just a matter of following the rules. Indeed, the teachers seem to impose a series of abstract rules about written products even when some of them are not appropriate for the specific text the student is creating.[3] For instance, the student author of our sample paragraph presented above is commanded to follow the conventional rules for writing a five-paragraph essay — to begin the introductory paragraph by telling his reader what he is going to say and to end the paragraph with a thesis sentence. Somehow these abstract rules about what five-paragraph products should look like do not seem applicable to the problems this student must confront when revising, nor are the rules specific strategies he could use when revising. There are many inchoate ideas ready to be exploited in this paragraph, but the rules do not help the student to take stock of his (or her) ideas and use the opportunity he has, during revision, to develop those ideas.

The problem here is a confusion of process and product; what one has to say about the process is different from what one has to say about the product. Teachers who use this method of commenting are formulating their comments as if these drafts were finished drafts and were not going to be revised. Their commenting vocabularies have not been adapted to revision and they comment on first drafts as if they were justifying a grade or as if the first draft were the final draft.

Our summary finding, therefore, from this research on styles of commenting is that the news from the classroom is not good. For the most part, teachers do not respond to student writing with the kind of thoughtful commentary which will help students to engage with the issues they are writing about or which will help them think about their purposes and goals in writing a specific text. In defense of our teachers, however, they told us that responding to student writing was rarely stressed in their teacher-training or in writing workshops; they had been trained in various prewriting techniques, in constructing assignments, and in evaluating papers for grades, but rarely in the process of reading a student text for meaning or in offering commentary to motivate revision. The problem is that most of us as teachers of writing have been trained to read and interpret literary texts for meaning, but, unfortunately, we have not been trained to act upon the same set of assumptions in reading student texts as we follow in reading literary texts.[4] Thus, we read student texts with biases about what the writer should have said or about what he or she should have written, and our biases determine how we will comprehend the text. We read with our preconceptions and preoccupations, expecting to find errors, and the result is that we find errors and misread our students' texts.[5] We find what we look for; instead of reading and responding to the meaning of a text, we correct our students' writing. We need to reverse this approach. Instead of finding errors or showing students how to patch up parts of their texts, we need to sabotage our students' conviction that the drafts they have written are complete and coherent. Our comments need to offer students revision tasks of a different order of complexity and sophistication from the ones that they themselves identify, by forcing students back into the chaos, back to the point where they are shaping and restructuring their meaning.[6]

For if the content of a student text is lacking in substance and meaning, if the order of the parts must be rearranged significantly in the next draft, if paragraphs must be restructured for logic and clarity, then many sentences are likely to be changed or deleted anyway. There seems to be no point in having students correct usage errors or condense sentences that are likely to disappear before the next draft is completed. In fact, to identify such problems in a text at this early first-draft stage, when such problems are likely to abound, can give a student a disproportionate sense of their importance at this stage in the writing process.[7] In responding to our students' writing, we should be guided by the recognition that it is not spelling or usage problems that we as writers first worry about when drafting and revising our texts.

We need to develop an appropriate level of response for commenting on a first draft, and to differentiate that from the level suitable to a second or third draft. Our comments need to be suited to the draft we are reading. In a first or second draft, we need to respond as any reader would, registering questions, reflecting befuddlement, and noting places where we are puzzled about the meaning of the text. Comments should point to breaks in logic, disruptions in meaning, or missing information. Our goal in commenting on early drafts should be to engage students with the issues they are considering and help them clarify their purposes and reasons in writing their specific text.

For instance, the major rhetorical problem of the essay written by the student who wrote the first paragraph (the paragraph on nuclear power) quoted above was that the student had two principal arguments running through his text, each of which brought the other into question. On the one hand, he argued that we must use nuclear power, unpleasant as it is, because we have nothing else to use; though nuclear energy is a problematic source of energy, it is the best of a bad lot. On the other hand, he also argued that nuclear energy is really quite safe and therefore should be our primary resource. Comments on this student's first draft need to point out this break in logic and show the student that if we accept his first argument, then his second argument sounds fishy. But if we accept his second argument, his first argument sounds contradictory. The teacher's comments need to engage this student writer with this basic rhetorical and conceptual problem in his first draft rather than impose a series of abstract commands and rules upon his text.

Written comments need to be viewed not as an end in themselves — a way for teachers to satisfy themselves that they have done their jobs — but rather as a means for helping students to become more effective writers. As a means for helping students, they have limitations; they are, in fact, disembodied remarks — one absent writer responding to another absent writer. The key to successful commenting is to have what is said in the comments and what is done in the classroom mutually reinforce and enrich each other. Commenting on papers assists the writing course in achieving its purpose; classroom activities and the comments we write to our students need to be connected. Written comments need to be an extension of the teacher's voice — an extension of the teacher as reader. Exercises in such activities as revising a whole text or individual paragraphs together in class, noting how the sense of the whole dictates the smaller changes, looking at options, evaluating actual choices, and then discussing the effect of these changes on revised drafts — such exercises need to be designed to take students through the cycles of revising and to help them overcome their anxiety about revising: that anxiety we all feel at reducing what looks like a finished draft into fragments and chaos.

The challenge we face as teachers is to develop comments which will provide an inherent reason for students to revise; it is a sense of revision as discovery, as a repeated process of beginning again, as starting out new, that our students have not learned. We need to show our students how to seek, in the possibility of revision, the dissonances of discovery — to show them through our comments why new choices would positively change their texts, and thus to show them the potential for development implicit in their own writing.

Notes

[1]C. H. Knoblach and Lil Brannon, "Teacher Commentary on Student Writing: The State of the Art," *Freshman English News* 10 (Fall 1981): 1–3.

[2]For an extended discussion of revision strategies of student writers see Nancy Sommers, "Revision Strategies of Student Writers and Experienced Adult Writers," *College Composition and Communication* 31 (Dec. 1980): 378–88.

[3]Nancy Sommers and Ronald Schleifer, "Means and Ends: Some Assumptions of Student Writers," *Composition and Teaching* 2 (Dec. 1980): 69–76.

[4]Janet Emig and Robert P. Parker, Jr., "Responding to Student Writing: Building a Theory of the Evaluating Process," paper, Rutgers University.

[5]For an extended discussion of this problem see Joseph Williams, "The Phenomenology of Error," *College Composition and Communication* 32 (May 1981): 152–68.

[6]Ann Berthoff, *The Making of Meaning* (Upper Montclair: Boynton, 1981).

[7]W. U. McDonald, "The Revising Process and the Marking of Student Papers," *College Composition and Communication* 24 (May 1978): 167–70.

Sommers's Insights as a Resource for Your Teaching

1. Sommers clearly advises multiple readings of student writing. She indicates that reading a student text to understand its meaning and to provide commentary that can motivate revision is critical to students' growth as writers. Don't be daunted by the paper load. If you focus your commentary on what happens as you read and respond to the meaning of a text, you'll find that what may have distracted you at the lexical level has disappeared from or changed substantively in the draft submitted for evaluation and grading. You may be spending the same amount of time or even less time overall when you read early and late drafts.

   Revision conferences also provide opportunities for you to offer thoughtful commentary. They force you to make text-specific comments. Advise your students to take advantage of the discovery checklists and revision checklists in *The Bedford Guide for College Writers* to supplement your specific conversation about revision.

2. Ask a colleague teaching the same course to work with you reading some early drafts. Trade a set of drafts. Write your comments about revision on a separate sheet of paper; exchange and compare your comments, paying particular attention to the specificity of each comment and to precision of language. You'll both profit from the discussion and may find your reading of the text enhanced by this "external assessor."

   You might also use this technique when you evaluate late drafts. The ensuing conversation about your evaluative comments and criteria for evaluation will certainly give you both perspective on and confidence about your process of evaluating and grading.

3. The increasing access to computer technology provides you new opportunities for assisting writers in their processes of revision. Check out campus resources for networked classrooms where you can read student drafts even as they generate or rework them. Ask students to give you a draft on disk and write marginal or interlinear comments in italics or boldface. Order software such as *Daedalus* that gives you read/write access to individual and group texts.

Sommers's Insights as a Resource for the Writing Classroom

1. Ask students to write from recall about the commentary they received or receive outside your writing classroom on their writing (this would be a good

exercise for Chapter 1, "Writing from Recall"). Ask them to explain, in journal entries or in fifteen-minute writing sessions, how a comment prompted or inhibited deep-level revising. One caution: because such an assignment can trigger painful or angry memories, advise the students not to name the person who wrote comments that obstructed revision. Explain that the "text" of the comment can be analyzed for its effect without your having to know the author. If the students want to laud the instructor whose comments motivated them to revise for wholeness, suggest they write that instructor a fan letter.

2. Peer editors might fall into these same styles of commentary. Bring in a sampler of peer editing comments and ask the class as a whole or in groups to analyze how well they prompt revision. Direct their attention to the peer commentary incorporated in *The Bedford Guide for College Writers* on page 449.

3. Use one of the peer editing checklists from *The Bedford Guide for College Writers* or one that your class has constructed in response to a shared writing task for an in-class evaluation session. Ask students to write sentence-length, specific comments about issues of meaning and attention to the readers' concerns. Move from writer to writer and read the comments. Tell each peer editor if his or her comments would motivate you to revise.

4. Ask class members to identify commentary that has assisted them in deep revision when they write a self-assessment to accompany a submitted draft. Ask a question like "What advice did your peer readers give and what did you do with the advice?"

RICHARD BEACH   *Demonstrating Techniques for Assessing Writing in the Writing Conference*

Richard Beach reports on a variety of techniques that he uses to assist student writers to assess their writing and to detect "dissonance" between their goals and their texts. Like Sommers, he believes that the "dissonances of discovery" will motivate revision.

The article describes ways to demonstrate to students how to assess their own drafts and to use that self-assessment for revision. Beach models techniques for describing a draft, judging its success, and selecting appropriate revisions. He emphasizes that the writing instructor must be a careful listener, implying that the instructor must guard against "appropriating" the writer's work when demonstrating how he or she, acting as the writer, would pose self-assessment questions. You'll find many useful and specific questions that you would be likely to ask in a conference. In the conclusion of the essay, Beach explains that, in any one conference with a student, he uses only two or three of the conferencing techniques he describes.

Beach recommends that you begin conferences by asking the writers to tell you their reactions to their difficulties with a draft. The "guided assessing form" that the writers prepare before conferences is a particularly effective way to make them take responsibility for the conferences.

Notice how Beach has worked to shift the focus of the conference from the teacher describing the writing and its success to the writer assessing his or her own work. Beach indicates that such self-assessment is a new experience that must often be demonstrated so that the writer can practice it.

For further advice on handling the writing conference, see Chapter 2, "Creating a Writing Community," in Teaching with THE BEDFORD GUIDE FOR COLLEGE WRITERS. *1. Practical Suggestions.*

In a conference, I ask a student to tell me how she feels about her draft. "Oh, I feel pretty good about it" is her response; "maybe it needs a few more details." Having read the draft, I know that it's riddled with more serious problems than lack of details.

How can this student be taught to critically assess her writing? As experienced teachers know, simply telling the students what their problems are and what to do about those problems doesn't help them learn to become their own best readers. It teaches them only how to follow instructions.

Moreover, in giving students "reader-based feedback" — how I respond as a reader — which presumably implies to students that certain problems exist, I must assume that they are capable of defining the implied problem, which is often not the case. The majority of students who have difficulty assessing their own writing need some instruction in how to assess. Teachers typically demonstrate techniques for assessing writing by discussing rhetorical or logical problems in published and/or students' texts. Unfortunately, students often have difficulty applying this instruction to assessment of problems in their own texts. For these students, a teacher may then need to augment classroom instruction in assessing techniques by demonstrating these techniques in writing conferences — showing them how to assess their own unique problems — and then having them practice this assessing in the conference.

This more individualized approach to teaching assessing in conferences involves the following steps:

1. determining a student's own particular difficulty by analyzing his or her use of certain assessing techniques;

2. demonstrating the stages of assessing: describing, judging, and selecting appropriate revisions;

3. describing the different components of the rhetorical context — purpose, rhetorical strategies, organization, and audience, showing students how each component implies criteria for judging drafts and selecting appropriate revisions;

4. having students practice the technique that was just demonstrated.

Techniques of Assessing

In order to discuss ways of demonstrating different assessing techniques, I propose a model of assessing. As illustrated in the chart [Figure 1], assessing involves three basic stages: describing, judging, and selecting/testing out revisions. I will briefly define each of these stages and then, for the remainder of this paper, discuss how I demonstrate these techniques in a conference.

As depicted in this chart, each of the first two stages implies a subsequent stage. By *describing* their goals, strategies, or audience, writers have some basis for making judgments about their drafts. For example, a writer describes his strategy — that in the beginning of his story, he is "setting the scene in order to show what a small-town world is like." He describes his audience — noting that the audience probably knows little about that particular setting. Now he can infer appropriate criteria for judging his setting — whether he has included enough information to convey the sense of a "small-town world" to his reader. This judgment, in turn, helps him in the final stage, *selecting appropriate revisions* — in this case, adding more information about the setting.

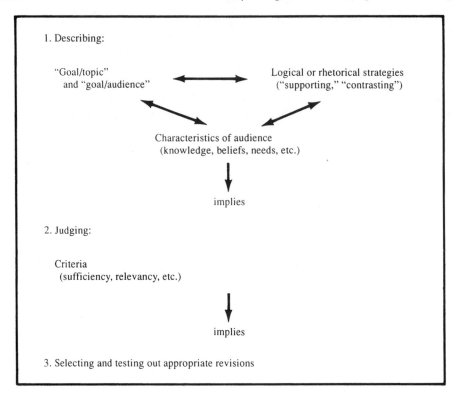

Figure 1. Stages of the assessing process

In demonstrating assessing techniques, I am therefore showing students more than how to use a specific technique. I am also showing them that describing audience implies criteria for judging or that defining a problem implies criteria for selecting revisions. These demonstrations help students appreciate the value of describing and judging in helping them make revisions.

One benefit of a conference is that it provides a forum for students to practice their assessing with a teacher. The teacher can then note instances in which a student is having difficulty and, instead of simply telling the student how to improve her assessing, demonstrate how to assess. The student then has a concrete guide for trying out a certain assessing technique.

Determining Difficulties in Assessing

In order to know which technique to demonstrate, I try to pinpoint a student's difficulty in using a particular technique. I therefore have students begin the conference by giving me their reactions to and sense of the difficulties in describing, judging, or selecting revisions. However, given the brevity of many conferences, I often can't diagnose students' difficulties by relying solely on their comments in the conference. I therefore use guided assessing forms, which students complete prior to the conference.

The questions on these forms are based on the three assessing stages, as listed below:

The Guided Assessing Form

Describing

1. What are you trying to say or show in this section?

2. What are you trying to do in this section?

3. What are some specific characteristics of your audience?

4. What are you trying to get your audience to do or think?

Judging

5. What are some problems you perceive in achieving 1, 2, and 4?

Selecting Appropriate Revisions

6. What are some changes you can make to deal with these problems?

In using the forms, students divide their draft into sections, answering the questions on the form for each section. The students don't necessarily need to begin with the "describing" questions; they may begin by noting problems and then working back to the describing stage.

By reading over the form in the beginning of the conference and by listening to their reactions to the draft I try to determine a student's particular difficulty in assessing her draft. If, for example, for each of three sections in her draft a student has difficulty describing what she is "trying to say or show," I might conclude that she has difficulty defining her intentions. The fact that she's also had difficulty answering my questions about goals further suggests that inferring intentions is a problem for her.

I then demonstrate how I would identify intentions. Rather than using my own writing, which the student isn't familiar with, I use the student's writing. I adopt the student's role or persona, demonstrating how I, from her perspective, would infer intentions. I stress to the student that while I am showing her how I would infer intentions, I am not implying that my approach is the "one correct way." I also *avoid* telling the students what they ought to be saying, for example, by telling them what I think they are "really trying to say." Rather, I am showing students how to do something rather than telling them what to say.

After I demonstrate a certain technique, I then ask the student to make her own inferences. If she continues to have difficulty, I demonstrate that technique further.

All of this requires careful attention to clues suggesting difficulties, as well as a conceptual framework for sorting out and isolating certain strategies. Based on my own experience and research on assessing, I will now discuss how I demonstrate each of the stages of the assessing process — describing, judging, and selecting revisions.

The Describing Stage

The describing stage consists of describing goals for content (What am I trying to say?), audience (What do I want my audience to do or think?), logical or rhetorical strategies (What am I trying to do: supporting, contrasting, shifting to a different point?), and audience characteristics (knowledge, traits, needs, etc.). Writers obviously use goals as criteria for judging whether their text says or does what they want it to say or do. Once they identify their goals, they can detect dissonance between their goals and their text, dissonance that leads to judgments about problems in achieving their goals.

This is not to imply that writers must always articulate their goals in order to assess their writing. Writers often have only a "felt sense" of their intentions without ever articulating them, but they know how to use their unarticulated intentions to determine that something is amiss and to decide what to do about their problems.

In a conference, it is often useful to have students articulate their goals because those goals are necessary for judging, for determining the extent to which those goals have or have not been fulfilled. If students are to be able to make these judgments, they may need help articulating goals.

Difficulties in describing goal/topic and goal/audience. In my research on use of the guided assessing forms, I asked students to describe what they were trying to say or show ("goal/topic") or what they wanted their audience to do or think ("goal/audience") in each of several sections of their draft.[1] Many students in these studies have difficulty stating what it is that they are trying to say or show. They often simply restate their text *verbatim* rather than stating their intended topic or idea. For example, in writing an analysis of citizen participation in the government of her hometown, a student described her draft section as saying that "a lot of citizens in the town don't vote and there often aren't enough candidates to run for local offices," almost a verbatim restatement of what she was saying in the draft. She did not go beyond that restatement to recognize a point of that section, her "goal/topic" — that citizens aren't involved in town government. She also had difficulty identifying her "goal/audience," what she wanted her audience to do or think having read her essay. Because she had difficulty identifying these goals, she had difficulty judging her draft.

To some degree, identifying these goals is difficult, particularly if students don't perceive the purpose for defining goals — to further assess their draft. I therefore try to show students that clearly defining goals helps them in judging their draft.

In demonstrating definitions of goal/topic, I demonstrate the difference between simply restating the content of a section of their draft and recognizing the goal or purpose of that section. In working with the student writing about her local government, I first take her restatement of the text, "that citizens don't vote and there aren't enough candidates" and, playing the role of the "dumb reader," to use Walker Gibson's term, ask the question "what's the point?" I then infer a goal statement — that the citizens aren't involved — and show her that, in contrast to her restatement, I can use this goal statement to pinpoint disparities between goal and text.

Another problem with students' identifications of goal/topic is that they are often so global that they are not very useful for perceiving disparities between goals and text.[2] For example, in writing an autobiographical narrative about a series of shoplifting incidents, a student states that he was "trying to show what I was like when I was a teenager." This description is too global for assessing what it is he wants to show about this past self. The student needs to identify what the incidents show about his past self.

Having diagnosed the student's goals as too global, I then propose, using his other comments in the conference, a more precise goal statement: "in portraying my shoplifting, I'm trying to show that I was so lonely that I would do anything to be popular with my peers." I then use this inferred goal to review the shoplifting episodes, judging whether or not the descriptions of the student's behavior in each episode convey his need for friendship. Again, I am demonstrating the value of goal statements, particularly precise goal statements.

Difficulties in describing rhetorical or logical strategies. In describing rhetorical or logical strategies, writers are defining what they are doing in their texts — supporting, defining, stating, requesting, contrasting, describing, evaluating, specifying, etc. In naming these strategies, writers go beyond simply summarizing what they are trying to say, to identifying what they are trying to do, conceiving of their text from a functional or pragmatic perspective.

Each of these strategies implies certain criteria for assessing the success or failure of that strategy. By describing these strategies, writers evoke the particular criteria necessary for judging the use of that strategy. Writers then narrow down the criteria in light of their particular goals and the characteristics of their audience. For example, the strategy, supporting, implies the criteria, *sufficiency, relevancy,* or *specificity of support:* do I have enough support? is my support relevant to my thesis? is my support specific enough? Given an audience which the writer assumes knows little about the topic, the writer is particularly concerned about the sufficiency of information — is there enough supportive information for that audience to understand a point? Or, in requesting, as suggested by speech-act theorists, I am concerned about my power, right, or ability to make a request; my reader's ability to fulfill my request; and my reader's perception of my sincerity in making a request. Given a reader who may doubt my right to make a request, I'm particularly concerned that my request implies that I have the right to make such a request.

For example, the administration at my university has decided to reduce my program, but without giving any clear rationale for the proposed reduction. In writing to the administration requesting some clarification of their rationale, I somewhat cynically anticipate their response — that I have no right to make such a request. I argue that I have the right to ask for clarification because further reductions would jeopardize my program and my job. I therefore clearly define my affiliation with the program in order to imply my right to make such a request.

Describing strategies and inferring implied criteria is a complicated process that requires a pragmatic perspective on writing — conceiving of writing as doing things rather than simply conveying information. It also requires tacit knowledge of the conditions governing the use of these strategies. It is therefore not surprising that, as our analysis of the assessing forms indicated, many students had difficulty describing their strategies and inferring implied criteria.[3] When asked to describe their strategies, students often had difficulty going beyond describing what they were trying to "say" to inferring what it is they were trying to "do." They frequently restated content — "I am writing about my high school and college courses," rather than inferring strategy — "I am contrasting my high school and college courses." These students, with only a restatement of content, then had difficulty making judgments about their text. Those students who identified a strategy were more likely to make a judgment because they were able to successfully contrast high school and college courses.

In demonstrating the difference between a summary of content and a description of strategy I again demonstrate how descriptions of strategies can be used to imply criteria. For example, having inferred that the student is contrasting high school and college classes, I then note that "contrasting" implies, among other criteria, the importance of information relevant to the contrast and the validity of the contrast — whether or not the information constitutes valid evidence for a contrast.

Difficulties in describing characteristics of audience. Making inferences about characteristics of audience is also a complex process. There is much debate regarding the conflicting evidence about how much writers actually think about their audience.[4]

I would argue that, rather than conceiving of audience as a unified global construct, writers infer or create specific prototypical characteristics such as what and how much members of an audience know about a topic, what they believe about a topic, and their needs, status, power, attitudes, or expectations. For example, in writing a set of directions for windsurfing, a writer may conceive of her audience as "someone who knows little about windsurfing." Or, in arguing the case for nationalizing the steel industry, a writer conceives of his audience as "someone who is opposed to my belief about nationalization." These conceptions are prototypical because writers often never know, even with familiar audiences, exactly what their audience knows, believes, needs, etc. They must therefore rely on prototypical constructs derived from approximations of their audience.

Writers also derive these characteristics from their defined goals and strategies. In giving a set of directions for windsurfing, a writer knows that she needs to consider what her audience may or may not know about windsurfing, because that characteristic is particularly useful for judging the relevancy and sufficiency of information in her directions. Writers therefore infer these prototypical constructs because, as with decisions about goals and strategies, the constructs imply relevant criteria for judging their writing.

Inferring these characteristics of audience also allows writers to adopt a reader's schema, as they must in order to distance themselves from their text. Having created the construct, "someone who is opposed to nationalizing the steel industry," they can then assess the text from that perspective.

When, in our research, Sarah Eaton and I asked students to infer characteristics of their audience on their assessing form, most of the students made few if any references to specific audience characteristics.[5] Most of their inferences consisted of anticipated emotional responses such as "my reader should like this beginning" or "my audience will be bothered by this section," inferences reflecting an egocentric orientation. They were more concerned with how their audience would react to their writing than with how to adapt their text to their audience.

When I sense that students are having difficulty inferring characteristics of audience, I demonstrate how I infer these characteristics from my description of strategies or goals. For example, in writing her paper about the lack of citizen participation in affairs of her hometown, the student previously cited began her paper by describing the town's government, noting that she's trying to "provide background information in order to set the scene." However, she has difficulty judging her use of this defined strategy — setting the scene — because she has difficulty inferring audience.

Using her description of her "backgrounding" strategy, I note that in giving background information, I need to determine how much her audience may know about her hometown. Once I've isolated the appropriate attribute — knowledge — I create the construct, "someone who knows little about the town." I then use that construct to judge her descriptions of the town.

The Judging Stage

Sensing dissonance. Having described these components of the rhetorical context, writers then judge their text. In judging, a writer needs to sense dissonance between goals and the text, dissonance that serves as an incentive to revise. However, many students in our research had difficulty sensing dissonance because they had difficulty adopting a reader's perspective. In order to demonstrate ways of sensing dissonance, I go back and describe goals, strategies, characteristics, for example, "someone who knows little about book publishing." I, as instructor, then cite instances in which I, as a reader, didn't have enough background information to understand the draft. Given my goal, as the writer, of informing my reader about book publishing, I know that, from the reader's perspective, something is amiss.

Applying criteria. Once writers sense the dissonance, they need to specify the reason for the problem, why something is amiss.

Students often have difficulty specifying reasons for their problems. They may say that "this is awkward" or "this doesn't flow"; but these judgments often don't point towards any predicted solutions, because they are too vague. In contrast, judgments such as, "I don't have enough examples to support my thesis," imply some specific directions: add more examples.

One reason students aren't able to specify their reasons is that they simply don't know or don't know how to apply criteria such as sufficiency, relevancy, validity, clarity, appropriateness, or coherence. For example, a student thinks that there is a problem with her extended illustration of an ineffective teaching technique, but she can't define the reason for the problem. I then show her how to define a reason for her problem. Having defined her strategy, *giving examples*, I infer implied criteria — relevancy, sufficiency, or clarity of the information in terms of illustrating the point. I then ask the question — given the goals and characteristics of audience, is this a problem of relevancy, sufficiency, or clarity? I then note that, from my perspective as reader, the illustration is too long. This suggests that sufficiency of information serves as a useful criterion for selecting and testing out appropriate revisions. One can hope that the student will then recognize the value of specifying criteria in order to make revisions.

Selecting and Testing Out Appropriate Revisions

Once writers have defined their problem, they select and test out those revisions that will best solve the problem. A writer may select a certain revision strategy — adding, deleting, modifying, rewording, etc. — and/or formulate the content involved in using that revision strategy ("I will add more information about the appearance of the house").

Difficulties in selecting revisions. Just as writers' descriptions imply judgments, their judgments imply appropriate revisions. If their information is irrelevant, then they need to delete that information or make it more relevant. However, when students in our study were asked to answer the question on the form, "What are you going to do about your problem?" many had difficulty identifying possible revisions because they hadn't clearly defined their problem or the reasons for their problem.[6]

In these instances, I go back to the judging stage and demonstrate how specifying problems and reasons for problems implies revisions.

Difficulties in testing out optional revisions. Once students select a revision, they often assume that that revision will do the job, failing to consider why or how that revision works according to their goals, strategies, and characteristics of audience. For example, in writing about police corruption, a student notes that he wants to add some more examples of police corruption, but he doesn't know why he's adding the examples. I then show him how to review his revisions in terms of his goals, strategies, or audience characteristics. The student then realizes that the additional examples help bolster his charge — his central point — that the police corruption exists in all areas of society. Having reaffirmed his goal, he can test out whether each additional example supports his contention that "corruption is everywhere."

In showing students how to justify their revisions by considering their goals, strategies, or audience characteristics, I am illustrating that in assessing, it is essential to constantly cycle back to conceptions of the rhetorical context in order to reaffirm, clarify, or modify those conceptions in light of their advancing comprehension of that context as they write.

Diagnosing Students' Response to Modeling: Comprehending and Applying

These, then, are some of the techniques of assessing that I demonstrate in the conference. In most cases, I demonstrate no more than one or two of these techniques in any one conference. Otherwise, I end up dominating the conference rather than having the students practice their own assessing. After I complete my demonstration, I ask the students whether or not they understood the technique I was demonstrating. If a student didn't understand the technique, I repeat the demonstration until I am confident that the student not only understood the technique but also could actually employ that technique.

In subsequent conferences, I often find that my demonstrations have benefitted students in that they are able to use these techniques on their own, either in the conferences or on the guided assessing forms. In an attempt to determine the influence of the demonstrations, I conducted a study of one teacher's use of demonstration with a group of eight college freshman students enrolled in a remedial composition course.[7] I analyzed (1) the transcripts of conferences and the students' assessing forms for evidence of students' use of assessing techniques, and (2) the students' revisions from the beginning to the end of the course. Over time, most of the students demonstrated marked changes, particularly in their ability to describe goals and strategies and to use those descriptions to judge their drafts and make revisions that improved their writing.

If learning to assess drafts is central to learning to revise and improve writing quality, then demonstrating these assessing techniques assumes a central role in composition instruction.

Notes

[1]Richard Beach and Sarah Eaton, "Factors Influencing Self-assessing and Revising of College Freshmen," *New Directions in Composition Research,* ed. Richard Beach and Lillian Bridwell (New York: Guilford, 1984) 149–70.

[2]Beach and Eaton.

[3]Beach and Eaton.

[4]Donald Rubin, Gene Piché, Michael Michlin, and Fern Johnson, "Social-Cognitive Ability as a Predictor of the Quality of Fourth-Graders' Written Narratives," *New Directions;* Brant Burleson and Katherine Rowan, "Are Social-Cognitive Ability and Narrative Writing Skill Related?" *Written Communication* 2 (Jan. 1985): 25–43.

[5]Beach and Eaton.

[6]Beach and Eaton.

[7]Richard Beach, "The Self-assessing Strategies of Remedial College Students," paper presented at the annual meeting of the American Educational Research Association, New York, 1977.

Beach's Insights as a Resource for Your Teaching

1. Preparing for revision conferences is critical to your success with them. Before you hold your first set of conferences, role-play with a colleague. Use a sample of your own writing and Beach's "Guided Assessing Form" to prepare. Practice the roles both of apprehensive and "silent" student and nondirective reader. Discuss with your colleague the insights you gained from playing each role.

2. Tape-record or videotape a series of conferences with writers. Analyze your questions. Do you ask the writer to self-assess? Do you demonstrate how writers can assess their drafts? Do you ask questions that show writers a process or strategy to use without slipping into "how I would rewrite this draft"?

Beach's Insights as a Resource for the Writing Classroom

1. Hold mini-conferences (two or three minutes long) during in-class drafting. Ask each student one or two of the describing questions Beach uses. Most students will be able to answer specifically and return to drafting. The student who is uncertain could use some "intervention" and assistance with generating purpose or thinking about audience.

2. Help students design self-assessment questionnaires for each of the major assignments. Many of the discovery and revision checklists in *The Bedford Guide* provide excellent questions for such a questionnaire. Require each student to reflect on his or her draft and to complete the questionnaire. Often that process prompts the writer to additional revision and redrafting before submitting the manuscript. Often it "primes" the conversation you have in a conference. Some students can recognize difficulties in a draft through a self-assessment questionnaire but need to talk with a more practiced reader-writer to discuss options or to find direction for selecting revisions.

3. Workshops can also prompt self-assessment that leads to revision. Help groups generate assessment questions that they ask each other during a workshop. Often, group members can assist the writer by describing what they understood as his or her purpose and how they reacted as readers. This generates "data" that the writer needs to judge the draft.

JEFFREY SOMMERS *Bringing Practice in Line with Theory: Using Portfolio Grading in the Composition Classroom*

Sommers emphasizes that portfolio grading in the composition classroom — an increasingly frequent teaching and learning option — presents a unique opportunity to connect the practice of responding to and evaluating student writing with an individual's beliefs about writing and about teaching writing. He demonstrates that a portfolio assignment encourages students to revise and helps them discover writing as learning.

Sommers argues that portfolio grading will aid both the learner and the instructor only if the reflective teaching practitioner identifies and works out appropriate answers to the hard questions that such an assessment practice prompts. He describes three portfolio models: representative sampling, holistic perspective, and developmental perspective. Sommers speculates about the interconnections among each model and assessment criteria, grading standards, the student-instructor relationship in the writing classroom, and effects on paper load. The essay is one of twenty-three collected in Portfolios: Process and Product *edited by Belanoff and Dickson.*

Portfolio assessment in the composition classroom offers not a methodology but a framework for response. Rather than provide definitive answers to questions about grading criteria and standards, the relationship between teacher and student, and increased paper loads, the portfolio approach presents an opportunity for instructors to bring their practice in responding to student writing in line with their theories of composing and pedagogy. My essay proposes to take an exploratory look at how portfolio evaluation compels instructors to address a number of important, and long-lived, issues underlying response to student writing. When an instructor chooses to use a portfolio system, certain other decisions must inevitably follow, and it is the implications of these decisions that I propose to examine most closely.

As the writing process has become the focus of composition classes over the past three decades, it seems an almost natural evolution for portfolio evaluation to have entered the classroom. Emphasizing the importance of revision to the composing process — regardless of which theoretical view of composing one takes — ought to lead to a classroom practice that permits, even encourages, students to revise. While such revision can, of course, occur in a classroom in which the writing portfolio is not in use, the portfolio itself tends to encourage students to revise because it suggests that writing occurs over time, not in a single sitting, just as the portfolio itself grows over time and cannot be created in a single sitting. Elbow and Belanoff argue that a portfolio system evaluates student writing "in ways that better reflect the complexities of the writing process: with time for freewriting, planning, discussion with instructors and peers, revising, and copyediting. It lets students put these activities together in a way most productive for them" (14).

Additionally, the portfolio approach can help students discover that writing is indeed a form of learning. Janet Emig has argued that writing "provides [a] record of evolution of thought since writing is epigenetic as process-and-product" (128). Portfolios provide a record of that record. Emig also describes writing as "active, engaged, personal — notably, self-rhythmed" (128). The notion that writing occurs over time in response to the rhythms created by the individual writer — a notion that makes eminent sense when one considers that no two writers seem to work at precisely the same pace and that no two pieces of writing seem to take form at the same pace even for the same writer — is another excellent argument for using portfolios. The portfolio approach allows writers to assemble an *oeuvre* at their own pace, within the structure of the writing course and its assignments, of course. Nevertheless, the portfolio by its very nature suggests self-rhythm because some pieces will require more drafts than others, even if explicit deadlines are prompting their composition.

For good cause then have portfolio systems of evaluation become commonplace in composition classrooms. But with these portfolios also come serious issues about grading standards and criteria, about how teachers and students relate to one another, about how teachers handle increased paper loads. Before examining how these issues might be resolved, perhaps it is time to acknowledge that this essay has yet to define portfolio. I have deliberately avoided doing so for two reasons: first, *portfolio* is a familiar-enough term and not really all that mysterious, and thus what I have written so far should be comprehensible to my readers; second, no consensus exists about just what a *portfolio* is or should be, however familiar the concept may seem. In fact, two distinctly different models of portfolios exist, each compelling its adherents to address the central issues of response in very different theoretical ways.

The first model is described well by James E. Ford and Gregory Larkin, who use as an analogy an artist's portfolio. Each student's work is "collected, like the best representative work of an artist, into a 'portfolio' " (951). We are to see students in the role of free-lance commercial artists, approaching an art director at an advertising agency with a large portfolio case containing their "best representative work." Such a model is easily transferred into the writing classroom. Students in the writing course produce a certain number of written documents during the term, agreeing in advance that only a specified number of those documents will be graded by the instructor. Commercial artists would never compile a portfolio that consisted of every piece of work they had done and neither do the students; the idea is to select a representative sampling that shows the creators at their best.

This portfolio model most likely grows out of instructors' concern with grading criteria and standards. Ford and Larkin, as the title of their article suggests, came to the portfolio as a means of guaranteeing grading standards. Instructors are justified in upholding rigorous standards of excellence because their students have been able to revise their work and select their best writing for evaluation. As Ford and Larkin comment, "A student can 'blow' an occasional assignment without disastrous effect" (952), suggesting that the instructor is being eminently fair. Elbow and Belanoff, in the context of a programmatic portfolio-assessment project, make a similar argument, one equally applicable to the individual classroom. "By giving students a chance to be examined on their best writing — by giving them an opportunity for more help — we are also able to demand their best writing" (13). This portfolio system "encourages high standards from the start, thereby encouraging maximum development" (Burnham 137).

To Ford and Larkin, Burnham, and Elbow and Belanoff, a portfolio is a sampling of finished products selected by the student for evaluation. Although the instructor using this model may very well be concerned with the students' development as writers, as Burnham's remark indicates, essentially this portfolio model is grade driven and could be accurately labeled a *portfolio grading system*. It is grade driven because the rationale for using the portfolio framework grows out of an understanding that the student's written work will ultimately be evaluated.

However, portfolio grading, paradoxically, not only grows out of a concern for eroding standards, but also out of a concern for the overemphasis upon grades in writing courses. Christopher Burnham calls the students' "obsession" with grades a "major stumbling block" (125) to effective learning in the composition classroom and turns to portfolio grading as a means of mitigating the students' obsession with grades. Burnham concludes that the portfolio system "establishes a writing environment rather than a grading environment in the classroom" (137).

Thus, by addressing the issue of responding to the student's writing, Burnham wants to change the relationship between the student and the instructor. He wants to create a more facilitative role for the instructor, in accordance with suggestions about response from Donald Murray, Nancy Sommers, and Lil Brannon and C. H. Knoblauch. He not only wants to allow students to retain the rights to their own writing, he wants them to assume responsibility for their writing, asserting that portfolio grading "creates independent writers and learners" (136).

The question then of when and what to grade becomes quite significant. Although grading criteria must be established by instructors who employ portfolio grading, new criteria for grading the final drafts do not generally need to be developed. Presumably, instructors will bring to bear an already developed set of criteria for grading, applying these criteria rigorously to designated papers, thus protecting the integrity of their standards.[1] Nonetheless, a crucial question arises: when will student work receive a grade: at midterm, only at the end of the term, with each submission? Some instructors grade every draft and revision as students submit them, some grade only the revisions, some grade only papers designated as final drafts. In some portfolio-grading systems, the students select a specified number of final drafts at midterm and a second set at end of the term, while in other systems, all grading occurs at the end of the term.

Instructors using portfolio grading must decide when to offer grades. Grading every draft keeps the students informed, but, because even a temporary grade has an air of finality to many students simply because it is a grade, this policy may undercut the idea that each draft may potentially develop into a finished product. Grading revisions only may encourage the grade-obsessed student to revise if only to obtain a grade, thus introducing revision to some students who otherwise lack the motivation to revise, but also reinforcing the primacy of grades.

By deferring grades until the end of the term, instructors can extend the duration of the "writing environment" that Burnham hopes to substitute for the "grading environment" in the course. However, if students are indeed obsessed with grades, as he argues, then it seems likely that for a substantial number of students, or perhaps for all of the students to varying extents, there will always be a grading environment lurking beneath the writing environment of the course. If instructors respond effectively and frequently and confer with students individually, they can keep students informed of their approximate standing in the course, possibly deflecting their grade anxiety, but it is disingenuous to claim that portfolio grading removes grade obsession. If the portfolio ultimately produces an accumulation of individual grades, grade obsession cannot really be eliminated although it certainly can be reduced.

Yet a larger issue arises, an issue related to one's pedagogical assumptions about the significance of grades. Burnham discusses the portfolio system as a means of leading to student development, a development inevitably measured by the final grades earned by the student's portfolio. Inherent in this model is the idea that students can improve the writing, and thus the grade, by revising and selecting their best work. Inevitably, then, instructors using portfolio grading must address the issue of grade inflation. Although one of the motivating forces behind portfolio grading, as we have seen, is protecting grading standards, the system itself is designed to promote better writing by the students, and it stands to reason that many students are going to be submitting portfolios that consist of writing better than they might be able to produce in a classroom employing a traditional grading system. Will instructors raise the standards so high that even the improved writing in the portfolios falls into the usual grading curve? Or, and this seems much more likely, will the grades themselves on the whole be somewhat higher because of the portfolio approach despite higher standards? Should higher grades be of significant concern to instructors? Do higher grades mean "grade inflation"? What is the role of grades in writing courses? Portfolio grading compels instructors to consider these important questions.

Finally, portfolio grading presents problems to instructors in handling the paper load. Since most programs suggest or stipulate a certain number of assignments per term, instructors using the portfolio system must determine how they will count assignments. Will newly revised papers count as new assignments? By doing so, the instructor can keep the paper load from mushrooming. Let's focus on a course that requires seven papers in a semester (the situation at my institution), with the understanding that the portfolio will consist of four final drafts selected by the student. If instructors count revisions of papers 1 and 2 as papers 3 and 4, their paper load will be less because students will still only produce seven drafts for them to read. On the other hand, the students' options at the end of the term will be reduced by this method of counting; they will have to select four final drafts from only five different pieces in progress.

To ensure students the full choice of seven, however, instructors commit themselves to more responding. In our hypothetical case, they will read at least nine drafts, seven first drafts, and revisions of the first two papers. Thus a routine decision actually has important pedagogical implications.

Several methods of controlling the paper load do exist. One is to divide the term in half, asking students to produce two miniportfolios. At midterm, for instance, in the situation already described, students are required to submit two final drafts for grading out of the first four assigned papers. At the end of the term, students must select two of the final three assigned papers for grading. Thus the paper load is under greater control because the students cannot continue work on the first four papers after midterm. On the other hand, Burnham's desire to create a writing environment rather than a grading environment will be affected because grades will become of primary concern not once but twice during the term.

Another method for controlling the paper load is to limit the number of drafts students may write of individual papers. Without such a limit, some students will rewrite and resubmit papers almost weekly, adding greatly to the paper load; of course, one can argue that such students are developing as writers in an important way. Deadlines for revisions of papers can also be used to control the paper load since "real" writers always work under deadlines. They may revise and revise and revise, but ultimately they must conclude. Instructors may allow students to revise a given assignment as often as they wish but within a designated period of time. Another method of controlling the paper is to limit the number of revisions students may submit at one time or to designate specific times when revisions may be submitted. Late in the term, industrious students may have revisions of three or four different assignments ready to be submitted; some limit on the number they may hand in at one time can help instructors manage the course more effectively. Stipulating that revisions can be handed in only on certain days can allow instructors to plan their time for responding more efficiently.

Eventually, the end of the term arrives, and for many instructors using portfolio grading, the paper load explodes. Portfolios of four papers or more per student come in at the end of the term and must be graded quickly in order to submit final grades on time. Holistic grading can make the paper load manageable as instructors offer no comments but just a letter grade on each final draft. Grading portfolios at the end of the term undeniably requires more time than grading a single final exam or final paper would. However mundane these questions of handling the paper load may seem, the answers one supplies affect the entire portfolio grading system because many of these decisions may influence the relationship between students and their instructors, and some may influence, or be influenced by, instructors' grading criteria and standards.

To sum up then, a portfolio grading system defines a portfolio as a sampling of students' finished writing selected by the students for evaluation. Portfolio grading offers instructors a means of keeping their grading standards high while employing their usual grading criteria, it presents one potential method for reducing students' obsession with grades and transforming the classroom environment into one more engaged with writing than grading, and it increases instructors' paper loads. Instructors' decisions about when to grade and how to manage the paper load raise complications because they affect the relationship between instructors and their students. Thus, teachers planning on implementing portfolio grading need to consider carefully how they will do so in a way that will keep their practice in line with their own theoretical assumptions about writing and about composition pedagogy.

The second, newer, portfolio system model I will call the "holistic portfolio." The holistic portfolio is a response to continued theorizing about the nature of the composing process. Louise Wetherbee Phelps argues that theories underlying teaching practices evolve toward greater depth, and she sketches a hierarchy of response models to student writing beginning with one she labels "evaluative attitude, closed text" (49). In this model, the instructor treats the student text as "self-contained, complete in itself. . . . a discrete discourse episode to be experienced more or less decontextually" (50). This concept of response to a text views reading as evaluation; instructors responding in this model may speak of "grading a stack of papers." The next response model described by Phelps is one she calls "formative attitude, evolving text" (51). Instructors read students' drafts as part of a process of evolution, thus entering into and influencing the students' composing process. In this model of response, instructors locate "learning largely in the actual composing process" (53).

Phelps describes a third model of response as "developmental attitude, portfolio of work": "Whereas the first group of teachers reads a 'stack' of papers and the second reads collected bits, scraps, and drafts of the composing process, the third reads a 'portfolio' of work by one student" (53). Phelps elaborates on two ways to work with portfolios, describing first the portfolio grading model we have already examined, which she dubs "the weak form." In this approach, she writes, "teachers continue to read and grade individual papers, attempting to help students perfect each one" (53). As Phelps has described the models of response, we can see that she has first described portfolio assessment used in a programmatic approach to large-scale decision making about student proficiency and placement. Her second model fairly accurately describes the portfolio-grading approach of Ford and Larkin and Burnham, elaborated upon somewhat in her depiction of "the weak form" of her third response model.

In the second method of using portfolios, Phelps also describes a different portfolio system. Some instructors employ portfolios because they wish to respond from a *"developmental* perspective." From this perspective, the student writing "blurs as an individual entity" and is treated as a sample "excerpted from a stream of writing stimulated by the writing class, part of the 'life text' each literate person continually produces" (53). Phelps concludes:

> The reader's function is [to read] through the text to the writer's developing cognitive, linguistic, and social capacities as they bear on writing activities. The set of a single writer's texts to which the reader has access, either literally or through memory, is the corpus from which the reader tries to construct a speculative profile of the writer's developmental history and current maturity. (53)

This definition of portfolio no longer serves as an analogy to the commercial artist's carefully assembled portfolio of a representative sampling of her best work. Instead it more closely resembles an archivist's collection of a writer's entire *oeuvre*. Instructors do not deal with selected writings but evaluate the entire output of the student writer. The implications of such a definition are quite different from those of the portfolio grading model defined by Ford and Larkin, Burnham, and Elbow and Belanoff.

While portfolio grading systems are driven by pedagogic concerns with fair grading as well as with composing process theory, the holistic portfolio system is primarily driven by a pedagogical concern with composing process theory. Although Knoblauch and Brannon's polemic *Rhetorical Traditions and the Teaching of Writing* does not discuss portfolio evaluation, its view of the composing process might very readily lead to it. Knoblauch and Brannon describe the "myth of improvement" that has stifled writing instruction by focusing on the kind of evaluation Phelps details in her first model of response (evaluative attitude, closed text). Knoblauch and Brannon suggest that "the most debilitating illusion associated with writing instruction is the belief that teachers can, or at least ought to be able to, control writers' maturation, causing it to occur as the explicit consequence of something they do or ought to do" (165). This illusion is reductionist, leading to a view of the writing course "in minimal functionalist terms" (165). This "myth of improvement" has produced a definition of teaching and curricular success that stresses "trivial but readily demonstrable short-term 'skill' acquisitions" and has led some teachers "to imagine it is fair to 'grade on improvement,' mistaking a willingness to follow orders for real development" (165).

While Knoblauch and Brannon's book remains controversial, their critique of "the myth of improvement" cogently articulates many instructors' reservations about grading practices based on the artificial academic calendar, a system that demands students learn at a given pace, defined by a ten-week quarter, a fourteen-week trimester, or a sixteen-week semester. Knoblauch and Brannon conclude by arguing that "symptoms of growth — the willingness to take risks, to profit from advice, to revise, to make recommendations to others — may appear quickly, even if improved *performance* takes longer" (169).

For instructors whose conception of the composing process is compatible with the developmental schemes underlying Knoblauch and Brannon's book and Phelp's third model of response, the holistic portfolio should have great appeal. It presents these instructors with difficult decisions, however, in the same areas that the portfolio grading system presented its practitioners: grading criteria and standards, the teacher-student relationship, and handling the paper load.

While upholding grading standards was the catalyst for portfolio grading, holistic portfolio systems appear to be less concerned with the notion of grading standards, at least in traditional terms. Because the holistic portfolio system does not focus instructors' attention on specific final drafts, it does present instructors with some major decisions about criteria for the final evaluation.

Several possibilities exist. Instructors may create a grading system that weights final drafts but also grades draft materials, notes, peer commentary, and so on. Counting the number of drafts or the variety of included material is a way to "grade" preliminary materials. However, any counting method might distort the course's emphasis on development by encouraging students to create "phony" drafts, drafts written after the fact simply to pad the portfolio (just as many of us used to compose outlines after completing high school term papers as a way of meeting a course requirement).

Another way to grade the final portfolio is more holistic, and thus probably "purer" in the sense that it avoids treating individual drafts as "collected bits, scraps, and drafts" and portfolios as part of "the life text" (Phelps 53). The instructor looks for "symptoms of growth," to borrow Knoblauch and Brannon's phrase — "the willingness to take risks, to profit from advice, to revise, to make recommendations to others." Those students who demonstrate the greatest growth receive the highest grades, assuming that the instructor has developed a scale that measures growth — no small assumption.

While the holistic portfolio can fit very nicely into a developmental view of the composing process, it presents great difficulties in fitting at all into a traditional academic grading system and poses serious questions for instructors about how they see their writing courses fitting into the academy. This method of evaluation works most readily in a pass/no pass grading situation, indeed is an argument for such a grading system. But pass/no pass writing courses are the exception rather than the rule. Unfortunately, neither Knoblauch and Brannon nor Phelps really addresses the issue of how to grade in a writing course that emphasizes a developmental perspective on writing. It is conceivable that an instructor holistically evaluating a set of portfolios could assign an entire class of industrious students grades of A, having developed grading criteria that emphasize "symptoms of growth"; such an instructor can have rigorous standards in that only those students who have made the effort and demonstrated the growth receive the A's. However, one suspects this instructor would face a one-to-one meeting with a concerned writing program administrator or department chair sometime after submitting the final grades.

Some compromise or accommodation must undoubtedly be made by instructors, perhaps along the lines discussed earlier of weighting final drafts. The important point to make here is that instructors should be aware of how the grading criteria they develop correlate with the theory underlying their use of portfolio evaluation.

Given the problematic nature of grading holistic portfolios, why would instructors adopt this model of the portfolio system? The holistic portfolio system offers distinct advantages in defining a healthy teacher-student relationship. Burnham's hopes of creating a writing environment rather than a grading environment are more readily realized in the holistic portfolio system. Because the final portfolio will not be graded in any traditional sense, because individual grades on drafts do not occur, in theory the classroom using the holistic portfolio can indeed become a writing environment, since there is no reason for it to become a grading environment, and the instructor can truly doff the evaluator's role and don instead the facilitator's role.

Burnham praises portfolio grading for encouraging students to assume responsibility for their learning; portfolio grading "creates independent writers and learners," he concludes (137). His point is that when students know that they can control their grades through extra effort in revising and through the selection process available to them prior to final evaluation, they become more responsible and more independent; in today's terminology, they become "empowered." However, the motivation comes from a concern with grades.

In the holistic portfolio system, the students are also afforded the opportunity to become more responsible, not for their grades so much as for their development. They can indeed become independent learners, independent of traditional grading obsessions as well. The teacher and student can become "co-writers," in Phelps's phrase. The emphasis in the course falls not on improving texts as a means of improving a grade but instead falls on developing as a writer, understanding that this development is more important than grades on individual texts.

Both models of portfolios, then, hope to free students of the tyranny of the grade. The portfolio grading system does so temporarily, but also readily accommodates the traditional institutional need for grades. The holistic portfolio system can indeed free students to become learners and writers for the duration of a writing course but only if instructors have resolved the essential conflict between their course and the institution's demand for traditionally meaningful grades.

In the final area of paper load, it seems most likely that the holistic portfolio system will produce a heavier paper load than the portfolio grading system will. Any schemes to limit students' output would likely conflict with the theoretical assumptions that lead to using the holistic portfolio system. Thus students' portfolios are likely to grow in length as well as in the hoped-for depth of development. At the end of the term, instructors must read not merely a specific number of selected final drafts, but entire portfolios, certainly a slower process. Periodic reading of the growing portfolios — which instructors taking such a developmental perspective will probably wish to do — may reduce the paper load at the end of the course since instructors can scan the familiar materials in the portfolio, but it will not significantly reduce the paper load so much as spread it out over the course of the term.

Instructors contemplating a portfolio system of either sort, or a hybrid version of the two models described, are faced with the need to answer some important questions for themselves before incorporating the system into their writing classes. Louise Weatherbee Phelps concludes her discussion by commenting that her depiction of response models represents an increasing growth on the part of instructors. She argues that "experience itself presses teachers toward increasingly generous and flexible conceptions of the text and the reading task" (59). If she is correct, as I think she is, then the movement in composition classrooms toward portfolio systems of one sort or another will accelerate as the emphasis on the composing process as central to writing courses continues.

As the profession continues to refine its thinking about composition pedagogy, portfolio systems seem destined to proliferate in use and grow in significance. The portfolio system of evaluation has tremendous advantages, which are described throughout the rest of this book, but it also requires great thought on the part of instructors because a portfolio system implemented in a scattershot manner may well undercut the goals of a writing course. The portfolio offers instructors wonderful opportunities to bring their teaching practice in line with their theoretical assumptions about writing and about teaching, but that convergence can only occur if instructors ask themselves the right — and the tough — questions and work out the answers that best provide what both instructors and students need in the writing course.

Note

[1] I am assuming that instructors themselves will grade the papers. Ford and Larkin describe a programmatic use of portfolio grading wherein the portfolios are graded by a team of graders not including the students' instructor. My interest in this essay, however, is in the issues faced by individual instructors who do not have the power to implement such grading practice but must conduct their own evaluations.

Works Cited

Belanoff, Pat, and Marcia Dickson, eds. *Portfolios: Process and Product.* Portsmouth: Boynton, 1991.

Brannon, Lil, and C. H. Knoblauch. "On Students' Rights to Their Own Texts: A Model of Teacher Response." *College Composition and Communication* 33 (1982): 157–66.

Burnham, Christopher. "Portfolio Evaluation: Room to Breathe and Grow." *Training the New Teacher of College Composition.* Ed. Charles Bridges. Urbana: NCTE, 1986.

Elbow, Peter, and Pat Belanoff. "State University of New York at Stony Brook Portfolio-Based Evaluation Program." *New Methods in College Writing Programs.* Ed. Paul Connolly and Teresa Vilardi. New York: MLA, 1986. Reprinted in Belanoff and Dickson.

Emig, Janet. "Writing as a Mode of Learning." *College Composition and Communication* 28 (1977): 122–28.

Ford, James E., and Gregory Larkin. "The Portfolio System: An End to Backsliding Writing Standards." *College English* 39 (1978): 950–55.

Knoblauch, C.H., and Lil Brannon. *Rhetorical Traditions and the Teaching of Writing.* Portsmouth: Boynton, 1984.

Murray, Donald. "Teaching the Other Self: The Writer's First Reader." *College Composition and Communication* 33 (1982): 140–47.

Phelps, Louise Wetherbee. "Images of Student Writing: The Deep Structure of Teacher Response." *Writing and Response: Theory, Practice, and Research.* Ed. Chris M. Anson. Urbana: NCTE, 1989.

Sommers, Nancy. "Responding to Student Writing." *College Composition and Communication* 33 (1982): 148–56.

Sommers's Insights as a Resource for Your Teaching

1. Sommers emphasizes the serious inquiry a writing teacher should undertake before and while introducing portfolio grading in a writing classroom. If you've kept a reflective journal, scan it for passages where you've clarified your beliefs about the student-instructor relationship you desire and about assessment criteria and grading standards. Work out your portfolio policy from those stances.

2. Pat Belanoff and Peter Elbow have written collaboratively and frequently about what they learned from a portfolio-based evaluation program at the State University of New York at Stony Brook. They emphasize the collaborative learning and the feeling of community that result when writing instructors trade and evaluate student portfolios. To benefit most from using portfolio grading, work with one or two colleagues. Read the portfolios holistically, writing down general impressions and overall strengths and weaknesses. Then talk about how those features influence your responses and grading systems. Such conversation can help you clarify your teaching philosophy and gain confidence about your ways of responding to student writing.

3. The "teaching portfolio" cited throughout this ancillary is, of course, a "developmental portfolio." You will accrue the same benefits of ownership, empowerment, and autonomous learning from your teaching portfolio as can your students from their writing portfolios.

Sommers's Insights as a Resource for the Writing Classroom

1. It's possible to combine the representative and developmental portfolio models so that students can "own" the process and also become more able to identify the ways they have grown as writers. Negotiate with the class the minimum number of writing samples that should be submitted. Require that, for each submission and for the arrangement of the portfolio, students describe the entire process that led to the submitted writing, identify its strengths, and discuss why they view the work as "representative." Ask students to write a cover letter for the portfolio that applies shared criteria — such as an analysis of the "reflectiveness" or "growth" of the writer as demonstrated by the portfolio. Ask for a discussion of goal setting for continuous growth as a writer and learner. Such self-assessment can lead even the most grade-conscious writers into some independence.

2. Invite class members to think about the writings they have peer edited and offer advice to the writers about works they would recommend including in a portfolio.

3. Plan a conference or two with individual writers in which each can talk about the works and the decisions being made about submissions. Some students will be apprehensive about a portfolio assignment; some will dive in.

4. Encourage students to look at all they wrote during the term, including writing across the curriculum, in assessing their work and planning submissions.

LIZ HAMP-LYONS
AND WILLIAM CONDON

Questioning Assumptions about Portfolio-Based Assessment

Teacher-researchers Liz Hamp-Lyons and William Condon focused on class portfolios collected for a large-scale writing assessment to study the judgments that faculty readers made about portfolios. They concluded that any portfolio-based writing assessment must be continuously monitored, questioned, and revised in light of new uses and discoveries by students and faculty. The materials in the portfolio and the processes of judging the portfolio as a whole will generate new questions about student achievement, as well as new directions for faculty discussion and development. In effect, Hamp-Lyons, Condon, and their colleagues concluded that portfolio assessment was less a system than a highly recursive process.

Through collaborative research, Hamp-Lyons and Condon became aware of a set of assumptions about portfolio-based assessment, which they shared with their colleagues and with teachers who work with large-scale portfolio assessment at other institutions. The assumptions informed the initial design of the assessment project; they became criteria by which the researchers could analyze and evaluate the data they collected from their study of reader responses. The faculty assumed that because portfolios provide more texts (more evidence of student performance) and multiple genres, this broader basis for judgment would make decisions easier. The data did not demonstrate that students organized portfolios in ways that provided a broad base for judgment; the data also suggested that faculty readers arrived at a score for the whole portfolio early in the reading process. In response, the researchers are thinking seriously about how to clarify expected outcomes and how to revise the assessment to achieve those outcomes.

Similarly, the data indicated that for the processes of eliciting portfolios and responding to them much potential remains to be developed. Process was not easier to see in portfolios than in timed essays, although it could become more so if two needs are met: one, students need clear directions about how to present their portfolios; and two, readers need reliable and valid evaluation processes. With these changes, pedagogical and curricular values can be thematized as part of the process of evaluating, perhaps leading the community of readers to the assumed outcome of consensus in assessing and teaching writing. What at first glance seems no more than a report from one institution becomes a useful lens for faculty and individual writing instructors to use in reviewing, reflecting on, and improving their assessment practices.

Interest in and commitment to portfolios for assessing college writing have swelled enormously in the past decade and are still growing. In "Using Portfolios," Pat Belanoff and Peter Elbow wrote extensively about the benefits portfolios brought to the freshman composition program they ran at SUNY–Stony Brook. Anson and Brown have written, in "Large-Scale Portfolio Assessment in the Research University," about the efforts of faculty at the University of Minnesota toward large-scale portfolio collection at entry which, while they ultimately sank under the weight of campus-wide politics, inspired similar efforts at places such as the University of Alaska (Wauters). As the use of portfolios for purposes ranging from entry-level writing assessment (at Miami University: see Daiker) to campus-wide curriculum development (Larsen) becomes common, evaluation by portfolio method is increasingly accepted as an enriched evaluation and thus a better evaluation. Our own experience with portfolios at the University of Michigan (Condon and Hamp-Lyons) confirms that portfolio-based assessment does enrich the process of assessing writing; further, it enriches the process of teaching writing, of developing curriculum and faculty in a writing program, of collecting data about the program's effectiveness, and much, much more. The benefits of portfolio assessment are real, and the indications are that its potential has hardly begun to develop.

We write, then, from the perspective of a commitment to portfolio assessment, but also from the perspective of teacher-researchers who seek to understand all we do, even when it is successful. A great deal is still unknown about what portfolios do and, perhaps even more interestingly, about the nature of the role and activities we, as teachers and readers, engage in during portfolio assessment. In order to explore some of the issues involved in how teacher-evaluators use, perceive, and react to the portfolios they collect in their classes, we conducted a study of how they handle the cognitive task of making what we had initially thought would be a "holistic" judgment of the multiple texts in portfolios in one composition program. The insights we gained from viewing the reading of a portfolio from a kind of reader-response perspective caused us to question some of the major assumptions behind most portfolio assessments, including our own, and to find ways of working with portfolios that would take these new insights into account.[1]

The first stage of our work with portfolios, begun in 1987, taught us that what had looked originally like a system that we could put into place was actually a process, iterative in nature and different in each iteration (Condon and Hamp-Lyons), a discovery echoed by Roemer, Schultz, and Durst as they worked with portfolios and discovered "processes of change," and doubtless by many colleagues across college writing programs. While the first stage taught us many exciting, challenging, and worthwhile lessons, this second study taught us many new lessons. It led us to the realization that a portfolio-based system of writing assessment must continually be questioned, and must continually grow in response to new discoveries and to new phenomena, phenomena often engendered by the portfolio evaluation process itself. As a result, we realized that we needed to move to another stage of thinking about portfolios within a writing program, a kind of thinking that would prepare us to incorporate the new knowledge we gained from our study while maintaining the carefully-wrought strengths of the system we had developed. To achieve this difficult balancing act, the portfolio assessment process itself must provide mechanisms for (1) prompting readers to be aware of the process they are going through, (2) gathering appropriate data about that process, and (3) making the changes or accommodations which each new iteration shows are necessary. Our study of teacher-evaluators' reading and judging of portfolios demonstrated that portfolio assessments require maintenance that may be different in kind from that required for traditional writing assessments, but which at least equals them in intensity. In the remainder of this paper we point out that certain commonly-assumed benefits of portfolio assessment — ones which had informed our own adoption and design of this method — are not inherent to portfolio assessment but come only as a result of the same kind of care and attention that allow a holistic assessment to achieve reliability and validity. We continue to assert that portfolio-based assessment is vastly superior to traditional holistic assessment because of the many programmatic benefits it brings with it. But we must also assert that, like all beneficial innovations, its greatest benefits come when it is not entered into lightly or unquestioningly, but when critical eyes are brought to bear on it, demanding enlightenment and thereby helping to ensure excellence.

Setting up a portfolio-based writing assessment requires a great deal of planning and a great deal of work. It is also by its nature a highly contextualized operation, an aspect that we see as a strength rather than a weakness. In the University of Michigan's English Composition Board, approximately 12 percent of entering students receive entry assessment scores which place them in Practicum, scores based on a standard holistic reading of fifty-minute impromptu argumentative essays, which students produce during their orientation sessions. Practicum — an intensive half-term course limited to sixteen students per section, each of whom has a half-hour individual conference with the instructor each week — is an introductory course in academic writing, focusing on argumentation. At the end of this course, students prepare portfolios of the best writing they have done in the course. Each portfolio contains four pieces: two revised essays, one of which must be an argument; one impromptu essay, written in class; a reflective piece, written in class, that deals in some way with the writing in the portfolio (metacognition); plus a table of contents. Students also take a post-test in which they write a fifty-minute impromptu essay that is not part of the portfolio but which may in rare cases of major disagreements figure into the student's exit placement.[2] The outcome of this credit/no credit course, rather than a grade, is a placement: Repeat Practicum, Introductory Composition, or Exempt from Introductory Composition.

The system for arriving at decisions about portfolios at Michigan has been carefully developed, but like those in other portfolio assessment contexts, we found our imponderables in the human dimensions of portfolio assessment (see, for example, Roemer, Schultz, and Durst; or Smit, Kolonosky, and Seltzer). As we tried to answer our colleagues' questions about "how" they should arrive at a judgment of a portfolio, we discovered that the procedural changes involved in converting from the essay test to the portfolio for assessment are simple compared to the cognitive changes implicated in the conversion from reading single, fifty-minute impromptu arguments from each writer to reading portfolios consisting of several different pieces of writing produced by different writers from different sections of the same course. Portfolio assessment involves a "people-oriented" kind of self-examination. We were satisfied that we understood the needs and responses of the writers to the portfolio approach in these courses: with only sixteen students and a one-on-one half-hour conference weekly, all instructors come to know their students well. But we realized we needed to know more about what another key group of people, the portfolio readers, were doing and how what they were doing affected student outcomes. Therefore, we wanted to look as closely as we could at the process of reading a portfolio. At the same time, we did not want to set up an experimental study, or to intrude into the complex process by which a class instructor who has worked with a student throughout a course reads the student's work again from an evaluative perspective. Similarly, we did not want to intrude, if we could avoid it, into the process by which instructors read portfolios from students in other sections of the program.

Therefore, we began by giving copies of five portfolios from past classes to all our faculty/readers, and asking them to read the portfolios and keep a log of their reading so that we might first check our assumptions about some easily definable "problem" areas. We gave readers some general guidelines for what to note and comment on, based on the discussions we had had about portfolios in faculty meetings, but left the activity fairly open. Reading these logs allowed us to see the need to understand more about two areas: the criteria readers used to make their judgments, and the processes by which they applied those criteria as they read.

We next asked our faculty to repeat the reading log activity, but this time with a more conscious focus on these two key areas, and with the "live" portfolios they were reading from their own class and a colleague's. As we worked with the data from this second stage, we identified for the faculty several facets of writing that seemed to be especially salient to their reading: evidence of awareness of viewpoints other than the writer's own; recognition of complexity in the issues the writer discusses; coherent presentation of support which accommodates the issues the author raises; adequate transitions; and consistent voice. These facets, of course, grow out of the local values of our program, and we do not suggest that they would be appropriate in a different writing program with different values. Drawing also from the vast quantity of data generated by the first and second stages, we began to see some aspects of the portfolio reading process we should ask readers to examine: whether a portfolio is seen as a unit or as parts which must somehow be weighed; at what point judgment (i.e., scoring) occurs; the differences between reading our own students' portfolios versus those from another class; whether standards are stricter in a portfolio than on a timed post-test.

In the next stage, therefore, we constructed a more formal kind of reading log that at the same time limited the amount of work we asked readers to do — for readers were unanimous that the intense self-reflection we were asking of them was extremely time-consuming. Readers completed this log on selected portfolios during actual portfolio reading sessions. This "Reader Response Questionnaire" attempted to get at such questions as how and when a reader makes the decision about a score on a portfolio, what standards readers feel they are bringing into play, what divergent evidence among texts lead them to a score decision, and so on. We gave the questionnaire to groups of readers on different exit assessment occasions, so that some readers completed several over an academic year, while others completed only one. On different occasions, readers were asked to complete the survey on portfolios from their own class, from another instructor's class, or on a batch of portfolios chosen to be common to them all.

Because our faculty members are well-trained and experienced in formal writing assessment, their expectations of formal characteristics of assessment for the portfolio process were quite high. For them, it was critical that we go as far as possible in establishing criteria and standards for judging the portfolios. Thus, during the year and a half that we were collecting these data, we also began holding standardizing sessions, though the purposes here were somewhat different from the purposes for the traditional standardizing sessions in holistic assessment. Since we found no discussion of standardizing in the literature on portfolio assessment, we needed, in the first place, to find out what standardizing for portfolios should be like, how it differed from that other kind of standardizing session, and what the goals of standardizing should be (e.g., to what extent we should strive for agreement in score levels, how similar our criteria needed to be, how much portfolios can differ and still be generally recognized as fulfilling the requirements of the course). Getting people to read and score portfolios and to talk about their processes for doing so and the standards they were applying made the reading itself a more public activity, exposing each of us to the methods others were using to make their judgments, and the perceptions we shared about portfolio assessment in general and about individual portfolios in particular. These standardizing sessions added enormously to our understanding of the data we were collecting in the various stages of our reader-response study.

Identifying and Questioning Assumptions about Portfolios

As we moved through the stages of reader-response data collection described above, and as we attended to the discussions in standardizing sessions, we became conscious of some of our own assumptions about portfolio-based assessment, assumptions that we seemed to share with our colleagues and with people in other programs that employ portfolio assessment. We identified five areas where our study of readers' responses to portfolios during their reading led us to question those assumptions. In what follows, we first explain each assumption, relating it to the questions raised by our data; then we consider how a portfolio assessment program may respond to these insights.

Assumption One: Because a portfolio contains more texts than a timed essay examination, it provides more evidence and therefore a broader basis for judgment, making decisions easier.

This assumption contradicts the widely held belief that teachers read holistically: a larger number of texts only offers a broader basis for judgment if quality varies from text to text, and readers can only take a variation of quality into account if they read non-holistically. Our surveys of reader behavior suggest that holistic reading, in the case of portfolios, is highly unlikely, if not impossible. Multiple texts, unless texts are so close in kind and quality that they are virtually identical, inevitably force readers to consider one text in the light of another, to weigh one against the other, and to make a decision that, while representing a judgment about the whole portfolio, is grounded in a weighing of the parts, rather than in a dominant impression of the whole. In such cases, decisions become harder, not easier, as the portfolio presents a more complex, more comprehensive "snapshot" of the writer's ability. And even this more comprehensive decision requires that readers make use of all the evidence the portfolio provides, an issue we shall examine at greater length in our discussion of common aspects of Assumptions One and Two.

Assumption Two: A portfolio will contain texts of more than one genre, and multiple genres also lead to a broader basis for judgments, making decisions easier.

Here we can see two underlying assumptions: first, that writing quality will vary from genre to genre, and second, that a portfolio will necessarily contain texts of more than one genre. While we can expect, for example, that writing a personal narrative is different from writing a critical analysis (since those forms make different demands on the writer's skills), it does not necessarily follow that a student will do well on one and poorly on the other. If writing quality does not vary from one genre to another, there is no assessment argument for including multiple genres (though there may be pedagogical reasons), since they do not actually broaden the basis for the decision. And if writing quality *does* vary from one genre to the other, then the decision is harder, and the reader is thrown back into the dilemma of holistic versus non-holistic reading described above. In addition, in a system like ours that leaves the contents of a writer's portfolio in the writer's hands as far as possible, there is no guarantee that genres will vary. We had specified that *one* of the revised essays had to be an argument, and the prompts for in-class essays cued students to write arguments. The genre for the second revised essay was left open, but in practice it was almost uniformly another argument. Introducing the requirement that a student include a reflective piece in the portfolio was in part a reaction against the perception that too many of our students' portfolios contained only one genre, argumentation.

Our data also reveal that, for these readers in this context, the influence of multiple genres, when they occurred, seemed to be minor. There was nothing in any of the reading logs about writing performance on one genre rather than another. Never did a reader say, "This student knows how to present a point of view, but can't handle reporting the views of others," for example, or even, "This student can write an effective narrative, but has a good deal of trouble with more complex forms of discourse." Rather than finding that different genres offered readers different kinds of evidence, we discovered that revised texts seemed to offer different evidence from the impromptu texts, even though those texts were almost always the same genre. Often, we saw in the readers' logs occasions where readers had to backtrack and reread a revised piece in the light of what they were seeing in the impromptu. And when readers did comment on weighing the evidence of one text against another, it seemed to be that the different kinds of evidence, rather than anything else, caused them problems. As far as we could see, knowing more made the decision harder, not easier.

But behind all this, and behind Assumption One, is an assumption that readers will attend to all the text they see; that is, if readers are given more text to read, they will read it all as intensely as they would the limited text generated during a single essay-test session. We have found again and again in portfolios of different kinds, at different times, from different readers, a clear suggestion that readers do not attend equally to the entire portfolio. Although the portfolios in our study contain four texts from a course of instruction, each of which has the potential to offer conflicting evidence to the other three, readers' self-reports indicate that readers arrived at a score during their reading of the first paper. A few readers reached a tentative score after the first or second paragraph of the first piece of text. Some readers postponed any decision until the second piece, but moved to a score rather soon within it. Readers seemed to go through a process of seeking a "center of gravity" and then read for confirmation or contradiction of that sense. The following reading log extract shows a process that is typical:

What is the first thing you read in full?
The cover sheet.

Where do you go from there?
I read in page order.

At what point does a possible score occur to you?
Pretty much in the middle of paper 1, but I try to keep an open mind. . . .

Do you revise the score you first thought of?
I move more toward a "2-" on the impromptu.

At what point do you become certain of the score?
After the impromptu, but I look at the third paper briefly.

These data question the assumption that portfolios provide a broader basis upon which readers can make judgments. On the basis of the reader-response questionnaires, for example, perhaps four pieces are not needed in the portfolio, and some other configuration (perhaps an impromptu and a revised piece with all its prior drafts) might be more constructive. These insights have also led us to advise instructors to tell their students to organize the pieces they put in their portfolio in descending order of quality, i.e., to put what they think is their best piece first. Students who use the technique of saving the best for last and bracketing their worst in the middle may lose out in the reading process.

Perhaps discovering that some of our assumptions were unfounded should have led us to abandon the notion of portfolio-based assessment — but there are many reasons for moving to portfolio assessment, many of which we have discussed at length elsewhere (Condon and Hamp-Lyons). Our response was not to abandon the approach, but to give serious thought to what we wanted from exit assessments, and how we could achieve those results.

Clearly, if we are interested in whether the quality of a student's writing varies from genre to genre, we need to ensure that each portfolio contains multiple genres, a move that would simply mean redesigning the instructions to students about the contents of the portfolio. However, even the seemingly simple and unambiguous step of requiring multiple genres has far-reaching implications for the ethos of a writing program, since it requires teachers to redesign their goals to fit the portfolio expectations — in our case, for example, to value other written genres in addition to argumentation. Making such a pedagogical decision is a matter for the whole writing faculty, and indeed is likely to go beyond the writing program. In our case, for example, the focus on argumentation was established as the result of several research studies which highlighted the importance of the genre within the specific University of Michigan context (Keller-Cohen and Wolfe; Hamp-Lyons and Reed). Studying our reader-response data, then, made us more aware of the values upon which the writing program was built.

And if the change to multiple genres occurs, the question whether different genres necessarily result in evidence of different writing qualities or competencies remains. Even if it is true that a portfolio contains more than one genre, we must doubt whether this will indeed provide a broader basis for a decision. Our data show that many readers are not conscious of genre as a factor, or are unconsciously compensating for variation due to genre. If we wanted to hold to Assumption Two, then, we would need to provide explicit response criteria that differ from genre to genre, and require faculty to use these criteria while reading (not to mention while teaching). This in turn means that writers would have to state the genre of each of their texts in the cover sheets of their portfolios. This seems to us an unlikely scenario. But we reiterate our questioning of the assumption that having a broader basis for evaluation will make evaluation easier; we have become convinced that it is likely to make decisions more complex and difficult.

A problem with many of the suggestions we have sketched out above for both Assumptions One and Two is that the response sheets — and the processes expected of readers — would be extremely complex and time-consuming. Readers do not normally follow the procedures set out for them using the predicted processes when they read evaluatively (Huot; Cooper and Hamp-Lyons; Hamp-Lyons). Our studies have already suggested that readers tend to reduce the cognitive — and time — load in portfolio reading by finding short cuts to decisions; indeed, it is often these short cut strategies that raise the issues we are seeking to resolve. We believe this is a human trait and not unique or idiosyncratic to our situation or our readers, who are professional and well-trained in assessment reading. It is impracticable to seek to solve a problem with a solution more cumbersome than the original plan. But what we have learned about our inability to validate Assumptions One and Two raises the specter of readers not reading the whole portfolio — of this wonderful mechanism, this excellent pedagogical tool, losing some of its assessment value because readers are missing some portion of what is there. The superiority of portfolios as an assessment tool is dependent on readers reading, judging, and valuing *all* the texts. Hence, we believe we should be able to resolve our problems with Assumptions One and Two together, since they are so closely related. We have considered three possibilities.

Perhaps a practical solution would be to require readers to answer a couple of questions on each portfolio, designed to place subsequent texts in the context of the first piece in the portfolio, e.g., "Specify the strengths present in this text which make it better than the first text"; "Specify the characteristics of this text that make it less competent than the first piece in the portfolio"; "Specify the ways in which this text appears to be of the same quality as the first." An alternative might require the readers to generate some kind of feedback that demands commenting intelligently on the portfolio as a whole, which would at least ensure that readers pay more careful attention to all the pieces in the portfolio, attention which would probably translate into different scoring behaviors as well. Finally, if we adopt the assumption that readers read a portfolio holistically — which, so far at least, would be no more than a convenient fiction — we might combine these approaches and design criteria that force readers to make judgments about whether the quality of the pieces in the portfolio was consistently or inconsistently high (or low, or medium), and provide a means for generic feedback tied to those criteria. A different kind of solution addresses our finding that readers attend to differences between revised and impromptu texts; portfolios could contain fewer texts and more stages. Would readers pay more attention to multiple versions of one text than they do to multiple separate texts? We don't know at this stage, but, again, removing one of the two revised texts in exchange for a draft or two of the other, which means trading one type of evidence for another, is a solution that could be simply accomplished, but which raises complex questions of curriculum and values. Such a solution requires, at least, the participation of the faculty as a whole, and if the decision is to be an informed one, it will require more information than we have at present. It seems that, in order to ensure that readers read the student's whole text, responses must go beyond merely putting a score down on a piece of paper. We hope that the next stage of our investigation of portfolio reading will begin to answer questions concerning which if any of these proposed strategies may be successful.

Assumption Three: Portfolios will make process easier to see in a student's writing and enable instructors to reward evidence of the ability to bring one's own text significantly forward in quality.

As soon as we articulated this assumption — before we looked at any data — it was obvious to us that this assumption necessitates that drafts (i.e., evidence of the writing processes prior to the product) be included in the portfolio. A system requiring multiple texts is not inherently based on multiple passes at any of those texts, and if it is not, process will not be "easy to see." We had expected to find (given the earlier assumptions about what readers do) that instructors would reward evidence of the student's ability to bring her or his own text significantly forward in quality. But as we studied the reading logs we realized that inferring process from the contrast between formal, finished papers and impromptu writing is too restrictive to enable readers to see and reward effective applications of processes and clear improvement in texts. In fact, we found several instances where readers' perceptions of greater competence in the revised texts than in the impromptu led them to place greater emphasis on the lack of skill in the impromptu. It seemed from readers' self-reflections that they were aware of the part they had played *as instructors* in improving *their own* students' texts, and that this led them to be suspicious when they saw significantly better revised texts than impromptu writing in portfolios from other classes. Perhaps this means that the readers were seeing the improvement as the instructor's work rather than the student's. Some readers' self-reports, in fact, indicated this very belief. A reader might say something like: "The two revised essays look very competent but I know how hard we [NB: "we"] worked on them; I think the impromptu shows more accurately the kinds of problems this student has." Thus, a reader might place the student "Repeat Practicum" while accepting that two of the four papers are at a level that warrants placement into Introductory Composition. This problem would, we believe, have been considerably lessened if the portfolios had contained multiple drafts of at least one of the revised papers. If readers have only product data to evaluate, and if the instructional context does not necessarily require students to write more than one draft, portfolios cannot support process pedagogy.

Assumption Three, then, is rather easy to validate: we need to encourage, even require, students to include drafts in their portfolios. Nothing else can happen here if readers don't have drafts to respond to. We stress drafting, conferencing, and multiple revision in our courses, but currently our portfolios fail to reflect our pedagogical values in this vital respect. Thus, while our "taught" curriculum emphasizes revision and process, our "tested" curriculum explicitly requires only product, leaving students free to ignore what their teachers tell them about process. Given the full context of the Practicum course, with its class meetings, regular weekly conferences, and so forth, avoiding revision would not be easy, but the portfolio, in theory, allows students to complete the course without having to revise, and some students have done so. Expanding the portfolio to include drafts is the first and most important change the second stage of our study has resulted in. Future studies will explore whether and how readers use the information provided by the inclusion of process evidence in a student's portfolio.

Assumption Four: Portfolio assessment allows pedagogical and curricular values to be taken into account.

Assumption Four posits, first, that possessing contextual knowledge helps the reader to make decisions, and second, that decisions made in light of that knowledge are better decisions. In this way, Assumption Four represents the common argument that portfolios somehow automatically represent a closer connection with curricular values. Here, too, we have come to believe that this can only be true if the connection between curriculum and portfolio is carefully and consistently built. The mere existence of a portfolio method of assessment does not assure it. Through the creation of portfolio reading teams, the requirement of sharing assignments among members of a team, the meetings of portfolio readers in small teams, and the general portfolio standardization for all faculty, we have striven to ensure that our portfolio system represents our pedagogical values.

Portfolio assessment allows pedagogical and curricular values to be taken into account when a teaching program provides ways for faculty to interact. The interactions must extend beyond coming together for portfolio standardizing sessions; they must run deep enough for every member of the community to feel that s/he completely understands the values and teaching goals of the program, and to feel that s/he can influence what happens and how it happens. This level of interaction will be easiest when programs provide a close working environment and plenty of informal opportunities for interaction; a carefully-constructed and monitored portfolio assessment system with portfolio groups, calibrating sessions, etc.; and a well-developed professional structure where faculty meet to consider both pedagogy and research on a regular basis. In making decisions about individual portfolios, faculty must have strong input, not only through the scores they give but through an internal appeal procedure. In the program we studied, instructors are notified of the proposed outcome for every student in their sections and have an opportunity to request a change, explaining why and producing additional evidence. These are the minimum requirements if a program is to ensure that the portfolios the students prepare and the scores the faculty give actually reflect the pedagogical and curricular values of that program and, more importantly, that those pedagogical and curricular values are subject to revision as a result of the evidence the portfolios present. To the extent that a program does not have these attributes, it must either develop them or develop other mechanisms for assuring that its pedagogical and curricular values will be expressed in the portfolios; such expression will not occur without careful program-wide attention.

Assumption Five: Portfolio assessment aids in building consensus in assessment and in instruction.

Assumption Five suggests that more information, more data, will lead a group of faculty more easily to consensus. To the extent that faculty are aware of their values and willing to take them out in public and look at them, portfolio assessment can aid in building consensus about instruction. We believe we have gone further in this direction than most, but we can't say we've produced consensus and clarity about instructional goals and methods. We have found some instances where discussions over portfolios have revealed differences among faculty over pedagogical goals, differences that discussion in the small portfolio teams that meet regularly during the semester could not resolve. Our experience, our close investigation, has shown us that to make portfolio assessment aid in building consensus in assessment and instruction, we have to go much further than we first thought. Yes, portfolios do build community and consensus more effectively and dynamically than impromptu writing assessments, but even here there are no easy outcomes. A community is not a group of people who all agree with each other. Communities have to work continually to find their grounds for agreement and to find ways to compromise on areas where they disagree. Some of our faculty, for example, privilege "academic writing" more than others; some define argument quite narrowly, others rather widely; some are more troubled by final drafts with errors in traditional grammar than others are. We have learned that maintaining a strong portfolio-based assessment program requires us to (a) seek out issues that demand consensus and (b) provide forums for building consensus. The process doesn't stop with the first consensus-building stage. If a portfolio evaluation is introduced but not maintained, no matter how thoughtfully it was established, consensus will disappear and the community will find itself with more discord than under less pervasive methods of assessment.

The Need for Criteria

We hadn't made many passes through the portfolio assessment process before we realized that portfolio reading requires as much of an evaluative stance as a traditional essay-test reading does, despite the portfolio reading's contextualized nature. Readers still had to make decisions, and we still expected that we would be able to identify and, ultimately, define a standard for a passing portfolio and for an outstanding one. Indeed, this quest to establish external, written criteria provided the impetus for what became our inquiry into readers' responses to portfolios, which turned into our analysis of common assumptions about portfolio assessment, above. Our readers have told us over and over that they feel the need for criteria and standards against which to measure portfolios, both those from other classes and from their own. This need is real, yet it is a difficult need to address, for it confronts one of the differences between traditional, holistic essay assessment (a proficiency test) and portfolio assessment (an achievement test): the relationship of criteria to the reading and scoring process. In essay assessment, the criteria are external to the goals of a writing program's curriculum. The context within which the writer produces the essay is essentially separate from the criteria by which the essay will be judged. For such an entry assessment, criteria are based on expectations of the academy as a whole. Thus, explicit, written criteria are important to the holistic scoring process; training readers, establishing reliability and validity, standing up to public scrutiny — all would be impossible without these explicit, external criteria.

On the other hand, in the portfolio exit assessment context of which we write, the criteria are grounded in the curriculum of the course in which the portfolio is produced. As students move through the course, they discover important features of writing and the writing process. In other words, what students learn in the class, among many other things, is a gradual revealing of the criteria, and that knowledge in turn informs the student's preparation of the portfolio. And because the scoring criteria are implicit in the whole system of writing instruction that leads up to the completion of the portfolio, the instructor's contextual knowledge of that system guides her/his process of reading and scoring the portfolios. In such a situation, the absence of external standards and external criteria for portfolios makes standardizing sessions central to the portfolio judgment process. In these sessions, all the faculty have worked together to search out the criteria we should apply to portfolios and the language we could best use to talk about them, continually discovering new kinds of portfolios and new kinds of problems and continually needing to redefine and re-draw our expectations about portfolios and how we respond to them. In other words, as the context for making a judgment changes, so do the implicit criteria for making the judgment, and the standardizing sessions become the locus for identifying those changes and "fixing" them for the duration of the current reading. Such a system of continually developing criteria appeals to the romantic side of human nature, yielding criteria that remind us of Tennyson's Camelot:

> For an ye heard a music, like enow
> They are building still, seeing the city is built
> To music, therefore never built at all,
> And therefore built for ever. (33)

Yet the classical side of us yearns for hard and fast criteria, for permanence, for "rules" readers as teachers can point to and say, "Here. Look at this. This is why you need to continue in Practicum." Furthermore, our classical side tells us that in order for a program to be fully accountable for its decisions, it must have explicable, sharable, consistent criteria. To date, portfolio assessments have relied on common values, on a shared sense of what competence is and what excellence is. Developing explicit criteria would require codifying our common values, while probably setting aside the individual emphases which have on occasion brought two readers to an impasse. Making values external also makes them less subject to change as the goals of a writing program change. We must search for an approach that permits criteria that are constantly open to negotiation, open to the changes that a recursive process of teaching and reading portfolios must involve. At the same time, perhaps there is strength in formalizing a method that would reflect the best of what readers already do, seeking to guide all-toward those "good reader" processes. We perceive that the issues we have to resolve center on our emerging understanding that using portfolios to make exit decisions from our courses calls for an evaluative stance, as does traditional direct writing assessment, but that the evaluative stance it calls forth is of a different kind. We see a difficult balancing act ahead, but one that will become necessary to all portfolio assessment programs as they grow toward maturity.

Conclusion

Like the portfolio-based assessment we established, this article has undergone many transformations. It began as a project that would help our faculty reach consensus about what they meant by argumentation, a necessary step considering that two of the four items in our portfolios are arguments. Out of that project grew an effort to define criteria for assessing portfolios, a project that led us to ask readers to describe their practice of coming to a decision about portfolios. In the process, we came up hard against the assumptions we have examined in this article, assumptions which we found were common to portfolio-based assessments. Like most writing programs, we shifted to portfolios because we thought they provided a more accurate assessment of writing. After examining our assumptions, however, we have found that increased accuracy is not an inherent virtue of portfolio assessment; while it stands to reason that including more writing and a wider variety of writing as the basis for a judgment would make that judgment more accurate, our research indicates that these improvements come not as a result of using portfolios, but as a result of how a faculty or a program approaches the task of portfolio assessment. Over the last five years, we have discovered that portfolio assessment brings many benefits to a writing program: it promotes communication among faculty; it promotes faculty training and development as a natural outgrowth of the teaching experience; it democratizes a faculty, allowing the grizzled veterans of the composition wars to learn from the raw recruits, as well as allowing the inexperienced access to the advice, support, and knowledge of our most experienced faculty; it promotes consensus and collaboration; the list could go on and on. Ironically, the reason we adopted portfolio assessment in the first place is the one reason our research calls into question: the assessment reason. Further research into the problems we have encountered with these common assumptions will help establish whether portfolio assessment is better *qua* assessment; its other benefits, in our experience, make it a worthwhile endeavor, even if we are never able to prove that it is a better *assessment* than a timed writing holistically scored.

We have tried to show in our study both our commitment to portfolio assessment and our determination to question it closely and use what we learn to make the weak stronger and the good even better. We believe this can only happen when we confront our own assumptions. For us, this is neither the beginning nor the end, but a stage in a continuing process of learning and growth as we try to find ways of affirming what our students can do with writing.

Notes

[1] We must offer our appreciation to all the colleagues who participated in the portfolio assessment and in particular in the reader-response study during this period: Jan Armon, Cheryl Cassidy, Francelia Clark, George Cooper, Kathy Dixon, Louise Freyman, Helen Isaacson, Emily Jessup, Martina Kohl, Phyllis Lassner, Mark McPhail, Eleanor McKenna, Barbra Morris, Kenn Pierson, Sharon Quiroz, Martin Rosenberg, Bill Shea, Kim Silfven, and Maureen Taylor.

[2] At the time this study was conducted, the post-test was still administered and scored; the success of the portfolio-based exit assessment has since allowed us to discontinue the post-test.

Works Cited

Anson, Chris, and Robert L. Brown. "Large-Scale Portfolio Assessment in the Research University: Stories of Problems and Success." *Notes from the National Testing Network in Writing* 19 (Mar. 1990): 8–9.

Belanoff, Pat, and Peter Elbow. "Using Portfolios to Increase Collaboration and Community in a Writing Program." *Journal of Writing Program Administration* 9 (Spring 1986): 27–39.

Condon, William, and Liz Hamp-Lyons. "Introducing a Portfolio-Based Writing Assessment: Progress through Problems." *Portfolios: Process and Product.* Ed. Pat Belanoff and Marcia Dickson. Portsmouth: Boynton, 1991. 231–47.

Cooper, George, and Liz Hamp-Lyons. *Looking in on Essay Readers.* Ann Arbor: English Composition Board, 1988.

Daiker, Donald A., Jeffrey Sommers, Gail Stygall, and Laurel Black. *The Best of Miami's Portfolios.* Oxford: Miami UP, 1990.

Hamp-Lyons, Liz. "Reconstructing Academic Writing Proficiency." *Assessing Second Language Writing in Academic Settings.* Ed. Liz Hamp-Lyons. Norwood: Ablex, 1991. 127–53.

Hamp-Lyons, Liz, and Rebecca Reed. *Development of the New Michigan Writing Assessment: Report to the College of LS and A.* Ann Arbor: English Composition Board, 1990.

Huot, Brian. "Reliability, Validity, and Holistic Scoring: What We Know and What We Need to Know." *College Composition and Communication* 41 (Feb. 1990): 201–13.

Keller-Cohen, Deborah, and Arthur Wolfe. *Extended Writing in the College of Literature, Science, and the Arts: Report on a Faculty Survey.* Ann Arbor: English Composition Board, 1987.

Larsen, Richard L. "Using Portfolios in the Assessment of Writing in the Academic Disciplines." *Portfolios: Process and Product.* Ed. Pat Belanoff and Marcia Dickson. Portsmouth: Boynton, 1991. 137–50.

Roemer, Marjorie, Lucille M. Schultz, and Russel K. Durst. "Portfolios and the Process of

Change." *College Composition and Communication* 42 (Dec. 1991): 455–69.

Smit, David, Patricia Kolonosky, and Kathryn Seltzer. "Implementing a Portfolio System." *Portfolios: Process and Product.* Ed. Pat Belanoff and Marcia Dickson. Portsmouth: Boynton, 1991. 46–56.

Tennyson, Lord Alfred. *Idylls of the King.* New York: New American Library, 1961.

Wauters, Joan K. "Evaluation for Empowerment: A Portfolio Proposal for Alaska." *Portfolios: Process and Product.* Ed. Pat Belanoff and Marcia Dickson. Portsmouth: Boynton, 1991. 57–68.

Hamp-Lyons and Condon's Insights as a Resource for Your Teaching

1. The shared reading of student portfolios prompts spontaneous and seren-dipitous conversation about student learning, assignments, classroom strat-egies, and syllabus design. If you teach in a program where portfolio assess-ment is not used, experiment with it. Even if you are the only instructor experimenting with an end-of-term portfolio, ask two or three colleagues to assist you in reading and making judgments about the portfolio as a snap-shot of the student writer. Share the other readers' responses with the writer.

2. Portfolios can provide a broader basis for judgment of student achievement, but we must direct students in putting portfolios together. We must also as-sist them in the self-assessment processes that are necessary for them to as-semble a portfolio that represents them more fully than does a series of writ-ten texts alone. Ideally, in a course portfolio a writer can show his or her process of constructing or amplifying an identity as a writer. A portfolio should be the "multiple voices" and the "multiple selves" of a writer: the writer creating a text, the writer as the "best reader" of his or her text, the writer/reader retrospecting and assessing both individual texts and the "story" implicit in the collection of texts.

   To help your students, introduce them early in the semester to the con-cept of the portfolio as a reflective genre. Give them opportunities with each submitted manuscript to assess their work and reflect on what they learned through the process of writing the paper. Hold conferences on a "mini port-folio" in which the writer selects one work and writes a letter discussing how it was generated and why it represents the writer in process. Ask stu-dents to submit at least one set of drafts that demonstrate competence in or growth with the process of revising. Ask for a letter of introduction describ-ing the portfolio to multiple readers and an essay of reflection explaining how the selections work together in demonstrating the writer.

   Elbow has described ways to use a portfolio for assessment and to grade the portfolio at the end of the term. An alternative, which might prove help-ful to students unaccustomed to self-assessment, would be awarding course credit for the portfolio as an end-of-semester capstone. If the portfolio counts in the overall course grade for at least one grade-level difference and if stu-dents have feedback during the semester about building a portfolio, they learn to use the process of assembling portfolio to monitor and to set goals for their learning.

Hamp-Lyons and Condon's Insights as a Resource for the Writing Classroom

1. With the portfolio as with any writing assignment, there's always the danger that students will generate what they perceive the teacher wants rather than write for themselves. Encourage students to have peers read and respond to the portfolios during the process of creating a portfolio. This gives you more basis for judging the "whole" of the learner. Ask peers to write letters in response to the whole portfolio, commenting on their impressions of the texts and of the writer. Often in these letters they will mention some change they

observed in the writer during the course. Often they will comment on the improvements they see in the final drafts of texts they critiqued.

2. Assign a mini-portfolio about one-third of the way into the semester: tell students to select something that demonstrates change for them as learners since they arrived on campus and to submit it with a letter of self-assessment that explains how the artifact represents this change. Don't stipulate a written product or positive change; most students will use a writing or set of drafts but some will take the opportunity to submit another artifact and explain in the self-assessment letter why it is significant to their perception of change. The broad prompt permits use of imagination and encourages students to look at both curricular and cocurricular sites for learning. Evaluate how well the self-assessment letter communicates reflective and personal thought to a public reader.

JOSEPH M. WILLIAMS *The Phenomenology of Error*

In this essay, Williams explores the "deep psychic forces" that affect the ways we approach errors in student writing. Williams claims that no two people have quite the same conception of what error is and that people detect error only when they are explicitly looking for and expect to find it. The implications of these insights are quite profound — and, indeed, not without a certain political significance. If no one really knows what error is and if everyone sees error only when actively looking for it, then perhaps a certain prejudice informs our encounters with student writing — a prejudice that has no coherent intellectual basis.

I am often puzzled by what we call errors of grammar and usage, errors such as *different than, between you and I*, a *which* for a *that*, and so on. I am puzzled by what motive could underlie the unusual ferocity which an *irregardless* or a *hopefully* or a singular *media* can elicit. In his second edition of *On Writing Well* (New York[:HarperCollins], 1980), for example, William Zinsser, an otherwise amiable man I'm sure, uses, and quotes not disapprovingly, words like *detestable vulgarity* (43), *garbage* (44), *atrocity* (46), *horrible* (48), *oaf* (42), *idiot* (43), and *simple illiteracy* (46), to comment on usages like *OK, hopefully*, the affix *-wise*, and *myself* in *He invited Mary and myself to dinner*.

The last thing I want to seem is sanctimonious. But as I am sure Zinsser would agree, what happens in Cambodia and Afghanistan could more reasonably be called horrible atrocities. The likes of Idi Amin qualify as legitimate oafs. Idiots we have more than enough of in our state institutions. And while simple illiteracy is the condition of billions, it does not characterize those who use *disinterested* in its original sense.[1]

I am puzzled why some errors should excite this seeming fury while others, not obviously different in kind, seem to excite only moderate disapproval. And I am puzzled why some of us can regard any particular item as a more or less serious error, while others, equally perceptive, and acknowledging that the same item may in some sense be an "error," seem to invest in their observation no emotion at all.

At first glance, we ought to be able to explain some of these anomalies by subsuming errors of grammar and usage in a more general account of defective social behavior, the sort of account constructed so brilliantly by Erving Goffman.[2] But errors of social behavior differ from errors of "good usage": Social errors that excite feelings commensurate with judgments like "horrible," "atrocious," "oaf(ish)," and "detestable" are usually errors that grossly violate our personal space: We break wind at a dinner party and then vomit on the person next to us. We spill coffee in their lap, then step on a toe when we get up to apologize. It's the Inspector Clouseau routine. Or the error metaphorically violates psychic space: We utter an inappropriate obscenity, mention our painful hemorrhoids, tell a racist joke, and snigger at the fat woman across the table who turns out to be our hostess. Because all of these actions crudely violate one's personal space we are justified in calling them "oafish"; all of them require that we apologize, or at least offer an excuse.

This way of thinking about social error turns our attention from error as a discrete entity, frozen at the moment of its commission, to error as part of a flawed transaction, originating in ignorance or incompetence or accident, manifesting itself as an invasion of another's personal space, eliciting a judgment ranging from silent disapproval to "atrocious" and "horrible," and requiring either an explicit "I'm sorry" and correction, or a simple acknowledgment and a tacit agreement not to do it again.[3]

To address errors of grammar and usage in this way, it is also necessary to shift our attention from error treated strictly as an isolated item on a page, to error perceived as a flawed verbal transaction between a writer and a reader. When we do this, the matter of error turns less on a handbook definition than on the reader's response, because it is that response — "detestable," "horrible" — that defines the seriousness of the error and its expected amendment.

But if we do compare serious nonlinguistic gaffes to errors of usage, how can we not be puzzled over why so much heat is invested in condemning a violation whose consequence impinges not at all on our personal space? The language some use to condemn linguistic error seems far more intense than the language they use to describe more consequential social errors — a hard bump on the arm, for example — that require a sincere but not especially effusive apology. But no matter how "atrocious" or "horrible" or "illiterate" we think an error like *irregardless* or a *like* for an *as* might be, it does not jolt my ear in the same way an elbow might; a *between you and I* does not offend me, at least not in the ordinary sense of offend. Moreover, unlike social errors, linguistic errors do not ordinarily require that we apologize for them.[4] When we make *media* a singular or dangle a participle, and are then made aware of our mistake, we are expected to acknowledge the error, and, if we have the opportunity, to amend it. But I don't think that we are expected to say, "Oh, I'm sorry!" The objective consequences of the error simply do not equal those of an atrocity, or even of clumsiness.

It may be that to fully account for the contempt that some errors of usage arouse, we will have to understand better than we do the relationship between language, order, and those deep psychic forces that perceived linguistic violations seem to arouse in otherwise amiable people.[5] But if we cannot yet fully account for the psychological source of those feelings, or why they are so intense, we should be able to account better than we do for the variety of responses that different "errors" elicit. It is a subject that should be susceptible to research. And indeed, one kind of research in this area has a long tradition: In this century, at least five major surveys of English usage have been conducted to determine how respondents feel about various matters of usage. Sterling Leonard, Albert Marckwardt, Raymond Crisp, the Institute of Education English Research Group at the University of Newcastle upon Tyne, and the *American Heritage Dictionary* have questioned hundreds of teachers and editors and writers and scholars about their attitudes toward matters of usage ranging from *which* referring to a whole clause to split infinitives to *enthuse* as a verb.[6]

The trouble with this kind of research, though, with asking people whether they think *finalize* is or is not good usage, is that they are likely to answer. As William Labov and others have demonstrated,[7] we are not always our own best informants about our habits of speech. Indeed, we are likely to give answers that misrepresent our talking and writing, usually in the direction of more rather than less conservative values. Thus when the editors of the *American Heritage Dictionary* asks its Usage Panel to decide the acceptability of *impact* as a verb, we can predict how they will react: Merely by being asked, it becomes manifest to them that they have been invested with an institutional responsibility that will require them to judge usage by the standards they think they are supposed to uphold. So we cannot be surprised that when asked, Zinsser rejects *impact* as a verb, despite the fact that *impact* has been used as a verb at least since 1601.

The problem is self-evident: Since we can ask an indefinite number of questions about an indefinite number of items of usage, we can, merely by asking, accumulate an indefinite number of errors, simply because whoever we ask will feel compelled to answer. So while it may seem useful for us to ask one another whether we think X is an error, we have to be skeptical about our answers, because we will invariably end up with more errors than we began with, certainly more than we ever feel on our nerves when we read in the ways we ordinarily do.

In fact, it is this unreflective feeling on the nerves in our ordinary reading that interests me the most, the way we respond — or not — to error when we do not make error a part of our conscious field of attention. It is the difference between reading for typographical errors and reading for content. When we read for typos, letters constitute the field of attention; content becomes virtually inaccessible. When we read for content, semantic structures constitute the field of attention; letters — for the most part — recede from our consciousness.

I became curious about this kind of perception three years ago when I was consulting with a government agency that had been using English teachers to edit reports but was not sure they were getting their money's worth. When I asked to see some samples of editing by their consultants, I found that one very common notation was "faulty parallelism" at spots that only by the most conservative interpretation could be judged faulty. I asked the person who had hired me whether faulty parallelism was a problem in his staff's ability to write clearly enough to be understood quickly, but with enough authority to be taken seriously. He replied, "If the teacher says so."

Now I was a little taken aback by this response, because it seemed to me that one ought not have to appeal to a teacher to decide whether something like faulty parallelism was a real problem in communication. The places where faulty parallelism occurred should have been at least felt as problems, if not recognized as a felt difficulty whose specific source was faulty parallelism.

About a year later, as I sat listening to a paper describing some matters of error analysis in evaluating compositions, the same thing happened. When I looked at examples of some of the errors, sentences containing alleged dangling participles, faulty parallelism, vague pronoun reference, and a few other items,[8] I was struck by the fact that, at least in some of the examples, I saw some infelicity, but no out-and-out grammatical error. When I asked the person who had done the research whether these examples were typical of errors she looked for to measure the results of extensive training in sentence combining, I was told that the definition of error had been taken from a popular handbook, on the assumption, I guess, that that answered the question.

About a year ago, it happened again, when a publisher and I began circulating a manuscript that in a peripheral way deals with some of the errors I've mentioned here, suggesting that some errors are less serious than others. With one exception, the reviewers, all teachers at universities, agreed that an intelligent treatment of error would be useful, and that this manuscript was at least in the ballpark. But almost every reader took exception to one item of usage that they thought I had been too soft on, that I should have unequivocally condemned as a violation of good usage. Unfortunately, each of them mentioned a different item.

Well, it is all very puzzling: Great variation in our definition of error, great variation in our emotional investment in defining and condemning error, great variation in the perceived seriousness of individual errors. The categories of error all seem like they should be yes-no, but the feelings associated with the categories seem much more complex.

If we think about these responses for a moment we can identify one source of the problem: We were all locating error in very different places. For all of us, obviously enough, error is in the essay, on the page, because that is where it physically exists. But of course, to be in the essay, it first has to be in the student. But before that, it has to be listed in a book somewhere. And before that in the mind of the writer of the handbook. And finally, a form of the error has to be in the teacher who resonated — or not — to the error on the page on the basis of the error listed in the handbook.

This way of thinking about error locates error in two different physical locations (the student's paper and the grammarian's handbook) and in three different experiences: the experience of the writer who creates the error; in the experience of the teacher who catches it; and in the mind of the grammarian — the E. B. White or Jacques Barzun or H. W. Fowler — who proposes it. Because error seems to exist in so many places, we should not be surprised that we do not agree among ourselves about how to identify it, or that we do not respond to the same error uniformly.

But we might be surprised — and perhaps instructed — by those cases where the two places occur in texts by the same author — and where all three experiences reside in the same person. It is, in fact, these cases that I would like to examine for a moment, because they raise such interesting questions about the experience of error.

For example, E. B. White presumably believed what he (and Strunk) said in *Elements of Style* (New York[: Macmillan], 1979) about faulty parallelism and *which* vs. *that*:

> Express coordinate ideas in similar form. This principle, that of parallel construction, requires that expressions similar in content and function be outwardly similar. (26)
>
> *That. which. That* is the defining or restrictive pronoun, *which* the non-defining or non-restrictive. . . . The careful writer . . . removes the defining *whiches,* and by so doing improves his work. (59)

Yet in the last paragraph of "Death of a Pig,"[9] White has two faulty parallelisms, and according to his rules, an incorrect *which*:

> . . . the premature expiration of a pig is, I soon discovered, a departure which the community marks solemnly on its calendar. . . . I have written this account in penitence and in grief, as a man who failed to raise his pig, and to explain my deviation from the classic course of so many raised pigs. The grave in the woods is unmarked, but Fred can direct the mourner to it unerringly and with immense good will, and I know he and I shall often revisit it, singly and together, . . .

Now I want to be clear: I am not at all interested in the trivial fact that E. B. White violated one or two of his own trivial rules. That would be a trivial observation. We could simply say that he miswrote in the same way he might have mistyped and thereby committed a typographical error. Nor at the moment am I interested in the particular problem of parallelism, or of *which* vs. *that,* any more than I would be interested in the particular typo. What I am interested in is the fact that no one, E. B. White least of all, seemed to notice that E. B. White had made an error. What I'm interested in here is the noticing or the not noticing by the same person who stipulates what should be noticed, and why anyone would surely have noticed if White had written,

I knows me and him will often revisit it, . . .

Of course, it may be that I am stretching things just a bit far to point out a trivial error of usage in one publication on the basis of a rule asserted in another. But this next example is one in which the two co-exist between the same covers:

Were (sing.) is, then, a recognizable subjunctive, & applicable not to past facts, but to present or future non-facts. (576)

Another suffix that is not a living one, but is sometimes treated as if it was, is *-al* . . . (242)

H. W. Fowler, *A Dictionary of Modern English Usage.* Oxford[: Oxford UP], 1957.

Now again, Fowler may have just made a slip here; when he read these entries, certainly at widely separate intervals, the *was* in the second just slipped by. And yet how many others have also read that passage, and also never noticed?

The next example may be a bit more instructive. Here, the rule is asserted in the middle of one page:

In conclusion, I recommend using *that* with defining clauses except when stylistic reasons interpose. Quite often, not a mere pair of *that's* but a threesome or foursome, including the demonstrative *that,* will come in the same sentence and justify *which* to all writers with an ear. (68)

and violated at the top of the next:

Next is a typical situation which a practiced writer corrects for style virtually by reflex action. (69)
                    Jacques Barzun, *Simple and Direct.* New York[: Harper], 1976.

Now again, it is not the error as such that I am concerned with here, but rather the fact that after Barzun stated the rule, and almost immediately violated it, no one noticed — not Barzun himself who must certainly have read the manuscript several times, not a colleague to whom he probably gave the manuscript before he sent it to the publisher, not the copy editor who worked over the manuscript, not the proof reader who read the galleys, not Barzun who probably read the galleys after them, apparently not even anyone in the reading public, since that *which* hasn't been corrected in any of the subsequent printings. To characterize this failure to respond as mere carelessness seems to miss something important.

This kind of contradiction between the conscious directive and the unreflexive experience becomes even more intense in the next three examples, examples that, to be sure, involve matters of style rather than grammar and usage:

Negative constructions are often wordy and sometimes pretentious.

1. wordy   Housing for married students is not unworthy of consideration.

    concise   Housing for married students is worthy of consideration.

    better   The trustees should earmark funds for married students' housing. (Probably what the author meant)

2. wordy   After reading the second paragraph you aren't left with an immediate reaction as to how the story will end.

    concise   The first two paragraphs create suspense.

The following example from a syndicated column is not untypical:

> Sylvan Barnet and Marcia Stubbs, *Practical Guide to Writing*. Boston [: Little, Brown], 1977, 280.

Now Barnet and Stubbs may be indulging in a bit of self-parody here. But I don't think so. In this next example, Orwell, in the very act of criticising the passive, not only casts his proscription against it in the passive, but almost all the sentences around it, as well:

> I list below, with notes and examples, various of the tricks by means of which the work of prose construction is habitually dodged. . . . *Operators* or *verbal false limbs*. These save the trouble of picking out appropriate verbs and nouns, and at the same time pad each sentence with extra syllables which give it an appearance of symmetry. . . . the passive voice is wherever possible used in preference to the active, and noun constructions are used instead of gerunds. . . . The range of verbs if further cut down . . . and the banal statements are given an appearance of profundity by means of the *not un* formation. Simple conjunctions are replaced by . . . the ends of sentences are saved by . . .
>
>   "Politics and the English Language"

Again, I am not concerned with the fact that Orwell wrote in the passive or used nominalizations where he could have used verbs.[10] Rather, I am bemused by the apparent fact that three generations of teachers have used this essay without there arising among us a general wry amusement that Orwell violated his own rules in the act of stating them.

And if you want to argue (I think mistakenly) that Orwell was indulging in parody, then consider this last example — one that cannot possibly be parodic, at least intentionally:

> Emphasis is often achieved by the use of verbs rather than nouns formed from them, and by the use of verbs in the active rather than in the passive voice.
>
> *A Style Manual for Technical Writers and Editors*, ed. S. J. Reisman. New York[: ?], 1972. 6–11.

In this single sentence, in a single moment, we have all five potential locations of error folded together: As the rule is stated in a handbook, it is simultaneously violated in its text; as the editor expresses in the sentence that is part of the handbook a rule that must first have existed in his mind, in his role as writer he simultaneously violates it. And in the instant he ends the sentence, he becomes a critical reader who should — but does not — resonate to the error. Nor, apparently, did anyone else.

The point is this: We can discuss error in two ways: we can discuss it at a level of consciousness that places that error at the very center of our consciousness. Or we can talk about how we experience (or not) what we popularly call errors of usage as they occur in the ordinary course of our reading a text.

In the first, the most common way, we separate the objective material text from its usual role in uniting a subject (us) and that more abstract "content" of the object, the text, in order to make the sentences and words the objects of consciousness. We isolate error as a frozen, instantiated object. In the second way of discussing error, a way we virtually never follow, we must treat error not as something that is simply on the surface of the page, "out there," nor as part of an inventory of negative responses "in here," but rather as a variably experienced union of item and response, controlled by the intention to read a text in the way we ordinarily read texts like newspapers, journals, and books. If error is no longer in the handbook, or on the page, or in the writer — or even purely in the reader — if instead we locate it at an intersection of those places, then we can explain why Barzun could write — or read — one thing and then immediately experience another, why his colleagues and editors and audience could read about one way of reflexively experiencing language and then immediately experience it in another.

But when I decided to intend to read Barzun and White and Orwell and Fowler in, for all practical purposes, the way they seem to invite me to read — as an editor looking for the errors they have been urging me to search out — then I inform my experience, I deliberately begin reading, with an intention to experience the material constitution of the text. It is as if a type-designer invited me to look at the design of his type as he discussed type-design.

In short, if we read any text the way we read freshman essays, we will find many of the same kind of errors we routinely expect to find and therefore do find. But if we could read those student essays unreflexively, if we could make the ordinary kind of contract with those texts that we make with other kinds of texts, then we could find many fewer errors.

When we approach error from this point of view, from the point of view of our pre-reflexive experience of error, we have to define categories of error other than those defined by systems of grammar or a theory of social class. We require a system whose presiding terms would turn on the nature of our response to violations of grammatical rules.

At the most basic level, the categories must organize themselves around two variables: Has a rule been violated? And do we respond? Each of these variables has two conditions: A rule is violated or a rule is not violated. And to either of those variables, we respond, or we do not respond. We thus have four possibilities [see Figure 1]:

1a. A rule is violated, and we respond to the violation.

1b. A rule is violated, and we do not respond to its violation.

2a. A rule is not violated, and we do not respond.

2b. A rule is not violated, and we do respond.

Now, our experiencing or noticing of any given grammatical rule has to be cross-categorized by the variable of our noticing or not noticing whether it is or is not violated. That is, if we violate rule X, a reader may note it or not. But we must also determine whether, if we do *not* violate rule X, the same reader will or will not no-

Figure 1

	[+ response]	[– response]
[+ response]		
[– response]		

tice that we have violated it. Theoretically, then, this gives us four possible sets of consequences for any given rule. They can be represented on a feature matrix like [Figure 2]. That is, the first kind of rule, indicated by the line marked 1, is of the following kind: When violated, [+V], we respond to the violation, [+R]. When it is not violated, [−V], we do not respond, [−R]. Thus the same rule results in combinations of features indicated by (a–d). Rule type 2 is characterized by a rule that when violated, [+V], we do not notice, [−R]. But when we do not violate it, [−V], we do not notice it either, [−R]. Thus the single rule combines features indicated by (b–d). The other rules follow the same kind of grid relationships. (As I will point out later, the problem is actually much more complex than this, but this will do as a first approximation.)

I do not assert that the particular items I will list as examples of these rules are universally experienced in the way indicated. These categories are based on personal responses, and it is possible that your responses are quite different than mine. But in fact, on the basis of some preliminary research that I shall report later, I would argue that most readers respond in the ways reflected by these categories, regardless of how they might claim they react.

The most obviousest set of rules be those whose violation we instantly notes, but whose observation we entirely ignore. They are the rules that define bedrock standard English. No reader of this journal can fail to distinguish these two passages:

> There hasn't been no trainees who withdrawed from the program since them and the Director met to discuss the instructional methods, if they met earlier, they could of seen that problems was beginning to appear and the need to take care of them immediate. (+V, +R)

> There haven't been any trainees who have withdrawn from the program since they and the Director met to discuss the instructional methods. If they had met earlier, they could have seen that problems were beginning to appear and that they needed to take care of them immediately. (−V, −R)

Among the rules whose violation we readily note but whose observance we do not are double negatives, incorrect verb forms, many incorrect pronoun forms, pleonastic subjects, double comparatives and superlatives, most subject-verb disagreements, certain faulty parallelisms,[11] certain dangling modifiers,[12] etc.

The next most obvious set of rules are those whose observation we also entirely ignore, but whose violation we ignore too. Because we note neither their observation nor their violation, they constitute a kind of folklore of usage, rules which we can find in some handbook somewhere, but which have, for the most part, lost their force with our readers. For most readers, these two passages differ very little from one another; for many readers, not at all:

Figure 2

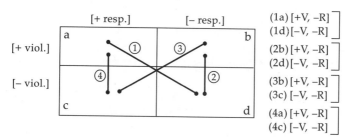

Since the members of the committee had discussed with each other all of the questions which had been raised earlier, we decided to conduct the meeting as openly as possible and with a concern for the opinions of everyone that might be there. And to ensure that all opinions would be heard, it was suggested that we not limit the length of the meeting. By opening up the debate in this way, there would be no chance that someone might be inadvertently prevented from speaking, which has happened in the past. (+V, –R)

Because the members of the committee had discussed with one another all the questions that had been raised earlier, we decided to conduct the meeting in a way that was as open as possible and concerned with the opinion of everyone who might be there. To ensure that all opinions would be heard, someone suggested that we not limit the length of the meeting. By opening up the debate in this way, we would not take the chance that someone might be inadvertently prevented from speaking, something which has happened in the past. (–V, –R)

I appreciate the fact that some readers will view my lack of sensitivity to some of these errors as evidence of an incorrigibly careless mind. Which errors go in which category, however, is entirely beside the point.[13] The point is the existence of a *category* of "rules" to whose violation we respond as indifferently as we respond to their observance.

A third category of rules includes those whose violation we largely ignore but whose observance we do not. These are rules which, when followed, impose themselves on the reader's consciousness either subliminally, or overtly and specifically. You can sense the consequence of observing these rules in this next "minimal pair":

I will not attempt to broadly defend specific matters of evidence that one might rest his case on. If it was advisable to substantially modify the arguments, he would have to re-examine those patients the original group treated and extend the clinical trials whose original plan was eventually altered. (+V, –R)

I shall not attempt broadly to defend specific matters of evidence on which one might rest one's case. Were it advisable substantially to modify the arguments, one should have to re-examine those patients whom the original research group treated and extend the clinical trials the original plan of which was eventually altered. (–V, +R)

I appreciate that many of you believe that you notice split infinitives as quickly as you notice a subject-verb error, and that both should be equally condemned in careful prose. At the end of this paper, I will try to offer an argument to the contrary — that in fact many — not all — of you who make that claim are mistaken.

The exceptions are probably those for whom there is the fourth category of error, that paradoxical but logically entailed category defined by those rules whose violation we note, and whose observance we also note. I think that very few of us are sensitive to this category, and I think for those very few, the number of items that belong in the category must, fortunately, be very small. Were the number of items large, we would be constantly distracted by noticing that which should not be noticed. We would be afflicted with a kind of linguistic hyperesthesia, noticing with exquisite pleasure that every word we read is spelled correctly, that every subject agrees with its verb, that every article precedes its noun, and so on. Many of us may be surprised when we get a paper with no mispelled words, but that pleasure does not derive from our noticing that each word in turn is correctly spelled, but rather in the absence of mispelled words.

In my own case, I think I note equally when an infinitive is split, and when it is not. In recent months, I also seem to be noticing when someone uses *that* in the way that the "rule" stipulates, and I notice when a writer uses *which* in the way which the "rule" prohibits. I hope I add no more.

I suspect that some readers put into this category the *regardless/irregardless* pair, *media* as a singular and as a plural, perhaps *disinterested/uninterested.* I offer no pair of contrasting examples because the membership of the category is probably so idiosyncratic that such a pair would not be useful.

Now in fact, all this is a bit more complicated than my four categories suggest, albeit trivially so. The two-state condition of response: [+/−], is too crude to distinguish different qualities of response. Responses can be unfavorable, as the ordinary speaker of standard English would respond unfavorably to

Can't nobody tell what be happening four year from now.

if it appeared in a text whose conventions called for standard English. A response can be favorable, as in the right context, we might regard as appropriate the formality of

Had I known the basis on which these data were analyzed, I should not have attempted immediately to dissuade those among you whom others have . . .

(We could, of course, define a context in which we would respond to this unfavorably.)

Since only the category of [+ response] can imply a type of response, we categorize favorable and unfavorable response [+/− favorable], across only [+ response]. This gives us four more simple categories:

[− violate, − favorable]

[− violate, + favorable]

[− violate, + favorable]

[− violate, − favorable]

The first two I have already illustrated:

[−v, −f]: He knowed what I meaned.

[−v, + f]: Had I known the basis on which . . . I should not etc.

This leaves two slightly paradoxical categories, which, like Category IV: those rules whose violations we notice and whose observations we notice too, are populated by a very small number of items, and function as part of our responses only idiosyncratically. In the category [− violate, − favorable], I suspect that many of us would place *It is I,* along with some occurrences of *whom,* perhaps.

The other paradoxical category, [+ violate, + favorable] is *not* illustrated by *It's me.* because for most of us, this is an unremarked violation. If it elicits a response at all, it would almost invariably be [− favorable], but only among those for whom the *me* is a bête noir. In fact, I can only think of one violation that I respond to favorably: It is the *than* after *different(ly)* when what follows is a clause rather than a noun:

This country feels differently about the energy crisis than it did in 1973.

I respond to this favorably because the alternative,

This country feels differently about the energy crisis from the way it did in 1973.

is wordier, and on principles that transcend idiosyncratic items of usage, I prefer the two less words and the more certain and direct movement of the phrase. My *noticing* any of this, however, is entirely idiosyncratic.

As I said, though, these last distinctions are increasingly trivial. That is why I refrain from pursuing another yet more finely drawn distinction: Those responses, favorable or unfavorable, that we consciously, overtly, knowingly experience, and those that are more subliminal, undefined, and unspecific. That is, when I read

It don't matter.

I know precisely what I am responding to. When most of us read a *shall* and a shifted preposition, I suspect that we do not consciously identify those items as the source of any heightened feeling of formality. The response, favorable or unfavorable, is usually less specific, more holistic.

Now what follows from all this? One thing that does not follow is a rejection of all rules of grammar. Some who have read this far are undoubtedly ready to call up the underground grammarians to do one more battle against those who would rip out the Mother Tongue and tear down Civilized Western Values. But need I really have to assert that, just because many rules of grammar lack practical force, it is hardly the case that none of them have substance?

Certainly, how we mark and grade papers might change. We need not believe that just because a rule of grammar finds its way into some handbook of usage, we have to honor it. Which we honor and which we do not is a problem of research. We have to determine in some unobtrusive way which rules of grammar the significant majority of careful readers notice and which they do not. One way to do this research is to publish an article in a journal such as this, an article into which have been built certain errors of grammar and usage. The researcher would then ask his readers to report which errors jumped out at them *on the first reading*. Those that you did not notice should then not be among those we look for first when we read a student's paper.

One curious consequence of this way of thinking about error is that we no longer have to worry about defining, rejecting, quibbling over the existence of a rule. We simply accept as a rule anything that anyone wants to offer, no matter how bizarre or archaic. Should anyone re-assert the nineteenth-century rule against the progressive passive, fine. Upon inspection it will turn out that the rule belongs in the category of those rules whose violation no one notices, and whose observation no one notices either. As I said, it may be that you and I will find that for any particular rule, we experience its violation in different ways. But that is an empirical question, not a matter of value. Value becomes a consideration only when we address the matter of which errors we should notice.

Done carefully, this kind of classification might also encourage some dictionary makers to amend their more egregious errors in labeling points of usage. The *AHD*, for example, uses "non-standard" to label

> . . . forms that do not belong in any standard educated speech. Such words are recognized as non-standard not only by those whose speech is standard, but even by those who regularly use non-standard expressions. ( )

The *AHD* staff has labeled as non-standard, *ain't, seen* as the past tense of *see*, and *don't* with a singular subject. It has also labeled as non-standard *irregardless, like* for *as, disinterested* for *uninterested*, and *see where*, as in the construction, *I see where. . . .* Thus we are led to believe that a speaker who would utter this:

> I see where the President has said that, irregardless of what happens with the gasoline shortage, he'll still be against rationing, just like he has been in the past. He seems disinterested in what's going on in the country.

would be just as likely to continue with this:

> I ain't sure that he seen the polls before he said that. He don't seem to know that people are fed up.

Indeed, we would have to infer from this kind of labeling that a speaker who said "I ain't sure he seen . . ." would also be sensitive to mistakes such as *disinterested* for *uninterested* or *like* for *as*. In matters such as this, we see too clearly the very slight scholarly basis upon which so much of this labeling rests.

Finally, I think that most of this essay is an exercise in futility. In these matters, the self-conscious report of what should be counted as an error is certainly an unreliable index to the unself-conscious experience. But it is by far a more satisfying emotion. When those of us who believe ourselves educated and literate and defenders of good usage think about language, our zealous defense of "good writing" feels more authentic than our experience of the same items in unreflective experience of a text. Indeed, we do not experience many of them at all. And no matter how wrong we might discover we are about our unreflective feelings, I suspect we could be endlessly lectured on how we do not respond to a *less* in front of a count noun, as in *less people*, but we would still express our horror and disgust in the belief that *less* is wrong when used in that way. It simply feels more authentic when we condemn error and enforce a rule. And after all, what good is learning a rule if all we can do is obey it?

If by this point you have not seen the game, I rest my case. If you have, I invite you to participate in the kind of research I suggested before. I have deposited with the Maxine Hairston of the University of Texas at Austin (Austin, Texas 78712), a member of the Editorial Board of this journal, a manuscript with the errors of grammar and usage that I deliberately inserted into this paper specifically marked. How can I ask this next question without seeming to distrust you? If you had to report right now what errors you noticed, what would they be? Don't go back and reread, looking for errors, at least not before you recall what errors you found the first time through. If you would send your list (better yet, a copy of the article with errors noted on first reading circled in red) to Professor Hairston, she will see that a tally of the errors is compiled, and in a later issue will report on who noticed what.

If you want to go through a second time and look for errors, better yet. Just make clear, if you would, that your list is the result of a deliberate search. I will be particularly interested in those errors I didn't mean to include. There are, incidentally, about one hundred errors.

Notes

[1] I don't know whether it is fair or unfair to quote Zinsser on this same matter:

> OVERSTATEMENT. "The living room looked as if an atomic bomb had gone off there," writes the inexperienced writer, describing what he saw on Sunday morning after a Saturday night party that got out of hand. Well, we all know that he's exaggerating to make a droll point, but we also know that an atomic bomb didn't go off there, or any other bomb except maybe a water bomb. . . . These verbal high jinks can get just so high — and I'm already well over the limit — before the reader feels an overpowering drowsiness. . . . Don't overstate. (108)

[2] Erving Goffman, *Frame Analysis: An Essay on the Organization of Experience* (New York: Harper, 1974).

[3] Some social errors are strictly formal and so ordinarily do not require an apology, even though some might judge them "horrible": a white wedding gown and a veil on a twice-

divorced and eight-month pregnant bride, brown shoes with a dinner jacket, a printed calling card.

⁴Some special situations do require an apology: When we prepare a document that some-one else must take responsibility for, and we make a mistake in usage, we are expected to apologize, in the same way we would apologize for incorrectly adding up a column of figures. And when some newspaper columnists violate some small point of usage and their readers write in to point it out, the columnists will often acknowledge the error and offer some sort of apology. I think William Safire in the *New York Times* has done this occasionally.

⁵Two other kinds of purely linguistic behavior do arouse hostile feelings. One kind in-cludes obscenities and profanities. It may be that both are rooted in some sense of fouling that which should be kept clean: obscenities foul the mouth, the mouth fouls the name of a deity. The other kind of linguistic behavior that arouses hostility in some includes bad puns and baby talk by those who are too old for it. Curiously, Freud discusses puns in his *Wit and the Relation to the Unconscious* (under "Technique of Wit") but does not in "The Tendencies of Wit" address the faint sense of revulsion we feel at a bad pun.

⁶Sterling Leonard, *Current English Usage*, English Monograph No. 1 (Champaign: NCTE, Chicago, 1932); Albert H. Marckwardt and Fred Walcott, *Facts about Current English Usage*, English Monograph No. 7 (Champaign: NCTE, New York, 1938); Raymond Crisp, "Changes in Attitudes toward English Usage," diss., U Illinois, 1971; W. H. Mittins, Mary Salu, Mary Edminson, Sheila Coyne, *Attitudes to English Usage* (London: Oxford UP, 1970); *The American Heritage Dictionary of the English Language* (New York: Dell, 1979). Thomas J. Cresswell's *Usage in Dictionaries and Dictionaries of Usage*, Publication of the American Dialect Society, Nos. 63–64 (University: U Alabama P, 1975), should be required reading for anyone interested in these matters. It amply demonstrates the slight scholarly basis on which so much research on usage rests.

⁷William Labov, *The Social Stratification of English in New York City* (Washington, DC: Center for Applied Linguistics, 1966), 455–81.

⁸Elaine P. Maimon and Barbara F. Nodine, "Words Enough and Time: Syntax and Error One Year After," in *Sentence Combining and the Teaching of Writing*, ed. Donald Daiker, Andrew Kerek, and Max Morenberg (Akron: U Akron P, 1979) 101–8. This is considered a dangling verbal: *For example, considering the way Hamlet treats Ophelia, there is almost corruptness in his mind.* Clumsy yes, but *considering* is an absolute, or more exactly, meta-discourse. See note 12. This is considered a vague pronoun reference: *The theme of poisoning begins with the death of old King Hamlet, who was murdered by his brother when a leperous distillment was poured into his ear while he slept.* Infelicitous, to be sure, but who can possibly doubt who's pouring what in whose ear (103)? Counting items such as these as errors and then using those counts to determine competence, progress, or maturity would seem to raise problems of another, more substantive, kind.

⁹*Essays of E. B. White* (New York: Harper, 1977), 24.

¹⁰Orwell's last rule: *Break any of these rules sooner than say anything outright barbarous*, does not apply to this passage. Indeed, it would improve if it had conformed to his rules:

> I list below, with notes and examples, various of the tricks by means of which a writer can dodge the work of prose construction. . . . such writers prefer wherever possible the passive voice to the active, and noun constructions instead of gerunds. . . . they further cut down the range of verbs. . . . they make their banal statements seem profound by means of the *not un*-formation. They replace simple conjunctions by. . . . they save the ends of sentences. . . .

Should anyone object that this is a monotonous series of sentences beginning with the same subject, I could point to example after example of the same kind of thing in good modern prose. But perhaps an example from the same essay, near the end, will serve best (my emphasis):

> When *you* think of a concrete object, *you* think wordlessly, and then, if *you* want to describe the thing *you* have been visualizing, *you* probably hunt about till *you* find the exact *words* that seem to fit it. When *you* think of something abstract *you* are more inclined to use words from the start, and unless *you* make a conscious effort to prevent it, the existing dialect will come rushing in and do the job for *you*. . . .

Nine out of ten clauses begin with *you*, and in a space much more confined than the passage I rewrote.

[11]Virtually all handbooks overgeneralize about faulty parallelism. Two "violations" occur so often in the best prose that we could not include them in this Category I. One is the kind illustrated by the E. B. White passage: the coordination of adverbials: . . . *unerringly and with immense good will*. The other is the coordination of noun phrases and WH-clauses: *We are studying the origins of this species and why it died out*. Even that range of exceptions is too broadly stated, but to explain the matter adequately would require more space than would be appropriate here.

[12]Handbooks also overgeneralize on dangling constructions. The generalization can best be stated like this: When the implied subject of an introductory element is different from the overt subject of its immediately following clause, the introductory element dangles. Examples in handbooks are always so ludicrous that the generalization seems sound:

> Running down the street, the bus pulled away from the curb before I got there.

> To prepare for the wedding, the cake was baked the day before.

Some handbooks list exceptions, often called absolutes:

> Considering the trouble we're in, it's not surprising you are worried.

> To summarize, the hall is rented, the cake is baked, and we're ready to go.

These exceptions can be subsumed into a more general rule: When either the introductory element *or* the subject of the sentence consists of *meta-discourse*, the introductory element will not always appear to dangle. By meta-discourse I mean words and phrases that refer not to the primary content of the discourse, to the reference "out there" in the world, the writer's subject matter, but rather to the process of discoursing, to those directions that steer a reader through a discourse, those filler words that allow a writer to shift emphasis *(it, there, what)*, and so on, words such as *it is important to note, to summarize, considering these issues, as you know, to begin with, there is,* etc. That's why an introductory element such as the following occurs so often in the prose of educated writers, and does not seem to dangle (meta-discourse is in [italics]):

> To succeed in this matter, *it is important* for you to support as fully as possible . . .

> Realizing the seriousness of the situation, *it can be seen that* we must cut back on . . .

As I will point out later, the categories I am suggesting here are too broadly drawn to account for a number of finer nuances of error. Some violations, for example, clearly identify social and educational background:

> He didn't have no way to know what I seen.

But some violations that might be invariably noted by some observers do not invariably, or even regularly, reflect either social or educational background. Usages such as *irregardless, like* for *as, different than,* etc. occur so often in the speech and writing of entirely educated speakers and writers that we cannot group them with double negatives and non-standard verb forms, even if we do unfailingly respond to both kinds of errors. The usage note in the *American Heritage Dictionary* (Dell Paperback Edition, 1976; third printing, November 1980) that *irregardless* is non-standard and "is only acceptable when the intent is clearly humorous" is more testimony to the problems of accurately representing the speech and writing of educated speakers. On February 20, 1981, the moderator on *Washington Week in Review,* a Public Broadcasting System news program, reported that a viewer had written to the program, objecting to the use of *irregardless* by one of the panelists. To claim that the person who used *irregardless* would also use *knowed* for *knew* or an obvious double negative would be simply wrong. (I pass by silently the position of *only* in that usage note. See note 13, item 9.) The counter-argument that the mere occurrence of these items in the speech and writing of some is sufficient testimony that they are not in fact educated is captious.

[13]Here are some of the rules which I believe belong in this Category II: (1) Beginning sentences with *and* or *but;* (2) beginning sentences with *because* (a rule that appears in no handbook that I know of, but that seems to have a popular currency); (3) *which/that* in regard to

restrictive relative clauses; (4) *each other* for two, *one another* for more than two; (5) *which* to refer to a whole clause (when not obviously ambiguous); (6) *between* for two, *among* for more than two. These next ones most readers of this journal may disagree with personally; I can only assert on the basis of considerable reading that they occur too frequently to be put in any other category for most readers: (7) *less* for *fewer*; (8) *due to* for *because*; (9) the strict placement of *only*; (10) the strict placement of *not only, neither*, etc. before only that phrase or clause that perfectly balances the *nor*. The usage of several disputed words must also suggest this category for most readers: *disinterested/uninterested, continuous/continual, alternative* for more than two. Since I have no intention of arguing which rules *should* go into any category, I offer these only as examples of my observations. Whether they are accurate for you is in principle irrelevant to the argument. Nor is it an exhaustive list.

¹⁴The rules that go into Category III would, I believe, include these. Again, they serve only to illustrate. I have no brief in regard to where they *should* go. (1) *shall/will*, (2) *who/whom*, (3) unsplit infinitives, (4) fronted prepositions, (5) subjunctive form of *be*, (6) *whose/of which* as possessives for inanimate nouns, (7) repeated *one* instead of a referring pronoun *he/his/him*, (8) plural *data* and *media*, singular verb after none.

Williams's Insight as a Resource for Your Teaching

1. What is your own definition of error? Where does it come from? Make a list of the two or three infractions that are most significant to you, and describe how you came to feel that way about them. How do you respond when you find them in student writing? Does your typical pattern of response to these errors lessen their frequency? What are some other patterns of response you could test in the classroom?

2. What do you make of the surprising turn Williams takes at the end of his essay? Many readers catch only a handful of errors on their first reading and are stunned by the revelation that he has deliberately loaded a hundred into his prose. What are the implications of this surprise with respect to your response to error in student writing? How do you suppose the error got there in the first place?

Williams's Insight as a Resource for Your Classroom

1. Ask your students to discuss their feelings about grammatical correctness. Share with them some of the histrionics that Williams notes in the opening of his essay, and ask them to brainstorm for ideas about where this emotional violence comes from.

2. Explore what you and your students know — and don't know — about error. If Williams is right, you will discover a wide range of disagreement about what "error" means. In class, establish a handful of basic rules that will be considered important criteria of correctness. Then type them up and distribute them to the class. Have the students practice using these rules on their classmates' drafts.

ELAINE O. LEES *Proofreading as Reading, Errors as Embarrassments*

In this follow-up to Joseph Williams's essay ("The Phenomenology of Error"; see above), Elaine Lees argues that although "error" originates in the writer, it actually exists in the reader. Lees suggests that proofreading is largely an interpretive activity, a struggle of meaning-making, in which the proofreader judges the writer's level of literacy and the communities to which the writer can and cannot belong. An error can be experienced as a flaw in "social display" and an invitation to exclude the writer from the writing community he or she has sought to enter. An error is therefore an embarrassment, a fracturing of one's social identity, and, as such, its source is the reader who points it out — a conclusion that directs us to consider the meanings of error and error analysis in a new, political light.

> But *physically* [in the case of a printed page], what is there are atoms in motion, not paper and small mounds of ink. Paper and small mounds of ink are elements in the human world.
>
> — Hubert L. Dreyfus, *What Computers Can't Do*

> A single event cannot be embarrassing, shameful, irresponsible, or foolish in isolation, but only as an act in the biography of a whole, historical individual — a person whose personality it reflects and whose self-image it threatens. Only a being that cares about who it is, as some sort of enduring whole, can care about guilt or folly, self-respect or achievement, life or death. And only such a being can read.
>
> — John Haugeland, "Understanding Natural Language"

It's happened so often, I've begun to accept it. I'm a guest at a party, or I'm next to a stranger on a train. I strike up conversation. Sooner or later my companion asks, "What do you do?"

"I teach English."

"Ahhh — I'd better watch what I say."

Errors, when people locate them, locate people; and so we're wary of them. We try to search them out, like fleas, in our texts, and pinch them away before anyone notices. Our language about proofreading suggests how we picture it: we "catch" mistakes; we "clean up" drafts; we get rid of problems in a text's "surface." To enhance our chance of bagging every error, we make things to help us: handbooks, style sheets, usage manuals, and, lately, programs that edit. The fact that machines appear to find "mechanical errors" for us complements our view of proofreading as hunting and errors as verminous prey. We've been tool-builders a long time.

But the hunt for errors proves tricky. In his excellent paper "The Phenomenology of Error," Joseph Williams names five different places where the errors teachers notice can be said to be located. He subcategorizes these places as "two different physical locations (the student's paper and the grammarian's handbook)" and "three different experiences: the experience of the writer who creates the error; . . . the experience of the teacher who catches it; and . . . the mind of the grammarian . . . who proposes it." (155–56). To demonstrate that these locations are distinct, Williams cites instances in which writers on grammar and usage — writers such as Jacques Barzun, E. B. White, and George Orwell — violate their own precepts: some within the same volume; some within the same chapter; and a few in the act of stating the precepts themselves. Williams thereby raises the question of what "recognizing an error" means, if one can commit an error in the act of decrying it and one's readers appear not to notice.

To account for this puzzle, Williams identifies two ways to read texts and discuss errors: ways that correspond, roughly, to considering them as a proofreader or editor might and considering them as an "ordinary" reader might. In distinguishing these ways of reading, Williams begins to suggest some of the complexities at work in the perception of error:

> In short, if we read any text the way we read freshman essays, we will find many of the same kinds of errors we routinely expect to find and therefore do find. But if we could read those student essays unreflexively, if we could make the ordinary kind of contract with those texts that we make with other kinds of texts, then we could find many fewer errors. (159)

In his essay Williams' major concern is with the second, "unreflexive," experience of error; mine here is with the first, error known through the deliberate attempt to find it, error identified through the activities we call editing and proofreading.[1] I believe, however, that though some such distinction as Williams makes between ways of reading surely holds — as Williams wittily argues by burying a hundred "errors" for readers to overlook in his own essay — his second description of reading applies, more fully than the preceding passage suggests, to what occurs in deliberate error hunting: readers (even college English teachers focusing their attention on finding errors in a fairly brief student paper) *normally* fail to experience some instances of what others (or even they) agree are textual errors, vary in their classifications of the errors they do experience, and thus differ in their assessments of a single paper's errors.[2]

I'd like to begin my discussion of error by adapting Williams' error-location categories slightly, abandoning for a time his references to grammarians and grammar books, in order to consider further the three remaining sites he proposes for error: the text, the writer, and the reader. Encapsulated in this trinity we have, I think, a history of error studies.

The traditional place to locate error among these entities, it seems to me, is the text. The text, in fact, is where even Williams says we can all agree error resides: "For all of us, obviously enough, error is in the essay, on the page, because that is where it physically exists" (155). Because it has been customary to view errors as existing physically on pages, it has also been easy to imagine them as unambiguously countable and classifiable, like particles of foreign matter in a beverage, as though the vital issue were determining how many and what kinds were there. Thus error counts and classifications have dominated error studies since at least the late nineteenth century (Hull 6–12), and error counting and classifying have continued into recent years in such projects as the National Assessment of Educational Progress's "Writing Mechanics" measurement (Mellon 29–33).

In addition, the tradition of imagining errors as physical features of texts has strengthened our inclination to regard proofreading as a mechanical exercise, a matter of looking closely at details, paying attention to "what's really on the page" rather than to what we believe is there. Because we tend to regard errors as basic features of texts, we tend to think of proofreading as simpler than other writing processes — less in need of study and less complex to teach. Yet more than a few writers in college in the last few decades have failed to master the arts of noticing and repairing errors their teachers saw in their work, though these writers were motivated to improve their editing, stood to gain substantial rewards by doing so, and willingly accepted the instruction they were offered. Within the customary view of proofreading as seeing what's before one's eyes, the troubles these writers encountered appear all but inexplicable.

Recently, error analysis (borrowed from second-language pedagogy) has shifted our notion of where errors exist away from texts and toward writers: In error analysis, one identifies patterns of error in an individual writer's work and thereby attempts to learn something about what's "in" the writer. One looks in the writer for an unconventional rule, a mistaken generalization about linguistic patterns, and then one tries to change not so much the product as the producer, by substituting a new rule for the old one.[3] Once patterns of error in a writer's work have been identified, the writer, aware of their existence, can begin to substitute conventional forms for unconventional ones. In this view, error is individual, subject to idiosyncrasy, unclassifiable through reference to the characteristics of texts alone.[4]

What is new, and exciting, about Williams' approach to error is the degree to which it locates error in readers. Though Williams explicitly places error (at least in one of his ways to discuss it) at an intersection of text, reader, handbook, and writer, and though he elsewhere affirms error's physical existence in texts, his emphasis and principal interest in "The Phenomenology of Error" appear to lie in examining error's dynamics in readers' experience.

I intend here to draw on the work of Stanley Fish to explore further what it means to imagine errors as existing in readers. But before I focus on Fish's ideas, I'd like to suggest what errors are not, by pointing out ways in which errors can't be said to exist "physically," as errors, in either texts or writers.

To begin with, we can't say errors exist as discrete physical objects in texts, for errors seem not to affect texts' physical aspects at all. Errors do not alter texts' physical surface, that is, in the way lumps of correction fluid or erasure holes do. We might not call them errors if they did. What we call an error in a text must be recognizable, it seems, as part of a failed attempt to perform a convention-bound, linguistic act. For errors to be recognizable as products of such attempts, they must possess most of the attributes, including the physical attributes, of the things they're intended to be. If irregularities in texts cease to be thus recognizable, they cease to seem like errors and appear to be something else: acts of zaniness, perhaps, or works of art.

We encounter problems, too, when we try to locate writers' errors, for errors do not appear to exist as definable units in writers' bodies or behavior. To an outsider, writers do not seem engaged in different sorts of activity when they make errors and when they don't; the production of an error is indistinguishable from the production of its correct neighbors. Moreover, as a matter of definition, we assume writers themselves can't tell when they're making errors,[5] and thus it follows that writers can't deliberately produce them. As soon as "error" production becomes deliberate — as soon as a writer attempts to load a text, as Williams does, with what he believes are violations of usage and grammar rules — the activity becomes less like "making errors" and more like playing a game or trick. If we are to claim that error resides "in writers" at all, then, we'll have to claim it's there in a special way, as something other than error, as a thing that achieves its identity as "error" by being read — interpreted — by someone else.

When errors have physical manifestations, they have them most often in readers. During the past five years, for a series of studies I've conducted, I've had occasion to watch more than fifty writers as they proofread. With these proofreaders the detection of an error was frequently an observable event, accompanied by such symptoms as raised eyebrows, grimaces, vocal "ahas," rapid moves to correct, and in the most pronounced instances, a kind of pouncing in which the proofreader's whole body lunged toward the page. Something happens to readers — never to texts, almost never to writers — in their encounters with error; they are changed by error, as error, in ways writers and texts are not.

To suggest terms in which we might understand these encounters, I'll here give them a "reading": I'll borrow language from recent literary theory, particularly from the works of Fish, and describe proofreading as an interpretive activity, an act of meaning-construction, a type of criticism — differing from others not in its being more "basic" or "literal," but in the kinds of interpretations it produces.

Let me suggest that a proofreader — and by "proofreader," I mean any person skillfully hunting for errors, not necessarily a professional — is a person who (like New Critics, Jungians, structuralists, and others) uses texts as occasions for constructing particular sorts of meanings — in this case, meanings that support conventional judgments of literacy. Proofreaders thus may be said to form what Fish calls "interpretive communities" (167–73), groups of readers who "share interpretive strategies not for reading (in the conventional sense) but for writing texts, for constituting their properties and assigning their intentions" (171). Such strategies, according to Fish, "exist prior to the act of reading and therefore determine the shape of what is read" (171). They "give texts their shape, making them rather than, as it is usually assumed, arising from them" (168).

That is, the members of an interpretive community share a way of thinking (Fish would say the way of thinking shares the members of the community) which "implicates" the members of the community "in a world of already-in-place objects, purposes, goals, procedures, values, and so on" (304). The members of the community agree on the existence and meaning of objects, then, not because such objects are units of the real world, but because the members of the community share a way of "reading" phenomena that brings such objects into being. The community can recognize its objects because it participates in a "universe of discourse that also includes stipulations as to what [will] count as an identifying mark, and ways of arguing that such a mark is or is not there" (Fish 304). The norms for assigning meanings to texts, according to Fish, "are not embedded in the language (where they may be read out by anyone with sufficiently clear, . . . unbiased, eyes) but inhere in an institutional structure within which one hears utterances as already organized with reference to certain assumed purposes and goals" (306).

Viewed from such a perspective, proofreading, like other sorts of reading, becomes an act of interpretation and criticism carried out within a cultural group. The meanings proofreaders construct allow the discovery of error, as the meanings Jungians construct allow the discovery of archetypes; structuralists, binary oppositions; and biographicalists, allusions to the author's life. In the same way we might describe Jungian reading as a readiness to construct archetypes, if possible, out of the materials offered by a text, so we might describe proofreading as a readiness to construct errors, if possible, out of the same materials. Errors can no more be said to be physically "there" or "not there" on a page, then, than Christ figures or autobiographical allusions can. All are created by readers' enacting interpretive frameworks.

One consequence of this way of viewing proofreading is that it allows us to see error as no more part of a text's physical or "fundamental" features than its other meanings are. Students who proofread their own work unsuccessfully may be viewed not so much as "missing what's there" on the surface of their texts as constructing, or to use Fish's term, "writing," those texts differently from the way other, powerful readers do. Though a student may compose a text in which a teacher finds errors, we cannot assume that the student constructs, or can construct, a text that reveals those errors as he or she reads.

If errors are no more on the surface of texts than archetypes and ironies are, it may appear odd that more readers agree about the existence of specific errors in a text than about the existence of other meanings in it. This fact seems less puzzling when we consider that nearly all readers have learned to behave, at least some of the time, as proofreaders — many more than have learned to be Jungians or New Critics. As interpretive communities go, the community of proofreaders of Edited American English (for example) is very large. Error-hunting is perhaps the only form of textual criticism in which virtually every successfully schooled person has received lengthy training. Moreover, large groups of readers have learned to behave as proofreaders at the same mothers' knees: in educational systems where methods of teaching reading and writing are widely shared and therefore likely to produce large numbers of readers who share ways of constructing errors in texts they read. Thus, though the ability to perceive a "literal" or "surface" level of texts may not be genuinely basic to reading,[6] learning to construct what we term texts' "literal" or "surface" level is a significant part of basic education.

From this education, we learn to agree about (if not always to experience) the relevant features of words, sentences, paragraphs, and whole texts — as those features are defined by members of the prevailing interpretive community of proofreaders. The lack of this ability to "constitute the properties" of texts, to share the conventional view of what matters in words and sentences is, I think, what Patricia Laurence alludes to when she suggests that her Basic Writing students are "out of touch with words and sentences *as they are*" [italics Laurence's (28)]. Students can't see words and sentences "as they are" (none of us do that); the pedagogical problem is that some students consistently fail to see the textual features we believe are relevant — not so much to our purposes, as to the students' own.[7] These students may not know how to read into their texts the details necessary for proofreading in a freshman English class; they may not know how to order those features into systems and hierarchies that will enable them to succeed as students in a university. As a result, when they proofread, the students don't "create" the texts — even the so-called surface-level texts — that their teachers do. Such students do not possess interpretive frameworks that enable them to "see" the same errors in their writing that their teachers see. The students are not full members of the teachers' interpretive communities.

Blissful ignorance does not necessarily mark such a student's condition, however. The following passage, taken from a paper by a freshman in a Basic Writing course, suggests the anguish a writer experiences when he realizes his texts differ, mostly on the "surface," from texts considered acceptable in the community he wishes to join. In the passage, the writer begins by commenting on a distinction made by Howard Gardner in his book *Art, Mind, and Brain* between "First-Draft Creativity" (characteristic of the work of preschool children) and "Mature Creativity" (characteristic of the work of those who have passed through what Gardner terms the "Literal Stage," a period in which one learns the norms of one's society) (94–102). We may note, as we read, how our own membership in what I've called the "community of proofreaders of Edited American English" affects our sense of what the text means and who the writer is.

> [A]lthough the person work can be understooded by society it must go under many other revision when the person gets older, so it will be under the exceptable way of the society.
>
> By the person reworking his works from the first draft to become a mature creator, he must take some risks in finding out the excepted literature views that he must use in his society. This means that he must use punctuation marks by the way the society wants it to be used, not by the way he wants it. In my opinion the person goes through these risks as a trial and error method. He tries different methods to find out which makes society understand his work. He tries to reach this goal, so he can be on the border line of what society wants and what he wants. . . .
>
> But if the trial and error does not work, and he is in my position of not knowing how to express himself my using the exceptive method of the society, he would have pity for himself, he would be up late at nights asking God for his help. The person who is stuck in the literal stage, his written would be unorganized, and he would make simple mistakes. He cares about the mistakes, but it would hurt him so bad that he would just don't know what to do. While the writer that is not stuck would have some freedom in the way he wrote his works. . . .[8]

Definitions of error abound: Errors have been seen as simple mistakes, as sins or willful violations of received rules of conduct, as involuntary wanderings from the path one has chosen. All of these views of error assume the relevance of the error-maker's state of mind: In each, error can be identified only in the context of an individual's attempt to place him- or herself within a group, a culture. The group, the "readers," offer candidates roles and positions to aspire to; errors are defined against the background of these aspirations.

Williams touches on the social nature of error by considering whether written error can be viewed as a flawed transaction between writer and reader, in which a reader is affronted by a writer's lapse. Williams grounds his discussion of error as social offense on the terms in which "otherwise amiable" people, like William Zinsser, denounce certain errors of grammar and usage. Williams cites Zinsser's apparent endorsement of terms like *"detestable vulgarity . . . garbage . . . atrocity . . . horrible . . . oaf . . . idiot . . .* and *simple illiteracy . . .* to comment on usages like *OK, hopefully,* the affix *-wise,* and *myself* in *he invited Mary and myself to dinner"* (152). Williams concludes that "errors of social behavior differ from errors of 'good usage,'" in that "social errors that excite feelings commensurate with judgments like 'horrible'" are usually personal affronts to one's companions. Because such actions "crudely violate one's personal space we are justified in calling them 'oafish'; all of them require that we apologize, or at least offer an excuse" (152–53).

Though recognizing advantages in considering "error as part of a flawed transaction" (153), Williams also notes the contrast between the consequences of linguistic and nonlinguistic social lapses:

> If we do compare serious nonlinguistic gaffes to errors of usage, how can we not be puzzled over why so much heat is invested in condemning a violation whose consequence impinges not at all on our personal space? The language some use to condemn linguistic error seems far more intense than the language they use to describe more consequential social errors — a hard bump on the arm, for example — that require a sincere but not especially effusive apology. (153)

What intrigues me in Williams' discussion are the double references of the terms he quotes to show readers' scorn for linguistic errors. Most of the epithets Williams cites — terms such as *vulgarity, oaf, idiot,* and *simple illiteracy* — refer more directly to beha*vers* than beha*viors*; they are assertions of social location, not statements pinpointing effects of actions. The terms recall the social standing of those expected to perform such acts, rather than ways the acts affect others.

How do such terms operate, then? Their thrust at first seems to indicate they exist to put error-makers in their places, to protect privileged groups from incursions by groups less privileged, to use language forms as social controls. The error-hunter's prey, initially identified as the traces of outsideness, turn out to be outsiders themselves. But the vehemence and ubiquity of social epithets in discussions of error suggest further that though we — and by "we" I mean those who manage the ways of conventional literacy with reasonable success — may disdain the company of those we consider oafs, illiterates, idiots, or vulgar persons, even more intensely we fear to *be* such persons. Error-makers may be people whom aspirants to education feel it's worse to *become* than to *know.*[9]

Written errors, then, may be experienced as flaws in a social display, a display whose "readers" judge performance against ideals they hold for their own behavior. No apology is necessary when one makes an error, for one's companions have not been injured. The error-maker, if made aware of the error, feels not guilty, but embarrassed, because his or her social confidence has been called into question or diminished. We do not regard our textual errors as affronts to readers (except in some very special circumstances noted by Williams 166), but rather diminutions of, embarrassing exposures of, ourselves. We need not seek others' forgiveness for our sentence-level errors; in making them, we've harmed none of our fellows. In the social economy of error, the error-maker is the injured party.

It's not surprising, then, that the disposition to correct errors in one's writing appears early and lasts long. Given means and opportunity, preschool children — people of every age — hasten to correct what they view as errors in work they take seriously, notwithstanding variations in what they view as errors. As Flower and Hayes note, evaluating and revising are among the three writing processes that "share the special distinction of being able to interrupt any other process and occur at any time in the act of writing" (374). Because we care about our appearance in the world, about who we are and how our acts reflect upon us, we act immediately to eradicate what we perceive as flaws in our work.[10]

Nor is it surprising that we've set our wits to making error-detecting implements, tools that help us catch what we otherwise couldn't find. Most of these implements fit under one of three headings: rules, tricks, or games. *Rules* (e.g., statements like "capitalize the first letters of sentences") serve us by specifying ways to overpower idiosyncrasy, creating or reinforcing a culture. *Tricks* (e.g., reading a text from end to beginning; reading a text aloud) serve us by overpowering rules, breaking through perceptions that arise from our approaching texts in the usual or "obvious" ways. *Games,* a hybrid form, link rules with tricks. "Parse," for instance, is a game in which players rename all a sentence's words (a trick) and then see whether they can still call the product a sentence (following rules that define the name-strings constituting sentences).

People find errors by combining their limited strength as rule-followers with a vast inclination to play games and tricks.[11] People may also be aided in finding errors in another's writing by their ability to imagine how others feel and wish to behave in a given situation: the roles one might intend to take, the conventions one might intend to observe, and the leeway the culture allows one in observing those conventions. We can grasp what parts of another's display are probably unintended slips, deviations from conventional form that would embarrass a writer with the desires and ambitions we've attributed. To exercise these capacities, we draw on more sorts of rules, if *rules* is the word for them, than those usually associated with the correctness of writing.

Let me pause here to clarify. I'm not suggesting that we can't formulate grammatical or usage rules to account for most of the error-correcting we do. We can; we have. What I am arguing is that we call up and apply those rules, when we use them, in a profoundly social context, informed by our sense of the goals people have in situations. Most of the time we can take milieu, situation, for granted. But sometimes it causes us to alter the rules.

Take misspellings. Spelling errors seem at first the simplest of the simple, a particularly clear-cut case among types of error. If the string of letters in a word doesn't appear in the dictionary, or if it appears next to an inappropriate meaning or part of speech, then we've got a misspelling. An oaf, a machine, can handle that; and in fact spelling-checkers were among the earliest and most successful features of commercial editing software.

But the preceding definition of *misspelling* breaks down quickly when we get to cases. There's a cafeteria near my office, for instance, that calls itself "The Salad Company," and its employees wear, emblazoned across their chests, the motto "Lettuce serve you." From one point of view — from the preceding definition — that motto contains a misspelling, a thing that might, in a different context, be termed a "homonym substitution," not unlike *there* for *they're* or *affect* for *effect*. But no one familiar with American advertising would read that *lettuce* as other than exactly what the writer intended, no matter how perfectly it also fit a definition of misspelling.

We might account for our reading of *lettuce* by postulating rules of a different sort, rules that specify a discourse type and what is appropriate to it. We can, in other words, add a set of genre rules to our definition of misspelling — something like "apply this definition of misspelling in reading student papers, but not in reading commercial slogans"; or, "in advertising slogans, homonym substitutions do not count as misspellings if they make relevant puns." Then, provided we can recognize the genre of the thing we're reading, we can apply spelling rules more deftly. This insight, I think, underlies Hayes and Flower's early description of the editing process as a production system:

> We assume that the EDITING process has the form of a production system. The conditions of the productions have two parts. The first part specifies the kind of language to which the editing production applies, e.g., formal sentences, notes, etc. The second is a fault detector for such problems as grammatical errors, incorrect words, and missing context. When the conditions of a production are met, e.g., a grammatical error is found in a formal sentence, the action that is triggered is a procedure for fixing the fault.
>
> Consider the following production:
>
> [(formal sentence) (first letter of sentence lower case) _ change first letter to upper case]
>
> If the writer is producing formal sentences, this production will detect and correct errors in initial capitalization. However, if the writer is only producing notes, the conditions of the production will not be met and capitalization will be ignored. (17)

Such a view of editing, by acknowledging the importance of context in identifying error, curbs our inclination to view errors as violations of timeless principles, as textually contained linguistic flaws.

But even rules specifying discourse types aren't enough to account for readers' identification of some errors. Consider the following sentence, taken from an essay in a Basic Writing student's final folder — one among several hundred files of essays read, in a day-long event known as Folder Day, by my university's composition staff to determine whether marginal Basic Writing students should pass their courses. The student, discussing techniques used to manipulate consumers, wrote:

> People nowadays are using sex to sell things all the time (such as in movies, TV, and pubic advertising).[12]

Here, to judge from the reactions of the staff members who saw it, is a sentence containing a mistake; and I think it's reasonable to claim the problem involves a misspelling. I feel confident, too, that had I polled staff members, I'd have discovered high consensus about what the writer's "intended text" was. But notice how all of the factors previously mentioned work against our reading "pubic" as an error: the misspelling is itself a legitimate word, an appropriate part of speech, whose meaning fits the written context in which it appears. Part of a piece of academic writing, it makes suitably decorous reference to the subject at issue and, coupled with "advertising," forms a concise label for the practice of "using sex to sell things all the time."

Yet we know it's a misspelling. We grasp what the writer intends to *say*, I think, because — given the situation — we grasp what the writer intends to *be*; we know the writer wouldn't want to write that sentence as it appears — to create the response that sentence creates in readers — in an essay destined to be read by a group of English teachers. And not for fear of flunking, either.

We know error, at the outset, as chagrin: errors are failures in the candidacies we undertake. They reveal our imperfect mastery of the behavior considered appropriate to communities we wish to join or roles we wish to fulfill. When we perceive our errors, and realize others may have done so, we lose some of our sense of who we are. That's why errors annoy and embarrass us; that's why their echoes keep us company late at night.

Errors, then, are departures from textual convention that have the power to embarrass authors by calling into question their social identities. One consequence of defining error as a threat to social identity is that we may begin to look in new places to understand proofreading. The study of proofreading may become in part sociological, a study of how readers acquire the ability to assess texts' conventionality, to "construct" errors conventionally in the writing they examine.

Activities like reading, writing, listening, and talking — as well as studying precepts for acceptability and paradigm cases of acceptable and unacceptable forms — appear to shape the way one evaluates texts' conventionality. All of these activities are community-shapers, activities that promote and reinforce a common way of viewing or interpreting a world and that create a "conformed set of readers," an "interpretive community." They are also, however, activities whose results may vary systematically, once variations among subcommunities occur — variations, for instance, in conventions articulated and taught, in speech patterns, in kinds of writing and reading encouraged. These and other diversities then contribute to diversities in the ways individuals identify errors as they read.

Adopting what might be called a sociological view of error may also lead us to examine the constraints a community sets on the kinds of "editing rules," including deviant editing rules, its writers use to discover textual error. Though the range of deviant rules seems almost endless when one attempts to catalogue them, perhaps it is not. Perhaps the rules that constrain editing are themselves constrained by characteristic approaches a community takes toward handling language.

One shaper of editing rules, both conventional and deviant, is the very language used to socialize writers — the formulas, maxims, and slogans of the English class. In what might be called "induced errors,"[13] we find the metaphors and figures of teacher-talk made manifest, animated in ways their first users never intended. For instance, we can better understand a novice writer's adding indentations at the top of every page when we recall that students are sometimes told to paragraph at the beginning of new sections of papers.

Finally, and most important, the view of proofreading and error I've outlined may cast light on why some writers experience so much difficulty learning to detect what others regard as errors in their work. In learning to identify a familiar form as an error — whether that form be a pattern borrowed from spoken language, a common misspelling, or an idiosyncratic rule a writer has long followed — a learner not only moves *into* an interpretive community, but moves *out of* one as well: a person cannot, as Fish recognizes, move into a situation from anything but another situation (172, 316, 376–77). To make such a move at all, it appears the learner must give up a system, a set of assumptions, a way of proceeding: one that already works, or seems to.

But it's not clear that a person can entirely give up, entirely abandon, an interpretive system he or she has mastered, if to do so means to surrender the power to use it. Expertise in an interpretive system consists exactly of being able to experience the world of objects and meanings that the system makes possible, rather than of attending to conventions generating those objects and meanings. The crucial difference between an interpretive system mastered and a system being learned, then, may well lie not so much in the patterned differences between rules in the two systems as in the fact that the first system, if the learner is expert in it, is *used* rather than seen.[14] The user has mastered the first system's way of creating meanings and now experiences those meanings as adhering to objects (also constituted through the interpretive community), rather than generated by specific interpretive strategies.

I'm not sure one ever leaves an interpretive community, in fact, if to leave it means to lose the capacity to create its objects and meanings. That is, I'm not sure one surrenders the ability to enter into and instantly practice an interpretive system one has previously mastered. A Marxist who formerly practiced Jungian interpretation does not experience bafflement when he or she subsequently encounters Jungian readings of texts. No intelligibility problem occurs, as would be the case if the reader had genuinely "ceased doing" Jungian readings. The reader need not even experience an interval of "figuring out" the Jungian interpretation, as a novice learning the system would. Instead, there is instant understanding, though now, perhaps, accompanied by classification ("There's a Jungian") and judgment ("whose approach to reading is reductive"). But the previous reader remains in some sense accessible to the present one; the previous interpretive system remains intelligible to the interpreter.

When one changes interpretive communities,[15] then, one may retain power to generate readings sponsored by another system. If this view is correct, the human reader familiar with two interpretive systems always has access to, always holds in abeyance, a different text from the one he or she is "writing" at the time. For short, we may describe such a reader as heterotextual. When we note that proofreading and meaning-reading tend to interrupt and derail each other, we are simply noting a familiar instance of heterotextuality at work. "Literate" readers, by virtue of their having learned to read for error as well as gist, always have the capacity to construct at least one alternate reading of a text.[16] And, in this case, the alternate readings appear to break out of abeyance readily.

For writers whose history provides them with expertise in multiple interpretive systems, the situation appears doubly complex: if they have learned more than one set of conventions for assigning judgments of error and correctness, they may at times — for reasons different from usual reasons like fatigue, uncertainty, cognitive overload, partial learning, and the like — overlook what in other circumstances they would identify as errors. For example, Mary Epes writes of students who, in one sense, "knew" standard verb endings well but could not edit verb errors in their own texts. When Epes underlined verbs at random in their papers, however, these students could identify verbs that had "correct" endings and repair the others. But before Epes underlined verbs, the same writers could not see the same errors (21).

I doubt that Epes' students needed lessons on verb endings, or more practice exercises, or even more lessons on "reading carefully," at least as such lessons are usually taught. Epes' students knew verb errors when they saw them; the trouble was, instead, that they couldn't see verb errors when they knew them. Skillful language users in a community where verb inflections differed from standard, the students were negotiating a path through their expertise in two inflectional systems.

As long as underlinings cued the students to read as if they were completing exercises in standard verb forms, they performed that role well. But without such cues, they did not automatically perform verb exercises as they read, nor did they perceive the verbs before them as somehow "odd."

As a teacher, I'm not sure what to make of all this. Error and editing — things that at first seemed mechanical and commonplace — now appear outrageous and strange. Today I take less comfort than I once did in reassurances that my students — with practice, as they gain "increasing familiarity" with written forms — will eventually become relaxed and expert editors. I believe some will. But I also suspect some will not, despite their best efforts and mine. And I'm not yet sure what makes the difference.

I don't think that traditional editing exercises are an answer for these writers — witness the evanescence of Epes' students' ability to edit when their papers lacked textbooklike cues.[17] Error detection may be least problematic (though perhaps not most accurate) for writers who possess a kind of innocence, a limitation on the number of systems of "correctness" they've learned to trust. Once that innocence is gone, once a writer becomes competent in multiple interpretive systems, the activity of editing may change its nature radically.

But I also hesitate to conclude we can offer only "trial-and-error" navigational methods to writers who have at stake their chance to locate, and occupy, a borderline between "what society wants" and what they want. Such writers may always need to edit texts specially — by using a checklist or formula or machine editor or some such prop — when they need to locate all forms regarded as errors by a particular audience. This, it seems to me, should not be read as a sign of failure, but rather as a concomitant of competence. In some circumstances, the ability to miss an error may simply be confirmation that for human beings writing isn't univocal.

It may be possible to design mechanical aids that reduce, temporarily, readers' heterotextuality, allowing them to apply more of the editing expertise they possess. Word processors that highlight potential trouble spots so editors may review and evaluate them or that sound out and pronounce texts aloud so editors may listen for anomalies would begin to offer assistance of the kind I mean. Such instruments would not operate by catching errors for their users (the users would have to decide what to catch), but would instead assist editing by stabilizing texts.

As long as errors threaten social identities, however, writers and readers will attempt to catch them. What I'm suggesting here is that the hunt may take us places we had never planned to go.

Notes

[1]I will use the terms *editing* and *proofreading* interchangeably here to refer to the processes of reading and alteration by means of which writers eliminate what they believe to be errors in their texts.

[2]These claims are based on observations I've made while directing graduate teaching seminars in composition and on the preliminary findings of a study a colleague and I conducted in which ten teachers identified the errors in two student papers.

[3]For discussions of error analysis' applications to the teaching of writing, see Kroll and Schafer, and Bartholomae.

[4]For a discussion of the value of consulting learners when assessing their errors, see Corder, "Error Analysis" 206.

[5]The exceptions to this generalization are skilled typists, who often "know in their fingers" when they have typed wrong, or the wrong number of, letters for a word. Typographical errors are, in error analysis' terminology, "mistakes" rather than "errors," however.

[6]For an overview of this position, see Smith 3–9. See also Goodman 57–65.

[7]For a lengthy discussion of the relation between features and situation, see Dreyfus, 206–24. A related argument, addressing issues in literary criticism, appears in Fish 326–27.

[8]I am grateful to Christopher S. Cammock for permission to reproduce this passage.

[9]William Labov notes that some teachers' reactions to children's linguistic errors are most violent when the errors are those the teachers themselves must work hard not to make ("the very pattern which they so sharply correct in themselves" 28). It's also worth remarking here that, despite Williams' claim, "social errors" can "excite feelings commensurate with judgments like 'horrible'" when the errors are one's own. In that case, as every adolescent knows, offenses far less serious than knocking someone on the arm can produce exquisite misery in the offender.

[10]See Haugeland for the argument that caring about one's identity is essential in comprehending natural language.

[11]Computers, on the other hand, find errors by combining vast strength at rule-following with a limited capacity to play games. (Computers can't play "Parse" now as well as we do, perhaps because computers lack our capacity to understand tricks.) So, from time to time, error-hunting computers catch things that aren't our prey and miss things that are our prey. Their game is not quite our game.

[12]I am indebted to Syd Coppersmith, Laura Dice, and Susan Gelburd for help in recalling this sentence.

[13]For a related use of this term, see Stenson.

[14]See Dreyfus and Dreyfus for a discussion of stages in the development of expertise.

[15]Here I also include those idiosyncratic interpretive "communities" containing only one member: those stabilized but highly personal systems of meaning-construction one sometimes encounters in inexperienced readers and writers.

[16]Computers have an advantage over us in single-minded reading, for they are able to construct — to "write" and "read" — one text at a time. Perhaps this capacity will make them useful, in the future, to writers struggling with multiple interpretive systems. But it's doubtful, for the reasons discussed earlier, that computers will ever prove better at detecting some types of errors than human proofreaders are.

[17]Mary Epes and her colleagues Carolyn Kirkpatrick and Michael Southwell have developed an interesting series of nontraditional exercises for students who have error problems. See their self-instructional workbook *The Comp-Lab Exercises*.

Works Cited

Bartholomae, David. "The Study of Error." *College Composition and Communication* 31 (1980): 253–69.

Corder, S. P. "Error Analysis, Interlanguage and Second Language Acquisition." *Language Teaching and Linguistics: Abstracts* 8 (1975): 201–18.

———. "The Significance of Learners' Errors." *IRAL* V/4 (1967). Rpt. in *Error Analysis: Perspectives on Second Language Acquisition*. Ed. Jack C. Richards. London: Longman, 1974. 19–27.

Dreyfus, Hubert L. *What Computers Can't Do: The Limits of Artificial Intelligence*. Rev. ed. New York: Harper, 1979.

Dreyfuss, Hubert L., and Stuart E. Dreyfus. *Mind over Machine*. New York: Free Press, 1988.

Epes, Mary. "Tracing Errors to Their Sources: A Study of the Encoding Processes of Adult Basic Writers." *Journal of Basic Writing* 4 (1985): 4–33.

Epes, Mary, Carolyn Kirkpatrick, and Michael Southwell. *The Comp-Lab Exercises*. Englewood Cliffs: Prentice, 1980.

Fish, Stanley. *Is There a Text in This Class? The Authority of Interpretive Communities*. Cambridge: Harvard UP, 1980.

Flower, Linda, and John R. Hayes. "A Cognitive Process Theory of Writing." *College Composition and Communication* 32 (1981): 365–87.

Gardner, Howard. *Art, Mind, and Brain: A Cognitive Approach to Creativity*. New York: Basic, 1982.

Goodman, Kenneth S. "What We Know about Reading." *Findings of Research in Miscue Analysis: Classroom Implications*. Ed. P. David Allen and Dorothy J. Watson. Urbana: ERIC and NCTE, 1976. 57–70.

Haugeland, John. "Understanding Natural Language." *Journal of Philosophy* 76 (1979): 619–32.

Hayes, John R., and Linda S. Flower. "Identifying the Organization of Writing Processes." *Cognitive Processes in Writing*. Ed. Lee W. Gregg and Erwin R. Steinberg. Hillsdale: Erlbaum, 1980. 3–30.

Hull, Glynda A. "The Editing Process in Writing: A Performance Study of Experts and Novices." Diss. U of Pittsburgh, 1983.

Kroll, Barry M., and John C. Schafer. "Error-Analysis and the Teaching of Composition." *College Composition and Communication* 29 (1978): 242–48.

Labov, William. *The Study of Nonstandard English*. Urbana: NCTE, 1978.

Laurence, Patricia. "Error's Endless Train: Why Students Don't Perceive Errors." *Journal of Basic Writing* 1.1 (1975): 23–42.

Mellon, John C. *National Assessment and the Teaching of English: Results of the First National Assessment of Educational Progress in Writing, Reading, and Literature — Implications for Teaching and Measurement in the English Language Arts*. Urbana: NCTE, 1975.

Smith, Frank. *Understanding Reading: A Psycholinguistic Analysis of Reading and Learning to Read*. New York: Holt, 1971.

Stenson, Nancy. "Induced Errors." *New Frontiers in Second Language Learning*. Ed. John H. Schumann and Nancy Stenson. Rowley, MA: Newbury, 1974. 54–70.

Williams, Joseph M. "The Phenomenology of Error." *College Composition and Communication* 32 (1981): 152–68.

Lees's Insights as a Resource for Your Teaching

1. In a journal, reflect on the history of your own relationship with error in light of what Lees discusses in her essay. Matters of grammar and spelling, according to Lees, are the flashpoints by which we either gain access or are denied access to particular communities. Your reflection on your own relations with error are necessarily a reflection on the formation of your own social identity. What key experiences stand forth here?

2. What implications follow from Lees's insight with respect to your own handling of error in the classroom? If error is embarrassment, then surely this embarrassment bears a significant relation to the anxiety and frustration that Mike Rose identifies (in the following article) as a key source for writer's block. Although it may be impossible to address error in student writing in ways that are not embarrassing (in Lees's sense), try to devise strategies to defuse this destructive force. Perhaps devise journal assignments that invite students to draw connections between error and "ethos" and to the political issues of community and social identity.

Lees's Insight as a Resource for the Writing Classroom

1. If you have access to a video recorder, duplicate with your students the study that Lees conducted with proofreaders: videotape the students' reaction to error when they proofread other classmates' work. Present Lees's theory to them, show the tape, and have them discuss it. If the discussion goes well, it might generate essay assignments or even collaborative assignments about community membership and social identity.

2. Ask students to freewrite about how they feel when someone spots an error in something they've written or said. Have them then compare their feelings about these moments. Write the major patterns of agreement on the board, and then ask them to freewrite about these general patterns: What do the groups' responses imply? From here, draw connections to "ethos," social identity, or persona and the gate-keeping role that readers play. Have students brainstorm ways of discussing error that minimizes embarrassment.

MIKE ROSE   *Rigid Rules, Inflexible Plans, and the Stifling of Language: A Cognitivist Analysis of Writer's Block*

What's really going on when a student writer can't write, even when an assignment's deadline looms closer and closer? In this study, Mike Rose finds ten students at UCLA who struggle with writer's block and compares their composing processes with those of students who do not have writer's block. Students are often blocked by very specific cognitive objects: they are stifled by rigid dos and don'ts of writing, and their inflexible plans never match what they finally produce on the page. Writers who do not struggle with writer's block, on the other hand, are unimpeded by any such hypersensitivity to rules and plans: they just write, knowing that they can revise or retract later.

Ruth will labor over the first paragraph of an essay for hours. She'll write a sentence, then erase it. Try another, then scratch part of it out. Finally, as the evening winds on toward ten o'clock and Ruth, anxious about tomorrow's deadline, begins to wind into herself, she'll compose that first paragraph only to sit back and level her favorite exasperated interdiction at herself and her page: "No. You can't say that. You'll bore them to death."

Ruth is one of ten UCLA undergraduates with whom I discussed writer's block, that frustrating, self-defeating inability to generate the next line, the right phrase, the sentence that will release the flow of words once again. These ten people represented a fair cross-section of the UCLA student community: lower-middle-class to upper-middle-class backgrounds and high schools, third-world and Caucasian origins, biology to fine arts majors, C+ to A– grade point averages, enthusiastic to blasé attitudes toward school. They were set off from the community by the twin facts that all ten could write competently, and all were currently enrolled in at least one course that required a significant amount of writing. They were set off among themselves by the fact that five of them wrote with relative to enviable ease while the other five experienced moderate to nearly immobilizing writer's block. This blocking usually resulted in rushed, often late papers and resultant grades that did not truly reflect these students' writing ability. And then, of course, there were other less measurable but probably more serious results: a growing distrust of their abilities and an aversion toward the composing process itself.

What separated the five students who blocked from those who didn't? It wasn't skill; that was held fairly constant. The answer could have rested in the emotional realm — anxiety, fear of evaluation, insecurity, etc. Or perhaps blocking in some way resulted from variation in cognitive style. Perhaps, too, blocking originated in and typified a melding of emotion and cognition not unlike the relationship posited by Shapiro between neurotic feeling and neurotic thinking.[1] Each of these was possible. Extended clinical interviews and testing could have teased out the answer. But there was one answer that surfaced readily in brief explorations of these students' writing processes. It was not profoundly emotional, nor was it embedded in that still unclear construct of cognitive style. It was constant, surprising, almost amusing if its results weren't so troublesome, and, in the final analysis, obvious: the five students who experienced blocking were all operating either with writing rules or with planning strategies that impeded rather than enhanced the composing process. The five students who were not hampered by writer's block also utilized rules, but they were less rigid ones, and thus more appropriate to a complex process like writing. Also, the plans these non-blockers brought to the writing process were more functional, more flexible, more open to information from the outside.

These observations are the result of one to three interviews with each student. I used recent notes, drafts, and finished compositions to direct and hone my questions. This procedure is admittedly non-experimental, certainly more clinical than scientific; still, it did lead to several inferences that lay the foundation for future, more rigorous investigation: (a) composing is a highly complex problem-solving process[2] and (b) certain disruptions of that process can be explained with cognitive psychology's problem-solving framework. Such investigation might include a study using "stimulated recall" techniques to validate or disconfirm these hunches. In such a study, blockers and non-blockers would write essays. Their activity would be videotaped and, immediately after writing, they would be shown their respective tapes and questioned about the rules, plans, and beliefs operating in their writing behavior. This procedure would bring us close to the composing process (the writers' recall is stimulated by their viewing the tape), yet would not interfere with actual composing.

In the next section I will introduce several key concepts in the problem-solving literature. In section three I will let the students speak for themselves. Fourth, I will offer a cognitivist analysis of blockers' and non-blockers' grace or torpor. I will close with a brief note on treatment.

Selected Concepts in Problem Solving: Rules and Plans

As diverse as theories of problem solving are, they share certain basic assumptions and characteristics. Each posits an *introductory period* during which a problem is presented, and all theorists, from Behaviorist to Gestalt to Information Processing, admit that certain aspects, stimuli, or "functions" of the problem must become or be made salient and attended to in certain ways if successful problem-solving processes are to be engaged. Theorists also believe that some conflict, some stress, some gap in information in these perceived "aspects" seems to trigger problem-solving behavior. Next comes a *processing period*, and for all the variance of opinion about this critical stage, theorists recognize the necessity of its existence — recognize that man, at the least, somehow "weighs" possible solutions as they are stumbled upon and, at the most, goes through an elaborate and sophisticated information-processing routine to achieve problem solution. Furthermore, theorists believe — to varying degrees — that past learning and the particular "set," direction, or orientation that the problem solver takes in dealing with past experience and present stimuli have critical bearing on the efficacy of solution. Finally, all theorists admit to a *solution period*, an end-state of the process where "stress" and "search" terminate, an answer is attained, and a sense of completion or "closure" is experienced.

These are the gross similarities, and the framework they offer will be useful in understanding the problem-solving behavior of the students discussed in this paper. But since this paper is primarily concerned with the second stage of problem-solving operations, it would be most useful to focus this introduction on two critical constructs in the processing period: rules and plans.

Rules

Robert M. Gagné defines "rule" as "an inferred capability that enables the individual to respond to a class of stimulus situations with a class of performances."[3] Rules can be learned directly[4] or by inference through experience.[5] But, in either case, most problem-solving theorists would affirm Gagné's dictum that "rules are probably the major organizing factor, and quite possibly the primary one, in intellectual functioning."[6] As Gagné implies, we wouldn't be able to function without rules; they guide response to the myriad stimuli that confront us daily, and might even be the central element in complex problem-solving behavior.

Dunker, Polya, and Miller, Galanter, and Pribram offer a very useful distinction between two general kinds of rules: algorithms and heuristics.[7] Algorithms are precise rules that will always result in a specific answer if applied to an appropriate problem. Most mathematical rules, for example, are algorithms. Functions are constant (e.g., pi), procedures are routine (squaring the radius), and outcomes are completely predictable. However, few day-to-day situations are mathematically circumscribed enough to warrant the application of algorithms. Most often we function with the aid of fairly general heuristics or "rules of thumb," guidelines that allow varying degrees of flexibility when approaching problems. Rather than operating with algorithmic precision and certainty, we search, critically, through alternatives, using our heuristic as a divining rod — "if a math problem stumps you, try working backwards to solution"; "if the car won't start, check X, Y, or Z," and so forth. Heuristics won't allow the precision or the certitude afforded by algorithmic operations; heuristics can even be so "loose" as to be vague. But in a world where tasks and problems are rarely mathematically precise, heuristic rules become the most appropriate, the most functional rules available to us: "a heuristic does not guarantee the optimal solution or, indeed, any solution at all; rather, heuristics offer solutions that are good enough most of the time."[8]

Plans

People don't proceed through problem situations, in or out of a laboratory, without some set of internalized instructions to the self, some program, some course of action that, even roughly, takes goals and possible paths to that goal into consideration. Miller, Galanter, and Pribram have referred to this course of action as a plan: "A plan is any hierarchical process in the organism that can control the order in which a sequence of operations is to be performed" (16). They name the fundamental plan in human problem-solving behavior the TOTE, with the initial T representing a *test* that matches a possible solution against the perceived end-goal of problem completion. O represents the clearance to *operate* if the comparison between solution and goal indicates that the solution is a sensible one. The second T represents a further, post-operation, *test* or comparison of solution with goal, and if the two mesh and problem solution is at hand the person *exits* (E) from problem-solving behavior. If the second test presents further discordance between solution and goal, a further solution is attempted in TOTE-fashion. Such plans can be both long-term and global and, as problem solving is underway, short-term and immediate.[9] Though the mechanicality of this information-processing model renders it simplistic and, possibly, unreal, the central notion of a plan and an operating procedure is an important one in problem-solving theory; it at least attempts to metaphorically explain what earlier cognitive psychologists could not — the mental procedures (see 390–91) underlying problem-solving behavior.

Before concluding this section, a distinction between heuristic rules and plans should be attempted; it is a distinction often blurred in the literature, blurred because, after all, we are very much in the area of gestating theory and preliminary models. Heuristic rules seem to function with the flexibility of plans. Is, for example, "If the car won't start, try X, Y, or Z" a heuristic or a plan? It could be either, though two qualifications will mark it as heuristic rather than plan. (A) Plans subsume and sequence heuristic and algorithmic rules. Rules are usually "smaller," more discrete cognitive capabilities; plans can become quite large and complex, composed of a series of ordered algorithms, heuristics, and further planning "sub-routines." (B)

Plans, as was mentioned earlier, include criteria to determine successful goal-attainment and, as well, include "feedback" processes — ways to incorporate and use information gained from "tests" of potential solutions against desired goals.

One other distinction should be made: that is, between "set" and plan. Set, also called "determining tendency" or "readiness,"[10] refers to the fact that people often approach problems with habitual ways of reacting, a predisposition, a tendency to perceive or function in one way rather than another. Set, which can be established through instructions or, consciously or unconsciously, through experience, can assist performance if it is appropriate to a specific problem,[11] but much of the literature on set has shown its rigidifying, dysfunctional effects.[12] Set differs from plan in that set represents a limiting and narrowing of response alternatives with no inherent process to shift alternatives. It is a kind of cognitive habit that can limit perception, not a course of action with multiple paths that directs and sequences response possibilities.

The constructs of rules and plans advance the understanding of problem solving beyond that possible with earlier, less developed formulations. Still, critical problems remain. Though mathematical and computer models move one toward more complex (and thus more real) problems than the earlier research, they are still too neat, too rigidly sequenced to approximate the stunning complexity of day-to-day (not to mention highly creative) problem-solving behavior. Also, information-processing models of problem-solving are built on logic theorems, chess strategies, and simple planning tasks. Even Gagné seems to feel more comfortable with illustrations from mathematics and science rather than with social science and humanities problems. So although these complex models and constructs tell us a good deal about problem-solving behavior, they are still laboratory simulations, still invoked from the outside rather than self-generated, and still founded on the mathematico-logical.

Two Carnegie-Mellon researchers, however, have recently extended the above into a truly real, amorphous, unmathematical problem-solving process — writing. Relying on protocol analysis (thinking aloud while solving problems), Linda Flower and John Hayes have attempted to tease out the role of heuristic rules and plans in writing behavior.[13] Their research pushes problem-solving investigations to the real and complex and pushes, from the other end, the often mysterious process of writing toward the explainable. The latter is important, for at least since Plotinus many have viewed the composing process as unexplainable, inspired, infused with the transcendent. But Flower and Hayes are beginning, anyway, to show how writing generates from a problem-solving process with rich heuristic rules and plans of its own. They show, as well, how many writing problems arise from a paucity of heuristics and suggest an intervention that provides such rules.

This paper, too, treats writing as a problem-solving process, focusing, however, on what happens when the process dead-ends in writer's block. It will further suggest that, as opposed to Flower and Hayes' students who need more rules and plans, blockers may well be stymied by possessing rigid or inappropriate rules, or inflexible or confused plans. Ironically enough, these are occasionally instilled by the composition teacher or gleaned from the writing textbook.

"Always Grab Your Audience" — The Blockers

In high school, *Ruth* was told and told again that a good essay always grabs a reader's attention immediately. Until you can make your essay do that, her teachers and textbooks putatively declaimed, there is no need to go on. For Ruth, this means that beginning bland and seeing what emerges as one generates prose is unacceptable. The beginning is everything. And what exactly is the audience seeking that reads this beginning? The rule, or Ruth's use of it, doesn't provide for such investigation. She has an edict with no determiners. Ruth operates with another rule that restricts her productions as well: if sentences aren't grammatically "correct," they aren't useful. This keeps Ruth from toying with ideas on paper, from the kind of linguistic play that often frees up the flow of prose. These two rules converge in a way that pretty effectively restricts Ruth's composing process.

The first two papers I received from *Laurel* were weeks overdue. Sections of them were well written; there were even moments of stylistic flair. But the papers were late and, overall, the prose seemed rushed. Furthermore, one paper included a paragraph on an issue that was never mentioned in the topic paragraph. This was the kind of mistake that someone with Laurel's apparent ability doesn't make. I asked her about this irrelevant passage. She knew very well that it didn't fit, but believed she had to include it to round out the paper. "You must always make three or more points in an essay. If the essay has less, then it's not strong." Laurel had been taught this rule both in high school and in her first college English class; no wonder, then, that she accepted its validity.

As opposed to Laurel, *Martha* possesses a whole arsenal of plans and rules with which to approach a humanities writing assignment, and, considering her background in biology, I wonder how many of them were formed out of the assumptions and procedures endemic to the physical sciences.[14] Martha will not put pen to first draft until she has spent up to two days generating an outline of remarkable complexity. I saw one of these outlines and it looked more like a diagram of protein synthesis or DNA structure than the time-worn pattern offered in composition textbooks. I must admit I was intrigued by the aura of process (vs. the static appearance of essay outlines) such diagrams offer, but for Martha these "outlines" only led to self-defeat: the outline would become so complex that all of its elements could never be included in a short essay. In other words, her plan locked her into the first stage of the composing process. Martha would struggle with the conversion of her outline into prose only to scrap the whole venture when deadlines passed and a paper had to be rushed together.

Martha's "rage for order" extends beyond the outlining process. She also believes that elements of a story or poem must evince a fairly linear structure and thematic clarity, or — perhaps bringing us closer to the issue — that analysis of a story or poem must provide the linearity or clarity that seems to be absent in the text. Martha, therefore, will bend the logic of her analysis to reason ambiguity out of existence. When I asked her about a strained paragraph in her paper on Camus' "The Guest," she said, "I didn't want to admit that it [the story's conclusion] was just hanging. I tried to force it into meaning."

Martha uses another rule, one that is not only problematical in itself, but one that often clashes directly with the elaborate plan and obsessive rule above. She believes that humanities papers must scintillate with insight, must present an array of images, ideas, ironies gleaned from the literature under examination. A problem arises, of course, when Martha tries to incorporate her myriad "neat little things," often inherently unrelated, into a tightly structured, carefully sequenced essay. Plans and rules that govern the construction of impressionistic, associational prose would be appropriate to Martha's desire, but her composing process is heavily constrained by the non-impressionistic and nonassociational. Put another way, the plans and rules that govern her exploration of text are not at all synchronous with the plans and rules she uses to discuss her exploration. It is interesting to note here, however, that as recently as three years ago Martha was absorbed in creative writing and was publishing poetry in high school magazines. Given what we know about the complex associational, often non-neatly-sequential nature of the poet's creative process, we can infer that Martha was either free of the plans and rules discussed earlier or they were not as intense. One wonders, as well, if the exposure to three years of university physical science either established or intensified Martha's concern with structure. Whatever the case, she now is hamstrung by conflicting rules when composing papers for the humanities.

Mike's difficulties, too, are rooted in a distortion of the problem-solving process. When the time of the week for the assignment of writing topics draws near, Mike begins to prepare material, strategies, and plans that he believes will be appropriate. If the assignment matches his expectations, he has done a good job of analyzing the professor's intentions. If the assignment *doesn't* match his expectations, however, he cannot easily shift approaches. He feels trapped inside his original plans, cannot generate alternatives, and blocks. As the deadline draws near, he will write something, forcing the assignment to fit his conceptual procrustian bed. Since Mike is a smart man, he will offer a good deal of information, but only some of it ends up being appropriate to the assignment. This entire situation is made all the worse when the time between assignment of topic and generation of product is attenuated further, as in an essay examination. Mike believes (correctly) that one must have a plan, a strategy of some sort in order to solve a problem. He further believes, however, that such a plan, once formulated, becomes an exact structural and substantive blueprint that cannot be violated. The plan offers no alternatives, no "subroutines." So, whereas Ruth's, Laurel's, and some of Martha's difficulties seem to be rule-specific ("always catch your audience," "write grammatically"), Mike's troubles are more global. He may have strategies that are appropriate for various writing situations (e.g., "for this kind of political science assignment write a compare/contrast essay"), but his entire approach to formulating plans and carrying them through to problem solution is too mechanical. It is probable that Mike's behavior is governed by an explicitly learned or inferred rule: "Always try to 'psych out' a professor." But in this case this rule initiates a problem-solving procedure that is clearly dysfunctional.

While Ruth and Laureal use rules that impede their writing process and Mike utilizes a problem-solving procedure that hamstrings him, *Sylvia* has trouble deciding which of the many rules she possesses to use. Her problem can be characterized as cognitive perplexity: some of her rules are inappropriate, others are functional; some mesh nicely with her own definitions of good writing, others don't. She has multiple rules to invoke, multiple paths to follow, and that very complexity of choice virtually paralyzes her. More so than with the previous four students, there is probably a strong emotional dimension to Sylvia's blocking, but the cognitive difficulties are clear and perhaps modifiable.

Sylvia, somewhat like Ruth and Laurel, puts tremendous weight on the crafting of her first paragraph. If it is good, she believes the rest of the essay will be good. Therefore, she will spend up to five hours on the initial paragraph: "I won't go on until I get that first paragraph down." Clearly, this rule — or the strength of it — blocks Sylvia's production. This is one problem. Another is that Sylvia has other equally potent rules that she sees as separate, uncomplementary injunctions: one achieves "flow" in one's writing through the use of adequate transitions; one achieves substance to one's writing through the use of evidence. Sylvia perceives both rules to be "true," but several times followed one to the exclusion of the other. Furthermore, as I talked to Sylvia, many other rules, guidelines, definitions were offered, but none with conviction. While she *is* committed to one rule about initial paragraphs, and that rule is dysfunctional, she seems very uncertain about the weight and hierarchy of the remaining rules in her cognitive repertoire.

"If It Won't Fit My Work, I'll Change It" — The Non-blockers

Dale, Ellen, Debbie, Susan, and Miles all write with the aid of rules. But their rules differ from blockers' rules in significant ways. If similar in content, they are expressed less absolutely — e.g., "*Try* to keep audience in mind." If dissimilar, they are still expressed less absolutely, more heuristically — e.g., "I can use as many ideas in my thesis paragraph as I need and then develop paragraphs for each idea." Our non-blockers do express some rules with firm assurance, but these tend to be simple injunctions that free up rather than restrict the composing process, e.g., "When stuck, write!" or "I'll write what I can." And finally, at least three of the students openly shun the very textbook rules that some blockers adhere to: e.g., "Rules like 'write only what you know about' just aren't true. I ignore those." These three, in effect, have formulated a further rule that expresses something like: "If a rule conflicts with what is sensible or with experience, reject it."

On the broader level of plans and strategies, these five students also differ from at least three of the five blockers in that they all possess problem-solving plans that are quite functional. Interestingly, on first exploration these plans seem to be too broad or fluid to be useful and, in some cases, can barely be expressed with any precision. Ellen, for example, admits that she has a general "outline in [her] head about how a topic paragraph should look" but could not describe much about its structure. Susan also has a general plan to follow, but, if stymied, will quickly attempt to conceptualize the assignment in different ways: "If my original idea won't work, then I need to proceed differently." Whether or not these plans operate in TOTE-fashion, I can't say. But they do operate with the operate-test fluidity of TOTEs.

True, our non-blockers have their religiously adhered-to rules: e.g., "When stuck, write," and plans, "I couldn't imagine writing without this pattern," but as noted above, these are few and functional. Otherwise, these non-blockers operate with fluid, easily modified, even easily discarded rules and plans (Ellen: "I can throw things out") that are sometimes expressed with a vagueness that could almost be interpreted as ignorance. There lies the irony. Students that offer the least precise rules and plans have the least trouble composing. Perhaps this very lack of precision characterizes the functional composing plan. But perhaps this lack of precision simply masks habitually enacted alternatives and sub-routines. This is clearly an area that needs the illumination of further research.

And then there is feedback. At least three of the five non-blockers are an Information-Processor's dream. They get to know their audience, ask professors and T.A.s specific questions about assignments, bring half-finished products in for evaluation, etc. Like Ruth, they realize the importance of audience, but unlike her, they have specific strategies for obtaining and utilizing feedback. And this penchant for testing writing plans against the needs of the audience can lead to modification of rules and plans. Listen to Debbie:

> In high school I was given a formula that stated that you must write a thesis paragraph with *only* three points in it, and then develop each of those points. When I hit college I was given longer assignments. That stuck me for a bit, but then realized that I could use as many ideas in my thesis paragraph as I needed and then develop paragraphs for each one. I asked someone about this and then tried it. I didn't get any negative feedback, so I figured it was o.k.

Debbie's statement brings one last difference between our blockers and non-blockers into focus; it has been implied above, but needs specific formulation: the goals these people have, and the plans they generate to attain these goals, are quite mutable. Part of the mutability comes from the fluid way the goals and plans are conceived, and part of it arises from the effective impact of feedback on these goals and plans.

Analyzing Writer's Block

Algorithms Rather Than Heuristics

In most cases, the rules our blockers use are not "wrong" or "incorrect" — it is good practice, for example, to "grab your audience with a catchy opening" or "craft a solid first paragraph before going on." The problem is that these rules seem to be followed as though they were algorithms, absolute dicta, rather than the loose heuristics that they were intended to be. Either through instruction, or the power of the textbook, or the predilections of some of our blockers for absolutes, or all three, these useful rules of thumb have been transformed into near-algorithmic urgencies. The result, to paraphrase Karl Dunker, is that these rules do not allow a flexible penetration into the nature of the problem. It is this transformation of heuristic into algorithm that contributes to the writer's block of Ruth and Laurel.

Questionable Heuristics Made Algorithmic

Whereas "grab your audience" could be a useful heuristic, "always make three or more points in an essay" is a pretty questionable one. Any such rule, though probably taught to aid the writer who needs structure, ultimately transforms a highly fluid process like writing into a mechanical lockstep. As heuristics, such rules can be troublesome. As algorithms, they are simply incorrect.

Set

As with any problem-solving task, students approach writing assignments with a variety of orientations or sets. Some are functional, others are not. Martha and Jane (see note 14), coming out of the life sciences and social sciences respectively, bring certain methodological orientations with them — certain sets or "directions" that make composing for the humanities a difficult, sometimes confusing, task. In fact, this orientation may cause them to misperceive the task. Martha has formulated a planning strategy from her predisposition to see processes in terms of linear, interrelated steps in a system. Jane doesn't realize that she can revise the statement that "committed" her to the direction her essay has taken. Both of these students are stymied because of formative experiences associated with their majors — experiences, perhaps, that nicely reinforce our very strong tendency to organize experiences temporally.

The Plan That Is Not a Plan

If fluidity and multi-directionality are central to the nature of plans, then the plans that Mike formulates are not true plans at all but, rather, inflexible and static cognitive blueprints.[15] Put another way, Mike's "plans" represent a restricted "closed system" (vs. "open system") kind of thinking, where closed system thinking is defined as focusing on "a limited number of units or items, or members, and those properties of the members which are to be used are known to begin with and do not change as the thinking proceeds," and open system thinking is characterized by an "adventurous exploration of multiple alternatives with strategies that allow redirection once 'dead ends' are encountered."[16] Composing calls for open, even adventurous thinking, not for constrained, no-exit cognition.

Feedback

The above difficulties are made all the more problematic by the fact that they seem resistant to or isolated from corrective feedback. One of the most striking things about Dale, Debbie, and Miles is the ease with which they seek out, interpret, and apply feedback on their rules, plans, and productions. They "operate" and then they "test," and the testing is not only against some internalized goal, but against the requirements of external audience as well.

Too Many Rules — "Conceptual Conflict"

According to D. E. Berlyne, one of the primary forces that motivate problem-solving behavior is a curiosity that arises from conceptual conflict — the convergence of incompatible beliefs or ideas. In *Structure and Direction in Thinking,*[17] Berlyne presents six major types of conceptual conflict, the second of which he terms "perplexity":

> This kind of conflict occurs when there are factors including the subject toward each of a set of mutually exclusive beliefs. (257)

If one substitutes "rules" for "beliefs" in the above definition, perplexity becomes a useful notion here. Because perplexity is unpleasant, people are motivated to reduce it by problem-solving behavior that can result in "disequalization":

> Degree of conflict will be reduced if either the number of competing . . . [rules] or their nearness to equality of strength is reduced. (259)

But "disequalization" is not automatic. As I have suggested, Martha and Sylvia hold to rules that conflict, but their perplexity does *not* lead to curiosity and resultant problem-solving behavior. Their perplexity, contra Berlyne, leads to immobilization. Thus "disequalization" will have to be effected from without. The importance of each of, particularly, Sylvia's rules needs an evaluation that will aid her in rejecting some rules and balancing and sequencing others.

A Note on Treatment

Rather than get embroiled in a blocker's misery, the teacher or tutor might interview the student in order to build a writing history and profile: How much and what kind of writing was done in high school? What is the student's major? What kind of writing does it require? How does the student compose? Are there rough drafts or outlines available? By what rules does the student operate? How would he or she define "good" writing? etc. This sort of interview reveals an incredible amount of information about individual composing processes. Furthermore, it often reveals the rigid rule or the inflexible plan that may lie at the base of the student's writing problem. That was precisely what happened with the five blockers. And with Ruth, Laurel, and Martha (and Jane) what was revealed made virtually immediate remedy possible. Dysfunctional rules are easily replaced with or counter-balanced by functional ones if there is no emotional reason to hold onto that which simply doesn't work. Furthermore, students can be trained to select, to "know which rules are appropriate for which problems."[18] Mike's difficulties, perhaps because plans are more complex and pervasive than rules, took longer to correct. But inflexible plans, too, can be remedied by pointing out their dysfunctional qualities and by assisting the student in developing appropriate and flexible alternatives. Operating this way, I was successful with Mike. Sylvia's story, however, did not end as smoothly. Though I had three forty-five minute contacts with her, I was not able to appreciably alter her behavior. Berlyne's theory bore results with Martha but not with Sylvia. Her rules were in conflict, and perhaps that conflict was not exclusively cognitive. Her case keeps analyses like these honest; it reminds us that the cognitive often melds with, and can be overpowered by, the affective. So while Ruth, Laurel, Martha, and Mike could profit from tutorials that explore the rules and plans in their writing behavior, students like Sylvia may need more extended, more affectively oriented counseling sessions that blend the instructional with the psychodynamic.

Notes

[1]David Shapiro, *Neurotic Styles* (New York: Basic, 1965).

[2]Barbara Hayes-Ruth, a Rand cognitive psychologist, and I are currently developing an information-processing model of the composing process. A good deal of work has already been done by Linda Flower and John Hayes (see note 13 and surrounding text). I have just received — and recommend — their "Writing as Problem Solving" (paper presented at American Educational Research Association, April 1979).

[3]Robert M. Gagné, *The Conditions of Learning* (New York: Holt, 1970) 193.

[4]E. James Archer, "The Psychological Nature of Concepts," *Analysis of Concept Learning*, ed. H. J. Klausmeier and C. W. Harris (New York: Academic P, 1966), 37–44; David P. Ausubel, *The Psychology of Meaningful Verbal Behavior* (New York: Grune, 1963); Robert M. Gagné, "Problem Solving," *Categories of Human Learning*, ed. Arthur W. Melton (New York: Academic P, 1964) 293–317; George A. Miller, *Language and Communication* (New York: McGraw, 1951).

[5]George Katona, *Organizing and Memorizing* (New York: Columbia UP, 1940); Roger N. Shepard, Carl I. Hovland, and Herbert M. Jenkins, "Learning and Memorization of Classifications," *Psychological Monographs.* 75.13 (1961) (entire no. 517); Robert S. Woodworth, *Dynamics of Behavior* (New York: Holt, 1958) chs. 10–12.

[6]Gagné, *The Conditions of Learning*, 190–91.

[7]Karl Dunker, "On Problem Solving," *Psychological Monographs*, 58.5 (1945) (entire no. 270); George A. Polya, *How to Solve It* (Princeton: Princeton UP, 1945); George A. Miller, Eugene Galanter, and Karl H. Pribram, *Plans and the Structure of Behavior* (New York: Holt, 1960).

[8]Lyle E. Bourne, Jr., Bruce R. Ekstrand, and Roger L. Dominowski, *The Psychology of Thinking* (Englewood Cliffs: Prentice, 1971).

[9]John R. Hayes, "Problem Topology and the Solution Process," *Thinking: Current Experimental Studies*, ed. Carl P. Duncan (Philadelphia: Lippincott, 1967) 167–81.

[10]Hulda J. Rees and Harold E. Israel, "An Investigation of the Establishment and Operation of Mental Sets," *Psychological Monographs.* 46 (1925) (entire no. 210).

[11]Ibid.; Melvin H. Marx, Wilton W. Murphy, and Aaron J. Brownstein, "Recognition of Complex Visual Stimuli as a Function of Training with Abstracted Patterns," *Journal of Experimental Psychology* 62 (1961): 456–60.

[12]James L. Adams, *Conceptual Blockbusting* (San Francisco: Freeman, 1974); Edward DeBono, *New Think* (New York: Basic, 1958); Ronald H. Forgus, *Perception* (New York: McGraw, 1966) ch. 13; Abraham Luchins and Edith Hirsch Luchins, *Rigidity of Behavior* (Eugene: U of Oregon Books, 1959); N. R. F. Maier, "Reasoning in Humans. I. On Direction," *Journal of Comparative Psychology* 10 (1920): 115–43.

[13]Linda Flower and John Hayes, "Plans and the Cognitive Process of Writing," paper presented at the National Institute of Education Writing Conference, June 1977; "Problem Solving Strategies and the Writing Process," *College English* 39 (1977): 449–61. See also note 2.

[14]Jane, a student not discussed in this paper, was surprised to find out that a topic paragraph can be rewritten after a paper's conclusion to make that paragraph reflect what the essay truly contains. She had gotten so indoctrinated with Psychology's (her major) insistence that a hypothesis be formulated and then left untouched before an experiment begins that she thought revision of one's "major premise" was somehow illegal. She had formed a rule out of her exposure to social science methodology, and the rule was totally inappropriate for most writing situations.

[15]Cf. "A plan is flexible if the order of execution of its parts can be easily interchanged without affecting the feasibility of the plan . . . the flexible planner might tend to think of lists of things he had to do; the inflexible planner would have his time planned like a sequence of cause-effect relations. The former could rearrange his lists to suit his opportunities, but the latter would be unable to strike while the iron was hot and would generally require consider-

able 'lead-time' before he could incorporate any alternative sub-plans" (Miller, Galanter, and Pribram, 120).

[16]Frederic Bartlett, *Thinking* (New York: Basic, 1958) 74–76.

[17]*Structure and Direction in Thinking* (New York: Wiley, 1965) 255.

[18]Flower and Hayes, "Plans and the Cognitive Process of Writing" 26.

Rose's Insights as a Resource for Your Teaching

1. Consider the risks in teaching students how to write: invariably, a few students will be cowed by your authority and will internalize even the most idle and perfunctory observations that you make. Worse yet, they will treat them not simply as useful tips but as some sort of holy edict. When they do, their ability to compose will be curtailed. In a journal, reflect on ways to prevent your overly earnest students from damaging themselves this way. What are some strategies you might devise to teach in a way that minimizes this risk?

2. How do you help students who have come into your classroom blocked by mishandled writing advice? What can you say to them? Can you use some of Freire's theory when giving advice to students who have already mishandled the advice given them in the past?

Rose's Insights as a Resource for the Writing Classroom

1. Consider the juxtaposition of the essays by Williams and Rose. Could a zealous marking of "incorrect" spots in a paper be a contributing factor to what Rose identifies as an overly zealous conscientiousness about following the rules? How might these two essays modify the ways you comment on student writing?

2. Ask students to meet in small groups and make a list of the five most important dos and don'ts of writing. Then have them write their lists on the board. As you discuss them, emphasize their tentative nature, and encourage students to take all of them with a grain of salt. Explain to them that to be overly concerned with such matters can undermine the process of getting thoughts down on paper.

DEBORAH MCCUTCHEN,	*Editing Strategies and*
GLYNDA A. HULL,	*Error Correction*
AND WILLIAM L. SMITH	*in Basic Writing*

Why do some students submit papers that are loaded with obvious errors, while other students turn in papers that are almost error free? This article suggests that the first group has problems detecting error in their work, which prevents them from editing or "cleaning up" the text. McCutchen, Hull, and Smith suggest that there are two distinct processes at work in error detection or editing: a consulting strategy and an intuiting strategy. When students use a consulting strategy, they defer to memorized rules to decide whether they have a problem in their text. When students use an intuiting strategy, they proceed in a more naturalistic way, consulting not memorized rules but rather their own intuitions as native speakers of the language. Unfortunately, the overwhelming majority of errors are of the sort that can be detected only via the consulting strategy. While repeated drilling of grammar generates no appreciable gains in a student's ability to use the consulting strategy, a computer program that addresses errors in particular work samples does give the student greater command of the consulting strategy.

Much has been written about the systematicity of basic writers (BW)[1] errors (Bartholomae; Hull; Shaughnessy). By understanding this systematicity, writing instructors can gain new insight into student writing. However, instructors must do more than understand the source and systematicity of errors made by basic writers; they must teach these students strategies that enable them to correct those errors. To do that, writing instructors must look beyond error as the end product of some process, and they must look to the processes (i.e., strategies) required to detect and correct those errors.

We must realize, as Perl has pointed out, that basic writers are not completely without strategies when they enter the classroom. One BW student stated his basic strategy this way: "When all fails, stick a comma in and see what happens." Clearly, not all their strategies are worthy of cultivation and refinement through instruction, but there are data to suggest that BW students have some strategies that can serve them quite well, especially in the case of certain kinds of error.

Intuiting and Consulting Strategies

Hull identified two strategies that BW students frequently use in editing: an *intuiting* strategy, which students use when they check the sound of a piece of text when read, and a *consulting* strategy, which students use when they make reference to some learned rules of grammar, spelling, punctuation, and so on. (Hull also described a *comprehending* strategy, which students use when they find a problem in the meaning of a piece of text. This strategy might, however, be thought of as a special case of the intuiting strategy and is not discussed here.) These are far from all the strategies that BW students use while editing. They are, however, strategies that a large number of BW students bring with them to the classroom. Furthermore, when applied correctly by students, these strategies can be effective ways to edit certain errors. They are not, however, interchangeable options; certain errors lend themselves to correction via one strategy or the other. Given the sentence *The building in which the children ran into*, BW students can often "hear," or intuit, the syntactic problem, and they say things such as "That just doesn't sound right" or "I'll try to make that sound better." However, given the intended possessive phrase *the geniuses word*, students cannot detect the error by judging how the phrase sounds. Indeed, the phrase sounds fine. The apostrophe error can be detected only by consulting some rule about possession in nouns being marked by an apostrophe followed by *s*. In short, errors that can be corrected with the intuiting strategy are those that can be detected aurally given a true verbatim reading of the text (e.g., blurred syntactic patterns, incorrect word choice, missing words). That is, they violate lexical or syntactic constraints of the language. Errors that are amenable to the consulting strategy, on the other hand, violate only rules of *written*, not spoken, language (e.g., misspellings and incorrect punctuation, such as sentence boundary errors and missing apostrophes). Thus editing these errors requires knowledge of written language conventions, not just a native speaker's linguistic intuitions.[2]

Using paper-and-pencil editing tasks, Hull found that BW students were better at correcting errors that required the intuiting strategy than errors requiring the consulting strategy. Since this was true for their own texts as well as for texts written by others, their advantage with the intuiting strategy cannot be discounted simply as students being able to detect problematic phrasings that they themselves never produce. Rather, the effect seems due to the different demands made by the two strategies. The consulting strategy demands referencing rules of standard written English, rules these students may not know because of their limited exposure to print. The intuiting strategy, on the other hand, involves a more "naturalistic," holistic analysis of phrasing, a process that might more easily transfer from the students' experience with spoken language.

If students' differential success with the two strategies is due to the nature of the strategies themselves, the effect should be robust enough to replicate in various editing situations; but more important, such robustness would suggest that these strategies should perhaps be considered in editing instruction. The present studies were attempts to replicate Hull's findings in different editing situations. They were carried out as part of a larger study of the effects of word processing and computer-assisted instruction on BW editing skills. Certainly, editing on a computer is different from editing on paper in many ways, two obvious differences being the printed format and the ease of editing. Not only does the student see printed text rather than handwritten scrawls but minor changes in the text no longer necessitate the burdensome chore of rewriting entire pages. If students' strategies remain constant while the editing situation changes so markedly, we might validly argue that those strategies must be taken into account in writing instruction.

Study 1

Study 1 was a pilot study, designed to assess the impact of word processing on BW students and their writing. Prior to the beginning of the school term, BW students were given instruction on using word processors and were given access to microcomputers on which they wrote their class assignments. In addition, students were asked, three times during the fifteen-week term, to do special editing tasks using the word processors. The students were asked to complete one during the third week of the term, one during the seventh week, and one during the eleventh. The texts the students were to edit had been written by basic writers in previous terms, and they contained a variety of errors. An excerpt from one of the texts is presented in Figure 1. (Some changes had been made in the texts to equate errors across the three different texts, but the texts remained typical of student writing.) The students were instructed to correct errors in "spelling, punctuation, or typing" but not to concern themselves with "changes in word choice or paragraphing or the arrangement of sentences." That is, students were instructed to *edit* the texts, not to *revise* them.

The students viewed the texts on the CRT screen of a microcomputer and made their changes using the word processor that they used on their own assignments. Brief procedural checks were done to make sure that the students could successfully use the word processors to effect their changes. Even by the third week of the term, students were quite facile making the kinds of changes typically required in editing (adding text, removing text, rearranging text, and so on). While some students developed idiosyncratic procedures that were somewhat inelegant, all students were quite competent using the word processors.

Since participation was voluntary, not all students completed all editing tasks. Thirteen completed the first session, nine the second, and five the third. Due to the small number of students, statistical analyses were not performed on these data. The data consist of the percentage of text errors that the students detected and attempted to correct. While successful editing requires error correction as well as error detection, the data reflect editing attempts, regardless of their complete success. However, since so few error detections resulted in only partial corrections (fewer than 5 percent of the errors detected were not corrected perfectly), the liberal scoring does little to distort the results.

The mean accuracy scores revealed less than perfect performance by the students. In session one, the group (n = 13) scored a mean of 54 percent correct across

Truly, one of most creative moments was one in which occurred in the spring of '76. My entire family went on a camping trip to Lost River, West Virginia. The campsite sat atop a large mountain, and we were surrounded by thick woods. The entire area was densely populated with large trees, many as old as 500 to 600 years. Not only was the area surrounded by bears as well.

The first few days were relatively uneventful. However, on the third night we were all awakened by a loud noise behind our tent. My father and I quickly rose to our our feet to see what it was, sure enough, it was a large brown bear. Frightened out of my wits, I ran to the car. My father quickly woke my sister and mother as the bear ran past our tent and into the road. Quickly, I put the keys into the ignition and put the car into reverse, unknowingly hitting the bear.

Crazy as it sounds, we had a bear in which was stuck under our car. Unable to go forward or backward, we were all stupified as to what to do. Suddenly, I had an idea. . . .

Figure 1. Excerpt from a text that students were to correct

---

all error types. In session two, the group (n = 9) scored 62 percent correct, and in session three (n = 5), 52 percent correct. Because of possible self-selection factors influencing which students went on to complete session two, a second analysis was done to compare only the accuracy of students who completed both sessions one and two. The subset of nine students who completed both the first and second editing tasks scored similarly on each (62 percent correct on each). Thus the lower performance rate of session one reflects a lower scoring set of students who did not go on to complete session two.

Since only five students completed the third editing task, the data for this session should not be considered conclusive. Still, the apparent decrease in performance (down to 52 percent correct) was interesting. When the performance of the five students in session three was compared with their performance in sessions one and two, small differences remained (59 percent correct in sessions one and two compared with 52 percent correct in session three). There is doubt whether this decrease in performance should be taken seriously, but clearly there is no *increase* in the students' error correction across the term.

An analysis of Hull's error categories provides some additional insight. The three texts that the students edited contained several types of errors (e.g., sentence boundary errors, syntactic errors, missing verb inflections, missing apostrophes, misspellings, repeated words, and word confusions). Some of these errors (especially syntactic errors and word confusion) could be corrected using the intuiting strategy, while others (notably misspellings and missing apostrophes) could be corrected only by the students consulting a rule. Students were more likely to correct intuiting errors than consulting errors in the first two sessions (64 percent and 72 percent correct, respectively, for intuiting errors compared with 56 percent and 54 percent correct for consulting errors). This difference replicates Hull's (in press) findings.

For the five students who completed the third editing task, the picture (tentative as it might be) looks somewhat different. In the third session, overall performance decreased primarily due to decreased performance on intuiting errors. Students corrected only 43 percent of the intuiting errors, while they corrected 57 percent of the consulting errors. An examination of the performance of those five students in editing sessions one and two revealed that in the earlier sessions they had shown the same advantage with intuiting errors as had the rest of the group. In sessions one and two, they had corrected a larger percentage of intuiting errors (80 percent and 70 percent, respectively) than consulting errors (46 percent and 54 percent). Thus their accuracy on intuiting errors had decreased between the first two sessions (three and seven weeks into the term) and the third session (eleven weeks into the term).

Since it is based on so few subjects, such a result may need no explanation. In addition, texts were not counterbalanced across sessions, so the result may perhaps be due to increased difficulty of the third text. Still, the pilot data were interesting enough to warrant further investigation.

Protocol Support

In order to see first-hand how students interacted with the word processors, we had followed a small number of these BW students throughout the term and had collected protocols as they worked on their own assignments and as they worked on the three editing tasks. Again, there is support in the protocols for different editing strategies being used by the students as they go about the editing task.

There were individual differences in how explicit students were about their use of the intuiting strategy. Some students, like HT (false initials), simply reread sections of text over and over, trying possible alternatives until the text sounded right. Consider HT as he read a section of text and mulled over a word confusion error: "got in my truck and took off so the guys in the engine wouldn't respect . . . wouldn't *expect* . . . wouldn't *suspect* . . . wouldn't *suspect* anything." In contrast, other students were much more explicit of their use of the "sounds-okay" intuiting strategy, students such as MD whose protocol excerpt follows:

> [reads from the text shown in Figure 1] campsite sat atop a large mountain. [to himself] That sounds okay. [reads] And we were surrounded by thick woods. The entire area was densely populated with large trees, many as old as 500 to 600 years. Not only was the area surrounded . . . not only the area . . . the area was also surrounded by bears . . . surrounded by bears. [Backs up] My entire family went on a camping trip to Lost River, West Virginia. The campsite sat atop a large mountain and we were surrounded by thick woods. The entire area was densely populated by large trees, many as old as 500 to 600 years. The area was also surrounded by . . . [to himself] something about that doesn't sound right. . . .

While MD, like HT, reread often, he was more explicit in his use of the intuiting strategy, frequently saying things such as "Let's see how it sounds" and "It doesn't sound right at all" as he reread.

Both students also used the consulting strategy, and their protocol statements clearly distinguish the two strategies. For example, while considering an unnecessary comma, MD remarked "since it's like two things, you don't need a comma after that." Similarly, HT's statement, "I think *high school* is capitalized," shows his reference to rules and illustrates how the consulting strategy differs from the intuiting "sounds okay" strategy.

Since we followed only four students in protocol sessions, we again can point only to trends in the data. Still, a consistent picture emerges. Over the course of the term, students seemed to rely less on their "sounds okay" intuiting strategy and more on consulting strategies. MD was very explicit about his "sounds-okay" intuiting strategy in the third week of the term, but in later sessions his references to the sound of phrases decreased markedly. He still reread, but he no longer explicitly stated that he was checking how the text sounded. HT had been less explicit about his use of the intuiting strategy all along, but by the third session his editing behavior had changed. He had become very concerned with rules, especially rules concerning commas. In that session, he removed commas from adjective series and from before modifying phrases. He corrected two comma splice errors by replacing commas with periods, but he also created two sentence fragments when he did the same thing with commas that attached elaborative phrases to their main clauses. So despite HT's increased concern with rules late in the term, he was still applying those rules with less than complete success.

Summary of Study 1

Combining the protocol evidence with the error correction data from the larger group, we can draw two conclusions. First, word processing alone did not dramatically alter BW students' ability to edit errors in texts (and judging from student performance on the editing tasks in this study, neither did a writing course[3]). There was no increase in the percentage of errors corrected between session one in the third week of the term and session three in the eleventh week. Second, Hull's distinction between intuiting and consulting strategies was supported, both in terms of the different cognitive processes the two strategies employ and in the differential success BW students have in using them. As in Hull's studies, BW students were more successful (in the first two sessions, at least) correcting intuiting errors than consulting errors.

A third point emerged from the data, but so far it is much more appropriately termed a "suggestion" rather than a "conclusion." Students did not improve much in their use of consulting strategy by the end of the term (they corrected about 56 percent of the consulting errors both at the beginning of the term and at the end), although the protocols suggest that they came to use the consulting strategy more. They became very attentive to rules and rule applications, even when they did not have a firm grasp of those rules. Furthermore, by the end of the term, students seemed to rely less on their intuiting strategies, thus replacing a strategy that they used relatively well with one they used less well. This is not to say that the intuiting strategy is all that students need to correct errors in their texts. The intuiting strategy cannot *replace* rule-consulting strategies, but it certainly can supplement them, especially with certain kinds of errors.

Study 2

Despite the problems of Study 1, we were enough intrigued by the data's suggestiveness to include a better-controlled version in a later study. In Study 2, we had BW students correct errors in two passages, one early in the term and one later in the term, again stressing editing over revision. The three texts from Study 1 were again used, this time counterbalanced across subjects and order of presentation. For Study 2, however, some slight modifications of the texts were made. Each text was edited so as to contain sixteen errors, eight intuiting errors (two examples of four different intuiting errors) and eight consulting errors (two examples of four consulting errors).

By the time Study 2 was begun, we had designed an interactive editor that supplemented the word-processing program and gave students feedback on their changes as well as help in focusing on the error.[4] The interactive editor is described in detail elsewhere (Hull and Smith; Smith, Hull, and McCutchen), so it is described here only briefly. As in Study 1, students viewed the text on the CRT screen of a microcomputer, and they effected their changes using a word processor with which they were familiar. (The interactive editor had embedded within it the word processor that students used throughout the term to prepare their class assignments.) Students were free to move through the text at will, making changes when they detected an error. When students attempted a correction, a message on the bottom of the screen informed them whether or not they had corrected the error, and when students made two incorrect changes of the same error, the general area of the text pertinent to the error was highlighted in bold text on the computer screen. If on the third attempt students again failed to correct the error, a smaller segment of text was highlighted, further focusing students on the location of the error. If students failed to correct the error in four attempts, a correction was displayed for them, and they went on with the remainder of the text.

Thus Study 2 differed from Study 1 in that students used the interactive editor to help correct the errors in the texts. Also, the texts, presented this time in counterbalanced orders, were slightly modified to contain only sixteen errors, eight of which were clearly intuiting errors and eight of which were consulting errors. Study 2 also involved enough students (thirty-four students completed both editing tasks) so that statistical analyses were possible.

Of special interest was the effect of the interactive editor on students' editing strategies. Certainly feedback on the accuracy of their changes should help students with editing of any sort, but would their intuiting and consulting strategies be affected equally? If students are less successful with the consulting strategy because they lack familiarity with many of the rules of written English, then highlighting the specific area of text containing the error may be especially useful in the case of consulting errors. While students may not have enough control over certain rules to monitor text for possible violations, when an area is highlighted as an error, students may be able to experiment with possible rule applications and, given feedback on those experimental changes, finally come up with the appropriate correction. However, aside from calling attention to a piece of text, highlighting may not be as helpful with the intuiting strategy. Highlighting may, in fact, force the student out of a holistic "sounds okay" intuiting strategy and into a rule consulting strategy. For intuiting errors this may be especially problematic, since the "rules" of syntax and phrasing are less accessible than those of punctuation and spelling.

Since students had four opportunities to correct each error, the error correction data can be analyzed in a variety of ways. Some, however, are more meaningful than others, and Table 1 presents the data partitioned in a way that may best answer the important questions. In this table, the data are presented by error type (consulting and intuiting) and by session. Within each session, however, the mean percentage correct (shown in parentheses) is partitioned into percentage of errors corrected on the first attempt (that is, before the student had any special help from the interactive editor with a particular error) and percentage corrected on attempts after the first (that is, after the student received all the help he or she needed to correct the error, not counting the computer-supplied corrections). The first mean in each cell (labeled *No Help* in Table 1) gives an indication of how well the students do on their own with the errors, while the second (labeled *+Help*) involves some indication of the helpfulness of the editor's feedback and highlighting.

Two sets of data were submitted to an analysis of variance (ANOVA). The first analysis was performed on total percentage correct, that is, on the percentage of errors that the BW students corrected appropriately, regardless of whether they had help or corrected an error on the first try. As is evident in the means in Table 1, the only significant difference was between the two error types. Students were more successful correcting intuiting errors than consulting errors, $F(1, 33) = 6.03$, $p < 05$. They corrected 89.6 percent of the intuiting errors compared with 83.9 percent of the

Table 1
Percentage Error Corrections Made by BW Students

Error Category	Session 1			Session 2			Mean by Error Type
	No Help	+Help	(Total)	No Help	+Help	(Total)	
Consulting	51.5	30.9	(82.4)	56.6	28.7	(85.3)	83.9
Intuiting	69.5	19.9	(89.4)	69.1	20.6	(89.7)	89.6
Mean by Session		85.9			87.5		

consulting errors. There was no difference, however, between the first and second sessions, $F < 1$. Students corrected 85.9 percent of the errors in the first session and 87.5 percent in the second. Also there was no interaction between error types and sessions, $F < 1$.

As Table 1 shows, student performance with no help from the interactive editor mirrors the analysis just reported, with differences between the error types but no differences between sessions. Without help from the interactive editor, the overall level of performance was lower, 51.5 percent correction rate with consulting errors and 69.5 percent correction rate with intuiting errors, but this is comparable to the performance of students in Study 1, who also had no help with the editing task. Thus with no help, these students perform much like those in Study 1.

The percentage of errors corrected *with help*, however, shows a somewhat different picture, and these data were submitted to a second analysis of variance. Again, there was no difference between the two sessions, $F < 1$, but there was a difference between the error types, this time in the opposite direction. Help from the interactive editor was more beneficial to the students in the case of consulting errors, $F(1, 33) = 11.7$, $p < .01$. With the editor's help, students corrected an additional 29.8 percent of the consulting errors, while they corrected only an additional 20.2 percent of the intuiting errors. It should be noted that, because of students' higher initial success with intuiting errors, there were fewer intuiting errors remaining to be corrected in subsequent attempts. However, since students' 89.6 percent total accuracy rate with intuiting errors was still well below perfect performance, the difference between intuiting and consulting errors does not seem entirely due to a ceiling effect. Thus, as we initially suspected, feedback from the interactive editor may be more beneficial in students' successive attempts to correct consulting errors.

Summary of Study 2

The most striking result of Study 2 was the improvement in students' error correction given the help of the interactive editor. Students corrected 60 percent of the errors (summed across the two error types) with no help from the interactive editor and nearly 86 percent with help when needed. Feedback usually improves performance, and this generality held true in these editing tasks. This result seems more striking, however, when we recall that the feedback consisted *only* of highlighting error locations, not in providing information on how errors might be corrected. Again, this finding replicates Hull (in press). There still was no improvement in error correction across the two sessions, but once again there was a clear difference in students' success with intuiting and consulting errors. Students were significantly more accurate correcting intuiting errors. An especially important benefit of the interactive editor, however, is the aid it gives students with consulting errors, the errors with which they have the most trouble when left with only their own strategies and no feedback.

General Conclusions

In two studies, with two very different procedures, we have seen evidence of two strategies at work as BW students go about correcting sentence-level errors. One strategy (intuiting) seems more tied to native speakers' linguistic intuitions about the form and structure of their language, while another strategy (consulting) relies more on knowledge of the conventions of standard *written* English — knowledge that is typically acquired through experience with formal written language. Given the distinction between the knowledge required by the two strategies, it is not surprising that BW students are less successful editing consulting errors than intuiting errors. Basic writers often have had insufficient experience with print and, as a result, may have impoverished knowledge of the written conventions required for successful application of the consulting strategy. These students are, however, native speakers of English for the most part, and thus have adequate knowledge (albeit primarily implicit) of the linguistic structures required for successful application of the intuiting strategy.[5] Thus students' knowledge of oral language more easily maps into the intuiting strategy.

In light of the data from the two studies reported here, some interesting speculations can be offered concerning student editing strategies and instruction. Much of what goes on in a BW classroom is devoted to acquainting students, at least implicitly, with the rules and conventions of written English. This seems appropriate, especially since students' rule-consulting strategies are the ones they use with least success. The results of Study 1, however, suggest that the classroom emphasis on consulting strategies does not necessarily improve students' performance with those strategies. There remains much room for improvement in students' correction of consulting errors, and the results of Study 2 suggest that our computer-assisted instruction, while generally helpful, is especially helpful in increasing students' success with consulting errors.

Students come into the classroom, however, also possessing an intuiting strategy for editing that involves checking whether a text "sounds okay" based on general linguistic intuitions. This strategy is effective in detecting certain kinds of errors, but our protocols suggest that during the course of their writing instruction (and perhaps because of that instruction), students may come to focus more and more on their consulting strategies, sometimes to the neglect of their intuiting strategies.

We should take care that we are not unwittingly discouraging students from using the intuiting strategy to exploit the linguistic knowledge they possess as native speakers, thereby taking away one tool that they already use with some success (albeit in limited contexts). Successful editing requires attention to multiple levels of text; thus both intuiting and consulting strategies can be useful to writing students. Rather than present the rule-based consulting strategy to students as an *alternative* editing strategy, perhaps writing instruction should present the consulting strategy as an *additional* strategy. Instruction might then help students improve intuiting strategies as well as consulting strategies, while also helping students recognize appropriate contexts for each. In that way, writing instruction could provide students with strategies to deal with one level of error while also improving strategies they already possess to deal with another level of error.

Furthermore, this analysis of editing strategies provides one example of how we might think about the cognitive processes and requisite knowledge involved in writing (in this case, *editing* in particular). By moving beyond the errors themselves to the processes involved in correcting them (or even producing them), we might better inform students about the process of writing and learning to write, rather than simply respond to their written products. Our interactive editor, which helps model for students the close reading required during editing, might be considered a step in this process-focused direction. Enabling students to fine-tune editing strategies that they seem to use naturally might be another.

Notes

[1]We are aware that "basic writer" is a label that has different meanings depending on who is using it. However, lacking a better term, we adopt it in this article to mean those students who come to college underprepared for the writing tasks they encounter. The basic writing students who were subjects in studies we report here scored a 2 on a 4-point holistic scale in a university's timed-writing placement test.

[2]Within this discussion we will refer to *intuiting errors* and *consulting errors,* but these are merely shorthand references. These errors should be understood in terms of the strategies adequate to correct them — intuiting strategies in one case and consulting strategies in the other. Our focus, then, is on the editing strategy rather than the error. These two sorts of errors certainly do not account for all the errors that students make, nor are they necessarily mutually exclusive, except in our experimental materials. However, errors amenable to these two strategies do account for a sizable proportion of the errors BW students make. Thus helping students to apply these strategies successfully could go a long way in helping students edit sentence level errors.

[3]It could be that with a term of writing instruction, students did improve in editing their own writing, but that the improvement did not transfer to the editing tasks we presented to them. This runs counter, however, to Hull's (in press) finding that BW students were more successful correcting errors in texts by other writers.

[4]The interactive editor described here developed out of the collaborative work of many researchers from the University of Pittsburgh departments of English, linguistics, and psychology and from the Learning Research and Development Center.

[5]Certainly this does not hold for those students in BW classrooms whose native language is something other than English. These students have knowledge of other linguistic structures, and this knowledge frequently affects their writing of English (sometimes adversely).

References

Bartholomae, D. "The Study of Error." *College Composition and Communication* 31 (1980): 253–69.

Hull, G. A. "The Editing Process in Writing: A Performance Study of More Skilled and Less Skilled Writers." *Research in the Teaching of English* 9 (June 1983).

Hull, G. A., and W. L. Smith. "Error Correction and Computing." *Writing On-line: Using Computers in the Teaching of Writing,* ed. J. L. Collins and E. A. Sommers. Upper Montclair: Boynton, 89–101.

Perl, S. "The Composing Processes of Unskilled College Writers." *Research in the Teaching of English* 13 (1979): 317–36.

Shaughnessy, M. *Errors and Expectations: A Guide for the Teacher of Basic Writing.* New York: Oxford UP, 1977.

Smith, W. L., G. A. Hull, and D. McCutchen. "Computer-Controlled Editing: A First Study of Effect and Affect." Paper presented at the conference of the National Council of Teachers of English, Philadelphia, November 1985.

McCutchen, Hull, and Smith's Insights as a Resource for Your Teaching

1. Computer programs offer students something that repeated drilling does not. Why is the computer more successful? How might drilling students on consulting strategies backfire and undermine their linguistic intuition as native speakers? What insights into this situation can you glean from Mike Rose's article (preceding selection)?

2. How might you strive to duplicate this computer program's success in your teaching practices? What ways can you devise to intercede in students' processes without creating the personalized anxiety that leads to writer's block?

McCutchen, Hull, and Smith's Insights as a Resource for the Writing Classroom

1. Draft an essay that is filled with errors of both intuiting and consulting. Photocopy it for your students, and have them work through it in groups, correcting as they go. Find out exactly what they know and don't know. Decide which consulting strategies to give them more practice with by asking them to plant such errors in their papers for each other to find. This way of teaching consulting strategies avoids tedious drill work and contextualizes the relevant issues in ways that should enable the students to grow more adept in addressing them.

2. Describe the McCutchen, Hull, and Smith study to your students. Have them reflect in their journals about their own experiences with learning to detect errors and edit their texts. Afterwards, ask the students to discuss what they've written and find significant patterns in their accounts. Large-level reflection about their development as writers gives them a sense of the issues that they are struggling to master and, in so doing, facilitates that mastery.

4. Issues in Writing Pedagogy: Institutional Politics and the Other

Check the table of contents of journals like *Rhetoric Review, Journal of Teaching Writing,* or *College English*; scan a program of the Conference on College Composition and Communication; use the Internet to subscribe to <listserv@vm.cc. purdue.edu>; browse in the "new acquisitions" section of your library; or pick up the weekly *Chronicle of Higher Education.* You will find vigorous discussion of multiple issues that influence and grow out of the teaching of writing at the college level. One of these issues, the extension of writing as learning across the curriculum, has become part of campus conversations and is quickly becoming a "given" for institutional reform. Of the many issues that challenge and encourage teachers of writing, two currently receive the strongest focus: How might writing teachers acknowledge the diversity of our students' experience? How can we use writing assessment to nourish our teaching?

The readings in Chapter 4 are portals to the larger discussions on diversity, assessment, teaching, and student learning. Each reading provides both an entry to the discussion and reading paths to follow when you decide to broaden and deepen your engagement.

Paradigms of writing, language acquisition, and reading as recursive processes have led to recognition of and respect for the individual engaged in learning. This recognition and respect has in turn informed the discussion, research, and practice in many areas: admissions policies; the teaching of writing, English as a second language, and composition as cultural critique; collaborative learning; whole-language learning; the "feminization" of composition; and assessment. There is also greater awareness of multicultural perspectives on writing, reading, and the gaining of wisdom.

Nouns such as *literacy, diversity, feminism, multiculturalism, social construction, negotiation, discourse communities,* and *postmodernism* resonate in our professional conversations. We simultaneously individualize instruction and "acculturate" students to discourse communities. We attempt to balance recognition of and tolerance for diversity with recognition of and tolerance for common ground and "universal" beliefs and values.

Terms such as *literacy, diversity,* and *multiculturalism* seem descriptive. However, competing definitions are offered daily. We hear national, state, local, and institutional mandates for increasing and enhancing literacy, for acknowledging and respecting diversity, and for broadening our awareness of and inquiry into the multiple perspectives, issues, and cultures (ethnic, regional, social, political, gender-linked, religious, and so on) that make up the mosaic of "America" and of the world community. Equally often, we hear critical voices stipulate alternative definitions for literacy (lowering standards, weakening education), for diversity (exclusivity and prejudice), and for multiculturalism (attempts by the "other" to break down the coherent tradition and value system of the "majority").

The community of writers with whom we work brings together individuals who have traditionally been welcomed to and included in knowledge communities and individuals who have been excluded. We teach these students in times of vigorous debate about how education could and should serve all these learners. The task is daunting and exciting. Look to the Annotated Bibliography for more readings to guide you in reflecting on your practices within this environment.

MIKE ROSE   *Crossing Boundaries*

This excerpt from Lives on the Boundary: The Struggles and Achievements of America's Underprepared *is eloquent, precise, and inspiriting. In the concluding chapter, "Crossing Boundaries," Rose calls for a "revised store of images of educational excellence, ones closer to egalitarian ideas — ones that embody the reward and turmoil of education in a democracy, that celebrate the plural, messy human reality of it." Obviously, we couldn't reprint the entire book, but we suspect that after reading and reflecting on this chapter you'll decide to go and read it yourself.*

Through all of my experiences with people struggling to learn, the one thing that strikes me most is the ease with which we misperceive failed performance and the degree to which this misperception both reflects and reinforces the social order. Class and culture erect boundaries that hinder our vision — blind us to the logic of error and the everpresent stirring of language — and encourage the designation of otherness, difference, deficiency. And the longer I stay in education, the clearer it becomes to me that some of our basic orientations toward the teaching and testing of literacy contribute to our inability to see. To truly educate in America, then, to reach the full sweep of our citizenry, we need to question received perception, shift continually from the standard lens. . . .

> The humanities presume particular methods of expression and inquiry — language, dialogue, reflection, imagination, and metaphor . . . [and] remain dedicated to the disciplined development of verbal, perceptual, and imaginative skills needed to understand experience.
> – The Humanities in American Life, Report of the
> Rockefeller Commission on the Humanities[1]

Two young men have walked in late and are standing around the back of the classroom, halfheartedly looking for seats. One wears a faded letterman's jacket, the other is bundled up in a bright red sweater and a long overcoat. A third student has plopped his books by the door and is hunkering down against the wall. This is Developmental English in a state college in Ohio. It is December, and the radiators are turned up high. Occasional clanks are emitted by some distant valve. The room is stuffy with dry heat. The teacher directs the latecomers to some seats in the front, and he begins the lesson. The class is working on pronoun agreement. They have worked on it for a week and will continue to work on it for another. The windows are frosted at the edges. In the distance, a tall smokestack releases a curling black stream diagonally across the sky.

Students designated "developmental" at this school must take a year's worth of very basic English before they can move into standard Freshman Comp. Their year is broken into two semesters. During the first semester they inch through a thick workbook filled with grammar exercises: "Circle the correct pronoun in this sentence: That was her/she in the lecture hall" or "Supply the correct pronoun for the following sentence: The recruits were upset by _____ scores on the fitness tests." Some of this they do at home. Most of it they do in class. That way, the teacher can be sure they are doing it. They hand in their workbooks regularly to have the teacher check their answers.

The course involves very little writing, except for words and phrases the students must scribble in the blanks on the pages. Some class discussion is generated when the teacher has the students read their answers. Periodically he will explain a rule or illustrate its use on the blackboard. Young men along the back wall fill in a blank now and then; the rest of the time, they're eyeballing the teacher and talking softly. A girl is filing her nails. Students in the middle of the room are bent over their workbooks, penciling in answers, erasing them, looking up and out the frosted windows. A skinny boy in the front is going down the page as mechanically as Melville's pallid scrivener.

There are sentences being written in this class, but not by mandate of the dean of instruction. Two girls close to the door have been passing notes all hour; they are producing the class's most extended discourse. Students are not asked to write here because it is assumed — as it is assumed in many such basic courses — that they must first get all their workbook pronouns to agree with their workbook antecedents. When they reach the second semester, they will, for fifteen weeks, do some small amount of writing, but that writing will be limited to single sentences. At this school, and many others, the English department and the program that coordinates remedial courses are philosophically and administratively separated. Different schools have different histories, but often — as was the case here — the separation was strongly influenced by the English department's desire to be freed from basic instruction. The two departments at this school, though, have an unusually stringent agreement: anything longer than the sentence (even two or three sentences strung together) is considered *writing*, and the teaching of writing shall be the province of the English Department. Anything at the sentence level or smaller (like filling words and phrases into a workbook) is to be considered grammar review, and that falls within the domain of the remedial program. For one academic year, then, students who desperately need to improve their writing will not be writing anything longer than the sentence. This particular slicing of the pedagogical pie is extreme in its execution, but the assumptions about error, remediation, and the linguistic capabilities of poorly prepared students that undergird it remain widespread in America — and they influence everything from lesson plans to the sectioning of academic territory. Given the pervasiveness of these assumptions, it would be valuable to consider, for a moment, their origins.[2]

A good place to begin is with the encounter of educational psychology and schooling. Turn-of-the-century English education was built on a Latin- and Greek-influenced grammar, primarily a set of prescriptions for conducting socially acceptable discourse. So when psychologists began investigating the teaching of writing, they found a pedagogy of memory and drill, one concentrating on the often arcane dos and don'ts of usage. They also found reports like those issuing from the Harvard faculty in the 1890s that called attention to the presence of errors in handwriting, spelling, and grammar in the writing of that university's entering freshmen. The twentieth-century writing curriculum, then, was focused on the particulars of usage, grammar, and mechanics. Correctness became, in James Berlin's words, the era's "most significant measure of accomplished prose."[3]

Such a focus suited educational researchers' approach to language: a mechanistic orientation that studied language by reducing it to discrete behaviors and that defined growth as the accretion of these particulars. Quantification and measurement were central to the researchers' method, so the focus on error — which seemed eminently measurable — found justification in a model of mind that was ascending in American academic psychology. This approach was further supported and advanced by what Raymond Callahan has called "the cult of efficiency," a strong push to apply to education the principles of industrial scientific management.[4] Educational gains were defined as products, and the output of products could be measured. Pedagogical effectiveness — which meant cost-effectiveness — could be determined with "scientific" accuracy. What emerges, finally, is a combination of positivism, efficiency, and a focus on grammar that would have a profound influence on pedagogy and research.

Textbooks as well as workbooks reflected this orientation. One textbook for teachers presented an entire unit on the colon. A text for students devoted seven pages to the use of a capital letter to indicate a proper noun. Research, too, focused on the details of language, especially on listing and tabulating error. You rarely find consideration of the social context of error, or of its significance in the growth of the writer. Instead you find studies like those of W. S. Guiler's tally of the percentages of 350 students who, in misspelling *mortgage,* erred by omitting the *t* versus those who dropped the first *g*.[5]

Despite the fact that the assumptions about language and learning informing these approaches to teaching and research began to be challenged by the late 1930s, the procedures of the earlier era have remained with us. This trend has the staying power it does for a number of reasons: it gives a method — a putatively objective one — to the strong desire of our society to maintain correct language use. It is very American in its seeming efficiency. And it offers a simple, understandable view of complex linguistic problems. The trend reemerges most forcefully in times of crisis: when budgets crunch and accountability looms or, particularly, when "nontraditional" students flood our institutions. A reduction of complexity has great appeal in institutional decision making, especially in difficult times: a scientific-atomistic approach to language, with its attendant tallies and charts, nicely fits an economic decision-making model. When in doubt or when scared or when pressed, count.

This orientation to language complements the way we conceive of remediation.

The designation *remedial* has powerful implications in education — to be remedial is to be substandard, inadequate — and, because of the origins of the term, the inadequacy is metaphorically connected to disease and mental defectiveness. The etymology of the word *remedial* places its origins in law and medicine, and by the late nineteenth century the term generally fell into the medical domain. It was then applied to education, to children who were thought to have neurological problems. But *remedial* quickly generalized beyond the description of such students to those with broader, though special, educational problems and then to those learners who were from backgrounds that did not provide optimal environmental and educational opportunities.

As increasing access to education brought more and more children into the schools, the medical vocabulary — with its implied medical model — remained dominant. People tried to *diagnose* various *disabilities, defects, deficits, deficiencies,* and *handicaps,* then tried to remedy them. So you start to see all sorts of reading and writing problems clustered together and addressed with this language. For example, William S. Gray's important monograph, *Remedial Cases in Reading: Their Diagnosis and Treatment,* listed as "specific causes of failure in reading" inferior learning capacity, congenital word blindness, poor auditory memory, defective vision, a narrow span of recognition, ineffective eye movements, inadequate training in phonetics, inadequate attention to the content, an inadequate speaking vocabulary, a small meaning vocabulary, speech defects, lack of interest, and timidity.[6] The remedial paradigm was beginning to include those who had troubles as varied as bad eyes, second language interference, and shyness. The semantic net of *remedial* was expanding and expanding.

It is likely that the appeal of medical-remedial language had much to do with its associations with scientific objectivity and accuracy — powerful currency in the efficiency-minded 1920s and 1930s. Consider, as illustration, this passage from Albert Lang's 1930 textbook, *Modern Methods in Written Examinations.* The medical model is explicit:

> Teaching bears a resemblance to the practice of medicine. Like a successful physician, the good teacher must be something of a diagnostician. The physician by means of a general examination singles out the individual whose physical defects require a more thorough testing. He critically scrutinizes the special cases until he recognizes the specific troubles. After a careful diagnosis he is able to prescribe intelligently the best remedial or corrective measures.[7]

The theoretical and pedagogical model that was available for "corrective teaching" led educators to view literacy problems from a medical-remedial perspective. Thus they set out to diagnose as precisely as possible the errors (defects) in a student's paper — which they saw as symptomatic of equally isolable defects in the student's linguistic capacity — and devise drills and exercises to remedy them. (One of the 1930s nicknames for remedial sections was "sick sections." During the next decade they would be tagged "hospital sections.") Such corrective teaching was, in the words of one educator, "the most logical as well as the most scientific method."

Though we have, over the last fifty years, developed a richer understanding of reading and writing difficulties, the reductive view of error and the language of medicine is still with us. A recent letter from the senate of a local liberal arts college is sitting on my desk. It discusses a "program in remedial writing for . . . [those] entering freshmen suffering from severe writing handicaps." We seem entrapped by this language, this view of students and learning. We still talk of writers as suffering from specifiable, locatable defects, deficits, and handicaps that can be localized, circumscribed, and remedied. Such talk carries with it the etymological wisps and traces of disease and serves to exclude from the academic community those who are so labeled. They sit in scholastic quarantine until their disease can be diagnosed and remedied.

This atomistic, medical model of language is simply not supported by more recent research in language and cognition. But because the teaching of writing — particularly teaching designated remedial — has been conceptually and, as with the Ohio program, administratively segmented from the rich theoretical investigation that characterizes other humanistic study, these assumptions have rarely been subjected to rigorous and comprehensive scrutiny. *The Humanities in American Life,* the important position paper from which the epigraph to this section is drawn, argues passionately for the wide relevance of the humanities and urges the serious engagement of humanists in teacher training, industry, and adult basic education — areas they, for the most part, have abandoned. But until the traditional orientations to error and remediation are examined to their core, until the teaching of writing and reading to underprepared students is fundamentally reconceived, then the spirited plea of the Rockefeller Commission will be, for many in America, just another empty homiletic. Consider, after all, what those students in Developmental English are really learning.

The curriculum in Developmental English breeds a deep social and intellectual isolation from print; it fosters attitudes and beliefs about written language that, more than anything, *keep* students from becoming fully, richly literate. The curriculum teaches students that when it comes to written language use, they are children: they can only perform the most constrained and ordered of tasks, and they must do so under the regimented guidance of a teacher. It teaches them that the most important thing about writing — the very essence of writing — is grammatical correctness, not the communication of something meaningful, or the generative struggle with ideas . . . not even word play. It's a curriculum that rarely raises students' heads from the workbook page to consider the many uses of written language that surround them in their schools, jobs, and neighborhoods. Finally, by its tedium, the curriculum teaches them that writing is a crushing bore. These students traverse course after remedial course, becoming increasingly turned off to writing, increasingly convinced that they are hopelessly inadequate. "Writing," one of the students tells me. "Man, I've never been any good at writing." "English," says another, "is not my thing." . . .

We seem to have a need as a society to explain poor performance by reaching deep into the basic stuff of those designated as other: into their souls, or into the deep recesses of their minds, or into the very ligature of their language. It seems harder for us to keep focus on the politics and sociology of intellectual failure, to keep before our eyes the negative power of the unfamiliar, the way information poverty constrains performance, the effect of despair on cognition.

"I was so busy looking for 'psychopathology,' . . ." says Robert Coles of his early investigations of childhood morality, "that I brushed aside the most startling incidents, the most instructive examples of ethical alertness in the young people I was getting to know."[8] How much we don't see when we look only for deficiency, when we tally up all that people can't do. Many of the students in this book display the gradual or abrupt emergence of an intellectual acuity or literate capacity that just wasn't thought to be there. This is not to deny that awful limits still exist: so much knowledge and so many procedures never learned; such a long, cumbersome history of relative failure. But this must not obscure the equally important fact that if you set up the right conditions, try as best you can to cross class and cultural boundaries, figure out what's needed to encourage performance, that if you watch and listen, again and again there will emerge evidence of ability that escapes those who dwell on differences.

Ironically, it's often the reports themselves of our educational inadequacies — the position papers and media alarms on illiteracy in America — that help blind us to cognitive and linguistic possibility. Their rhetorical thrust and their metaphor conjure up disease or decay or economic and military defeat: a malignancy has run wild, an evil power is consuming us from within. (And here reemerges that nineteenth-century moral terror.) It takes such declamation to turn the moneyed wheels of government, to catch public attention and entice the givers of grants, but there's a dark side to this political reality. The character of the alarms and, too often, the character of the responses spark in us the urge to punish, to extirpate, to return to a precancerous golden age rather than build on the rich capacity that already exists. The reports urge responses that reduce literate possibility and constrain growth, that focus on pathology rather than on possibility. Philosophy, said Aristotle, begins to wonder. So does education. . . .

There is a strong impulse in American education — curious in a country with such an ornery streak of antitraditionalism — to define achievement and excellence in terms of the acquisition of a historically validated body of knowledge, an authoritative list of books and allusions, a canon. We seek a certification of our national intelligence, indeed, our national virtue, in how diligently our children can display this central corpus of information. This need for certification tends to emerge most dramatically in our educational policy debates during times of real or imagined threat: economic hard times, political crises, sudden increases in immigration.

Now is such a time, and it is reflected in a number of influential books and commission reports. E. D. Hirsch argues that a core national vocabulary, one oriented toward the English literate tradition — Alice in Wonderland to zeitgeist — will build a knowledge base that will foster the literacy of all Americans.[9] Diane Ravitch and Chester Finn call for a return to a traditional historical and literary curriculum: the valorous historical figures and the classical literature of the once-elite course of study. Allan Bloom, [former] Secretary of Education William Bennett, Mortimer Adler and the Paideia Group, and a number of others have affirmed, each in their very different ways, the necessity of the Great Books: Plato and Aristotle and Sophocles, Dante and Shakespeare and Locke, Dickens and Mann and Faulkner. We can call this orientation to educational achievement the canonical orientation.

At times in our past, the call for a shoring up of or return to a canonical curriculum was explicitly elitist, was driven by a fear that the education of the select was being compromised. Today, though, the majority of the calls are provocatively framed in the language of democracy. They assail the mediocre and grinding curriculum frequently found in remedial and vocational education. They are disdainful of the patronizing perceptions of student ability that further restrict the already restricted academic life of disadvantaged youngsters. They point out that the canon — its language, conventions, and allusions — is central to the discourse of power, and to keep it from poor kids is to assure their disenfranchisement all the more. The books of the canon, claim the proposals, the Great Books, are a window onto a common core of experience and civic ideals. There is, then, a spiritual, civic, and cognitive heritage here, and *all* our children should receive it. . . . This is a forceful call. It promises a still center in a turning world.

I see great value in being challenged to think of the curriculum of the many in the terms we have traditionally reserved for the few. . . . Too many people are kept from the books of the canon, the Great Books, because of misjudgments about their potential. Those books eventually proved important to me, and, as best I know how, I invite my students to engage them. But once we grant the desirability of equal curricular treatment and begin to consider what this equally distributed curriculum would contain, problems arise: If the canon itself is the answer to our educational inequities, why has it historically invited few and denied many? Would the canonical orientation provide adequate guidance as to how a democratic curriculum should be constructed and how it should be taught? . . .

Those who study the way literature becomes canonized, how linguistic creations are included or excluded from a tradition, claim that the canonical curriculum students would most likely receive would not, as is claimed, offer a common core of American experience.[10] The canon has tended to push to the margin much of the literature of our nation: from American Indian songs and chants to immigrant fiction to working-class narratives. The institutional messages that students receive in the books they're issued and the classes they take are powerful and, as I've witnessed since my Voc. Ed. days, quickly internalized. And to revise these messages and redress past wrongs would involve more than adding some new books to the existing canon — the very reasons for linguistic and cultural exclusion would have to become a focus of study in order to make the canon act as a democratizing force. Unless this happens, the democratic intent of the reformers will be undercut by the content of the curriculum they propose.

And if we move beyond content to consider basic assumptions about teaching and learning, a further problem arises, one that involves the very nature of the canonical orientation itself. The canonical orientation encourages a narrowing of focus from learning to that which must be learned: it simplifies the dynamic tension between student and text and reduces the psychological and social dimensions of instruction. The student's personal history recedes as the *what* of the classroom is valorized over the *how*. Thus it is that the encounter of student and text is often portrayed by canonists as a transmission. Information, wisdom, virtue will pass from the book to the student if the student gives the book the time it merits, carefully traces its argument or narrative or lyrical progression. Intellectual, even spiritual, growth will *necessarily* result from an encounter with Roman mythology, *Othello*, and "I heard a Fly buzz — when I died —," with biographies and historical sagas and patriotic lore. Learning is stripped of confusion and discord. It is stripped, as well, of strong human connection. My own initiators to the canon — Jack MacFarland, Dr. Carothers, and the rest — knew there was more to their work than their mastery of a tradition. What mattered most, I see now, were the relationships they established with me, the guidance they provided when I felt inadequate or threatened. This mentoring was part of my entry into that solemn library of Western thought — and even with such support, there were still times of confusion, anger, and fear. It is telling, I think, that once that rich social network slid away, once I was in graduate school in intense, solitary encounter with that tradition, I abandoned it for other sources of nurturance and knowledge.

The model of learning implicit in the canonical orientation seems, at times, more religious than cognitive or social: truth resides in the printed texts, and if they are presented by someone who knows them well and respects them, that truth will be revealed. Of all the advocates of the canon, Mortimer Adler has given most attention to pedagogy — and his Paideia books contain valuable discussions of instruction, coaching, and questioning. But even here, and this is doubly true in the other manifestos, there is little acknowledgment that the material in the canon can be not only difficult but foreign, alienating, overwhelming.

We need an orientation to instruction that provides guidance on how to determine and honor the beliefs and stories, enthusiasms, and apprehensions that students reveal. How to build on them, and when they clash with our curriculum — as I saw so often in the Tutorial Center at UCLA — when they clash, how to encourage a discussion that will lead to reflection on what students bring and what they're currently confronting. Canonical lists imply canonical answers, but the manifestos offer little discussion of what to do when students fail. If students have been exposed to at least some elements of the canon before — as many have — why didn't it take? If they're encountering it for the first time and they're lost, how can we determine where they're located — and what do we do then?

Each member of a teacher's class, poor *or* advantaged, gives rise to endless decisions, day-to-day determinations about a child's reading and writing: decisions on how to tap strength, plumb confusion, foster growth. The richer your conception of learning and your understanding of its social and psychological dimensions, the more insightful and effective your judgments will be. . . .

To understand the nature and development of literacy we need to consider the social context in which it occurs — the political, economic, and cultural forces that encourage or inhibit it. The canonical orientation discourages deep analysis of the way these forces may be affecting performance. The canonists ask that schools transmit a coherent traditional knowledge to an ever-changing, frequently uprooted community. This discordance between message and audience is seldom examined. Although a ghetto child can rise on the lilt of a Homeric line — books can spark dreams — appeals to elevated texts can also divert attention from the conditions that keep a population from realizing its dreams. The literacy curriculum is being asked to do what our politics and our economics have failed to do: diminish differences in achievement, narrow our gaps, bring us together. Instead of analysis of the complex web of causes of poor performance, we are offered a faith in the unifying power of a body of knowledge, whose infusion will bring the rich and the poor, the longtime disaffected and the uprooted newcomers into cultural unanimity. If this vision is democratic, it is simplistically so, reductive, not an invitation for people truly to engage each other at the point where cultures and classes intersect.

I worry about the effects a canonical approach to education could have on cultural dialogue and transaction — on the involvement of an abandoned underclass and on the movement of immigrants . . . into our nation. A canonical uniformity promotes rigor and quality control; it can also squelch new thinking, diffuse the generative tension between the old and the new. It is significant that the canonical orientation is voiced with most force during times of challenge and uncertainty, for it promises the authority of tradition, the seeming stability of the past. But the authority is fictive, gained from a misreading of American cultural history. No period of that history was harmoniously stable; the invocation of a golden age is a mythologizing act. Democratic culture is, by definition, vibrant and dynamic, discomforting and unpredictable. It gives rise to apprehension; freedom is not always calming. And, yes, it can yield fragmentation, though often as not the source of fragmentation is intolerant misunderstanding of diverse traditions rather than the desire of members of those traditions to remain hermetically separate. A truly democrative vision of knowledge and social structure would honor this complexity. The vision might not be soothing, but it would provide guidance as to how to live and teach in a country made up of many cultural traditions.

We are in the middle of an extraordinary social experiment: the attempt to provide education for all members of a vast pluralistic democracy. To have any prayer of success, we'll need many conceptual blessings: A philosophy of language and literacy that affirms the diverse sources of linguistic competence and deepens our understanding of the ways class and culture blind us to the richness of those sources. A perspective on failure that lays open the logic of error. An orientation toward the interaction of poverty and ability that undercuts simple polarities, that enables us to see simultaneously the constraints poverty places on the play of mind and the actual mind at play within those constraints. We'll need a pedagogy that encourages us to step back and consider the threat of the standard classroom and that shows us, having stepped back, how to step forward to invite a student across the boundaries of that powerful room. Finally, we'll need a revised store of images of educational excellence, ones closer to egalitarian ideals — ones that embody the reward and turmoil of education in a democracy, that celebrate the plural, messy human reality of it. At heart, we'll need a guiding set of principles that do not encourage us to retreat from, but move us closer to, an understanding of the rich mix of speech and ritual and story that is America.

Notes

[1]Report of the Commission on the Humanities, *The Humanities in American Life* (Berkeley: U of California P, 1980) 2.

[2]The discussion of error and remediation is condensed from Mike Rose, "The Language of Exclusion: Writing Instruction at the University," *College English* 47 (Apr. 1985): 341–59.

[3]James Berlin, *Writing Instruction in Nineteenth-Century American Colleges* (Carbondale: Southern Illinois UP, 1984) 73.

[4]Raymond Callahan, *Education and the Cult of Efficiency* (Chicago: U of Chicago P, 1962).

[5]W. S. Guiler, "Background Deficiencies," *Journal of Higher Education* 3 (1932): 371.

[6]William S. Gray, *Remedial Cases in Reading: Their Diagnosis and Treatment* (Chicago: U of Chicago P, 1922).

[7]Albert Lang, *Modern Methods in Written Examinations* (Boston: Houghton, 1930) 38.

[8]Robert Coles, in Sherry Kafka and Robert Coles, *I Will Always Stay Me: Writings of Migrant Children* (Austin: Texas Monthly P, 1982), 134.

[9]E. D. Hirsch, *Cultural Literacy: What Every American Needs to Know* (Boston: Houghton, 1987); Diane Ravitch and Chester E. Finn, Jr., *What Do Our Seventeen-Year-Olds Know?* (New York: Harper, 1987); Allan Bloom, *The Closing of the American Mind: How Higher Education Has Failed Democracy and Impoverished the Souls of Today's Students* (New York: Simon, 1987); William J. Bennett, *To Reclaim a Legacy* (Washington: National Endowment for the Humanities, 1984); Mortimer J. Adler, *The Paideia Proposal* (New York: Colliers, 1982), Paideia: *Problems and Possibilities* (New York: Macmillan, 1983), and *The Paideia Program* (New York: Macmillan, 1984).

[10]For a critical discussion of literary canon formation, see Paul Lauter, ed., *Reconstructing American Literature* (Old Westbury: Feminist, 1983).

Rose's Insights as a Resource for Your Teaching

1. In the synthesizing of personal narrative, research, teaching practice, and broad reading, Rose clearly models the importance to any professional of writing down the specific events, sudden insights, reflective speculations, and discouragements of practicing the profession. We haven't learned how Rose generated his text, but we recommend that you use the dialectical journal or teaching portfolio to generate your texts.

2. In *Lives on the Boundary* Rose cites "stories" of his students to build his argument. Case studies are very persuasive data. For each writing course you teach, set yourself the writing task of keeping notes about three students that could be developed into case studies. Over the course of several semesters, you will discover that certain themes or intuitions about how you could more effectively teach will emerge as you reflect on the case studies and, by association, on your own learning and that of other students.

3. In *Lives on the Boundary* Rose identifies himself as one of the underprepared students whom education does not yet serve adequately. Many writing teachers begin as well-prepared and successful students who never had to struggle as fiercely with learning as many of their students. For this reason, it's critical that writing teachers begin and continue their work with very careful "listening" to their students and with interdisciplinary research and reading of philosophical perspectives and pedagogic strategies. Persist.

Rose's Insights as a Resource for the Writing Classroom

1. Students on the "boundaries" in your classroom may have less skill than mainstream students for "inventing the university," David Bartholomae's phrase for the process of initiation into academic discourse and culture. Bartholomae insists English 101 needs to assist novices to imitate and practice the perspectives, habits of thought, and language that are expected at colleges and universities.

   Design journal entries and writing assignments that invite all students to reflect on the difficulties and successes they have in the courses they are taking besides the writing course. Use conferences, small-group discussion, or class discussion for writers to share their experiences and collaborate in "demystifying" the academic discourse community.

2. Students will have strong opinions about the canonical model of education. Organize discussion sessions followed by writings that move from personal reflection to analysis to a "What If" writing about what should be read by "educated persons" and why.

SUSAN MILLER   *The Sad Women in the Basement: Images of Composition Teaching*

Susan Miller is interested in the institutional politics that affect writing instruction. While composition courses generate the overwhelming share of the money in English departments, the teachers of these courses are usually the lowest paid and receive no benefits, sabbaticals, or tenure, unlike their colleagues who teach literature and generate less revenue. Historically, the drudgework of teaching writing has been the province of women, while the easier and more lucrative task of teaching literature courses has been the province of men. These injustices inform the entire structure of literate practice in this country.

One of the chief characteristics of composition, at least of composition perceived as teaching, has been that it fills the time that others take to build theories. Creating a process paradigm, despite its incompleteness, has been a monumental achievement because its existence *as* theory historically marks a new era in which composition professionals have room of their own, space to write their own story and become included in "history," not just to pore over student writing to find its faults.

But it remains to speculate about why a space for research and theory building has been filled with assertions that professional teachers of composition, taken and taking themselves seriously, work in a symbol system described as a "paradigm." That specific form takes them even further from the immediate and powerful community around them, their colleagues in literary study. It might be argued that this choice was made because such a model for observing writing lay ready for application and that composition professionals took it up because they agreed that writing is a "behavior" of autonomous individuals. But other models for studying other conceptions of writing were equally available. The choice to describe the past and present in composition as "current-traditional" and "process" paradigms, explanations of writing as a set of observable actions, is very much like the choice of "rhetoric" to explain composition history. Its particular sort of authority also invites interpretation.

We cannot refuse this invitation, for as Gerda Lerner stressed in *The Creation of Patriarchy*, already established symbol systems are provisions that even enslaved and socially powerless males commonly adopt to identify with other males who have power and wealth. She comments that historically, "what was decisive for the individual was the ability to identify him/herself with a state different from that of enslavement or subordination" (222). But as they established their research, composition professionals did not choose to identify their work with the traditions of those who held power in their immediate surroundings. Their choice to risk a move even further from literary studies is, in English studies, both "different" and suspiciously, because overtly, "scientific." Its alienation from root metaphors in literary study can help us further understand the subordinated identity that it was meant to remedy, the established identity of those who teach composition.

At least one contrast between theories presented as a "paradigm" and promoted or objected to as they relate to "science" and early identities of composition teaching is their difference in regard to traditional images of masculinity. Words like *hard* (data, science), *tough-minded,* and *rigorous,* like the word *test,* fall on the right side of our most common images of power. Not "everyone" in composition consciously chose these distinctive metaphors over another symbolic code they might have applied from a broad "English" or from specifically literary study. Many have taken exception to it; many are appalled by its "difference," if not entirely by its symbolic forcefulness. But everyone in composition has in some measure benefitted from this symbolic choice, just as all women have (again, in some measure) benefitted from feminist theories that decisively separate them from earlier, traditional representations.

This choice attaches composition to a form of power that clarifies the more traditional and accepted identity of the composition teacher, an identity deeply embedded in traditional views of women's roles. Apart from self-evident statistics about the "feminization" of composition (Holbrook), many theoretical positions and the self-perceptions of individual composition teachers confirm that composition teaching has been taken to be "worthy" but not "theoretically" based, culturally privileged, work. To overcome this ancillary status, composition professionals have found it entirely reasonable, if not entirely successful, to redefine their hitherto blurred identity in more crisply masculine, scientific, terms.

As the last chapter suggested with the example of "motherhood," individuals are "placed," or given the status of subjects, by ideological constructions that tie them to fantasized functions and activities, not to their actual situations. These ideological constructions mask very real needs to organize societies in particular ways. For example (here, *the* example), the identity of the female person was created as "woman," the opposite, complement, extension, and especially the supplement to male identity. This traducement was first necessary to organize cultures for their survival. A female's particularity or her ignorance of such category formation could not at first, and has not later, excused her from a cultural identity devised to ensure group survival. She responds by virtue of the call for womanhood, not consciously *to* it. This particular "hood" cloaks, suppresses, and finally organizes individual female particularity.

Similarly, when we look at the particularity of people (of both sexes) who teach composition, we may find enormous variations in their interests, education, experience, and self-images as teachers. But when we examine the ideological "call" to create these individuals as a special form of subjectivity for composition teaching, we see them in a definitive set of imaginary relationships to their students and colleagues. Particularities are masked by an ideologically constructed identity for the teacher of composition.

The female coding of this identity is, in fact, the most accurate choice if a choice between sexes is made at all, although the large proportion of women hired to teach composition does not simply cause — or simply result from — cultural associations that link nurturance to teaching "skills" of writing. But we cannot overlook the facts. As Sue Ellen Holbrook infers from her statistical analysis of this "Women's Work," it is likely that about two-thirds of those who teach writing are women (9). In 1980, 65 percent of the participants in the NCTE College Section were women, in comparison to 45 percent women participants in MLA (10). Drops in doctoral enrollments in the 1970s and 1980s have been decreases in *male numbers,* not in numbers of females, so concurrent drops in full-time tenurable appointments have affected women most directly. Women, by and large, fill the temporary jobs teaching composition that are the residue from declines in "regular" appointments.

In composition research, the hierarchy that places women in a subordinate status is maintained: men appear to publish a greater percentage of articles submitted to *College English* (65 percent); books by men dominate in selective bibliographies (approximately 70 percent); male authors overwhelmingly dominate in "theoretical" (as against nurturant, pedagogical) publication categories (Holbrook 12–13). Holbrook's analysis of these demonstrable proportions and of the historical position of women as faculty members in universities gives her good ground for infer-ring that "men develop knowledge and have higher status; women teach, applying knowledge and serving the needs of others, and have lower status" (7–8).

Economic determiners obviously have had a great deal to do with these dispo-sitions among the actual genders of composition teachers. But imaginary relation-ships of all teachers of composition to their students and colleagues are complex, not simple results of a one-to-one correspondence between kinds of "work" and patriarchal images of men and women. For instance, no one can take issue with evidence that the origins of English studies required that those who taught compo-sition would contribute to the survival of a whole group. Just as "it was absolutely necessary for group survival that most nubile women devote most of their adult-hood to pregnancy" (Lerner 41), it was absolutely necessary that the earliest English departments devote a significant portion of their energy to fulfilling the vision of them Eliot imagined at Harvard and that others took up: offering quasi-religious literary principles *and* a test of composition.

As I have said, we cannot be reductive here: composition teaching is not pre-cisely, at least not only, "imaginary" womanhood, as I will explain. But the infer-ence suggested by evidence of early huge composition classes, of the few people appointed to conduct their teaching, and of "leadership" in composition programs from one person over multitudes of students (like A. S. Hill's at Harvard or of "Miss Dumas and the staff" at Georgia) is that a great deal of delivery from a very small (conceptual) input was required of English departments from the outset.

It is interesting in this regard that we also have heard so much and so often about the "victory" of Francis Child at Harvard in giving over rhetoric for literature

---

Relation of Promotion to Field of Specialization

When asked if promotion is related to field of specialization in their de-partments, sixty-two (71 percent of the eighty-seven who answered this ques-tion) replied no. One qualified by stating that "it is, I believe, related to sex." (Four did not answer; seven were unsure.) The fourteen respondents who re-plied yes (22 percent) included two who stated that composition appears to create a privilege for promotion. Three described their departments as accus-tomed to differentially evaluating work in "the many mansions" of scholar-ship; one said that "the department must promote to full professor in five years, no matter what"; and one echoed responses to questions about tenure difficul-ties with "no, not yet." Four others, however, spoke of various kinds of normal and extraordinary field-related prejudices:

1. Yes, partially due to relative new entry of composition; we have no full professor in composition.

2. Some departments will never change their negative attitude toward com-position as a specialty. . . . They [people in composition] have grudgingly been afforded a certain status. The central administration is very aware of our strength in the composition/rhetoric area and is extremely support-ive.

3. The Chair debated the authenticity of a national award that a . . . book . . . had won (but not the award won by a poetry book of a colleague). Thus, he denied my promotion but supported that of my colleague.

4. While work in composition is worthwhile, literature is better.

when he threatened to leave for Johns Hopkins in 1875 (e.g., Corbett 625–26; Kitzhaber 55; Graff 40–41). A. S. Hill was brought in from his newspaper career to manage composition in 1876 so that others' literary study would not symbolically sink under its weight. His task was to manage the actual "work" that Richard Ohmann has described ("Reading"), in a position that became a symbol of the management of "work" itself. In this regard, it is unlikely that presidents in new, vocationally justified land grant institutions, or anyone else, would have permitted English departments to thrive without well-managed labor from composition teaching. Along with evidence in discussions like William Riley Parker's, Wallace Douglas's, or James Berlin's of "where English departments come from," the small sizes of early departments in comparison to the numbers of students to whom they were required to teach composition point out that this teaching, if only at first, helped justify new English departments. It was loud in their ideological "call."

All of this evidence points toward how a cooperative brotherhood within English studies first *necessarily* separated and subordinated the teacher of composition in those departments that were well enough supported to establish a division of necessary labor. This division would by definition be inequitable, considering the ideological motivations for including composition in literary English that explain its rise. And in smaller settings, where work could not be divided among different people, the work of composition could be compartmentalized from the leisure or "play" of literature. Single individuals, those who have taught both subjects in largely undergraduate institutions, have identified themselves as members of "literature."

Francis Child's rearrangement of his teaching duties to include research and to focus exclusively on literature thus also became part of an emerging symbol system in English. Escaping rhetoric and composition teaching was an early sign of an institution's ardent regard for individuals. Using Lerner's terms, we can describe this privilege as a symbol in the "American Academic Dream," an internalized goal for those who felt themselves enslaved and poor or who accepted the association of composition with all of the "low" qualities that had been meant to apply to its students. But the important point is that, like women in early communities that depended on their production of live births, composition teachers were at first necessarily placed where they would accrue subordinate associations that were no less binding than those still imposed on women.

Obviously, this historically created role for composition teaching also loads the identity of its teachers with larger biases that were first associated with the whole of English literary study. The cultural identity of anyone in English shared the upstart, nonserious, vulgar (as in vernacular), dilettantish, and certainly nonscientific qualities ascribed to their new pursuits. But as performers in a site for illegitimate and transgressive textual activities that are inextricably linked to, but only placed beside, a newly established and unsophisticated community, composition teachers would not have been separately recognized at all in the larger academic world. The students in the course that I have called a course in silence were taught by those for whom a separate and recognized "profession" of composition was "unspeakable." Outsiders to English did not recognize composition as separate, as they still do not. Among insiders, it was a deniable subtext in a new discipline that was inevitably competing for publicity among established fields and hoping to be regarded as the guardian of national "ideals" with a worthy claim on time for academic research.

Consequently, the work of correcting spelling was at least partially uncompetitive with other symbolically constructed functions for English. Its mundane nature overcame any of its potentially positive associations with morality or serious intelligence in the "new" secular university. And this work was actually threatening to the time necessary to compete for symbolic academic rewards. Like any group or individual widely thought to be *nouveau*, literary studies needed to ignore an embarrassing root under a new family tree if that tree was to grow. The Teaching of Writing Division of the inclusive MLA was established only in 1973, well after a distinct insider group of self-identified composition teachers had formed the Conference on College Composition and Communication in 1949.

We have, therefore, at least two historicized identities from which associations with composition teaching would stem. In actuality, composition teaching was work, and work of a particularly subordinate kind that *by definition within English studies* preceded the students' later exposure to cultural ideals in literature. It was literally "ground work." Ideologically, composition teaching had no claim on professional legitimacy, for it was not grammatical instruction in classical languages to transmit the Hegelian "spirit" of the past. The supposed low quality of its students and their writing, and its own mechanistic practices, had been constituted by the ideology of English to be illegitimate counterparts to ideals of content and perfections of execution that increasingly defined literary textuality. Over time, catalogues that describe developing English curricula in this century show that as even faint associations with classical grammatical instruction grew dimmer, composition was increasingly diminished and simplified. Concurrently, literary studies grew and became more complex.

These actual and imagined historical identities for composition teaching and its teachers have entrenched the imaginary identity around composition teachers. Their power over actual activities, like the power of womanhood over females, is not lessened by new facts. Although composition teachers now teach small classes relative to the majority of classes in other college-level subjects, their new ability to compete for research time, their publications, or the comparatively high salaries that some receive among their colleagues in literature do not automatically improve images held over from entirely different historical conditions.

The teacher of composition thus inevitably has at least some attributes of the stigmatized individual whom Erving Goffman describes in *Stigma: Notes on the Management of Spoiled Identity.* Goffman is a sociologist whose analysis focuses on interactions among stigmatized and normal individuals and groups within the same social situations, an arrangement that occurs in one department where ego identities from both literature and composition complexly conflict as privileged and subordinate, or healthy and "spoiled," identities. He is also a structuralist whose system of analysis identifies the stigmatized by their *relationships* with "normals," not by their intrinsic qualities.

The "central feature" of these relationships is, Goffman says, "acceptance," which in fact appears to be the primary issue that current composition professionals identify when they discuss accomplished and hoped-for changes in their status. The stigmatized individual is treated so that "those who have dealings with him fail to accord him the respect and regard which the uncontaminated aspects of his social identity have led them to anticipate extending, and have led him to anticipate receiving" (8–9). The otherwise physical normalcy of the deaf, the apparent masculinity of a male homosexual, and by extension the Ph.D. in literature of a part-time composition teacher will lead their associates and each of them to expect acceptance in the group who share their larger "ego" identity, a "felt" identity (105). But contamination from deafness, sexual practices, or trivialized teaching responsibilities also means that they will receive treatment from others that powerfully contradicts these expectations.

Research Awards

Respondents overwhelmingly reported that their institutions and/or departments regularly provide one or another sort of support for research. Of 106 responding to the first questions, eighty-five (80 percent) answered yes or "occasionally"; two responded that support comes only from outside the institution. Thirteen respondents (12 percent) were in institutions where research support is unavailable.

The frequency of applications and success of the eighty-nine who answered the three parts of the question about their own applications for research support show that ninety-three applications for research (not all to investigate problems defined as composition topics) had been made by this group in the previous ten years. One additional person indicated that she had "outside funding." Some respondents had applied and been turned down before later success; some had received more than one award. Although no control group from English or another humanistic department was used to measure this level of activity and four of these respondents defined themselves as "in" literature or as receiving grants toward research in it, a two-thirds (66 percent) rate of awards among this group defines them as aware of funding opportunities, active in pursuing them, and capable of competing successfully when they do.

In addition, those responding to these questions appear to believe that research awards in composition are made as often as in other fields.

Goffman lists a number of typical responses to such treatment from stigmatized persons: they attempt to correct the flaw; they use the stigma for "secondary gains," such as an excuse for failures in other areas; they see the stigma as a disguised blessing; they reassess the value of being "normal"; they avoid "normals"; and they develop anxieties, hostilities, suspicions, and depression. We can find obvious instances of some of these responses from composition teachers who apply for full-time positions in literature, who imitate the elevation of Francis Child by defining themselves as primarily graduate faculty and researchers, or who avoid the Modern Language Association because it remains "irrelevant" to their interests. Naturally, each of these possible and actual strategies for coping colors encounters with normals and their groups.

Applying this analysis, we must emphasize that no feature *intrinsic* to composition teaching urges stigma on its participants. The *discrepancy* between a felt identity and social treatments of those who allow themselves to be perceived as "in" composition causes stigmatized relations. Thus when it is "normal" to teach both composition and literature, as it is for faculty in undergraduate four-year or junior colleges, or normal to teach composition while engaging in graduate studies in literature or in creative writing, the stigmatic discrepancy need not develop. Even when all graduate students must teach composition and some faculty occasionally take it on, the larger cultural or academic attitude toward composition does not prevent it from being considered a perverse or abnormal endeavor, one marginal to the "true" identity of members of these groups. In these settings, however, some can treat it as a joke, a source of shared good humor and complaints, or as a temporary initiation ritual that "everyone" must endure, a mark of maturation in trial by fire.

Perceptions of the Relative Status of Fields in English

The survey asked respondents to rank, on a scale of one to nine, eight fields (literature, literary theory, composition, rhetoric, linguistics, feminist studies, film, and folklore) and an open category ("other") according to their perceptions of these fields' relative status in their departments. . . .

The respondents clearly perceived literature to have the highest status in their departments. They most often placed literary theory in second place, and they placed composition or rhetoric (or the two combined) in third place, where it (or they) received thirty-one mentions (34 percent of ninety ranking these fields). . . .

Composition and rhetoric also held sixth place in these rankings. The seventh rank went to film studies, which was placed at that level twelve times. Folklore held eighth place, receiving thirteen mentions (23 percent), and ninth place was held by "other."

Evaluated this way, data from these respondents suggest the following levels of status among fields:

1. Literature
2. Literary theory
3. Composition/rhetoric
4. Literary theory and composition/rhetoric
5. Linguistics
6. Composition/rhetoric
7. Film
8. Folklore
9. Other

That is, below the clear leader (literature), literary theory and composition/rhetoric appear to be vying for position in many settings, but composition/rhetoric has relatively low status (in sixth place) in many others. . . .

We can infer that these respondents recognized composition/rhetoric as a field as often as they did literature and that they appeared to be aware of recent elevations in its status. Rankings from three respondents were excluded from these data because they provided dualistic, past and future, rankings; these rankings commented directly on the changes perceived by the respondents. One only noted, "*I perceive rhetoric and composition highly. The literature people don't.*"

It is easy to see, therefore, that only individual composition teachers in a certain relationship to "normalcy" would be seriously stigmatized by this identity. While the entire activity of composition teaching is stigmatized in its historicized relation to literary centralism, many who engage in it can contain it, neutralize it, ignore it, and otherwise make it "all right." Temporary deafness, cross-dressing on Halloween, being assigned one composition course a year, or holding a graduate assistantship while completing a degree in Shakespeare do not permanently disable relations with the normal.

But it is one thing to go to the circus each year for entertainment, or even as part of one's family duty, and another thing entirely to run off to *join* the circus that composition was constituted to be. Openly displaying the signs that associate an individual with stigmatized groups, like openly engaging in any interaction taken to be peripheral to institutional purposes, inevitably disrupts normal social interactions.

We might infer from this distinction between the results of partial and full participation in a stigmatized, transgressive activity that one of the clearest operations of composition teaching is the cultural regulation and repression through stigma of particular kinds of otherwise normal activities — teaching and learning. Composition courses, from all of the evidence we have of their history, of the identity of their students, and of their choice of a research paradigm, *automatically* raise the issue of legitimacy. By this I mean that these courses and their teaching raise the issue of how an *actual* identity can take on imaginary associations that serve either privileged *or* marginalized cultural roles. The actual activities of someone who is learning to write, or of someone who is teaching composition, inevitably become implicated in a relationship to the imaginary perfection of literary texts. Both literary production and literary products are composition's "Other," the second terms in discrepancies between "the raw and the cooked" or "savage and domesticated" texts.

Given this foundational structure, we can extend Lerner's analysis of the operations of patriarchy to agree that a surplus of women or of live births, and perhaps a surplus of English Ph.D.s in literature, can make available human resources that have traditionally been closely regulated to guarantee that their scarcity will dispose them only in competitive and "proper" social circumstances. A surplus of females as slaves may in fact instigate prostitution, wherein commercialized sexual activity can fulfill symbolic (unlicensed, subnormal) cultural needs (see Lerner 133). But such a surplus can instead become the basis for newly normalized relationships, which a culture can afford to leave "unnamed" or even to elevate to the special status of "independence," "freedom," and "self-determination." In either case, permitting actions by this sort of surplus to remain outside established designations for proper and improper activities — that is, not calling its sexual activity prostitution — will mask the *actual* extracultural or extrafamilial situations of this surplus. Excess women, and perhaps excess Ph.D.s, may take on new roles that cloak their real status as surplus.

Consequently, it is even further possible that a surplus Ph.D. or a Ph.D. candidate in literature will take one of two paths: openly to choose the unlicensed, subnormal identity associated with composition, as many recently have, or more covertly to provide this teaching on a part-time, ad hoc basis while implicitly retaining a "normal" ego identity in a claim that "self-determination" or "independence" are his or her motives. This analysis from Goffman is in no way meant to belie the sincerity of such identity claims. But his structuralist model does explain one way that a group of individuals might *actually* derive their identities from composition teaching but also avoid its stigma through new and *imaginary* legitimizations for it.

Additionally, as Goffman points out, an imagined exemption from a stigma like this one can even further affect the actual conditions around stigmatized status. The surplus of Ph.D.s who have taken up composition teaching as one way to engage in transgressive behavior without actually joining the circus now have special professional grants, organizational fee structures, organizations, and support from professional position papers like the Wyoming Conference Resolution on the status of part-time composition teachers (Slevin 50). All show that normal people may respond to a new imaginary identity for the deviant. Dominant, already accepted groups may, that is, provide new *actual* relations that are within a "normal" range. These dispensations and expressions of concern have resulted from imagining normalcy for marginalized groups of part-time, traveling "gypsy" scholars. New institutional structures incorporate purveyors of the carnival into larger cultural systems, so that it always remains outside and suburban to an established city, not an independent force that might become parallel to it or competitive with it.

Such responses do change actual conditions for one kind of composition teacher, just as feminist theories have contributed to actual benefits for women by urging social services and legislation to benefit those who are marginalized by virtue of being single, divorced, or lesbian. As earlier references to Althusser indicate, ideologies emerge from a struggle *between* classes; they are not positions that a class will inevitably take from within itself.

But no new actuality can entirely revise the identity state of those who choose the first path, openly devoting themselves to a deviant identity as composition teachers or further becoming researchers in composition. Again, Goffman helpfully points toward the condition of this person:

> Even while the stigmatized individual is told that he is a human being like everyone else, he is being told that it would be unwise to pass or to let down "his" group. In brief, he is told he is like anyone else and that he isn't — although there is little agreement among spokesmen as to how much of each he should claim to be. This contradiction and joke is his fate and his destiny. . . . The stigmatized individual thus finds himself in an arena of detailed argument and discussion concerning what he ought to think of himself, that is, his ego identity. To his other troubles he must add that of being simultaneously pushed in several directions by professionals who tell him what he should do and feel about what he is and isn't, and all this purportedly in his best interests. (124–25)

Goffman hereby suggests that we look even more closely at the situation of these individuals who overtly claim to be *in* composition as its teachers and who are academically placed where they could not be imagined before model building, and finally paradigm construction, were undertaken (see Berlin chap. 7). The professionals surrounding these teachers — their colleagues, their (usually male) privileged theorists, and administrators who form and enact institutional structures — all contribute to a particular kind of blurring in their experienced identity, the conflict that Goffman quite accurately describes as both a contradiction and a joke. As Stallybrass and White say of the "Maid and the Family Romance," both "service" and "motherhood" converge in the call to this group from traditional ideology.

But composition teaching is not simple "motherhood," in service to father texts. The social identity of the composition teacher is intricately blurred in a matrix of functions that we can understand through the instructive example of Freud's description of the "feminine," which was formed at about the same time that composition courses and their teaching first achieved presence in the new university. Despite the problematics feminists point out in his work, Freud's description of associations that contain ambivalently situated women can be seen as a reliable account of nineteenth-century sexual mythologies, offering us historical access to early and continuing images of the gender-coding of composition teaching.

Freud dreamed of his family nurse, whom he later transformed into "mother." The nurse in the dream "initiated the young Freud in sexual matters" (Stallybrass and White 157). But later, in Freud's writing about "femininity," "the nurse has been displaced by the mother" (157). In a series of statements, Freud by turns associated seduction and bodily hygiene with motherhood and the maid, at one time calling the maid the most intimate participant in his initiations and fantasies, and at another thinking of these matters in relation to perfect motherhood. Stallybrass and White infer that because the nineteenth-century bourgeois family relegated child care to nurses, the maid both performed intimate educational functions and had power over the child. "Because of his size, his dependency, his fumbling attempts at language, his inability to control his bodily functions" (158), the child could be

---

Difficulties with Tenure in Composition

Among the thirty-four who answered that they had perceived problems with tenure related to composition as a field, only one attributed the difficulty to problems with the quality of a particular person's work. . . .

Among responses classified in table A-8, twelve respondents explained specific instances of difficulties that they perceive as related to having composition as a field. Very difficult personal situations were revealed: two were promoted before tenure, then suffered from second thoughts of colleagues about actually tenuring people in composition; two people reported results from an institution that, they say, "routinely passes over people who spend too much time on composition"; one reported that she "made changes in the program," then left her position after warnings about receiving tenure; three reported similar difficulties when appointments to administer composition were later not "counted" for tenure; one said that she had, in an unprecedented departmental action, been put up for review two years after the beginning of her appointment; two other less specific cases involved releasing all of the people in composition, or some of them, while retaining others in literature. One person was told at hiring that he would never be promoted or allowed to serve on committees because he had been hired to teach writing courses. But he witnessed changes from this situation in his department to active hiring in composition. Nonetheless, he reported that a more junior colleague in composition had been reviewed first by the usual three outside reviewers, then by three more because the first group was perceived as "too complimentary."

---

shamed and humiliated by the maid. But paradoxically, it is more acceptable to desire the mother than the maid, who is "hired help," so that actual interactions with a nurse/maid might be fantasized as having occurred with the mother.

Without stressing prurient comparisons between the "low" work of composition and this representation of intimate bodily and other educational functions (although in nineteenth-century sociopathology they were certainly there to be drawn) it is fair to suggest that this symbolic blurring still encodes the role of teachers of composition. It explains some otherwise troubling contradictions in their habitually conceived identities. The bourgeois mother and maid, that is, both represent comfort and power. The mother was the source Freud turned to for explanatory information about the maid; the mother was also, with the father, an authority. The maid was an ambivalently perceived site for dealing with low, unruly, even anarchic desires and as yet uncontrolled personal development.

Even down to the reported problematic of leaving the "home" language in a requirement to "'forget' the baby-talk of the body" (Stallybrass and White 166), a developmental stage associated with the maid, we can see an oscillation between images of mother and maid. Leaving the maid represents foregoing infantile freedoms for the embarrassments that the mother/power figure is likely to represent, as she did when the child moved on to formal Latin lessons in the process of leaving the governess for the schoolmaster (a process that Freud's Wolf Man found crucial). By the obvious analogy with learning vernacular language again, as a formalized system, the composition student's teacher combines the two images of mother and maid. This powerful but displaced person blurs anxieties over maturation that must inevitably accompany a move toward public language.

Consequently, one figure of a composition teacher is overloaded with symbolic as well as actual functions. These functions include the dual (or even triple) roles that are washed together in these teachers: the nurse who cares for and tempts her young charge toward "adult" uses of language that will not "count" because they are, for now, engaged in only with hired help; the "mother" (tongue) that is an ideal/ idol and can humiliate, regulate, and suppress the child's desires; and finally the disciplinarian, now not a father figure but a sadomasochistic Barbarella version of either maid or mother.

By virtue of all the institutional placements of composition teaching that were described earlier, it is clear that the individual composition teacher is a culturally designated "initiator," much like a temple priest/ess who functions to pass along secret knowledge but not to participate freely in a culture that depends on that knowledge. Strict regulations, analogous to those devised to keep "hired help" in its place, prevent those who introduce the young to the culture's religious values and rites from leaving their particular and special status. These mediators between natural and regulated impulses are tied to vows, enclosed living spaces, and/or certain kinds of dress (see Lerner 123–41).

But this initiating role, whether it is described in terms of religious/sexual initiations or as the groundwork under discursive practices, is unstable in any context. It was never worked out in regard to codified culture even in ancient times, when the socially separated *grammaticus* and *rhetor* argued over who should initiate students into rhetorical composition. Thus the teacher of composition is not assigned only the role of initiator, which might involve the care, pedagogic seduction, and practice for adult roles provided by nurses in bourgeois homes. In addition, this teacher must withhold unquestioned acceptance, represent established means of discriminating and evaluating students, and embody primary ideals/idols of language. This initiator, who traditionally has a great deal at stake in the model-correctness of his or her own language, must also *be* the culture to which the student is introduced.

This embodiment in rules and practice exercises, the rituals of language, displaces actual discourse. It requires the student to keep a distance. If there is an Oedipal situation in regard to working out an imagined young student's entitlements to full participation in cultural "principles," the composition teacher is the Jocasta figure, the desired and desiring but always displaced representation of maturity. In the terminology of psychopathology, this teacher is called into an inverted neurotic situation, one that displays the *social* irruption of *psychic* processes, not the more usual "*psychic* irruption of *social* processes" (Stallybrass and White 176).

Some might counter that this structure contains the imaginary identity called for from any teacher of any introductory course claiming to initiate students into "essential" cultural knowledge. But the composition teacher consciously and unconsciously initiates students into the culture's discourse on *language,* which is always at one with action, emotion, and regulatory establishments. This teacher is always engaged in initiations to the textual fabric of society and thus will always be in a particular and difficult relation to the powers that overtly regulate that society. Although the fairs that permeated social life in Europe were broken up and discontinued in the process of regulations like the Fairs Act of 1871 in England (Stallybrass and White 177), actual carnivals do not disappear. "Fragmentation, marginalization, sublimation, and repression" (178) keep them alive. Similarly, the identity first imposed on teachers of composition is held over, even after their mechanistic and very obviously regulatory earliest roles are revised and are in fact contradicted by many stated goals, practices, and actual situations.

Doubts about the plausibility of this explanation of the composition teacher's blurred identity may be lessened by common responses to these teachers, which should reveal its force. Like the carnival, composition teaching still is often acknowledged as "an underground self with the upper hand" (Stallybrass and White 4). It is an employment that in the majority of its individual cases is both demeaned by its continuing ad hoc relation to status, security, and financial rewards, yet given overwhelming authority by students, institutions, and the public, who expect even the most inexperienced composition teacher to critize and "correct" them in settings entirely removed from the academy. The perduring image of the composition teacher is of a figure at once powerless and sharply authoritarian, occupying the transgressive, low-status site from which language may be arbitrated.

Continuing associations of composition teachers with "Miss Grundyism" also reinforce this claim that as an identity, composition teaching codes the individual of either sex as a woman, the inheritor of the "pink sunsets" image of literary initiation that has in the last quarter-century largely been removed from the self-perceptions of literary professionals by their own "theory." In this way also, the existence of composition within English permits literature to displace and translate an older social identity onto only one of its parts. Composition is a site for residues and traces from earlier literary identities that first coded English as "female" among "hard" disciplines.

If we return to the original question I posed in this chapter, the question of why composition professionals would have chosen a "process paradigm" that appears to estrange them from English studies, we may answer that this choice emerges from their blurred identity and from strategies for coping with its nonetheless clear stigma. The choice of a "process" "paradigm" for research appears to, but finally does not, represent a contradiction in terms. On the one hand, associations with "process" extend and in fact enlarge the subjectivity for its own sake that removes students and their teachers from the need to verify, validate, and find significance in "results." "Process" thereby reinforces the composition professional's claim on a "normal" identity among colleagues in literature, expressing a desire that is difficult to shake. But on the other hand, associations with a scientific "paradigm" give value only to verified, valid, significant "results" from research. This member of the pair of terms reveals yet another mechanism for coping with stigma, in the form of a desire to elevate stigmatized status to a place that is imagined to be above the identity of the "normal."

The juxtaposition of these terms does not, I would argue, unconsciously preserve androgyny and thereby give equal privileges to two terms of a pair that is symbolically female and male, yin and yang. Instead, the choice of this seemingly contradictory pair in a new description of composition teaching and theory contains two equal preservations of the historical (traditional, hegemonic) situation of composition. *Process* practices extend and preserve literary subjectivity, while their explanation in a *paradigm* theory extends and preserves the anxiety about status that has always been associated with English studies, both in regard to the perfection of elitist texts and as a professional concern about identity in relation to older, "harder" disciplines.

As in other examples, composition professionals inevitably re-create the conditions that first established their identities. Persistent attempts to change these conditions without changing the basic structure of high and low that sustain them leave composition in new versions of traditional values. Stallybrass and White summarize such moves in a judgment whose importance cannot be overstated: "The point is that the exclusion necessary to the formation of social identity is simultaneously a *production* at the level of the Imaginary, and a production, what is more, of a complex hybrid fantasy emerging out of the very attempt to demarcate boundaries, to unite and purify the social collectivity" (193). They claim, that is, that by separating itself from an objectionable entity — the stigma, for example, of "mere" teachers of composition engaged in "grotesque" untheorized work — a group necessarily produces a "new grotesque."

We see this process in action in regard to composition teaching and theorizing, both of which have appeared to exclude formerly acceptable literary agendas as well as "soft," unorganized theories of composition or interpretations based on work that is not really "in" the field. But the production that occurs simultaneously with this attempt to mark boundaries, unite, and purify a field of composition also is a process of exclusion, the very process that otherwise dedicated teachers of composition object to and take as their motive for change. Consequently, the theories I have applied to the identity of the composition teacher may appear to describe a condition that is past or clearly passing, not one that is held over in a complex set of continuing interactions that slowly move the teacher out of a sweat shop and into respectable professional modes. Nonetheless, the nature of this movement is too clearly implicated in reproducing the conditions it wishes to revise to be celebrated with unqualified assertions that "change" has occurred, as new institutional blurrings of the identity of composition also demonstrate.

Works Cited

Berlin, James. *Rhetoric and Reality: Writing Instruction in American Colleges, 1900–1985.* Carbondale: Southern Illinois UP, 1987.

Corbett, Edward P. J. *Classical Rhetoric for the Modern Student.* New York: Oxford UP, 1971.

Goffman, Erving. *Frame Analysis.* New York: Harper, 1974.

Graff, Gerald. *Professing Literature: An Institutional History.* Chicago: U of Chicago P, 1987.

Holbrook, Sue Ellen. "Women's Work: The Feminizing of Composition." Presentation, CCCC. St. Louis, March 1988.

Kitzhaber, Albert. "Rhetoric in American Colleges, 1850–1900." Diss. U of Washington, 1953.

Lerner, Gerda. *The Creation of Patriarchy.* New York: Oxford UP, 1986.

Ohmann, Richard. "Reading and Writing, Work and Leisure," from *Only Connect: Uniting Reading and Writing.* Ed. Thomas Newkirk. Upper Montclair: Boynton-Cook, 1986.

Slevin, James. "A Note on the Wyoming Resolution and ADE." *ADE Bulletin* 87 (1987): 50.

Stallybrass, Peter, and Allon White. *The Politics and Poetics of Transgression.* Ithaca: Cornell UP, 1986.

Miller's Insights as a Resource for Your Teaching

1. Miller's analysis of writing instruction in American colleges suggests that to teach writing is to work in a ghetto within the university. This injustice varies from institution to institution, but everyone can reflect on the power dynamics at work in his or her institution and explore strategies for diplomatically thematizing the ghettoization of writing instruction in individual classrooms.

2. In a journal, reflect on the ways that your frustration with writing instruction might affect your own day-to-day morale and, in turn, the morale of your students. Can you think of readings to assign that might boost morale and reduce the somber tedium with which most institutions encode the scene of writing instruction? Narratives about the extraordinary joy and power that come from winning literacy are helpful. Consider the *Narrative of the Life of Frederick Douglass, an American Slave*, for example.

Miller's Insights as a Resource for the Writing Classroom

1. Ask students to freewrite about the differences between their composition class and, say, a class on Shakespeare or Virginia Woolf. By discussing these perceived differences, students can become aware of the special goals of the course that is designed to teach them to write. By becoming more attuned to these goals, they stand a better chance of reaching them.

2. Assign a literary text in your classroom, and then juxtapose this text with texts written by students or with other nonliterary writing, such as journalism, popular fiction, or song lyrics. Ask the students to discuss and write about the cultural dynamics that envelope each of these texts, and explore how the writing process is affected by the institutional norms that perpetuate and entrench those dynamics.

MURIEL HARRIS AND   *Tutoring ESL Students:*
TONY SILVA   *Issues and Options*

Muriel Harris, a writing center administrator and theorist, and Tony Silva, an English as a Second Language specialist, wrote this piece for colleagues who train tutors to work with ESL writers. However, the essay also provides composition teachers a clear overview of issues and practical teaching strategies for working with ESL writers. The questions that nag new peer tutors and their responses to texts written by ESL students differ only by degree of apprehension from the questions and reading responses of writing teachers. The "tutorial principles" cited are also standard teaching practices of writing instructors. The recommended readings are useful additions to the professional library of a writing instructor. Use this essay as a jumping-in point for thinking about, and planning to work with, students who compose in English as their second — or third or fourth — language.

For students whose first language is not English, the writing classroom cannot provide all the instructional assistance that is needed to become proficient writers. For a variety of reasons, these students need the kind of individualized attention that tutors offer, instruction that casts no aspersions on the adequacy of the classroom or the ability of the student. We should recognize that along with different linguistic backgrounds, ESL students have a diversity of concerns that can only be dealt with in the one-to-one setting where the focus of attention is on that particular student and his or her questions, concerns, cultural presuppositions, writing processes, language learning experiences, and conceptions of what writing in English is all about. Typically, the tutorial assistance available for these students is provided by writing centers, and much of the personal help available there is precisely the same as for any native speaker of English: the goal of tutors who work in the center is to attend to the individual concerns of every writer who walks in the door — writing process questions, reader feedback, planning conversations, and so on. But also typically, tutors, who bring to their work a background of experience and knowledge in interacting effectively with native speakers of English, are not adequately equipped to deal with some additional concerns of non-native speakers of English — the unfamiliar grammatical errors, the sometimes bewilderingly different rhetorical patterns and conventions of other languages, and the expectations that accompany ESL writers when they come to the writing center. Tutors can be reduced to stunned silence when they try to explain why "I have many homeworks to completed" is wrong or why we say "on Monday" but "in June."

Tutors need some perspective on rhetorical approaches other than those they expect to find, such as a direct statement of the topic or discourse with a linear development. When tutors find, instead, an implicitly stated point or when they become lost in a long, seemingly meandering introduction or digressions that appear irrelevant, they flounder, not recognizing that implicitness and digressions may be acceptable rhetorical strategies in the writing of some other cultures. Because the need to learn more about how to work with ESL writers in tutorials is immediate and real, one of the authors of this essay, a writing center director, asked the other author, the coordinator of ESL writing courses at our university, for help. The conversations that ensued are summarized here in terms of the questions that guided our discussion of various issues and options, and our hope is that our exchanges will be of interest to others who train tutors to work with ESL students. We also hope that composition teachers looking for guidance when conferencing with ESL students will find useful suggestions for their own interactions with these students.

Plunging In: How Do We Prioritize among Errors?

In the peer tutor training course in our writing center, peer tutors are especially eager to meet and work with ESL students, but their initial contacts can be somewhat frightening because some unfamiliar concerns crop up. To the untrained tutor's eye what is most immediately noticeable is that a draft written by an ESL student looks so different. Vocabulary choices might be confusing, familiar elements of essays are missing, and sentences exhibit a variety of errors — some we can categorize, some we cannot. Tutors' first concern is often a matter of wanting some guidance about where to plunge in. Where should they start? New tutors who have not yet completely internalized the concept of the tutorial as focusing only on one or two concerns think initially it is their responsibility to help the writer fix everything in the draft in front of them. As tutors learn the pedagogy of the tutorial, they become more comfortable with selecting something to work on for that session, but they still need suggestions for a hierarchy and some sense of what is most important.

When tutors ask how to prioritize among errors, they should be encouraged to begin by looking for what has been done well in the paper, acknowledge that, and go from there. Such a suggestion fits in well with the tutorial principle of beginning all interaction with writers on a positive note and reminds us that ESL writers should not be separated out as different or unlike other students in this regard. And tutors should also be encouraged to let their students know that errors are a natural part of language learning and that most readers will be interested primarily in what writers have to say. So tutors need to distinguish between errors that will interfere with the intended reader's understanding of the text (global errors) and those that will not (local errors) and to give priority to the former. To illustrate for tutors this notion of global vs. local errors at the sentence level, the following example can help. Suppose an ESL student, attempting to describe some classmates as uninspired by a particular lecture, wrote: "Those students are boring" instead of "Those students are bored." This would constitute a global error. On the other hand, a construction such as "Those student are bored" would represent a local error.

Using Research: How Helpful Is It to Look for Patterns?

With our heightened awareness of multiculturalism, we are also more aware of cultural preferences that are reflected in writing, such as the often-cited Asian preference for indirection. The question in working one-to-one with ESL students is how helpful such generalizations really are. Work in contrastive rhetoric would seem to be particularly valuable because it describes patterns of rhetorical preferences in other cultures, patterns which may explain the seemingly inappropriate rhetorical strategies used by ESL students. But to what degree is such knowledge useful? To what extent should we help tutors become aware of such differences? On the one hand, there is a danger that they can begin to use general patterns as givens, expecting all speakers of other languages to fit the models they have learned. On the other hand, without any knowledge of cultural preferences tutors are likely to see differences as weaknesses and to assume that the ESL student needs basic writing help. For example, instead of introducing the American intolerance of digression as culturally appropriate for American discourse, a tutor might treat an ESL student purposefully using digression as an inadequate writer who has problems with organization. If the tutor assumes that student is deficient, the tutor's tendency might be to work on outlining and to leave aside any rationale for why digressions should be avoided. Tutors need to introduce preferences and conventions of American discourse for what they are — alternate conventions and preferences.

However, to consider the extent to which such knowledge is helpful, we have to begin with some background information. The study of first-language transfer at or below the sentence level, typically referred to as "contrastive analysis" (see Brown 153–63 for a concise summary of this work), and the study of differences in rhetorical preferences among various cultures, usually termed "contrastive rhetoric" (see, for example, Grabe and Kaplan; Leki), have given us useful insights into how the writing of ESL students may differ from accepted standards of American discourse. The question of the transfer of first-language (L1) linguistic and rhetorical patterns to second-language (L2) writing has been a central and contentious issue in ESL studies since the beginning of work in this area. In the early days it was believed that L1 transfer (then called interference) was the primary if not exclusive cause of L2 problems. Therefore, it was felt that if one could catalog the differences between a student's L1 and L2, one could anticipate — and thus be prepared to deal with — any problems that student might encounter in the L2. However, research showed that this was not the case. There were many problems that could not be accounted for by L1 interference. Other factors, such as cognitive development, prior language and/or writing instruction, and experience were also implicated. Today, it is generally believed that transfer can be positive or negative and that it is only one of the potential causes of L2 writing problems. Thus we have to approach the question of the use of such knowledge with some hedging. On one hand, being cognizant of typical problems associated with particular groups of ESL students can be helpful — especially if tutors work largely with one or two particular groups. At the very least, this would make tutors very familiar with these problems and perhaps enhance their ability to deal with them. However, tutors need to keep two things in mind: (1) not all members of a particular group may manifest all of the problems or cultural preferences associated with that group; and (2) not all problems will be a result of transfer of L1 patterns.

A related issue is that of culturally conditioned patterns of behavior, some articulated, some not. In the Writing Lab's tutor-training course, we dip into Edward Hall's work to help tutors-to-be become aware of the variety of human behaviors which are conditioned, consciously or unconsciously, by one's culture. Since some of these behaviors can impede communication in a tutorial, it's important to recognize that such differences occur. A few favorite topics among the tutors-in-training are their reactions to the preference for or avoidance of eye contact, the differences among cultures in regard to the amount of space that people expect to maintain between themselves and others, the acceptability of touching between strangers, and so on. The cautionary advice about not doing too much large-scale or whole-group predicting is worth recalling here, but we also have to be aware that we might make unconscious judgments about others based on our expectations about such behaviors. In addition, we have to deal with different cultural assumptions about time, keeping appointments vs. showing up (if at all) much later, and so on. Understanding and accommodating cultural differences is, to a great extent, what ESL instruction is all about. This is especially true when working with students who are very new to and not very cognizant of the workings of American culture.

Recognizing Differences: How Do We Distinguish Language Learning from Writing Process Needs?

There is a tendency to think about ESL students as if they're all alike when obviously they're not. And in writing centers our focus is on working with individual differences of all kinds. So when the tutor and student negotiate the agenda of what they'll work on, the tutor has to do some assessment about a variety of things, including some sense of what skills the student has or doesn't have — not an easy matter when it might be that the writer's low level of language proficiency, not weak writing skills, is causing the problem. For example, does the thin, undeveloped two-paragraph essay an ESL student brings in indicate the need to talk about how to develop topics or is the student's lack of language proficiency in English keeping her from expressing a rich internal sense of what she wants to write about? As tutors we know that our conversation would take on a somewhat different emphasis depending on our analysis of the situation. The question then becomes one of how to decide whether the student needs help with language or with writing processes.

While the distinction between language proficiency and writing ability is not clear cut, it is crucial to make such a distinction in order to understand and address a given ESL writer's problems (see Barbara Kroll's "The Rhetoric and Syntax Split" for an excellent discussion of this issue). In some cases, a very low level of English proficiency will prevent a student from producing any kind of coherent prose. For such a student some basic language instruction, preceding or accompanying writing instruction, would be indicated. Then there is the student with enough English proficiency to make it unclear whether problems result primarily from rhetorical or linguistic difficulties or from both. There are a number of ways tutors can proceed when trying to ascertain the cause of the problem — assuming they will see the student more than once. They can try to locate the student's results on general English proficiency tests or tests of English writing ability. They can consult with an ESL professional. They can analyze some samples of the student's writing and make a judgment of their own. They can ask the student's opinion about what the basic difficulty is.

Exploring Writing Process Differences: Do ESL Writers Compose Differently?

A rather small but growing body of research, reviewed and synthesized by Silva, compares the composing of ESL and native English speaking (NES) writers. The findings of this research suggest that while the composing processes of these two groups are similar in their broad outlines, that is, for both groups writing is a recursive activity involving planning, writing, and revising, there are some salient and important differences. The findings (and these should be seen as very tentative) suggest that adult ESL writers plan less, write with more difficulty (primarily due to a lack of lexical resources), reread what they have written less, and exhibit less facility in revising by ear, that is, in an intuitive manner — on the basis of what "sounds" right, than their NES peers. One implication that can be drawn from this research is that those who deal with ESL writers might find it helpful to stretch out the composing process: (1) to include more work on planning — to generate ideas, text structure, and language — so as to make the actual writing more manageable; (2) to have their ESL students write in stages, e.g., focusing on content and organization in one draft and focusing on linguistic concerns in another subsequent draft; and (3) to separate their treatments of revising (rhetorical) and editing (linguistic) and provide realistic strategies for each, strategies that do not rely on intuitions ESL writers may not have.

Confronting Error:
Does It Help to Categorize Sentence-Level Concerns?

When working on grammar with native speakers, tutors categorize types of error so that they can address seemingly disparate problems by focusing on a larger language principle at work. While it's useful to know how to do this so that one can figure out what the problem is and explain it in an effective way to the student, such categorization in the writing of ESL students is often difficult. To do such categorizing well, tutors may need to take a course in the grammar of modern English. Or maybe a short in-service seminar or self-study would do the trick. In any case, a merely intuitive understanding of how English works would not be sufficient for helping ESL writers — who do not share the tutor's native speaker intuitions and who often need explicit explanations. We should also remember that the "rules" of English vary in terms of level of usefulness. Most don't work all the time; some have as many exceptions as cases covered by the rule. So knowing the rules can help tutors a lot; but they can't count on the rules solving their problems in every case. Such advice should make tutors feel more comfortable with their role as writing collaborators rather than as grammarians whose function it is to spout rules. Tutors are there to help with the whole spectrum of writing processes, not to be talking grammar handbooks.

Although tutors do not work primarily on grammar and mechanics, some ESL writers — especially those whose first acquaintance with English was as a foreign language taught in classrooms in other countries — have a tendency to want to know rules. For example, in a tutorial with a native speaker of English or a student born in the United States who spoke another language before entering school, the student might ask "Is this sentence OK?" or "How do I fix this sentence?" But an ESL student who comes to the United States after studying English as a foreign language in another country is more likely to ask "Why is this wrong?" Such students seem to have a strong inclination toward organizing their knowledge of English by rules. Though things are changing, many foreign language classes (and this includes foreign language classes in the United States) privilege the learning of grammatical rules, of learning about the language as an object, and neglect the learning of how to actually communicate, orally or in writing, in the foreign language. Certainly, this can make learners very rule-oriented in their outlook. However, there is something else that may also contribute to an ESL student's seeming preoccupation with rules. It's necessary to keep in mind that non-native speakers of a language (especially ones with lower levels of second language proficiency) simply don't have the intuitions about the language that native speakers do; that is, it is harder for them to recognize when something "sounds good." Therefore, in lieu of these intuitions, these students will have to rely on explicit rules to a certain extent.

Adjusting Expectations:
How Do We Withstand the Pressure to Correct Every Error?

ESL writers often come to the writing center seeking an editor, someone who will mark and correct their errors and help them fix the paper. On one hand, as tutors we are collaborators who listen to the student's concerns when setting the tutorial agenda. On the other hand, as tutors we also want to begin with rhetorical concerns before looking at sentence-level matters. This causes delicate negotiating between tutor and student when these differing preferences for the agenda collide. But tutors should be firm about dealing with rhetorical matters before linguistic ones (recognizing that sometimes this distinction is hard to make), a sequence as beneficial for ESL writers as it is for native speakers. Tutors should remind ESL writers that their linguistic options may be determined to a large degree by the rhetorical requirements of their papers and that, correlatively, it doesn't make sense to focus initially on grammatical or mechanical problems which may disappear as a result of rhetorically based revisions.

A related problem is that when ESL students are particularly insistent on having tutors correct all grammatical errors in a paper, tutors are at a loss to explain in meaningful ways why this is not productive. Resisting such pressure is very difficult, especially when ESL students are writing papers for other courses where they think the paper should be "correct." One way to address this is for tutors to adjust expectations. Tutors need to tell ESL writers that it is unrealistic for them to expect to be able to write like native speakers of English — especially when it comes to the small but persistent problems like articles and prepositions. Tutors can explain that even non-native speakers of English who live in an English speaking area for many years and write regularly in English maintain a written accent. It might help to compare this to a foreign accent in pronunciation and to remind ESL students that most native speakers (their professors included) will probably not penalize them much or at all for minor problems in their writing. It also helps to remind such students to focus on substance and not worry so much about style. But there are faculty who do have unrealistic demands about the level of correctness, who expect non-native speakers of English to write error-free prose — not to have a written accent, so to speak. If an ESL student's teacher has such unrealistic expectations, then the student is justified in seeking out editing help, and a native English speaking colleague, friend, or tutor is justified in providing such help.

Another way that tutors can deal with students' insistence on having all errors corrected is to explain the role of a tutor. ESL students need to know that tutors are expected to help them with strategies that will make them effective, independent writers. We need to explicitly state that tutors are supposed to be educators, not personal editors. This problem is often a result of a mismatch between the assumptions and expectations of tutors and students, though tutors do tend to hang on to their kind-hearted desire to help the student turn in a good paper. Writing center specialists endlessly quote Steve North's now famous one-liner that the tutor's job "is to produce better writers, not better writing" (438). But we still suffer pangs when the student leaves with less than an "A" paper in hand. Offering editorial services is not a learning experience — except for the editor, of course — and tutors need to resist their impulse to help as much as ESL students need to resist their desire to have every grammatical error corrected.

Setting Goals: What Can We Accomplish?

Since second-language learning is typically a long, slow process, tutors have to confront the realities of the time constraints they face in tutorials. Sometimes tutors meet briefly with ESL writers who are about to hand in a paper, sometimes tutors may have a few more leisurely tutorials with the same student, and sometimes tutors are able to meet over a more extended period of time, including sessions when the student is not working on a particular paper. The question then becomes one of deciding what can reasonably be done in the varying situations tutors find themselves in. In terms of last-minute encounters, a tutor can't do much with a paper that is about to be handed in — except act as a proofreader or offer moral support. And neither of these has much instructional value in the long run. However, dealing with an early or intermediate draft of a paper at one or more short sessions can be very useful if tutors can resist trying to deal with all of a draft's problems at once. It is more realistic and more useful to focus on one or two salient difficulties, the things that strike the tutor as most problematic for the reader. To do more would probably overload and frustrate the student and wind up being counterproductive. Going this slowly will probably not result in great improvements in a particular paper, but is more likely to facilitate real learning and writing improvement over time.

When tutors are able to meet with ESL students over a period of time and meet when the student is not working on a particular paper, there are several kinds of tutorial activities that might be useful in helping the student build language proficiency. To begin this sequence, a tutor should first look at one or more samples of the student's writing to get a feel for what linguistic features need to be addressed and in what order (global first, local later). Then, always working with a text the student has written previously or writes in the tutorial, the tutor can help the student identify and remedy errors or help the student generate lexical and/or syntactic options that would improve the student's text. This sort of procedure would help with building language proficiency and might also help the student develop effective personalized strategies for generating language, revising, and editing. Such an approach also harmonizes with the writing center philosophy that what we do particularly well in the tutorial setting is to help writers develop strategies individually matched to their own preferences and differences. Because the tutorial is also especially well suited to working through writing processes, to engaging in various processes such as planning, organizing, revising, and editing with the writer, working through various texts the ESL writer is drafting and revising is easily accomplished in a one-to-one setting.

Resisting the Urge to "Tell":
How Do We Stop Supplying All the Answers?

Since writing center pedagogy has given high priority to working collaboratively and interactively, a major goal of a tutor is to help students find their own solutions. Tutors thus don't see themselves as "instructors" who "tell" things. Yet the ESL student cannot easily come to some of the realizations that native speakers can as a result of tutorial questioning and collaboration. To confound the problem even more, while the tutor is uncomfortable straying from the role of collaborator, ESL writers are likely to find such a situation strange or uncomfortable when they come from cultures/educational systems where teachers are expected to be "tellers," where those who don't "tell" are seen as poor teachers, or where such casual interaction with relative strangers is seen as odd or inappropriate. This means that tutors cannot assume that a pattern of interaction that is common and accepted in their culture will be familiar or comfortable for their ESL students. Therefore, tutors might find it useful to make sure that they and their ESL students understand each other's goals and expectations vis-a-vis their tutoring sessions.

In terms of the tutor's role, there may have to be adjustments in their pedagogical orientation. Tutors who work with ESL students may have to be "tellers" to some extent because they will probably need to provide cultural, rhetorical, and/or linguistic information which native speakers intuitively possess and which ESL students do not have, but need to have to complete their writing assignments effectively. That is, regardless of their level of skill in collaboration or interpersonal interaction, tutors will not be able to elicit knowledge from ESL students if the students don't have that knowledge in the first place. This is not to suggest that "telling" should become a tutor's primary style of interacting with ESL writers; they should use it when they feel it would be necessary or appropriate, just as they assume the role of informant occasionally when working with native speakers of English. Tutors can also make minor accommodations in their tutoring style when working with ESL writers. For example, with non-native students who are used to hearing directive statements from teachers, Judith Kilborn has suggested that where it is appropriate, tutors modify the normal mode of asking questions so that instead of asking "Why . . . " or "How . . . ," tutors can, for example, say, "Please explain. . . ." An answer to a relatively open-ended request for explanation might be more useful and enlightening for both the ESL student and the tutor.

Making Hierarchies: What Aspects of Grammar Are Most Important?

Although tutorials should begin with discussions of larger rhetorical concerns, at some point ESL students will want help with grammatical correctness. When tutors do confront working with grammar, problems with verb endings and tenses, prepositions, and deleted articles often are the most noticeable. But are these the most useful things to start with? One way to define the most important areas is functionally; that is, the ones most important to address are those that most interfere with the reader's understanding of what the writer wants to say (global errors) regardless of their structural characteristics. Research suggests that ESL writers most commonly make the following errors:

Verbs

> Inflectional morphology (agreement with nouns in person, number, etc.)
>
> Verbal forms (participials, infinitives, gerunds)
>
> Verb complementation (the types of clauses or constructions that must follow a particular verb)

Nouns

> Inflection (especially in terms of singular/plural and count/mass distinctions)
>
> Derivation (deriving nouns from other parts of speech, e.g., *quick — quickness*, which often seems quite arbitrary to non-native speakers)

Articles (related to problems in classifying nouns)

> Use of wrong article
>
> Missing article
>
> Use of an article when none is necessary or appropriate

Prepositions (primarily a result of limited lexical resources)

> Knowing which one goes with a particular noun, verb, adjective, or adverb

These four error types account for most of the errors made by ESL writers with a fairly high level of English proficiency; ESL writers with lower levels of proficiency may also exhibit more problems with basic sentence, clause and phrase structure — which (when combined with vocabulary limitations) result in writing that is very difficult to decipher. Article problems can be important, too; that is, they can seriously obscure meaning in some contexts. But they generally do not cause readers any serious difficulties, and because they are so hard to eradicate, they should not be a high priority for tutors. It might help both tutors and ESL writers to think of article problems in writing as akin to a slight foreign accent in writing — something that doesn't pose serious difficulties and disappears only gradually — if at all.

When working with the complicated matter of articles and prepositions and non-rule-governed matters such as idioms, tutors need some new pedagogies as well as guidance for explaining topics not normally discussed in grammar handbooks. But, while we can develop an explanation of article use in English, such an explanation will not be simple by any means. It would involve making sequential decisions about the noun phrase that an article modifies — common or proper, count or non-count, singular or plural, definite or indefinite. Then, of course, there are the several classes of special cases and the many outright exceptions to the rules (Ann Raimes's *Grammar Troublespots* is helpful here; see 85–92). ESL writers could understand such explanations — but it's not clear that this understanding would translate into greatly improved performance in making correct article decisions while actually writing. Article use can improve gradually with increased exposure to English, but it's not realistic to expect that an ESL writer will ever use articles like a native speaker does. ESL students should be encouraged to do the best they can and then get a native speaker to proofread their work — if proofreading is absolutely necessary. As for preposition problems, they are lexical rather than grammatical problems. We either know the correct preposition in a given context or we don't — there are really no rules we can appeal to. Therefore, ESL writers need to learn prepositions the same way they learn other vocabulary items — through study or exposure to the language. Idioms are also a lexical rather than a grammatical matter. Second language learners usually have a keen interest in idiomatic expressions and are eager to learn and use them. Tutors can capitalize on this interest by providing students with idiomatic options for words and expressions they have used in their text. Both tutor and student might find this a useful and enjoyable activity. One proviso: When introducing an idiom, tutors need to also supply information about the appropriate context for the use of that idiom in order to avoid putting the student in a potentially embarrassing situation.

Encouraging Proofreading: What Strategies Work Well?

With native English speakers we are often successful in helping them learn to edit for correctness by reading aloud, something some ESL students can also learn how to do. Some are able to find their own mistakes, even add omitted articles, and it really works. But for other ESL students, this doesn't seem to be an effective strategy. ESL writers who can't successfully edit "by ear" aren't proficient enough in English to have a "feel" for what is correct and what isn't. It follows that those with higher levels of proficiency will have more success with reading aloud, but even the most proficient aren't likely to display native-speaker-like intuitions. Therefore, some recourse to more mechanical rule-based proofreading strategies or to outside help, such as a native speaker reader, will probably be necessary.

Adding Resources: What Are Useful Readings for Tutors?

Since many tutors and directors would like to better prepare themselves to work with ESL students but have limited time to spend, we will limit our suggestions for further reading to a small fraction of the abundant literature produced in recent years on ESL writing and ESL writers. The resources described in this section were chosen on the basis of their timeliness, breadth, and accessibility.

The first resources are book-length treatments of issues in ESL writing and writing instruction. One is Ilona Leki's, *Understanding ESL Writers: A Guide for Teachers.* This introductory book addresses the history of ESL writing instruction, relevant models of second language acquisition, differences between basic writers and ESL writers, personal characteristics of ESL writers, ESL writers' expectations, writing behaviors, and composing processes, contrastive rhetoric, common sentence level errors, and responding to ESL writing. The second is Joy M. Reid's *Teaching ESL Writing.* This work deals with the special problems and concerns that distinguish first and second language writing instruction, addressing in particular the variables of language and cultural background, prior education, gender, age, and language proficiency. Reid also provides an overview of different ESL composition teaching methodologies and offers specific information on developing curricula, syllabi and lesson plans for basic, intermediate, and advanced ESL writing classes. Also useful are two collections covering a broad range of issues in ESL writing. The first is Barbara Kroll's *Second Language Writing: Research Insights for the Classroom,* which contains thirteen papers in two major sections. The papers in the first section address theories of L2 writing and provide overviews of research in a number of basic areas of ESL composition. The second section is comprised of reports of empirical research on current issues in L2 writing instruction. The second collection, Donna M. Johnson and Duane H. Roen's *Richness in Writing: Empowering ESL Students,* includes eighteen papers in three sections which deal respectively with contexts for ESL writing, specific rhetorical concerns of L2 writers, and cultural issues in the writing of ESL students.

Two additional resources are the *Journal of Second Language Writing,* a scholarly journal which publishes reports of research and discussions of issues in second and foreign language writing and writing instruction, and *Resources for CCCC Members Who Want to Learn about Writing in English as a Second Language,* a fact sheet of information about professional organizations, conferences, publications, and educational and employment opportunities for those interested in working with ESL writers. (For a copy of the *Resources* fact sheet, write to Tony Silva, Chair, CCCC Committee on ESL, Department of English, Heavilon Hall, Purdue University, West Lafayette, Indiana 47907-1356.)

Conclusion

ESL instructors and writing center people need to keep interacting with and learning from each other. We each have insights, methods, research, and experiences to share. For those of us in writing centers, it's useful to know that writing center tutors can draw on both research and language teaching approaches used in ESL classrooms. Writing center directors can share with ESL teachers one-to-one pedagogies that work in the writing center as well as our perceptions of how individual differences interact with various classroom pedagogies on different students. We can also share our awareness of the kinds of questions students really ask, our first-hand observations of how students cope with writing assignments and teacher responses, and our encounters with non-native differences that interfere with learning how to write in American classrooms. Such information can only serve to illuminate the work of ESL teachers. Similarly, insights from ESL writing theory, research, and practice can help writing centers, and mainstream composition in general, to deal effectively with their increasingly multilingual and multicultural student populations.

Works Cited

Brown, H. Douglas. *Principles of Language Learning and Teaching.* 2nd ed. Englewood Cliffs: Prentice, 1987.

CCCC Committee on ESL. *Resources for CCCC Members Who Want to Learn about Writing in English as a Second Language (ESL).* Urbana: NCTE, 1992.

Grabe, William, and Robert B. Kaplan. "Writing in a Second Language: Contrastive Rhetoric." *Richness in Writing: Empowering ESL Students.* Ed. Donna Johnson and Duane Roen. New York: Longman, 1989. 263–83.

Hall, Edward. *The Silent Language.* New York: Doubleday, 1959.

Johnson, Donna M., and Duane H. Roen, eds. *Richness in Writing: Empowering ESL Students.* New York: Longman, 1989.

Kilborn, Judith. "Tutoring ESL Students: Addressing Differences in Cultural Schemata and Rhetorical Patterns in Reading and Writing." Minnesota, TESOL Conference. St. Paul, 2 May 1992.

Kroll, Barbara. "The Rhetoric and Syntax Split: Designing a Curriculum for ESL Students." *Journal of Basic Writing* 9 (Spring 1990): 40–45.

———, ed. *Second Language Writing: Research Insights for the Classroom.* New York: Cambridge UP, 1990.

Leki, Ilona. "Twenty-Five Years of Contrastive Rhetoric: Text Analysis and Writing Pedagogies." *TESOL Quarterly* 25 (Spring 1991): 123–43.

———. *Understanding ESL Writers: A Guide for Teachers.* Portsmouth: Boynton, 1992.

North, Stephen. "The Idea of a Writing Center." *College English* 46 (Sep. 1984): 433–46.

Raimes, Ann. *Grammar Troublespots: An Editing Guide for Students.* 2nd ed. New York: St. Martin's, 1992.

Reid, Joy M. *Teaching ESL Writing.* Englewood Cliffs: Regents, 1993.

Silva, Tony. "Differences in ESL and Native Speaker Writing." *Writing in Multicultural Settings.* Ed. Johnnella Butler, Juan Guerra, and Carol Severino. New York: MLA, 1997.

Harris and Silva's Insights as a Resource for Your Teaching

1. Harris and Silva's advice that ESL tutors distinguish global errors from local errors is also a rule of thumb for writing teachers. The authors remind us that many ESL students have a product-centered introduction to writing in English and assume "correctness" will be the writing teacher's first criterion for evaluation. Emphasize in your comments on drafts or in your conferences with ESL writers that your first concern is with the message and that you will focus primarily on errors that impede you in understanding what the writer wants to say. Remind them that, as they revise for ideas and structure, some of their global errors will disappear. Remind them to separate revising (rhetorical concerns) from editing (linguistic concerns).

2. Early in the semester, invite all your students to write you letters describing their histories as writers and learners and detailing anything you need to know about them to work with them as writers. In conferences with individual writers, use your reading of and response to an early writing assignment, journal entries, and the letter to initiate a conversation about the ESL student's writing experiences and about his or her confidence and fluency in spoken and written English. Anticipate that some ESL students — perhaps because of their fluency level or lack of proficiency with basic communication skills in English or perhaps because of cultural communication patterns — will need to become comfortable with one-to-one conferences. They may not articulate their concerns and questions clearly in a first conference or may send verbal and nonverbal messages that they comprehend what you say when in fact they don't. Anticipate that some students will be silent in classroom discussions because they fear speaking incorrectly or they lack cognitive readiness.

Harris and Silva's Insights as a Resource for the Writing Classroom

1. Both ESL students and students with learning disabilities benefit from work that emphasizes planning, pacing of activities, and writing in stages. Guide students through various heuristics in class and in double-entry journals to help them acquire or refine skills in planning texts. (The scaffolding exercise described in the next article is a particularly useful heuristic.) Invite all writers to submit drafts in stages: a discovery draft, a draft focused on ideas and organization, a draft revised to attend to audience, and a draft revised for linguistic concerns. (Many ESL students, most students with learning disabilities, some apprehensive students, and some inexperienced writers will respond to the opportunity.) Set up deadlines, and write up your reader's response and "needs" for the first two drafts. Draft three should go to peer critics; draft four may be shared with peer tutors in your writing centers. Direct writers to submit all drafts along with the "finished" text, so you can comment on their drafting and revising process.

2. Collaborative activities are high-risk experiences for some ESL students and familiar experiences for others. To introduce small-group discussions or projects and peer critique, ask class members to write a three-minute letter about their expectations for and fears about working collaboratively. Merge the letters and make a handout for large-group discussion. Ask the class to agree on some shared responsibilities for collaborative activities. On self-assessment protocols afterward, ask students to evaluate how well these responsibilities were met. (Return the letter and protocols and ask students to keep them to use in conferences when they assess their work in groups later in the semester.)

CARYL K. SILLS   *Success for Learning-Disabled Writers across the Curriculum*

In this article from the useful journal College Teaching, *Caryl K. Sills draws on her expertise as a writing teacher and director of a writing program to advise colleagues across the curriculum in their work with writers with learning disabilities. She offers specific and practical strategies for assisting these writers with the same processes that all writers engage in. She indicates that all students can at some point profit from the methods and attitudes that she has identified: "more learning and teaching time, pacing, encouragement from the teacher, and a positive self-concept." Her list of works cited provides a quick entry into the research and the conversation about working with writers with learning disabilities.*

Despite major gains in identifying and helping students with learning disabilities, the disorder remains inadequately defined. Consequently, some students are labeled perceptually impaired and are thus entitled to support services, while others are dismissed as low achievers and denied the same considerations (Wilczenski and Gillespie-Silver 202). Certainly low achievement can be the result of family, motivational, and other psychological variables, but neurological or physiological deficiencies may also be contributing to the student's poor academic performance (Berninger, Mizokawa, and Bragg 69).

It is this latter explanation that I intend to explore in order to help professors across the curriculum promote success in writing for their students. Teachers must become aware that among the variables related to learning, the following are relevant to improving writing skills: more learning and teaching time, pacing, encouragement from the teacher, and a positive self-concept (Leinhardt and Pallay 572). In other words, although most identified learning-disabled students are provided some form of counseling and tutoring, they, like any student, are most likely to succeed in a supportive classroom. There are methods and attitudes by which we can help all low-achieving students to realize their full academic potential.

In fact, these strategies can be useful to all students at some time or another.

What Is a Learning Disability?

Parents and teachers have recognized for a long time that some students are slow learners despite their apparent intelligence and willingness to work hard (Berninger, Hart, Abbott, and Karovsky 104). In fact, a study of college academic performance reported by Wilczenski and Gillespie-Silver found "no statistically significant differences in college GPA for students identified as learning disabled and students identified as not learning disabled" (199). However, despite average or above average intellectual ability, students with a perceptual impairment have varying degrees of difficulty in receiving and/or expressing information. The problem is usually a result of a permanent central nervous system dysfunction that causes the learner to receive inaccurate information through his or her senses and then to have trouble processing that information (Farnham-Diggory 175). Nevertheless, many students with learning disabilities succeed despite this dysfunction, most probably with the help of patient and dedicated teachers and counselors.

In the majority of cases, students with learning problems display weaknesses in reading and writing. Sometimes, but not always, they also have trouble with speech. "Such disorders have been recognized medically for a long time, and are termed dyslexia (referring to reading), dysgraphia (writing and spelling), and aphasia (understanding and producing speech)" (90).

Even though they have been identified as learning disabled, some students will be unwilling to admit their condition to the instructor. Others appear to be unaware that their problems with writing similarly plague other writers. Both categories of weak writers are unaware or unconvinced that specific strategies and accommodations offered by specialists in learning disabilities can help them.

Privacy laws do not allow us to take the most direct route and ask a student if he or she is disabled. However, we might inquire indirectly by saying, "Do you often have a problem when you have to write under pressure? Have you received special tutoring in the past? Has spelling always been a problem for you?" (Vacchiano). If asked in a supportive manner, these kinds of questions can lead the student to appreciate the type of help available, including diagnostic procedures.

Available services vary widely among colleges, but even if they are limited for the learning disabled at your institution, there are sound strategies that you can use. These will focus on the symptoms of the problem (poor spelling, poor organization, unfinished work, discontinuities). Although the following strategies and accommodations were designed by learning disabilities specialists, every unskilled writer will benefit from them.

Estimates of people with learning disabilities "range from 10 to 15 percent of the population" (Berninger, Hart, Abbott, and Karovsky 110). In addition to perceptual difficulties, these people often have poor self-esteem, are easily frustrated, have poor study/note-taking skills, are anxious about tests, and lack social skills. In addition, students with dysgraphia, by the time they enter college, have become overanxious about any writing assignment because of their early frustration with the production of alphabet letters. This apprehension can usually be traced to their difficulty in grammar school in integrating visual and fine-motor functions to produce written words (Berninger, Mizokawa, and Bragg 61, 64). Thus, at the most visible level, handwriting becomes an impediment to communication (spacing between words and letters may be inconsistent: writing may have an extreme up or down slant on an unlined page).

Also, some students may have difficulty with phonological codes (such as writing *reson* for *reason* or *diffrent* for *different*) or orthographic codes that guide letter formation and the ordering of letter clusters into words. Spelling thus becomes tangled, with letter transpositions (*aminal* for *animal*) or dropped endings (*an* for *and* or leaving off *ed* or *s*) or word substitution (*were* for *where* or *bell* for *ball*). Other errors include omission of low information load words, such as auxiliaries, modals, prepositions, pronouns, or conjunctions; distorted word order; lack of punctuation; limited word choice; and problems using multiple meanings of words. The result is that even though some students have oral fluency, their writing is characterized by immature simplicity.

It is important to note that many ESOL students may also have these writing problems, and teachers should not jump to conclusions that they may be learning disabled.

Another area of weakness for students with a writing deficiency is at the sentence level. When given a sentence combining exercise with nongrammatical guiding cues, most basic writers do fine. For example, students might be asked to combine the following four simple sentences into a single complex sentence using the guiding cues in the parentheses:

> You got beyond those pious utterances about his concern for the weak and oppressed. *(WHEN)* You realized *(SOMETHING)*. He was quite simply an egomaniac. *(THAT)* He had no other concern but his own selfish ambition. (Gregg 337)

Nevertheless, even with these cues, learning-disabled writers will have difficulty combining the simple sentences so that they make sense (334).

Finally, writers with a physiological or neurological deficiency are also weak in planning, translating, and revising a piece of writing (Berninger, Mizokawa, and Bragg 66). For example, they will likely have difficulty ordering their random thoughts in freewriting and putting ideas into sequence. Such writers may also have trouble identifying the connections between ideas, such as cause-result relationships or oppositions. When revising and editing, they often cannot recognize irrelevant information or where omissions disrupt the logic of an argument.

Difficulties with writing do not necessarily mean that the student will also have problems with math or computer science. Nevertheless, writing ability is a basic skill important in all disciplines; therefore, specific deficiencies that characterize a physiologically or neurologically based learning disability are important to recognize.

In other words, a person with perceptual impairment will have unusual difficulty with some academic tasks, but not others. In this way, we know that the individual has a learning disability as opposed to general retardation (Farnham-Diggory 90). In blunt words, most students with writing weaknesses are not unintelligent, and they can learn to overcome their poor performance.

According to Public Law 94-142 (and its recent update, PL 99-457), a learning disability is a "disorder in one or more of the basic psychological processes involved in understanding or using language, spoken or written, which may manifest itself in an imperfect ability to listen, think, speak, read, write, spell, or do mathematical calculations" (Berninger, Mizokawa, and Bragg 57). Although PL 94-142 does not pertain to colleges and universities, another federal law does: the Rehabilitation Act of 1973. Section 504 of this act specifies that institutions, including colleges and universities, must make reasonable accommodations for handicapped students (Farnham-Diggory 101).

It is worth remembering that providing reasonable accommodations does not mean changing or lowering performance standards on the basis of the student's disability. We would probably all agree that a student with extremely weak vision should be allowed to sit close to the blackboard or have access to a computer monitor with large print capability. Accommodations for students with a learning dysfunction are no less reasonable and necessary, such as support services that include tutoring, personal counseling and advising, as well as special arrangements for test taking (such as privacy, an extended time limit, or a reader).

Nevertheless, in addition to institutional support services, there is a great deal individual teachers can do in the classroom.

Promoting Success for All Writers

Extra Effort for Clear Communication

Learners can be classified as visual, auditory, and kinesthetic. Some of us need to see in writing exactly what we are expected to do; others need to hear and then vocalize instructions, and some need to add a physical expression such as gestures, writing down or assembling parts of an assignment, moving into a small group, or working on a computer or at a chalkboard. Making assignments and conducting class discussions that accommodate all three perceptions are the surest ways to reach every student. For example, visual learners need written assignments even when class time is devoted to oral instructions and explanations. Also, important points covered in class discussions can be visually reinforced by printing the information on the board or typing it onto a computer display.

For auditory learners, the instructor or a student can read assignments aloud and prompt discussion of each aspect. Instructors can emphasize vital points through repetition or by simply saying, "this is important." Finally, each class session should include some physical relief for kinesthetic learners, as they can have difficulty concentrating if required to sit in one place for an hour or more. In fact, several short activities during each class hour, rather than a single long activity, can help students focus more effectively and better retain what they have learned.

In addition, teachers can ask individual students to state their understanding of an assignment in order to check their comprehension. This is helpful for all class members when done in whole class discussion, but for students with learning impediments it is essential. Also, teachers should be available outside of class for additional questions. Correcting misperceptions up-front saves both student and instructor from weakly focused or vague writing.

Teachers in every discipline can help students understand reading material by providing a reading guide and by modeling close-reading techniques, such as annotating text or outlining major points. If a written response to the reading is assigned, the students and instructor can together design a proofreading checklist. These simple aids can help students with weak reading or writing skills become better prepared to discuss reading assignments and then to respond intelligently in writing.

Students who read with difficulty need written comments on their writing assignments or essay examinations in printed letters rather than cursive writing (and need to be told to provide adequate margins so that comments can be close to the text in question). It is not always possible to go over all papers with students individually. However, on the day a written assignment or examination is returned, the teacher can arrange to talk individually with students. Another tactic is not to put a grade on a very poor paper and to require the student to discuss revisions later, in your office. During individual consultations, it is helpful to encourage students to work with tutors available in a writing center.

Writing Mechanics

Handicapped writers have difficulty writing logically and conforming to standard English grammar, syntax, and spelling. However, strategies that work with unskilled writers are also effective for disabled students. The following exercises work well with whole class, small group, or individual instruction.

Although many fine writers are atrocious spellers, perceptually impaired writers often spell words differently within the same paper or copy quoted material inaccurately. Simple memorization of spelling rules will rarely help this situation. Instead, writers need to work with spelling programs that emphasize word families or structural spelling patterns, such as word anagram exercises, which ask the student to unscramble letters to create correctly spelled words (Berninger, Mizokawa, and Bragg 71).

When students spell words incorrectly, circle the error but do not correct it; require the student to look up the correct spelling in a dictionary and revise the paper accordingly. All students, but especially chronic misspellers, can benefit from keeping a list of terms that appear frequently in course readings or that the instructor uses, including the correct spelling of any variations (*physiology, physiological*) as well as brief definitions. They should be encouraged to use this list whenever they write.

At the sentence level, students can do exercises that combine sentences or that ask them to unscramble words or add words to a base phrase to form a good sentence. These sentence-combining exercises help develop innate language skills of native English speakers, but they are skills that perceptually handicapped writers may not be able to achieve without instruction and practice. Sentence combining enriches vocabulary at the same time that it reinforces knowledge and control of sentence structures (Gregg 336).

Coherence

Mina Shaughnessy cautioned us some time ago that "some writers, inhibited by their fear of error, produce but a few lines an hour or keep trying to begin, crossing out one try after another until the sentence is hopelessly tangled" (7). How aptly this describes students with a writing deficiency who, having once achieved "correctness" in writing simple sentences, are afraid to try other forms. The above exercises can set these students free.

Teachers might also try paragraph anagrams on course content to focus on the ties that link ideas. For example, writers can unscramble sentences to form a logical paragraph. Another activity is drawing arrows from any word or phrase in a sentence that refers to a previous word or phrase to demonstrate how ideas are connected by grammatical repetitions or transformations (Berninger, Mizokawa, and Bragg 72).

A more difficult problem in achieving coherence is explained by Mike Rose: if students can't structure an essay or take a story apart in the way most of us educated in the United States have been trained to do, their difficulties may be related more to immaturity and inexperience than to their inability to structure or analyze whatever experience is available (275). Such a viewpoint implies that instruction and experience can help writers "see" their own or others' writing as a set of integrated units that make sense best when combined in one way as opposed to others.

For many college students, this may be true. However, for learning-disabled writers, the opposite is often true: some deficit in their ability to structure experience is the cause of their inability to achieve coherence. For example, the writer's thoughts may wander, or be incomplete, or out of sequence. Therefore, specific strategies to help develop a writer's ability to perceive and then produce coherence should focus on ways to plan and organize a particular piece of writing.

Planning and Organizing

We traditionally encourage writers to generate ideas by brainstorming or freewriting and then to organize the information in some form of outline that may vary from a brief scratch outline of phrases to a formal presentation in sentence form. However, people who perceive best auditorily will benefit from taping their ideas and then transcribing the spoken words into writing by replaying small portions of it. "This approach frees the [student] to focus on written spelling, capitalization, and punctuation without the added burden of generating ideas and organization simultaneously" (Berninger, Mizokawa, and Bragg 72).

Nevertheless, once ideas have been generated, they must be logically ordered. It is often helpful to write each outline point on a separate file card that can be moved about to try out different patterns. The cards should then be numbered for reference as the writer drafts the paper. Students should also choose from a list of transitions to express appropriate relationships between their ideas (and eventually paragraphs).

Of course, this approach is unsuited to essay examinations or in-class writings that are limited to one or more class periods. However, Richard H. Haswell proposes that the few logical structures that appear in "lean" in-class writings can be diagrammed. While the writers continue developing these or related ideas in informal writing, the diagram can serve as a plan for a more fully elaborated piece of writing (312). Giving writers time to consider alternatives within a supportive environment, where the instructor's comments and encouragement are freely offered, can make a world of difference in the students' understanding and in their ability to write coherently.

Nevertheless, "unless students are trained in the thinking strategies that underlie expository composition . . . writing instruction alone may not ensure LD students' writing independence" (Englert et al. 365). On the basis of a study reported in 1991, Carol Englert and a team of researchers at Michigan State University recommend that teachers model these thinking strategies through "classroom dialogues that focus upon the writer's inner thinking and the writing process" (338).

We need to provide models of appropriate text structures to help students organize their thoughts. For example, if the paper assignment asks students to compare and contrast, instructors can demonstrate how to set up a comparison/contrast grid; if the paper asks students to show an understanding of a particular cause/effect relationship, teachers can diagram various possibilities (using arrows or tree diagrams) of how a single cause can generate diverse results or how a particular result can be traced back to multiple causes. Such models offer sequential steps for students to follow, and when students use these structures in small groups to help focus each other's plans, writing is transformed from a solitary to a social activity, which often increases potential for success.

Englert et al. also suggest that effective preparation for writing should include scaffolding techniques to support the learners' development of new skills and abilities (339). A scaffold is a writing instruction tool that holds the task constant while adjusting the nature of students' participation through graduated assistance. For example, teachers can scaffold a writing task by asking a series of graduated questions to guide students to appropriate conclusions. The following questions can help students link and integrate separate ideas in order to understand the psychological dimensions of altruism: What is helping behavior? Can you think of two or three real or hypothetical examples of helping behavior? What is the negative state relief model? How does it explain altruistic behavior? What is the empathy-altruism model? How does it explain altruism? Are the two theories mutually exclusive? Why or why not?

Revising

For surface revision, learning-disabled writers must reread their writing several times, each time with a specific game plan. For example, the first proofing can focus on content; the next on organization, forms of sentences and links; and finally on spelling, capitalization, and punctuation. Students with a writing deficiency often benefit from keeping a list of their own most commonly misspelled words and referring to it during the proofreading stage of every piece of writing.

SCAN is an acronym for a global-level proofreading exercise that focuses on the overall coherence and clarity of the piece of writing. Instructors can encourage students to use SCAN before they hand in an essay exam or the final draft of a paper. It includes the following questions, which students ask themselves one at a time while rereading each sentence.

S = does it make sense?

C = is it connected?

A = can I add more?

N = do I note errors?

Another technique for developing detection and correction skills is guided or précis composition that requires students to manipulate prewritten material while keeping a sense of essay structure. This kind of controlled composition demands accuracy in both transcription and manipulation, and therefore focuses the students' attention on correct spelling and sentence structure (Gregg 336). Using texts for guided composition that contribute to the students' knowledge and understanding of the content of a particular course offers an obvious double benefit.

Peer feedback is just as important for writers with a learning disability as it is for the rest of us. Honest efforts to improve one's writing skills are respected by most other students, and those with learning deficiencies are usually positively motivated by their peers.

Finally, although some writers on learning disabilities have recommended the teaching of a few strategies sequentially and thoroughly in order to improve students' writing, rather than presenting simultaneously the multiple components of the process, Englert et al. found that an integrated approach to instruction is as effective with learning-disabled writers as with able writers (364–65). In other words, writers need to attend to both the local and global aspects of writing to ensure that their intended meaning is clear and unobstructed by mistakes in spelling, grammar, punctuation, or word choice.

Confident Writing in Class

Most learning disabilities programs allow untimed test-taking in a relatively stress-free environment. Even without this official accommodation, we can structure an environment for student success.

What I do in my composition classes, at all levels, can be helpful to student writers in a test situation in any course. For example, students are given material to read in advance, and we discuss the material. I encourage my students to suggest questions for the test, and we also discuss possible responses. The practice in writing and in using analytical strategies helps them in the actual test. In a basic writing class, I will often read the questions aloud with them to clarify what is being asked and what is expected in their response (thus, again, reinforcing the visual with an auditory supplement). Because of the advance preparation, all of the students have something worthwhile to say, and because we discuss possible questions and how to respond, most students can plan and reorganize their essay quickly, and have ample time to draft and edit their writing.

It is essential that students understand what various direction words mean, such as *analyze, compare, criticize, define, discuss, evaluate, prove,* and *summarize.* Providing a concise explanation of what the students are being asked to do is the surest way to promote their success in doing it. For example, instead of just asking them to criticize a theory or incident, instruct them to "give your judgment of both good points and limitations and provide evidence for each."

I teach in a computer lab that has a separate, traditional seating area. This has been especially helpful for my learning disabled students. For in-class writing assignments, students choose whether or not to write on the computer. I encourage dyslexic students to learn touch typing and take advantage of word processing with style and spell checkers. Sylvia Farnham-Diggory explains the advantages as follows:

> Their fingers can be trained to spell automatically. That is, fingers can be trained to bypass the letter sound correspondence disconnections and snarls that plague dyslexics. For this to happen, the visual-motor letter patterns must become automated. As automaticity (Mrs. King calls it "motor memory") is established, the student's writing almost miraculously improves. (107–08)

For those who are still more comfortable writing longhand, I provide an on-line dictionary/thesaurus on the instructor's computer and allow hand-held spelling/style checkers. Students are also encouraged to consult a proofreading guide we have developed together for the particular assignment. There is a small anteroom just outside the computer lab for students who need a more quiet space. When possible, I also offer learning impaired students extra time to complete an in-class assignment or send them to the Writing Center to finish the assignment under supervision. Therefore, although I cannot offer a totally untimed in-class writing — because of the logistics as well as the necessity for college students eventually to learn to cope with timed tests — I can remove some of the stress.

Students' Stories

What is it like to be learning disabled? Try the following: read and summarize an article printed in 8-point, or smaller type which looks like this; copy a passage that reads: *sdrawkcab.* Now listen to how two of my students in a basic writing course described the process of writing encumbered by a learning disability:

> *Jill:* In the third grade I was identified as having a learning disability. For reading and math I would go to a special classroom, and some of the other kids

would make fun of me. I hated going to that room. . . . My high school teachers gave me very easy work so I was sure to pass and graduate. I liked getting away with all of that in high school, but not now. Since high school set me aside and let me squeak by, I did not learn enough. Now I am so glad to be at college, but at the same time I do not think that I can do it.

Martin: I have always had a difficult time with my education, which has made it far from enjoyable. When I was in forth [sic] grade I was diagnosed with dyslexia. This meant that I needed special attention when doing my work. I began working in a resource room with a tutor. . . . The tutoring did help, but I had to get up and leave the class to get to the tutor. This subjected me to other students pointing and whispering. This made me embarrassed and I hated having to get up to leave. Lunch time was even worse. I had to listen to other kids call me nasty names like stupid. . . . My teachers never gave me any work that required much thinking and I seemingly drifted through high school. . . . My education has been an uphill struggle all the way. Basically it's been disappointing and has had few rewards.

Both of these students are now struggling with college-level writing and succeeding, but it takes a lot of determination and the ability to turn obstacles into challenges.

Joe's story is also typical. Joe is learning disabled and has transferred from a community college where he had performed adequately. He received transfer credit for both semesters of College English under an articulation agreement, although he was well aware of his weaknesses in composition. His junior year at Monmouth he got a C- and a D in the two-semester World Masterpiece requirement, and he failed the writing proficiency examination. In courses other than English, Joe did reasonably well: he got a C+ in Critical Discourse (oral argumentation) and some Bs and a few As (Business Statistics) in his business major. His GPA at the end of his junior year was 2.561.

Even more significant for Joe is that he passed the writing proficiency examination on the second try — but not without a lot of hard work. Joe took my one-credit Writing Reasoned Arguments course, which gives supplemental practice. Joe had a very hard time in the course, and I suggested that he take an Incomplete and work for an additional semester with a writing tutor. He did, and took the dreaded writing proficiency examination after he had completed the requirements I had set for him. Joe's success is typical because it illustrates the amount of instruction and hard work that many learning-disabled students are willing to undertake in order to achieve their full potential.

When we understand the challenges faced by writers with learning deficiencies and the possible accommodations for their disability, we will be better prepared to help learning-disabled writers to succeed. As Englert et al. conclude:

With repeated instruction and practice in the successive text structures, students [with learning disabilities] gradually internalized the strategies and self-talk modeled by teachers. On this basis, it seems that the writing process need not be decomposed or reduced to a sequential set of strategies that are learned and practiced in isolation. With the proper degree of instructional scaffolding (e.g., teachers' dialogue and procedural facilitation), the writing process can be held constant while adjusting the nature of students' participation through graduated assistance. (368–69)

Finally, I hope to have demonstrated that caring intervention in the processes of planning, writing, and editing/proofreading a piece of writing can result in significant improvement. Most important, we need not lower standards or look the other way in order for these students to succeed in our composition courses or in any others that require writing. Providing accommodations and instruction for the needs of writers with a learning dysfunction will allow them to meet the standards set for our regular students, even if it takes them a little longer. Success is its own best motivation.

Works Cited

Berninger, V. W., D. T. Mizokawa, and R. Bragg. "Theory-Based Diagnosis and Remediation of Writing Disabilities." *Journal of School Psychology* 29(1991): 57–79.

Berninger, V. W., T. Hart, R. A. Abbott and P. Karovsky. "Defining Reading and Writing Disabilities with and without IQ: A Flexible, Developmental Perspective." *Learning Disabled Journal* 15(1992): 103–18.

Englert, C. S., T. E. Raphael, I. M. Anderson, H. M. Anthony, and D. D. Stevens. "Making Strategies and Self-Talk Visible: Writing Instruction in Regular and Special Education Classrooms." *American Educational Research Journal* 28(1991): 337–72.

Farnham-Diggory, S. *The Learning Disabled Child.* Cambridge: Harvard UP, 1992.

Gregg, N. "College Learning Disabled Writers: Error Patterns and Instructional Alternatives." *Journal of Learning Disabilities* 6(1983): 334–38.

Haswell, R. H. "Dark Shadows: The Fate of Writers at the Bottom." *College Composition and Communication* 39(1988): 303–15.

Leinhardt, G., and A. Pallay. "Restrictive Educational Settings: Exile or Haven?" *Review of Educational Research* 2(1982): 557–78.

Rose, M. "Narrowing the Mind and Page: Remedial Writers and Cognitive Reductionism." *College Composition and Communication* 39(1988): 267–302.

Shaughnessy, M. P. *Errors and Expectations.* New York: Oxford UP, 1977.

Vacchiano, J. "Monmouth College English Department Policy on Learning Disabled." West Long Branch, NJ, 1988.

Wilczenski, F. L., and P. Gillespie-Silver. "Challenging the Norm: Academic Performance of University Students with Learning Disabilities." *Journal of Student Development* 33(1992): 197–202.

Sills's Insights as a Resource for Your Teaching

1. Find out if your campus resources (writing center, reading lab, etc.) include tutorial services or developmental courses for basic writers, ESL students, and students with learning disabilities. Often, consultants in these programs can work with students for whom faculty have designed individualized instruction to assist students to spend more "time on task." These consultants can also supplement the one-on-one conferences you might hold with writers with learning disabilities.

2. Sills quotes two students who describe the long-term effects of being "special" students. Both struggle to achieve a positive self-concept and to catch up on learning that was not made accessible to them. Some students with learning disabilities will hesitate to tell you they need "reasonable accommodations." Early on, ask all students to write you letters in which they relate their histories as writers and learners. Prompt them to detail anything that you need to know to work with them individually: Are any of them working full-time? Apprehensive about writing? "Nontraditional" students? Follow up with a conference in which you discuss an early in-class writing, the writer's history, and class events. The encouragement and comfort level you build with these activities enables many students to work more confidently and successfully.

3. The teaching strategies suggested by Sills are routinely shared in writing-across-the-curriculum workshops and are central to writing classrooms: delivering assignments in three modes to accommodate student learning styles; organizing collaborative activities and peer critique sessions; holding conferences with individual students about their writing and learning experi-

ences; structuring preparation for timed writing or test-taking; writing prompts that cue students to the cognitive task and to your expectations of scope or coverage; and providing access to word-processing. Using these ideas, write a "teaching strategies inventory" that you can use for self-evaluation. Set one goal per strategy, and assess your achievement through student evaluations and reflection in your dialectical journal.

Sills's Insights as a Resource for the Writing Classroom

1. Experiment with a scaffolding technique to prompt a discovery draft. Invite students to discuss possible readings from *The Bedford Guide for College Writers* and to negotiate on one reading for use in an essay-exam simulation. Use an overhead transparency or a computer display to show students a series of writing prompts used for essay exams in a variety of courses. Ask students to discuss how they "decode" each prompt and to explain what, minimally, they would do in an essay-exam situation to satisfy each prompt. Indicate that they will spend the next class in guided prewriting. Organize a series of graduated questions (a scaffolding) that guides them to a broader question that calls for analysis and evaluation. Conduct the essay-exam simulation with a prompt that requires analysis and evaluation. Distribute a self-assessment protocol in which writers describe their process of writing to the prompt: what they perceive as strengths, what they might do with the essay had they more time, and what they learned about writing on demand. Grade the paper as an essay exam with a focus on whether and how well the writer analyzed and evaluated the substance of the reading. Return the graded essays with a description of what traits differentiated an A from a B, a B from a C, and so on. The grade is information only — unless the student decides to use it in a portfolio or negotiates with you for credit.

SUZANNE CLARK *Review: Women, Rhetoric, Teaching*

The phrases "feminist theory" and "feminist composition" refer to issues that have been problematized over the last twenty-five years to such a degree that many cite "feminist composition" as a subfield in the discipline of composition studies. Discussion of the "feminization of composition" comprises many issues, such as gender-inclusive language, gendered rhetoric, and "women's ways" of knowing (Mary Belenky and others on cognitive development of voice, self, and identity); of valuing (Carol Gilligan on moral development); of discourse (Gesa E. Kirsch on women's academic writing); and of teaching.

In a careful review of five recent texts, Suzanne Clark provides an overview of current discussion of feminism and rhetoric, tensions between feminist pedagogy and critical pedagogy, and the emerging visibility of women's work and leadership in composition and rhetoric.

Kirsch, Gesa E. *Women Writing the Academy: Audience, Authority, and Transformation.* Foreword by John Trimbur. Carbondale: Southern Illinois UP, 1993. 168 pp. $12.95 (paper).

Larrabee, Mary Jeanne, ed. *An Ethic of Care: Feminist and Interdisciplinary Perspectives.* New York: Routledge, 1992. 288 pp. $49.95 (cloth); $16.95 (paper).

Luke, Carmen, and Jennifer Gore. *Feminisms and Critical Pedagogy.* Foreword by Maxine Greene. New York: Routledge, 1992. 224 pp. $49.95 (cloth); $15.95 (paper).

Phelps, Louise Wetherbee and Janet Emig, ed. *Feminine Principles and Women's Experience in American Composition and Rhetoric.* Pittsburgh: U of Pittsburgh P, 1995. 424 pp. $59.95 (cloth); $22.95 (paper).

Singley, Carol J., and Susan Elizabeth Sweeney. *Anxious Power: Reading, Writing, and Ambivalence in Narrative by Women.* Albany: State U of New York P, 1993. 256 pp. $49.50 (cloth); $16.95 (paper).

Feminist theory has become in the last two decades a complex, even difficult, subject. What is a useful approach for feminist teachers of rhetoric and composition? It is not an easy question to answer. Until very recently, the field of rhetoric and composition has had more women within it — and less conscious discussion about the feminine (and feminism) — than other disciplines of the humanities or of social sciences. The books I am reviewing here address this gap, but they have important methodological differences, with much at stake for the classroom. Although all share the desire to see how gender affects knowledge, the stance various editors and authors take and their degree of critical awareness varies considerably. Do women have any special or privileged knowledge about teaching? Isn't there something blindly self-serving about such an argument? On the other hand, rhetoric has been a notoriously misogynist discipline. Exposing the gendering in rhetoric might enable men as well as women teachers to question the chief methodology of the classroom, which is rhetorical inquiry. Teaching is, after all — like writing — a language art.

Not all of these books foreground rhetoric as a method of inquiry, however. The figure of a caring responsive mother/teacher emerges as a model in three of these works, which valorize experience and relationship as if they were, to use the terms Louise Wetherbee Phelps and Janet Emig provide, "feminine principles." There are recognizable affinities here with a social science tradition of women's studies, with the set of gendered approaches identified by Mary Belenky and her associates as "women's ways of knowing," and with the gendered ethics defined by Carol Gilligan, a tradition explored in *The Ethic of Care.* Gesa Kirsch makes the writing practices of academic women the object of her study, suggesting the possibility that their pedagogy (more "connective") and their writing (more personal) might reflect such feminine principles. She does not, perhaps, emphasize enough the implication: that a study of rhetoric and gender needs to inform the thinking of other disciplines too — that the way women write and speak about their research might produce a different knowledge.

Feminists, however, are not in agreement about this. Do the conventions and associations of present-day American culture necessarily represent enduring or generalizable gender differences? Is it helpful to the teaching of writing to find out? Feminism has always worked at some level not as a maternal but as a critical discourse, doubling other discourses; to speak as woman is not to speak as an ungendered, unproblematic subject. Carmen Luke and Jennifer Gore, in *Feminisms and Critical Pedagogy,* use the leverage provided by feminist viewpoints to unsettle what they see as a troubling dogmatism in the developments of the critical pedagogy movements. In a book on women's narratives that also emphasizes the unsettling aspect of the feminine, *Anxious Power,* Carol Singley and Susan E. Sweeney theorize that women's literacy includes not only "reading and writing" but also "ambivalence." Although this book might seem more concerned with literary texts, I include it here because it clearly illustrates how a study of women's writing pushes the boundaries of literature to include all writing, and because it provides an examination of narrative and gender that could be very helpful in rhetoric and composition classrooms. But the fact that feminism has only recently appeared in rhetoric and composition, and that a field which at some levels is dominated by women is so late in taking up their cause raises important questions about the relationship of theory and practice — and may account for the complexity of the feminisms appearing in this field.

What kind of influence upon a discipline does the practice of teaching exert? The answer to this question is of special importance to the women in rhetoric and composition. First, this is because the field of composition studies has been defined in the decades since the 1960s, growing as programs in writing have grown, and staffed by a female majority, mostly of exploited, underpaid workers. Those who claim that experience and practice ought to be the sources of our disciplinary knowledge — and those who have practical expertise with little extra time to develop a theoretical sophistication — are apt to be women. Furthermore the field has retained its connection through NCTE and the theme of teaching to education in elementary and secondary schools, with the motherly connotations of teaching children thereby made available. This has also meant that the empirical methods of research associated with education rather than English departments enter into rhetoric and composition, and may enter with a feminized gendering.

This is not to say that critical feminists are not interested in practice — many have political commitments which may include literacy work and teaching basic writers, and many make practices the object of their analysis: think of Patricia Bizzell, Susan Miller, or Linda Brodkey. However, critical feminists would seriously contest the epistemological assumption that one's practical classroom experience may provide the knowledge that's required to talk about writing, or the ethical assumption that "care" provides a guide for moral judgments. Rather, what worries them is precisely the extensive involvement of teachers in reproducing — as opposed to transforming — social values. The historical exploitation of women by institutional processes makes many feminists want to gain critical distance from the repetitions of practice. So a critical feminist may regard the idea of basing knowledge upon practice alone with a certain horror. If some feminists embrace the nurturing mother as a figure, others seek the means to resist traditional feminine roles in social reproduction.

Louise Wetherbee Phelps and Janet Emig assert in their collection, *Feminine Principles and Women's Experience in American Composition and Rhetoric,* that what they call a "feminist populism" has been associated with the development of rhetoric and composition. They give an unusual degree of primacy to personal experience, which they see as reflecting innate sexual differences "inevitably embodied and biologically derived." The principles of this feminist populism influenced the choice of essays in this volume, based upon a maternal ethos of responsibility and nurture, equity of discourses, and a democratic inclusiveness of contributors. The most important assumption of the editors is that this volume ought to appeal to readers who are teachers. It is addressed to those who read in the teacherly mode of thinking about practice, about models, and about their professional lives. However, it relies dangerously on the appeal of personal stories and of affirming feminine strengths alone, rather than also including thorough examinations of the arguments in the field.

In addition to her introductory comments, Louise Wetherbee Phelps includes a strong essay urging women in composition to work for a transformation not just of the field but of higher education. In "Becoming a Warrior: Lessons of the Feminist Workplace," Phelps takes to task those who connect the feminization of composition studies with low status, stigma, and marginalization because they don't see the opportunities for having an impact — for example, through writing across the curriculum, educational reform in teacher evaluation, and through the new pedagogics. She positions herself in particular against the left: "I reject both the despair and the adversarial, deeply pessimistic characterization of American education and American society that many leftist intellectuals hold." Even though the stereotypical virtues of relatedness, nurturing, and compassion may have been imposed by a particular ideology, Phelps argues that they become feminist as they are freely chosen and made the subject of debate. Phelps uses her own experiences as director of the writing program at Syracuse to ask: "How can we become warriors unafraid of our own power?" She recounts the terrible contradictions that a reformist director of a writing program is likely to face, given the facts of an exploited faculty who may be asked to spend greater time developing curriculum and doing research in the service of a utopian project. Her essay — though buried in the middle of the volume because she and Emig have arranged the book according to alphabetical order — provides the most forceful example of the volume's plea for affirmation. The only problem with this truly personal assertion is a lack of context — not only in this volume, but in history, institutions, or scholarship which might help readers make clearer connections to their own situations. Readers who do indeed wish to learn from the experience of other women may not be certain about which lessons might apply.

Two other essays in the volume take up the question of feminine authority, but with greater attention to this question of rhetorical context. Patricia Bizzell in "Praising Folly: Constructing a Postmodern Rhetorical Authority as a Woman" proposes a figure of a rhetorical authority not afraid to appear foolish or sentimental in affirming egalitarian values, feminist without being limited to the biology of gender or race. Her fool would, like Erasmus' Folly, belong to the discourse of skepticism, persuading through *phronesis* or arguments about probable knowledge, but also expressing a utopian compassion. Nancy Sommers, in "Between the Drafts," uses a personal story to argue that revision negotiates between authority and the personal. She suggests, then, asking students to work with sources of their own to complicate academic sources, as her own essay models. Thus her authority is revisionary in a double sense.

In general, the volume emphasizes personal narrative and a maternal ethos. Several of the essays are explicit elaborations of a perspective related to the "ethic of care." Emily Jessup and Marion Lardner, for example, advocate a maternal perspective in "Teaching Other People's Children," and, they say firmly, criticisms of such a maternal attitude are misogynist. Janice Hays argues in "Intellectual Parenting and a Developmental Feminist Pedagogy of Writing" that college instructors also need to act in a parental relationship to students, helping them to develop out of dualistic thinking, which separates feeling from intellect, and toward committed relativism, the stage William Perry thinks college students should reach as they mature. In "Collaboration, Conversation, and the Politics of Gender," Evelyn Ashton-Jones asks whether feminist practices of collaboration are in danger of simply reproducing the very structures of gender that feminism puts into question. Ashton-Jones wants to take from Chodorow, Gilligan, and Belenky and her associates the lesson that women and men have been socialized differently. If interactive styles are gender-specific, collaborative groups will not be pedagogics of equity and will simply repeat the problems of women students.

Studies of literacy outside the institutions of higher education characterize some of the most engaging essays in the collection. Myrna Harrienger writes a case study of Grace, age eighty, stroke victim in "Writing a Life: The Composing of Grace." Writing here is a practice which accompanies and defines a daily life, including the difficulties of sickness and old age. Harrienger uses Phelps' argument that writing is more than school composition; it is a means of reflection which produces meaning — and composition studies should make that function an object of inquiry. This is a theme for quite another stage in life in the essay written by Sara Dalmas Jonsberg, with Marie Salgado and the Women of the Next Step, "Composing the Multiple Self: Teen Mothers Rewrite Their Roles." This article is written about teen pregnancies from the point of view of narrative theory, with the idea that part, at least, of the problem is the way the young women's lives have been plotted, and part of the solution is a rewriting. Christine Holm Kline, in "Rockshelf Further Forming: Women, Writing, and Teaching the Young," portrays the double-blind for women in teaching by focussing on elementary teachers talking about their work. If they are expert, they are also treated as immature, in need of the direction and control exerted by texts, curriculum, standardized tests, and other forms of institutional domination. Another effort to represent women's experience with literacy is Mary Kay Tirrell's "Interview with Son Kim Vo: The Role of Vietnamese Women in Literacy Processes." Son Vo, an "educator-mother," teaches Vietnamese students who are losing touch in the United States with their language and culture. Son Kim Vo is utterly unconflicted about playing a motherly role in her relationships to students; her notion of morality and community is very much bound up with such a position.

With the pervasive attention to teaching in this volume, not much consideration is given to feminist theories of language or even to the interactions of gender and rhetorical convention. Two essays take up these questions. Lillian Bridwell-Bowles, believing that we need new kinds of writing to confront the conventions of academic thought, asks students at all levels to invent new forms in "Discourse and Diversity: Experimental Writing Within the Academy." She specifically disagrees with those who think students must master the forms of argument, preferring to think of students entering into a dialogue with the still-powerful conventions of academic discourse by experimenting with a yet undefined "other" discourse.

But perhaps this "other" discourse is, like the purloined letter, hidden in plain view, as Cinthia Gannett's essay suggests: "The Stories of Our Lives Become Our Lives: Journals, Diaries, and Academic Discourse." Gannett thinks the objections to journals (for example, that they encourage incorrect writing and too-personal topics) might come from their association with the very personal "diaries" which are a kind of "girl's writing," a gendering which marks the genre's development, so the tensions are between marginalized discourse communities and the traditionally dominant. As Gannett described the form, it resembles the notion of an écriture féminine: fragmented, recursive, cumulative, fluid, connected to women's lives and women's bodies. Finally, she sees journals as a way to serve Belenky's idea of "coming to voice."

The two historical essays in the book are very different. Mitzi Myers writes less to define the feminine than to restore a history of women's instruction and thus contributes helpfully to our much-needed sense of cultural context. In "Of Mice and Mothers: Mrs. Barbauld's 'New Walk' and Gendered Codes in Children's Literature," she argues that women's didactic literature in the late eighteenth century, and Barbauld in particular, had an important influence on literacy practices, presenting a new model of education written in the form of mother-child dialogues about everyday experiences which taught children to interpret the world around them, and counseled sympathy for the plight of animals and others. Myers argues that the powerful, even if overlooked, influence of this juvenile writing enabled women to participate in cultural construction. She does not consider that the maternal might be defined as well by this practice — that a particular version of sentimental femininity has been created by this association with juvenile writing. Describing Barbauld's teaching texts as "participatory, dialogic, vernacular, quotidian, empathetic, relational, nurturing" — belonging to what she calls the "mother tongue" — Myers seems at moments to use the concept as if it denoted a maternality beyond history. However, her research on the history of didactic literature suggests that current assumptions about the relationship of women to teaching practices can be traced in part to the influence of Barbaud and other women writers. Writing from a middle-class domesticity, they constructed a version of the mother-teacher which continues to exert influence. The other historical essay goes much further in asserting a continuous feminization in rhetorical history: Robert J. Connors' "Women's Reclamation of Rhetoric in Nineteenth-century America" does not, however, offer much help in understanding the nuances of gender's influence. Before the nineteenth century, he claims, rhetoric was an agonistic, competitive discipline which taught public speaking only to men in educational institutions characterized by extremely combative relationships between faculty and students. Then it became, as women entered schools, an irenic, cooperative discipline teaching a private practice of writing to women as well as men, in newly coeducational institutions which emphasized nurturing forms of instruction. The old abstractions, necessary to the construction of ethical arguments, gave way to the expression of personal experience. While his history tries to persuade us that rhetoric has changed its gender, he seems, finally, to be critical of such a feminized discipline. His history, alas, gives the victory over to women much more swiftly and totally than most feminist historians would accept, and thereby serves to reinforce a reductive notion of how the feminine might appear.

The emphasis on teaching in this Phelps/Emig volume is appropriate to a feminist inquiry, even though the methodologies included are rather limited. To the extent that it claims to represent "principles," however, the book distorts the current state of feminist scholarship, obscuring the much broader spectrum of important research being contributed by women in the field. While the anthology will be widely interesting, it is not representative of feminism as it now exists in the profession of English — indeed, pointedly ignores, both in references and bibliography, most of the larger feminist debate. Even more worrisome, the book is not really a multicultural collection; either the authors' call for papers generated a rather narrow range of response or they were narrow in their selections. However, the book is important precisely because it does address the question of pedagogy and women's experience in composition.

Feminism has been widely influenced by the discussion around Carol Gilligan's work since 1982, and a further understanding of this debate is especially important for a feminist pedagogy. Mary Jeanne Larrabee has done an excellent job of providing a thorough approach to the arguments through the essays collected in *An Ethic of Care*. The publication of Gilligan's *In a Different Voice* challenged the hierarchy of Lawrence Kohlberg's widely accepted theory of moral development, asserting the significance of responsibility, relationship, and practice against an ethic of rights and justice. The subsequent discussion of Gilligan's work also thematized woman's difference as a matter of finding a voice for an ethic of care. The essays in this volume do not simply elaborate a uniform understanding of such an ethic, however. They argue for and against, from within feminism and without, from a narrow methodological perspective but also from wide-ranging historical, critical, and philosophical perspectives, enabling us to take another look at Gilligan's work and its implications. Larrabee's introduction points out the web of complications for feminists that arise from addressing the question of ethics — questions that circle around the influence of gender, race/ethnicity, and class on human development, but also questions about the impact of an ethic of care on feminist practice.

The first part of the book provides an introduction to the basic issues of Gilligan's work in relationship to Kohlberg, and even here the complexity of the views emerge very successfully. Annette Baier writes about the woman-directed quality of this moral theory; Mary Brabeck situates Gilligan within the traditions of stereotyping women's morality in relationship to male reason; Lawrence Blum examines Gilligan together with the "impartialist" view of moral philosophy to which Kohlberg belongs; and Owen Flanagan and Kathryn Jackson move from the philosophical differences over care and justice to question the very idea of morality as a unitary domain. Several of these essays worry about limiting the debate to two ethics. In Part Two, the discussion is extended to include other feminist issues. Linda Nicholson inserts the moral development argument into the history of gender, in effect suggesting that it might be reduced to the conflict of public and private spheres; and reflect the separation of a feminized emotion or subjectivity from masculine reason and objectivity. Linda Kerber worries about romanticizing women's morality. An essay by Carol Stack points out that Gilligan overlooks African-American moral experience, which doesn't fit the gendered dichotomy or either ethic, and John Broughton criticizes Gilligan for her gender dualism. Part Three then opens up a thorough methodological critique of the theory, starting with Gertrud Nunner-Winkler's challenge to the notion that the moral differences at issue are sex-specific. Lawrence Walker examines the research literature and concludes that Kohlberg's work has not resulted in a significant bias against the moral reasoning of women, contrary to Gilligan's allegations — that the reasoning of men and women has turned out to be very similar. Diana Baumrind replies that these critiques are flawed and argues that Kohlberg is biased at the level of theory, giving priority to abstract reasoning over concrete, pragmatic views. But other essays also question Gilligan's methodology.

In the final section, Gilligan herself responds to critics by underlining the different approach to morality she has taken. By foregrounding *voice*, she argues, she has reconceived scholarship in a way that is not necessarily gendered even though it is an approach favored by women over men. An essay by Bill Puka outlines some of the enduring feminist concerns about the way the care ethic seems to reinforce conventional feminine orientations rather than women's more liberatory aspirations. One of the most useful essays in the book for researchers in rhetoric and composition is Joan Tronto's thoughtful consideration of a feminist ethics. Taking into account the dangers of a Eurocentric bias, a conservatism, or a relativism, she thinks about the ways that an ethic of care might be translated into action. Finally, Marilyn Friedman asks whether justice and care are distinguished in practice and thinks about how to move ethics away from the traditions of gender division that both segregate and denigrate women. Thus the volume begins and ends with a critical approach to feminist theory which resists the too-easy characterizations that have made the ethic of care seem at once essentialist and ethnocentric. The attention to practice is important for rhetoric and composition, not only because it has implications for teaching, but less obviously because it overlaps with a rhetorical understanding of ethical issues, as contrasted to the Kantian abstractions associated with moral philosophy. This book makes the connection at once clearer and more complex, rescuing Gilligan's thought from the reductive binaries of gender debates but also elaborating a thorough list of problems attending the discussion.

In her book on *Women Writing the Academy*, Gesa Kirsch sympathetically relates the struggles of women to find a voice of authority in higher education. The book is based on a series of interviews with women professors and students in five disciplines: history, anthropology, education, psychology, and nursing. Selections from these interviews are interspersed with chapters of analysis. Kirsch does not critique the idea that women bring different habits and values to the academy, though she worries at length about the problem of essentialism. While she is particularly interested in women's writing, she wants to investigate women's experience in higher education, what helps them succeed and what challenges they face. Kirsch thinks the primary difficulty for feminism arises from the contradictory motives that inevitably accompany women's position as "other": On the one hand, in order to succeed, women must learn the ways of the institution, but, on the other hand, women need to critique these very conventions if feminism is to make any kind of difference. Women's emphasis on connection adds another complication, informing the tendency to choose interdisciplinary study, to engage in new, more engaged forms of pedagogy, as well as to experience lives often made even more complex by relationships. Kirsch is writing about the utopian aspirations as well as the difficulties of women's academic life. She is especially concerned with the possibility for a feminist transformation of conventional disciplinary discourses. Can women's writing not only qualify them for academic life, but also help to change it?

In addition to the vivid examples provided by individual stories, Gesa Kirsch's book provides useful analyses of feminist issues in rhetoric and composition as introductions to the more specific descriptions of her research results. Her chapter on authority, "Working against Tradition," for example, begins by bringing familiar ideas about the need for students to master conventions together with the complications introduced by gender. "Expanding Communities" talks about audience, summarizing problems women have with authority that many have noted, and adding the important problem brought about by feminist desires to address larger audiences, to go outside the academy with their message. "Crossing Disciplinary Boundaries" notes the limitations of interdisciplinary research as well as its promise to change knowledge. Together with Pat Sullivan, Gesa Kirsch established a feminist workshop at CCCC several years ago which helped bring academic women together to talk about their work. Her book serves a similar introductory function, laying the groundwork for women to examine their lives in the academy.

The notion that the stories of women's lives are different lies behind all three of the above books. Indeed, developmental theories like Gilligan's depend upon some kind of underlying narrative, including the assertion that women's stories are more cyclical, less linear than those of men. Narrative is also important to feminist argument, which turns to personal story, citing frustration with abstract models. A frequent assumption is that traditional forms of argument do not account for the differences women experience. Yet stories as well may reveal how thoroughly women are both caught and excluded by tradition, and the narrative of frustration itself defines a common feminist trope. *Anxious Power,* edited by Carol Singley and Susan Sweeney, examines issues of ambivalence in women's narrative. The lineage for the book is literary as well as rhetorical and many of the essays take poststructuralist critiques of the subject into account. As defined here, feminine narrative expands literary tradition to include fairy tales, oral stories, diaries and autobiographies, ghost stories, epistolary fiction, dystopic fiction, poetry, cross-genre writing such as narrative/autobiography, and criticism. This suggests how women's narratives open literature up to rhetoric. The book posits a series of historical stages in women's relationships to writing: that from the middle ages to the eighteenth century, women writers were anxious authors; that nineteenth century women expressed the desire to write in terms of romance; that modernist women were more confrontive about differences, not only of gender; and that postmodern women are both revisionary and inventive, trying to define a feminine tradition. The essays in this volume address women's narratives from various perspectives, but they include an effort to specify the strategies which express the anxiety of writing — strategies familiar in the literature on women and language, such as dialogics, metafiction, refusals of closure, crossing generic lines, writing under erasure, disrupting sequence, making a collage or patchwork, collaborating, destabilizing traditions through irony, marking uncertainty, struggling with the inadequacy of language. The volume, in general, represents a much more extensive reading of feminist theory than those reviewed above. That is, the authors situate their discussions of, for example, the selfhood of women within the debate about essentialism and subjectivity, so they do not seem to rely without acknowledgement on categories that others have called into question.

Carol Singley believes that women's difficult relationship to language stems from a selfhood that is made fragile, not autonomous or authoritative (she occludes, however, the difficult question of masculine selfhood, presumably operating with a sense of authority that is deeply indebted to language, and hence illusory). Susan Sweeney argues that women write differently than men because they are responding to a tradition composed by men, not by women. Sweeney thinks she finds "a peculiarly feminine ambivalence toward narrative authority" in the "multiplicity of narrative voices." Other essays in the book examine the feminine in particular writers representing the four stages of women's narrative, including Christine de Pisan, Amelia Lanyer, Mary Sidney, Marie-Catherine D'Aulnoy, Jane Barker, Jane Austen, Mary Guion, Harriet Jacobs, Charlotte Brontë, Sarah Grand, Edith Wharton, Willa Cather, Joyce Carol Oates, Clarice Lispector, Toni Morrison, Maxine Hong Kingston, Sandra Cisneros, Doris Lessing, Fanny Howe, Margaret Atwood. In the final, capstone essay Diane Freedman articulates the theory of a female tradition shaping the book: "It may be that the female writer's ambivalence — her sense of being both self and other, both writer and reader, both powerful and anxious — is the matrix for a distinctly female narrative tradition, in which voices and genres combine without cancelling each other out."

Trying to define what might be distinctly female is a rather different problem than using the perspective of feminism to engage in critique. In rhetoric and composition, the articulation of feminine principles or of a women's history reclaims a gendered set of values for writing, a gendered ethic for pedagogy. A feminist critique, on the other hand, might work to raise questions about unconscious dogmatisms without necessarily installing an alternative (gendered) set of standards. This, at least, is the hope of Carmen Luke and Jennifer Gore for their collection of essays, *Feminisms and Critical Pedagogy*. Their aims are widely shared by others in the critical pedagogy movement — to empower students, challenge canonical thinking, and show the relations of domination. But this book was written, they say in the introduction, as an "uneasy" reading of critical pedagogy, uneasy as a consequence of their teaching practices. In *Feminisms and Critical Pedagogy*, the specific chapters record various kinds of unease, based on what one might call "experience," a category that is already under pressure in the discourse of critical pedagogy. There is always the possibility that such resistance will be discounted ahead of time. That is why it is particularly important for these writers to insist at once upon a resistance called experience and upon their location within discourses which have passed "experience" through a critical examination.

Valerie Walkerdine, in "Progressive Pedagogy and Political Struggle," worries about the "sham" of a progressive classroom. Imagining the students as free individuals, working under the "soft benevolence" of a mother-teacher, seems to enable them to escape the authoritarianism associated with more "patriarchal" instruction, even though it makes their freedom depend on the teacher's care. But a Foucauldian analysis of authority would locate the power, rather, in normalizing practices and surveillance. The history of reform associated with a feminized education made love a way of disciplining. But the power relations are denied — and the mother/teacher must pay the cost of playing servant to the child. Thus, she argues, such progressive pedagogy validates masculine sexuality, and violence, through the excessive attention paid by the teacher. And in each case, the woman must take the irrationality upon herself. Thus progressivism does not empower students or teacher, but rather makes powerlessness invisible. Carmen Luke, in "Feminist Politics in Radical Pedagogy," deconstructs the metanarratives of education — in particular, here, those of critical or radical pedagogy. She does this by analysing radical pedagogy's construction of the subject, which does not theorize gender and therefore simply reinstates the historically masculine metanarrative. Critical pedagogy fails to acknowledge the gendered history of speaking critically. It also constructs a colorless, genderless "individual" which is based upon liberal ideas of a disembodied subject, and valorizes experience without taking account of its situation in discourses. She calls for a strategic essentialism — claiming a feminism which might engage in a politics of affinity rather than identity. Similarly advocating greater reflexivity about the self as subject, Jennifer Gore points out that specific authors are prominent in critical pedagogy (Giroux, McClaren, Freire, Schor), while feminist criticism is defined by the opposition of liberal and radical traditions. A critical pedagogue such as Giroux is in danger of setting himself apart from critique — "he wants teachers to be self-reflexive but is not himself."

This collection differs most markedly from that of Phelps/Emig and Kirsch in its questioning of identity politics. Not only are these writers critical of the idea that empowering students means a search for some kind of natural identity, story, or "voice," they work to unsettle claims about what a feminine self might be, and claims that the effort to empower student selves can be easy or straightforward. As Jane Kenway and Helen Modra put it, these essayists share an unease not with what a complexly analyzed feminism might bring to pedagogy, but with the narrow and reductive ways that a feminist pedagogy seems to be imagined in higher education. Mimi Omer points out that poststructuralist feminism sees the ostensible fragility of identity as a powerful source of change. Furthermore, the concept of voice, she argues, does not necessarily empower students but may, rather, leave them without the resources to be self-critical. The point is not to discover an authentic individual, but to denaturalize assumptions that are, in fact, conventional — to dislodge the sense of fixity. Like Shoshana Felman, she argues that what disrupts expectations in a classroom may be valuable. "For feminist poststructuralists, it is the gaps and ruptures in practice — the breaks, confusion, and contradiction that are always a part of the interplay in teaching — that offer the greatest insight and possibilities for change . . . the return of the repressed, the uncanny." Furthermore, the assumption that the instructor knows what is best for students is no more liberating when the instructor is on the left. "How do the micro-politics of the 'emancipatory' classroom differ from the macro-politics of imperialism?" (87) We need, in other words, to rethink power relations in the classroom, to acknowledge the complexity of the situation.

In spite of the enormous theoretical gap between writers in this volume and Phelps/Emig or Kirsch — and therefore the different valences attached to the vocabulary — at the last there is some kind of agreement that feminists must talk about teaching and about the experiences of women in academic institutions. The essay by Patti Lather offers a helpful analysis of the problem, reviewing the charges Ellsworth levels against critical pedagogy together with responses from McLaren and Giroux. If critical pedagogics work to interrupt the oppressions of a certain cultural history, nevertheless too often they have failed to think about the way liberation is something done to someone defined as "other." But does this mean the educator is silenced or must disengage politically? At issue is the tendency — for Enlightenment thought, but also for feminist discourse — to seize the moral high ground by attacking others. Lather chooses to read Ellsworth not as attacking, however, but as offering an unsettling view, from classroom experience, which functions to deconstruct unexamined assumptions of critical pedagogy — a brave view, moreover, given the vitriolic responses she elicited. Like Gayatri Spivak, Lather argues that feminist deconstructive critique does not necessarily disable practice by propelling us into continuous revision. She sees the possibilities for post-critical intellectuals — abandoning crusading rhetoric — to open up difference, "to refigure community, to include ways of disagreeing productively among ourselves" (132). Magda Lewis points out that feminist teachers must acknowledge how critique reproduces the practices we are critiquing, that we need to pay attention to classroom dynamics. And Luke and Gore conclude the volume with a return to the daily routines of academic work, to personal narratives and academic careers kept private which, they argue, should be part of the public dimension of feminist practice.

I would like to acknowledge also a sense of uneasiness about the politics of discussions about both feminist pedagogy and critical pedagogy. This unease arises because the discussion of differences seems currently so powerless to make useful distinctions, complicating and exposing the multilayered effects of a feminist analysis. The danger that feminist inquiry continues to confront is not that disputes among feminists could weaken feminism — to the contrary, feminism has gathered strength as it has continued to acknowledge and describe the significance of differences, notable turns in its history as it opened up to the evidence of its inadequacy enforced by the testimony of women around the world, and as it discussed the questions around sexuality propelled especially by lesbian women. No, the danger is that reactionary and "backlash" movements continue to enforce a kind of massification on "feminism." Ellen Goodman has written about the "straw feminist" effect. We have all debated "essentialism." The truth is that essentialism is not so much a danger within as without, the danger of reductionism imposed by unfriendly writers who insist on writing as if feminism were just one thing, a simple movement. As if feminists could "get over it" before anti-feminists are at last led by our continued efforts to "get it." In particular, the campaign against the "politically correct" has seemed (in a too-familiar way) to reduce the left to an unreasonable and hysterical feminism, its hidden emblem the figure of the schoolmarm teaching, this time, not how to write correctly but how to vote correctly, and thus exceeding her domestic entitlement. Bringing to bear the paranoid logic of the cold war on feminist projects, such attacks go on succeeding in their most important aim: to reduce feminist work on writing and education to a single stereotype and then to claim that that is what feminists themselves most devoutly wish.

My task in this review, then, has been to suggest the complex and multiple-layered analysis that feminists are now contributing to the evolving field of rhetoric and composition. And I wish to insist on the doubleness of women's relationship to the field; their particularly striking appearance, their lengthy absence from notice. In particular, feminism is struggling with power, and with the figure of the nurturing mother. Instruction has always implicated rhetoric in the difficulty of taking over the parental role and instilling an ethical as well as pragmatic dimension to learning. This parental role always involves us in that difficult moment of deciding something for someone else — an imbalance of power, if you will, that requires not giving the power away but trying to be responsible about the decision. An important problem, and one that all of the volumes under review help to alleviate, is that women's significant work and real authority in the classroom and the institution has been invisible. The new visibility of feminist writing in rhetoric and composition will finally add gender as an important subject in the fund of disciplinary knowledge. The discussion about what that means has only just begun.

Clark's Insights as a Resource for Your Teaching

1. What may have been the effects of gender on you as a student of writing? Use your recall and observations to freewrite about your student and adult experiences of writing. In the second entry of your "dialogue" on gender and writing, reflect on these questions: What are issues for you or your colleagues? Do these confirm, challenge, or intersect with themes and issues Clark describes in her review essay? Decide on one or two questions you have about the "feminization of composition," and use those to guide some of your reflection about the writing community, student behaviors, student texts, and your responses to texts.

2. Initiate conversations with veteran women writing faculty about theories or claims you find when you read further about "feminist composition." Compare notes on teaching practice, trade "practitioner's lore," and share information about useful readings on pedagogy and writing theory.

Clark's Insights as a Resource for the Writing Classroom

1. In the conclusion of her essay, Clark expresses concern about the political climate, which derides and trivializes the issues presented and argued in the texts reviewed. The neologism *feminazi* and the term *politial correctness* are examples of this derision that your students may recognize. Generate a list of similarly dismissive terms, phrases, or stereotypes from the popular culture, and organize small groups to conduct research on two or three terms selected from the list. Direct the groups to determine, if possible, the etymology, history, connotations, denotations, and usage of each term and to prepare written reports for a class "glossary." Introduce the concept of stipulative definitions during class discussion of language change and influence. Ask for journal entries reflecting on any kinds of derisive or pejorative language students have observed.

2. It's inevitable that some students in your class will complain about certain readings in *The Bedford Guide for College Writers* as "feminist" or "male-bashing" (or "whining about" racism, sexism, homophobia, classism, etc.). Organize a "censorship panel" or a forum debate in which one group of students criticizes and another defends one such essay. Ask all students to read the essay a second time and write journal entries identifying issues or arguments and analyzing the purpose and perspective of the writer. Assign or have students volunteer for three-person panels. The remainder of the students are to listen carefully to the panelists or debaters, take notes, and ask questions during rebuttal. Save ten minutes for closure; ask each team to identify the strongest arguments made by their opponents, and ask the audience to identify what they heard that made them rethink a position or gave them new insights. Send students off to reflect on the discussion in journal entries. By establishing a forum where "sound bites" can be turned into analysis and critique, you provide students an opportunity to learn that an opinion might be more acceptable to multiple listeners when it is fully and carefully communicated.

EILEEN E. SCHELL   *The Costs of Caring:*
"Feminism" and
Contingent Women Workers
in Composition Studies

In this selection, Eileen Schell elaborates on a feminist discourse about teaching that is rooted in an explicitly "feminine" system of caring and nurturing rather than judging and criticizing, in connectedness and empathy rather than abstractions and edicts. This maternalistic mode, however, often conflicts with the desires of women to be taken seriously as teachers and intellectuals. Moreover, it directly corroborates the gender inequities that push women toward lower-paying and less secure jobs than their male colleagues. Women have less time to devote to scholarly activity and reflective inquiry into their practice. As a result, the body of knowledge generated about writing instruction is a distinctly masculine one.

Lorie Goodman Batson contends that when we speak of women in composition studies — their varying interests, desires, motivations, and political affiliations — we often appeal to a common female identity that levels differences and creates alliances where there may be divergences (207–08). As identity categories become increasingly fragmented and contested in postmodern thought, it is important for feminists in composition "to begin challenging the privileging of singular political identities" (Wicke and Ferguson 7). Poststructuralist and postmodern critiques of identity politics necessitate that we reexamine previously unchallenged assumptions about women students and women teachers.

In particular, the argument that feminists in composition should favor what Elizabeth Flynn refers to as "femininst" principles or the "recuperation of those modes of thinking within the field that are compatible with a feminine epistemology" ("Studies" 143) needs to be reexamined. According to Flynn, a feminine epistemology is an approach to language study "characterized by modalities of relatedness and mutuality, indistinct boundaries, flexibility, and non-oppositional styles" (147). In this essay, I examine the limits of femininist thought; I critique arguments that advocate a feminist pedagogy based on an "ethic of care," which is a set of principles that Nel Noddings refers to as a reliance on an ethical subject's "feelings, needs, situational conditions," as a "personal ideal rather than universal ethical principles and their application" (96). It is my contention that femininist pedagogy, although compelling, may reinforce rather than critique or transform patriarchal structures by reinscribing what Magda Lewis calls the "woman as caretaker ideology," the "psychological investment women are required to make in the emotional well-being of men [and others] — an investment that goes well beyond the classroom into the private spaces of women's lives" (174). While I do not wish to discredit femininist pedagogy, I do wish to question the ways that an ethic of care may prevent feminists from addressing one of the most serious gender problems we face in composition studies: the relegating of women to contingent (part-time and non-tenure-track) writing instructorships.

"Feminism" in Composition Studies

Beginning in the latter half of the 1980s, feminists in composition have created a discourse on pedagogy that perpetuates feminine values and principles (Caywood and Overing; Phelps and Emig; Flynn, "Composing" and "Studies"; Frey,

"Equity"; Rubin). In 1987, Cynthia Caywood and Gillian Overing coedited the anthology *Teaching Writing: Pedagogy, Gender, and Equity,* the first book-length work on feminist writing pedagogy. Drawing on the work of feminists Nancy Chodorow, Carol Gilligan, and Sara Ruddick, several volume contributors (Daumer and Runzo; Frey; Goulston; Stanger) advocate a pedagogical approach rooted in Nodding's ethic of care: a process of ethical decision making based on interrelationships and connectedness rather than on universalized and individualized rules and rights.[1] Weaving together strands of liberal and cultural feminisms, the editors contend that feminist pedagogy revalues the experience of women students and encourages individual voice and personal growth in the writing classroom (Caywood and Overing xi). In "Transforming the Composition Classroom," Elisabeth Daumer and Sandra Runzo urge feminist teachers to help their students "unearth" their authentic voices by encouraging them to "search out untraditional sources, often the forms of writing which have not been granted the status of literature because they are either personal (journals, letters, diaries) or community-based (Blues, spirituals, work songs)" (56). In this formulation, female students' subjectivities are represented as buried treasure, which must be brought to light with the assistance of the feminist teacher. Thus the theory of subjectivity in *Teaching Writing* is grounded in Enlightenment notions of the self-governing, autonomous individual.

Cultural feminism, as represented in *Teaching Writing,* entails a radical transformation of pedagogical relationships. "Cultural feminism," writes Linda Alcoff, "is the ideology of a female nature or female essence reappropriated by feminists themselves in an effort to revalidate undervalued female attributes" ("Feminism" 408). Following nineteenth-century ideals of femininity, cultural feminists argue that feminine values have been denigrated and superseded by masculine values such as aggressiveness, confrontation, control, competition, domination, and physical violence. To reverse the perpetuation of harmful masculine values, cultural feminists contend that all people — men and women alike — should emulate feminine values: nurturance, supportiveness, interdependence, and nondominance. In addition, cultural feminists deemphasize a model of communication based on argumentation and endorse a rhetoric of mediation, conciliation, and shared authority. Alcoff warns that, although many women have developed invaluable skills and abilities in response to patriarchal restrictions, feminists should be wary of advocating "the restrictive conditions that give rise to those attributes: forced parenting, lack of physical autonomy, dependency for survival on mediation skills" (414). Furthermore, Devoney Looser cautions that theories of gender identity that presume "a stable and/or recoverable homogenized" female subject "present costs that feminist compositionists may not be ready to pay" (55).

The happy marriage between cultural feminism and expressivist composition studies, however, is evident in many of the essays in *Teaching Writing.* As Wendy Goulston indicates, process theories of composing rely on qualities associated with a "female style" (25). In fact, Caywood and Overing locate their volume at the "recurrent intersection" between feminist theory and expressivist writing theory: the privileging of process over product; the encouragement of inner voice, exploratory or discovery writing; collaboration; and the decentering of teacherly authority (xii–xiii). Caywood and Overing find that "the process model, insofar as it facilitates and legitimizes the fullest expression of individual voice, is compatible with the feminist revisioning of hierarchy, if not essential to it" (xiv).

Unlike expressivist pedagogy, femininist pedagogy consciously embraces "maternal thinking," a term borrowed from Sara Ruddick's landmark essay "Maternal Thinking" (Daumer and Runzo 54). According to Ruddick, feminists should strive to bring the patterns of thinking characteristic of the social practices and intellectual capacities of the mother "in[to] the public realm, to make the preservation and growth of all children a work of public conscience and legislation" (361). In Ruddick's theory of ethics, maternal thinking is governed by three interests: preserving the life of the child, fostering the child's growth, and shaping an acceptable child (348–57). To accomplish these maternal interests, the mother must exercise a capacity for "attentive love," the supportive love and caring that allows a child to persevere and grow (357–58). Applied broadly to human relations, maternal thinking offers a radical alternative to a theory of ethics based on a concept of individual rights (see Perry).

Applied broadly to the feminist writing classroom, maternal thinking encourages writing teachers to create a supportive, nonhierarchical environment responsive to students' individual needs and cultural contexts (Daumer and Runzo 50). The maternal writing teacher "empowers and liberates students" by serving as a facilitator, a midwife to students' ideas; she individualizes her teaching by fostering "self-sponsored writing"; she decenters her authority by encouraging collaborative learning among peers (49). In "The Sexual Politics of the One-to-One Tutorial Approach," Carol Stanger borrows Gilligan's theory of women's moral development to argue for a model of collaborative learning that encourages students to build knowledge through consensus, not competition (41). In "Equity and Peace in the New Writing Classroom," Olivia Frey, like Stanger, endorses a "peaceful classroom" based on "understanding and cooperation," not on competition and aggression: "Group work and peer inquiry . . . discourage harmful confrontation since through cooperative learning students discover how to resolve conflict creatively and effectively" (100). Both Stanger and Frey eschew hierarchical forms of discourse in favor of discourses grounded in mediation and negotiation.

Overall, contributors to *Teaching Writing* suggest that a classroom based on an ethic of care can counteract patriarchal pedagogy's "emphasis on hierarchy, competition, and control" (Gore 70). They also appear to agree with the premise that feminists are better equipped to achieve a nonhierarchical and noncompetitive classroom because they possess the nurturing, maternal qualities to facilitate such a change (70). Yet will the maternal stance work for all women teachers and students, including those who are white and working-class, African American, Latina, or Asian? Caywood and Overing admit that their volume "may not meet some of the particular needs of minority students" (xv), implying that maternal teaching is best suited for white middle-class women. Although the volume omits the important perspectives of minority women and teachers, it nevertheless has served as the starting point for conversation about feminist pedagogy in composition studies (xv) and an inspiration for further feminist pedagogical models based on an ethic of care.

But what are the ethical, emotional, and material costs of a pedagogy based on an ethic of care? If teaching writing is considered women's work — underpaid and underrecognized — how might feminist pedagogy make it difficult for feminists in composition to address gender inequities in academic work, particularly the preponderance of women in part-time and non-tenure-track positions?

The Hidden Costs of an Ethic of Care

Ethnographic studies and surveys of feminist classrooms demonstrate that students, both male and female, expect their women teachers to act as nurturing mother figures (Friedman, "Authority" 205). There is often conflict between that expectation and the teacher's need to be taken seriously as a teacher and intellectual (205). Research on gender bias in student rating of women teachers, conducted by Diane Kierstead, Patti D'Agostino, and Heidi Dill, reveals that

> if female instructors want to obtain high student ratings, they must be not only highly competent with regard to factors directly related to teaching but also careful to act in accordance with traditional sex-role expectations. In particular . . . male and female instructors will earn equal student ratings for equal professional work only if the women also display stereotypically feminine behavior.
>
> (Kierstead et al. qtd. in Koblitz)

If a feminist teacher adopts a maternal stance, she may better conform to her students' expectations. But what if her pedagogy favors critical challenge and intellectual rigor, not overt encouragement and nurturance (Friedman, "Authority" 207)? Neal Koblitz reports that if women teachers give challenging assignments and exams and follow rigorous grading policies, students are more inclined to give them lower ratings. A study of teaching evaluations at the University of Dayton indicates that "college students of both sexes judged female authority figures who engaged in punitive behavior more harshly than they judged punitive males" (Elaine Martin qtd. in Koblitz).

The research that Koblitz cites shows that for women teachers caring is not merely a natural instinct or impulse, it is a socially and historically mandated behavior. "Caring," writes the feminist philosopher Joan C. Tronto, "may be a reflection of a survival mechanism for women or others who are dealing with oppressive conditions, rather than a quality of intrinsic value on its own" ("Women" 184). Women who do not occupy positions of power often adopt a posture of attentiveness or caring accompanied by "deferential mannerisms (e.g., differences in speech, smiling, other forms of body language, etc.)" as a way to appease and anticipate the needs of those in power (184).[2] Rather than view caring as solely a natural act, we can productively view it as a form of "emotional labor," a category that the feminist philosopher Sandra Bartky defines as the "emotional sustenance that women supply to others." It is the labor of "feeding egos" and "tending wounds": "The aim of this supporting and sustaining is to produce or to maintain in the one supported and sustained a conviction of the value and importance of his own chosen projects, hence of the value and importance of his own person" (102). Bartky characterizes emotional labor as a continuum occupied on the one end by commercial caregivers, who perform "perfunctory and routinized [caregiving] relationships," and on the other end by "sincere caregivers," who direct "wholehearted acceptance" and emotional support toward the objects of their caregiving (116).

Not surprisingly, academic women often feel compelled to direct their energy into caring labor: teaching, advising students, and performing lower-level administrative duties. As one tenured woman faculty member observes in Angela Simeone's study of academic women:

> I think the great trap of young women today is that there is a sort of subtle pressure to be compliant, to not assert themselves intellectually, to spend . . . more time with students than the men do, to be motherly and nurturing, to be on a million committees, not to be a power within the university but to just do the drudgery that has to be done, to be compliant in every way. And then they don't get tenure and they fail. They don't say no to these demands, and these demands are demands that are much more put on women. (36)

Many administrators and full-time faculty members believe that women make ideal candidates for teaching writing because the same qualities necessary for motherhood — patience, enthusiasm, and the ability to juggle multiple tasks — are qualities that effective writing teachers possess (Holbrook 207). The belief that women's essential nature is to marry and mother is reinforced consciously and unconsciously throughout the institutions of hegemonic culture: the schools, government, religion, and family life. These institutions — or ideological state apparatuses, to use Louis Althusser's term — structure the social relations that interpellate human subjects (81). Through sexual-role socialization in the family, schools, and churches, women learn to channel their energies into nurturing forms of labor: teaching, nursing, social work, and mothering.

This sexual division of labor charts a predetermined pattern for many women's lives, what Nadya Aisenberg and Mona Harrington call the "marriage plot": "The central tenet of the plot, of course, is that a proper goal is marriage, or, more generally, the woman's sphere is private and domestic. Her proper role within the sphere is to provide support for the male at the head of the household of which she forms a part" (6). The marriage plot carries over into the public sphere, where a woman's proper role "is still to be supportive — either to an employer . . . or in some cases to a cause" (6). The marriage plot requires that women's roles, even in academic work, be supportive and nurturing. Women should be satisfied and fulfilled by low-paying, low-status teaching jobs.

The marriage plot is particularly pervasive in composition studies, where a large group of contingent women workers "nurture" beginning writers for salaries that rival those of underpaid waitresses. Sue Ellen Holbrook's history "Women's Work: The Feminizing of Composition Studies" and Susan Miller's "The Feminization of Composition" and *Textual Carnivals* call attention to the prevalence of this caretaker ideology. Miller's metaphorical analysis of the hierarchical, gendered constructions of teaching illuminates how institutional scripts cast women teachers as nurturers (*Carnivals* 137), thus making it problematic for feminists to continue advocating nurturant behavior as a form of empowerment.

According to Judith Gappa and David Leslie, women make up only 27 percent of all full-time, tenure-track faculty members in American colleges and universities, yet they make up 67 percent of all part-time faculty members. In the humanities, 67 percent of part-time positions are filled by women, whereas 33 percent of full-time positions are filled by women (25; see also Burns 21). Bettina Huber reports that of a cohort of 1,674 women who received Ph.D.s in English between 1981 and 1986, 56 percent found tenure-track appointments by 1987, whereas of a cohort of 1,475 men, 77.8 percent did (62). Some women choose to teach part-time because it affords them the flexibility to raise a family or care for aging parents, to pursue a writing or artistic career, or to run a home business. Others are less than happy with their contingent status. Some women turn down full-time employment to avoid relocating a family or a partner already holding a full-time job. Others seek part-time work (often several part-time jobs pieced together) because they cannot find full-time work in an overcrowded job market.

Although conditions of employment vary, universities and colleges often hire contingent writing faculty members on a semester-to-semester basis through "informal interviewing and appointment procedures" and without the benefit of contractual job security (Wallace 11). Many administrators hire contingent faculty members a few weeks or even days before the semester begins, as soon as enrollment numbers materialize for first-year composition. When part-time faculty members are hired, their "research, creativity," or previous academic employment is often not valued (11). Once hired, these teachers may receive little or no training or work orientation. And the criteria for assessing their teaching are often ill-defined (13).

Keeping in mind these grim facts about the gendered nature of contingent writing instruction, we need to assess how theories of femininist pedagogy based on an ethic of care may reinforce the labor patterns that feminists critique. Socialist feminist analyses of women's work in nurturant occupations may help in that assessment.

Socialist Feminism and Sex-Affective Production

Like cultural feminists and liberal feminists, socialist feminists examine how patriarchal socioeconomic relations subordinate women's interests to the interests of men. Unlike cultural and liberal feminists, however, socialist feminists (Michele Barrett, Sandra Lee Bartky, Zillah Eisenstein, Ann Ferguson, Heidi Hartmann, Alison Jaggar) argue that sex, class, and racial oppression maintain the gendered division of labor. Moreover, socialist feminists critically examine women's labor, analyzing the costs and benefits of the ideology of nurturance. The socialist feminist philosopher Ann Ferguson has argued that contemporary American women, despite differences of race, class, and sexual orientation, have in common "a sex/class connection organized by the sexual division of unpaid labor in the family household as well as wage labor, the gender bias of the patriarchal state, the mass media and the public/private split of family household and economy" (8). Although Ferguson seemingly essentializes women's labor, she emphasizes that class identity highlights differences among women, since individual women belong to overlapping classes that are often in conflict with one another: family class, sex class (organized around the gendered division of labor), race class, and economic class (119). Within these different class positions, women are expected to engage in forms of labor that involve the function of caring or sex-affective production, "that human physical and social interaction which is common to human sexuality, parenting, kin and family relations, nurturance and social bonding" (7–8).

Sex-affective production is characterized by "unequal exchange," in which women often receive "less of the goods produced than men" although they work harder and spend more time producing those goods: "The relations between men and women can be considered exploitative because the men are able to appropriate more of women's labor time for their own uses and also receive more of the goods produced" (132). Since sex-affective modes of production are largely unpaid, underpaid, and underrecognized forms of labor — such as mothering, nursing, and teaching — they are essential to the successful functioning of a late-capitalist economy. Moreover, women's involvement in nurturant labor is made to seem natural by discourses on gender and work claiming that women choose "inferior work status" (Bergmann, "Feminism" 23). The feminist economist Barbara Bergmann explains:

> If a person doing the [career] choosing is female, the person's choices are seen as powerfully conditioned by her "home responsibilities." This line of thinking leads to the view of women's inferior position in paid work as a benign and necessary adaptation to biological and social realities, and in no way due to biased and malign behavior on the part of employers. (23)

Maria Markus describes a "second tier" of work for women in the "less attractive, less creative, and usually less well-paid branches" of the professions. Women who end up in the second tier tend to be "'accused' of not 'planning their careers,' of not 'keeping their eyes open to the next step' but instead of burying themselves in the current tasks and awaiting 'natural justice' to reward them for working hard." Furthermore, women's lesser "agility" in professional careers includes their "lower mobility" as a result of family attachments and women's tendency to focus on human relations (105, 106).

In English studies, a second tier of work exists for women in the form of contingent writing instructorships, and such positions epitomize the paradox of sex-affective production. On the one hand, emotional rewards — a "psychic income"[3] — keep women invested in teaching; on the other hand, many contingent women writing instructors recount experiences of exploitation and express feelings of alienation. This paradox supports Bartky's claim that women may be epistemically and ethically disempowered by providing nurturance for others while they receive little compensation — emotional and material — in return (117). Women's so-called innate, instinctual desire to nurture and care for others brings them a psychic income — personal fulfillment and satisfaction — yet that psychic income is "the blood at the root" (A. Ferguson) of women's exploitation as underpaid workers.

To understand the costs as well as benefits of an ethic of care in feminist writing pedagogy, I conducted primary research on contingent women writing instructors' attitudes toward their work, exploring the contradictory forces that surround their involvement in writing instruction. My research reveals that a pedagogy based on an ethic of care is simultaneously empowering and disempowering: it offers psychic rewards while exacting a distinct emotional and material price from women workers.

Contingent Labor as Sex-Affective Production

In the fall of 1992 and spring of 1993, I interviewed a dozen lecturers (both full- and part-time) who held semester-to-semester teaching contracts in the first-year writing program at the University of Wisconsin, Milwaukee, where I worked as a teaching assistant and assistant writing program coordinator. The interviewees were white women ranging in ages from twenty-five to fifty-five; most had master's degrees in literature or education, and some had completed credits toward the doctoral degree. The women of ages twenty-five to thirty-five had five to seven years of teaching experience in community colleges or state universities; the women of ages thirty-five to fifty-five had taught for ten to fifteen years in community colleges, state universities, or public and private elementary and secondary schools. I conducted the interviews in an open-ended manner, allowing the responses to determine the order of the questions. Each interview lasted approximately ninety minutes and was taped and partially transcribed. To allow these women to speak candidly and without fear of institutional reprisal, I have omitted their identities. (I also surveyed essays and articles on women's experiences as part-time and non-tenure-track faculty members to broaden the perspective of my interview project. And as a former part-time faculty member, I drew on my own experiences.)

In the interviews, I investigated how contingent women faculty members describe the costs and benefits of their work, and I paid particular attention to their "workplace emotions," a term used by Carol Stearns and Peter Stearns, who research "emotionology," the history and sociology of the emotions (7–8). Stearns and Stearns define emotions as socially constructed, historically specific responses rather than as transhistorical and transcultural essences. In a separate essay, Peter Stearns describes how nineteenth-century industrialization brought technological displacement, inflation, management impersonality, white-middle-class downward mobility, and the increasing isolation of unskilled workers (149–50). In the early twentieth-century office, management began to suppress anger and impose a standard of surface friendliness, particularly among white-collar workers and those who worked "in a variety of service industries including the airlines and branches of social work" (156). Because of societal expectations and management policies that mandate friendliness and nurturant behavior, workers in caring professions increasingly experience emotions like anger, cynicism, and frustration in response to a loss of autonomy, increased work hierarchies, management domination and surveillance, job instability, lack of promotion, and specific forms of workplace discrimination.[4]

In my interviews with part-time women writing instructors, the concept of workplace emotion helped illuminate a split between the instructors' feelings about their classrooms and their feelings about the institutions that employed them. Both the interviewees and the writers of published narratives revealed that while they liked, even loved, to teach, they nearly all had negative feelings about their working conditions and their relation to the institution at large. In the classroom, they felt in control, valued, and alive; in the institution, they often felt invisible and alienated.

The separation between institutional space and classroom space mirrors the attitude that teaching is a private or individual activity and research a public activity. In an account of her experiences as a part-time writing instructor at the State University of New York, Stony Brook, Clare Frost characterizes this public-private split: "I may be a misfit in the academy but not in my classroom. For me it's not a job, it's a calling. The pain of being an adjunct is not inflicted in the classroom, but in the hallowed halls of academe. My struggle to be seen and heard in this discipline is also a struggle to have faith in myself and what I'm doing" (66).

In both the published narratives and the interviews I conducted, women writing instructors reported passionate feelings about teaching and described a sense of connection and satisfaction; they identified their teaching roles as supportive, nurturing, and facilitative. One interviewee characterized herself as a midwife: "I think they've got little baby writers in them that are going to be born. I'm helping the student who has had *x* number of bad encounters with writing give birth to that infant writer inside." Many of the interviewees remarked that they continue to endure exploitative working conditions because they enjoy teaching. Frost writes:

> I love the teaching of composition. I enjoy seeing my students use writing to tap into themselves, some for the first time in their lives. I glow when some of their final evaluations say that the course was better than they expected it or that their attitudes about writing have improved. For me, getting to know a new group of young people each semester and seeing what they can accomplish in a few short months is exhilarating. I don't find their writing boring, because I don't find them boring. (66)

One woman, in her late forties and with over ten years of teaching experience, argued that the students, not the institutional setting, offered her psychic rewards: "The students give a lot back to me. The institution doesn't give me much. I get a paycheck, I get an office, I get a nine-year-old computer. I don't get much support from the institution." The attachment to teaching is bittersweet because many contingent teachers are isolated from professional networks. Nancy Grimm, a formerly part-time writing teacher at Michigan Technological University, describes the unstable nature of part-time labor:

> For seven years I have taught part-time. I give conference presentations. I publish a little. I even direct the local site of the National Writing Project — one of the department's few graduate level offerings. But at this university I will never be full-time, and I will never be hired for more than a year at a time. My part-time teaching load fluctuates each year. More than once, I have made less money than I made the year before. My teaching load — and consequently my salary — depends on how many gaps the department has to fill. I am going nowhere, but to work effectively I can't let myself confront the issue too often. (14)

The key issue for contingent women faculty members who wish to participate in research and scholarship is "work time" — the way in which students and teachers circulate in the organizational structure of English (Watkins 4–6). In composition studies, the work time of intellectuals (specialists, practitioners) is directly affected by the research-teaching division, a split predicated on the difference between the creation of knowledge and the perpetuation of already existing knowledge or know-how. Teachers perpetuate what Antonio Gramsci has characterized as the "pre-existing traditional, accumulated intellectual wealth," whereas scholars create new forms of knowledge (307). Scholars, Evan Watkins writes, are classified as professionals "understood to work at the very frontiers of knowledge, at the edge of a 'heart of darkness' where expertise . . . [is] tested in the most demanding situations" (104).

Teaching writing, of course, resides on the low end of the research-teaching binary. Not only is writing instruction devalued, but it also requires substantial time and emotional energy from the teacher. The CCCC "Statement on Principles and Standards for the Postsecondary Teaching of Writing" acknowledges that writing instruction is labor-intensive:

> The improvement of an individual student's writing requires persistent and frequent contact between teacher and student both inside and outside the classroom. It requires assigning far more papers than are usually assigned in other college classrooms; it requires reading them and commenting on them not simply to justify a grade, but to offer guidance and suggestions for improvement; and it requires spending a great deal of time with individual students, helping them not just to improve particular papers but to understand fundamental principles of effective writing that will enable them to continue learning throughout their lives. (335)

The labor-intensive nature of writing instruction makes it difficult for contingent faculty members in composition to take part in scholarly conversations. Mary Kupiec Cayton argues, "The material conditions of participating in the conversation that is academic scholarship include the ability to devote oneself to it wholeheartedly — at least at certain points in time." Borrowing Kenneth Burke's metaphor that scholarship resembles a parlor conversation, Cayton likens contingent faculty members to parlor maids who are busy "attending to the necessary chores that will free the guests for conversing." Because their teaching responsibilities — and often family responsibilities — remove them from the parlor conversation that is academic scholarship, contingent women faculty members often "play a supporting role rather than the role of the participant," and as a result they hear and understand less "of what is transpiring inside the parlor" (655). Frost attests to the difficult choices they must make regarding their work time:

> After family responsibilities and more than thirty hours a week spent directly on the teaching of three sections of composition, I have to think carefully and pragmatically about how I'm going to spend the precious remaining time. . . . For the sad truth is that even if I become more knowledgeable — read theorists, attend conferences, present papers, take additional courses — I will receive no additional institutional recognition of any sort. I will not receive a penny more in remuneration for the courses I currently teach, nor will I become eligible for a full-time position or additional employee benefits. In fact, no practical or professional benefit will result. (63–64)

One of the interviewees, an experienced instructor with a background in ESL and teaching experience at several institutions, commented that, while she felt the writing program administrator and his assistant valued and respected her work as a teacher, she was invisible to the rest of the university: "As far as the rest of the school goes, I don't even think they know who I am. I'm just someone filling a hole, and they don't know about my experiences, they don't know about my ideas, I know they don't know who I am, they don't care who I am, they just want someone in there teaching classes."

She referred to herself as an interchangeable part, "not even a person — just a cog" in the university machine. Another interviewee described the university as a machine that consumes human labor: "A friend of mine once said the institution wants to chew you up and when they're done with you, they'll spit you out." She commented on her expendability: "You know there will be five more people standing in line to do what I do, and they'll love doing what they're doing just like I love doing what I'm doing."

For those interviewees who had been working for many years as contingent writing instructors, the overwhelming response to their professional situation was a growing and hardening cynicism. One woman stated that she had learned not to expect any rewards or recognition from the university: "I think I'm just very hardnosed and resigned. I just say 'I like my job, I'm good at my job,' but I don't have any expectations. I don't expect any recognition. I'm just jaded and sort of hardened to anything like that." As Cynthia Tuell relates, contingent faculty members are like handmaids:

> We clean up the comma splices. We organize the discourse of our students as though straightening a closet. When it's straight the "regular" professors teaching "regular" courses don't have to pick through the clutter and can quickly find the suit that suits them. When we can't manage to scrub them clean, we are called on to flunk out the great unwashed before they sully the orderly classrooms of the upper divisions. As handmaids, we are replaceable and interchangeable. . . . As handmaids, we serve the needs of our masters, not the vision we may have of ourselves, of our work, or of our students. (126)

For many women, the cycle of contingent teaching constitutes a form of exploitation sweetened by emotional or psychic rewards.

Although teaching composition has been thought of as women's work for the past seventy years, we have only begun to question the larger socioeconomic structures that channel women into contingent work.[5] As feminists in composition studies, we need to understand how femininist arguments for an ethic of care may reinforce the cycle of sex-affective production, in which women work hard but appropriate few professional rewards for themselves. By studying women's work narratives, we can gain alternative visions of our disciplinary realities and begin to rethink fundamental assumptions about our disciplinary identities and the structure of academic work. Ultimately, we can work on multiple levels — national and local — to organize coalitions that improve the working conditions of our colleagues who are non-tenure-track writing instructors.

Addressing Professional Inequities

Although we — feminist teachers and intellectuals — may exercise an ethic of care in our writing classrooms, we may fail to exhibit an analogous ethic in our relations with non-tenure-track faculty members. Unlike Susan Miller's "sad women in the basement" (*Carnivals* 121), some of us work on the first floors of English departments, where we serve as writing program administrators and as directors of writing centers, writing-across-the-curriculum programs, and graduate programs in rhetoric and composition. Many of us train and supervise graduate teaching assistants and serve as dissertation advisers, holding power and prestige unimaginable to women writing teachers of previous generations.

But our privilege does not mean that we are exempt from the threat of sexual discrimination and sexual harassment. Some of us on the tenure track feel exploited and underappreciated; some of us have been denied tenure and feel that our work in writing pedagogy and rhetorical theory has been undervalued; some of us have been pushed into administering writing programs as untenured assistant professors and must fight to maintain time for our scholarly work. Our experiences resonate with those of the women scholars who pioneered composition studies and who tell us of the great personal and professional price they paid to achieve professional recognition in a fledgling subdiscipline (see Crowley, "Three Heroines").

Empowered financially and professionally yet subject to sexual discrimination and sexual harassment, women academics occupy contradictory roles (see Luke and Gore, "Women"). Evelyn Fox Keller and Helene Moglen find that academic women, because of their historically marginal positions in higher education, "continue to feel the oppression of past struggles and the ongoing burdens of tokenism" (26). Uncomfortable with newly won power and embattled by the criticisms of hostile colleagues, they may not realize the privileges or advantages they do have (28). Nor are they "immune to the problem of competition"; in an economy of scarce resources, where "influence and power are by definition in limited supply," women must compete with one another for positions, committee and teaching assignments, teaching awards, and book contracts (22). Academic women also directly and indirectly benefit from the exploitation of other women's labor, particularly the labor of non-tenure-track faculty members. Even as I write this essay, I am benefiting from the exploitation of contingent faculty members at my institution. My research load — and the research load of three dozen other tenure-track faculty members — is made possible by the labor of approximately forty part-time and full-time non-tenure-track writing faculty members, two-thirds of whom are women. I call attention to this issue to illustrate the deep contradictions — tensions and discontinuities — of academic life. While many of us work to alleviate inequities in our classrooms, we are nevertheless complicit in gendered inequities that are often invisible or appear natural to us. Feminist research in composition studies, however, can serve as a site for exposing, questioning, and changing academic hierarchies that are considered natural. The continuing presence of women in contingent writing instructorships can become a site of activisim for feminists in composition.

I am not alone in calling for better working conditions for contingent writing instructors. The CCCC has addressed the problem of contingent labor through its 1989 "Statement of Principles and Standards for Postsecondary Writing Instruction." Adapted from the 1986 "Wyoming Conference Resolution" — a grass-roots petition calling for improvements in the working conditions for exploited writing faculty members — the CCCC statement is "based on the assumption that the responsibility for the academy's most serious mission, helping students to develop their critical powers as readers and writers, should be vested in tenure-line faculty" (330).[6]

Although the statement acknowledges that "most teachers of writing are women and that many more of them are people of color than are tenure-line faculty" (CCCC Committee 336), it does not address the specific barriers to success women face in academic work: racial and sexual discrimination, sexual harassment, and the gendered division of labor.[7] Neither the "Wyoming Conference Resolution" nor the CCCC statement deals with the larger social and economic structures that channel women into contingent labor. The problem of contingent labor in composition studies is not just a professional issue that we can correct by eliminating contingent positions and hiring more full-time faculty members; it is a gender issue, and thus a feminist issue, tied to larger systems of exploitation. To ignore this problem is to ignore one of the largest gender inequities in English studies.

Feminists in composition must find ways to alleviate this problem through collective action. Two groups in the CCCC, the Committee on the Status of Women in the Profession and the Coalition of Women Scholars in the History of Rhetoric and Composition, offer sites for promoting the professional development and equitable treatment of women faculty members in composition. In addition, the yearly CCCC feminist workshop offers a forum for women to meet and discuss feminist research, pedagogy, and professional issues. At the 1995 CCCC feminist workshop, Women in the Academy: Can a Feminist Agenda Transform the Illusion of Equity into Reality?, presenters spoke about family and partner choices, part-time labor, administrative work, ageism, sexual orientation, race, ethnicity, and class issues. Workshop leaders Jody Millward and Susan Hahn distributed a mission statement entitled "Other Choices, Other Voices: Solutions to Gender Issues" and proposed that the CCCC, NCTE, American Association of University Women, and MLA conduct an investigative survey of the employment, underemployment, and professional choices of women in ESL, essential skills, and composition. They urged the organizations to establish an ethical code of hiring that would consider the traditional practice of hiring from the outside rather than promoting from within; the high teaching load and lack of institutional support for nonliterary fields; the overreliance of institutions on temporary contracts and part-time positions; recommendations for health and retirement benefits; recommendations for flexible careers, including job sharing, part-time tenure, and flexibility of tenure deadlines; maternal-leave policies and spousal hiring; the establishment and enforcement of sexual harassment policies; the enforcement of policies to prohibit discrimination based on ethnicity, age, marital status, sexual orientation, and number of children. In addition, members of the workshop drafted a statement on affirmative action to be presented to the CCCC Executive Committee.

Efforts to combat the problem of gender and contingent labor on a national level emphasize consciousness-raising and general organizing strategies, but local organizing may be a better way to change specific institutional climates. On university campuses across the country, faculty women's coalitions have offered many academic women the opportunity to act collectively and speak out against sex discrimination, sexual harassment, and the general exploitation of women faculty members.[8] For instance, on nonunionized campuses a local departmental or university-wide women's coalition could conduct a study of the working conditions of non-tenure-track women faculty members across campus, offering both a statistical analysis and testimonial accounts of hiring practices, salaries, evaluation procedures, contract renewal, fringe benefits, and professional development opportunities. Armed with such a report and a comparative analysis of working conditions at peer institutions, a women's coalition could influence departmental and university administrators to improve the working conditions, salary, benefits, and professional development opportunities for non-tenure-track women. Moreover, faculty women's coalitions provide psychological support for women, a designated space for women to meet and receive professional advice and mentoring (for coalition models see Childers et al.).

A major obstacle confronting women's coalition building is the meritocracy ideal — the individualist "work hard and you will succeed" mentality that fails to acknowledge power relations and hierarchies among women. Many powerful women faculty members see their achievements as individual efforts and hesitate to help other women, particularly non-tenure-track faculty members. Bernice Johnson Reagon characterizes the problem: "Sometimes you get comfortable in your little barred room and you decide you in fact are going to live there and carry out all of your stuff in there. And you gonna take care of everything that needs to be taken care of in the barred room" (358). For women the academy can operate as a barred room where a few enter while others are left outside. As we feminists in composition studies gain intellectual capital and institutional clout, we must not merely advance our individual careers and unquestioningly perpetuate the hierarchies and inequities of disciplinary culture; we must find ways to critique and transform the inequitable labor situation for non-tenure-track women faculty members, many of whom are our former students. While working at the material level — in local university and college settings and through professional organizations — we also need to reassess the theories that guide our feminist practices. Although femininist writing pedagogy deserves recognition and praise, we must ask if an ethic of care will enable us to improve and transform the working conditions and material realities of writing teachers. We need models of feminist thought that reassess rather than reinscribe the costs and benefits of the ideology of nurturance. Socialist feminist analyses enable us to see the costs of nurturant labor and help us make self-conscious choices about our investment in femininist pedagogies. Without acknowledging differences among women, the costs of maternal pedagogy, and the gendered constructions of teaching, theories of femininist pedagogy may reinscribe the woman-teacher-as-caretaker ideology, a time-honored role that has often limited and circumscribed women's mobility and creativity.

Notes

I thank Lynn Worsham for the term "contingent workers" and for her intellectual guidance in the formulation of this essay.

[1]See Mary Field Belenky, Blythe McVicker Clinchy, Nancy Rule Goldberger, and Jill Mattuck Tarule's description of a "caring" or "connected" pedagogy in chapter 10 of *Women's Ways of Knowing* ("Connected Teaching "). See also Noddings.

[2]See also Tronto's analysis of an ethic of care in *Moral Boundaries*. For a general overview of the philosophical and political debates over an "ethic of care," see Larrabee.

[3]"Psychic income" is a term used in economic theory to describe the non-monetary rewards of labor. For a feminist assessment of the psychic costs of a psychic income, see Gillam.

[4]For an insightful discussion of pedagogy and schooling as a site for the education of emotion, see Worsham, "Emotion and Pedagogic Violence."

[5]For an informative survey of the problem of part-time labor in composition studies, see Slevin. For general accounts of contingent academic employment across the disciplines, see Emily Abel; Gappa and Leslie; Leslie, Kellams, and Gunne; Tuckman and Tuckman; Tuckman, Vogler, and Caldwell.

[6]The CCCC statement advises that no more than ten percent of a department's course sections be staffed by part-time faculty members (CCCC Executive Committee 333). The statement, however, has been criticized by part-time teachers who object to the recommendation that departments transform part-time lines into tenure-track positions and impose "severe limits on the ratio of part-time to full-time faculty" (333). Part-time faculty teachers accused the statement of favoring research faculty members and discrediting practitioners, "those whose expertise has developed outside the typical, traditional scholarly track" (Gunner, "Fate" 117). They argue that the Wyoming resolution has been transformed from an argument for improved working conditions for contingent faculty members to an argument for hiring Ph.D.s in rhetoric and composition. But neither side has fully examined the implications of the relation between gender and part-time status, and this is where feminists can make an important intervention.

[7]Regardless of my criticisms of the CCCC "Statement," I would like to acknowledge the important work of Sharon Crowley, James Slevin, and other former members of the CCCC Committee on Professional Standards who have brought the issue of non-tenure-track labor to the attention of tenured faculty and administrators.

[8]Faculty members who wish to address the problem of gender and part-time labor should consult the professional statements about reasonable contingent working conditions: Modern Language Association; AAUP Committee; AAUP Subcommittee; CCCC Executive Committee; CCCC Committee; Robertson, Crowley, and Lentricchia (on the "Wyoming Conference Resolution"); Wyche-Smith and Rose (on the "Wyoming Conference Resolution"). General guides to improving the working conditions of part-time faculty members through organizing efforts can be found in Gappa; Gappa and Leslie; Tuckman and Biles; Wallace. Journals and newsletters devoted exclusively to contingent instructors and the improvement of their working conditions are the *Adjunct Advocate, Professing: An Organ for Those Who Teach Undergraduates,* and *Forum: The Newsletter of the Part-Time Faculty Forum for the CCCC.* Helpful general guides to organizing women's coalitions are Bannerji et al.; DeSole and Hoffmann.

Works Cited

Aisenberg, Nadya and Mona Harrington. *Women of Academe: Outsiders in the Sacred Grove.* Amherst: U of Massachusetts P, 1988.

Alcoff, Linda. "Cultural Feminism versus Post-structuralism: The Identity Crisis in Feminist Theory." *Signs: Journal of Women in Culture and Society* (1988): 405–36.

Althusser, Louis. "Ideology and Ideological State Apparatuses." *Contemporary Critical Theory.* Ed. Dan Latimer. San Diego: Hartcourt, 1989, 61–102.

Bartky, Sandra Lee. *Femininity and Domination: Studies in the Phenomenology of Oppression.* New York: Routledge, 1990.

Batson, Lorie Goodman. "Defining Ourselves as Women (in the Profession)." *Pre/Text: A Journal of Rhetorical Theory* (1988): 207–09.

Bergmann, Barbara R. "Feminism and Economics." *Academe* (Sept.-Oct. 1983): 22–25.

Burns, Margie. "Service Courses: Doing Women a Disservice." *Academe* (May-June 1983): 18–21.

Caylon, Mary Kupiec. "Writing as Outsiders: Academic Discourse and Marginalized Faculty." *College English* 53 (1991): 647–60.

Caywood, Cynthia L., and Gillian R. Overing. Introduction. Caywood and Overing, *Teaching* xi–xvi.

Childers, Karen, et al. "A Network of One's Own." DeSole and Hoffmann 117–227.

Crowley, Sharon. "Three Heroines: An Oral History." *Pre/Text: A Journal of Rhetorical Theory* (1988): 202–06.

Daumer, Elisabeth, and Sandra Runzo. "Transforming the Composition Classroom." Caywood and Overing, *Teaching* 45–62.

Ferguson, Ann. *Blood at the Root: Motherhood, Sexuality, and Male Dominance.* London: Pandora, 1989.

Flynn, Elizabeth A. "Composing as a Woman." *College Composition and Communication* 39 (1988): 423–35.

Friedman, Susan Stanford. "Authority in the Feminist Classroom: A Contradiction in Terms." *Gendered Subjects: The Dynamics of Feminist Teaching.* Ed. Margo Culley and Catherine Portugues. New York: Routledge, 1985. 203–08.

Frost, Clare. "Looking for a Gate in the Fence." Fontaine and Hunter 59–69.

Frye, Marilyn. "On Being White: Thinking toward a Feminist Understanding of Race and Race Supremacy." *The Politics of Reality.* Freedom: Crossing, 1983, 110–27.

Gappa, Judith, and David Leslie. *The Invisible Faculty: Improving the Status of Part-Timers in Higher Education.* San Francisco: Jossey-Bass, 1993.

Gore, Jennifer M. *The Struggle for Pedagogies: Critical and Feminist Discourses as Regimes of Truth.* New York: Routledge, 1993.

Goulston, Wendy. "Women Writing." Caywood and Overing. *Teaching* 19–30.

Gramsci, Antonio. *An Antonio Gramsci Reader: Selected Writings, 1916–1935.* Ed. David Forgacs. New York: Schocken, 1988.

Grimm, Nancy. Account. "The Part-Time Problem: Four Voices." By Elizabeth A. Flynn, John F. Flynn, Nancy Grimm, and Ted Lockhart. *Academe* Jan-Feb. 1986: 14–15.

Holbrook, Sue Ellen. "Women's Work: The Feminizing of Composition Studies." *Rhetorical Review* 9 (1991): 201–29.

Huber, Bettina. "Women in the Modern Languages, 1970–90." *Profession* 90. New York: MLA, 1990. 58–73.

Keller, Evelyn Fox, and Helene Moglen. "Competition: A Problem for Academic Women." Miner and Longino 21–37.

Koblitz, Neal. "Bias and Other Factors in Student Ratings." *Chronicle of Higher Education* 1 Sept. 1993: B3.

Lewis, Magda. "Interrupting Patriarchy: Politics, Resistance, and Transformation in the Feminist Classroom." Luke and Gore, *Feminisms* 167–91.

Looser, Devoney. "Composing as an 'Essentialist'? New Directions for Feminist Composition Theories." *Rhetoric Review* 12 (1993): 54–69.

Luke, Carmen, and Jennifer Gore, eds. *Feminisms and Critical Pedagogy.* New York: Routledge, 1992.

Markus, Maria. "Women, Success, and Civil Society: Submission to, or Subversion of, the Achievement Principle." *Feminism as Critique: Essays on the Politics of Gender in Late-Capitalist Societies.* Ed. Seyla Benhabib and Drucilla Cornell. Cambridge: Blackwell, 1987. 96–109.

Miller, Susan. "The Feminization of Composition." Bullock and Trimbur 39–53.

Noddings, Nel. *Caring: A Feminine Approach to Ethics and Moral Education.* Berkeley: U of California P, 1984.

Perry, William G. *Forms of Intellectual and Ethical Development in the College Years.* New York: Holt, Rinehart, 1970.

Phelps, Louise Wetherbee. "A Constrained Vision of the Writing Classroom." *Profession 93.* New York: MLA, 1993. 46–54.

Reagon, Bernice Johnson. "Coalition Politics: Turning the Century." B. Smith. *Girls* 356–68.

Rubin, Donnalee. *Gender Influences: Reading Student Texts.* Carbondale: Southern Illinois UP, 1993.

Simeone, Angela. *Academic Women: Working towards Equality.* Boston: Bergin, 1987.

Stanger, Carol. "The Sexual Politics of the One-to-One Tutorial Approach and Collaborative Learning." Caywood and Overing, *Teaching* 31–44.

Stearns, Carol Zisowitz, and Peter N. Stearns. Introduction. *Emotion and Social Change: Toward a New Psychohistory.* Ed. Stearns and Stearns. New York: Homes, 1988. 1–21.

Tronto, Joan C. *Moral Boundaries: A Political Argument for an Ethic of Care.* New York: Routledge, 1993.

Tuell, Cynthia. "Composition Teaching as 'Women's Work': Daughters, Handmaids, Whores, and Mothers." Fontaine and Hunter 123–39.

Wallace, M. Elizabeth. "Who Are These Part-Time Faculty Anyway?" *Part Time Academic Employment in the Humanities.* Ed. Wallace. New York: MLA, 1984. 3–29.

Watkins, Evan. *Work Time: English Departments and Circulation of Cultural Value.* Stanford: Stanford UP, 1989.

Wicke, Jennifer, and Margaret Ferguson. "Introduction: Feminism and Postmodernism; or The Way We Live Now." *Feminism and Postmodernism.* Ed. Wicke and Ferguson. Durham: Duke UP, 1994. 10–33.

Schell's Insights as a Resource for Your Teaching

1. In your journal, consider how sexual-identity politics inform your own classroom practice. Reflect on the tension between a "maternalistic" process and its masculine opposite. Which process predominates in your classroom? Which do the students seem to solicit? Which does your institution solicit? How do these solicitations work out in your day-to-day practice?

2. Schell suggests that there is a strong, though incomplete, link between what Berlin (356) calls the expressivist approach and her description of maternalistic processes. How might you modify Schell's claims about the particular ideologies that inform the gender dynamics of the composition classroom?

Schell's Insights as a Resource for the Writing Classroom

1. Discuss gender stereotypes that surround the study of literate practices with your students. Broadly speaking, girls are supposed to be good at English, whereas boys are supposed to be good at science — and yet the standard conception of the great writer is typically male. Have them explore these stereotypes, where they come from, and how they affect the struggle to teach and learn writing. Use Schell's arguments to organize your own questions for the students to answer.

2. Ask the students to write in their journals and then discuss in small groups their understanding of the role of writing instruction within the larger curriculum of their school. Ask them to consider the importance of writing with respect to their chances of success or failure in the world. What role does writing play in one's career? How significant is one's gender? How important is writing within the curriculum of your school? Do gender dynamics govern writing instruction? Are there conflicts or inequities to discuss?

JAMES A. BERLIN   *Poststructuralism, Cultural Studies, and the Composition Classroom: Postmodern Theory in Practice*

Rhetorician James A. Berlin (1942–1993) wrote extensively about the history and theory of rhetoric and composition over time and in American institutions. He served the disciplines of rhetoric and composition studies with his explorations of the interconnections of rhetoric, ideology, and pedagogy. In "Rhetoric and Ideology in the Writing Classroom" (reprinted in Chapter 1) Berlin identifies three major kinds of rhetorics that have influenced current theory and practice of teaching writing: he has named the practitioners "expressivists" (Elbow, McCrorie, and Murray), "cognitivists" (Flower, Hayes, and Lunsford), and "social-epistemicists" (Freire and Shor).

In this article, Berlin defends the use of postmodern theory in rhetoric and composition studies: "It is clear to me that rhetoric and composition studies has arrived as a serious field of study because it has taken into account the best that has been thought and said about its concerns from the past and the present, and I have found that postmodern work in historical and contemporary rhetorical theory has done much to further this effort." He traces a convergence of postmodern speculation and rhetorical studies — most particularly, social-epistemic rhetoric.

Recognizing the difficulty of the body of thought and its discourse conventions, Berlin gears the discussion toward "the overworked composition teacher or the new graduate student" as he discusses some postmodern concepts that he views as counterparts to ideas in social-epistemic rhetoric. Berlin offers a fourth way to see English 101. Cultural studies, cultural critique, and postmodern insights intersecting in a social-epistemic rhetoric have a purpose that Berlin defines as "finally political, an effort to prepare students for critical citizenship in a democracy."

The uses of postmodern theory in rhetoric and composition studies have been the object of considerable abuse of late. Figures of some repute in the field — the likes of Maxine Hairston and Peter Elbow — as well as anonymous voices from the Burkean Parlor section of *Rhetoric Review* — most recently, TS, a graduate student, and KF, a voice speaking for "a general English teacher audience" (192) — have joined the chorus of protest. The charges have included willful obscurity, self-indulgence, elitism, pomposity, intellectual impoverishment, and a host of related offenses. Although my name usually appears among the accused, I am sympathetic with those undergoing the difficulties of the first encounter with this discussion. (I exclude Professor Hairston in her irresponsible charge that its recent contributors in *College English* are "low-risk Marxists who write very badly" [695] and who should be banned from NCTE publications.) I experienced the same frustration when I first encountered the different but closely related language of rhetoric and composition studies some fifteen years ago. I wondered, for example, if I would ever grasp the complexities of Aristotle or Quintilian or Kenneth Burke or I. A. Richards, not to mention the new language of the writing process. A bit later I was introduced to French poststructuralism, and once again I found myself wandering in strange seas, and this time alone. In reading rhetoric, after all, I had the benefit of numerous commentators to help me along — the work of Kinneavy and Lauer and Corbett and Emig, for example. In reading Foucault and Derrida in the late seventies, on the other hand, I was largely on my own since the commentaries were as difficult as the originals, and those few that were readable were often (as even I could see) wrong. Nonetheless, with the help of informal reading groups made up of colleagues and students, I persisted in my efforts to come to terms with this difficult body of thought.

I was then, as now, convinced that both rhetorical studies and postmodern specula-tion offered strikingly convergent and remarkably compelling visions for conduct-ing my life as a teacher and a citizen. It is clear to me that rhetoric and composition studies has arrived as a serious field of study because it has taken into account the best that has been thought and said about its concerns from the past and the present, and I have found that postmodern work in historical and contemporary rhetorical theory has done much to further this effort.

I will readily admit that discussants in postmodern theories of rhetoric have been more concerned with advancing this immensely rich vein of speculation than they have with communicating with the novice. But I think it is a mistake to con-demn them for this. Contrary to what KF, the hard-working general English teacher, has asserted, teaching writing is not a "relatively simple and straightforward task" (192). As the intense effort that has been given this activity in the 2500-year history of Western education indicates, communication is at once extremely important in the life of a society and extremely complex (see the histories of Kennedy or Corbett or Vickers, for example). Those who wish to come to grips with this complexity cannot be expected to write exclusively for the uninitiated, a move that would hope-lessly retard the development of any discussion. A new rhetoric requires a new lan-guage if we are to develop devices for producing and interpreting discourse that are adequate to our historical moment. I would argue that those working today at the intersections of rhetoric and postmodern theory are beginning to generate rhetorics that in conception and pedagogical application promise to be counterparts to the greatest accomplishments of the past — of an Aristotle (who once sounded strange next to Plato) or an Isocrates (who sounded strange next to Gorgias) or to Campbell (who sounded strange next to Ward). Eventually (and sooner than we might imag-ine, I expect), those interested in rhetoric will be talking and thinking in the new terminologies emerging today, finding them just as comfortable as the language of cognitive rhetoric or expressionist rhetoric. Still, this does not help the overworked composition teacher or the new graduate student who is eager to explore the sig-nificance of this new speculation for theory and the classroom but is not sure where to start.

In this essay I want to present as clearly as I know how some of the central features of postmodern theory that workers in rhetoric have found especially rel-evant to their efforts. Since covering the field as whole would require more space than I have here, however, I want to restrict myself to considering the ways these postmodern conceptions are counterparts to discussions in social-epistemic rheto-ric. I will also include a description of a freshman course I have designed that is the result of my theoretical studies, a course that combines methods of cultural studies (itself a product of postmodern thought coupled with a progressive politics) with the methods of social-epistemic rhetoric in a beginning composition class. My in-tent is to demonstrate that the complexities of theory have immediate pedagogical applications, and that one of the efforts of composition teachers must be to discover these. Indeed, I will argue that the merger of theory and classroom practice in a uniquely new relation is one of the results of (what I should perhaps now call) postmodern rhetorical theory.

The Postmodern

John Schilb has explained that postmodernism "can designate a critique of tra-ditional epistemology, a set of artistic practices, and an ensemble of larger social conditions" (174). Here the focus will be on the first, particularly on that body of thought that has emerged in what is loosely called structuralist and poststructuralist theory (sometimes called the "language division" of postmodern speculation). In

"Rhetoric Programs after World War II: Ideology, Power, and Conflict," I attempt to outline the ways certain branches of rhetorical studies in the US, particularly of the epistemic variety, have paralleled the trajectory of structuralist and poststructuralist developments both at home and abroad. In this section I would like to explore the important features of postmodernism in which this is most apparent; in the next I will trace their uses in social-epistemic rhetoric. The significant postmodern developments fall into three general categories: the status of the subject; the characteristics of signifying practices; the role of master theories in explaining human affairs.

The unified, coherent, autonomous, self-present subject of the Enlightenment has been the centerpiece of liberal humanism. From this perspective the subject is a transcendent consciousness that functions unencumbered by social and material conditions of experience, acting as a free and rational agent who adjudicates competing claims for action. In other words, the individual is regarded as the author of all her actions, moving in complete freedom in deciding how she will live. This perception has been challenged by the postmodern conception of the subject as the product of social and material conditions. Here the subject is considered the construction of the various signifying practices, the uses of language, of a given historical moment (see, for example, Benveniste, Barthes, Foucault). This means that each person is formed by the various discourses, sign systems, that surround her. These include both everyday uses of language in the home, school, the media, and other institutions, as well as the material conditions that are arranged in the manner of languages — that is, semiotically (like a sign system), such as the clothes we wear, the way we carry our bodies, the way our school and home environments are arranged. These signifying practices then are languages that tell us who we are and how we should behave in terms of such categories as gender, race, class, age, ethnicity, and the like. The result is that each of us is heterogeneously made up of various competing discourses, conflicted and contradictory scripts, that make our consciousness anything but unified, coherent, and autonomous. At the most everyday level; for example, the discourses of the school and the home about appropriate gender behavior ("Just say 'No'!") are frequently at odds with the discourse provided by peers and the media ("Go for it"). The result is that we are made up of subject formations or subject positions that do not always square with each other.

Signifying practices then are at the center of the formation of the "subject" and of "subjectivities" — terms made necessary to avoid all the liberal humanist implications of talking about the "individual." But the conception of signifying practices, of language, is itself radically altered in this scheme. A given language is no longer taken to be a transparent medium that records an externally present thing-in-itself, that is, it is not a simple signaling device that stands for and corresponds to the separate realities that lend it meaning. Language is instead taken to be a pluralistic and complex system of signifying practices that construct realities rather than simply presenting or re-presenting them. Our conception of material and social phenomena then are fabrications of signifying, the products of culturally coded signs. Saussure, the prime originator of structuralism in Europe, first demonstrated the ways language functions as a set of differences: Signifiers derive meaning not in relation to signifieds, to external referents, but in relation to other signifiers, the semiotic systems in which they are functioning. For example, just as the sound "t" is significant in English because it contrasts with *d* — making for a difference in meaning between *to* and *do* — a term, such as *man*, has significance in a given discourse because it contrasts with another term, such as *woman* or *boy* or *ape*. And just as the sounds of a language are culturally variable, so are its terms and their structural relations. A sign thus has meaning by virtue of its position relative to another sign or signs within a given system, not to externally verifiable certainties. Most important, these signs are arranged in a hierarchy so that one is "privileged," that is, considered more important than its related term. For example, Alleen Pace Nilsen has shown that terms in English that are gender specific almost invariably involve positive connotations in the case of males and negative connotation in the case of females (*master/mistress, sir/madam, chef/cook,* for example). Such hierarchies, once again, are not universal but are culturally specific.

Roland Barthes has shown the ways that signs form systems (semiotic systems) that extend beyond natural language to all realms of a culture, for example, film, television, photography, food, fashion, automobiles, and on and on (see *Mythologies*). He presents a method for analyzing and discussing the semiosis (sign production) of texts as they appear in virtually all features of human behavior. Michel Foucault has indicated the manner in which different "discursive regimes," elaborate systems of signifying systems, forge knowledge/power formations that govern action during successive stages of history. (He does so, furthermore, while denying any master regime or narrative unfolding over time, a matter to be considered shortly.) Finally, Jacques Derrida has shown the attempt of philosophy to establish a foundation, an essential presence, for its systems in a realm outside of language, an effort to avoid the role of signification, of discourse, in all human undertakings. From the postmodern perspective, then, signifying practices shape the subject, the social, and the material — the perceiver and the perceived.

These antifoundational, antiessentialist assaults on Enlightenment conceptions of the subjects and objects of experience are extended to postulates of grand narratives of the past or present — that is, the stories we tell about our experiences that attempt to account for all features of it (its totality) in a comprehensive way. Jean-François Lyotard has been the central figure in denying the possibility of any grand metanarrative that might exhaustively account for human conditions in the past or present. Like Foucault, he renounces the totalizing discourse of such schemes as Hegelianism or Marxism or the faith in scientific progress or the invisible hand of economic law. All are declared language games that are inherently partial and interested, intended to endorse particular relations of power and to privilege certain groups in historical struggles. Against this totalizing move, Lyotard argues for a plurality of particular narratives, limited and localized accounts that attempt to explain features of experience that grand narratives exclude. The structuralist and poststructuralist analyses of sign systems look for the binary opposites of key terms, the marginalized terms that often go unmentioned. (This is why they use the term *foreground:* it refers to putting the concealed and unacknowledged term in a binary structure forward so that the *complete* significance of the term can be examined in a given discourse.) Similarly, postmodern studies of cultures of the past and present look for what is left out, what exists on the unspoken margins of the culture. This moves attention to such categories as class, race, gender, and ethnicity in the unfolding of historical events. This is often history from the bottom up, telling the stories of the people and events normally excluded from totalizing accounts.

Social-Epistemic Rhetoric

Those familiar with social-epistemic rhetoric can readily see its convergence with postmodern conclusions about language and culture. I have discussed this rhetoric at length in *Rhetoric and Reality,* "Rhetoric and Ideology in the Writing Class," and elsewhere. Here I wish to offer a look at the ways in which it converges with postmodern speculation in providing a mutually enriching theoretical synthesis. To say this differently, poststructuralism provides a way of more fully discussing elements of social-epistemic rhetoric that are fully operative within it; at the same time, social-epistemic rhetoric provides poststructuralism with methods for discussing the production and reception of texts — and especially the former — that have been a part of its effort. I will show these convergences in discussing the elements of the rhetorical situation — interlocutor, conceptions of the real, audience, and language — as they are being conceived in social-epistemic rhetoric informed by poststructuralism. I should also mention that this development is bringing social-epistemic rhetoric, particularly, as I will show, in the classroom, very close to the work of cultural studies as it has been discussed by the Birmingham Center for Contemporary Cultural Studies.

We have already seen that the subject of the rhetorical act cannot be regarded as the unified, coherent, autonomous, transcendent subject of liberal humanism. The subject is instead multiple and conflicted, composed of numerous subject formations or positions. From one perspective this is a standard feature of many historical rhetorics in their concern with the *ethos* of the speaker, her presentation of the appropriate image of her character through language, voice, bearing, and the like. For a contemporary rhetoric, the writer and reader, the speaker and listener (and more of their commutability of function shortly), must likewise be aware that the subject (the producer) of discourse is a construction, a fabrication, established through the devices of signifying practices. This means that great care must be taken in choosing the subject position that the interlocutor wishes to present, and equally great care must be taken in teaching students the way this is done. In other words, it will not do to say, "Be yourself," since all of us possess multiple selves, not all of which are appropriate for the particular discourse situation. This is not, it should be noted, to deny that all of us display a measure of singularity. As Paul Smith argues, the unique place of each of us in the network of intersecting discourses assures differences among us as well as possibilities for originality and political agency. This does not mean, however, that anyone can totally escape the discursive regimes, the power/knowledge formations, of the historical moment. Political agency but never complete autonomy is the guiding formulation here.

But if the subject, the sender, is a construct of signifying practices in social-epistemic rhetoric, so are the material conditions to which the subject responds, the prime constituents of the message of discourse. (I am of course relying on Burke's formulation of language as symbolic action to be distinguished from the sheer motion of the material, as well as on the work of Barthes and Foucault). This is not to deny the force of the material in human affairs: people do need to provide for physiological needs, to arrange refuge from the elements, and to deal with eventual physical extinction. However, all of these material experiences are mediated through signifying practices. Only through language do we know and act upon the conditions of our experience. Ways of living and dying are finally negotiated through discourse, the cultural codes that are part of our historical conditions. These conditions are of an economic, social, and political nature, and they change over time. But they too can only be known and acted upon through the discourses available at any historical moment. Thus the subject who experiences and the material and social conditions experienced are discursively constituted in historically specific terms.

The mediation of signifying practices in the relations of subjects to material conditions is especially crucial. From the perspective offered here, signifying practices are always at the center of conflict and contention. In the effort to name experience, different groups are constantly vying for supremacy, for ownership and control of terms and their meanings in any discourse situation. As Stuart Hall, a past director of the Birmingham Center, has pointed out, a given language or discourse does not automatically belong to any class, race, or gender. Following Volosinov and Gramsci, he argues that language is always an arena of struggle to make certain meanings — certain ideological formulations — prevail. Cultural codes thus are constantly in conflict: they contend for hegemony in defining and directing the material conditions of experience as well as consciousness itself. The signifying practices of different groups thus compete in forwarding different agendas for the ways people are to regard their historical conditions and their modes of responding to them, and these signifying practices are thus always a scene of battle (Hall, "The Rediscovery of 'Ideology'").

The receiver of messages, the audience of discourse, obviously cannot escape the consequences of signifying practices. The audience's possible responses to texts are in part a function of its discursively constituted social roles. These roles are often constructed with some measure of specificity as membership in a specific discourse community — in a particular union or profession, for example. But these roles are never discretely separate from other subject positions the members of an audience may share or, on the other hand, occupy independent of each other. In other words, members of an audience cannot simply activate one subject position and switch off all others. Thus, audiences must be considered both as members of communities and as separate subject formations. The result is that the responses of the audience as a collective and as separate subjects are never totally predictable, never completely in the control of the sender of a coded message or of the coded message itself. As Stuart Hall has demonstrated, audiences are capable of a range of possible responses to any message. They can simply accommodate the message, sharing in the codes of the sender and assenting to them. The audience can completely resist the message, rejecting its codes and purposes and turning them to other ends. Finally, the receiver can engage in a process of negotiation, neither accommodating alone nor resisting alone, instead engaging in a measure of both (Hall, "Encoding/Decoding").

The work of rhetoric, then, is to study the production and reception of these historically specific signifying practices. In other words, social-epistemic rhetoric will enable senders and receivers to arrive at a formulation of the conception of the entire rhetorical context in any given discourse situation, and this will be done through an analysis of the signifying practices operating within it. Thus in composing a text, a writer will engage in an analysis of the cultural codes operating in defining her role, the roles of the audience, and the constructions of the matter to be considered. These function in a dialectical relation to each other so that the writer must engage in complex decision making in shaping the text to be presented. By dialectic I mean they change in response to each other in ways that are not mechanically predictable — not presenting, for example, simply a cause-effect relation but a shifting affiliation in which causes and effects are mutually interactive, with effects becoming causes and causes effects simultaneously. The reader of the text must also engage in a dialectical process involving coded conceptions of the writer, the matter under consideration, and the role of the receiver of the text in arriving at an interpretation of the text. Writing and reading are thus both acts of textual interpretation and construction, and both are central to social-epistemic rhetoric. More of this reading/writing relationship will be taken up later. First I would like to consider the role of ideology in rhetoric.

As I have indicated throughout, signifying practices are never innocent: they are always involved in ideological designations, conceptions of economic, social, political, and cultural arrangements and their relations to the subjects of history within concrete power relations. Ideology is not here declared a mystification to be placed in binary opposition to truth or science. The formulation invoked is instead derived from Louis Althusser as elaborated in Goran Therborn's *The Ideology of Power and the Power of Ideology*. This conception places ideology within the category of discourse, describing it as an inevitable feature of all signifying practices. Ideology then becomes closely imbricated with rhetoric, the two inseparably overlapped however distinguished for purposes of discussion. From this perspective, no claims can be offered as absolute, timeless truths since all are historically specific, arising in response to the conditions of a particular time and place. Choices in the economic, social, political, and cultural are thus based on discursive practices that are interpretations — not mere transcriptions of some external, verifiable certainty. Thus the choice is never between ideology and absolute truth, but between different ideologies. Some are finally judged better ("truer") than others on the basis of their ability to fulfill the promises of democracy at all levels of experience — the economic, social, political, and cultural — providing an equal share of authority in decision making and a tolerance for difference.

Ideology addresses or interpellates human beings. It provides the language to define the subject, other subjects, the material and social, and the relation of all of these to each other. Ideology addresses three questions: what exists, what is good, what is possible? The first, explains Therborn, tells us "who we are, what the world is, what nature, society, men and women are like. In this way we acquire a sense of identity, becoming conscious of what is real and true." Ideology also provides the subject with standards for making ethical and aesthetic decisions: "*what is good*, right, just, beautiful, attractive, enjoyable, and its opposites. In this way our desires become structured and normalized." The very configurations of our desires, what we will long for and pursue, are thus shaped by ideology. Finally, ideology defines the elements of expectation: "*what is possible* and impossible: our sense of the mutability of our being-in-the-world and the consequences of change are hereby patterned, and our hopes, ambitions, and fears given shape" (18). This is especially important since the recognition of the existence of a condition (homelessness, for example) and the desire for its change will go for nothing if ideology indicates that a change is simply not possible (the homeless freely choose to live in the street and cannot be forced to come inside). All three are further implicated in power relations in groups and in society, in deciding who has power and in determining what power can be expected to achieve.

Finally, ideology always brings with it strong social and cultural reinforcement, so that what we take to exist, to have value, and to be possible seems necessary, normal, and inevitable — in the nature of things. And this goes for power as well since ideology naturalizes certain authority regimes — those of class, race, and gender, for example — and renders alternatives unthinkable, in this way determining who can act and what can be accomplished. Finally, ideology is always inscribed in the discourses of daily practice and is pluralistic and conflicted. Any historical moment displays a wide variety of competing ideologies and each subject displays permutations of these conflicts, although the overall effect is to support the hegemony of dominant groups.

All of this has great consequences for the writing classroom. Given the ubiquitous role of discourse in human affairs, instructors cannot be content to focus exclusively on teaching the production of academic texts. Our business must be to instruct students in signifying practices broadly conceived — to see not only the rhetoric of the college essay but the rhetoric of the institution of schooling, of the workplace, and of the media. We must take as our province the production and reception of semiotic codes broadly conceived, providing students with the heuristics to penetrate these codes and their ideological designs on our formation as the subjects of our experience. Students must come to see that the languages they are expected to speak, write, and embrace as ways of thinking and acting are never disinterested, always bringing with them strictures on the existent, the good, the possible, and regimes of power.

If rhetoric is to be a consideration of signifying practices and their ideological involvement — that is, their imbrication in economic, social, political, and cultural conditions and subject formation — then the study of signs will of course be central. A large part of the business of this rhetoric will be to provide methods for describing and analyzing the operations of signification. Just as successive rhetorics for centuries furnished the terms to name the elements involved in text production and interpretation for the past (inventional devices, arrangement schemes, stylistic labels for tropes and figures), social-epistemic rhetoric will offer a terminology to discuss these activities for contemporary conditions and conceptual formulations. Structuralism, poststructuralism, and rhetoric have all begun this effort, and workers in semiotics have profited from them. It is composition teachers, however, who are best situated to develop ways of analyzing and discussing discourse to enable students to become better writers and readers. (After all, most of the important rhetorics of the past were written by teachers: Socrates, Plato, and Aristotle all taught the counterpart of freshman composition.) This leads to a consideration of the relation of reading and writing, of text production and text interpretation.

As I have already indicated, social-epistemic rhetoric demands revised models of reading and writing. Both composing and interpreting texts become instances of discourse analysis and, significantly, negotiation. Indeed, the very acts of writing and reading are themselves verbally coded discursive procedures which guide the production and interpretation of meanings, making a certain range more likely to appear and others more improbable. This exclusionary coding is apparent, for example, in reflecting on the directives for text production and reception provided in certain expressionist rhetorics. For these, only personal and metaphoric accounts can be regarded as authentic discourse, and, unlike current-traditional rhetoric, any attempt to be rational, objective, and dispassionate is considered a violation of the self and of genuine writing. In addition, for social-epistemic rhetoric, writing and reading become acts of discourse analysis as both the sender and receiver attempt to negotiate the semiotic codes in which each is situated — that is, the signifying practices that make up the entire rhetorical context. Composing and reception are thus interactive since both are performances of production, requiring the active construction of meaning according to one or another coded procedure. The opposition between the active writer and the passive reader is displaced since both reading and writing are considered constructive. It will be the work of rhetoric and composition teachers, then, to develop lexicons to articulate the complex coding activity involved in writing and reading, and this leads us to the classroom.

The Classroom

The recommendations of the new rhetoric proposed here become clearest in considering pedagogy. For social-epistemic rhetoric, teaching is central, not an afterthought through which practice is made to conform with the more important work of theory. Instead, the classroom becomes the point at which theory and practice engage in a dialectical interaction, working out a rhetoric more adequate to the historical moment and the actual conditions of teacher and students. From this perspective, all teachers of rhetoric and composition are regarded as intellectuals engaging in theoretical and empirical research, the two coming to fruition in their interaction within the classroom. Indeed, as Patricia Donahue and Ellen Quandahl have argued, composition teachers are through this interaction striving to create a new variety of academic discourse. The teacher's duty here is to bring to bear rhetorical theory as broadly defined in this essay within the conditions of her students' lives. The teacher will in this act develop methods for producing and receiving texts, including strategies for negotiating and resisting signifying practices, that are best suited for the situations of her students. These of course will be recommended to other teachers, but only as example and guideline, not pronouncements from on (theoretical) high. The uses of postmodern theory in rhetoric will then be in the hands of teachers, not prescribed in advance by "outside experts."

This role as intellectual, furthermore, has an important political dimension, involving the transformation and improvement of present social and political arrangements. As I have emphasized elsewhere, social-epistemic rhetoric grows out of the experience of democracy in the US, carrying with it a strong antifoundational impulse (*Rhetoric and Reality; "*Rhetoric and Ideology*"*). Knowledge/power relationships are regarded as human constructions, not natural and inevitable facts of life. All institutional arrangements are humanly made and so can be unmade, and the core of this productive act is found in democracy and open discussion.

The social-epistemic classroom thus offers a lesson in democracy intended to prepare students for critical participation in public life. It is dedicated to making schools places for individual and social empowerment. Schools after all are places, as Aronowitz and Giroux remind us, "of struggle over what forms of authority, orders of representation, forms of moral regulation, and versions of the past should be legitimated, passed on, and debated" (32). The teacher must then recognize and resist inequities in our society — the economic and social injustices inscribed in race, ethnic, and gender relations, relations that privilege the few and discriminate against the many. This classroom is dialogic, situating learning within the realities of the students' own experience, particularly their political experience. The dialogic classroom is designed to encourage students to become transformative intellectuals in their own right. Studying signifying practices will require a "critical literacy." As Ira Shor explains: "Critical literacy invites teachers and students to *problematize* all subjects of study, that is, to understand existing knowledge as historical products deeply invested with the value of those who developed such knowledge." For this teacher, all learning is based in ideology, and signifying practices — the production and reception of texts — must challenge dominant ideological formations. In Shor's terms, the study of discourse must go "beneath the surface to understand the origin, structure, and consequences of any body of knowledge, technical process, or object under study" (24). Students thus research their own language, their own society, their own learning, examining the values inscribed in them and the ways these values are shaping their subjectivities and their conceptions of their material and social conditions.

The Course

I would now like to turn to a course in freshman composition that will demonstrate the operations of the social-epistemic rhetoric described here. This effort locates the composing process within its social context, combining the methods of semiotic analysis in considering cultural codes with the recommendations of the rhetoric I have outlined. As will be apparent, it is allied with attempts to refigure English studies along the lines of cultural studies, a matter I have discussed in "Composition Studies and Cultural Studies" and "Composition and Cultural Studies: Collapsing the Boundaries." Since I devised the syllabus for this course to be shared with teaching assistants in my mentor group at Purdue and since my report here is based on our shared experience over the past three years, I will use the plural pronoun in referring to the effort. (I would also like to thank them for their cooperation throughout.)

The course is organized around an examination of the cultural codes — the social semiotics — that are working themselves out in shaping consciousness in our students and ourselves. We start with the personal experience of the students, but the emphasis is on the position of this experience within its formative context. Our main concern is the relation of current signifying practices to the structuring of subjectivities — of race, class, and gender formations, for example — in our students and ourselves. The effort is to make students aware of cultural codes, the competing discourses that are influencing their formations as the subjects of experience. Our larger purpose is to encourage students to resist and to negotiate these codes — these hegemonic discourses — in order to bring about more democratic and personally humane economic, social, and political arrangements. From our perspective, only in this way can they become genuinely competent writers and readers.

We thus guide students to locate in their experience the points at which they are now engaging in resistance and negotiation with the cultural codes they daily encounter. These are then used as avenues of departure for a dialogue. It is our hope that students who can demystify the subtle devices of persuasion in these cultural codes will be motivated to begin the re-forming of subjectivities and social arrangements, a re-forming which is a normal part of democratic political arrangements. We also want to explore the wide range of codes that students confront daily — print, film, television — in order to prepare them to critique their experiences with these codes. As Donald Morton and Mas'ud Zavarzadeh explain, this "critique (not to be confused with criticism) is an investigation of the enabling conditions of discursive practices" (7). Its purpose is to locate the ideological predispositions of the semiotic codes that we encounter and enact in our lives, seeing their commitment to certain conceptions of the existent, the good, and the possible. The course then explores these coded discourses in the institutional forms — the family, the school, the work place, the media — that make them seem natural and timeless rather than historically situated social constructions.

The course consists of six units: advertising, work, play, education, gender, and individuality. Each unit begins with a reading of essays dealing with competing versions of the significance of the topic of the unit. For example, the unit on education includes an analysis of US schools by a diverse range of observers: William Bennett, Jonathon Kozol, John Dewey, and James Thurber. These essays are often followed with a film dealing with school experiences — for example, *Risky Business* or *Sixteen Candles* or *The Breakfast Club*. A videotape of a current television program about schools — for example, *Beverly Hills, 90210* — is also often included. The important consideration is not the texts in themselves but the texts in relation to certain methods of interpreting them.

Students are provided a set of heuristics (invention strategies) that grow out of the interaction of rhetoric, structuralism, poststructuralism, semiotics, and cultural studies (again, especially of the Birmingham Center variety). While those outlined here have been developed as a result of reading in Saussure, Peirce, Lévi-Strauss, Barthes, Gramsci, Raymond Williams, Stuart Hall, and others, an excellent introduction to them for teachers and students can be found in John Fiske's *Introduction to Communication Studies*. (Diana George and John Trimbur's *Reading Culture* will perform a similar function for composition classrooms.) In examining any text — print, film, television — students are asked to locate the key terms in the discourse and to situate these within the structure of meaning of which they form a part. These terms of course are made up of the central preoccupations of the text, but to determine how they are working to constitute experience their functions as parts of coded structures — a semiotic system — must be examined. The terms are first set in relation to their binary opposites as suggested by the text itself. (This of course follows Saussure's description of the central place of contrast in signification and Lévi-Strauss's application of it.) Sometimes this opposition is indicated explicitly, but often it is not. It is also important to note that a term commonly occupies a position in opposition to more than one other term.

For example, we sometimes begin with a 1981 essay from the *Wall Street Journal*, "The Days of a Cowboy Are Marked by Danger, Drudgery, and Low Pay," by William Blundell. (This essay is most appropriate for the unit on work, but its codes are at once so varied and so accessible to students that it is a useful introduction to any unit.) We first consider the context of the piece, exploring the characteristics of the readership of the newspaper and the historical events surrounding the essay's production, particularly as indicated within the text. The purpose of this is to decide what probably acted as key terms for the original readers. The essay focuses on the cowboss, the ranch foreman who runs the cattle operation. The meaning of "cowboss" is established by seeing it in binary opposition to the cowboys who work for him as well as the owners who work away from the ranch in cities. At other times in the essay, the cowboss is grouped together with the cowboys in opposition to office workers. Through the description of labor relations on the ranch, the cowboys are also situated in contrast to urban union workers, but the latter are never explicitly mentioned. Finally, the exclusively masculine nature of ranching is suggested only at the end of the essay when the cowboss's wife is described in passing as living apart from the ranch on the cowboss's own small spread, creating *male/female* domain binary. All of these binaries suggest others, such as the opposition of *nature/civilization, country/city, cowboy/urban cowboy,* and the like. Students begin to see that these binaries are arranged hierarchically, with one term privileged over the other. They also see how unstable these hierarchies can be, however, with a term frequently shifting valences as it moves from one binary to another — for example, *cowboy/union worker* but *cowboss/cowboy.* It is also important to point out that this location of binaries is of course not an exact operation and that great diversity appears as students negotiate the text differently. Their reasons for doing so become clear at the next level of analysis.

These terms are then placed within the narrative structural forms suggested by the text, the culturally coded stories about patterns of behavior appropriate for people within certain situations. These codes deal with such social designations as race, class, gender, age, ethnicity, and the like. The position of the key terms within these socially constructed narrative codes are analyzed, discussed, and written about. It is not too difficult to imagine how these are at work in the binaries indicated above. The narratives that cluster around the figure of the cowboy in our culture are quickly detected in this essay — for example, patterns of behavior involving individuality, freedom, and independence. These, however, are simultaneously coupled with self-discipline, respect for authority (good cowboys never complain), and submission to the will of the cowboss. Students have little difficulty in pointing out the ways these narratives are conflicted while concurrently reinforcing differences in class and gender role expectations. Of particular value is to see the way the essay employs narratives that at once disparage the *Wall Street Journal* readers because they are urban office workers while enabling them to identify with the rugged freedom and adventure of the cowboys, seeing themselves as metaphorically enacting the masculine narrative of the cowboss in their separate domains. In other words, students discover that the essay attempts to position the reader in the role of a certain kind of masculine subject.

These narrative patterns at the level of the social role are then situated within larger narrative structures that have to do with economic, political, and cultural formulations. Here students examine capitalist economic narratives as demonstrated in this essay and their consequences for class, gender, and race relations and roles both in the workplace and elsewhere. They look, for example, at the distribution of work in beef production with its divisions between managers and workers, thinkers and doers, producers and consumers. They also consider the place of narratives of democracy in the essay, discussing the nature of the political relations that are implied in the hierarchies of terms and social relations presented. It should be clear that at these two narrative levels considerable debate results as students disagree about the narratives that ought to be invoked in interpreting the text, their relative worth as models for emulation, and the degree to which these narratives are conflicted. In other words, the discussion emerging from the use of these heuristics is itself conflicted and unpredictable.

Thus, the term as it is designated within a hierarchial binary is situated within narratives of social roles, and these roles are located within more comprehensive narratives of economic and political formations in the larger society. The point of the interpretation is to see that texts — whether rhetorical or poetic — are ideologically invested in the construction of subjectivities within recommended economic, social, and political arrangements. Finally, as should now be clear, this hermeneutic process is open-ended, leading in diverse and unpredictable directions in the classroom. And this is one of its strengths as it encourages open debate and wide-ranging speculation.

After some experience with written and video texts, students apply these heuristics to their personal experiences in order to analyze in essay form the effect of an important cultural code on their lives. The students select the topic and content of the essay, but they must do so within the context of the larger theme of each unit. Thus, in the unit on education, students must choose some feature of their school experience from the past or present that has been of particular personal significance. The students must then locate points of conflict and dissonance in the cultural codes discovered, although they are not expected to resolve them. For example, students often choose to write about their experiences in high school athletics in order to discuss the conflicted codes involved in the emphasis on personal versus team success, winning versus learning to accept defeat, discipline versus play, and the like. The roles the students learn to assume in sports are examined in terms of such categories as gender, age, race, and group membership. Some students have explored the differences in the experiences of male and female athletes. Here they commonly examine the narratives appropriate to the behavior of each as recommended by dominant cultural codes about sports. These role definitions and performances are then placed within larger narratives having to do with life experiences, such as vocational aspirations, career objectives, marriage plans, and the like. Students at this point often discover the parallels between the contrasting experiences of males and females in high school sports and the contrasting experiences of males and females in career tracks. Once again, the various levels of conflict are explored, both within the expectations for each gender and across the genders, although, once again, students are not expected to resolve them. It should also be noted that conflicts also appear as students disagree in discussions about the codes that are being recommended within these sports activities. These incidents reinforce the point that cultural codes are always negotiated so that students produce them as well as simply re-produce them; that is, students do not always simply submit to these codes, often reshaping them to serve their own agendas. And of course incidents of resistance are frequently discussed as students report their defiance of required roles — for example, refusing to engage in some humiliating hazing ritual against those declared "losers."

As students develop material through the use of the heuristic and begin to write initial drafts of their essays, they discover the culturally coded character of all parts of composing. Students must learn to arrange their materials to conform to the genre codes of the form of the essay they are writing — the personal essay, the academic essay, the newspaper essay, for example. (Students could also be asked to create other kinds of texts — short stories, poems, videos — although we have not done so in our composition course. Here the genre codes of each would again be foregrounded.) These essay genres conform to socially indicated formal codes that students must identify and enact, and they, of course, carry great consequences for meaning. A given genre encourages certain kinds of messages while discouraging others. Next, at the level of the sentence, stylistic form comes into play, and the student must again learn to generate sentence structures and patterns of diction that are expected of the genre employed. It is important that students be made aware of the purposes of these codes, both practical and ideological. In other words, expecting certain formal and stylistic patterns is not always a matter of securing "clear and effective communication." As all writing teachers know, most errors in grammar and spelling do not in themselves interfere with the reader's understanding. The use of *who* for *whom*, for example, seldom creates any confusion in reference. These errors instead create interferences of a social and political nature.

Finally, I would like to restate a point on the interchangability of reading and writing made earlier. In enacting the composing process, students are learning that all experience is situated within signifying practices, and that learning to understand personal and social experience involves acts of discourse production and interpretation, the two acting reciprocally in reading and writing codes. Students in the class come to see that interpretation involves production as well as reproduction, and is as constructive as composing itself. At the same time, they discover that the more one knows about a text — its author, place of publication, audience, historical context — the less indeterminate it becomes and the more confident the reader can be in interpreting and negotiating its intentions. Similarly, the more the writer understands the entire semiotic context in which she is functioning, the greater will be the likelihood that her text will serve as a successful intervention in an ongoing discussion. After all, despite the inevitable slippages that appear in the production and interpretation of codes, people do in fact communicate with each other daily to get all sorts of work done effectively. At the same time, even these "effective" exchanges can be seen to harbor contradictions that are concealed or ignored. These contradictions are important to discover for the reader and writer because they foreground the political unconscious of decision making, a level of unspoken assumptions that are often repressed in ordinary discourse. It is here that the betrayals of democracy and the value of the individual are discovered despite the more obvious claims to the contrary.

The purpose of social-epistemic rhetoric is finally political, an effort to prepare students for critical citizenship in a democracy. We want students to begin to understand that language is never innocent, instead constituting a terrain of ideological battle. Language — textuality — is thus the terrain on which different conceptions of economic, social, and political conditions are contested with consequences for the formation of the subjects of history, the very consciousness of the historical agent. We are thus committed to teaching writing as an inescapably political act, the working out of contested cultural codes that affect every feature of experience. This involves teachers in an effort to problematize students' experiences, requiring them to challenge the ideological codes they bring to college by placing their signifying practices against alternatives. Sometimes this is done in a cooperative effort with teachers and students agreeing about the conflicts that are apparent in considering a particular cultural formation — for example, the elitist and often ruthlessly competitive organization of varsity sports in high schools. Students are able to locate points of personal resistance and negotiation in dealing with the injustices of this common social practice. At other times, students and teachers are at odds with each other or, just as often, the students are themselves divided about the operation and effects of conflicting codes. This often results in spirited exchange. The role of the teacher is to act as a mediator while ensuring that no code, including her own, goes unchallenged.

This has been a lengthy introduction to the intersections of postmodern discourse theory and rhetoric. Even so, it only begins to explore the possibilities, as can be seen, for example, in the excellent new collection, *Contending with Words: Composition and Rhetoric in a Postmodern Age,* edited by Patricia Harkin and John Schilb. (This volume arrived while I was putting the finishing touches on this piece.) These essays share with mine the confidence that postmodern speculation has much to offer writing teachers. None, furthermore, suggests that it is a savior come to redeem us from our fallen ways. All see rhetoric and composition as engaged in a dialectic with the new speculation, the result being the enrichment of both. Indeed, these essays confirm what I have long maintained: The postmodern turn in recent discussions in the academy is an attempt to restore the place of rhetoric in the human sciences. In it we find an ally in our work of creating a critically literate citizenry, and we ought not to reject it just because it speaks a nonstandard dialect.

Works Cited

Aronowitz, Stanley, and Henry A. Giroux. *Education under Siege.* South Hadley: Bergin, 1985.

Barthes, Roland. *Mythologies.* Trans. Annette Lavers. New York: Hill, 1972.

Benveniste, Emil. *Problems in General Linguistics.* Trans. Mary Elizabeth Meek. Coral Gables: U of Miami P, 1971.

Berlin, James A. "Composition and Cultural Studies." *Composition and Resistance.* Ed. Mark Hurlbert and Michael Blitz. Portsmouth, NH: Heinemann, 1991. 47–55.

———. "Composition Studies and Cultural Studies: Collapsing the Boundaries." *Into the Field: The Site of Composition Studies.* Ed. Anne Ruggles Gere. New York: MLA, 1992.

———. "Rhetoric and Ideology in the Writing Class." *College English* 50 (1988): 477–94.

———. *Rhetoric and Reality: Writing Instruction in American Colleges, 1900–1985.* Carbondale: Southern Illinois UP, 1987.

———. "Rhetoric Programs after World War II: Ideology, Power, and Conflict." *Rhetoric and Ideology: Compositions and Criticisms of Power.* Ed. Charles W. Kneupper. Arlington: Rhetoric Society of America, 1989.

Blundell, William E. "The Days of a Cowboy Are Marked by Danger, Drudgery, and Low Pay." *Wall Street Journal* 10 June 1981, sec. A1:1.

Burke, Kenneth. *Language as Symbolic Action.* Berkeley: U of California P, 1966.

Corbett, Edward P.J. *Classical Rhetoric for the Modern Student.* New York: Oxford UP, 1965.

Derrida, Jacques. *Of Grammatology.* Trans. Gayatri Spivak. Baltimore: Johns Hopkins UP, 1976.

Donahue, Patricia, and Ellen Quandahl. *Reclaiming Pedagogy: The Rhetoric of the Classroom.* Carbondale: Southern Illinois UP, 1989.

Dowst, Kenneth. "The Epistemic Approach: Writing, Knowing, and Learning." *Eight Approaches to Teaching Composition.* Ed. Timothy Donovan and Ben W. McClelland. Urbana: NCTE, 1980.

Elbow, Peter. "Reflections on Academic Discourse." *College English* 53 (1991): 135–55.

Fiske, John. *Introduction to Communication Studies.* 2nd ed. London: Routledge, 1990.

Foucault, Michel. *Power/Knowledge: Selected Interviews and Other Writings, 1972–1977.* Ed. Colin Gordon. Trans. Colin Gordon et al. New York: Pantheon, 1980.

George, Diana, and John Trimbur. *Reading Culture.* New York: HarperCollins, 1992.

Hairston, Maxine C. "Comment and Response." *College English* 52 (1990): 694–96.

Hall, Stuart. "Encoding/Decoding." *Culture, Media, Language.* Ed. Stuart Hall et al. London: Hutchinson, 1980.

———. "The Rediscovery of 'Ideology': Return of the Repressed in Media Studies." *Culture, Society and the Media.* Ed. Michael Gurevitch et al. London: Routledge, 1982.

Harkin, Patricia, and John Schilb, eds. *Contending with Words: Composition and Rhetoric in a Postmodern Age.* New York: MLA, 1991.

Hodge, Robert, and Gunther Kress. *Social Semiotics.* Ithaca: Cornell UP, 1988.

Johnson, Richard. "What Is Cultural Studies Anyway?" *Social Text* 16 (1986–87): 38–80.

Kennedy, George A. *Classical Rhetoric and Its Christian and Secular Tradition from Ancient to Modern Times.* Chapel Hill: U of North Carolina P, 1980.

KF. "Putting on the Dog: Heuristics, Paradigms, and Hermeneutics." *Rhetoric Review* 10 (1991): 187–93.

Knoblauch, C. H., and Lil Brannon. *Rhetorical Traditions and the Teaching of Writing.* Upper Montclair: Boynton, 1984.

Morton, Donald, and Mas'ud Zavarzadeh. *Theory/Pedagogy/Politics: Texts for Change.* Urbana: U of Illinois P, 1991.

Nilsen, Alleen Pace. "Sexism in English: A Feminist View." *Perspectives: Turning Reading into Writing.* Ed. Joseph J. Comprone. Boston: Houghton, 1987.

Schilb, John. "Cultural Studies, Postmodernism, and Composition." *Contending with Words: Composition and Rhetoric in a Postmodern Age.* Ed. Patricia Harkin and John Schilb. New York: MLA, 1991. 173–88.

Scott, Robert L. "On Viewing Rhetoric as Epistemic." *Central States Speech Journal* 18 (1967): 9–16.

Shor, Ira. "Educating the Educators: A Freirean Approach to the Crisis in Education." *Freire for the Classroom.* Ed. Ira Shor. Portsmouth: Heinemann, 1987. 7–32.

Smith, Paul. *Discerning the Subject.* Minneapolis: U of Minnesota P, 1988.

Therborn, Goran. *The Ideology of Power and the Power of Ideology.* London: Verso, 1980.

TS. "Joining the Conversation." *Rhetoric Review* 10 (1991): 175–86.

Vickers, Brian. *In Defence of Rhetoric.* Oxford: Clarendon, 1988.

Berlin's Insights as a Resource for Your Teaching

1. Berlin cites a long history of education as preparation for citizenry. To explore your stance on "critical citizenship," freewrite or return to the draft of your philosophy of composition and expand a section that discusses the reasons why you want to teach writing.

2. The essay provides a good opportunity to model active reading to your students. If you consciously use the double-entry journal as you read and reread this article, you could select a difficult passage from Berlin and show students how you came to understand the passage, using a transparency of the "dialogical thinking" in the entries as you "say aloud" what you did and what you thought as your read the passage the first time and then a second time.

Berlin's Insights as a Resource for the Writing Classroom

1. Daily, critics charge that college classrooms have been inappropriately politicized. Berlin states that all pedagogic choices have been and are political but may not have been acknowledged as such. When instructors "foreground" the political, cultural critique often becomes the major theme and focus of reading and writing assignments. Tasks like analysis, critique, and argument might seem to dominate writing assignments. However, students can engage in cultural critique in personal narrative as well as dialectical journals. Invite students to write "intellectual histories." In a second or third draft, encourage them to highlight the intersections of some "social construction" — such as race, ethnicity, class, or gender — with their lives as learners.

2. The concept of "constructing knowledge" rather than receiving knowledge may intimidate some of your students. An assignment focused on their initial college experiences could lead to class construction of a definition of "writing community" or "college writing." Assign a series of journal entries

focused on observing and reflecting on class activities, discussions, peer goups, and so on. Ask the class to generate topics for an essay to be written collaboratively by groups of three writers. List topics on a chalkboard, over-head transparency, or computer display, and prompt a class discussion of each topic.

Encourage the class members to clarify the thinking, writing task, and genre(s) implicit in each topic. Add criteria, if needed, to accommodate your course objectives or syllabus design.

Follow up with class discussion of the "prompts" they have written for the topics. Ask the class to negotiate a short list of topics from which each group will select one. Give the groups two weeks to use the resources for writers (recall, observation, reading, conversation, and imagination), gener-ate drafts collaboratively, review and revise drafts, and publish copies of the group essay for review and peer criticism from other groups.

During the two-week sequence, have individual writers use three-minute writings or journal entries to record and reflect on the group processes of constructing knowledge through a collaborative writing project. Ask the group to write a "short history of writing together" and each individual to write a short meditation on what he or she learned from the processes of co-authoring a text.

DAVID ROTHGERY   *"So What Do We Do Now?" Necessary Directionality as the Writing Teacher's Response to Racist, Sexist, Homophobic Papers*

David Rothgery meditates on a quandary familiar to all teachers of writing or literature courses and particulary those who have learned to analyze texts rhetorically with the in-sights of contemporary theory. Contemporary "anti-foundational" theorists like Bakhtin and Derrida posit that humans cannot gain certainty about their existence, behavior, per-spectives, or knowledge from universal principles or transcending truths. Any certainty about human experience comes from looking at the situation and examining the conditions of the historical moment, the institutional site, the power structure, the culture within which an event or phenomenon happens. Any "truth" is situational and judged as appropriate, functional, understandable, and reasonable within that situation; foundational moral cer-tainty is illusive and moral pluralism is safe ground.

When teachers read student or professional texts that seem to them morally reprehen-sible, analysis of "discursive formation" of the text seems insufficient. Rothgery finds no satisfaction in the suggestion that "usable" truths may exist even though transcendent truths do not. Rothgery believes there is a continuum by which teachers, learners, and other citi-zens can measure moral convictions and arrive at a "sense of a necessary direction — one of less cruelty to ourselves and the rest of humankind."

Then he waited, marshaling his thoughts and brooding over his still untested powers. For though he was master of the world, he was not quite sure what to do next.

But he would think of something. (221)

So ends Arthur Clarke's classic *2001: A Space Odyssey,* and, as David Bowman contemplates with some dismay his seeming mastery of the universe, his unstated question is one the contemporary writing or literature teacher might well appropri-

ate for his or her own contemporary pedagogical dilemma: So what do I do now
with my students? It is the question a high-school English teacher once asked me as
she read some Derrida and Nietzsche as part of a required Contemporary Theory
and Pedagogy class I was teaching. Her pedagogical quandary was not an isolated
one. I answered her with another question: "What if a student in your freshman
writing class submits to you a rough draft of a paper which you consider to be racist
— very racist? Would you, or should you, with that paper — or perhaps one that
asserts that it is the duty of Christians to ferret out every gay and 'beat some sense
into him' — mark it as any other paper?"

She seemed to squirm in her seat. She had, in fact, once gotten a racist paper,
and her response had been unequivocal: she did not allow the paper and "sat the
student down and set him right." Whatever truth there is to Foucault's assertion
that each "society has its régime of truth, its 'general politics' of truth — i.e. the
types of discourse which it accepts and makes function as true" ("Truth" 131), and
whatever personal power agendas are working subtly at the heart of any particular
discourse, still, to that teacher that morning, there were some things you could be
certain about. In the case of a racist paper, some seemingly universal principle far
beyond "political correctness," beyond situational truths, was at issue.

Still, as she struggled through some of the assigned readings for the course, it
was clear she was having some difficulty reconciling her own moral fervor with
what Bakhtin, Derrida, and other theorists of the "anti-foundational" persuasion
were arguing: that the human condition does not permit certainty regarding any
"Transcendent Truths" as our moral underpinnings, but rather some "truth" in a far
less fundamental sense, no matter what we may "feel."

Patricia Bizzell, in restating the dilemma, points to a resolution which works
for her and which has implications for any classroom teacher:

> We have not yet taken the next, crucially important step in our rhetorical turn.
> We have not yet acknowledged that if no unimpeachable authority and tran-
> scendent truth exist, this does not mean that no *respectable* authority and no
> *usable* truth exist. (665; emphasis added)

She implies that teachers must proceed by these "usable" truths and center pedagogical discussions not so much on how one piece of discourse can be made less
value-laden, but rather on how all discourse *is* value-laden and therefore political.
Dale Bauer, sensitive to a too "authoritative rhetoric" in the classroom, one necessarily tied to a "political position" (391), directs students' attention to "how signs
can be manipulated" (391) so as to insure a "mastery that is not oppressive" (395).
On the surface, just as foundationalism in its search for the objective principle is an
appealing way to go, so too the kind of anti-foundationalism represented by Bizzell
and Bauer — with its recognition that we really can't be certain that any principle
is "objective" beyond our saying it is — is appealing in a post-Nietzschean world
wherein we have become acutely aware of the linguistic fictional nature of our "non-
fictional truths" (consider, e.g., the Margaret Mead version of Samoa). It's all part of
the same game. We knock out the big "T" (Truth or Transcendent Truth) but remain,
nevertheless, committed to a "respectable authority," a "reasonable truth," an analysis of how power agendas "manipulate signs," and, while showing how our deep-
seated aversions to racism, sexism, and homophobia can be subjected to the same
process, we, nevertheless, push forward with our convictions. Surely we can and
will do this. We will continue to evaluate student papers as to mechanics/usage,
style, organization, thesis, and by way of thesis development we will surely "do in"
our dangerously myopic, intellectually backward students with appropriately low

grades. Our "situational truth" is, if not transcendently valid, certainly more valid than the kind of truth such students promote.

Something about this approach, however, smacks too much of "having our cake and eating it too": there are no Transcendent Truths, but rather "usable truths", which we, as teachers, will make serve as our moral underpinnings. I am uncomfortable. And if I refuse to buy off entirely on the anti-foundationalist argument, I do not believe that makes me a victim of wishful thinking, of a refusal to accept in some way the reality of our essential rhetoricity. Admittedly, the fundamental "situatedness" of the human condition does not allow for the certainty of Transcendent Principles emblazoned across the sky, but neither does it allow for the certainty of there *not* being universals which suggest a direction.

Again and again I have heard professors admit (not in these terms of course, for it is not quite academic to make such admissions) that pedagogical *practice* and contemporary *theory* have to be inconsistent. That is, if it is true we must now discard forever notions of universal principles, it is also true we cannot live (and teach) as though no universal principles underlie anything. In the classroom we encourage a healthy conviction because it leads to the purposefulness which, in turn, increases the probabilities for more creative and powerful rhetoric. This inconsistency is to me, though, as indefensible as an auto manufacturer's claim that it "builds the strongest car possible" when in fact it does not.

On the one hand, the teacher who received the racist paper could have evaluated the rough draft by way of the usual criteria: thesis or essential argument, validity and relevance of supporting evidence, logic and hierarchy of ideas. What better approach than letting the student demonstrate for himself or herself the untenable nature of racist arguments? Such an approach surely works with the arguments, untenable or not, set forth in any paper from "American Management Styles: Finest in the World" to "Survival of Our Wetlands: More Priority, Please." After all, even with these papers we could argue that, in each case, something bordering on "fundamental" is at work: in the first paper, respect for the laborer perhaps; in the second, concern for our children's children. Still, teachers are not likely, with such papers, to react as our teacher did to the racist paper, which she regarded as a paper of an entirely different species. I suppose we could include in that extreme "different species" category (whether we ever receive them or not) papers which argue that we burn epileptics as devils, raze gay bars, lynch Blacks who dare to date White women, burn cats in satanic rites, or return women to their proper roles as child-rearers and sex toys.

My point in invoking these extreme examples is that, indeed, there is a *continuum*, a "more fundamental" at work, a sense of directionality. I take issue with those who believe we can buy into a universe of "situational ethics" or "usable" truths — that is, until we are willing to grant there is nothing to be gained in striving toward "fundamental" or "transcendent" principles which such papers violate in promoting cruel behavior towards humankind and the other creatures which populate the earth. Burning epileptics at the stake, abusing children, promoting by willful neglect the extinction of an animal species — such acts don't properly merit some gradation of ethical value relative to a particular culture or period of time.

Rarely do we come across extremely reprehensible papers — such as those which do openly promote cruel behavior. But our writing classes do become the setting for argument about capital punishment, euthanasia, abortion, women's rights. If we regard these discussions as having at most only "situational" weight — a "this time and place" payoff — then the dynamics of shared ideas is not allowed its proper role in the *necessary directionality* for the human condition and the condition of the planet we inhabit — that of alleviating suffering and cruelty, physical, mental, and spiritual — no matter which status the cosmic deities or demons accord such cruelty.

What is this "continuum," this "necessary directionality"? Consider the subject of racism. At one end of the continuum are non-racist papers arguing the merits of affirmative action, and at the other end are Skinhead-oriented papers arguing the supremacy of the White race. In between are many kinds of papers, such as one I once received which questioned why White students must be forced to mingle in small-group discussions with Hispanics and Blacks. Surely, for most teachers, something *more* fundamental is at stake in the Skinhead paper, and something *less* fundamental is at stake in the paper on classroom grouping. But this "more"/"less" continuum is, for the teacher, a different vision of ethics than "usable truth," which by its very nature admits of no true sense of continuum. My point is "more fundamental" and "usable" cannot inhabit the same world. At what point, for example, does the seemingly fundamental truth about cruelty and insensitivity to those of different color become the "usable" truth of arrangement of students within classroom groups or the "reasonable" and "situational ethic" of "Does Affirmative Action Succeed in Its Goals?"?

I am certainly *not* arguing that a teacher could not legitimately deal with papers presenting reprehensible ideas by way of the usual criteria of structure, logic, grammar, and style. The question I pose is this: Has contemporary theory, with its insights into the "situatedness" of our existence and perspectives, left us any sense of a valid — indeed, a *necessary*, "we-can-no-longer-go-back-to-that" — directionality by way of shared ideas? Can we indeed go back to treating women as objects, African-Americans as possessions, homosexuals as freaks, epileptics as devils?

Stanley Fish argues, in *Doing What Comes Naturally*, that

> questions of fact, truth, correctness, validity, and clarity can neither be posed nor answered with reference to some extracontextual, a historical, nonsituational reality, or rule, or law, or value; rather, anti-foundationalism asserts, all these matters are intelligible and debatable only within the precincts of the contexts or situations or paradigms or communities that give them their local and changeable shape. (344)

Fish speaks only of what he can be certain. He cannot be certain of Transcendent Truths. Nor can we. But does this mean we cannot be committed to moving toward truths which are *so comprehensive* that their force cannot be ignored?

Necessary Direction away from cruelty is just such a truth. The question is not so much whether or not we must assign to these "truths" the status of "undeniable absolutes," but whether we must assign to them some essence which is *so fundamental*, so clearly pointing to a necessary direction, that *we must insist that, pedagogically, an unqualified moral conviction must assert itself.* As long as "better" is given its proper "transcendent" due, a true moral purpose remains, and a true moral conviction in the classroom can continue. The confrontation of values, of situational ethics, that defines any composition classroom dynamics is not a naive affective or fictional game that we as teachers must continue to play to produce what Stanley Fish calls the "small . . . yield" of a "few worn and familiar bromides" (355); on the contrary, it is a confrontation founded in our sense of a *necessary* direction — one of less cruelty to ourselves and the rest of humankind.

This is not a starry-eyed meliorism or naive social evolutionism. Surely we do need in our classrooms the kind of discursive analysis the anti-foundationalists call for. A deconstructionist reading of *Mein Kampf* could not have been all bad. But Fish and Bizzell leave us too precarious an anchoring. Without that sense of a *necessary direction*, hate crimes such as the burning of crosses will necessarily be prosecuted only as vandalism, and the Andersonville and Auschwitz behavior will be defended by way of "following orders." We have moved *beyond* that. Indeed, humankind's condition seems to be defined in great measure by "situatedness." But what is functional and reasonable for one time and place must always push against other times and places — other situations on a greater scale. Racist and sexist behavior of any sort that promotes unnecessary cruelty must never be afforded the justification a too-unexamined moral pluralism may allow.

Otherwise, the kind of phenomena I experienced in my Writing Theory class in the spring of 1992 will be the norm. We were discussing Michel Foucault's *The Archaeology of Knowledge*. I had written on the board the sentence "Saddam Hussein is a Hitler." On the one hand, I recognized, as did the students, that the politically "correct" position on this (or on Hussein and the Gulf War in general) would vary greatly from campus to campus. Furthermore, Fish's comment that anti-foundationalism's super-self-consciousness is not a way out, that

> any claim in which the notion of situatedness is said to be a lever that allows us to get a purchase on situations is finally a claim to have *escaped situatedness*, and is therefore nothing more or less than a reinvention of foundationalism by the very form of thought that has supposedly reduced it to ruins (348–49 emphasis added),

still seemed valid here. Thus, the immediate reaction to the "Saddam Hussein is a Hitler" sentence in my class of relatively sophisticated rhetorical-theory students was in line with Foucault (and Fish): that we had to look at who said it and other dimensions of the "enunciative modalities," what "institutional sites" were being represented, and so on. The students suggested several such "sites" each with its own particular "political" baggage, its own appropriation of the statement, and I put them on the board:

Bush	Hussein	*NY Times* Editors	Soldier's Mother

"SADDAM HUSSEIN IS A HITLER." — REALITY?

W.W. II Veteran	Berkeley Anti-War Activist	Kurds

Our "situating" of a bit of discourse was, for a while, only an *academic* exercise — much as composition classes, I fear, tend to be for anti-foundationalist teachers. But when we finished congratulating ourselves on the incisiveness of our dissection, I put the chalk down and took a different approach. "But what if Hussein really *is* a kind of Hitler?" I asked. "What of the *very real possibility* that Hussein was *greatly* responsible for the unnecessary and perhaps cruel deaths of thousands of Kurds? What then? That is, what do we do now beyond analyzing the 'discursive formation' of that sentence?"

The students were literally unable to speak for almost a minute. It had not occurred to any of the students, all of them very bright, that *even in the classroom* there are questions that require more than being asked — that must be *answered*. I was not asking my students to take arms against Hussein but to sort out for themselves the truths regarding the possibility of a very real atrocity.

The classroom may be a laboratory, but it is a laboratory for the world we live in. Analysis and determination of power zones is of course essential, and too little of that has been done in our classrooms in the past. But when the *only* result for the classroom of anti-foundationalist and post-modernist insights is a discursive analysis which takes on the character of some linguistic Rubic's Cube, then we have plunged into the same idiocy that allowed learning theory to transform classrooms into robotical M and M dispenser systems.

As writers and teachers of writing, we must continue to grope in the recognition that our moral convictions do not translate as self-contained situational ethics alone, that they will continue to be measured along greater and greater scales — scales so large we must of necessity grant *some* of them a "highest order" status. "Better" — though it may and will be misappropriated and misapplied by the inexperienced, the uneducated, the cowardly, the wicked — must continue to be an operational term. We must continue to act, to "do," to "write" not only *as though* our writing is just one more version of Foucault's "discursive formations," emanating from this "institutional site" or that, but indeed *because* some of our convictions *are* more true, *are* better — because we can now discard *forever* some situational ethics.

What is the "new pedagogy" for our composition classrooms? Can it reside in "style," in anti-foundationalist situational truths which do not even consider the possibility of necessary directions (i.e., directions defined by *what can no longer be acceptable*)? That is indeed a "small yield," and the resulting classroom environment will produce too many students with a "small yield" attitude about not only their papers but the convictions which underlie them. Whatever naiveté there may be in the persistent groping in the dark for "first" principles to understand our universe, the real force of the greatest literature, or of that "one in a hundred" student composition, lies in that *groping* beyond the imprisonment of our situatedness. And a pedagogy that chooses to ignore the moral sweat, if you will, does a disservice of the profoundest order to the appreciation of good writing, of great writing. Yes, the groping between student and teacher may clash, but in the areas of racism, sexism, homophobia, the clash should be loud and morally meaningful in recognition that Necessary Directionality remains a valid concept.

Works Cited

Bauer, Dale. "The Other 'F' Word: The Feminist in the Classroom." *College English* 52 (Apr. 1990): 385–96.

Bizzell, Patricia. "Beyond Anti-Foundationalism to Rhetorical Authority: Problems Defining Cultural Literacy." *College English* 52 (Oct. 1990): 661–75.

Clarke, Arthur C. *2001: A Space Odyssey*. New York: Signet, 1968.

Fish, Stanley. *Doing What Comes Naturally: Change, Rhetoric, and the Practice of Theory in Literary and Legal Studies*. Durham: Duke UP, 1989.

Foucault, Michel. *The Archaeology of Knowledge*. Trans. A. M. Sheridan Smith. New York: Pantheon, 1972.

———. "Truth and Power." *Power/Knowledge: Selected Interviews and Other Writings, 1972–77*. Trans. Colin Gordon, Leo Marshall, John Mepham, and Kate Soper. Ed. Colin Gordon. New York: Pantheon, 1980. 109–33.

Rothgery's Insights as a Resource for Your Teaching

1. Without a clear definition of "necessary directionality," it can be difficult to distinguish what causes a personal reaction against the moral reasoning of a text. Whatever beliefs teachers hold about controversial issues such as abortion, capital punishment, or animal rights, censoring those isssues as paper topics clearly denies students opportunities for discovering or defining their own beliefs and for learning how to present their beliefs to an audience that may disagree. Share Rothgery's essay with teaching colleagues and suggest a "brown bag" discussion. Ask colleagues how they work with texts and students to accommodate not only multiple perspectives but also shared convictions or perspectives "we cannot go back to."

2. Rothgery acknowledges that a teacher might evaluate reprehensible texts more rigorously than other texts, using only rhetorical analysis to define the quality of those papers. If you receive a text that repulses you, first draft a letter in which you describe all the strengths of the paper and any problems with it. Put the letter aside and ask three or four veteran instructors to read the text "holistically," citing strengths and weaknesses they find in the "discursive formation." Compare your letter with their feedback as a way to provide the student with a "fair" reading of the text. Then ask those colleagues how/if/why they would deal with what makes the essay reprehensible to you.

Rothgery's Insights as a Resource for the Writing Classroom

1. Texts that are reprehensible to you will also disturb many of your students. Before you model peer criticism, bring in a text that triggers moral repulsion and pose the question, "If a peer wrote a text that was intentionally or unintentionally stepping beyond what you believe 'must not happen,' how would you help that writer understand your reaction?" Organize small groups of three or four and follow up with reports to the large group. Ask class members to identify common themes from the discussions and to write in their journals about those themes.

2. Swift's "A Modest Proposal" is "canonical" in composition texts partly because the satire deliberately triggers what to Swift was a "transcendent truth" and what Rothgery would describe as a "necessary directionality." Many students will not have read the satire and will be repulsed, sometimes missing the ironic juxtaposition of the two voices in the text. Organize a class discussion of the text in terms of the traditional argument: demonstration of a problem, formal statement of solution, explanation of the solution, and refutation of alternative solutions. Use the chalkboard to outline the satire twice, side by side: first from the voice of the "modest proposal" and then from the covert voice of Swift as it undercuts and broadens the description of the problem and solutions. Expect that class members will be able to think about how Swift manipulated their early reactions (e.g., "This is sick").

   The class conversation will come to focus on the proposer's criteria of evaluation ("fair, cheap, and easy") against the implied criteria of Swift. Assign follow-up journal entries, asking students to analyze the use of "fair, cheap, and easy" criteria in modern or contemporary world events and comment on the moral criteria that perhaps are used or could be used on a "larger scale" over time, across concepts of nation, race, gender, and so on.

Annotated Bibliography

Research and reflection about writers, writing, and our practices of working with writers have proliferated over the last two decades. Ph.D. programs in rhetoric and composition theory have increased. You can find multiple resources to assist you as you teach yourself more about working with writers: many sourcebooks and introductions to teaching writing are available; journals and NCTE (National Council of Teachers of English, <http://www.ncte.org>) anthologies offer additional theoretical and pedagogical perspectives on the range of topics addressed in this ancillary. Supplementing the works cited in the individual readings, this brief and selective bibliography offers you a starting point for broadening and deepening your thinking about writers and about ways to work with writers.

Bruffee, Kenneth A. *Collaborative Learning: Higher Education, Interdependence and the Authority of Knowledge*. Johns Hopkins UP, 1993. Bruffee presents a tightly woven analysis. He argues for change in higher education through collaborative learning. Specific analyses of collaborative practice across disciplines provide additional insights and advice to writing teachers who foster collaborative learning.

———. *A Short Course in Writing: Composition, Collaborative Learning, and Constructive Reading*. 4th ed. New York: Harper, 1995. This textbook with prompts for creative and transactional writing can be used in classrooms or by an individual for self-teaching. Bruffee's introduction offers a clear description of the relationships among writing, reading, teaching, and social construction as a needed direction in higher education.

Enos, Theresa, ed. *A Sourcebook for Basic Writing Teachers*. Manchester, NJ: McGraw, 1987. Thirty-nine essays extend the discussion of basic writing. The collection focuses on the sociolinguistic dimensions of literacy and shows the range of contemporary research, theory, and practice, building on the foundation laid by Mina Shaughnessy in *Errors and Expectations*.

Freire, Paulo. *Pedagogy of the Oppressed*. Trans. Myra Bergman Ramos. New York: Herder, 1972. Freire argues that literacy empowers the individual and that through the process of "naming his world," a person becomes free. His discussion of learner and master-learner collaborating in dialogue and action provides a useful model for writing as process pedagogy.

Gotswami, Dixie, ed. *Reclaiming the Classroom: Teacher Research as an Agency of Change*. Upper Montclair: Boynton, 1987. This book of essays describes reasons for and methods of conducting research in the classroom. Its scope is impressive, both in variety of research projects and methodologies and in discussions of the effects on instructors and students. The editor has pulled together important — and often original — essays by the leading teacher-scholars in composition and rhetoric.

Graves, Richard. *Rhetoric and Composition: A Sourcebook for Teachers and Writers*. 3rd ed. Upper Montclair: Boynton, 1990. Graves organized this sourcebook for writing teachers of all levels. The thirty-eight selections by well-known theorists and researchers document the energetic growth in the discipline of writing since 1963. Five chapters introduce the novice instructor to and update the veteran instructor about the growth and health of the scholarly discipline; practicing teachers' reports and "lore"; strategies to motivate student writers; questions about style; and "new perspectives, new horizons."

Irmscher, William F. *Teaching Expository Writing*. New York: Holt, 1979. The first text written for teachers of writing, this book poses the central questions every new teacher has. Irmscher writes from all the writer's resources: recall of his decades of teaching writing and his status as the "most senior" director of a composition program; humanistic observation of students as writers; conversation with writers and writing specialists; continuous reading in the discipline; and a lively imagination.

Lindemann, Erika. *A Rhetoric for Writing Teachers* 3rd ed. New York: Oxford UP, 1995. Lindemann does not supplant Irmscher but enriches the reading about teaching writing. Her text reports both theory and practice.

Myers, Miles. *The Teacher-Researcher: How to Study Writing in the Classroom.* Urbana: NCTE, 1985. An introduction to classroom writing assessment and research into writing processes, this book reviews procedures for teacher research and theoretical frameworks. It shows teachers — from kindergarten through college — ways to study writing in the classroom using specific examples of research.

Shaughnessy, Mina P. *Errors and Expectations: A Guide for the Teacher of Basic Writing.* New York: Oxford UP, 1979. Shaughnessy was the first to demonstrate a respect for an understanding of the processes that "basic writers" experience. This landmark study helps clarify the philosophy of teaching basic writers and design curriculum and classroom practice to assist these writers to develop into mature writers.

Skon, Linda, David W. Johnson, and Roger T. Johnson. "Cooperative Peer Interaction versus Individual Competition and Individualistic Efforts: Effects on the Acquisition of Cognitive Reasoning Strategies." *Journal of Educational Psychology* 73 (1981): 83–92. The researchers compared the effects of cooperative, competitive, and individualistic goal structures on what students achieve and what higher-order cognitive reasoning strategies they learned. The results indicate that cooperative goal structures and the resulting collaboration prompt higher achievement and more discovery of higher-order cognitive reasoning strategies.

Tate, Gary, and Edward P. J. Corbett, eds. *The Writing Teacher's Sourcebook.* 3rd ed. New York: Oxford UP, 1994. With each edition, the editing team adds new articles to a "canon" of essential discussions. These new articles extend theory and perspective or, as with readings about writers and computers, introduce the teaching strategies that had been considered on the "borders" or not central to teaching practice and have now become necessary strategies.

Trimbur, John. "Consensus and Difference in Collaborative Learning." *College English* 51 (Oct. 1989): 602–17. Trimbur extends the conversation about Bruffee's writing on collaborative learning and responds to critical counterclaims by emphasizing the practical realities of collaborative learning.

Wiener, Harvey S. *The Writing Room: A Resource Book for Teachers of English.* New York: Oxford UP, 1981. Like Irmscher and Lindemann, Wiener offers advice about teaching writing from day one. His focus is the basic writing classroom and his discussion is informed — like Shaughnessy's — by his classroom experiences in an open-doors writing program.

Teaching Writing: Concepts and Philosophies for Reflective Practice

Berthoff, Ann E. *Reclaiming the Imagination: Philosophical Perspectives for Writers and Teachers of Writers.* Upper Montclair: Boynton, 1983. Berthoff's theme of "reclaiming the imagination" reflects her philosophy and practice of encouraging writing as dialectical and reflective action.

Bruffee, Kenneth A. "Social Construction, Language, and the Authority of Knowledge: A Bibliographical Essay." *College English* 48 (Dec. 1986): 773–90. This introduction to social constructivist thought in literary criticism and history with its connections to composition studies lays out a foundation of a "social-epistemic" approach to teaching writing. Bruffee provides a bibliography to help other writing teachers explore these philosophical underpinnings.

Emig, Janet. "Writing as a Mode of Learning." *College Composition and Communication* 28.2 (May 1977): 122–27. Emig asserts a "first principle" that informs both contemporary practice in composition classrooms and writing-across-the-curriculum initiatives and programs.

Fulkerson, Richard. "Four Philosophies of Composition." *College Composition and Communication* 30 (Dec. 1979): 342–48. Fulkerson proposed the terms *expressive, mimetic, rhetorical,* and *formalist* to describe philosophies of composition current in the late 1970s and has continued to reflect on and discuss philosophies and concepts that have evolved further. The piece is not dated because of the range of assumptions and practices that students, new instructors, and veteran instructors bring to the writing classroom.

Hillocks, George, Jr. "What Works in Teaching Composition: A Meta-Analysis of Experimental Treatment Studies." *American Journal of Education* 93 (Nov. 1984): 133–70. Hillocks reviews experimental treatment studies of the teaching of composition over twenty years. While assessing effectiveness of different modes and focuses of instruction, he found that a writing-as-process focus within an "environmental mode" was more effective than other approaches to composition. His discussion of the implications of the research is especially useful.

Myers, Miles, and James Gray. *Theory and Practice in the Teaching of Composition.* Urbana: NCTE, 1983. The text has a double audience: it shows teachers how their strategies for teaching writing connect to and reflect an area of research, and it shows researchers that what teachers do intuitively can often be validated by research. The organization of readings by the teaching methods of processing, distancing, and modeling is especially useful.

North, Stephen. *The Making of Knowledge in Composition: Portrait of an Emerging Field.* Upper Montclair: Boynton, 1987. North discusses the place of "practitioner's lore," and the development of new research methodologies to study questions generated by reflection on the writing experiences of diverse students.

Raymond, James C. "What Good Is All This Heady, Esoteric Theory?" *Teaching English in the Two-Year College* (Feb. 1990): 11–15. Raymond answers this question (often posed by writing teachers who are busy with the daily tasks of working with writers). He "translates" poststructural theory into practical applications.

Smith, Frank. "Myths of Writing." *Language Arts* 58.7 (Oct. 1981): 792–98. Smith describes and clarifies twenty-one misconceptions that students, faculty, and the public hold about what writing is, how it is learned, and who can teach it.

Thinking about the Writing Process

Generating a Draft

Fulwiler, Toby. *The Journal Book.* Portsmouth, NH: Boynton, 1987. Forty-two essays discuss the use of journals for discovery and invention in writing classrooms and in other disciplines across the curriculum.

Hilbert, Betsy S. "It Was a Dark and Nasty Night It Was a Dark and You Would Not Believe How Dark It Was a Hard Beginning." *College Composition and Communication* 43.1 (Feb. 1992): 75–80. Hilbert writes from lengthy experience as a writing instructor about beginning a new semester with new writers and predictable difficulties. The essay is tonic and a healthy reminder to us about staying focused on why we teach writing as we enter or return to the classroom.

Rose, Mike. *When a Writer Can't Write: Studies in Writer's Block and Other Composing-Process Problems.* New York: Guilford, 1985. Eleven essays identify and analyze cognitive and affective dimensions of writing apprehension. The range of discussion emphasizes the effects of the environment and writing situations on the writer: novice writers, ESL writers, graduate students, and professional writers are all affected by writing apprehension at various times.

———. *Writer's Block: The Cognitive Dimension.* Carbondale: Southern Illinois UP, 1984. This landmark book researching and analyzing writer's block emphasizes that a variety of cognitive difficulties are behind the problem. Case studies and the report of research results offer useful insights about ways to teach writing that will enable writers to get beyond blocks.

Revising a Draft

Bartholomae, David. "The Study of Error." *College Composition and Communication* 31 (Oct. 1980): 253–69. Bartholomae encourages a study of how students revise texts as they speak aloud about them. He connects the phenomenon to his definition of basic writing as a kind of writing produced as students learn the knowledge of a new discourse community.

Flower, Linda, John R. Hayes, Linda Carey, Karen Schriver, and James Stratman. "Detection, Diagnosis, and the Strategies of Revision." *College Composition and Communication* 37 (Feb. 1986): 16–55. This article, produced through collaborative research and writing, describes some of the important intellectual activities that underlie and affect the process of revision. The article presents a working model for revision, for identifying "problems," and for generating solutions.

Harris, Muriel. "Composing Behaviors of One- and Multi-Draft Writers." *College English* 51 (Feb. 1989): 174–91. This study of eight experienced writers who described themselves as one-draft or multidraft writers provides useful materials for individualizing the processes of rewriting for students.

Sommers, Nancy. "Between the Drafts." *College Composition and Communication* 43 (Nov. 1992): 23–31. Nancy Sommers models the use of personal narrative as another kind of "evidence" to support or argue points in academic writing. She suggests that we should encourage and help students to use personal narrative in academic writing when they can. Use of personal narrative along with the traditional sources is a recurring theme in discussions of assisting writers as they rethink purpose, readership, and identity during the process of revising and re-visioning text.

Sudol, Ronald A., ed. *Revising: New Essays for Teachers of Writing.* Urbana: NCTE, 1982. Useful essays describing both the practice and the theory of revising strategies and processes.

Teaching Critical Reading and Writing

Berthoff, Ann. "Is Teaching Still Possible? Writing, Meaning, and Higher-Order Reasoning." *College English* 46.6 (Dec. 1984): 743–55. Berthoff surveys and evaluates models of cognitive development and their connections to positivist perspectives on language. She discusses alternative perspectives on language and learning that emphasize reading and writing as interpretation and as the making of meaning.

Elbow, Peter. "Teaching Thinking by Teaching Writing." *Change* 15.6 (Sept. 1983): 37–40. Elbow's argument that "first-order creative, intuitive thinking and second-order critical thinking" can and should be encouraged in writing instruction, could be used for writing-across-the-curriculum initiatives.

Flower, Linda, and John R. Hayes. "The Cognition of Discovery: Defining a Rhetorical Problem." *College Composition and Communication* 31.1 (Feb. 1980): 21–32. The researchers used protocol analysis to study the differences between writers engaged in problem-solving cognitive processes.

Karbach, Joan. "Using Toulmin's Model of Argumentation." *Journal of Teaching Writing* 6.1 (Spring 1987): 81–91. This article illustrates the use of Toulmin's three-part model of argumentation: data, warrant, and claim. While describing heuristic procedures, Karbach proposes this informal logic as a strategy for teaching inductive and deductive logic within any writing assignment.

Kneupper, Charles. "Argument: A Social Constructivist Perspective." *Journal of the American Forensic Association* 17.4 (Spring 1981): 183–89. A communication specialist analyzes argumentation theory from the perspective of social constructionism. He examines uses and connections between argument as structure and argument as process along with their socio-epistemic implications.

Lunsford, Andrea. "Cognitive Development and the Basic Writer." *College English* 41 (Sept. 1979): 39–46. After reviewing theories of cognitive development, Lunsford demonstrates that many basic writers operate below the stage of forming concepts and have difficulty in "decentering." She recommends strategies and writing assignments to help basic writers practice and acquire more complex cognitive skills.

———. "The Content of Basic Writers' Essays." *College Composition and Communication* 31.3 (Oct. 1980): 278–90. Lunsford reports that three factors affect word choice and linguistic flexibility of basic writers: the level of writing skill they bring to a classroom, their stages of cognitive development, and their self-concepts.

Shor, Ira. *Critical Teaching and Everyday Life.* Chicago: U Chicago P, 1987. Influenced by Paulo Freire's pedagogical theories, Shor emphasizes learning through dialogue. His analysis of education is inclusive: open admissions teaching of writing, traditional and nontraditional students and learning environments, elite and nonelite educational missions, and "liberatory" teaching modes that challenge social limits of thought and action and encourage cultural literacy. Cognitive skills are acquired and enhanced through collaborative problem solving and reflection leading to action.

Teaching Writing with Computers

Bruce, Bertram, Joy Kreefy Peyton, and Trent Batson. *Network-Based Classrooms: Promises and Realities.* New York: Cambridge UP, 1993. The collaborative technology of "electronic networks for interaction" accommodates and prompts the social construction of knowledge. The collection ranges from descriptions of "how to" to "effects." Caveat: the rapid development and redesign of the technology and the advent of the World Wide Web may make the nuts and bolts obsolete, so focus on themes, issues, and significance to writing improvement.

Hawisher, Gail, and Paul LeBlanc, ed. *Re-Imagining Computers and Composition: Teaching and Research in the Virtual Age.* Portsmouth, NH: Boynton, 1992. The editors selected twelve essays to describe and speculate about theoretical, research, and pedagogical implications of the dramatically increased use of electronic technology for composition.

Hawisher, Gail E., and Charles Moran. "Electronic Mail and the Writing Instructor." *College English.* 55.6 (Oct. 1993): 627–43. The writers describe advantages and effects of introducing electronic communication to a composition course. The essay gives practical advice to newcomers.

Lanham, Richard. *The Electronic Word: Democracy, Technology, and the Arts.* Chicago: U of Chicago P, 1993. In a reader-based study, rhetorician Lanham analyzes the creative potential of electronic writing for coming closer to these long-standing goals: access, unfettered imagination, and effective communication. He views the electronic word as dramatically and healthily changing the construction and experience of "knowledge."

Responding to and Evaluating Student Writing

Anson, Chris. *Writing and Response: Theory, Practice, and Research.* Urbana: NCTE, 1989. The essays include discussion of responding to student journal writing, responding via electronic media, and responding in conferences. Theoretical perspectives and instructional practice are intermixed.

Belanoff, Patricia, and Marcia Dickson, eds. *Portfolios: Process and Product.* Portsmouth, NH: Boynton, 1991. In the first comprehensive collection of writings on using portfolios for classroom and portfolio assessment, the editors called for "practitioners' lore" and research. This is the book to start with when considering use of writing portfolios.

Berthoff, Ann. *Thinking, Writing: The Composing Imagination.* Portsmouth, NH: Heinemann, 1982. Berthoff focuses on the reading-writing relationship within a course organized around the central task of teaching composition. Insights and practical suggestions abound.

Brooke, Robert E. *Writing and Sense of Self: Identity Negotiation in Writing Workshops.* Urbana: NCTE, 1991. Brooke describes the effects of responding in the context of writing through workshops: effects on the kinds of writing projects students risked and effects on their processes of negotiating identities as writers.

Cooper, Charles R., and Lee Odell, eds. *Evaluating Writing: Describing, Measuring, Judging.* Urbana: NCTE, 1977. With its comprehensive survey of ways teachers can describe writing and measure the growth of writing, this remains a useful sourcebook. The discussion of involving students in the evaluation of writing includes individual goal setting, self-evaluation, and peer evaluation. Multiple responses to multiple processes and features of the writing are implicitly recommended.

Flower, Linda, and Thomas Hucking. "Reading for Points and Purposes." *Journal of Advanced Composition* 11.2 (Fall 1991): 347–62. By researching how undergraduate and graduate students use point-driven or purpose-driven reading strategies, the authors conclude that readers who use a point-driven strategy tend to stay at a less complex level of interpretation.

Freire, Paulo. *Education for Critical Consciousness.* New York: Seabury, 1973. Freire's argument for educational reform focuses on the need for the development of "critical consciousness" in learners, who thus become the agents rather than the subjects of their education. Freire's focus is congenial with social-epistemic rhetoric and emphasizes the social construction of knowledge through collaborative work.

Hamp-Lyons, Liz, ed. *Assessing Second Language Writing in Academic Contexts.* Norwood, NJ: Ablex, 1991. Twenty-one essays examine the multiple issues of assessing second language writing. Many of the articles focus on assessment design and decision making that affect ESL writers in an assessment program, but the principles of good assessment practices for diverse populations are clearly defined.

Hillocks, George, Jr. "The Interaction of Instruction, Teacher Comment, and Revision in Teaching the Composing Process." *Research in the Teaching of English* 16 (Oct. 1982): 261–82. An early study of the effects of instructor response on student revision and attitudes toward writing. The article points out that helpful commentary or conference discussion promotes a writer's growth.

Newkirk, Thomas, ed. *Only Connect: Uniting Reading and Writing.* Upper Montclair: Boynton, 1986. The fifteen articles in this collection by major scholars in the discipline of "English" explore the relationships of reading and literary study to composition.

Noguchi, Rei R. *Grammar and the Teaching of Writing: Limits and Possibilities.* Urbana: NCTE, 1991. Beginning with the shared conviction that grammar must be taught within the context and processes of drafting and revising, Noguchi helps writing teachers identify the sites where grammar and writing overlap and suggests productive ways to integrate grammar instruction with issues of meaning, organization, and style.

Odell, Lee. "Defining and Assessing Competence in Writing." *The Nature and Measurement of Competency in English.* Ed. Charles R. Cooper. Urbana: NCTE, 1981. Practical advice about clarifying what an instructor defines as writing competence along with descriptions of holistic and other assessment measures for both classroom and large-scale assessment.

Roseberry, Ann S., Linda Flower, Beth Warren, Betsy Bowen, Bertram Bruce, Margaret Kantz, and Ann M. Penrose. "The Problem-Solving Processes of Writers and Readers." *Collaboration through Writing and Reading: Exploring Possibilities:.* Ed. Anne Haas Dysott. Urbana: NCTE, 1989. 136–64.

Welch, Nancy. "One Student's Many Voices: Reading, Writing, and Responding with Bakhtin." *Journal of Advanced Composition* 13.2 (Fall 1993): 493–502. Welch demonstrates a "Bakhtinian" reading of a student text to argue that teachers should respond to the many voices in a student text for two reasons: to assist the writer to become aware of responding to a specific and effective text, and to let the student see and acknowledge the self — and the self in the process of becoming.

White, Edward M. *Assigning, Responding, Evaluating: A Writing Teacher's Guide.* New York: St. Martin's, 1992. For the "state of the art" in writing assessment, White surveys and evaluates the designs and applications of writing assessments and helps writing instructors use the information garnered through assessment to improve classroom instruction.

———. *Teaching and Assessing Writing.* San Francisco: Jossey, 1985. The publisher here is significant: in this first major discussion of the symbiosis of writing assessment and classroom teaching, the preeminent publisher of discourse in higher education agreed that this would be an important test. This should be the first book a new writing teacher uses to learn about contemporary research and practice in understanding, evaluating, and improving students' writing performance.

Yancey, Kathleen Blake, ed. *Portfolios in the Writing Classroom: An Introduction.* Urbana: NCTE, 1992. This collection focuses on the use of writing portfolios in secondary and higher education courses across the curriculum. The articles describe objectives and designs for the use of portfolios. Some theoretical discussion appears in assorted entries. Like most NCTE publications, this is a very useful introduction to the field.

Issues in Writing Pedagogy

Fostering Literacy

Dyson, Anne Haas, ed. *Collaboration through Reading and Writing: Exploring Possibilities.* Urbana: NCTE, 1989. The discussion of the interrelationships of reading, writing, and learning was first generated at a working conference of researchers and theorists concerned with literacy teaching and training. The strong interdisciplinary bent of the text is evident in each chapter.

Heath, Shirley Brice. "An Annotated Bibliography on Multicultural Writing and Literacy Issues." *Quarterly of the National Writing Project and the Center for the Study of Writing and Literacy* 12.1 (Winter 1990): 22–24. This bibliography lists and annotates sixteen books and articles that focus on multicultural writing and literacy issues, including bilingual education, English as a second language, writing instruction, literacy, and multicultural education.

Smith, Frank. *Essays into Literacy.* Portsmouth, NH: Heinemann, 1983. Smith's theory about literacy as the ability to make use of all available possibilities of written language informs thirteen essays written over a ten-year period. The research into and reflection on elementary and secondary reading and writing experiences produced insights that transfer easily to discussion of college-level literacies.

Fostering Diversity

Berlin, James, and Michael Vivion, eds. *Cultural Studies in the English Classroom.* Portsmouth, NH: Boynton, 1993. Berlin offers a comprehensive discussion of cultural critique as a purpose for writing and reading coursework, reminding readers that all pedagogic choices are political, whether they are foregrounded or implicit in course design and activities. Cultural critique necessarily examines and analyzes the power relationships within the multiple cultures of a dominant culture.

Eichorn, Jill, Sara Farris, Karen Hayes, Adriana Hernandez, Susan C. Jarratt, Karen Powers-Stubbs, and Marian M. Schiachitano. "A Symposium on Feminist Experiences in the Composition Classroom." *College Composition and Communication* 43 (Oct. 1992): 297–332. In describing their experiences using feminist composition pedagogies, the writers illustrate ways of respecting diversity within a writing community.

Flynn, Elizabeth A. "Feminist Theories/Feminist Composition." *College English* 57.2 (Feb. 1995): 201–12. Flynn reviews four book-length studies in "feminist composition," connecting them to theoretical perspectives and demonstrating the vigorous dialogue from many directions that feminist pedagogues and theorists have engendered.

Herrington, Anne. "Basic Writing: Moving the Voices on the Margin to the Center." *Harvard Educational Review* 60.4 (Nov. 1990): 489–96. Herrington describes the redesign of a basic writing course to give voice to marginalized minority students. After a shift to reading works by mostly nonwhite authors, students were encouraged to reflect in writing on those readings and on their experiences of marginalization.

Rose, Mike. *Lives on the Boundary: The Struggles and Achievements of America's Underprepared.* New York: Free, 1989. Through personal narrative and incisive analysis, Rose describes the underclass of students representing diverse cultures and subcultures who are considered underachieving, remedial, or illiterate. Rose speculates about the nature of literacy and liberal learning curricula that could empower these marginalized writers and learners.

Teaching ESL Students

Carson, Joan G. and Gayle L. Nelson. "Writing Groups: Cross-Cultural Issues." *Journal of Second Language Writing* 3.1 (1994): 17–30. Citing the dearth of research on communication assumptions and behaviors of Asian students in collaborative writing communities, Carson and Nelson call for additional studies of ways in which culturally specific beliefs and behaviors might affect cooperation and interaction in peer response groups and collaborative writing projects. Although no description of cultural constraints on learning to write can be applied universally, the discussion offers useful insights to possible barriers for ESL writers in collaborative groups.

Leki, Ilona. *Understanding ESL Writers: A Guide for Teachers.* Portsmouth, NH: Boynton, 1992. This is an excellent handbook for learning about the concerns, expectations, and errors of ESL students. Written for the double audience of ESL instructors and writing teachers, it provides useful advice about responding to the texts of ESL writers.

Raimes, Ann. "Language Proficiency, Writing Ability, and Composing Strategies: A Study of ESL College Student Writers." *Language Learning* 37.3 (Sept. 1987): 439–68. Raimes analyzed the writing strategies of ESL student writers from different levels of ESL instruction. She found that although both native and nonnative writers shared many strategies, ESL learners were less inhibited by attempts to correct their work.

Reid, Joy, and Barbara Kroll. "Designing and Assessing Effective Writing Assignments for NES and ESL Students." *Journal of Second Language Writing* 3.1 (1995): 17–41. Reid and

Kroll emphasize the need to design fair writing assignments that encourage students to learn from writing experiences as they demonstrate what course material they know and understand. They analyze successful and flawed writing prompts and assignments from the perspective of ESL writers; the practical advice they offer is as pertinent to mainstream composition teaching as to working with ESL writers or writers with learning disabilities.

Writing across the Curriculum

Anson, Chris, John Schwiebert, and Michael M. Williamson. *Writing across the Curriculum: An Annotated Bibliography.* Westport, CT: Greenwood, 1993. This very useful bibliography describes both scholarship in and pedagogic strategies for extending and using writing across the curriculum, whether the model is "writing as learning" or "writing in the discipline."

Fulwiler, Toby, and Art Young, eds. *Language Connections: Writing and Reading across the Curriculum.* Urbana: NCTE, 1982. This text, aimed at all college and university instructors, offers theoretical perspectives and practical activities to prompt writing as learning. The text encourages peer evaluation, conferences between instructors and students, and shared evaluation and includes a limited bibliography on cross-curricular language and learning.

Herrington, Anne. "Writing to Learn: Writing across the Disciplines." *College English* 43 (Apr. 1981): 379–87. This essay focuses on the design of writing assignments that can be connected to course objectives, whatever the discipline. Herrington encourages instructors to emphasize writing as discovery and learning in their responses to student writing.

Jeffrey Sommers, "Bringing Practice in Line with Theory: Using Portfolio Grading in the Composition Classroom." Reprinted by permission of Jeffrey Sommers. From *Portfolios, Process, and Product,* edited by Pat Belanoff and Marcia Dickson. Heinemann-Boynton/Cook Publishers, a subsidiary of Reed Elsevier Inc., Portsmouth, N.H., 1991.

Nancy Sommers, "Responding to Student Writing," *College Composition and Communication,* May 1982. Copyright 1982 by the National Council of Teachers of English. Reprinted with permission. "Revision Strategies of Student Writers and Experienced Adult Writers," *College Composition and Communication,* December 1980. Copyright 1980 by the National Council of Teachers of English. Reprinted with permission.

Patricia Webb, "Narratives of Self in Networked Communications," *Computers and Composition,* Volume 14, Number 1, 1997. Copyright 1997 by Ablex Publishing Corporation. Reprinted with permission.

Joseph Williams, "The Phenomenology of Error," *College Composition and Communication,* 1981. Copyright 1981 by the National Council of Teachers of English. Reprinted with permission.